The Voice of the People

The Voice of the People

Great Speeches from India's Parliament

Edited and compiled by
Smita Gupta

juggernaut

JUGGERNAUT BOOKS
C-I-128, First Floor, Sangam Vihar, Near Holi Chowk,
New Delhi 110080, India

First published by Juggernaut Books 2025

Speech starting on p. 59 has been reproduced from Parliamentary Debates, Rajya Sabha Official Report, session 54, vol. 54, 5 November 1965, from pp. 506–13.

Speech starting on p. 195 has been reproduced from Parliamentary Debates, Rajya Sabha Official Report, session 6, vol. 6, no. 1, 11 March 1954, from pp. 2,452–74.

Speech starting on p. 234 has been reproduced from Parliamentary Debates, Rajya Sabha Official Report, session 235, vol. 235, no. 2, 24 April 2015, from pp. 311–21.

Speech starting on p. 311 has been reproduced from Parliamentary Debates, Rajya Sabha Official Report, session 238, vol. 238, no. 16, 16 March 2016, from pp. 365–75.

Speech starting on p. 320 has been reproduced from Parliamentary Debates, Rajya Sabha Official Report, session 238, vol. 238, no. 16, 16 March 2016, from pp. 388–96.

Speech starting on p. 328 has been reproduced from Parliamentary Debates, Rajya Sabha Official Report, session 250, vol. 250, no. 18, 11 December 2019, from pp. 461–63.

Speech starting on p. 330 has been reproduced from Parliamentary Debates, Rajya Sabha Official Report, session 250, vol. 250, no. 18, 11 December 2019, p. 476.

Speech starting on p. 477 has been reproduced from Parliamentary Debates, Rajya Sabha Official Report, session 249, vol. 249, no. 33, 5 August 2019, from pp. 68–74.

Speech starting on p. 494 has been reproduced from Parliamentary Debates, Rajya Sabha Official Report, session 254, vol. 254, no. 2, 20 July 2021, from pp. 38–40.

10 9 8 7 6 5 4 3 2 1

P-ISBN: 9789353453336
E-ISBN: 9789353454258

Typeset in Adobe Caslon Pro by R. Ajith Kumar, Noida

Printed at Thomson Press India Ltd

Contents

Introduction

For over three decades, from 1987 to 2019, I reported on the proceedings of India's Parliament, especially that of the Lok Sabha. I had a ringside view as the never-ceasing drama of the world's largest democracy played out, the mood of its members changing with bewildering rapidity.

I sat in the Press Gallery, which overlooked the semi-circular green chamber of the Lok Sabha, of the old Parliament House. For close to ten years, as the *Times of India* correspondent, I sat directly above the Prime Minister (PM) of the day; and for another seven years or so, as *The Hindu*'s representative, I sat just above the Leader of the Opposition.

Theatre seats don't get any better than that!

So, three years ago, when I embarked on a project to put together a collection of the best speeches made in Parliament since Independence, I thought it would be a breeze. After all, I had myself covered almost half the period.

But when I got down to it, selecting speeches proved to be much harder than I had anticipated, and not just because learning to negotiate the Parliament Digital Library took longer than I had imagined. There was a problem of plenty – there was just too much to choose from.

My first instinct was to make a list of the best-known Members of Parliament (MPs) and then look for their most significant speeches, especially those that read well as written text. But it soon became apparent that speeches chosen randomly, merely for their excellence, whether in setting out new ideas or marking a historic moment, or, indeed, in their use of language, or even a combination of all four, would not tell the real story of India over the last seventy-eight years. For that story to be told effectively, there needed to be a criterion for the selection of speeches.

I decided, therefore, to draw up a list of big themes and pivotal events, whether they related to political and economic decisions or periodic episodes of religious unrest and social churning that had shaped and defined independent India's progress. I next searched for representative speeches which, when read together, would capture some of those conversations – and hopefully, the drama – thus allowing the history of that period to unfold and help to place major events in context.

In the process, many fine speeches had to be dropped as they did not fit into the plan that I had drawn up. For these omissions, I seek abject pardon of the many, many MPs whose words deserved to find a place in this book.

The other constraints in selection were space and, most importantly, language. Very few speeches made in languages other than English made the cut because they don't read as well in translation. In some cases, I ventured to improve the available translations but the rules regarding permission from Parliament authorities to reproduce these speeches demand a strict adherence to the official version. Indeed, I was told firmly that while I could use excerpts of the speeches, I could not touch anything else. That not only delayed the process but it has meant that there are speeches in this book which have grammatical errors, faulty syntax, typos, etc. – and there are speeches that had to be dropped entirely. For instance, in the case of a brilliant speech in Hindi made by Atal Behari Vajpayee after the creation of Bangladesh, the translation was a summary of the original. It, therefore, became pointless to include it.

Finally, editing the speeches to manageable lengths was difficult because, with very few exceptions, our MPs tend to be wordy – many don't warm up to their subject till the fifteenth minute or so! I have sought, wherever possible, to present both sides of the major debates that have taken place by including the voices of those in the Opposition at that point in time.

My choice of themes, selection of speeches and the way they have been arranged, are a reflection of my personal interests. Another individual, venturing on a similar project, would doubtless have made a different selection.

I had, initially, also decided to select speeches made only after the first general elections in 1952. But then, as I began to read the speeches, I felt there was a need to set the stage by including some speeches made between 1947 and 1952, for the stirring and varied events and the battle of ideas that would mark the years to follow.

It also seemed a shame to put together a collection of speeches made in the old Parliament House and not include Jawaharlal Nehru's 1947 'Tryst with Destiny' speech – undoubtedly one of the greatest speeches of the twentieth century. It also seemed appropriate, in the seventy-eighth year since this country became a free nation to recall the sacrifices made by those who won India its independence from colonial rule, and to articulate their fears and apprehensions of what might follow the establishment of a free nation.

And hence the speeches – also made at the midnight hour – by Dr Rajendra Prasad and Dr S. Radhakrishnan, who went on to become the country's first and second presidents. For lack of space, I had to drop the speech made by Chaudhury Khaliquzzaman, chosen to represent the Muslim voice in the Constituent Assembly. Sadly, he left for Pakistan by the end of 1947, an indication of those volatile and uncertain times.

This section also includes Dr B.R. Ambedkar's iconic 'Grammar of Anarchy' speech that critiqued the Constitution's critics, dwelt on the difficulties that lay ahead in sustaining the independence that had been won at such great cost, expanded on the idea of India as a 'nation' and the ideals and components of democracy.

What is significant about some of these speeches is that they are in many ways prescient, even prophetic, about the pitfalls ahead for the newly independent India. 'Should we not now correct our national faults of character, our domestic despotism, our intolerance which has assumed the different forms of obscurantism, of narrow-mindedness, of superstitious bigotry? Others were able to play on our weakness because we had them. I would like, ... to call for self-examination, for a searching of hearts. ... Political divisions, physical partitions, are external but the psychological divisions are deeper. The cultural cleavages are the more dangerous. We should not allow them to grow,' Radhakrishnan said in 1947, stressing, '...Swarajya is the development of that kind of tolerant attitude which sees in brother man the face Divine. Intolerance has been the greatest enemy of our progress. Tolerance of one another's views, thoughts and beliefs is the only remedy that we can possibly adopt.'

Close to eight decades on, his words resonate as sharply as they must have when they were uttered.

'... In a country like India – where democracy from its long disuse must be regarded as something quite new – there is danger of democracy giving place to dictatorship,' Ambedkar said two years later in 1949, adding, 'It is quite possible for this new born democracy to retain its form but give place to dictatorship in fact. If there is a landslide, the danger of the second possibility becoming actuality is much greater ... in India, Bhakti or what may be called the path of devotion or hero-worship, plays a part in its politics unequalled in magnitude by the part it plays in the politics of any other country in the world. Bhakti in religion may be a road to the salvation of the soul. But in politics, Bhakti or hero-worship is a sure road to degradation and to eventual dictatorship.'

Prescient and prophetic.

If the first section seeks to encapsulate the mood at the time of Independence, each of the remaining eleven sections, attempts to span as much as is possible of the ensuing decades. 'Dragon in the Room' has speeches starting with India's defeat in the India–China War in 1962 and ends with concern at the Chinese incursions across the still-disputed border over the last few years, highlighting how little progress has been made.

'The People Next Door' focuses on relations with another most significant neighbour, Pakistan. It begins in 1965 with the India–Pakistan War, takes note of the birth of Bangladesh and not just its political significance, but also includes an account of the human cost, through the heart-rending stories of the millions who were displaced. The section concludes with the historic bus ride the then Prime Minister Atal Behari Vajpayee undertook to Lahore in 1999, which was possibly the last occasion on which it was felt that there was a serious possibility of relations between the two countries improving.

If the second and third sections detail how critical relations with India's two major neighbours, China and Pakistan, would be to its own well-being, 'Pokhran and the India–United States Nuclear Deal' opens with Operation Smiling Buddha and Operation Shakti, the official names given to India's first two nuclear bomb tests in 1974 and 1998. The names reflect how the governments of the day viewed the events. The two tests irrevocably changed India's relations with the world at large and not just with its neighbours. The India–U.S. Civil Nuclear Agreement that was signed on 10 October 2008 marked a defining moment in the relations between the two countries and unmistakably altered India's position in the world. All three events also strengthened the three leaders behind the three decisions – Indira Gandhi, Atal Behari Vajpayee and Manmohan Singh.

'The Journey to a Liberalized Economy' – the fifth section – is dominated by budget speeches and, therefore, by the voice of the government of the day. The first speech reflects the concerns of a newly independent nation and addresses the challenges of the separation of India from Pakistan and that of creating a new narrative. Indira Gandhi's introduction of the nationalization of banks and Manmohan Singh's piloting of the opening of India's economy are clearly landmark speeches that changed the course of the country's economic history. The Opposition voice comes through in a speech by India's most influential Socialist leader Ram Manohar Lohia in which he takes on Jawaharlal Nehru directly.

The next section, 'Gender', covers the journey between the intense, heated debates on the Hindu Code Bill and the relatively smooth passage that the Transgender Bill had – even though it was moved as a Private Member's Bill – over sixty years later. This is perhaps a sign of the way times have changed. Sandwiched between those speeches are debates relating to women. These cover both the personal and the political. So there is the debate on legalizing abortion (1971), a law that helped women gain control not just over their bodies but also 'destiny', as a woman MP at the time said; the discussions (1985–86) that followed the Shah Bano verdict (dealing with maintenance for divorced Muslim women) in the Supreme Court and the Congress government's unconscionable flip-flop on the subject that was to have a long lasting impact on the Muslim vote; the Triple Talaq Law (2018), that far from empowering Muslim women, ended up only penalizing Muslim men; and the debate on The Commission of Sati (Prevention) Bill, 1987, shortly after a young widow, Roop Kanwar, jumped onto her husband's funeral pyre. There is also a speech on the contentious bill that took twenty-seven years to be made into law – the bill to reserve one-third of the seats in Parliament and legislative assemblies for women. The covert opposition from male MPs was understandable: when this law comes into effect, the balance of power between men and women at the highest level of decision-making will change irrevocably. To delay that process, perhaps, the Narendra Modi government announced that the bill (that was passed in 2023) would not be used in the general elections of 2024 but will have to wait to come into effect after delimitation of constituencies in 2026. Some have suggested that the ruling BJP hoped that this delaying tactic would ensure a larger share of women's votes in 2024 without annoying male MPs who might be unseated to accommodate female aspirants for seats in Parliament.

Then come the twin sections 'Deepening Democracy' and 'The Civic Space'. The first focuses on efforts by successive governments to spread equality and justice to all sections of a diverse society; the second has speeches by individuals – in this case, Opposition MPs – who pushed back to preserve the autonomy and freedom of the ordinary citizen.

In 'Deepening Democracy', the speeches heralding the giving of legal status to Mahatma Gandhi's dream of Panchayati Raj as the foundation of India's political system, strengthening the roots of democracy and the acceptance of the recommendations of the Mandal Commission Report in 1990 have been included. The latter decision – creating a 27 per cent quota for the Other Backward Castes (OBCs) in central government jobs and public sector undertakings – taken by the National Front (NF) government headed by Vishwanath Pratap Singh, was an act of great courage. It led, in the long run, to transformational change, particularly in the populous Hindi heartland, democratizing politics by propelling the OBCs upwards to challenge the hegemony of the less numerous upper castes. But in the short run, it provoked sharp and violent protests from upper caste students and became a primary and proximate cause of the fall of the V.P. Singh government. The other speeches in this section deal with governmental efforts to end crimes against Scheduled Castes and Scheduled Tribes, and the mood of the Muslim community during Manmohan Singh's tenure as prime minister: his emphasis on inclusive politics helped him to connect powerfully with the minorities.

In 'The Civic Space', there are speeches that vehemently oppose the notorious Maintenance of Internal Security Act (MISA) steered by the Congress in 1971;

frontally attack the imposition of the Emergency in 1976; firmly uphold the principle of diversity by defending the right to eat beef in 1996; and sharply castigate the BJP's 'narrow, selfish and arrogant' nationalism in 2016. The other speeches in this section critique the Aadhar project, oppose the controversial Citizenship Bill before it became an Act and defend the right to protest.

Religious conflict led to the Partition of India and its bitter aftermath. But the resurrection in recent decades of those divisions through the rise of Hindutva – of which the BJP government is a votary – made a section on 'The Religious Faultline' necessary. I have chosen to focus on only one event in post-Partition India that critically deepened that divide – the destruction of the Babri Masjid on 6 December 1992. In its immediate aftermath, there was shock, anger, consternation and communal violence in different parts of the country. The BJP, one of the principal protagonists of the Ram Janmabhoomi movement that led to the destruction of the mosque, oddly enough, decided to bring a no-confidence motion against the Congress government at the Centre, blaming it for not intervening in time in Ayodhya; simultaneously, it justified the destruction of the mosque. The speeches included touch on different aspects of the destruction of the mosque. One defends the felling of the Babri Masjid; another details its impact on the minorities; while a third is an official account of what happened, along with the limited options that lay before the government on that fateful day.

The destruction of the Babri Masjid was a turning point in India's post-Independence history. It accelerated the BJP's ascension to political power after decades on the fringes – barring a brief interregnum post-Emergency, when it was still known as the Bharatiya Jana Sangh (BJS) and was part of the Janata Party government. For the Congress, too, it marked a watershed for it was after this that the Muslims turned their backs on the party for not protecting the mosque. With the construction of a grand Ram temple at the site of the Babri Masjid by a BJP government more than three decades later in 2024, the message of 1992 has been re-emphasised. As a coda to this section, there is a solitary speech by a subaltern voice critical of the attempts to bring in the Uniform Civil Code, which remains part of the BJP's unfinished agenda.

A collection of Parliamentary speeches cannot do without a section purely on 'Politics' since that lies at the core of much of what is said and done. Ministerial resignations and Votes of Confidence that marked inflexion points in the history of free India's politics saw many of the speakers quoted here use the occasion to articulate the point of view of the losing side.

In 1951, B.R. Ambedkar, the Father of the Indian Constitution, resigned from Nehru's cabinet, primarily prompted by the latter's inability to push through the Hindu Code Bill. In 1969, Morarji Desai quit Indira Gandhi's government to protest against the nationalization of major banks through an ordinance. In 1996, Atal Behari Vajpayee preferred to put in his papers as prime minister before the trust vote he was up against could be voted on, instead of facing the ignominy of being defeated. Less than a year later, another Prime Minister H.D. Deve Gowda, sought a vote of confidence he knew he would lose so that he could use his exit speech to list his achievements for posterity. In 2018, Prime Minister Narendra Modi proved he still had the numbers in the Lok Sabha. But it was one of those rare occasions when the Congress's Rahul Gandhi set the tone, with an unequivocal message that love and tolerance, not hatred and lynchings, was the way forward for India. The section concludes with another speech by Narendra Modi that is a forceful critique of the Gandhi family. It was made on the occasion of the seventy-fifth anniversary of the acceptance of the Constitution.

'Trouble in Paradise' deals with Kashmir. If the region's integration with India at the time of Independence was marked by bloodshed and conflict, seventy-eight years later, it remains a major sticking point in the relations between India and Pakistan. Speeches by the two men who best articulated the opposing views on how Kashmir should be integrated with India have been excerpted here. India's first Prime Minister, Jawaharlal Nehru, gives a detailed account of the situation leading up to 1952, when the Delhi Agreement, a pact between the Indian and Kashmiri governments, was signed, formalizing the state's special status. The speech summarizes the international complications as well as the arrangements that had to be made between Kashmir and India regarding the future Constitution of Kashmir, underscoring the need for Article 370 in the Indian Constitution, a provision that defined the special relationship between Jammu and Kashmir and the Union of India. Then Nehru's foremost critic on the subject, BJS founder, Syama Prasad Mookerjee, effectively counters his arguments for the insertion of Article 370 in the Constitution. Sixty-seven years later, when Mookerjee's political heirs in the BJP abrogated Article 370, Ghulam Nabi Azad – at the time a senior Congress leader – made a moving speech opposing its revocation.

The book concludes on a sombre note, with 'Death, Disease and Famine'. In this section, a princess weighs in on whether a law should be enacted to prevent those certified as insane from having children; a Communist talks about 'hunger and death ... stalking various parts of the country'; and a Socialist speaks on behalf of the people about the devastating impact of the Covid pandemic.

As I trawled through the Parliament Digital Library, what struck me was not just the gradual waning of research that had gone into the crafting of the speeches –

and none of this had anything to do with ideology. Simultaneously, if earlier sharp differences on the floor of the House were expressed in a civilized fashion, gradually, the tone and tenor of some of the speeches became distinctly unparliamentary.

In the early decades, whether it was Nehru or his ideological adversaries like Syama Prasad Mookerjee, J.B. Kripalani or Ram Manohar Lohia, they had all clearly worked hard to place their world view before Parliament. Over the years, the number of MPs who were putting in that kind of work into their speeches has diminished. When I first began to cover Parliament in 1987, I recall that the study nooks set amidst the bookshelves in the Reading Room in the old Parliament House – earlier the Princes' Chamber, where the 102 emblems of the erstwhile Princely States, rimming the ceiling, remain reminders of a princely past – would be full of MPs researching and prepping for upcoming debates. Over the years, their numbers dwindled. Then, in 2002, a new Library Building was built: it has a superb collection of books and archival material. But not too many MPs use it even though its staff is very helpful. Of course, even today, there are some MPs who research their speeches diligently – and it shows.

Simultaneously, the increasing diversity in the two Houses and growth in political competition, has ensured a change in the sort of speeches made. Many MPs now often rely on folklore, mythology and rustic humour to bolster their arguments. Competing with the heirs of the patricians of old are the new subaltern voices. And then there are speeches that one might expect to hear at a public rally rather than on the floor of Parliament.

In India's pursuit of democracy, Parliament has made space for new voices, different kinds of voices and the speeches reflect that change, not just in subjects and priorities but also in the use of language.

Indeed, in my over three decades of covering Parliament, perhaps nothing brought home as sharply the changes that were taking place, as the sight, one day, of Saleem Sherwani and Phoolan Devi seated together in the Lok Sabha, engaged in what looked like a serious conversation.

Sherwani is the good-looking scion of an aristocratic Muslim landed family, a family friend of the Gandhis, an industrialist, hotelier and overseer of charitable works, twice a central minister and part of Delhi's glamorous page-three party-going set. Phoolan Devi, on the other hand, belonged to the lowly fisherfolk caste of Mallahs. She had battled all her life against the humble circumstances she had sprung from. Before she was murdered in 2001, she had looked poverty, oppression and rape squarely in the face and then turned dacoit to overcome those circumstances and endured a jail sentence.

It is unlikely that two persons from such widely divergent social backgrounds would have ever met – and, at any rate, not on terms of equality – had they not both been elected on the Samajwadi Party (SP) ticket to the eleventh and thirteenth Lok Sabhas.

That, for me, was the magic of Parliament: that unlike virtually any other forum in India, it is truly representative of the many linguistic, economic, religious and caste groups that populate the country. It may not be perfect, but it has a greater legitimacy than anything else in ruling on the public good.

In Phoolan Devi's case, she was unlettered, but she had 'a Ph.D. in life', Saroj Dubey, a Rajya Sabha MP, once told me after both went to Lucknow together as part of a team of MPs studying the condition of women prisoners. 'She was the one who asked the most searching questions. We were taken in by what the jail authorities were telling us but not Phoolan,' recalled Dubey. Indeed, she was an exemplary MP, learning much faster than many of her educated colleagues the art of posing questions related to her constituency and how to connect with MPs raising issues of interest to her constituents.

Parliament's importance lies in it providing an institutionalized context for discussion by people who do not just represent all sections of the people across the country but have reached that forum through an election. Their words and opinions have a greater legitimacy than those of the many other groups that have sprung up outside claiming to represent the people. Only elected MPs can truly claim to be the voice of the people.

The speeches included in this selection are, therefore, intended to give readers not just a sense of the major issues that our Parliamentarians have deliberated on for close to eight decades, spread across two centuries, but also, wherever possible, to reflect the just mentioned change in representation. But I am deeply conscious that the speeches in this book still represent a mere fraction of the total. I can only hope that this book will whet the readers' appetite for more – and will inspire them to check out the Parliament Digital Library.

I am also conscious that the speeches selected have been refracted through the lens of someone who lived through and covered the second half of those seventy-eight years.

Individuals as different in personality and world view as Rajiv Gandhi, V.P. Singh, Chandrashekhar, P.V. Narasimha Rao, H.D. Deve Gowda, Inder Kumar Gujral, Atal Behari Vajpayee, Manmohan Singh and Narendra Modi occupied the prime minister's seat during my stint as a Parliamentary correspondent.

A day – occasionally, even stretching into the early hours of the morning – spent in either of the two Houses was both an education and an entertainment. I would write daily on the proceedings when Parliament was in session: at the *Times of India*, I also did a weekly column, and many of those memories are still fresh in my mind.

The years when I covered Parliament were marked by epoch-making political changes. The V.P. Singh-led National Front (NF) government came to power in 1989, taking the BJP from two to over eighty seats in Parliament, thus marking the first real stirrings of a challenge to the Congress. In the decade that followed, two other events would fundamentally transform – in very different ways – the India that had won independence in 1947.

The process of economic liberalization and globalization – set in motion between 1991 and 1996 by the Narasimha Rao-led Congress government – changed India forever, creating an impatient, aspirational middle class, obsessed with its own well-being and improvement.

Simultaneously, the destruction of the Babri Masjid in Uttar Pradesh's Faizabad district on 6 December 1992 nudged the BJP even closer to the political centre-stage and led to the rise of Hindutva – an ideology that challenges many of the premises on which the Indian Republic was built. These economic and social changes led to a churning within society that was reflected in the conversations on the floor of Parliament.

That decade of the 1990s also witnessed the rise of subaltern politics, with Lalu Prasad Yadav, Mulayam Singh Yadav and Mayawati – the leaders of the Rashtriya Janata Dal (RJD), the Samajwadi Party (SP) and the Bahujan Samaj Party (BSP) – setting the political and social agendas in Bihar and Uttar Pradesh respectively. Those two states sent as many as 139 MPs to the Lok Sabha till the end of 2000, after which Uttarakhand and Jharkhand came into being. Even now, they send a collective 120 MPs to the Lok Sabha.

A majority of the representatives of these parties – the BSP, the RJD and the SP – belonged to sections of society that had long been suppressed, and the electoral upheavals that placed them in Parliament also placed them in the spotlight.

The Congress also had to contend with another national party, the BJP, which came to power at the head of the National Democratic Alliance (NDA) and remained in power between 1998 and 2004. Not just that, these two national parties had to deal with a range of largely regional parties snapping at their heels, and presenting new agendas and proffering new ideological convictions.

The idiom changed and politics became more competitive, as it suited those in the Opposition not to give the government of the day much time to state its case in Parliament or to inform the public about its achievements, legitimize its policies or demonstrate its leadership.

Faced with a hostile Opposition, uncooperative allies and an increasingly fractious environment, the Congress-led United Progressive Alliance government (2004–14) – like its predecessor, the BJP-led NDA under Vajpayee (1998–2004)

– retaliated by concentrating on the essentials, pushing through financial business and key laws.

Discussions among political parties continued to take place, but increasingly, these were private meetings between the government's parliamentary managers and Opposition leaders, the former trying to persuade and offering carrots, the latter seeking their pound of flesh. The two sides struck 'out-of-house' deals and, in the process, sacrificed the debates on the floor of the two Houses that are the heartbeat of democracy. With the focus shifting to deal-making outside the House, Parliament became barely functional and the number of laws being passed shrank.

While I was a witness to all this, the deterioration in Parliamentary practices began long before 2014. Unfortunately, these tendencies have only intensified in the years since then.

In the first decade after Independence, the first Lok Sabha Speaker, G.D. Mavalankar, even admonished Nehru for taking recourse to ordinances – which would later be ratified by Parliament – rather than bringing them to the House first, for instance. Of course, these were the early years, when everything was new. Later, when Indira Gandhi as prime minister imposed Emergency, concentrating powers in the Prime Minister's Secretariat rather than in the Cabinet, Parliament itself weakened.

With the arrival of the Narendra Modi-led BJP government in 2014, the easy conviviality outside the Houses that had earlier marked relations between MPs of opposing parties began to vanish.

The practice of sending controversial and complicated Bills to parliamentary committees – on which all political parties are represented – for detailed discussions to iron out differences has also been virtually abandoned.

To ensure that a Bill cannot be challenged in the Rajya Sabha, the BJP began the practice of labelling contentious Bills as Money Bills even though they may not qualify as such.

Those who only read newspaper accounts of what happens in Parliament – or at best watch the sanitized debates on Lok Sabha TV or Rajya Sabha TV – often blame the Opposition of the day for not spending enough time in discussion, not realizing that that is not entirely in their hands. The Chairs – the speaker of the Lok Sabha and the chairman of the Rajya Sabha – are supreme in the two Houses. The speaker, for instance, certifies whether a Bill can be labelled a Money Bill. Secondly, if the Opposition demands a discussion on a particular subject under a Parliamentary Rule that entails voting, the Chairs can decide whether the discussion should be permitted at all, and, if so, under which Parliamentary Rule. There are discussions that entail no voting; some that entail voting but where a defeat of the government amounts to censure by the House, not loss of government; and finally, there are votes of confidence where a defeat would lead to a collapse of the government.

In the old Lok Sabha, the Press, undoubtedly, had the best seats, facing the MPs. As a journalist, if you were attentive, you could spot not just every frown or smile on the faces of the MPs who were seated in an arc – with the Speaker facing them – but also observe the forging of friendships across the aisle and the blooming of fresh alliances across the House. I often wished I had developed the facility of being a lip-reader since I would have gleaned even more!

Body language and simply noting who was chatting with whom was often enough to give experienced journalists a clue as to the direction of political cross-currents. I recall once asking a Biju Janata Dal MP whether one of his colleagues was planning to leave the party: 'How did you know that? Very few people know,' he asked, looking surprised. And I said, 'I have been watching him from above.' He laughed and said, 'I guess we need to be careful what we do in the House.'

If the government was not sure of its numbers before an impending vote – whether that related to a Constitutional Amendment, a debate under a parliamentary rule in which a defeat would amount to a censure, or a no-confidence motion, where a loss would result in the fall of the government – it would not be unusual to see the Parliamentary Affairs Minister of the day and the ruling party Whips scurrying across the House to the Opposition benches, to make one last, fervent appeal for support.

One such occasion was 22 July 2008 when the Congress-led United Progressive Alliance (UPA) government faced its first confidence vote after the Left Front withdrew support to it over the India–US nuclear deal. Excitement was at an all-time high, with rumours of skulduggery swirling around the House.

The UPA had 226 MPs, of which 153 were from the Congress. But it needed another forty-six to win the motion in a House of 543. The Opposition, the National Democratic Alliance (NDA), on the other hand, had 170 MPs that included the BJP's 129. The UPA managers reached out to Mulayam Singh Yadav's Samajwadi Party, through his lieutenant, Amar Singh; his party had thirty-nine MPs.

Meanwhile, inside the House, there was high drama: three BJP MPs – Ashok Argal, Faggan Singh Kulaste and Mahaveer Bhagora – had stood up, waved bundles of cash in the House and accused the government of trying to buy their votes. This was the call for the BJP to rise en masse to demand the resignation of the Manmohan Singh government.

Offline – outside in the corridors – since the morning there had been 'talk' of video-taped evidence of the actual transaction, in which a senior Congress leader had apparently handed over the money to the three MPs in the lobby of a well-known five-star hotel situated close to Parliament House. To add to the excitement, there was news that a leading TV channel was going to play it just as the vote would take place in the House. As the hour approached and confusion reigned in the House, I recall stepping out at around 5 p.m. The first person I bumped into outside was a senior representative of that very channel. But he looked distraught, dishevelled, his shirt tails hanging out. To my question as to what time the incriminating video would be played, he just shook his head and muttered that no faces could be recognized on it. Apparently, the promised footage turned out to be too dark to incriminate anyone.

The vote went through and the UPA won the motion with 275 votes, three more than required; the NDA secured 256, and ten of their MPs, including five from the BJP, abstained. Those who voted for the government included thirty-two of the thirty-nine SP MPs, with the remaining seven voting against it. Four Opposition MPs, too, crossvoted for the UPA – they included two from the BJP, one from the Janata Dal-United and one from the Biju Janata Dal. Those who voted that day – on both sides of the floor – included MPs hauled out of sick beds and prison cells. It was a touch-and-go affair.

For journalists, of course, the action was always both 'onstage' and 'offstage', with time spent as much in the Press Gallery as in the offices of the Minister for Parliamentary Affairs, the Minister of State in the Prime Minister's Office or at those of the major political parties.

Till 2014, access wasn't a problem: although clearly some ministers and politicians were more inclined to talk than others. Of the political parties, the Janata Dal, the Telugu Desam Party (in its early days) kept an open house; even the BJP in the Vajpayee–Advani days would happily grant access to journalists.

Srikant Jena as the United Front (UF)'s Parliamentary Affairs Minister, literally, kept 'Open House', even permitting journalists to use his room to rest in. Three of his successors, Pramod Mahajan (in Vajpayee's government), Priya Ranjan Das Munsi and Pawan Kumar Bansal and Minister of State in the Prime Minister's Office Prithviraj Chavan (all in Dr Manmohan Singh's government) were also comparatively open.

In cases where it was less easy to gain entry, journalists resorted to the principle of strength in numbers. If you wanted a one-on-one interview with a minister, you took the official route. But when you needed some instant clarification on a government policy or something that had happened in the House, you went collectively to meet a minister.

Our collective visits to the room of Pranab Mukherjee – a Congress stalwart who had in his long political career held key ministerial portfolios and ended as president of India – almost always followed the same pattern. There would be some initial back and forth; eventually, we would be invited to enter the room. Once in, we would sit or stand in silence for at least five minutes, while Mukherjee remained deeply absorbed in his files. He would finally look up, as though surprised that his room had filled up. Then one brave soul would ask a question – the more tentative and apologetic it sounded, the greater the chance of a reply! A few more questions, the tea would arrive and everyone would relax – but what you had heard was held to be the true voice of the government.

And then there was Central Hall.

If that historic chamber – its walls hung with portraits of those who participated in the freedom struggle – is best known for being the site of the Transfer of Power in 1947, it is also where the president used to address the Joint Session of both Houses of Parliament, with journalists seated in the galleries that overlook the chamber. It is where the Constitution was drafted, the national anthem and tricolour adopted. It was central to the struggle for freedom.

Circular in shape, the three-storey high Central Hall has a distinctive dome, ninety-eight feet in diameter. The doors that lead off Central Hall, furnished with benches upholstered in green leather, open into the central courtyard and to corridors that end in the Old Library, the Lok Sabha or the Rajya Sabha. A smoking nook and a room for women MPs to take a break between sittings, if they wished to, were also carved out of Central Hall.

Over the years, Central Hall was also where MPs would take a break between debates, confabulate, discuss floor strategy and exchange gossip. It occasionally even provided neutral ground to resolve a tricky parliamentary issue when a minister's room appeared too restrictive. A limited number of senior journalists were also issued passes for Central Hall. During my seven years at *The Hindu*, in addition to the access I had to the Press Gallery, I also had a Central Hall Pass.

This was where you got the inside story, where you understood how and why a government policy was being crafted; it was where you could find out who was likely to be the next president; it was where you would learn what the glitches in a new Bill were. Over endless cups of tea – or coffee, if that was your preferred beverage – and hot buttered toast, provided by waiters employed by the Railway Ministry, you learnt what was happening in the backrooms of the world's largest democracy. Retired MPs – who have permanent entry to Central Hall – would come every day during Session to relive the old days and, more importantly from our perspective, help journalists who needed context for what was happening on a particular day.

For journalists of my generation, possibly the most dramatic moment took place in that chamber: the election of Vishwanath Pratap Singh as leader of the National Front, and prime minister, on 1 December 1989. V.P. Singh was the natural choice as that general election had been fought in his name, but that did not deter the other contenders – Devi Lal, who went on to become deputy prime minister and Chandrashekhar, who became prime minister two years later – from throwing their *pagdis* into the ring.

Journalists covering the beat showed up at Parliament House that day to find themselves staring at the doors of Central Hall – all barred. I don't know quite how it happened, but perhaps it was the mood of the moment, a heady mixture of hope and excitement, a belief in a new dawn and an end to corruption. Naïve, but there it was. We banged on the doors together and shouted to be let in – and lo and behold – the doors parted and we entered the holy precincts of Central Hall, the first time for a majority amongst us. The still photographers scrambled in, too – thankfully, there were no TV journalists at the time. One journalist actually scrambled up and climbed on to the chair of state, which is reserved for the president of India, to get a better view of the chamber; a member of the Watch and Ward staff looked on benevolently, merely saying: '*Yeh aapka din hain!*' (This is your day). Quite unimaginable today. And then I looked down: the carpet was a sea of empty Fuji, Kodak, Ilford and Orwo cartons that photographers had tossed onto it in their haste to load yet another roll of film in their cameras.

Then the drama unfolded. At the meeting of the Janata Dal Parliamentary Board, V.P. Singh proposed Devi Lal's name for prime minister, Chandrashekhar seconded it and Madhu Dandavate, the presiding officer, accepted it, as there were no other nominations. Then came the surprise: Devi Lal rose to thank V.P. Singh, but said he preferred to remain the Tau (Uncle) of Haryana, and proposed V.P. Singh's name instead. Dandavate immediately accepted the proposal, and Central Hall rang with the cheers of the MPs gathered there. The third contender, Chandrashekhar, was left fuming but helpless.

As we journalists rushed to get first responses from the leaders, the one that still rings in my ears was that of Surendra Mohan, one of our tallest Socialist leaders: 'Whatever else we cannot promise you, we promise you open government, and lots of stories.' But as Sir Arnold Robinson, the Cabinet Secretary, in 'Open Government', an episode in the popular BBC serial *Yes, Minister*, tells his junior – 'You can be open – or you can have government.'

In 11 months, the V.P. Singh government fell.

For the basic staff of Parliament House – and that included those who maintained the security, ensured the cleanliness of this vast building, cooked and served meals, and oversaw the libraries and museum – the work may have increased during the sessions, but this was their home. But for MPs and journalists, the first day of session was like the first day of term in school or college, with people greeting each other warmly, looking forward to being under the same roof, for five days a week, for the next month or months. During session-time, most governmental work tended to take place in Parliament House, as each minister and political party had an office on the premises, its size and location depending on the importance of the ministerial portfolio/number of MPs a particular party had. The news agencies, the Press Trust of India and the United News of India had offices on the first floor, close to the entrance to the Speakers' Gallery (where the Speaker's guests sat) and the Lok Sabha Press Gallery.

The chaiwallah who stood outside the offices of the two agencies dispensing tea was an institution. Over the years, he grew to know which of his daily customers liked milk and sugar in their tea and those who didn't. It was also the 'unofficial' spot for gathering or imparting news. MPs, and at times, even ministers – trying to look as though they had 'accidentally' chanced upon a throng of journalists – would stop by to ensure that what they had said on the floor of the House would be reported 'accurately'; some 'background' would be thrown in for additional clarity. It was also where journalists cross-checked quotes and information with each other.

While many non-journalists – even non-beat reporters – find it hard to believe that journalists exchange information, they do: in my days, it was part of 'the camaraderie of the beat'. 'Scoops' and 'special stories' were sacred, but the daily reports were more often than not a collective effort: our perspectives may have been different but what was filed was often enriched by our colleagues on the beat. There was a collegial feel to it.

In my early years as a parliamentary reporter, we were also permitted to have lunch in the dining rooms on the first floor, paying for our meals just as we did in Central Hall, and share a table with the MPs. There was an extensive menu and the dishes served reminded me of the kind of food served in the dining cars of trains when I was a child, a mix of Anglo-Indian and Indian fare – not surprising given that the food came from the catering service of the Indian Railways. We didn't realize what a privilege it was to dine at the MPs' dining room till it was taken away during the Vajpayee years, on the pretext that MPs often could not find a place. But my recollection of that period was that the MPs were generally pleased to be able to dispense their point of view to journalists in an informal setting. And when the Houses sat late, continuing till the early hours of the morning on some occasions, dinner was literally on the House.

That Parliament House no longer exists, even though the building still stands and some offices continue to be located within it, a reminder of the past. Its occupants have moved to a new triangular-shaped Parliament House within the same campus. The new complex has no Central Hall and the sense of continuity that it had provided because of its storied history has vanished. The link to the heroes of the freedom struggle, whose portraits stared down at you from its circular wall, has been broken. The neutral ground it provided to resolve difficult issues is gone.

But hopefully, the voices of our MPs, patrician and subaltern, men and women, the voices of courage and resistance, will live on, for some through the printed word, for others more fortunate like me, they will reverberate in our ears. Their voices will survive, beckoning not just to future generations, but also serving as inspiration for MPs, yet to be elected.

Section One

Setting the Stage

1

A New Dawn for India

Jawaharlal Nehru's *'Tryst with Destiny' is undoubtedly one of the greatest speeches of the twentieth century – eloquent, poetic, passionate, full of hope and yet tinged with sadness. But a clutch of noteworthy speeches, not as well known, were made by other stalwarts of the freedom struggle, as the 'midnight hour' approached on 14 August 1947.*

These transport the reader back to the early days of the Republic and the historic moments, when the sacrifices made by those who won India its independence were remembered. The fears, apprehensions and hopes of what might follow as India marched forward as a newly minted democracy, indeed the world's largest democracy, were also articulated.

Mahatma Gandhi was not physically present in the Central Hall of Parliament on the occasion. He was fasting in distant Calcutta in an effort to end the Hindu–Muslim violence that had broken out. But his role in the freedom struggle was recalled in these speeches.

Dr Rajendra Prasad*, India's first President, spoke first;* ***Jawaharlal Nehru****, the country's first Prime Minister, followed him, while* ***Dr Sarvepalli Radhakrishnan****, who would go on to become India's second President, in 1962, made the concluding speech. Sandwiched between Nehru and Radhakrishnan was Chaudhury Khaliquzzaman, a Congressman turned Muslim League member, who had been chosen to represent the Muslim voice in the Constituent Assembly.*

In his speech, Dr Rajendra Prasad exhorted his fellow citizens of free India to contribute to the 'building up of freedom for all and peace among mankind', sent his good wishes to Pakistan and expressed his sadness at the division of India and sent out a much-needed assurance to the minorities.

Nehru, on his part, made a 'pledge of dedication to the service of India and her people and larger cause of humanity'.

Radhakrishnan, describing Indians as 'ready victims' of 'separatist tendencies' asked his newly free countrymen 'to correct our national faults of character, our domestic despotism, our intolerance which has assumed different forms of obscurantism, of narrow-mindedness, of superstitious bigotry'.

Two women also participated in the ceremony that day, Sucheta Kripalani and Hansa Mehta; both had been members of the Constituent Assembly. Sucheta Kripalani would go on to become India's first woman chief minister (Uttar Pradesh). She also represented at different times New Delhi and Gonda in the Lok Sabha. Hansa Mehta was an acclaimed social reformer, feminist, writer and educationist. On the night of 14 August 1947, Sucheta Kripalani sang a few verses of 'Vande Mataram' at the beginning, and at the end the first few lines of two songs – designated as national songs – Iqbal's 'Sare Jahan Se Achcha Hindustan Hamara' and Rabindranath Tagore's 'Jana Gana Mana', the latter to become India's national anthem, while Hansa Mehta presented the National Flag on behalf of the women of India.

RAJENDRA PRASAD

14 August 1947

Build Freedom for All[1]

In this solemn hour of our history when, after many years of struggle, we are taking over the governance of this country, let us offer humble thanks to the Almighty Power that shapes the destinies of men and nations, and let us recall in grateful remembrance the services and sacrifices of all those men and women, known and unknown, who with smiles on their face walked to the gallows or faced bullets on their chests, who experience living death in the cells of the Andamans, or spent long years in the prisons of India, who preferred voluntary exile in foreign countries to a life of humiliation in their own, who not only lost wealth and property but cut themselves off from near and dear ones to devote themselves to the achievement of the great objective which we are witnessing today.

Let us also pay our tribute of love and reverence to Mahatma Gandhi who has been our beacon light, our guide and philosopher during the last thirty years or more. He represents that undying spirit in our culture ... which has kept India alive through vicissitudes of our history. He it is who pulled us out of the slough of despondency and despair and blew into us a spirit which enabled us to stand up for justice to claim our birthright of freedom and placed in our hands the matchless and unfailing weapon of truth and non-violence which, without arms and armaments, has won for us the invaluable prize of Swaraj at a price which, when the history of

[1] Editor's note: This is a translated version of President Rajendra Prasad's speech that was originally made in Hindi.

these times comes to be written, will be regarded as incredible for a vast country of our size and for the teeming millions of our population.

We were indifferent instruments that he had to work with but he led us with consummate skill, with unwavering determination, with an undying faith in our future, with faith in his weapon and above all with faith in God. Let us prove true to that faith. Let us hope that India will not, in the hour of her triumph, give up or minimize the value of the weapon which served not only to rouse and inspire her in her moments of depression but has also proved its efficacy. India has a great part to play in the shaping and moulding of the future of a war-distracted world. She can play that part not by mimicking, from a distance, what others are doing, or by joining in the race for armaments and competing with others in the discovery of the latest and most effective instruments of destruction. She has now the opportunity, and let us hope she will have the courage and strength to place, before the world for its acceptance, her infallible substitute for war and bloodshed, death and destruction. The world needs it and will welcome it, unless it is prepared to reel back into barbarism from which it boasts to have emerged.

Let us then assure all countries of the world that we propose to stick to our historic tradition to be on terms of friendship and amity with all, that we have no designs against any one and hope that none will have any against us. We have only one ambition and desire, that is, to make our contribution to the building up of freedom for all and peace among mankind.

The country, which was made by God and Nature to be one, stands divided today. Separation from near and dear ones, even from strangers after some association, is always painful. I would be untrue to myself if I did not at this moment confess to a sense of sorrow at this separation. But I wish to send on your behalf and my own our greetings and good wishes for success and the best of luck in the high endeavour of the government in which the people of Pakistan which, till today, has been a part and parcel of ourselves, will be engaged. To those who feel like us but are on the other side of the border we send a word of cheer. They should not give way to panic but should stick to their hearths and homes, their religion and culture and cultivate the qualities of courage and forbearance. They have no reason to fear that they will not get protection and just and fair treatment and they should not become victims of doubt and suspicion. They must accept the assurances publicly given and win their rightful place in the polity of the State, where they are placed, by their loyalty.

To all the minorities in India we give the assurance that they will receive fair and just treatment and there will be no discrimination in any form against them. Their religion, their culture and their language are safe and they will enjoy all the rights and privileges of citizenship, and will be expected in their turn to render loyalty to the country in which they live and to its Constitution.

To all we give the assurance that it will be our endeavour to end poverty and squalor and its companions, hunger and disease; to abolish distinction and exploitation and to ensure decent conditions of living. We are embarking on a great task. We hope that in this we shall have the unstinted service and cooperation of all our people and the sympathy and support of all the communities. We shall do our best to deserve it.

After this I propose that we all stand in silence to honour the memory of those who have died in the struggle for freedom in India and elsewhere.

(*The Assembly stood in silence for two minutes.*)

JAWAHARLAL NEHRU

14 August 1947

Tryst with Destiny

Long years ago we made a tryst with destiny, and now the time comes when we shall redeem our pledge, not wholly or in full measure, but very substantially. At the stroke of the midnight hour, when the world sleeps, India will awake to life and freedom. A moment comes, which comes but rarely in history, when we step out from the old to the new, when an age ends, and when the soul of a nation, long suppressed, finds utterance. It is fitting that at this solemn moment, we take the pledge of dedication to the service of India and her people and to the still larger cause of humanity.

At the dawn of history, India started on her unending quest, and trackless centuries are filled with her striving and grandeur of her success and failures. Through good and ill fortune alike, she has never lost sight of that quest, forgotten the ideals which gave her strength. We end today a period of misfortunes and India discovers herself again. The achievement we celebrate today is but a step, an opening of opportunity, to the greater triumphs and achievements that await us. Are we brave enough and wise enough to grasp this opportunity and accept the challenge of the future?

Freedom and power bring responsibility. The responsibility rests upon this Assembly, a sovereign body representing the sovereign people of India. Before the birth of freedom, we have endured all the pains of labour and our hearts are heavy with the memory of this sorrow. Some of those pains continue even now. Nevertheless, the past is over and it is the future that beckons us now.

That future is not one of ease or resting but of incessant striving so that we may fulfil the pledges we have so often taken and the one we shall take today. The service of India means the service of the millions who suffer. It means the ending of poverty and ignorance and disease and inequality of opportunity. The ambition of the greatest man of our generation has been to wipe every tear from every eye. That may be beyond us, but as long as there are tears and suffering, so long our work will not be over.

And so we have to labour and to work, and to work hard, to give reality to our dreams. Those dreams are for India, but they are also for the world, for all the nations and peoples are too closely knit together today for any one of them to imagine that it can live apart. Peace is said to be indivisible, so is freedom, so is prosperity now, and also is disaster in this one world that can no longer be split into isolated fragments.

To the people of India, whose representatives we are, we make an appeal to join us with faith and confidence in this great adventure. This is no time for petty and destructive criticism, no time for ill-will or blaming others. We have to build the noble mansion of free India where all her children may dwell.

I beg to move, Sir, that it be resolved that:

(1) After the last stroke of midnight, all members of the Constituent Assembly present on this occasion, do take the following pledge: 'At this solemn moment when the people of India, through suffering and sacrifice, have secured freedom, I … a member of the Constituent Assembly of India, do dedicate myself in all humility to the service of India and her people to the end that this ancient land attain her rightful place in the world and make her full and willing contribution to the promotion of world peace and the welfare of mankind';

(2) Members who are not present on this occasion do take the pledge (with such verbal changes as the President may prescribe) at the time they next attend a session of the Assembly. (Loud applause.)

SARVEPALLI RADHAKRISHNAN

(United Provinces: General)

14 August 1947

The Body Politic May Be Divided but the Body Historic Lives On

Mr. President, Sir, it is not necessary for me to speak at any great length on this Resolution so impressively moved by Pandit Jawaharlal Nehru and seconded by Mr. Khaliquzzaman. History and legend will grow round this day. It marks a milestone in the march of our democracy. A significant date it is in the drama of the Indian people who are trying to rebuild and transform themselves. Through a long night of waiting, a night full of fateful portents and silent prayers for the dawn of freedom, of haunting spectres of hunger and death, our sentinels kept watch, the lights were burning bright till at last the dawn is breaking, and we greet it with the utmost enthusiasm. When we are passing from a state of slavery and subjection to one of freedom and liberation, it is an occasion for rejoicing. That it is being effected in such an orderly and dignified way is a matter for gratification.

Mr. Attlee spoke with visible pride in the House of Commons when he said that this is the first great instance of a strong Imperialist power transferring its authority to a subject people whom it ruled with force and firmness for nearly two centuries. For a parallel, he cited the British withdrawal from South Africa; but it is nothing comparable in scale and circumstances to the British withdrawal from this country. When we see what the Dutch are doing in Indonesia, when we see how the French are clinging to their possessions, we cannot but admire the political sagacity and courage of the British people. (Cheers.)

We, on our side, have also added a chapter to the history of the World. Look at the way in which subject peoples in history won their freedom. Let us also consider the methods by which power was acquired. How did men like Washington, Napoleon, Cromwell, Lenin, Hitler and Mussolini get into power? Look at the methods of blood and steel, of terrorism and assassination, of bloodshed and anarchy by which these so-called great men of the world came into the possession of power. Here in this land under the leadership of one who will go down in history as perhaps the greatest man of our age (Loud cheers.) we have opposed patience to fury, quietness of spirit to bureaucratic tyranny and are acquiring power through peaceful and civilized methods. What is the result? The transition is being effected with the least bitterness, with utterly no kind of hatred at all. The very fact that we are appointing Lord Mountbatten as the Governor-General of India shows the spirit of understanding and friendliness in which this whole transition is being effected. (Cheers.)

You, Mr. President, referred to the sadness in our hearts, to the sorrow which also clouds our rejoicings. May I say that we are in an essential sense responsible for it also though not entirely. From 1600, Englishmen have come to this country – priests and nuns, merchants and adventurers, diplomats and statesmen, missionaries and idealists. They bought and sold, marched and fought, plotted and profited, helped and healed. The greatest among them wished to modernize the country, to raise its intellectual and moral standards, its political status. They wished to regenerate the whole people. But the small among them worked with sinister objectives. They tried to increase the disunion in the country, made the country poorer, weaker and more disunited. They also have had their chance now. The freedom we are attaining is the fulfilment of this dual tendency among British administrators. While India is attaining freedom, she is attaining it in a manner which does not produce joy in the hearts of people or a radiant smile on their faces. Some of those who were charged with the responsibility for the administration of this country, tried to accentuate communal consciousness and bring about the present result which is a logical outcome of the policies adopted by the lesser minds of Britain. But I would never blame them. Were we not victims, ready victims, so to say, of the separatist tendencies foisted on us? Should we not now correct our national faults of character, our domestic despotism, our intolerance which has assumed the different forms of obscurantism, of narrow-mindedness, of superstitious bigotry? Others were able to play on our weakness[es] because we had them. I would like, therefore, to take this opportunity to call for self-examination, for a searching of hearts. We have gained but we have not gained in the manner we wished to gain and if we have not done so, the responsibility is our own. And when this pledge says that we have to serve our country, we can best serve our country by removing these fundamental defects which have prevented us from gaining the objective of a free and united India. Now that India is divided, it is our duty not to indulge in words of anger. They lead us nowhere … The body politic may be divided but the body historic lives on. (Hear, hear.) Political divisions, physical partitions, are external but the psychological divisions are deeper. The cultural cleavages are the more dangerous. We should not allow them to grow. What we should do is to preserve those cultural ties, those spiritual bonds which knit our peoples together into one organic whole. Patient consideration, slow process of education, adjustment to one another's needs, the discovery of points of view which are common to both the dominions in the matter of Communications, Defence, Foreign Affairs, these are the things which should be allowed to grow in the daily business of life and administration. It is by developing such attitudes that we can once again draw near and gain the lost unity of this country …

Our opportunities are great but let me warn you that when power outstrips ability, we will fall on evil days. We should develop competence and ability which would help us to utilize the opportunities which are now open to us. From tomorrow morning – from midnight today – we cannot throw the blame on the Britisher. We have to assume the responsibility ourselves for what we do. A free India will be judged by the way in which it will serve the interests of the common man in the matter of food, clothing, shelter and the social services. Unless we destroy corruption in high places, root out every trace of nepotism, love of power, profiteering and black marketing which have spoiled the good name of this great country in recent times, we will not be able to raise the standards of efficiency in administration as well as in the production and distribution of the necessary goods of life.

Pandit Jawaharlal Nehru referred to the great contribution which this country will make to the promotion of world peace and the welfare of mankind. The Chakra, the Asokan wheel, which is there in the flag embodies for us a great idea. Asoka, the greatest of our emperors – look at the words of H.G. Wells regarding him, 'Highnesses, Magnificences, Excellencies, Serenities, Majesties – among them all, he shines alone a star – Asoka the greatest of all monarchs.' He cut into rock his message for the healing of discords. If there are differences, the way in which you can solve them is by promoting concord. Concord is the only way by which we can get rid of differences. There is no other method which is open to us.

Samavaya eva Sadhuh.[2]

We are lucky in having for our leader one who is a world citizen, who is essentially a humanist, who possesses a buoyant optimism and robust good sense in spite of the perversity of things and the hostility of human affairs. We see the way in which his Department interfered actively and in a timely manner in the Indonesian dispute. (Loud applause.) It shows that if India gains freedom, that freedom will be used not merely for the well-being of India but for Vishva Kalyana, i.e., world peace, the welfare of mankind.

Our pledge tells us that this ancient land shall attain her rightful and honoured place. We take pride in the antiquity of this land for it is a land which has seen nearly four or five millennia of history. It has passed through many vicissitudes and, at the moment, it stands, still responding to the thrill of the same great ideal. Civilization is a thing of the spirit, it is not something external, solid and mechanical. It is the dream in the people's hearts. It is the inward aspiration of the people's souls. It is the imaginative interpretation of the human life and the perception of the mystery of human existence. That is what civilization actually stands for. We should bear in mind these great ideals which have been transmitted to us across the ages. In this great time of our history we should bear ourselves humbly before God, brace ourselves to this supreme task which is confronting us and conduct ourselves in a manner that is worthy of the ageless spirit of India. If we do so, I have no doubt that the future of this land will be as great as its once glorious past.

Sarvabhutdisahamatmanam
Sarvabhutani catmani
Sampasyam atmayajivai
Saarwjyam adhigachati[3]

Swarajya is the development of that kind of tolerant attitude which sees in brother man the face Divine. Intolerance has been the greatest enemy of our progress. Tolerance of one another's views, thoughts and beliefs is the only remedy

[2] Editor's translation: Concord is good.

[3] Editor's translation: The self-sacrificer attains the universality of the self with all beings and all beings in the self to be worshipped.

that we can possibly adopt. Therefore, I support with very great pleasure this Resolution which asks us as the representatives of the people of India to conduct ourselves in all humility in the service of our country and the word 'Humility' here means that we are by ourselves very insignificant. Our efforts by themselves cannot carry us to a long distance. We should make ourselves dependent on that other than ourselves which makes for righteousness. The note of humility means the unimportance of the individual and the supreme importance of the unfolding purpose which we are called upon to serve. So in a mood of humility, in a spirit of dedication let us take this pledge as soon as the clock strikes 12.

2

A Constitution for the Masses

On 25 November 1949, when the Constituent Assembly of India met in the Constitution Hall of Parliament to have a final debate on the new Constitution, ***Dr Bhimrao Ramji Ambedkar****, Chairman of the Drafting Committee, delivered the closing speech.*

This has since become justly famous as the 'Grammar of Anarchy' speech, and it is a reference point in the evolution of Indian democracy. Ambedkar took on the Constitution's critics, talked of the difficulties that lay ahead in sustaining the independence that had been won at such great cost, expanded on the idea of India as a 'nation' and the ideals of democracy, which the Constitution enshrined.

This brilliant speech resonates even today, especially its statement that 'there can be no justification for … unconstitutional methods' as well as its warning against hero worship – 'Bhakti in religion may be a road to the salvation of the soul. But in politics, bhakti or hero worship is a sure shot road to degradation and to eventual dictatorship.'

It took over two years from Independence to the point where the new Constitution came into effect on 26 January 1950. India would then undertake the most ambitious democratic exercise ever carried out – the first general election (and concurrent state assembly elections). The polling for this took place between 25 October 1951 and 21 February 1952 and, given the Constitution's historic commitment to universal franchise, it gave 173 million voters a chance to pick their representatives.

BHIMRAO RAMJI AMBEDKAR

25 November 1949

Last Speech in the Constituent Assembly

… however good a Constitution may be, it is sure to turn out bad because those who are called to work it, happen to be a bad lot. However bad a Constitution may be, it may turn out to be good if those who are called to work it, happen to be a good lot. The working of a Constitution does not depend wholly upon the nature of the Constitution. The Constitution can provide only the organs of State such as the Legislature, the Executive and the Judiciary.

The factors on which the working of those organs of the State depend are the people and the political parties they will set up as their instruments to carry out their wishes and their politics. Who can say how the people of India and their parties will behave? Will they uphold constitutional methods of achieving their purposes or will they prefer revolutionary methods of achieving them? If they adopt revolutionary methods, however good the Constitution may be, it requires no prophet to say that it will fail. It is, therefore, futile to pass any judgment upon the Constitution without reference to the part which the people and their parties are likely to play.

The condemnation of the Constitution largely comes from two quarters, the Communist Party and the Socialist Party ... The Communist Party wants a Constitution based upon the principle of the Dictatorship of the Proletariat. They condemn the Constitution because it is based upon parliamentary democracy. The Socialists want two things. The first thing they want is that if they come into power, the Constitution must give them the freedom to nationalize or socialize all private property without payment of compensation. The second thing that the Socialists want is that the Fundamental Rights mentioned in the Constitution must be absolute and without any limitations so that if their Party fails to come into power, they would have the unfettered freedom not merely to criticize, but also to overthrow the State ...

I do not say that the principle of no acquisition of private property without compensation is so sacrosanct that there can be no departure from it. I do not say that Fundamental Rights can never be absolute and the limitations set upon them can never be lifted. What I do say is that the principles embodied in the Constitution are the views of the present generation or if you think this to be an overstatement, I say they are the views of the members of the Constituent Assembly. Why blame the Drafting Committee for embodying them in the Constitution? I say why blame even the Members of the Constituent Assembly?

Jefferson, the great American statesman who played so great a part in the making of the American Constitution, has expressed some very weighty views which makers of Constitution can never afford to ignore in one place. He has said: 'We may consider each generation as a distinct nation, with a right, by the will of the majority, to bind themselves, but none to bind the succeeding generation, more than the inhabitants of another country.' In another place, he has said: 'The idea that institutions established for the use of the nation cannot be touched or modified, even to make them answer their end, because of rights gratuitously supposed in those employed to manage them in the trust for the public, may perhaps be a salutary provision against the abuses of a monarch, but is most absurd against the nation itself. Yet our lawyers and priests generally inculcate this doctrine, and suppose that preceding generations held the earth more freely than we do; had a right to impose laws on us, unalterable by ourselves, and that we, in the like manner, can make laws and impose burdens on future generations, which they will have no right to alter; in fine, that the earth belongs to the dead and not the living.'

... what Jefferson has said is not merely true, but is absolutely true ... Had the Constituent Assembly departed from this principle laid down by Jefferson it would certainly be liable to blame, even to condemnation. But I ask, has it? Quite the contrary. One has only to examine the provision relating to the amendment of the Constitution. The Assembly has not only refrained from putting a seal of finality and infallibility upon this Constitution by denying to the people the right to amend the Constitution as in Canada or by making the amendment of the Constitution subject to the fulfilment of extraordinary terms and conditions as in America or Australia, but has provided a most facile procedure for amending the Constitution.

... Those who are dissatisfied with the (Indian) Constitution have only to obtain a two-thirds majority and if they cannot obtain even a two-thirds majority in the parliament elected on adult franchise in their favour, dissatisfaction with the Constitution cannot be deemed to be shared by the general public.

There is only one point of constitutional import to which I propose to make a reference. A serious complaint is made on the ground that there is too much ... centralization and that the 162 States have been reduced to Municipalities. It is clear that this view is not only an exaggeration, but is also founded on a misunderstanding of what exactly the Constitution contrives to do. As to the relation between the Centre and the States, it is necessary to bear in mind the fundamental principle on which it rests. The basic principle of Federalism is that the Legislative and Executive authority is partitioned between the Centre and the States not by any law to be made by the Centre but by the Constitution itself. This is what the Constitution does. The States under our Constitution are in no way dependent upon the Centre for their legislative or executive authority. The Centre and the States are co-equal in this matter. It is difficult to see how such a Constitution can be called centralism.

It may be that the Constitution assigns to the Centre too large a field for the operation of its legislative and executive authority than is to be found in any other federal Constitution. It may be that the residuary powers are given to the Centre and not to the States. But these features do not form the essence of federalism. The chief mark of federalism as I said lies in the partition of the legislative and executive authority between the Centre and the Units by the Constitution ... It is, therefore, wrong to say that the States have been placed under the Centre. Centre cannot by its own will alter the boundary of that partition. Nor can the Judiciary. ... Courts may modify, they cannot replace. They can revise earlier interpretations as new arguments, new points of view are presented, they can shift the dividing line in marginal cases, but there are barriers they cannot pass, definite assignments of power they cannot reallocate. They can give a broadening construction of existing powers, but they cannot assign to one authority powers explicitly granted to another. The first charge of centralization defeating federalism must therefore fall. The second charge is that the Centre has been given the power to override the States. This charge must be admitted, but before condemning the Constitution for containing such overriding powers, certain considerations must be borne in mind. The first is that these overriding powers do not form the normal feature of the Constitution. Their use and operation are expressly confined to emergencies only. The second consideration is: could we avoid giving overriding powers to the Centre when an emergency has arisen?

Those who do not admit the justification for such overriding powers to the Centre even in an emergency, do not seem to have a clear idea of the problem which lies at the root of the matter. The problem is so clearly set out by a writer in that well-known magazine *The Round Table* in its issue of December 1935 that I offer no apology for quoting the following extract from it. Says the writer: 'Political systems are a complex of rights and duties resting ultimately on the question, to whom, or to what authority does the citizen owe allegiance. In normal affairs the question is not present, for the law works smoothly, and a man goes about his business obeying one authority in this set of matters and another authority in that. But in a moment of crisis, a conflict of claims may arise, and it is then apparent that ultimate allegiance cannot be divided. The issue of allegiance cannot be determined in the last resort by a juristic interpretation of statutes. The law must conform to the facts or so much the worse for the law.'

When all formalism is stripped away, the bare question is, what authority commands the residual loyalty of the citizen? Is it the Centre or the Constituent State? The solution of this problem depends upon one's answer to this question which is the crux of the problem. There can be no doubt that in the opinion of the vast majority of the people, the residual loyalty of the citizen in an emergency must be to the Centre and not to the Constituent States. For it is only the Centre which can work for a common end and for the general interests of the country as a whole. Herein lies the justification for giving to the Centre certain overriding powers to be used in an emergency. And after all, what is the obligation imposed upon the Constituent States by these emergency powers? No more than this – that in an emergency, they should take into consideration alongside their own local interests, the opinions and interests of the nation as a whole. Only those who have not understood the problem, can complain against it.

Here I could have ended. But my mind is so full of the future of our country that I feel I ought to take this occasion to give expression to some of my reflections thereon. On 26th January 1950, India will be an independent country. What would happen to her independence? Will she maintain her independence or will she lose it again? This is the first thought that comes to my mind. It is not that India was never an independent country. The point is that she once lost the independence she had. Will she lose it a second time? It is this thought which makes me most anxious for the future.

What perturbs me greatly is the fact that not only India has once before lost her independence, but she lost it by the infidelity and treachery of some of her own people. In the invasion of Sind by Muhammad-bin-Qasim, the military commanders of King Dahar accepted bribes from the agents of Muhammad-bin-Qasim and refused to fight on the side of their King. It was Jaichand who invited Muhammad Ghori to invade India and fight against Prithvi Raj and promised him the help of himself and the Solanki kings. When Shivaji was fighting for the liberation of Hindus, the other Maratha noblemen and the Rajput kings were fighting the battle on the side of Moghul Emperors. When the British were trying to destroy the Sikh rulers, Gulab Singh, their principal commander, sat silent and did not help to save the Sikh kingdom. In 1857, when a large part of India had declared a war of independence against the British, the Sikhs stood and watched the event as silent spectators. Will history repeat itself? It is this thought which fills me with anxiety.

This anxiety is deepened by the realization of the fact that in addition to our old enemies in the form of castes and creeds we are going to have many political parties with diverse and opposing political creeds. Will Indians place the country above their creed or will they place creed above country? I do not know. But this much is certain that if the parties place creed above country, our independence will be put in jeopardy a second time and probably be lost for ever. This eventuality we must all resolutely guard against. We must be determined to defend our independence with the last drop of our blood.

On the 26th of January 1950, India would be a democratic country in the sense that India from that day would have a government of the people, by the people and for the people ... What would happen to her democratic Constitution? Will she be able to maintain it or will she lose it again? This is the second thought that comes to my mind and makes me as anxious as the first. It is not that India did not know what is democracy. There was a time when India was studded with republics, and even where there were monarchies, they were either elected or limited. They were never absolute. It is not that India did not know Parliaments or Parliamentary Procedure. A study of the Buddhist Bhikshu Sanghas disclosed that not only there were Parliaments – for the Sanghas were nothing but Parliaments, but the Sanghas knew and observed all the rules of Parliamentary Procedure known to modern times. They had rules regarding seating arrangements, rules regarding Motions, Resolutions, Quorum, Whip, Counting of Votes, Voting by Ballot, Censure Motion, Regularization, Res Judicata, etc. Although these rules of Parliamentary Procedure were applied by the Buddha to the meetings of the Sanghas, he must have borrowed them from the rules of the Political Assemblies functioning in the country in his time. This democratic system India lost. Will she lose it a second time? I do not know. But it is quite possible in a country like India – where democracy from its long disuse must be regarded as something quite new – there is danger of democracy giving place to dictatorship. It is quite possible for this newborn democracy to retain its form but give place to dictatorship in fact. If there is a landslide, the danger of the second possibility becoming actuality is much greater.

If we wish to maintain democracy not merely in form, but also in fact, what must we do? The first thing in my judgment we must do is to hold fast to constitutional methods of achieving our social and economic objectives. It means we must abandon the bloody methods of revolution. It means that we must abandon the method of civil disobedience, non-cooperation and satyagraha. When there was no way left for constitutional methods for achieving economic and social objectives, there was a great deal of justification for unconstitutional methods. But where constitutional methods are open, there can be no justification for these unconstitutional methods. These methods are nothing but the Grammar of Anarchy and the sooner they are abandoned, the better for us.

The second thing we must do is to observe the caution which John Stuart Mill has given to all who are interested in the maintenance of democracy, namely, not 'to lay their liberties at the feet of even a great man, or to trust him with powers which enable him to subvert their institutions'. There is nothing wrong in being grateful to great men who have rendered life-long services to the country. But there are limits to gratefulness. As has been well said by the Irish Patriot Daniel O'Connell, 'No man can be grateful at the cost of his honour, no woman can be grateful at the cost of her chastity and no nation can be grateful at the cost of its liberty.'

This caution is far more necessary in the case of India than in the case of any other country. For in India, Bhakti or what may be called the path of devotion or hero-worship, plays a part in its politics unequaled in magnitude by the part it plays in the politics of any other country in the world. Bhakti in religion may be a road to the salvation of the soul. But in politics, Bhakti or hero-worship is a sure road to degradation and to eventual dictatorship.

The third thing we must do is not to be content with mere political democracy. We must make our political democracy a social democracy as well. Political democracy cannot last unless there lies at the base of it social democracy. What does social democracy mean? It means a way of life which recognizes liberty, equality and fraternity as the principles of life. These principles … are not to be treated as separate items in a trinity. They form a union of trinity in the sense that to divorce one from the other is to defeat the very purpose of democracy. Liberty cannot be divorced from equality, equality cannot be divorced from liberty. Nor can liberty and equality be divorced from fraternity. Without equality, liberty would produce the supremacy of the few over the many. Equality without liberty would kill individual initiative. Without fraternity, liberty and equality could not become a natural course of things. It would require a constable to enforce them.

We must begin by acknowledging the fact that there is complete absence of two things in Indian Society. One of these is equality. On the social plane, we have in India a society based on the principle of graded inequality which means elevation for some and degradation for others. On the economic plane, we have a society in which there are some who have immense wealth as against many who live in abject poverty. On the 26th of January 1950, we are going to enter into a life of contradictions. In politics we will have equality and in social and economic life we will have inequality. In politics we will be recognizing the principle of one man one vote and one vote one value. In our social and economic life, we shall, by reason of our social and economic structure, continue to deny the principle of one man one value.

How long shall we continue to live this life of contradictions? How long shall we continue to deny equality in our social and economic life? If we continue to deny it for long, we will do so only by putting our political democracy in peril. We must remove this contradiction at the earliest possible moment or else those who suffer from inequality will blow up the structure of political democracy which this Assembly has so laboriously built up. The second thing we want is recognition of the principle of fraternity. What does fraternity mean? Fraternity means a sense of common brotherhood of all Indians – Indians being one people. It is the principle which gives unity and solidarity to social life. It is a difficult thing to achieve.

… I am of the opinion that in believing that we are a nation, we are cherishing a great delusion. How can people divided into several thousands of castes be a nation? The sooner we realize that we are not as yet a nation in the social and psychological sense of the word, the better for us. For then only we shall realize the necessity of becoming a nation and seriously think of ways and means of realizing the goal. The realization of this goal is going to be very difficult – far more difficult than it has been in the United States. The United States has no caste problem. In India there are castes. The castes are anti-national. In the first place because they bring about separation in social life. They are anti-national also because they generate jealousy and antipathy between caste and caste. But we must overcome all these difficulties if we wish to become a nation in reality. For fraternity can be a fact only when there is a nation.

Without fraternity, equality and liberty will be no deeper than coats of paint. These are my reflections about the tasks that lie ahead of us. They may not be very pleasant to some. But there can be no gainsaying that political power in this country has too long been the monopoly of a few and the many are not only beasts of burden, but also beasts of prey. This monopoly has not merely deprived them of their chance of betterment, it has sapped them of what may be called the significance of life. These downtrodden classes are tired of being governed. They are impatient to govern themselves. This urge for self-realization in the downtrodden classes must not be allowed to devolve into a class struggle or class war. It would lead to a division of the House. That would indeed be a day of disaster.

For, as has been well said by Abraham Lincoln, 'a House divided against itself cannot stand very long'. Therefore the sooner room is made for the realization of their aspiration, the better for the few, the better for the country, the better for the maintenance of its independence and the better for the continuance of its democratic structure. This can only be done by the establishment of equality and fraternity in all spheres of life. That is why I have laid so much stress on them.

... If we wish to preserve the Constitution in which we have sought to enshrine the principle of Government of the people, for the people and by the people, let us resolve not to be tardy in the recognition of the evils that lie across our path and which induce people to prefer Government for the people to Government by the people, nor to be weak in our initiative to remove them. That is the only way to serve the country. I know of no better.

Section Two

The Dragon in the Room

1

India Gets a Bloody Nose

After several years of increasingly violent border disputes, China invaded Ladakh and the North East Frontier Agency (or NEFA as Arunachal Pradesh was then known) on 20 October 1962. Apart from numerical superiority, China was better armed and equipped, and it made rapid advances, taking over much of the territory it claimed. Then, on 20 November 1962, China announced a unilateral ceasefire, and withdrew to what is now called the Line of Actual Control (LAC). Part of the fallout from this war was a reworking of India's geopolitical stances; the Soviet Union had been more supportive than the Western democracies in terms of providing arms as well as in its diplomatic efforts on India's behalf.

*Prime Minister **Jawaharlal Nehru** rose in Parliament on 8 November 1962, to seek the assent of the two Houses for the Emergency that had been declared by the President in the wake of defeat in the Indo-China war. This was possibly the lowest point in his tenure.*

The discussion in the Lok Sabha went on for several days and saw a record 165 MPs speaking on the subject. While both sides of the House supported the government's imposition of Emergency, Nehru was pilloried for his apparent blindness in not being able to see through the real intentions of the Chinese. In the speech given here, he answers his interlocutors, admitting his mistakes, underscoring the fact that the newly independent country was still grappling with the securing of arms and ammunition, and defends his preference for non-alignment in foreign policy and also his relationships with his Communist friends. There were multiple interruptions during the speech, and the then Speaker, Sardar Hukam Singh, had to quell these disturbances.

*The second speech from the same debate is that of **Umashankar Muljibhai Trivedi**, who left the Indian National Congress in 1951 to join the Bharatiya Jana Sangh. Trivedi, a barrister by training, was, along with Syama Prasad Mookerjee and Durga Charan Banerjee, among the three Jana Sangh members elected to the first Lok Sabha. He was with Mookerjee on his fateful visit to Kashmir. When the latter was detained, he moved a habeas corpus petition in the Kashmir High Court in Srinagar, but before it could be heard came the news of Mookerjee's death in confinement.*

Trivedi makes a powerful speech here, his arguments underscoring his party's hostility to Pakistan, Muslims and Communists, traits seen in the Jana Sangh's successor, the BJP.

JAWAHARLAL NEHRU

(Lok Sabha: Phulpur)

Lok Sabha: 8 November 1962

On Resolution Regarding the Proclamation of Emergency and Aggression by China

Mr. Speaker, Sir, I beg to move: 'This House approves the Proclamation of Emergency issued by the President on the 26th of October, 1962, under clause (1) of article 352 of the Constitution.'

Mr. Speaker: I shall place it before the House.

Resolution moved: 'This House approves the Proclamation of Emergency issued by the President on the 26th of October, 1962, under clause (1) of article 352 of the Constitution.' The Hon'ble Prime Minister may move the other resolution also.

Jawaharlal Nehru: I beg to move: 'This House notes with deep regret that in spite of the uniform gestures of goodwill and friendship by India towards the People's Government of China on the basis of recognition of each other's independence, non-aggression and non-interference, and peaceful coexistence, China has betrayed this goodwill and friendship and the principles of Panchsheel which had been agreed to between the two countries and has committed aggression and initiated a massive invasion of India by her armed forces. This House places on record its high appreciation of the valiant struggle of men and officers of our armed forces while defending our frontiers.

Several Hon'ble Members: Hear, hear.

Jawaharlal Nehru: ... and pays its respectful homage to the martyrs who have laid down their lives in defending the honour and integrity of our Motherland. This House also records its profound appreciation of the wonderful and spontaneous response of the people of India to the emergency and the crisis that has resulted from China's invasion of India. It notes with deep gratitude this mighty upsurge amongst all sections of our people for harnessing all our resources towards the organization of an all-out effort to meet this grave national emergency. The flame of liberty and sacrifice has been kindled anew and a fresh dedication has taken place to the cause of India's freedom and integrity.

This House gratefully acknowledges 'the sympathy and the moral and material support received from a large number of friendly countries in this grim hour of our struggle against aggression and invasion. With hope and faith, this House affirms the firm resolve of the Indian people to drive out the aggressor from the sacred soil of India, however long and hard the struggle may be.'

Mr. Speaker: I place this Resolution also before the House. Resolution moved: …

Jawaharlal Nehru: Mr. Speaker, Sir, we meet in Parliament today earlier than was intended, because of a grave crisis that has arisen. This House, and everybody in India, and the greater part of the world know that the People's Republic of China has invaded India with massive forces, and there have been some bloody battles resulting in considerable casualties on both sides. For five years, we have been the victims of Chinese aggression across our frontiers in the north. That aggression was, to begin with, rather furtive. Occasionally there were some incidents and conflicts. These conflicts might well be termed frontier incidents.

Today, we are facing a regular and massive invasion of our territory by very large forces. China, which has claimed and still claims to be anti-imperialist, is pursuing a course today for which comparisons can only be sought in the eighteenth and nineteenth centuries. In those past days, the European Powers, in the full flood of imperialist aggression and with strength and weapons given to them by the Industrial Revolution, took possession of large parts of Asia and Africa by force. That imperialism has abated now, and many of the colonies of European countries have been freed and are independent countries. But, curiously, the very champions of anti-imperialism, that is, the People's Government of China, are now following the course of aggression and expansion.

Some Hon'ble Members: Shame!

Hari Vishnu Kamath (Member from Hoshangabad): Down with China!

Jawaharlal Nehru: It is sad to think that we in India, who have pleaded for peace all over the world, and who have sought the friendship of China, and treated them with courtesy and consideration and pleaded their cause in the councils of the world should now ourselves be victims of new imperialism and expansionism by a country which says that it is against all imperialism.

This strange twist of history has brought us face to face with something that we have not experienced in this way for over a hundred years or more. We had taken it almost for granted that despite some lapses in recent years, as in the Suez Canal–China affair ... that this type of aggression was almost a thing of the past. Even the Chinese aggression on our borders during the last five years, bad as it was, and indicative of an expansionist tendency, though it troubled us greatly, hardly led us to the conclusion that China would indulge in a massive invasion of India.

Now, we have seen and experienced this very invasion and it has shocked us, as it has shocked a large number of countries. History has taken a new turn in Asia and perhaps the world, and we have to bear the brunt of it, to fight with all our might this menace to our freedom and integrity. Not only are we threatened by it, but all the standards of international behaviour have been upset and so all the world is affected by it, apart from the immediate consequences. No self-respecting country which loves its freedom, and its integrity can possibly submit to this challenge. Certainly, India, this dear land of ours, will never submit to it whatever the consequences. We accept the challenge in all its consequences, whatever they may be. It may be that this challenge is also an opportunity for us.

Indeed, the people of India in their millions have demonstrated that they accept this challenge and have shown a unity and an enthusiasm such as has been very seldom in evidence. A crisis has come and we have stood up to ... that crisis.

I have moved a Resolution seeking the approval of this House to the state of emergency that has been declared by the President. That was inevitable when foreign legions invaded India and our Constitution wisely provided for such a course to be followed by us in any serious crisis. I have no doubt that this House will approve of this declaration by the President and subsequently, I hope also of the Defence of India Ordinance and the other steps that are being taken to face this crisis.

I should like this House for a moment to look at this matter in some perspective. We stand, I do believe, at a turning point not only in the history of India but of Asia and possibly even of the world, because what happens in this conflict will affect it, obviously. It will affect Asia, of which two of the biggest countries are China and India. But it will affect the world also and, therefore, this conflict has very wide-reaching consequences. We should try to look at it from this point of view. For the moment, we are shocked at this cruel and crude invasion of another country. The world has also witnessed the response of the people of the country invaded, that is, our country, and the world will yet witness the way the people of India act when their freedom is threatened and their dear liberty is imperilled. So, we are shocked and in a state of high excitement. That is inevitable, and not surprising, but we have to remember that this turning point in history is not going to end soon. We may have to face this for a long period, for a number of years, I do not know how long, and we must train ourselves and the nation to be prepared to face it, however long the crisis may last.

It is in this mood ... that I ask this House to give a lead to the country. Chinese aggression on our frontiers is five years old and during these years, this House has discussed this matter repeatedly.

On the last occasion this discussion took place on the 12th August, 1962. Many White Papers have been issued, giving the long drawn-out correspondence between the Government of India and the Government of China. Only today I have placed another bunch of these papers contained in White Paper No. 7.

On the 22nd August, 1962, we sent a note to China. A reply was sent to this on the 13th September last. But before the reply was sent or received by us ... China's forces crossed the international boundary in the north-west corner of NEFA across the Thagla ridge and began to threaten the Indian post at Dhola. We had a number of posts near the northern frontier of NEFA adequate enough to meet any minor or normal incursion. We hoped that we would be able to meet this new aggression and immediately we took steps to strengthen our forces in that area.

Five days after this new aggression, on the 13th September, the Chinese Government sent us a threatening reply, asking for discussions on the boundary question. We have previously demonstrated by a mass of evidence that our boundary is what has been called the McMahon Line, but the boundary was not laid down even by Mr. McMahon, whoever is responsible for it ... It was a recognition of the long-standing frontier on the high ridge of the Himalayas which divided the two countries at the watershed. To some extent, though indirectly, the Chinese accepted this. Certainly they accepted the continuation of this line in Burma. But, apart from the constitutional or legal aspects, it is undoubted and cannot be challenged that no Chinese has ever been in that part on this side of the line, excepting, as the House knows, in a little border village called Longju.

Even the McMahon Line which the Chinese have called illegal was laid down 48 years ago, in 1914, and that was a confirmation of what was believed then. Legal or not, it has been a part of India for a long number of years and, certainly, let us say for 50 years or so, apart from its previous history which is also in our favour. Here then is a boundary which for nearly 50 years has been shown to be our northern frontier. I am limiting what I say to 50 years for the sake of argument; really, it was even before that. Even if the Chinese did not accept it – and I would like China to say that the objection they raised in 1913 to this treaty was not based on their objection to the McMahon Line; it was based on their objection to another part of the treaty which divided Inner Tibet and Outer Tibet, the McMahon Line did not come in that; however, it is a fact that they objected to the whole treaty because of that other objection – even if the Chinese did not accept it then, this has been in existence now ... in our practice, in our Constitution, in our organization, administration, etc., for nearly 50 years.

Even the non-acceptance of it, can it entitle them to undertake an armed invasion to upset it? Even the Chinese know and say that independent India has been in possession of this territory right up to the Himalayan watershed … Because, if any person takes the trouble to read through this vast correspondence, he will notice that their alleged frontier is a very mobile one; it changes. It is wherever they have laid the frontier and in this matter, too, they have stated many contradictory things. They have laid stress sometimes on the fact that we have occupied this area of NEFA or a large part of it since we became independent. That is a curious statement since, as I have said all along, it was fully recognized in 1913–14. Apart from that, when we became independent, we … naturally wanted these tribal people in the frontier areas to share our independence. The British largely left them to their own resources and interfered only when there was some trouble. But there is no doubt that the British considered their frontier to be the McMahon Line. They did not have a full-fledged administrative apparatus there.

On gaining independence, we were naturally anxious to develop these areas as we were trying to develop other areas of India. We tried, therefore, not only to introduce our administration there but schools, hospitals, roads, etc. It is this which the Chinese say represents our occupying that. Any person who sees these papers and the story behind them would easily say that we have occupied it in every sense, legally, constitutionally, administratively, practically for a large number of years. Now, the point is that whatever the legal and constitutional aspect of their claim might be … does that justify a sudden invasion of this kind?

The House will remember that we have discussed this matter many times previously; we discussed it largely in relation to their aggression in Ladakh because nothing had happened here except with the sole exception of the little frontier village, Longju. Repeatedly, in the course of talks sometimes they are reflected in these papers … we were given to understand something not absolutely, not clearly; as has now been discovered, always their phrases … could be interpreted any way, to assure us of something and later to deny that they had assured us.

I remember the long talk I had with the Chinese Prime Minister, specially about the McMahon Line … five years ago or six years ago … when he came to India. We had a long talk and immediately after … I put down in a note … the contents of our talk so that I might not forget it. That note is here in our office.

Much later, I sent an extract of my note of that talk to the Chinese Government and they denied the truth of it! I was very much surprised and hurt because I was quite certain. When we were talking it was not once I asked; I asked the same question two or three times and definitely the answer was given to me. He gave me to understand that although the Chinese Government considered the McMahon Line an illegal line and a British imperialist line, nevertheless because of the large number of facts, because of their desire to be friendly with us, they would be prepared to do this. That was the clearest impression that I got. He denied it later on. So, it becomes a little difficult to say what they stood by at a particular time.

Anyhow, my point is that whether they acknowledge the McMahon Line or not, undoubtedly it has been, till a few weeks ago, completely in our possession; the area on this side was completely in our possession; for generations past it has been in our possession; if you like it I can put a later date, 1913–14 …

How does it justify the Chinese Government to carry on an invasion of it, by any law, international standards of behaviour or for any other reason? … They go on saying that India attacked them and their frontier guards, as they are called, are merely defending themselves. I must confess that this complete perversion of facts and the attempt to make falsehood appear to be the truth, and the truth to be the falsehood has amazed me because nothing can be more utterly baseless …

Here is a single fact … they have invaded an area which has not been in their possession ever, ever in the history of the last 10,000 years. After all, the present Chinese Government came into existence 12 years ago or thereabouts. Any claim that they may directly make to this territory can only be made either in these 12 years or possibly previously through Tibet. So, it becomes a question of what they can claim through Tibet or through their domination over Tibet.

It is true that … there were some frontier questions between Tibet and India, even in British times. But all these questions were about little pockets or little frontier areas, small areas. Nobody has ever put forward, no Tibetan Government has ever put forward previously these large claims to what is tantamount to two thirds of NEFA, apart from the vast area in Ladakh. So, we arrive at one firm conclusion which is not capable of argument or denial; that is, the Chinese have come to this territory which, for a long time … has been included in India, and administered in a vague way and a little fully administered by India.

If they had any claim they could have discussed it and talked about it and adopted various means of peaceful settlement, appointed arbitrators or gone to The Hague Court … Here, I may say, it is fortunate, in this as in so many other cases, that the present Government of China is not represented in the United Nations. Hon. Members are surprised when we have supported the Chinese representation – the representation of the People's Government of China – in the United Nations. We have supported it in spite of this present invasion because … it is not a question of likes or dislikes. It is a question which will facilitate Chinese aggression; it will facilitate its misbehaviour in the future. It will make disarmament impossible in the world. You might disarm the whole world and leave China, a great, powerful country, fully armed to the teeth. It is inconceivable.

Therefore, in spite of our great resentment at what they have done, the great irritation and anger, still, I am glad to say that we kept some perspective about things and supported that even now. The difficulty is one cannot call them up before any tribunal or world court or anywhere. They are just wholly an irresponsible country believing, I believe, in war as the only way of settling anything, having no love of peace and … and with great power at their disposal. That is the dangerous state of affairs not only for India but for the rest of the world.

I am not going into the question, as some people do, of Communism or anti-Communism. I do not believe that that is a major issue in this matter or any other. Communism may help; but the major issue is an expansionist imperialist-minded country invading a new country …

… I do not know what the hon'ble Member has said. I am not entering into that argument. I am laying stress on this fact, because as some countries do, they explain everything in terms of Communism and anti-Communism. I think the remit is that they are unable to see many of the basic facts of the question. Communism may help or communism may hinder. Communism may give them a certain strength or weakness, whatever it may be.

But today we are facing a naked aggression, just the type of aggression which we saw in the 18th and 19th centuries; there was then no Communism anywhere.

… So, we have to face this: a new type of imperialism on our borders … and the whole world is concerned with that. For the moment, we are most concerned with it, and we have to face it and bear the burden ourselves, although some … friendly countries are certainly helping us and we are grateful to them for that help.

To say that we are committing all this aggression on Chinese territory is a kind of double talk which is very difficult for a man of my simple mind to understand …

… we commit aggression on the soil of our own country and they defend it by coming over the mountains into our territory! It is really extraordinary to what length people can go to justify their misdeeds. It is true that when we heard on the 8th September of their coming over the Thagla pass into our territory with some forces, we had quite adequate forces in our posts … to meet any incursion, but if large forces come over, an ordinary military post can hardly resist them.

We took immediate steps to send further forces to reinforce our posts. We sent them immediately as we had to … yet there was one unfortunate factor which normally should be remembered. That was, if we send our forces, who are tough, young and strong, nevertheless, we send them from the plains of India suddenly to 14,000 ft. high.

For any person, however strong he may be, it requires time to be acclimatized to these heights. But they went there. When they went there, then began a process; we sent some further forces and thought that they would be adequate to meet the Chinese menace … The Chinese also started increasing their forces there. Now, for them, it was a relatively easy matter, because they have vast forces in Tibet. I do not know how much they have. They used to have 11 divisions, and I am told they now have 13 or 14 divisions in Tibet … (Interruptions.)

I think, if the hon'ble Member feels keenly about it, we will send him to the frontier! Perhaps the Speeches may convince the Chinese. So, first of all, the Chinese armies were fully acclimatized, for long on the high plateau of Tibet. It was just not in the line with the ridge but only a little below the ridge. Secondly, the whole of Tibet has been covered in the last few years by roads and the roads there, in that extremely severe climate, mean simply levelling the ground, removing boulders, etc., because you do not require cement or anything at that height. The ground itself is so very hard. So, this is covered by roads, and they can travel perhaps at quick notice from one part to another in Tibet. So, they could bring large forces to the other side of the Thagla ridge.

They would not be immediately visible to us … although some forces were being added on by the Chinese crossing the Thagla ridge, they could not be seen … in the last few days of this battle that occurred there. On the 20th, they poured in masses of people … six, seven and eight times the number of troops that we had. They have thus logistic advantage not only of bringing troops but supplying everything that could be brought immediately on the other side of the Thagla ridge … We had a certain disadvantage … the logistic disadvantage of the people having been suddenly sent to those heights. Everything that they require has to be sent by air, and our Air Force has done a very fine piece of work there, in taking everything by air in spite, sometimes, of enemy fire and the difficulties that always occur in those high mountains …

May I add that there has been a great deal of attack about our unpreparedness. I think most of it is based on ignorance …

… I am glad of this generosity in not interrupting me. I say most of this talk is based on ignorance of facts. Some of it is true: first of all, it is perfectly true that we were not prepared to face two or three divisions of the Chinese army descending upon the forces there.

… I was talking about unpreparedness. It is perfectly true, as I said, that we were unprepared to meet a massive invasion of two or three divisions. But the other things that are said about roads, about blankets, etc. are very largely incorrect …

… It is really extraordinary that many persons here who know nothing about arms talk about arms.

Mr. Speaker: Let us hear the hon'ble Prime Minister. All sections shall have their opportunity to express themselves. We are now listening to the Prime Minister.

Jawaharlal Nehru: I do not wish to go into details. I merely wanted to indicate that the criticisms that are made, are partly justified, largely not justified. About arms, it is not a thing which one normally talks about in Parliament openly. But I would be glad to explain what we have done, what we have not done and the difficulties that we had to face …

The hon'ble House will remember that till independence, our defence department was entirely under the War Office, and the War Office not only laid down the policy, but insisted that everything as far as possible should be acquired through Whitehall. During the last Great War, because of the difficulties of acquiring war material from abroad, from the United Kingdom, some of our ordnance factories came up, but still they were rather elementary.

The first problem we have to solve, therefore, is to get out of this Whitehall atmosphere and the practice of our acquiring everything from there ... I think we have done rather well to build up in these years this industry. There is always a choice, and there has been a choice in this and other matters for us to buy arms from abroad or to make them ourselves. Obviously, it is ... better to make them ourselves, because that strengthens the country; industrially and otherwise; and secondly, you can't altogether rely on outside supplies; any moment they may fail you ... So, our practice has been to try to build up our arms industry ... in the country, and we have done fairly well. We might have done better; I do not know. All kinds of difficulties arise, because development of one industry depends on the whole industrial background of the country. We have laid stress on that. I would not go into that. A great deal was said about arms, automatic rifles, and the rest. For the last three or four years, we have been trying to make them and various difficulties arose about patents ... and, sometimes ... our own difficulties in finding enough foreign exchange ... Ultimately, we got over these difficulties and we started their manufacture ... sometime this year ...

The only alternative was previously for us to get a large number of those weapons from abroad. We hesitated; we wanted to make them ourselves. Undoubtedly, we could have got them, but remember this. If we tried to get all those weapons from abroad in what might be called relatively peacetime, we will have to spend enormous sums of money. Our whole planning, etc. will have gone, because when you talk of weapons in terms of war, you talk in terms of thousands of crores. It ... would have smashed our economy. It is a different matter when we have to face this tremendous crisis, which both our people feel so much and the world sees; we can get better terms to get the things and our people are prepared to spend much more.

I am merely pointing out something that may not be adequate explanation, but I want you to appreciate that every attempt has been made and continually being made to build up industry – an aircraft industry, an arms industry, etc., an up-to-date one. Obviously we cannot be up-to-date in the sense of competing, let us say, with America or the Soviet Union or England. It is just not possible for us to advance our basic industries and science so much. But we have made good advances scientifically. One of the most important features is that the defence science department that we have built up is a high-class affair, employing about

2,000 scientists ... if there were mistakes committed or delays committed, it is not for me to go into that now. It is not a good thing for us to apportion blame and say that such and such officer or such and such Minister, etc. is to blame. We are all to blame in a sense. (Interruptions.) ...

... ever since 1st October when I returned from abroad, every day I have been connected – previously I was connected through the Defence Ministry – but from the 1st October, I have been there every day. We, the Chiefs of Staff and others sat together and discussed the matters. And, naturally, it is for the experts, the Chiefs of Staff and their advisers to determine the tactics, the strategy, etc., of fighting, and not for me; I do not know enough about it. I can only put questions to them, make suggestions to them, leaving the final carrying out of it to their hands. We took several steps.

On the very next day, on 2nd October, we called back the Chief of the General Staff, General Kaul, who was on leave then. I want to mention his name specially because quite extraordinarily unjust things have been said about him. We sent for him and we changed the method of command, separating Naga Hills, etc., from NEFA. He went there practically within 24 hours. Some people say he had not had any experience of fighting. That is not correct. He had the experience of fighting in Burma. He was our Military Attaché in Washington when the trouble occurred in Kashmir, but he begged us to send him there. We sent him there and he was there. I doubt, knowing a good many of our officers and others – many of them are good in sheer courage and initiative and hard work – if we can find anybody to beat him. Anyhow, it is very unfair for our officers who are bearing a heavy burden, whether it be Kaul or anybody else, to be criticized in this way, criticized by foreign correspondents sending messages abroad. That is a highly improper, highly irresponsible thing to be done when they are bearing such a heavy burden.

Then, General Kaul, as soon as he went over there – he went there suddenly from here –14,000 feet daily, walked 16 to 20 miles from post to post over highly precipitous mountain areas. He fell ill and he came here to report after 4 or 5 days.

... I would like to point out to the House a fact ... that this invasion by the Chinese did not merely take place in NEFA on the 20th October. On that very day it was a coordinated attack all along the line from Ladakh to NEFA. Therefore, to say that because we had attacked them – we are perfectly justified in pushing them and attacking them – in NEFA, to make that an excuse and say that we had attacked them in NEFA and, therefore, they are attacking us on that day all along the line of Ladakh is ... manifestly a false statement ...

Now, a few days after the 20th October – I think it was 24th – a message was sent to the heads of Governments or heads of States in cases where it may be so, almost all of them, pointing out the background of the Chinese invasion and stating our firm resolve to resist it – a copy of it I have placed on the Table of the

House. We have received many replies, not from all yet but from many of them, extending their sympathy and support at the present crisis.

Just soon after, four or five days after this massive attack, the Chinese Prime Minister came out with, what is called, a 'three-point proposal' on which a ceasefire might be arrived ... It was not quite clear what he meant. But what appeared to us, and what appeared later on to us with further elucidation, was that it meant our not only acknowledging or partly acknowledging their right to be where they were on our territory, but our force retiring still further, some 20 kilometres or so; that is to say, although the Chinese armies would retire a little on our territory we would retire further and they would have an opportunity to build up their strength on our territory to attack us further later. It is an impossible thing for us to agree to. There has been some confusion about this in the countries, not only here but in other countries too, but as we have explained it most people have understood it – I am talking about other countries. We, in reply or independently, rather, proposed that they should retire to the line prior to the 8th September, that is behind the McMahon Line there and they should also retire the advances they had made since the 8th September in Ladakh.

Some of our friends have said that this was a weak proposal, we should have asked them to go out completely. Well, it is for the House to judge our weakness and strength, and the proposals must have some realities, because we have not only to abide by it but we have to convince all our friends elsewhere that we are making ... a proposal which is reasonable and which can be given effect to. The proposal was that they should retire to that line as it stood on 8th September both in NEFA and Ladakh. Then we were prepared to meet their representatives to consider what further steps should be taken to lessen tension, etc. Once that was agreed to, then would come as a third step our meeting together to consider the merits of the question. We have made that proposal and we stand by it. I think it is a reasonable proposal and certainly not in any sense a dishonourable or a weak one.

Then, meanwhile, many of our friends abroad, well-intentioned countries, made various efforts to bring about a cease-fire, stoppage of fighting and a consideration of the matter on the merits. Their efforts, or rather their desire, to help in stopping this fighting is very laudable, and we welcome their desire. But, not knowing all the detailed facts, sometimes, they made some proposals which had no great relevance to the situation.

I shall refer only to one of them and that was the reference made by President Nasser of the UAR. I must pay my tribute to President Nasser in this matter because he did not make a vague proposal in the air. People advise us to be good and peaceful, as if we are inclined to war. In fact, if we are anything, as the House well knows, we do not possess the war-like mentality and that is why for the purpose of war there is weakness. We may have developed it, but that is a different matter, I am talking of the past. So, people talking to us to be good boys and make up has no particular meaning, unless they come to grips with the particular issues involved. Now President Nasser took the trouble to understand the facts and thereafter issued a presidential decree or communique issued by the President-in-Council of the UAR in which he made certain proposals. These proposals were not exactly on the lines we had suggested but were largely in conformity with our proposals. They laid special stress on troops withdrawing to their lines where they stood prior to the 8th of September. That was a major thing. That fitted in with our proposal. China has rejected this proposal, made by President Nasser.

Now this crisis is not of our making or seeking. It is China which has sought to enforce its so-called territorial claims by military might. Indeed, she has advanced beyond the line of her territorial claims. As I said, their frontier is a mobile one; anything they could grasp becomes their frontier.

In this task, in defending our frontiers and our motherland, we have sought help from all friendly countries. I wish to express my gratitude for the prompt response to our appeal for sympathy and support which have been given to us by various countries. This help that is given is unconditional … It does not, therefore, affect directly our policy of non-alignment which we value. Those countries, which have helped us, have themselves recognized this and made it clear that they do not expect us to leave that policy. Help has been given to us swiftly by the United States, by the United Kingdom and by some other friendly countries. We are in touch with many others. We have also made approaches to other friendly countries like the Soviet Union and France for supply of equipment.

There is one other aspect which I should like to mention, which is not indirectly connected with this matter but directly connected, and that is our development plans and the Five-Year Plan. Some people have said, 'Let us give up these Plans so that we may concentrate on the war effort.' What is the war effort? People think of the soldiers on the front, which is perfectly right. They are bearing the brunt of the heat and danger. But in this matter, in the kind of struggle that we are involved in, every peasant in the field is a soldier, every worker in a factory is a soldier. Our work, our war effort essentially, apart from the actual fighting done, is in ever greater production in the field and factory. We must remember that it is an effort which depends greatly on our development. Today we are much more in a position to make that kind of effort in field and factory than, let us say, ten or twelve years ago; there is no doubt about that. We are not still adequately developed. I hope this very crisis will make us always remember that … a modern army fights with modern weapons which it has to manufacture itself in that country. It is based on the development of industry, and that industry must have an agricultural base if it is to succeed.

Therefore, we have to develop all-round, apart from agriculture and industry, which are the basic things in our Five-Year Plan. Then there is power, which is essential from the point of view of the war effort, from the point of view of industry ... even agriculture ... to talk of scrapping the Five-Year Plan is not to understand the real springs of our strength. We have to carry the Five-Year Plan and go beyond it in many respects. It may be in some matters which are considered non-essential we may tone down or leave them but in the major things of the Five-Year Plan, we have to make the fullest effort. Among the major things, agriculture is highly important. How can a country fight when it is lacking in food? ... We have to grow more and more, which is a difficult thing ... because of floods and all kinds of things.

Now, although we have fallen behind, I take it that we have to aim at higher targets than we have laid down even in the Third Plan ... We cannot get it so easily if we laid down certain targets ... in the Food Ministry. We must go down to the peasant, to the agriculturist and transform his present enthusiasm, his present energy into greater production. Nothing is more cheering and heartening than the reactions amongst people, amongst the peasants who have given their little mite. Let them transform them into greater production. I am sure they can, if we approach them rightly. So also with industry; so also with many other things like education, etc. We must look upon all of them as part of the war effort that we have to make. In this process I hope we shall not only build up our nation more swiftly but will make it stronger, make it more social-minded and lay the base of the socialist structure that we aim at ...

In effect we have to look at this matter as an effort of the whole nation. We may say – some people say – we want an armed people. That is true in a sense. But what we really want is the whole people mobilized for this effort doing their separate jobs whether it is in the field, the factory or the battlefield, thus combining together and strengthening the nation and bringing success to us. We have to be armed, therefore, not only by weapons of warfare but by weapons of agriculture, industry and all those as well.

We do not minimize our task. Let no man minimize it or have any illusions about it. It is not a thing which we can deal with by momentary enthusiasm, enthusiasm of the moment or lasting a month or two. It is a long effort that we require – a difficult effort – and we shall have to go out to do our utmost. It is not merely enough to pay something to the Defence Fund or to do something else. That is good in its own way. It is very welcome how people are paying them by straining every nerve to the utmost. We have to keep up our strength and our determination to the end. And that end may not be near. Therefore we have to prepare in every way to strengthen the nation not only for today and tomorrow but for the day after also to meet this menace. If we do that, I have no doubt that we shall be able to show the determination and fortitude that is required of our people. We have had a glimpse of it in their present enthusiasm which has been a most moving sight …

Now before I end I should like to say a word about our soldiers and airmen who are working under extraordinarily difficult circumstances. I want to send on your behalf our greetings and assurance of our full assistance. To those who have fallen in defence of the country we pay our homage. They will not be forgotten by us or by those who follow us. I am confident that all sides of this House will stand united in this great venture and will demonstrate to the world that free India which has stood for peace and will always stand for peace and friendship with other countries can never tolerate aggression and invasion. If we have worked for peace as we have done and we shall continue to do so, we can also work for war effectively if we are attacked as we have been. Sir, I commend these Resolutions to the House.

UMASHANKAR MULJIBHAI TRIVEDI

(Lok Sabha: Mandsaur)

Lok Sabha: 8 November 1962

On Resolution Regarding the Proclamation of Emergency and Aggression by China

Mr. Deputy Speaker, I have very consciously and carefully read the resolutions moved by the Prime Minister. I have felt in all humbleness that something is missing from these resolutions. Therefore, I feel that what has been dropped out of this resolution, inadvertently probably, is being supplied by my amendment.

It is really … very strange … that our government has found itself unprepared. Our Prime Minister did not like the idea of admitting unpreparedness. Opinions may differ, but for the last five years, this aggression against us, which Pandit Jawaharlal Nehru was pleased to call misbehaviour in the beginning, aggression at some later stage, and now he is pleased to call invasion, has been in progress. Knowing all these things and knowing the unpredictability of the Chinese nature, if we have not prepared ourselves for all these five years, I do not think that anything more can be said about this; I certainly do say that it is unpreparedness.

Our kindness, our goodness, our humanitarian outlook, our desire to be peace-loving – we have always been peace-loving – has been interpreted as the manifestation of our weakness and those who believe only in brute force have come down as tyrants of the old upon us, as wolves upon us. Upon whom? Upon a people who admittedly, all over the world, except for Pakistan, are known as a peace-loving nation …

Although our Prime Minister has made several mistakes, I shall not recapitulate them. We have agreed to forget our differences and finding faults, one way or the other. Just recapitulating them cannot put us in the solid position and solid front when we want to fight against the aggressors ...

We will have to hit back and hit hard and thrash the enemy relentlessly and mercilessly before we can drive him out from the sacred soil of our country. It appears that at the back of our mind we are still having a feeling that some sort of an amicable settlement by negotiations with China will come as a miracle and save us from all that war brings in its wake. None of us likes war, yet we cannot be complacent on that account. We cannot always go on thinking ... that negotiations will come through. They may come and you may welcome them when they do come, but for God's sake do not exert yourself in the direction of these negotiations. Exert yourself to drive out the invaders ... We do not want any piece of their land but put them where they belong. That would be enough for them.

Negotiations will come then, and there will be honourable negotiations. Nobody will stand in the way of negotiations, but the negotiations must be the negotiations of the *bahadur*, that is, of the brave and not the negotiations of the weak. It should be the negotiation of the *shoorveer*[1] and not the negotiation of the coward ... We will get ample opportunity to negotiate after the Chinese have been driven out from our sacred soil.

The atrocity of this invasion is all the more apparent when we remember that we were the one and ... only friendly nation so far as China was concerned. We took up China's cause ... Chou En-lai came here and we set up a mass hysteria. We welcomed him as we welcomed none else. We went about setting up clubs and societies. We set up the India–China Cultural Society and we had all along the saying, '*Hindi Chini Bhai Bhai*'.[2] All the time when this *bhai-bhai* business[3] was being carried on by us, the man was manoeuvring to stab us in the back ...

... We have been carrying on a solitary fight in the United Nations to get China ... into the organization. This friend who was thus treated with love and respect by us always has turned out to be our deadliest foe. No one has ever tried to invade us in this manner coming across the Himalayas from where nobody ever dared to come, and unprovoked at that. This morning I was reading a book which had a quotation from Pandit Jawaharlal Nehru. He said about the Himalayas: 'The Himalayas are not only near to us but also very dear; for they have always been part of our history and tradition, our thinking and our poetry; our worship and our devotion and mythologically the abode of our gods.' It is these Himalayas

---

1 Editor's translation: Warrior; man of valour.

2 Editor's translation: Indians and Chinese are brothers.

3 Editor's translation: Brotherly business.

that have been transgressed upon by the Chinese and it is these Chinese whom we want to throw back.

... those people who have committed this defilement of the Himalayas and who have polluted the sanctity of our country by treading upon it as murderers have ... to be driven out before we think of talking with them. I do not know how the change occurred in our hon'ble Prime Minister. We do remember that when he went ... to Italy he refused to shake hands with Mussolini only on the ground that Mussolini's hands were full of blood ... Yet, I do not know why the same sentiments did not strike him and deter him from shaking hands with Chou En-lai. Mistakes do occur but some ... mistakes are such that they cannot be easily forgotten.

When I repeat this ... I do not say this with any desire at criticism. I and my Party have determined to offer its full cooperation to the Government in this struggle but we must not forget ... the mistakes that we have committed.

My hon'ble friend, Seth Govind Das (Member of Parliament from Jabalpur), was bold enough to admit and said on the floor of the House that we did commit a Himalayan blunder when we allowed this Chinese monster to capture the Tibetans and to commit the genocide of the giant Khampas. None of us have seen the Khampas but those of us who have seen them know that to kill them was a great task for the Chinese. One Khampa ... is able to kill 20 Chinese. These people killed him outright and destroyed him completely from the soil of Tibet. We could show our anger about Algeria but we did not show sufficient anger when Tibet was subjugated and ... liquidated.

However, we must forget this ... The country is solidly standing behind Pandit Jawaharlal Nehru ... We do not see eye to eye, from group to group, party to party and State to State. The fissures of State against State, language against language, religion against religion, caste against caste, class against class and leanings towards money grabbing, power seeking, nepotism and the obnoxious corruption have been our banes. Yet, this invasion on our territory has enthused us to fight as one man and throw all differences deep down the well.

... the credit for this enthusiasm and ... oneness ... does not go to the Government but ... to the people at large. It is the people who have rallied round, who have forgotten the differences, who have felt the oneness, who have felt the upsurge and who are now standing, shoulder to shoulder to fight and throw back the Chinese. A great fellow-feeling arising from a common culture and heritage has suddenly catapulted the nation to a sense of responsibility and the urgent desire to maintain the hard-won freedom and has fettered the nation into one solid whole.

Our dissensions were thus merely superficial except that petty leaders thought in terms divisive. People are one and were one at all times. There was nothing wrong with the people except that they were being led in six different directions at once. The imminent danger and the emergency have wiped out those ills and the nation stands today as one man to fight the unholy invasion in our sacred territory.

But, with all that, we have still to face one factor … referred to by Shri Ranga … Shri U.N. Dhebar and Dr. Govind Das. This disturbing factor is the new international cult of communism. It has also got its tentacles in our country. The Russian paper, *Pravda*, has called upon the so-called progressive, meaning communist, elements to support the Chinese offer of negotiations. Who is *Pravda* to dictate these terms? What are the progressive groups that are there? May I ask my friends who believe in this international picture, have they not received a jolt? Have they not yet realized that their sense of communism and their sense of internationalism is incompatible with Indian nationalism and with patriotism to the country? The Communist Party and the fellow travellers do not seem to realize that patriotism and love of one's country are really incompatible with the conception of a foreign land being one's fatherland, and particularly that fatherland which is out to destroy our kith and kin and which has already succeeded in destroying a very large number of our young men at the front. With them, do we shake hands?

The Communist Party always proclaims itself to be a party of the poor, and the *jawans*[4] are not poor. There is no feeling for the *jawans*! They talk in terms of liberation. Whose liberation? I am not a slave. Nobody, none in my country is a slave. From whom do I seek liberation? I am already liberated. I am free. I do not want any further liberation. God save me from those liberators. It is in this perspective that we should try to remember and not forget in the future, who are our friends and who are not …

Dr. Nkrumah, President of Ghana, in writing to Mr. Macmillan, Prime Minister of England, says …'What has distressed me is your statement that the British Government would give India every help.' Why should this statement of Mr. Macmillan distress Dr. Nkrumah? He is in the Commonwealth. We are in the Commonwealth. Our Prime Minister is on good terms with him and he wants to talk with us as if he is our friend … Help given by one friend to another friend should distress another friend? Is that logic? Is it a thing which is expected from such a man? We must become very cautious about who are our friends. It is a very serious utterance coming from this so-called friend.

Then, there is Khawaja Nazimuddin who comes forward with the threat that we must accept his four conditions: (i) hold a plebiscite in Kashmir, (ii) remove our forces and put Kashmir in charge of United Nations forces, (iii) stop the imaginary persecution of the Mohammedans in India and (iv) stop other imaginary evictions of Muslims from India. Why does this man still go on talking like this?

Shri Ranga, with all his wisdom, wants to tell us that we must try to remove our differences with Pakistan. With whom can we remove differences? Are there

[4] Editor's translation: A male police constable or soldier.

differences? Where are the differences? We are just like a lamb. We have not done anything. But, the wolf says, you are spoiling the water although the water is coming from that side to this side. From this Pakistan, what do we expect? Let us have friendship with those who have extended friendship to us, whose hands are there to shake with us. The *Dawn* of Pakistan reports in its issue of 4th November, 1962 that large-scale shipments of armaments from Russia, Czechoslovakia and other communist powers have been arriving in China. I do not believe the *Dawn*. I never believe in that paper knowing that it writes falsehoods so far as India is concerned ... But, what hits me is the bold headlines given to this news which appears to gladden the heart of *Dawn*. We must not forget our relations with Pakistan all along, born of hatred and enmity, call it whichever way you like: always holding out enmity against us, always preaching enmity against the Hindus, driving them out and here we are in a majority.

... we must always be careful about those who cannot see eye to eye in this. Recent history would clearly indicate where we stand vis-à-vis Pakistan and its relations with China. We are only thankful to America that with the way it has manoeuvred to keep military stations in Pakistan, Pakistan dare not do any harm.

The question, therefore, for us to consider is who will give us support, moral, diplomatic and material. Our Prime Minister, in the Resolutions, has asked for moral and material support ... diplomatic support also is necessary in this world. Non-aligned people have already shown us our place and clearly indicated how they stand in relation to us. Russia is apathetic to us and decidedly sympathetic with China. Pakistan has been and is openly hostile. Ghana and Indonesia have given their own indication. The Prime Minister has conveyed to us that he is thankful to President Nasser for what he has done. We on this side and the public in general do not feel the same way about President Nasser. We wanted stronger words from President Nasser in our help. However, if the Prime Minister so feels, let him feel that way. We endorse his views for the present and we will watch things.

With all the provocations that we gave to the United Kingdom by our petty differences with it on the question of Goa, Nagaland, SEATO, Katanga, Central America, the Suez, etc., it has clearly put all those things in oblivion, and the spontaneous help rendered by the United Kingdom and by the USA and all other friendly nations including France and Germany are heartening pieces of news. We are in the British Commonwealth, and today we have to accept the wisdom of remaining in the Commonwealth, and that in the United Kingdom a great fellowship of nations has suddenly stirred the United Kingdom to a sense of responsibility for the security and freedom of one of its members.

Our Prime Minister, on the occasion of the reception given to Mr. Makarios, President of Cyprus, has asserted that he rules out the possibility of negotiations with the Chinese as long as they are in aggressive occupation. I think I understand him rightly when he says that there will be no negotiations till that aim has been achieved ... he ... means that he shall refuse to negotiate till the Chinese have been put behind the McMahon Line in the NEFA and behind the recognized borders in Ladakh also as recognized by law and history.

... It is good that Shri Krishna Menon has chosen to walk out of the Cabinet, which ought to have been done much earlier. The unpreparedness in which we have been caught has cost us much life and much money, and it has hurt our pride and prestige. We have the whole unhappy episode commencing from the end of July 1962 and going up to the 4th November 1962, of rabbit-fashion complacency and idiotic unpreparedness, a very sad commentary on our right to rule ourselves. I am told that we have been making tubs, bathtubs, and coffee percolators in our defence ordnance factories when we ought to have been improving our mortars and rifles.

The whole nation has arisen with a singleness of purpose to drive out the Chinese; yet, it saddens my heart to tell you that the day before yesterday when I passed by the recruiting office I found more than two thousand young men awaiting their turn to be examined by the recruiting officer, and some of them were waiting since 5 a.m. in the morning. Such callous behaviour, and particularly at this juncture, calls for very strong action against the offending officer or officers concerned, and any Minister who tolerates this or has tolerated it deserves the strongest condemnation in the strongest language from us.

May I make one suggestion here that recruitment must be carried out on a large-scale and trained officers or people chosen from amongst even the Members of Parliament be sent out to the villages, and daily recruitment of not less than 500 should be imposed as a minimum quota for recruitment upon such recruiting officers, and this task must be undertaken in the villages rather than in the cities, to guard against the infiltration of personnel of questionable loyalty?

I say so because I cannot forget what Mr. Kumaramangalam, a communist leader, has said, as reported in *The Statesman* of the 5th November, 1962, namely that: 'The defence production and mobilization efforts would be hampered if Communists were not included in the various committees formed to organize the country's defence.' ... Who is this man to threaten us like this? Are we going to tolerate this threat that comes from Mr. Kumaramangalam? May I, Sir, in all seriousness, ask the Government what delays the Government from taking action against persons who make such utterances and publish them to the detriment of the nation's effort and virtually threaten to sabotage the country's efforts to drive out the aggressors?

As one very fond of democratic rule, rather enamoured of democracy of the parliamentary type, I never agreed, and even today do not agree that in peace times we can have an act like the Preventive Detention Act. But, in this eventuality and in this emergency, I will call upon the Government not to hesitate in doing its duty by the nation without any consideration of personalities.

Finally, I would like to say a few more things before I resume my seat. Decency, dignity and self-respect require that we negotiate only after the barbarians are driven out ... and, therefore, again, I respectfully commend my amendment to the House. My amendment is in the following Resolution ... 'and to refuse to negotiate any terms with the aggressor till this end has been achieved'. So, I commend this amendment for the acceptance of the House.

... Let us now forget our differences, and in doing so, let us not forget to thank those friends who have rushed to our help in our hour of need. We express our deep sense of gratitude and our thanks for this act of kindness. Let us not also forget our jawans who have laid down their lives. In conclusion, I would say one last sentence. On behalf of my party, I assure the Government that every effort which the Government wants my party to put in for the successful termination of the hostilities against China will be made by my party jointly and severally by each one of the Members, and it will not consider any effort too great to secure the victory of our nation against the dark forces of invasion from China.

2

Trouble on the Line of Actual Control

For over six decades after India's humiliating defeat in the India–China war in 1962, the dispute over the border has continued. There were fierce artillery duels in Sikkim in 1967 when India held on to the key passes of Nathu La and Cho La. In 1975, there was an ambush at Tulung La in Arunachal Pradesh where four jawans of Assam Rifles were killed. That was followed by a long period of relative peace.

But then on 16 June 2020, an altercation between Indian and Chinese troops – that included jostling, throwing of stones and fighting with nail-studded batons – resulted in the first casualties along the Line of Actual Control since the ambush in Arunachal Pradesh in 1975. Twenty Indian soldiers were killed in the line of duty and China also suffered an undeclared number of casualties. A few months later, on 7 September 2020, shots were fired along the LAC for the first time in 45 years.

Eight days later, on 15 September, ***Rajnath Singh*** *(Union Defence Minister) – not Prime Minister Narendra Modi – made a statement on the subject in Parliament. He followed it up on 11 February 2021 with another statement in Parliament.*

However, unlike in 1962, and, indeed, in the years running up to it, when Parliament saw several extended debates on China, the ruling BJP did not permit any discussion on the subject in either House. Not just that, it did not even permit MPs from seeking clarifications in the Rajya Sabha, something that the rules permit.

RAJNATH SINGH

(Lok Sabha: Lucknow)

Lok Sabha: 15 September 2020

Redevelopments on Our Borders in Ladakh

Hon'ble Speaker, Sir, today I rise to brief this august House about the recent developments on our eastern borders in Ladakh. As you are aware that our Hon'ble Prime Minister, Shri Narendra Modi ji had recently visited Ladakh and met our brave soldiers to convey the message of solidarity of the nation behind their every action. I too have spent some time with our soldiers in Ladakh and I want to tell you that I have felt their indomitable courage, gallantry and valour. As you are aware, Col. Santosh Babu, along with his 19 brave soldiers, made the supreme sacrifice in the cause of defending the territorial integrity of India. Hon'ble Speaker, Sir, this House paid homage to them by observing two minutes silence yesterday.

At the outset, I would like to take some time to briefly provide some details of our boundary issues with China. As the House is aware, India and China are yet to resolve their boundary question. China does not accept the customary and traditional alignment of the boundary between India and China. We believe that this alignment is based on well-established geographical principles confirmed by treaties and agreements, as well as historical usages and practices, well known for centuries to both sides. The Chinese position, however, is that the boundary between the two countries has still not been formally delimited, that there exists a traditional customary line formed by the extent of jurisdiction that they claim was exercised historically by each side, and that the two sides have different interpretations of the position of the traditional customary line. The two countries had engaged in discussions during 1950s–60s but these efforts could not yield a mutually acceptable solution.

As the House is very well aware, China continues to be in illegal occupation of approximately 38,000 sq. km of the Indian territory in Ladakh. In addition, under the so-called 'Boundary Agreement' of 1963, Pakistan illegally ceded 5,180 sq. km of Indian territory in Pakistan Occupied Kashmir to China. China also claims approximately 90,000 sq. km of Indian territory adjacent to Arunachal Pradesh border as its own.

Both India and China have formally agreed that the boundary question is a complex issue which requires patience and have committed to seeking a fair, reasonable and mutually acceptable solution through dialogue and peaceful negotiations. In the interim, the two sides have also agreed that maintenance of peace and tranquility in the border areas is very essential for the further development of bilateral relations.

I would also like to mention here that as yet there is no commonly delineated Line of Actual Control in the border areas between India and China and two countries have different perceptions regarding the LAC. Therefore, in order to ensure peace and tranquility in the border areas, the two countries have concluded a number of agreements and protocols.

Under these agreements, the two sides have agreed to maintain peace and tranquility along the LAC without prejudice to their respective positions on the alignment of the LAC as well as on the boundary question. It is on this basis, that our bilateral relations also saw considerable progress since 1988. India's position is that while bilateral relations can continue to develop in parallel with discussions on resolving the boundary question, any serious disturbance in peace and tranquility along the LAC in the border areas is bound to have implications for the positive direction of bilateral relations.

Hon'ble Speaker, Sir, a key element of both the 1993 and the 1996 Agreements is that the two sides will keep their military forces in the areas along the Line of Actual Control to a minimum level. These agreements also mandate that pending an ultimate solution to the boundary question, the two sides shall strictly respect and adhere to the Line of Actual Control and it will not be violated in any condition. Furthermore, in these agreements, India and China also committed to clarification of the Line of Actual Control to reach a common understanding of the alignment. Thus, from the year 1990 to 2003, the two sides engaged in an exercise to reach a common understanding on the LAC. But, thereafter the Chinese side did not show a willingness to pursue this exercise. As a result, there are some areas where the Chinese and Indian perceptions of the LAC overlap. In these areas, as also with other sections of the border areas, the various agreements govern the manner in which troops of both sides should operate and deal with situations of face-offs to maintain peace and tranquility. Before I apprise the House of the current developments, let me inform that the Government has an elaborate and time tested coordination mechanism amongst different intelligence agencies including intelligence units of the Central Police Forces and the three armed forces. The technical and human intelligence is continuously gathered in a well coordinated manner. It is shared with the armed forces which helps them in taking decisions.

Hon'ble Speaker, Sir, let me now apprise the House of the developments this year. Since April, we had noticed a build-up of troops and armaments by the Chinese side in the border areas adjacent to Eastern Ladakh. In early May, the Chinese side had taken action to hinder the normal, traditional patrolling pattern of our troops in the Galwan Valley area, which resulted in a face-off. Even as this situation was being addressed by the Ground Commanders as per the provisions of our bilateral agreements and protocol, in mid-May the Chinese side made several attempts to transgress the LAC in other parts of the Western Sector. This included Kongka

La, Gogra and North Bank of Pangong Lake. These attempts were detected early and consequently responded to appropriately by our armed forces.

Hon'ble Speaker, Sir, we made it clear to the Chinese side both through diplomatic and military channels that China was, by such actions, attempting to unilaterally alter the status quo. It was categorically conveyed that this was unacceptable in any condition.

Hon'ble Speaker, Sir, given the growing friction along the LAC, the Army Commanders of the two sides held a meeting on 6th June, 2020 and agreed on a process of disengagement that involved reciprocal actions. Both sides also agreed to respect and abide by the LAC and not undertake any activity to alter the status quo. However, in violation of this, the Chinese side created a violent face off on 15th June at Galwan. Our brave soldiers laid down their lives and also inflicted costs including casualties on the Chinese side and succeeded in protecting our borders. The conduct of our armed forces throughout these incidents shows that while they maintained patience in the face of provocative actions, they also equally displayed valour when required to protect the territorial integrity of India.

Hon'ble Speaker, Sir, I would like the House to join me in recognizing the courage and valour of our soldiers, who undergo immense hardship in the most difficult conditions to keep us all safe and secure. While no one should doubt our determination to safeguard our borders, India believes that mutual respect and mutual sensitivity are the basis for peaceful relations with neighbours.

As we want to resolve the current situation through dialogue, we have maintained diplomatic and military engagement with the Chinese side. In these discussions, we have maintained the three key principles that determine our approach:

(i) both sides should strictly respect and observe the LAC;

(ii) neither side should attempt to alter the status quo unilaterally; and (iii) all agreements and understandings between the two sides must be fully abided by in their entirety. The Chinese side, on its part, took the position that the situation should be handled in a responsible manner and peace and tranquility should be ensured as per bilateral agreements and protocol.

Even as these discussions were going on, the Chinese side again engaged in provocative military manoeuvres on the night of 29th and 30th August in an attempt to change the status quo in the South Bank area of Pangong Lake. But yet again, due to timely and firm actions by our armed forces along the LAC, such attempts were thwarted.

Hon'ble Speaker, Sir, as it is clear from these events, the Chinese actions reflect a disregard of our various bilateral agreements. The amassing of the troops by China goes against the 1993 and 1996 Agreements. Respecting and strictly observing the Line of Actual Control is the basis for peace and tranquility in the border areas and it has been explicitly recognized in both the 1993 and 1996 Agreements. While our armed forces scrupulously abide by it, this has not been reciprocated by the Chinese side. Their actions have led to face-offs and frictions from time to time along the LAC. As I mentioned earlier, the agreements have detailed procedures and norms to deal with the situation of face-offs. However, in the recent incidents, this year, the violent conduct of Chinese forces has been in complete violation of all mutually agreed norms.

As of now, the Chinese side has mobilized a large number of troops and armaments along the LAC as well as in the depth areas. There are several friction areas in Eastern Ladakh including Gogra, Kongka La and North and South Banks of the Pangong Lake. In response to China's actions, our armed forces have also made appropriate counter deployments in these areas to ensure that India's security interests are fully protected.

Hon'ble Speaker, Sir, the House should have full confidence that our armed forces will always rise to the challenge. Furthermore, the manner in which our armed forces are taking actions and protecting the borders, we feel proud of them. This is still an ongoing situation and involves sensitive operational issues. Hon'ble Speaker, Sir, I would, therefore, not be able to give more details in public even if I want to, as I have my own limitation. I am sure that the House will understand this sensitivity.

Hon'ble Speaker, Sir, this rapid deployment by our armed forces including ITBP has taken place in a challenging time of Covid-19. Their efforts need to be appreciated. It has also been made possible by the high importance that the Government has placed for developing border infrastructure in the last few years. The House is aware that over the last many decades, China has undertaken significant infrastructure construction activity that has enhanced their deployment capabilities in the border areas. However, in response, our Government too has stepped up the budget for border infrastructure development to about more than double the previous levels. As a result, more roads and bridges have been constructed in the border areas. This has not only provided much needed connectivity to the local population, but has also provided better logistical support for our armed forces … (Interruptions.) This has enabled them to be more alert in the border areas …(Interruptions.)

Hon'ble Speaker, Sir, due to it, they can remain more alert and respond more effectively where required in the border areas. I would like to assure this House that in the coming years too, the Government will remain committed to this objective.

Hon'ble Speaker, Sir, I would like to emphasize that India remains committed to resolving the current issues in our border areas through peaceful dialogue and consultations. It was in pursuit of this objective that I met my Chinese counterpart on 4th September in Moscow and had an in-depth discussion with him. I conveyed in clear terms our concerns related to the actions of the Chinese side, including amassing of large number of troops, their aggressive behaviour and attempts to unilaterally alter the status quo. I also made it clear that even as we wanted to peacefully resolve the issue, we would like the Chinese side to work with us and we are determined to protect India's sovereignty and territorial integrity. My colleague, Shri Jai Shankar, the External Affairs Minister, has thereafter met the Chinese Foreign Minister in Moscow on 10th September. The two have reached an agreement that, if implemented sincerely and faithfully by the Chinese side, could lead to complete disengagement and restoration of peace and tranquility in the border areas.

As the Members are aware, in the past too we have had situations of prolonged stand-offs in our border areas with China which had been resolved peacefully. Even though the situation this year is very different both in terms of scale of troops involved or the number of friction points, we do remain committed to the peaceful resolution of the current situation. At the same time, I would like to assure the House that we are prepared to deal with all contingencies.

Hon'ble Speaker, Sir, this House has had a glorious tradition. Sir, I want to repeat that this House has had a glorious tradition that whenever the country is faced with a challenge, this House has always exhibited its strength and unity towards the resolve and determination of armed forces. This House has also reposed its full confidence in the indomitable spirit, gallantry and bravery of our armed forces deployed on our borders. I can assure you that the morale and motivation of our armed forces is very high. There should be no doubt about it. The reassuring visit by our PM has sent the message to our commanders and soldiers that 130 crore countrymen are with them. In view of the height of ice covered hills, the soldiers are being provided special types of warm clothes, specialized tents for staying and arms and ammunitions adequately. The determination of our soldiers is praiseworthy as at such great heights where there is scarcity of Oxygen and temperature is below zero degree, their motivation never goes down and they have been doing their duty for so many years on Siachen, Kargil and other high altitude destinations.

I have no hesitation in sharing with this august House that we are passing through a challenging phase in Ladakh and I would like to request this House to pass a resolution in support of our armed forces. The entire House is with the armed forces who defend our motherland in very inclement weather conditions at such great heights of the country without caring for their lives. Now, the time has come that this House must send a message to the armed forces that it has full faith in their courage and bravery and the entire country is with the armed forces which are continuously engaged in the defence of India's sovereignty and integrity.

Speaker, Sir, with these words I conclude my speech.

Section Three

The People Next Door

1

The India–Pakistan War of 1965

India and Pakistan have fought four major wars. The first involved Pakistan's attempt to grab the erstwhile princely state of Jammu and Kashmir by force in 1947–48.

In 1965, Pakistan launched several military actions over a period of several months. First, Pakistan launched an attack in the Rann of Kutch in April, which was rebuffed. Incidentally this led to the decision to create a specialized paramilitary outfit – the Border Security Force, for patrolling and defending the border.

Then Pakistan launched 'Operation Gibraltar' in August.

This involved sending in infiltrators dressed in mufti to try and precipitate an insurgency in Jammu and Kashmir – somewhat similar to the modus operandi that led to the Kargil conflict in 1999. That was followed by an invasion by regular troops.

The ensuing war resulted in massive casualties on both sides and witnessed the largest engagement of armoured vehicles and the biggest tank battles since the Second World War.

Hostilities ended after a ceasefire was declared through UNSC Resolution 211, following a diplomatic intervention by the Soviet Union and the United States, and the subsequent issuance of the Tashkent Declaration. At the time of the ceasefire, India had the upper hand – although the two countries fought to a standoff, the conflict is seen as a strategic and political defeat for Pakistan as it failed both to foment insurrection in Kashmir or to gain international support.

***Lal Bahadur Shastri**, Prime Minister at the time, provided stellar leadership, with some contemporary commentators describing the capture of the Haji Pir Pass, a key point of ingress, on 30 August 1965, as India's real 'surgical strike', a sly reference to the Narendra Modi-led government's claim that the strike on Uri in Pakistan in 2016 was the first time such an incident had taken place. As Pakistan, thereafter, increased the pressure on the chicken's neck connecting Jammu and Kashmir to the rest of India at Chamb and Akhnoor, Shastri ordered the Indian Air Force to assist the army, and gave permission for an attack in west Punjab across the international border towards Lahore.*

This caught Pakistan unawares and the Indian counter-thrust reached the suburbs of Lahore and the banks of the Ichogil Canal.

During that period, Shastri addressed Parliament several times. Here, he addresses the Rajya Sabha, after making a similar speech in the Lok Sabha on the continuing delicate situation in December 1965.

The country stood as one behind Shastri during that difficult period, but some Opposition leaders such as ***J.B. Kripalani*** *believed there was a need for a change in India's foreign policy to prevent a recurrence of war. On 24 September 1965 (a few months before Shastri made the speech excerpted here), following the announcement of the ceasefire, Kripalani expanded on this subject.*

On 10 January 1966, Shastri and President Ayub Khan of Pakistan signed the Tashkent Agreement, at the behest of diplomatic efforts hosted by the USSR. (Shastri died in Tashkent within hours of signing the agreement.)

Hopes of peace did not last. Within a few years, the third Indo-Pak war, which ended in the liberation of Bangladesh, would erupt.

J.B. KRIPALANI

(Lok Sabha: Amroha)

Lok Sabha: 24 September 1965

Discussion on UN Security Council Resolution Regarding Ceasefire Between India and Pakistan

Mr. Speaker, Sir, for years, our people have been suffering from many difficulties and inconveniences. But, in spite of that, when the country was in danger, they rose as one man and did what they possibly could do in the circumstances. Our fighting forces gave a splendid account of themselves. They performed deeds which were reminiscent of reckless Rajput bravery. Their bravery was sometimes suicidal. I hope that we are worthy of the great sacrifices that our fighting forces have made.

There are certain problems which we must rethink ... The conditions under which we are living require radical and revolutionary policies, if we are to get out of the troubles in which we find ourselves. We have, therefore, to rethink not only our foreign policy, but also our home policy. I have no objection if ... our government and Congressmen go on chanting hymns of non-alignment. Keep yourself as non-aligned as even China is. But for God's sake, keep your diplomacy, your strategy, your tactics in a fluid condition. These must change with the time, place and circumstances. We should have no permanent enemies, no permanent friends.

We have seen that though our cause was just, it was crystal clear that Pakistan had committed aggression, though it was clear that it had crossed the line … established by the United Nations at the time of the ceasefire, and although they crossed the international boundary, we found no friend except Malaysia.

An Honourable Member: Singapore.

J.B. Kripalani: Singapore. We are thankful to them but remember, they sided with us because it coincides with their self-interest; no nation sides with another unless their interests coincide. Unless we have some good understanding with people, and unless we cultivate friendship, we will find ourselves in the same position as we found ourselves in when this war began.

It is not difficult, at least for the democratic countries of the West to understand us as against Pakistan. The cry that Kashmir should go to Pakistan is based on communal lines. It should not be difficult for democratic countries to understand that if India is to be divided on communal lines, there can be no place for the 50 million Muslims in this country. This is such a simple thing that anybody can understand it, that is those who want to understand it, but they do not want to understand it.

It is also a fact that we have not properly explained to them the position in India. Who will be responsible for these 50 millions of people? Will the UNO be responsible for them if we hold that religion decides nationality? It is a good sign that the Muslims in India and in Kashmir even had shown that they do not believe in this theory of two nations. We never accepted it. We repudiated it. As a democratic set-up, we live by certain values which if the democratic countries of the West do not understand it means that they are prejudiced … they have … interests of their own which impel them to go not with truth but with untruth … I am glad that a member of the government also said that we must rethink our international policy. We should know where we have committed our mistakes and where we should correct ourselves …

It is said that we should be friendly to our friends and we should do only justice to our opponents and enemies. Beyond that, a nation cannot go. We cannot, maintaining an army, take shelter under the creed of the non-violence of Gandhiji. Even Gandhiji in his days did not say that free India will not keep an army and will not use it. We have to keep an army and we have to use it. We have to make it as powerful as we can. And while doing this, we must rely mostly on our resources. But there should be no opposition to relying on our resources and also getting things from outside. It appears to me that some people think … that there is a dichotomy between helping ourselves and our getting help from our friends. We must remember that no country in the world can defend itself alone. We must have friends but these friends must be such who are bound to us and help us in all emergencies, and are not friends of convenience, who take a neutral attitude when a critical situation arises in India.

I agree with Dr. Ram Manohar Lohia when he said that the United Nations Security Council is dominated by the big nations. It will be so dominated because it suffers from what is called power politics. It has passed a Resolution. We are glad that there is cessation of hostilities. But this cessation of hostilities took place 17 years ago also. What was the result? The problem was not solved. Today also the Security Council has shown no way of solving the problem. There are certain points in the Resolution of the Security Council which are dangerous and ominous, and I'm afraid that we may, in order to secure the goodwill of the world, which has shown no goodwill towards us, succumb to the implications of those two clauses, which say that we should move back to the old ceasefire line of 5th of August, and that this question is capable of a political solution, and that there should be a political solution.

I think there is danger in what Russia has said that the President of Pakistan and the Prime Minister of India should meet on the sacred soil of Russia. I think there ... can be no conversation between Pakistan and ourselves, considering what they have done even in the last 24 hours, considering the fire and brimstone that they are breathing from day to day, considering what comes on their radio ... There can be no talk unless they ... admit the proposition that nationality is not coextensive with religion, unless these basic principles are settled first, there would be no use in meeting together. I say that this line of 5th August was a line drawn ad hoc, I'm afraid, by people who did not know geography. If they had known geography, they would not have allowed the Haji Pir Pass to be in the hands of the Pakistanis. The line has not been drawn scientifically and from the military point of view. It was drawn in a hurry in order to placate world opinion. World opinion does not count and this United Nations Organization is only a little better than its predecessor, the League of Nations. It is dominated by power politics, it is dominated by a desire to keep the balance of power. As long as this idea of balance of power continues, as long as there is power politics, truth can never have its way. It will only be compromised and that compromise will land us again and again into difficulties. If we fix a new line, then also we will be again in difficulties. So we must make it clear to the Security Council, which is afraid of saying what is right and what is wrong, that when it cannot diagnose a disease, when it cannot give a remedy, when it is not prepared to say that this country is right and that country is wrong, its opinions are absolutely of no avail.

We referred the matter of aggression by Pakistan to them in 1948 and they brushed aside that question. They did not decide whether aggression had been committed or not. This time also they have refused to name Pakistan as the aggressor, when aggression was as clear as daylight. What do you expect from that Security

Council? I say you cannot expect any justice from that Council which is dominated by big nations and which is not prepared, even when there is a clear evidence of aggression, to say that there has been an aggression. Even if they had said that there had been an aggression, but that we should have peace in the world because the world could not afford a war, one could have understood it, one could have even appreciated it. But to evade that question is very dangerous … we must not put our trust in the Security Council, however anxious we may be to support it; in fact, we have shown our anxiety to support the United Nations on all occasions. Let us not rely upon it; let us rely upon our own strength. And if we have to rely upon our own strength, then we must reframe our foreign and internal policies.

We were relying upon the Arab world as our great friends; we were supporting them in everything that they did; we went so far as it gives their League the status of an international government. What has been the result? The utmost that they have done is that some of them are neutral in the struggle. To have expected that we should be supported by an Islamic country was a midday dream. We irritated people who were anxious to be friendly to us, for instance, Israel, from which we could have got … material help … technical help, whose agricultural problems are just like ours, who have been trying various experiments in cooperative farming; we could have learned from that country, but we never allowed it to approach us even. Why? Because we wanted to placate the Arab countries and it has given us no dividends at all. I think in this matter also, we must reconsider our foreign policy.

In our home policy, I say that, even though America is our friend, we must refuse to accept anything from them, be it money or economic aid or food. I assure you that just as people have risen this time, so would they rise to produce more food … You did not put your trust in them but preferred to get inferior food … that produces sickness. You go on asking for more and more. I say that we must stand on our own legs. What is our deficiency in food grains? If the government's figures say that it is only five per cent, we can make up that five per cent. If the cultivator is given good seeds … manure … money … water at proper time, and if there is no bureaucratic repression of the tenants, then I say with confidence that even with our present methods, the production can be increased by 30 per cent.

We forgo many things and send them to foreign countries … to earn foreign exchange. We do not cultivate the home market. We have an immense home market for tea, for jute and for everything that we have …

So we must not rely on outside help. I have been a friend to America but I see that we cannot rely even on America. We must progressively stop taking arms … economic aid from her and taking even food from her. We must rely upon our own resources. That was a lesson taught to us by Gandhiji. And this war should teach us … that we can rely upon no nation … we have to rely upon ourselves.

I'm glad that a member of the government has said that in this world, power alone counts and weakness is the greatest sin that a man or a nation can commit. What did Gandhiji do when he came to India? He first put strength among the people, strength against the British government of which we were afraid, strength against the Britisher before whom we trembled and we could not speak the truth, strength against the police and against the magistracy so that every urchin in the street could stand up and say, 'This is a satanic government and we want to destroy it.' That was the strength that he infused. And I saw what he did in Champaran and I saw it again in Punjab.

This strength can be infused only if our leaders are strong, if our leaders are determined, and there is no jockeying for positions and for power, if there are no quarrels among ourselves, if there are no quarrels among the members of the ruling party. If the ruling party is united, they will get the support of all the parties as they've got on this occasion. But I'm afraid and I hope I shall be proved wrong, that as soon as this danger is passed, we shall again go to sleep; as we went to sleep when the danger from China was past. The people gave an excellent exhibition of their enthusiasm and their spirit of sacrifice. They gave without any stint, and they gave without knowing whether they were going to give to the proper parties … men, women and children gave their all. I am sorry to say that up to now, no proper accounts have been given of the money and how it has been spent. I hope that this time at least we shall mobilize the enthusiasm of the country and the determination of the country to be free and independent. Let us build our hopes upon our people. What were we before Independence? We were a slave nation. But in a few years, strength was infused in us because Gandhiji believed in the common man. We refuse to trust the common man; we refuse to go to the common man and we think governments can go on without the support of the common man. The present crisis will pass and may pass; it cannot pass until we have been able to fix a new line of demarcation … Why should the Security Council talk of the old line of 5th August when its own observer has repudiated it? We must have a line which is scientifically defensible … militarily defensible. If we're not careful, we shall lose the battle that we have won and this great sacrifice of our young men and of our aviators will have gone in vain, and with it the response that has been given by the people. It is not for the first time that we have neglected this response of the people. If we do it this time, we may not get it again.

LAL BAHADUR SHASTRI

(Lok Sabha: Allahabad)

Rajya Sabha: 5 November 1965

Statement on Indo–Pakistan Relations

Mr. Chairman, in the statement which I made in this House on the 24th September, 1965, I had given an account of the developments culminating in a cease-fire coming into force between India and Pakistan at 3-30 a.m. on the 23rd September, 1965. I do not wish to take up the time of the House by going into details about subsequent happenings which have been fully reported in the press.

I would, instead, try to present the broad picture of the later developments and to share with the House Government's views and thoughts on the various issues that have yet to be resolved.

The cease-fire is still far from being fully effective. The main reason for this is the fact that Pakistani forces have continuously tried to occupy posts and areas which were not in their hands when the cease-fire came into effect. It is these violations by Pakistan that account for the uneasy conditions that prevail in areas where our troops are facing the Pakistan army. The House will recall that the actual hour of the cease-fire had to be put off by fifteen hours beyond the dead-line set in the Security Council Resolution of the 20th September, 1965 because Pakistan delayed its acceptance of the cease-fire till the last minute. During this period which elapsed between the acceptance of cease-fire by both countries and its actual coming into force, Pakistani forces were actively engaged in trying to occupy fresh territory wherever possible and particularly in South-West Rajasthan. Even after the cease-fire, Pakistani troops did occupy a few posts and villages in Rajasthan, which are separated from each other by long distances and are located in areas where there had been no fighting before. Apart from Rajasthan, in the Fazilka sector on the 24th and 25th September, in the Tithwal area on the 11th October, Pakistan launched major attacks in total disregard of the ceasefire. In the Chamb area, too, they have repeatedly tried to move forward after the cease-fire.

The Cease-fire Agreement cannot stand in the way of our troops regaining territory treacherously occupied after the cease-fire came into effect. Wherever such violations have occurred, we have obviously no choice left except to deal with the situation and foil the Pakistani designs. Our taking such remedial action cannot be considered a violation of the cease-fire. It is necessary that the Security Council should give serious thought to this aspect of the matter. We have been regularly drawing their attention to the cease-fire violations by Pakistan, the total number of which now add up to about a thousand. The Security Council must ensure that there are no more violations of the cease-fire, and that the places occupied after the cease-fire are vacated forthwith. If real progress is to be made on the road to peace, the cease-fire must be made truly effective. Until the cease-fire becomes effective, it is not possible to proceed to the subsequent step of withdrawal of armed personnel.

This was emphasized by me in a letter dated the 18th October, 1965, to the Secretary-General. I place on the Table of the House copies of communications exchanged between the Government of India and the UN Secretary General, and between our Permanent Representative on the UN and the President of the Security Council.

Another factor of the greatest importance in any discussion on withdrawals is the manner in which we can be assured that the infiltration which Pakistan initiated on the 5th August, 1965, will not be repeated again. I had emphasized this point in my discussions and correspondence with the Secretary-General even before the cease-fire came into being. As far as I am aware, no statement has been made by any Indian delegate to the UNO or to the UN Security Council, which has been inconsistent with whatever I have said in this House. I find it necessary to revert to this point with even greater emphasis because we have reports of a fresh build-up of infiltrators in Pakistan-occupied Kashmir and in the tribal areas.

The tragic events of the last few months should make the UN and the Security Council realize that prevention is not only better, but easier than cure. If firm action had been taken when infiltration began and General Nimmo reported on it, perhaps much of the tragic loss of life and property, which followed, could have been avoided. At that time, despite all our efforts, strong and prompt action was not taken. I do hope that the Secretary-General will start immediate investigations into what is going on in Pakistan-occupied Kashmir in preparation for unleashing a fresh wave of infiltrators.

I cannot help expressing the feeling that the world would be saved much trouble and misery if aggression is not countenanced anywhere, and objective efforts are made to identify the aggressor. In the recent conflict, the fact of Pakistani aggression could be seen by anyone who wanted to. The Chief UN Observer gave a clear and objective verdict. The Security Council itself referred to August 5 as the crucial date. On this date, India had taken no action. It was Pakistan that had started sending massive waves of infiltrators, and clearly she was the aggressor. Impliedly, Pakistan's aggression was noted, but this, certainly, was not enough: a clear verdict was necessary, and a body which is charged with the important responsibility of preserving world peace must necessarily be prepared to give a clear verdict. This is all the more necessary because a new technique is being adopted, under which invasions are launched in disguise, and forces of destruction are unleashed without the usual declaration of war. It is for this reason that India had been urging from the beginning that Pakistan should be identified as the aggressor. On its part, Pakistan has been denying all along its complicity in sending infiltrators into Kashmir. The actual position is, however, so clear that any impartial agency could testify to it. I would still like to suggest that the aggressor in the recent conflict be identified by some such method.

Pakistan, it seems, is not really interested either in a cease-fire, which it grudgingly accepted in form but not in substance, or in the subsequent steps which the Security Council Resolution on the subject contemplates, namely, the withdrawal of all armed personnel, which includes not only troops but also other infiltrators. Pakistan is pleading, instead, for immediate steps for bringing about, what it describes as, a political settlement. Translated into plain words, Pakistan wants the Security Council to give it what neither its armed infiltrators nor its regular troops could give it. With this object, Pakistan's Foreign Minister engineered a meeting of the Security Council and tried to have a discussion on the internal situation in Kashmir making all kinds of wild and baseless accusations.

Our Foreign Minister made it quite clear that, while we were ready to cooperate with the Security Council in the task of restoring peace, we would not participate in any discussion on matters relating to our internal affairs. When it became clear that Mr. Bhutto could not be restrained from raising matters pertaining to the internal administration of our State of Jammu and Kashmir, the Indian delegation abstained from taking part in subsequent meetings of the Security Council.

If Pakistan wants an end to the present tense situation, let it first honour and respect the Cease-Fire Agreement. Let it put an end to the daily violations of the cease-fire. Let it then withdraw its armed personnel from our territory, and we shall also withdraw our troops from the areas in Pakistan under our occupation. More important than any of these things, let Pakistan stop the various things which it is doing, apparently in preparation for a fresh trial of strength. Let it stop the recruitment of irregular forces in Pakistan-occupied Kashmir. Let it put a stop to the digging of trenches and putting up of military structures, which is going on at so many places just across the present cease-fire line. Let it give up its attempts to acquire arms and ammunition. Let it release the goods, the cargo, and the vessels it has seized. Let it also give up its collusion with China, which is based only on a common hatred of India, and is aimed at weakening and disintegrating this country. Let Pakistan, to put it briefly, first restore normal relations before we can discuss how to establish better relations.

Once Pakistan genuinely embarks upon the path of peace, the Government and the people of India will be ready to reciprocate. Unfortunately, all the evidence that we have about Pakistan's intentions shows no signs of any change of heart, any rethinking, any desire to prefer peace to war. In these circumstances, we have to shape our policy on two planes, as it were. On the one hand, we have to be careful not to allow ourselves to be swayed by the same atmosphere of hatred, which the Pakistani leaders have tried to build up, and not to depart from the fundamentals of our policy – of peace, of secularism and of economic development. On the other hand, we have to be vigilant and prepared to meet any threat at any time to any part of our territory.

In our relations with Pakistan we must continue to behave in accordance with the canons of civilized society. But Pakistan violated all diplomatic immunities by subjecting our High Commission in Pakistan to a search at the point of rifles and bayonets. Even though the movements and activities of the personnel of the Pakistan High Commission in Delhi were restricted, they enjoyed every protection, and lived in safety and without molestation of any kind. Rather than retaliate against them, we decided to recall our High Commissioner from Pakistan, and it is not our intention to send him back in the immediate future.

There has been a good deal of discussion with regard to the question of payment of our dues under the Indus Waters Treaty. The Minister of Irrigation and Power will soon be making a statement in this House in answer to a question, which will place the House in possession of the facts. We do not wish to go back on commitments solemnly entered into by us, whether in regard to the Indus Waters Treaty, or under the Kutch Agreement. While we are always ready to meet force with strength, we shall continue to honour our pledged word.

Regarding the seizure of our ships and cargo by Pakistan, the Minister for Transport has already made a statement in this House. On the plane of preparedness, we are doing all that is necessary. We are fully alive to the fact that at a time of their own choosing, Pakistan and its ally, China, might decide to act against us in concert, and we have, therefore, to be always on our guard against any eventuality. In our defence effort, we want to achieve self-reliance to the maximum extent possible and in the shortest possible time. Our soldiers who are fighting at the front are fully entitled to the best that this country can give them, and in this effort we do not intend to be found wanting.

A new Department of Defence Supplies has been created in the Ministry of Defence with the prime object of locating capacity within the country for those items, whether they are spare parts or components or complete equipment, needed for our defence for which we are dependent on imports. Even so, we may have to import, either arms or the machinery to produce them. It was this imperative need that made me appeal to our people to subscribe to the Gold Bond in a massive way. We have got to harness a substantial part of the gold reserves in this country, and put them to the service of the nation, if we are to be strong and self-reliant. We have given considerable thought to the new Defence Loans and the National Defence Gold Bond Scheme, which are now in operation, and we have tried to take a practical view and give whatever inducements are possible.

In themselves, these schemes are a useful investment, but what is more important, they represent a vital contribution to the nation's defence effort. Our countrymen today are imbued with a fierce determination to offer any sacrifice to make the country strong. I have every hope, therefore, that people will respond suitably to these schemes and especially that of the Gold Bonds in order to attain this objective.

The House would naturally want to know how we view the likely course of future events so far as Indo-Pakistan relations are concerned. Our own position is quite clear. We want to live in peace with Pakistan. We have never taken the initiative in forsaking the path of peace, nor shall we do so in future. We do not want to annex any part of Pakistan's territory. But, the restoration of peace and its future preservation can be assured only if Pakistan gives up the stormy course of wanton aggression. We cannot, Mr. Chairman, propitiate any aggressor. Threatened as we are, with a renewal of aggression, we have to be ever vigilant and ready.

Looking at all the circumstances, there is no doubt in my mind that the period of travel which began in August last will continue for a long time indeed. As a nation, we have to be prepared to meet this many-sided challenge. There is, therefore, no room for complacency.

At the same time, the experience of the recent past must fill us all with a new confidence. Hon'ble Members would be gratified to know that when I visited the forward areas in the Lahore and Sialkot sectors three weeks ago, I found the soldiers and the airmen imbued with the highest morale. Most of them had fought in the battlefield and had seen some of their colleagues laying down their lives heroically in defence of the motherland. On behalf of this House, and indeed on behalf of all the people of India, I conveyed to them our feeling of highest appreciation and deep gratitude and told them how the entire nation was united in its determination to fight the invader. I have also been able to go to other places and to see millions of persons, all resolved to meet any hardship and to make any sacrifice.

Undoubtedly, the people are facing difficulties, but these are not felt, nor mentioned. It seems that there is a regeneration, and millions of our countrymen are ready to give of their best to make the nation self-reliant and strong. Towards this single common purpose, I know that this House and this nation will flinch from no danger and count no sacrifice too great.

2

The Birth of Bangladesh

The creation of Bangladesh in 1971, and India's role in it, was the apogee of ***Indira Gandhi's*** *political career. Admirers at home included Opposition leader Atal Bihari Vajpayee, who would go on to become Prime Minister almost three decades later: he hailed her as Goddess Durga, the manifestation of strength and compassion. This marked a defining moment in the already fraught relations between India and Pakistan. For Pakistan, the coming into being of Bangladesh was a double humiliation: it was not just a military defeat, but a negation of the religious basis on which it had been carved out of erstwhile India. Under Indira Gandhi's leadership, the Indian Armed Forces won the India–Pakistan war decisively, and split Pakistan into two.*

This section has two speeches Indira Gandhi made as Prime Minister. In the first one, on 6 December 1971, three days after the start of the war, she announced that the Indian government had decided to grant recognition to Bangladesh; the second, on 16 December 1971, was made an hour after the fall of Dhaka, when Pakistani forces officially surrendered to their Indian counterparts.

On the first occasion, in the Lok Sabha, where Indira Gandhi made the statement, MPs cutting across political lines rose to congratulate her.

A leading Opposition leader of that time, ***Madhu Dandavate*** *(who would within six years become Union Railway Minister in the Janata Party government, and close to two decades later, Union Finance Minister in the National Front government) expressed his approbation in the speech excerpted here.*

The birth of Bangladesh struck such a chord that the then Lok Sabha Speaker, Gurdial Singh Dhillon – breaking with long-established practice – along with the members, thumped his table in appreciation of the new country being granted recognition.

On 16 December 1971, the Lok Sabha functioned normally, indeed conducting a great deal of legislative work. Nevertheless, MPs even as they participated in the scheduled discussions, repeatedly enquired of the Speaker whether reports coming in from Dhaka of an imminent surrender by the Pakistani forces were true, and when the Prime

Minister would come to the House. Noting the MPs' impatience, Indira Gandhi made a brief appearance in the Lok Sabha in the afternoon to say that she had heard that one Pakistani general had surrendered, but that she was waiting for the total capitulation before she could say anything definitive.

She returned at 5.30 p.m. to make the dramatic announcement that Dhaka was 'now the free capital of a free country'. There were no further speeches that day, but on 18 December, a Saturday, she was felicitated by fellow MPs in the historic Central Hall of Parliament.

Minutes before that celebration, in the Lok Sabha, Defence Minister ***Jagjivan Ram*** *– who many in the armed forces regard as India's finest defence minister – rose to give a blow-by-blow account of the war, not just on India's eastern frontier, but on the western front, too. In his telling, the 13-day war comes alive.*

But there was more than glory and guts; there was also the tragic and heart-rending story of the millions of Bangladeshis who were uprooted and forced to flee to India. ***Samar Guha****, an eternal rebel, shone a light on this aspect in a speech in the Lok Sabha on 16 June 1971, in the course of a discussion on the influx of refugees from Bangladesh.*

As a freedom fighter, Guha was jailed by the British; after Partition, in what was then East Pakistan, he was imprisoned in Dhaka Jail. After he moved to India, he was arrested and detained over twenty times by the Congress government. His last stint in jail was during the Emergency along with his other associates in the Janata Party. As a schoolboy, he joined the Bengal Revolutionary Party; as an adult, the Indian National Congress, followed by the Forward Bloc, the Praja Socialist Party, and the Socialist Party. At the time of his death, he was a member of the Janata Dal (Secular). A close associate of Subhas Chandra Bose, he participated in the Bangladesh liberation struggle, and is said to have been consulted by Indira Gandhi on the subject periodically. He was an MP between 1967 and 1980.

INDIRA GANDHI

(Lok Sabha: Rae Bareli)

Lok Sabha: 6 December 1971

Statement on Recognition to Bangladesh

The valiant struggle of the people of Bangladesh in the face of tremendous odds has opened a new chapter of heroism in the history of freedom movements.

Earlier, they had recorded a great democratic victory in their elections and even the President of Pakistan had conceded the right of Sheikh Mujibur Rahman to become Prime Minister of Pakistan. We shall never know what intervened to transform this benevolent mood and realistic approach, if it really was that, to deception and the posture of open hatred.

We are told that Sheikh Mujibur Rahman and his party, the Awami League, had planned a non-violent movement of resistance to the Government of West Pakistan. But they were caught unawares and overtaken by a brutal military assault. They had no alternative but to declare for independence. The East Pakistan Rifles and East Bengal Regiment became the Mukti Fauj and later the Mukti Bahini, which was joined by thousands of young East Bengalis, determined to sacrifice their lives for freedom and the right to fashion their future. The unity, determination and courage with which the entire population of Bangladesh is fighting have been recorded by the world Press. These events on our doorstep and the resulting flood of refugees into our territory could not but have far-reaching repercussions on our country. It was natural that our sympathy should be with the people of Bangladesh in their just struggle. But we did not act precipitately in the matter of recognition. Our decisions were not guided merely by emotion but by an assessment of prevailing and future realities.

With the unanimous revolt of the entire people of Bangladesh and the success of their struggle, it has become increasingly apparent that the so-called mother State of Pakistan is totally incapable of bringing the people of Bangladesh back under its control. As for the legitimacy of the Government of Bangladesh, the whole world is now aware that it reflects the will of the overwhelming majority of the people, which not many governments can claim to represent. In Jefferson's famous words to Governor Morris, the Government of Bangladesh is supported by the 'will of the nation, substantially expressed'. Applying this criterion, the military regime in Pakistan, which some States are so anxious to buttress, is hardly representative of its people even in West Pakistan.

Now that Pakistan is waging war against India, the normal hesitation on our part not to do anything which could come in the way of a peaceful solution, or which might be construed as intervention, has lost significance. The people of Bangladesh are battling for their very existence and the people of India fighting to defeat aggression now find themselves partisans in the same cause. I am glad to inform the House that in the light of the existing situation and in response to the repeated requests of the Government of Bangladesh, the Government of India have, after the most careful consideration, decided to grant recognition to the GANA PRAJA TANTRI BANGLAA DESH[1].

It is our hope that with the passage of time, more nations will grant recognition and that the GANA PRAJA TANTRI BANGLAA DESH will soon form part of the family of nations.

[1] Editor's translation: People's Republic of Bangladesh.

Our thoughts at this moment are with the father of this new State, Sheikh Mujibur Rahman. I am sure that this House would wish me to convey to their Excellencies the Acting President of Bangladesh and the Prime Minister and to their colleagues, our greetings and warm felicitations.

I am placing on the Table of the House copies of the communications which we have received from the Government of Bangladesh. Hon'ble Members will be glad to know that the Government of Bangladesh have proclaimed their basic principles of State policy to be democracy, socialism, secularism and the establishment of an egalitarian society in which there would be no discrimination on the basis of race, religion, sex or creed. In regard to foreign relations, the Bangladesh Government have expressed their determination to follow a policy of non-alignment, peaceful coexistence and opposition to colonialism, racialism and imperialism in all its manifestations. These are the ideals to which India also is dedicated.

The Bangladesh Government have reiterated their anxiety to organize the expeditious return of their citizens who have found temporary refuge in our country, and to restore their lands and belongings to them. We shall naturally help in every way in these arrangements. I am confident that in future the Governments and the peoples of India and Bangladesh, who share common ideals and sacrifices, will forge a relationship based on the principles of mutual respect for each other's sovereignty and territorial integrity, non-interference in internal affairs, equality and mutual benefit. Thus working together for freedom and democracy, we shall set an example of good neighbourliness which alone can ensure peace, stability and progress in this region. Our good wishes to Bangladesh.

MADHU DANDAVATE

(Lok Sabha: Rajapur)

Lok Sabha: 6 December 1971

Statement on Recognition to Bangladesh

Sir, the late Pandit Jawaharlal Nehru once said that freedom, like peace, is indivisible and a threat to freedom in one part of the world constitutes a threat to freedom elsewhere. I am glad the Prime Minister has listened to the voice of her father and in resounding terms, has accepted the freedom of Bangladesh, which is in consonance with the freedom of our country.

Today, the freedom fighters and martyrs of Bangladesh must have felt that their martyrdom has not gone in vain. They must have realized that the recognition of Bangladesh would not come at the diplomatic table, but it will emerge through the fire of revolution and struggle. And that way, the recognition of Bangladesh by India has come. For that reason, I congratulate the Prime Minister and also the country.

I do not wish to take much time. Today, the martyrs and the freedom fighters of Bangladesh must be remembering the words of the great Poet who said:

Oh! Liberty! Can man resign thee
Once having felt thy generous flame?
Can dungeon, bolts or bars
Confine thee or whip thy noble spirit tame?[2]

These were the words which illumined the path of many freedom fighters the world over. These are the words which will enliven and illumine the life and dedication of the freedom fighters of Bangladesh. I am glad the forces of freedom in India and in Bangladesh have tuned themselves in unison. That will be the picture of the world we will like to dream of and India will always stand for all those who are struggling for freedom. Our armies will never march on any country to conquer the land; our armies will always march to defend and uphold the freedom of the land, that is the tradition of our great country.

INDIRA GANDHI

(Lok Sabha: Rae Bareli)

Lok Sabha: 16 December 1971

Statement on Unconditional Surrender of West Pakistan Forces in Bangladesh

Mr. Speaker, Sir, I have an announcement to make, which I think the House has been waiting for, for some time. The West Pakistan forces have unconditionally surrendered in Bangladesh. The instrument of surrender was signed in Dacca at 16:31 hours IST today by Lt. Gen. A.A.K. Niazi on behalf of the Pakistan Eastern Command. Lt. Gen. Jagjit Singh Aurora, GOC-in-C[3] of the Indian and Bangladesh forces in the Eastern Theatre accepted the surrender. Dacca is now the free capital of a free country.

This House and the entire nation rejoice in this historic event. We hail the people of Bangladesh in their hour of triumph. We hail the brave young men and boys of the Mukti Bahini for their valour and dedication. We are proud of our own Army, Navy, Air Force and the Border Security Force, who have so magnificently demonstrated

[2] Editor's note: Part of the present French National Anthem.

[3] Editor's note: General Officer Commanding-in-Chief.

their quality and capacity. Their discipline and devotion to duty are well known. India will remember with gratitude the sacrifices of those who have laid down their lives, and our thoughts are with their families.

Our Armed Forces are under strict orders to treat Pakistani prisoners of war in accordance with the Geneva Convention, and to deal with all sections of the population of Bangladesh in a humane manner. The Commanders of the Mukti Bahini have issued similar orders to their forces. Although the Government of Bangladesh have not yet been given an opportunity to sign the Geneva Convention, they also have declared that they will fully abide by it. It will be the responsibility of the Government of Bangladesh, the Mukti Bahini and the Indian Armed Forces to prevent any reprisals. Our objectives were limited – to assist the gallant people of Bangladesh and their Mukti Bahini to liberate their country from a reign of terror and to resist aggression on our own land. Indian Armed Forces will not remain in Bangladesh any longer than is necessary.

The millions who were driven out of their homes across our borders have already begun trekking back. The rehabilitation of this war-torn land calls for dedicated team work by its Government and people.

We hope and trust that the Father of this new nation, Sheikh Mujibur Rahman, will take his rightful place among his own people and lead Bangladesh to peace, progress and prosperity. The time has come when they can together look forward to a meaningful future in their Shonar Bangla.[4] They have our good wishes. The triumph is not theirs alone. All nations who value the human spirit, will recognise it as a significant milestone in man's quest for liberty.

JAGJIVAN RAM

(Lok Sabha: Sasaram)

Lok Sabha: 18 December 1971

Statement Reviewing the Outcome of the Recent Armed Conflict Arising Out of Pakistani Aggression on India

Mr. Deputy-Speaker, Sir, I am sorry I have been late by a few minutes in coming to the House. I am rushing from Kanpur.

On Friday, December 3rd, around 5.40 p.m., Pakistan had unleashed its total war on India, with pre-emptive strikes at our airfields and heavy attacks on our defensive positions all along the western frontier. We were able to commence our counter action on the western front only around midnight.

[4] Editor's translation: Golden Bengal.

On the eastern frontier, we moved in the early hours of Saturday, December 4th, from different directions into what was then known as East Pakistan to act in concert with the Mukti Bahini and other elements of the National Liberation Forces of Bangla Desh. With the signing of the Instrument of Surrender by Lt. Gen. Niazi, Martial Law Administrator of Zone B, at 16.31 hours on Thursday, December 16th, the people of Bangla Desh were finally freed from West Pakistani subjugation of a quarter of a century and from the brutal terror that had gripped them since March 25, 1971.

The successful completion of this campaign of liberation, within a period of 12 days, across a vast expanse of land, crisscrossed with rivers and rivulets, inhabited by nearly 75 million people and held down by 93,000 regular and para-military forces of West Pakistani origin will rank in the annals of military history as a remarkable feat.

The strategy of our forces to bypass main cities to avoid civilian casualties and to prevent damage to national assets surprised the enemy.

The speed of our flanking movements and the determination with which they were pressed rendered the long prepared positions of the enemy untenable.

The Mukti Bahini fought shoulder to shoulder with our forces. The Freedom Fighters provided invaluable assistance by harassing the enemy in the rear and by enabling our forces to overcome numerous riverine obstacles.

The Indian Air Force achieved mastery of the vast airspace within the first twenty-four hours by completely annihilating the PAF[5] in Bangla Desh. The punishment inflicted from the air on military installations and positions caused tremendous havoc. The supply as well as escape routes by air were completely sealed.

Helicopters were extensively used to land our troops in the rear. A battalion of paratroopers was dropped at predetermined places north of Dacca. The link of these paratroopers with the ground forces of the Mukti Bahini and the Indian Army made it possible for us to reach the outskirts of Dacca on the eleventh day of the campaign.

Our Navy played a significant role. The Eastern Naval Command deployed our Aircraft Carrier VIKRANT with supporting ships and submarines to immobilize the port facilities at Chittagong and in the Khulna–Chalna–Mongla complex and to damage airfields and military installations on the southern periphery. Amphibious landings were carried out at Cox's Bazar to seal off a possible escape route for the enemy to Burma.

It appears that the Martial Law Administrator had lost operational control over his Divisional Commanders at an early stage of the battle. The Pakistani troops, however, fought gallantly. Their Commanders did not pay heed to the messages

[5] Editor's note: Pakistan Air Force.

addressed by General Manekshaw to save their lives. Major-General Rao Farman Ali's initiative was overruled by Pindi. It was only in the evening of December 15th that the wisdom of allowing further bloodshed dawned on the military rulers. (Interruptions.)

By then the tables had been turned on the aggressor on the Western front. Pakistan's massive offensive thrusts in the Poonch, Chhamb and Rajasthan sectors were effectively blunted. The fight to protect our sacred soil against Pakistan's furious onslaughts was fierce. Our jawans stood their ground with dogged determination and thrust the enemy back into his territory. Repeated attempts by the enemy to infiltrate behind our lines were frustrated. The local Kashmiris helped to round up straggling infiltrators. To protect our vital land communications in Jammu and Kashmir, we carried the war into the enemy's territory. To keep the enemy away from Rajasthan and Gujarat, we made significant gains in the Barmer and Kutch sectors. We succeeded in drawing the enemy's reserves into open battle and in scattering his attacking forces.

The Indian Air Force struck, without interruption, by day and by night, at aircraft on the ground, at airfield installations, runways and radar stations. Troop concentrations were broken up and armoured columns were scattered. Important installations of military value were severely damaged and the transportation system was disrupted. In addition, the IAF provided air cover to our ground forces and co-operated with them in destroying the enemy's tanks. Our air defence units took a heavy toll of the enemy's intruding aircraft. In the concluding stages of the conflict, the enemy's air activity was reduced to a fraction of ours.

The task of the Western Naval Command was to contain the Pakistani fleet and prevent it from hitting at our shipping and our ports.

The House is aware of the two daring attacks mounted by our Western fleet which damaged port and shore installations at Karachi and substantially reduced the strength of the Pakistani fleet. In consequence, the enemy was unable to interfere with our maritime shipping. While our ports functioned normally, our Navy completely succeeded in cutting off the enemy's supplies by sea.

The enemy has paid dearly for aggression. Pakistani losses in equipment are computed at 94 aircraft, 246 tanks, two warships, two submarines, two minesweepers and 16 gunboats, both in the Eastern and Western sectors. Vital installations of military significance have been severely damaged. Pakistani casualties are known to have been very heavy. Obviously, it is impossible to have the exact figures. A full tally of prisoners is not yet available. In Dacca alone, as many as 24,000 have surrendered.

The cease-fire on the Western front became effective yesterday at 8 p.m. At that hour, we were in occupation of numerous pockets of Pakistani territory. In Kargil, Gurais and Uri sector, our troops have occupied nearly 50 posts. In the Tithwal sector, a substantial portion of the Lipa valley is in our hands. Some commanding heights across the cease-fire line have been taken by us in the Poonch–Rajauri–Naushera sector. The whole of the Akhnur Dagger salient and a number of border posts in the Jammu sector are with us. We have crossed the Basantar River and the greatest part of the Shankargarh–Zafarwal salient is in our possession. The Dera Baba Nanak Enclave south of Ravi has been occupied by us. Several border posts in the Dera Baba Nanak–Ajnala–Amritsar–Khem Karan–Ferozepur–Mamdot and Fazilka sectors have been taken. In the Bikaner sector, Rukanpur, Ranhal and Bijanot have been captured. In the Jaisalmer–Islamgarh–Bhukhanwala Khu area, we are 4 to 8 miles inside Pak territory. Apart from a number of border posts on the border of Sind, including Chhad Bet, we have occupied the whole of Nagarparker Bulge and captured Chachro and Virawah. We have effective control right up to Naya Chor and Umarkot in the Pakistani province of Sind. The posts and the pockets in our possession ensure the security of our Western borders and provide full protection to our vital road links.

Our losses have been comparatively smaller. We lost 45 aircraft, 73 tanks and one frigate. All our installations are in full operational order.

For the liberation of Bangla Desh, 1,047 of our brave officers and men laid down their lives, 3,047 were wounded and 89 are missing.

On the Western front, 1,426 were killed, 3,611 were wounded and 2,149 are missing.

The area west of Munnawar Tawi was, at the time of cease-fire, in Pakistan's possession; so is the enclave west of Sutlej at Husainiwala. There is a very small lodgement in Pakistan's possession in the area in the west of Fazilka around village Pakka.

Pakistan's military adventure has recoiled on its military leaders. The experience of 14 days of fighting, the loss of territory and of manpower, together with the severe damage inflicted on equipment and installations would, as soon as the facts become known to them, convince the people of Pakistan of the disastrous consequences of unprovoked armed aggression.

On the evening of the December 16th, the Prime Minister announced a unilateral cease-fire. This would convince not only the people of Pakistan but the world at large in regard to our intentions. In our view, there is no dispute between our two countries which cannot be settled by friendly negotiation between ourselves.

We have no territorial ambitions. Our jawans who have fought so bravely and who have sacrificed their lives at the call of duty will, however, need to be assured that their sacrifices will yield results of lasting value to the peoples of India and Pakistan. They already have the satisfaction that they have contributed to the liberation of Bangla Desh and to the emergence of a Secular Democratic State on our Eastern Borders. It will now be our endeavour to forge, through bilateral negotiations, a new relationship with Pakistan, based not on conflict but on cooperation, guaranteeing to us the security of our borders and our vital road communications, and assuring to the peoples of the two countries freedom from fear of recurring wars and an opportunity to devote their full attention to economic and social progress.

We have to redeem the pledges we made to our people when we were elected to power. I am sure the people of Pakistan and Bangla Desh also ardently desire to devote their attention to similar tasks. Let us hope that the experience of fourteen days of armed conflict with Pakistan will help to usher an era of peace and prosperity for the subcontinent.

The House owes its gratitude to the vast number of men and women whose exertions and sacrifices have contributed to the success of our arms. We owe a special duty to the next of kin of those who have laid down their lives and to those who have been disabled by the conflict. We have also to make good the equipment we have lost. The tax-payer will, no doubt, do his part. The nation may, however, wish to give expression to its sentiments by organizing a massive voluntary effort to provide relief to those who have suffered and to provide to the armed forces equipment they have lost.

We could not have achieved this success but for the enthusiastic exertions of our farmers and our industrial workers. A special word of thanks is due to the railwaymen and truck drivers who kept supplies moving and to the personnel who manned our telecommunication network. The men in charge of our merchant shipping succeeded in keeping up a steady stream of supplies. I am also full of admiration for the courage and fortitude of the common man who carried on his normal tasks in the face of enemy gun-fire along our borders and around the airfields.

The nation can be proud of the devotion, the dedication, the determination, the skill and the efficiency of those of our citizens who fought, with all their might, on land, at sea, and in the air, the dark forces of aggression. Our military leadership rose to the occasion. The cooperation, understanding and cohesiveness achieved by the three services in planning and executing the joint operations have been gratifying. The Defence Forces of India are now a well-knit team, capable of guaranteeing the security of our motherland against external aggression. Their success on the battlefield should give us confidence in our war on poverty and want.

On behalf of the Defence Services and the Ministry of Defence, may I tender their grateful thanks for the generous appreciation by this august House, and indeed by the entire nation, of the efforts made by them to perform their national tasks to the best of their ability.

SAMAR GUHA

(Lok Sabha: Contai)

Lok Sabha: 16 June 1971

Discussion on Influx of Refugees from Bangladesh

Sir, when I rise to speak today, the faces of those emaciated skeletons who have crossed into Indian territory from Bangladesh flash into my mind's eye …

They are the people who have lost their near and dear ones.

… many of them have lost their near and dear ones in Bangla Desh. Many parents have lost their sons and daughters. Many sons and daughters have lost their parents. Many mothers and sisters – hundreds and thousands of them – have not only been dishonoured but thousands have been kidnapped and kept inside the cantonments and garrisons of the Pakistani army. Human history perhaps has no parallel to such a Titanic tragedy of uprooted humanity, millions of uprooted humanity, who face a terrible situation of total destitution, utter despair and boundless misery.

Yesterday, Shri Khadilkar quoted the figure of the Bangladesh refugees as 5.7 million. But that figure is wrong. Because, according to the statement issued by the Chief Minister of West Bengal, the figures are West Bengal: 45.6 lakhs, Tripura: 9.4 lakhs, Meghalaya: 3.4 lakhs and Assam: 8 lakhs … If you total all these, it is near about 7 million and this is the figure as on 11th June. Now it has already crossed the 7 million mark. According to Rev. Blum, an international gentleman, Director of 'War on Want', who visited almost all the borders, the figure has already touched the mark of 10 million.

The people who have come from Bangladesh … have not come as a result of natural calamity. They have come to seek shelter and protection in Indian territory as a result of the most brutal butchery, as a result of the conspiracy of the Government of Pakistan. It is a conspiracy of the Government of Pakistan not only to kill them, not only to butcher them, not only to commit genocide on the people of Bangladesh, but to push them … into the Indian soil, to subvert our own security, to shatter our economy, to create dislocation in our socio-economic matrix, to create communal tension here and to create a colossal problem for our own country.

These 7 million refugees from Bangladesh who have … been forced to enter into India as a result of the sordid conspiracy of a foreign government … Is it not aggression in disguise by Pakistan? If that is so, I want to remind the Government, by human touch alone, by giving them shelter and protection, you cannot resolve the problem of the Bangladesh refugees. Humanitarian touch may be essential to give them temporary shelter but the political problem, which is the real cause of uprooting millions … has to be faced with firm political determination and political action.

It was very nice yesterday to hear the Prime Minister say that we will go through hell to meet the situation in Bangladesh. She also rose very high when she said that she will not accept any political solution which will mean … death for Bangladesh. Very nice words, very encouraging words; but words do not mean anything unless followed by positive, firm and determined action. I want to know from the Government whether they can convince the people of India that this government, after the outbreak of national revolution in Bangladesh, has taken any positive action to … stop the worst kind of genocide that has been perpetrated on 7½ million people in Bangladesh, a thing that has never happened in any part of the world. What has happened to this government, a government which represents 55 crores of people, a government which represents a nation which is the second biggest in the world? … What is this, if it is not emasculation of the whole national being …

I do not want to dilate much on the subject … If this Government had any sense of responsibility, Shri Khadilkar, who is responsible for dealing with the refugee problem, when his presence in India was necessary every hour, would not have gone on a foreign tour … for nearly two weeks. Even when such an important discussion is being held in this House, he is not present here. He has left the responsibility to the Deputy Minister.

What did the Deputy Minister do? He made a naive statement, something like an astrological forecast. He said that they will be required to keep the Bangla Desh refugees only for six months. What is the basis of his calculation? How does he say that they will keep these refugees only for six months? Have they anything in mind, any positive programme or line of action? …

Shri Khadilkar should be sacked and relieved from the responsibility of this Ministry. He has not even gone to the border except once. On … the 23rd May evening, he flew to Calcutta and came back on the 24th May when Parliament opened, only for a few hours. After that, when people from the whole world are coming, this Rehabilitation Minister has not visited West Bengal, Tripura or any part of that area. Not even the Deputy Minister, none of the important Ministers has visited these refugee areas. This is the attitude …

… When you said that you would be required to keep the refugees only for six months, do you remember what taunting remark was made by the Speaker himself? The Speaker said, 'Do you really believe that they will go back?' It was a spontaneous reaction of the Speaker. The Speaker reflected the opinion of the people at large in our country and of all State Governments, because you have words, words and words – brave words, nice words, decent words, courageous words, words of confidence, but without an iota of positive action.

That is the reason why you have not been able to create any confidence either in the mind of Bangla Desh refugees or of any State Government or of the people of India that you really mean action and that these refugees will go back to Bangla Desh, their homeland. That is why the State Governments are reluctant to take these Bangla Desh refugees. Even after the Nehru-Liaquat Pact in 1950, Nehru had harboured the idea that after that Pact, the refugees would go back. But after 1956, he was completely disillusioned when not a single soul of a refugee went back on the assurance of Liaquat Ali. You can have an assurance but these assurances will have no meaning unless you take some positive action.

I will draw your attention to what the Meghalaya Government has done ... They have maltreated men and women. Refugees are treated as prisoners. 6,000 Bangla Desh refugees have been forced to go back to Sunamganj-Sylhet area out of sheer frustration. They said when they went back, 'We are being killed here; we will be killed there; let us be killed in our own homeland.' The Prime Minister went to visit Meghalaya ... You must enlighten this House about the condition there.

If you are really serious about sending the Bangla Desh refugees back to their homeland, I suggest that it is absolutely wrong to take them to different States. They should be kept in West Bengal, Tripura, Assam and Meghalaya. I remind you that at the time of partition, almost all refugees from West Pakistan were given temporary shelter in East Punjab in Government camps. It can be done in West Bengal and in all the border States ... If finance, management and supply can be assured by the Central Government, camps can be built in the interior areas of the border States. Why I say so? You must keep the Bangla Desh spirit amongst the refugees alive. Unless you keep the Bangladesh spirit alive, it will not be possible for you, even after a radical change in ... Bangla Desh, to send them back ... The Government should undertake the responsibility of financing and giving them supplies. These refugees can be put in the interior area of the border States.

The Chief Minister of West Bengal has made a statement that they have not been able to provide shelter to about 25 lakhs of refugees. They have only the sky above them, some water to drink, but no food. At the same time, the Minister says that those who are not in the camps will not be provided with ration. What a contradiction! You have not been able to give them shelter. You have not been able to set up camps. At the same time, you are denying them the ration. What a terrible thing! What an inhuman thing! ... You have admitted that 50 per cent of the refugees have not been provided any shelter either in the camps or any kind or improvised shelter. I demand that the rations be given to all, whether they are in camps or with their relatives or under the shade of trees or in the open with only sky above. Equal treatment should be given to all of them.

What is this ration that is given? It is only 400 grams of rice, 100 grams of dal, a few ... onions and potatoes. Is it not a fact that all these people have left everything behind in Bangla Desh? When they were coming here, even the last vestiges of their belongings were snatched away. They have come here only with bare skeleton. They have nothing with them. How will they cook? From where will they get utensils? From where will they get oil, fuel and all that? They have no clothings, no beddings, etc. The Government has not given them anything. I say, some cash allowance should be given to them so that they can purchase some clothings, beddings, etc.

About the management, and I do not know how many young men and women are there, the Government lacks imagination. Most of them are young men and women who have come … because their lives are in danger in Bangla Desh. Why have they not been recruited? Why don't you give them an opportunity to manage their own community kitchens, look after the sanitation and other things? It is to keep the spirit of Bangladesh alive in them. Why have you not done that? You should do that. Also, in all the camps, you should keep at least one leader a revolutionary of Bangla Desh so that they can keep up the spirit of Bangla Desh in them.

I would like to draw the attention of the hon'ble Minister to another point. The international help should be given not in cash but in kind. You know the reasons. The priority should be given for supplies of tents, tarpaulins, land and air transports, ambulance cars, tube-well equipment, dry foods, baby foods, milk powder, medicines, etc.

Lastly, I would like to say that Mr. Khadilkar, by his … lack of responsibility has amply proved that the Ministry of Rehabilitation and Labour and Employment should be separated immediately. If the Government really wants to tackle this gigantic problem, unprecedented problem of the refugees, immediately, a separate Ministry for Rehabilitation for dealing with refugees should be set up. They should set up immediately an office at Calcutta with either Minister of State or Deputy Minister who can take spot decisions.

It is a matter of shame for us that, when a delegation from UK is visiting Bangla Desh, and they will be coming to our country, the Government has not sponsored any delegation of the Members of Parliament to go to the border area to see things with their own eyes. I demand that the Government … immediately organize a delegation of Members of Parliament to go along to the border area to see things with their own eyes and help the Government in tackling this gigantic problem.

Lastly, I want that if the Government do not want to behave in a partisan way – it is a national problem and so long the Opposition has treated it as a national problem … they should immediately set up a Refugees Council with members of the Government Party as well as the Opposition and presided over by the Minister of Rehabilitation. Only then it will mean that the Government wants a national approach to the national crisis that we are facing today. Thank you, Sir.

3

The Bus to Lahore

*There was a short-lived thaw between India and Pakistan when **Atal Bihari Vajpayee,** as Prime Minister, took the bus to Lahore in February 1999. The image of Vajpayee hugging his Pakistani counterpart, Nawaz Sharif, led people to believe that it marked the dawn of a new era in Indo-Pak relations. 'I bring the goodwill and hope of my fellow Indians who seek abiding peace and harmony with Pakistan ... I am conscious that this is a defining moment in South Asian history and I hope we will be able to rise to the challenge,' Vajpayee said on his arrival in Lahore.*

But the goodwill generated by that visit did not last long: a few months later, the Pakistan Army undertook a covert operation to send troops into the Kargil area in Jammu and Kashmir. That led to a limited conflict that Pakistan lost. In December of the same year, IC-814 was hijacked and flown to Kandahar. India was forced to release terrorists in its custody in a swap for the return of the passengers taken hostage.

The Agra summit followed in 2001, when Vajpayee invited the then President Pervez Musharraf talks to India, in an effort to resume the talks. But the best that can be said of those talks, is that they concluded without any clear outcome. The terrorist attack on the Indian Parliament in December 2001 heralded a fresh phase of India–Pakistan tensions, which almost led to a fifth shooting war.

In May 2003, Vajpayee defended his record in dealing with Pakistan, days after he said, prophetically, that it would be the last time he would attempt to negotiate with that country. His party would lose the general elections a year on, in 2004.

*Earlier in the discussion, Congress leader **Sonia Gandhi,** while extending her party's support to any efforts to improve relations with Pakistan, raised a few questions in a well-crafted speech, ending with a pointed question on 'whether the Prime Minister has the support and the cooperation of his own ideological brotherhood'.*

ATAL BIHARI VAJPAYEE

(Lok Sabha: Lucknow)

Lok Sabha: 8 May 2003

Discussion Under Rule 193 on Indo–Pak Relations

Mr. Speaker, Sir, I would like to thank all those hon'ble Members who participated in the discussion. There are some issues on which there is a broad consensus in the House. The issue of our relation with Pakistan is one such issue. There may be difference of opinion among us, but inspite of that, we all work together to achieve the goal and our last goal is to ensure the victory, glory, fame and unity of India. A number of old issues have been raised in the discussion. It started from Lahore onwards. But I do not accept any blame for going to Lahore. (Interruptions.)

We have to live with our neighbour as a friend ... But we should not lose any opportunity of building good relations. Our development depends on internal and external peace. We do not want to buy weapons for war and to use our resources to buy such weapons, but when our freedom or integrity is in danger, we have to be ready to bear all costs and defend ourselves. I have told my Pakistani friends a number of times that we can change our friends but not our neighbours. None of us can get away from each other. We have to live here. Now one way of living together is to live like neighbours and friends and second way is to keep quarrelling and fighting, and give the world a chance to laugh at us and thus take the wrong way, as a result of misconstruing the emotions of our people. Therefore, we should be friends with our neighbours to the extent possible. That is why I went to Lahore. It would be wrong to say that no homework was prepared before the visit. This charge has also been made about the Agra talks. What does it mean? The structure of the government is very much intact, and my Government has not made any drastic change in the Ministry of External Affairs. I think that my friends would agree that the clever diplomats pass the buck on their officers, but the External Affairs Ministry protects its officers. We had full preparation, but in between the Kargil issue cropped up, which was essentially due to power struggle between their Government and army General. The Lahore Declaration signed by the two countries said the dialogue would be held and all issues will be solved peacefully. We had agreed on it. The Declaration was silent on Kashmir as in our discussion it was agreed that the Kashmir issue is a tangled one so it be deferred, and it would be better if we resolve other issues and go forward.

... I am referring to the talks that took place when General Musharraf came to Agra, during the discussion he did his best to have his way on Kashmir. Now he says that nothing of that sort took place. General Musharraf had to return ...

empty-handed from Agra. I am being held guilty of not preparing any home work. Had there been no preparation, we would not have been able to successfully repulse the Pakistani attack in Kargil. We did not allow Pakistan to succeed in its design. Their domestic troubles reached an extent that their Prime Minister had to resign. They could not work unitedly. I am saying all this only to underline the fact that our efforts are well-intentioned. Sometimes, it succeeds and sometimes it fails. Ceasefire has been declared a number of times. There is consensus that the two countries have friendly relations, especially, with regard to Jammu–Kashmir, but it could not be realized. Terrorist groups were split and differences surfaced among them. What is their condition today? I would not like to go in detail. Now it is being said that I had said that we would not talk with them unless cross border terrorism is stopped. Of course, I had said that, but my goal was to stop cross border terrorism. I decided to strive towards that goal and we worked so enthusiastically that, except a few countries, all countries of the world were of the opinion that cross-border terrorism should be stopped. We succeeded in turning world opinion in our favour. I do not say that our war against terrorism will be fought by others but it gave us scope for agreement and a way out was provided. Therefore, we decided that as the elections have taken place in Kashmir which is such a significant phenomenon and which, in my opinion, should be properly assessed.

Shrimati Soniaji did not ... mention ... elections in Jammu and Kashmir. Holding elections in Jammu and Kashmir has added a new chapter to Indian polity. People faced bullets and went for voting. All evil designs of Pakistan turned futile. I saw large gathering of the people that day. Though I had been to Kashmir earlier also. I have seen several types of welcome gathering in Kashmir but the meeting after the election in Jammu and Kashmir, wherein Mufti (Mohammad Sayeed) supported us and we welcomed him was ... unique ... That scene may have dumbfounded our neighbour country. Whether it was so or not, it created enthusiasm in our hearts that the public is with us: the venom of communalism will not work and people want peace. Many people were killed during the elections and many were injured. If one counts the total number ... one would realize that the people of Jammu and Kashmir have sacrificed a lot.

That day I felt that there is a need to take a new initiative. Meanwhile, an event of international importance took place, though I would not like to go in details over that. The way Iraq was attacked, neglecting and rendering the United Nations ineffective, compelled me to think that small developing and non-aligned nations need to think seriously about their future. I take it as a change in a new direction ... (Interruptions.)

... Mr. Speaker, Sir, that day I felt that there is a need to take a new initiative. In reply to his repeated query – whether terrorism has been controlled, if I say that it has come down then he would say, it will not do, it should be totally controlled.

Then I would say that all the terrorists do not belong to a single outfit, they are also divided. They are also playing different types of politics and all are not under one umbrella. It is quite a serious matter if it is so, but the reality is different. We got a hint that there is a wave of change and the people of Jammu and Kashmir have given a befitting reply. I found it was the right time to improve our relations, provided Pakistan stops cross-border terrorism and destroys terrorists' camps which have come up there. It is just a rehearsal and the talks are yet to start. When I had a telephonic talk with the Prime Minister of Pakistan, he invited me to play hockey in Pakistan. Then I told him that he had been a good player of hockey. I know that he has captained Pakistani Team and used to select his players. I asked him what will be the reaction in a situation when a hockey match between India and Pakistan is being witnessed by the entire town and meanwhile the news spreads that terrorists have massacred 50 innocent men, women and children in Jammu? What shall be the reaction to this? Will it create friendship? Therefore, I told that first terrorism should be stopped. I do not want to repeat what he said but he said that they are also fed up of this terrorism, and that they are fighting terrorism in their country, now we would fight it out unitedly. Only after that, we decided on the idea of exchange of views. I would assure the … Members that we will definitely tread the path cautiously.

If we become inactive, take no step or initiative and sit idle, it will not behove for a large country like India. India occupies a prominent position in the world. Everyone is aware of our feeling of dedication to peace. People have not supported Pakistan-sponsored terrorism; they have supported the elections in Jammu and Kashmir. Foreigners who came to watch the electoral process have realized that the people have expressed their opinion peacefully even in the face of bullets and the world should respect it. At least we should give them due importance. It is the beginning of a new chapter, let us extend it further.

None wants to lose Jammu and Kashmir. I do not know how Soniaji has said so. Who says Jammu and Kashmir will go to Pakistan? No, it will not go. Can a person saying so … afford to stay here? None has said so; I do not want to go into it. No one can divide Jammu and Kashmir. There are three parts, three separate divisions of Jammu and Kashmir. They have been staying together for the last several years and they would stay together under the new arrangement, also …

… Some more questions were raised. Pakistan is suggesting denuclearization of South Asia, which is not acceptable to us. The Pakistani Atomic Programme is India-specific whereas ours is not Pakistan-specific. We are not only concerned about Pakistan, we are concerned about our entire neighbourhood. We had adopted a nuclear doctrine and we have given an assurance that we will not attack first, whereas Pakistan has not made any such commitment. Not only that, it has refused to make any commitment to this effect. Then what is the meaning of a No-war-

Pact? Malhotra ji has quite rightly said that it should be, 'No proxy war pact'.

Mr. Speaker, Sir, other questions were also raised ... I would like to say that the entire world is facing a crisis, and in that situation, if no concrete decision is taken then crisis will deepen further.

It is not an offence to seek peace. Though it is another matter whether we succeed or not. Who wants failure? But with the apprehension that we may fail, we make no effort, that is not good. A large country like independent India cannot take this type of decision.

We had not opposed the Shimla Pact because it contained an element of friendship. That time I had opposed it because it did not resolve the Jammu and Kashmir issue.

We may have divergent views ... But when the world looks at India, it expects us to speak in one voice, that we would sit together and resolve our differences.

Mr. Speaker, Sir, I convey my thanks to all and expect that the consensus arrived at this juncture would be maintained.

SONIA GANDHI

(Lok Sabha: Rae Bareli)

Lok Sabha: 8 May 2003

Discussion Under Rule 193 on Indo–Pak Relations

Mr. Speaker, Sir, I rise to extend yet again the Congress Party's support to the Prime Minister in his search for a durable and enduring peace with Pakistan, but with all humility, Sir, allow me to say that the Congress's stand on dialogue with Pakistan has been finally vindicated. We only wish that the BJP-Ied NDA Government's policies in regard to Pakistan had clarity, conviction and consistency.

The Government's stance has vacillated from one extreme to another, giving rise occasionally to the impression that we are responding to external pressures. But, in spite of these inconsistencies, we have extended our broad and sustained support to the Government on matters relating to national security, to cross-border terrorism in Jammu and Kashmir, and Indo-Pak relations. But Sir, we are puzzled, and the country awaits an explanation for the inconsistent and contradictory statements made by the Prime Minister; by the Deputy Prime Minister; by the Foreign Affairs Minister from time to time on such a vital matter.

Repeatedly we have been told that there will be no resumption of talks with Pakistan so long as cross-border terrorism in Jammu and Kashmir continues. Here I would like to quote the Prime Minister from his speech in Gangtok, Sikkim, on the 14th April where he said, and I quote: 'To create a conducive atmosphere for talks it is imperative that cross-border terrorism is stopped immediately.' The implication here is quite clear. The Prime Minister here quite clearly implied that talks with Pakistan will be held only after it stopped cross-border terrorism. But then, the Prime Minister extended his hand of friendship to Pakistan in Srinagar, on 17th April, with the following words. Again I quote: 'We are again extending a hand of friendship, but hands should be extended from both sides. Both sides should decide to live together.' Here there is no mention, as far as I know – from all the reports that we saw coming out from Srinagar – of cross-border terrorism. Then again, the Prime Minister at the very end of his suo motu statement in the Lok Sabha on the 23rd April said, and again I quote: 'Stopping cross-border infiltration and destruction of terrorist infrastructure can open the doors for talks.'

This is not as categorical as in Gangtok, but it is nuanced, nevertheless. Therefore, are we now to understand that the Government has obtained firm commitments from Pakistan that its sponsorship of cross-border terrorism will cease? Are we to understand that this remains the pre-condition for the resumption of dialogue? Sir, as I have said before, the Congress's stand has been all along clear and unequivocal. It has been repeatedly articulated. We have also been repeatedly attacked by the BJP on this very issue, and particularly, when elections were close. But, we stood by our principles all along because we believe that they are in the interests of our country.

We have always said that the doors of diplomacy and the windows of dialogue – official or unofficial, formal or informal – must be kept open and active at all times and on all issues of mutual concern and interest.

Sir, India's and Pakistan's futures are linked. We need much closer and much more vibrant cultural contact; contacts between our educational institutions; cricket, hockey and other sporting institutions; relationships between political parties and civil society; organizations; tourism; economic and trade ties; and cooperation in many other vital areas. The Congress has also, for the past five years, been repeatedly advocating a transparent and verifiable set of confidence-building agreements on nuclear and missile issues.

Sir, the Shimla Agreement was signed in July 1972 and it provides the essential framework, essential architecture for fostering bilateral relationship. It is, if I may be permitted to say, a tribute to the noble instincts of Indiraji and her senior colleagues. Then, Indiraji offered a friendship pact to President Zia-ul-Haq. Subsequently, Shri Rajiv Gandhi travelled to Pakistan in 1988 and there was a brief moment of hope for both the countries. Among other things, Shri Rajiv Gandhi and Ms. Benazir Bhutto entered, at that time, into an agreement on non-attack on each other's nuclear installations. In the early 1990s, the Congress Government of Shri P.V. Narasimha Rao submitted to Pakistan a comprehensive set of confidence-building agreements.

Sir, we supported the Prime Minister's Lahore visit in February, 1999, but we were realistic enough not to go overboard as the then External Affairs Minister did when he termed it as a 'defining moment in Indo-Pak relations'. We all know, Mr. Speaker, Sir, that the defining moment was provided by the Kargil War, preparations for which were obviously going on, while our Prime Minister was being greeted in Lahore. After a long gap, the Government suddenly decided on the Agra Summit without much preparations, without any structured agenda. We watched the utter confusion with great amazement. We hoped for the best, but we were not surprised at the outcome. The Agra Summit was followed by a number of cease-fires.

We supported the Government at that time too. Then, Sir, we had sabre-rattling from both sides, another escalating war of words. We had the attack on Parliament. We had gruesome killings in Jammu and Kashmir. We had unprecedented troop mobilization followed by the usual kafila[1] of visitors from abroad and, then, a pullback. We are still baffled as to what the purpose of Operation Parakram was. What exactly did it accomplish? All of a sudden, then, the Prime Minister, once again, rolled the dice of peace from Srinagar three weeks back.

I believe that both the Parliament and the country are entitled to know why the Government conducted itself in such an ad hoc manner in such a sensitive area as India–Pakistan relations. What is the time-frame and the sequence that the Prime Minister has in mind for the resumption of this dialogue with Pakistan, and at what level are talks being contemplated? What steps are being taken to avoid a repeat of the Agra fiasco? Sir, the past has been painful. It has been complicated. it has been torturous, but let us not become prisoners of our memories.

The future beckons us. We have to make a new beginning, while protecting our interests. There is no question of partitioning Jammu and Kashmir. That is simply unacceptable. There is also no question of handing over Kashmir to Pakistan. That, too, is unacceptable. Let us be very clear of what we will not accept. Only then, we can move forward. I will now end by assuring the Prime Minister of our support. But, the real question is whether the Prime Minister has the enthusiastic and total support of NDA allies on his recently declared vision; whether the Prime Minister has the full backing of his own Cabinet and party colleagues; and, above all, whether the Prime Minister has the support and the cooperation of his own ideological brotherhood.

[1] Editor's translation: Convoy.

Section Four

Pokhran and the India–US Nuclear Deal

1

The Buddha Smiles

India conducted Operation Smiling Buddha, a successful test of an explosive nuclear device, at the Pokhran Test Range in Rajasthan on 18 May 1974. It was the first confirmed nuclear weapons test by a nation outside the five permanent members of the United Nations Security Council. (Taiwan [RoC] was the official Security Council member until the 1970s, and the People's Republic of China [PRC] conducted many nuclear tests before it became a Security Council member.)

Officially, the Indian Ministry of External Affairs described this test as a 'peaceful nuclear explosion'.

***Indira Gandhi**, the then Prime Minister of India, had already won huge acclaim after India's successful military campaign against Pakistan in 1971 that led to the creation of Bangladesh. The Pokhran test revived her popularity, which had flagged after the 1971 war. Indeed, the test led to the enhancement of the image of the Congress – and it was very well received in Parliament, with Indira Gandhi's critics all uniting to praise her role.*

In the speech excerpted here, Indira Gandhi announces the nuclear test, the rationale behind it, as well as some of the negative responses coming in from outside the country. She concludes her speech by saying, 'India does not accept the principle of apartheid in any matter and technology is no exception.'

If the test was received well at home, with India stating that the test was for peaceful purposes, it encountered opposition abroad. The Nuclear Suppliers Group (NSG) was formed in reaction to the Indian tests to check international nuclear proliferation. In 1992, the NSG decided to require full-scope International Atomic Energy Agency (IAEA) safeguards for any new nuclear export deals, which effectively ruled out nuclear exports to India. However, in 2008 it waived this restriction on nuclear trade with India as part of the India–US Civil Nuclear agreement. Pakistan, too, did not view the test as a 'peaceful nuclear explosion'. Pakistan's Prime Minister Zulfikar Ali Bhutto vowed in June 1974 that he would never succumb to 'nuclear blackmail' or accept 'Indian hegemony or domination over the subcontinent'.

INDIRA GANDHI

(Lok Sabha: Rae Bareli)

Lok Sabha: 22 July 1974

Nuclear Explosion Experiment

Hon'ble members are aware that at 08.05 hours on May 18, 1974, our Atomic Energy Commission successfully carried out an underground nuclear explosion experiment at a depth of more than 100 metres in the Rajasthan desert. This experiment was part of the research and development work which the Atomic Energy Commission has been carrying on, in pursuance of our national objective of harnessing atomic energy for peaceful purposes.

Hon'ble Members may recall that on November 15, 1972, I had stated in the Lok Sabha that the Atomic Energy Commission is studying conditions under which peaceful nuclear explosions carried out underground 'could be of economic benefit to India without causing environmental hazards'. Exactly one year later, on November 15, 1973, I informed Hon'ble Members of the Rajya Sabha of the continuing interest of the Atomic Energy Commission in this field and also stated that after satisfactory answers to the problems of the possible effects on environmental and ecological conditions are available, the question of actual underground tests for peaceful purposes could be considered.

I am glad to inform Hon'ble Members that this successful experiment on May 18 has not resulted in any way in radioactive contamination of the atmosphere. The radioactivity was so well contained that a party of scientists was able to fly 30 metres above the site and reach up to 250 metres on the ground within an hour of the experiment without encountering any radioactive contamination.

The Atomic Energy Commission is at present engaged in studying the result of the experiment. It is expected that this process will take about six months. In keeping with scientific tradition, the Atomic Energy Commission proposes to publish papers giving the results of the experiment for the benefit of the scientific world. All the material, equipment and the personnel in this project were totally Indian. India has not violated any international law or obligation or any commitment in this regard with any country. This experiment has evoked mixed responses from various countries.

While developing nations have, by and large, welcomed the experiment as a step in the research and development work carried on by India in the field of atomic energy for peaceful purposes, advanced nations, with some exceptions, have not shown equal understanding. The United States of America, while expressing satisfaction that the International Atomic Energy Agency's safeguards system has worked in regard to agreements with India and that the material used has not come from the United States, have reiterated that the policy of that Government is against nuclear proliferation. The USSR have noted that India has carried out a research programme striving to keep level with the world technology in the peaceful uses of nuclear explosion. The Chairman of the Indian Atomic Energy Commission has received a congratulatory message from the French Atomic Energy Commission on the success of the experiment. China officially reported the event without commenting on the explosion. The reaction of the Government of Japan has been to express regret for the experiment. Reactions from Canada and our neighbour, Pakistan, have been sharp.

While Canada is satisfied that India has not violated any agreement between the two countries, the Canadian Secretary of State for External Affairs has stated that the experiment represented a severe setback to efforts being made in the international community to prevent all nuclear testing and to inhibit the proliferation of nuclear explosion technology. The Government of India is unable to subscribe to the view expressed by the representatives of the Canadian Government in this regard. I have repeatedly reaffirmed our policy of using nuclear energy for peaceful purposes and have specifically stated that we have no intention of developing nuclear weapons. The Government of India sincerely hopes that the Government of Canada will appreciate and understand the background of this experiment. I have already mentioned in the earlier part of this statement the fact that our Atomic Energy Commission has been reviewing the progress in this technology from the theoretical and experimental angles. This intention was not kept secret and was made known to the world. If differences of interpretation have arisen between the Government of Canada and the Government of India, it is the Government of India's hope that they will be satisfactorily resolved in the discussions which are under way between the representatives of the two countries.

The Government of India is unable to comprehend the repeated talk of nuclear blackmail indulged in by the representatives of the Government of Pakistan. I have explained in my letter to Prime Minister Bhutto the peaceful nature and the economic purposes of this experiment and have also stated that India is willing to share her nuclear technology with Pakistan in the same way as she is willing to share it with other countries provided conditions for understanding and trust are created. I once again repeat this assurance and hope that the Government of Pakistan will accept India's position in this regard.

The Government of Pakistan has also made allegations about radioactivity having been carried to that country. I should like to take this opportunity of stating that this was impossible as there was no venting of radioactivity to the atmosphere and no formation of a radioactive cloud. Moreover, the wind was blowing in the opposite direction as it normally does at this time of the year and even in theory, any hypothetical radioactivity could never have gone to Pakistan. The wind pattern on May 18, 1974 was from … the south-west.

There are several published reports by scientists from advanced countries on the potential utilization of peaceful nuclear experiments. In 1970, 1971 and 1972, the International Atomic Energy Agency organized Panel Meetings on the peaceful uses of nuclear explosions and India attended all these meetings as a Panel Member. In the Foreword to the Peaceful Nuclear Explosions Phenomenology and Status Report, 1970, an indication has been given of the projects for which peaceful nuclear explosions could be used. The following quotation will be adequate in this regard: 'Fully contained nuclear explosions (those not breaking through to the ground surface) could be used for many projects. On an industrial level pilot-scale experiments have already been made on gas and oil stimulation, with encouraging results. In addition, the use of cavities created by such explosions appeared to have an economically attractive future for projects such as underground gas and oil storage, and the storage of radioactive wastes from nuclear power stations and chemical plants, for in situ retorting of oil from shale oil deposits, and for in situ leaching of low-grade ores broken up by the explosion. The latter application is of particular interest to one Member State, India, who could by this means use her very large low-grade non-ferrous metal ore deposits, thus making her more independent of imports of these metals and furthering the national economy.'

In view of the fact that we have just now carried out the experiment and the results will be available to us after six months, it is considered premature to talk of any particular technological application at a selected site. For any project of this nature to be considered economical and feasible, more experimental data must be available.

Hon'ble Members will notice that in the Panel discussions to which I have referred and in which most of the advanced countries have participated, it was emphasized that activities in the field of peaceful nuclear explosion are essentially research and development programmes. Against this background, the Government of India fails to understand why India is being criticized on the ground that the technology necessary for the peaceful nuclear explosion is no different from that necessary for a weapons programme. No technology is evil in itself; it is the use that nations make of technology which determines its character. India does not accept the principle of apartheid in any matter and technology is no exception.

2

Operation Shakti

In May 1998, India conducted a series of nuclear bomb tests at the Pokhran Test Range, in an exercise that's popularly known as Pokhran Two. The tests were said to have achieved their stated objective of giving India the capability to build 'suitcase' nukes with low yields as well as thermonuclear weapons with yields of up to 200 kilotons. (However, experts analysing the seismic signatures believe that the 'thermonuclear' or fusion device or so-called 'hydrogen bomb' did not work.)

Pokhran Two consisted of five detonations, and the tests were initiated on 11 May 1998, under the assigned code name Operation Shakti, with the detonation of one fusion and two fission devices. On 13 May 1998, two additional fission devices were detonated.

It may be pertinent to note that the tests were carried out by a 'lame-duck' caretaker government, which had lost a Vote of Confidence in April 1998. According to detractors, the tests may have had the political agenda of boosting that government's image with an eye to win votes in the upcoming general election.

The tests resulted in the imposition of sanctions against India by several countries, including Japan and the US.

The stock market registered significant gains, newspapers and television channels praised the government for its bold decision, and advocated the development of an operational nuclear arsenal for the armed forces. But the Opposition, led by the Congress, accused the BJP of using the tests for political ends.

The first speech in this section is by the Communist Party of India's **Indrajit Gupta**. *A towering figure in Indian politics in 1938, he returned with a Tripos from King's College, Cambridge, to join the peasants' and workers' movement, and lived the most spartan of life, even though he belonged to a family filled with Indian Civil Service officers. He was briefly Union Home Minister during the Prime Ministership of H.D. Deve Gowda. He holds the record till date of maximum number of terms in the Lok Sabha – 11. Here, he voices some of the Opposition's concerns, such as the fear of international isolation and of inviting retaliatory measures from hostile neighbours, as well as asks questions about the timing of the tests.*

*As Prime Minister at the time, **Atal Bihari Vajpayee** questions his critics, pointing out that Indira Gandhi too, at the time of Pokhran One, had not consulted other political parties. He also says that his government would not sign the The Comprehensive Nuclear-Test-Ban-Treaty (CTBT), since they realized 'that the superpowers of the world wanted to impose a discriminatory treaty on the world'.*

INDRAJIT GUPTA

(Lok Sabha: Midnapore)

Lok Sabha: 27 May 1998

On Recent Nuclear Test in Pokhran

Mr. Speaker, Sir, I have listened very attentively to the statement made by the hon'ble Prime Minister this morning, for which I think the whole country was waiting … there is a practically unanimous feeling in the country that the major share of credit for the scientific achievement which has been recorded must go to our scientists and our engineers, and cannot go to any political party … which may like to take credit in order to extract some political mileage out of it.

These scientists and engineers … demonstrated their capability in the nuclear field 24 years ago, not today … Twenty-four years ago, when the first blast took place in Pokhran, they had already demonstrated their capability and of course they have been updating their technology and now they have demonstrated in 1998 that they are capable of making an independent contribution … of the highest importance.

Incidentally, I would like to at this stage congratulate Dr. Abdul Kalam for getting the Bharat Ratna which he richly deserves.

As far as the sovereign right of a country is concerned … Nobody can question our right to go ahead with this type of testing … It is for us to explain why we are doing it, for what purpose we are doing it … But if some countries … talk … as if they are questioning our right, they have no business to do that because … an independent sovereign country certainly has got its own right.

The question that I would like to raise is why this testing has been done now … In his letter to President Clinton which I think was not meant to be publicised, but it was leaked to the Press, or the Press got hold of it somehow, the Prime Minister has attributed this sudden testing to what he calls the deteriorating security environment of India … he makes it quite clear that he is referring to a threat from China and this appears to be in tune with the anti-Chinese fulminations of the Defence Minister made a few days earlier.

In fact, the Defence Minister's rather aggressive remarks, I think, were meant … to prepare the ground for an official explanation which has now been made available in the Prime Minister's letter to the US President. I am not raising the question, at the moment, whether this type of letter should be considered as somewhat unusual or not. I do not know whether this kind of a letter, dealing with such a subject, addressed to the President of another country is proper or not in the field of international relations …

Sir, the question I am asking … is this: What was the sudden provocation, if any, at this stage? If it was from China's side, we would like to know what that provocation was. We have had our disputes with China for a long time and most of those disputes, perhaps, are not resolved yet. We all remember what happened in 1962. We remember that large tracts of Indian territory are in the possession of China and that the questions relating to the border have also not been resolved, but this is nothing new. This has been going on for so many years. I find that there is a statement which is connected with Starred Question number 20 to be answered today, the 27th of May in the Lok Sabha. This is a statement regarding neighbouring countries … It says:

'In recent years, India–China relations have developed steadily. The momentum of high level dialogue has been maintained and there is a growing functional cooperation between the two countries in diverse fields. The two countries have agreed to work towards a constructive and cooperative relationship oriented towards the 21st century. The bilateral trade reached US dollars 1.8 billion in 1997.

Various issues of mutual interest, including the boundary question, are being discussed in the framework of the India–China Joint Working Group and India–China Expert Group.'

Now, does this statement which has been submitted to the House on behalf of the Government give an impression that suddenly today there is a deterioration in India–China relations or that the bilateral mechanism which has been set up, the cooperation which is taking place, and the constructive dialogue which is taking place as mentioned here has suddenly been interrupted or sabotaged by China? I do not find it here in this statement.

Also, Sir, in this statement which was made by the honourable Prime Minister, there is paragraph number thirteen … It says that our policy towards our neighbours and other countries also have not changed … This is what was read out:

'India remains fully committed to the promotion of peace with stability, and resolution of all outstanding issues through bilateral dialogue and negotiations …

'… The Government will continue to remain engaged in substantive dialogue with our neighbours to improve relations and to expand the scope of our interactions in a mutually advantageous manner.'

I do not know whether all these statements are meant to indicate that China alone is an exception to this line and attitude that we, officially, here have said that we are taking and we want to continue to take. Nowhere it is mentioned that … China has suddenly … created a provocation … which has suddenly led us to take this decision of testing of nuclear weapons.

Therefore, I … would like some clarification … the Prime Minister should have even before the testing … taken at least the major political parties into confidence. They could have taken their own allies into confidence … that was not done. Now, when we are debating this matter in the House, certainly we have every right to ask this question as to what was the sudden provocation which led to this testing.

We all agree that there must be absolutely no relaxation of defence preparedness … of security measures, especially in our country where we have got a very troublesome environment along the borders … But … is it essential for our security that we should go in for production and deployment of nuclear weapons? Many countries, of course, as we know, have manufactured and stockpiled nuclear weapons in the name of security. But these are … weapons that … cannot be used. America which has the biggest stockpile of nuclear weapons was not able to use them against a poor and backward country like Vietnam. It fought Vietnam for 12 years in order to crush the liberation movement of the Vietnamese people. But it could not and dare not, in the face of the conscience of the world, use those weapons …

… what is more essential for our security in the long run is this. Firstly, what has been stated here in the Prime Minister's statement … 'building of good relations with our neighbouring countries and the creation of bilateral and regional mechanisms for that purpose'. These are weapons of mass destruction. He had quoted in the morning – approvingly, I suppose – from Pandit Jawaharlal Nehru who had said on 2nd April, 1954, in this House that 'nuclear, chemical and biological energy and power should not be used to forge weapons of mass destruction'.

We are now saying that we have now become a weaponized State, a nuclear weaponized State. So, I would like to know whether the weapons which we are engaged in researching and trying to manufacture can be used as weapons of mass destruction or not. Are they weapons of mass destruction or not? Of course, the Government must declare and has declared – I am glad to see – that we have no aggressive intentions towards anybody … But intrinsically, are they weapons of mass destruction or not? If they are, why are we giving up the line that we have pursued consistently for so many years …? … some provocation may have been there … from … Pakistan, because they suddenly developed this Ghauri missile and said that it has a long range of so many thousands of kilometres. This Ghauri missile may be interpreted as a threat to us.

So, if the Pakistan Government chooses to also go in for development of nuclear weapons, what would happen? The Prime Minister of Pakistan is reported to have said that the Indian experiments of underground testing are considered by Pakistan to be a threat to them and therefore, he has said that, within a few days, they would also test their own nuclear weapons. This means that a sort of competition and a race in nuclear arms is being triggered off and history has shown that this is … very risky … and … reckless … Even with the best of intentions, one cannot say where a mishap may occur.

Sir … it is not enough for the Prime Minister to have told President Clinton – I do not know whether the idea was to please the American rulers – that we consider the main threat to be from China. The Defence Minister, of course, is one of the outstanding champions of what is known as the Socialist International based in Amsterdam. He is one of the top leaders of that Socialist International which has always been a China baiter … But I do not expect the policy of the Amsterdam International to be taken over as the official policy of the Government of India …

… after Hiroshima and Nagasaki, the conscience of the world has renounced the use of nuclear weapons as weapons of mass destruction which cannot serve a military purpose. For example, the United Kingdom is one of the nuclear powers. But everybody knows that it has become a second class power … The mighty USSR got itself bankrupted by trying to chase nuclear parity with the United States and NATO … On the other hand, Japan and Germany are considered to be the powerful States. But they do not have nuclear weapons … but they are certainly not weak countries …

As I said, if Pakistan chooses to go in for what you may call a sort of tit-for-tat policy then there is a grave risk of a nuclear arms race being triggered off in this part of the continent.

The Prime Minister has said nothing about the economic cost of producing nuclear weapons. He has not specifically said anything about the impact of sanctions or the threat of sanctions. But I think … our Government, along with development of nuclear testing, should give a clear-cut commitment that we are not going to go in for the first use or the first strike of such weapons … and invite all other countries to join in this commitment and ask them to respond to it, and if they do not respond, they will automatically be exposed.

Sir, the United States sanctions may not cause irrecoverable damage to our economy because they are supposed to be coming mainly from the World Bank, the Asian Development Bank and so on. In fact, I find that there is perhaps a very far-sighted calculation even by our Government behind all this that these sanctions if they come – I think they have already started operating – will push forward the economic liberalization policy which we have been following since 1991. If the multinational corporations are assiduously wooed, then the private capital can replace the aid from the World Bank and the Asian Development Bank. It may even increase.

I find, Sir, that a well-informed paper like *The Economist* of London has pointed out that 'soon after the nuclear blasting, the Government of India has awarded 18 oil exploration contracts – 11 of them to American companies, whose projects had been in limbo for two years. It has cleared 34 exploration licences for onshore minerals in four States. Three foreign investments in power projects, which had been languishing for want of a Government guarantee, were suddenly approved and, according to newspaper reports, the Government is to allow foreign investors to own 100 per cent of the equity of housing companies against 40 per cent earlier and to raise hard currency loans for the first time.'

So, these American companies ... are very conscious of the huge market which exists here in India; even if the official agencies impose sanctions, nothing that we have done will dissuade or should dissuade the American private investors and multinational corporations from taking advantage of these various projects. So, on balance, we may not lose, we may even gain.

The Prime Minister mentioned this morning that they have declared a voluntary moratorium ... What exactly do you mean by this 'voluntary moratorium'? We have already said that we would consider signing some aspects of this CTBT. Nobody has clarified what is meant by 'some aspects of the CTBT'. One of the main conditionalities of the CTBT is that nuclear testing should be stopped. If we have already unilaterally declared that we are going to go in for a voluntary moratorium, now does it mean that one of the conditionalities of the CTBT is, in fact, being accepted by us by the back-door and that is the signal that we want to send out? Whatever it is, let the country and the Parliament be taken into confidence. There should be transparency now about these things.

So, Sir, I must say ... that the whole exercise appears to me to have been an exercise in futility. This type of weapon does not strengthen our security at all. Secondly, we have declared a moratorium. Thirdly, we do not know what is going to be the cost ... We have a pretty favourable standing in the international comity of nations. I do not know to what extent this thing will reduce our friends abroad and, perhaps, isolate us to some extent.

Fourthly, it is ... very ironical ... Sir, that in the Capital City of Delhi, thousands and lakhs of people are going without power and water, and we are going to go in for producing nuclear power now and saying that this is a great achievement ... just see what is going on. Yesterday, people from so many ... areas of Delhi have come out of their homes and staged angry demonstrations and they have even gheraoed the houses of some Councillors and other popular representatives of the ruling party because they have been given all sorts of assurances and those assurances have come to nothing. So, where does all this lead to? ...

... after a few days you will find there is little room left for enthusiasm ... except that our scientists have proved that they are second to none in the world. That is something of which I am proud. But beyond that, where do we go from here?

So, these are some of the questions which I would like the Prime Minister to deal with when he replies …

… It is quite heartening to find that in the recent conference of the non-aligned countries … in Cartagena, except for three or four countries, the overwhelming majority did not condemn India. They did not at all consider that India has done something which is against the spirit that has actuated the non-aligned countries all these years. That is a good thing …

Lastly, I would say the Prime Minister must take steps to see that his Ministers, if I may say so, do not speak in different voices … I broadly agree with what the Prime Minister says, the kind of line that he is trying to … advance because it is consistent with what we have been doing all these years. But we have got Ministers here who are making … bellicose and aggressive statements which are not calculated to strengthen peace or security, but which may provoke other people. We have neighbours who are not very friendly with us and this subject is something on which even some Ministers, I think, do not have any direct dealings at all. They also come out with statements. I do not know who has authorized them to do it. (Interruptions.) …

… on such a delicate and sensitive matter, official statements in the name of the Government should be confined to the Prime Minister who, in the past, as we know, was considered to be quite a renowned foreign policy expert even when he was not in the Government. When he was the Leader of the Opposition, the Government … sent him many times on foreign policy missions abroad because he was trusted as a competent and authoritative spokesman of the line which India had been following, and he conducted himself with great distinction … even in such meetings where we have confrontations directly with the Pakistanis in Geneva …

This is broadly what I want to say. I do not wish to take up more time. Thank you very much for the chance you have given me.

ATAL BIHARI VAJPAYEE

(Lok Sabha: Lucknow)

Lok Sabha: 29 May 1998

On Recent Nuclear Test in Pokhran

Mr. Speaker, Sir, the long discussion on nuclear tests conducted by India at Pokhran is about to conclude. I am grateful to the Hon'ble Members who took part in the debate. The House is unanimous in extending congratulations to the scientists, engineers, technicians and the jawans of our army for their significant contribution in conducting Pokhran tests.

There is also a consensus that if attempts are made to impose unreasonable restrictions on our economic sovereignty and if the inflow into our country of the aid coming from the world organizations is stopped, then we will face the situation unitedly.

Naturally, the need for conducting nuclear tests at Pokhran has been questioned during the discussions here. I am reminded of 1974 when discussion was held on Pokhran-1. At that time I was present. Comrade Indrajit Gupta was also present ... The words uttered by me during the debate in Parliament at the time of Pokhran-1 tests in 1974 are no different from what I am saying today. The whole country had welcomed Indiraji's decision of granting permission for conducting the tests. Her decision was not a collective decision. She did not consult the opposition for conducting the tests, but her decision was right and was in the interest of the country's security. Her decision was aimed at giving the opportunity to our scientists and, therefore, it was welcomed by all. I remember that Smt. Indira Gandhi did not make any speech in the discussion which was held at that time. On her behalf, on behalf of the government, another government minister had delivered a speech. The whole country was satisfied. Just now a hint has been given from our neighbour that in 1974 they were not ready and, therefore, they were silent, but now they are ready.

Some hon'ble members have said that Pakistan conducted the tests in response to India's tests. Is a nuclear test possible within a short period of 16 days? People who are aware of the complexities of conducting nuclear tests are present here, and they will testify that no country can make preparations for a nuclear test within a fortnight. This preparation has been going on for years together. Yesterday, we conducted nuclear test and today the news has come that Pakistan has conducted the test flight of a long range missile. Our leaders are well aware of the time since when this preparation has been going on, and they have prepared the country for it. It was not so that I have decided in one day and test was conducted. Today, I want to repeat what I had said earlier – that behind this nuclear test there is 50 years of research and hard work by our scientists and Jawans of our Army who kept on working in the scorching heat, hot sand and temperatures as high as 500 °C ... motivated by the sentiments of defending our country and enhancing the prestige of our nation. I don't think that there is any difference of opinion over this issue in the House. It is the characteristic of this country that whenever we have to face problems we forget all our differences. Ours is a democratic country – it is natural that people may have difference of opinion –

'Munde munde matah bhinna.'[1]

I was just going through a statement made by Shri Rajiv Gandhi in 1985 … on 11th October during the Press Conference in the Press Club, I would like to quote that:

'As I have said on a number of occasions, we have to consider our security and there is no question of allowing New Delhi or, for that matter, any other city in India to be flattened out. We will not allow that to happen. What is even more worrying about Pakistan's programme is that we are fairly sure that at least part of the finances of this programme have come from other countries. Now what we worry about is that the nuclear weapon when developed will also have to go to these countries. I did not say that we are going to wait on your decision, on your response. For Pakistan to explode their device I said that we have to take certain measures to protect ourselves. There are a number of measures, apart from making a nuclear weapon ourselves.'

…The Government was concerned and aware of the activities across the border. The superpowers, who have stockpiled nuclear weapons, were not ready to destroy all their weapons under a time-bound programme. That is why a unanimous decision was taken that we should not sign the CTBT, once we felt that the superpowers of the world wanted to impose a discriminatory treaty on the world. It was feared that we would be isolated.

At times, it becomes necessary to walk alone, but our decision has to be correct and then it would not matter much if we walk in isolation. We kept our option open but it appeared from the reports that came in later that it would be necessary to take some action in this regard. The scientists were also consulted … We see the nuclear weapons as the weapons of destruction. They are useful only for the purpose of defence or self-defence. Our opponents should realize that we possess nuclear weapons so that they do not dare to attack us … We have been attacked thrice in these 50 years. Our country is the messenger of peace. It never attacked anybody's land; it never attacked any country, rather it was subjected to attack. In fact, we were dispossessed of our land. Now we are trying to get it back. We are holding negotiations and it is possible only through negotiations. However, the country having a population of hundred crore cannot be put into a situation wherein it has to depend on the mercy of others for its defence.

We are peace-loving people and we want friendship based on justice and a friendship encouraging mutual interests. India is a vast country. It is strong and also prosperous … compared to the neighbouring countries; still, we never tried to take any undue advantage of our position. After all, this was the essence of the Gujral doctrine, but Shri Gujral should not shy away from admitting the fact that his

[1] Editor's translation: As many people, so many opinions.

doctrine did not succeed in the case of Pakistan … The infiltration of … terrorists inside our country continued and the border crisis also remained unresolved … I would like to reiterate the proposal that we are ready to hold further talks with Pakistan. Pakistan is our neighbouring country, hence we should sit down together to iron out our differences but Pakistan is not ready to go along with the consensus evolved at Dhaka or the subjects adopted for discussion in the Dhaka Resolution. The Prime Minister of Pakistan has repeated his proposal of being prepared for having talks with India. It is a good thing and the talks should be held.

I remember that once I had told a Pakistani leader that history may change but geography cannot be changed. Nor can we alter this fact that we are neighbours. It is good if we maintain friendly relations, but if the friendship is broken, we cannot simply change the neighbourhood as we are bound by this geographical fact of being neighbours.

On this occasion also, I would like to tell the friends of Pakistan: many people go to Pakistan and have friendly relations with the people of Pakistan. After coming back, they tell us that the insecurity of Pakistan stems from the apprehension that India has not accepted the separate existence of Pakistan, although there are no grounds for harbouring such a feeling. The country was divided, and Pakistan was formed. Now they should be happy, satisfied and gain prosperity. They should let us live in peace, and both of us should work together to root out poverty, unemployment, diseases, illiteracy not only from this region but from the face of the world.

We also envisage a world free from nuclear weapons. Now why did India have to take such a decision? Should we have ignored it yet again? Yesterday, I told journalists that I was not surprised at what had transpired. We knew that this was going to happen and we wanted to prevent it and that is why we took this step. However, it is being interpreted as if they conducted the test only because we had conducted it. Does that mean that they were preparing for it all along?

We are facing danger from some other quarters also. That country sees us as its sole enemy and their nuclear tests are directed at us …

When our country conducts the nuclear tests and also raises its voice along with other nations with regard to the nuclear tests, and also asks the superpowers to destroy their weapons … then it is stated that sincere attempts are not being made. Casting doubts on our sincerity will not help. We want Pakistan to join us in making this demand. It has been stated repeatedly yesterday that the nuclear weapons are the weapons of destruction, so why collective measures are not taken to destroy nuclear weapons? It is quite apparent from the widespread support lent by the third world countries in vocal and not so vocal terms for our nuclear tests that a substantial part of the world and a majority of people want permanent peace. They want a peace which is not violated by nuclear weapons. We would like to play a role in it, but we are also desirous of keeping our country safe … and … the safety of the world as a whole, is equally important for us.

But we should be heard. We should achieve such a position that others listen to us attentively. We do not want to create a situation in which we might hurt our own interests. Shri Deve Gowdaji is not present here … (Interruptions.)

An Hon'ble Member: He is present. He is sitting in the back seat.

Atal Bihari Vajpayee: I am having a look at the 1996 manifesto of Janata Dal. Perhaps the Janata Dal which I am referring to is the one to which Gowdaji is related.

'We will formally give a pledge of first non-use of nuclear capability against Pakistan.'

We are ready to … guarantee that we will not first use nuclear capability against Pakistan, but later on if there is a need, then we will use that. But for that, first we have to develop our nuclear capability.

This also lends support to the argument that all political parties have a unanimous opinion on this issue. When this was to be done? After whatever happened yesterday, there is no need to give any reply. Who had taken this decision and who should take the decision? It is for you to ponder over it. When some of my senior colleagues say that they were not aware of this, this does not mean that I have no trust upon them. Therefore, to talk of a unanimous decision or consultation is not proper. At that time, when a nuclear test had to be conducted, it was not possible to have consultations. Very limited people knew about it. As Advaniji said yesterday, everything gets leaked here, the entire report of the commission was published, but nobody could smell it. In foreign countries, this has been a subject of debate. It is also an indication of nation's determination.

It shows that if we want or the situation so demands and there is a challenge before our country, then the people of this country are ready to make bigger sacrifices and can take all precautions. This is an achievement. This should be duly acknowledged.

I felt hurt when an allegation was levelled that this was done for … political self-interest. I had said this earlier and today I would like to repeat it. I was in the opposition for 40 years and as a member of the opposition my role has always been appreciated and it has been said that I had not worked for party's interest but I worked for country's interest. Now that I am … Prime Minister or have been chosen to hold this prestigious office, shall I allow pettiness, selfishness and the party interests to come in my way? I can never stoop to such a level.

May God save me from committing such a sin. Some decisions may be wrong. There can be two opinions regarding the timing of a decision … but sincerity cannot be doubted. Why was a nuclear test conducted in 1974, we did not ask, people of the country did not ask, because it was the right step … Indiraji could have taken right step. Our friends from the Congress had honoured Smt. Indiraji at the time of the formation of Bangladesh … At that time we also honoured her. Entire country honoured her. After that decision was taken to conduct elections. We did not criticize this … We said that Indiraji did good work. My exact words were that an epoch-making step has been taken. If we lose the elections, it is all right, the elections are lost at times and won at other times.

Similarly, governments may come and governments may go. But the country should be united, should attain prosperity with pride and should be able to protect its precious freedom. However, this is not the responsibility of a single party or government alone. In the beginning of my speech at Pokhran, I had said that neither I nor my party take credit for this. Whatever was done was done in the country's interest. I was surprised when this question was raised that we had not worked according to our national agenda … We are pleased to know that there are several people who are keeping an eye on our national agenda. They have joined two parts of national agenda and have misinterpreted it. They will say that it was printed like this. But I will say that it has not been printed correctly. In that there are three issues – Combat effectiveness of Armed Forces.

'The state of preparedness, morale and combat effectiveness of the Armed Forces shall receive early attention and appropriate remedial action.'

In the next sentence, it has been stated that 'We will establish a National Security Council.' and its details have been given. In the end, it has been stated, in fact it should have been given in a separate letter to make the reading easier, however … there should not be any difficulty in understanding the meaning.

'Towards that end, we will re-evaluate the nuclear policy and exercise the option to induct nuclear weapons.'

It does not mean that first of all our armed forces will be strengthened, security council will be set up and after doing all this … if the situation demands to do it tomorrow, and even then we respond in the negative with an argument that our armed forces are not weaponized and the security council has not been formed. Nobody can ascribe such a meaning but attempts are being made to do so. Injustice has been done to us. I do not know whether such a discussion, consultation and meetings of scientists were ever held with the opposition on such an occasion. We fought the Bangladesh war, we were also involved in a war with China and conducted nuclear tests in Pokhran. But that was not any obligation on anyone. But I regret that our scientist Dr. Chidambaram failed to convince our politician, Shri Chidambaram.

Mr. Speaker, many other questions were raised during the discussion which lasted for a long duration. I am not going into the details of all these points. We have taken some decisions which have already been mentioned in brief.

We are disappointed that the US has displayed a lack of application of India's legitimate security concerns. I wish to reiterate Government's commitment to engage with all principal interlocutors in a responsible dialogue. We remain ready to discuss and explain our position.

Since 11th May, the government have taken certain initiatives which I'm going to enlist here.

1. We are already observing a voluntary moratorium and are ready to consider and discuss converting it into a de jure commitment.
2. We have volunteered to engage in negotiations on AFMCT.
3. India will undertake stringent controls on nuclear and missile-related technologies as well as those relating to other weapons of mass destruction.

We had already announced and reiterate our offer to discuss a 'No-First-Use' agreement with Pakistan and also with other countries bilaterally or in a multilateral forum.

Mr. Speaker, Sir, the policy of the government is to maintain friendly relations with China. China is our neighbouring country. Both the countries are in Asia and are big nations. It is required both the countries maintain friendship according to the principles of Panchsheel. There is some tension on the border issue. However, there is peace on the border these days. We want to solve the border issue through negotiation. Discussions ... should progress speedily to find ... a satisfactory solution. The way China helps Pakistan, is a matter of concern. This help could be used against us. It is required that China should take note of our concerns. Both India and China should work together with mutual cooperation which is in the interest of both the countries, Asia and the world as a whole. An attempt has been made to create some misunderstanding on the question of some statements. Once a distorted version of statements appears in the media, it is difficult to get the correct version to find a place in the print media and then the spicy material finds place in the headlines. Our policy is of friendship, development and to maintain peace in this Asian region. Besides preparing for our own security, our aim is to remain friendly with all countries. I'm confident that those who are our critics today will have a change in their attitude tomorrow. We have conducted a test, we did not create a war hysteria in our country. When the test was conducted the atmosphere in the country was normal. I myself visited Pokhran and remained there for several hours. There was no radioactivity there. A news item appeared that cases of nose bleeding have been reported. But from whose nose and how much blood came out of it, nobody is there to answer such questions.

However, this news item was published very prominently, especially in foreign countries. The soldiers are living there in those conditions.

There is no danger of radio-activity. There's also no question of getting political mileage out of it. We wish to make progress by formulating policies on the basis of consensus evolved with the cooperation of all the members.

I see it as my primary duty to effectively discharge the responsibility placed on my shoulders and everything else is secondary to that. It is not the issue concerning a person or family or group or community or religion. This country is multi-religious …

I was surprised to hear yesterday a very provocative speech delivered by the Prime Minister of our neighbouring country while addressing the nation on TV. He was provoking his people. He did not think of crores of people living in the neighbouring country … people who are followers of Islam are citizens of India and they are enjoying equal rights … However, such an occasion will never arise when I will feel like provoking the people of the country by addressing them through television and if at all such a day comes I would like to assure you that I will quit the very same day. I have got this opportunity to serve the nation and I wish to utilize this time properly … and I'm desirous of getting cooperation from all … quarters in this endeavour.

Some members had quoted from my speech delivered at the time Pokhran-1 tests were conducted. I had stated therein that the scientists and the soldiers had done their job, and now it was up to the politicians to do their bit. By politicians, I don't mean only politicians but all the people. What is required is that all of us should discharge our responsibilities …

3

Making Friends and Influencing People

The India–US Civil Nuclear Agreement marked a defining moment in the relations between the two countries. Under it, India agreed to separate its civil and military nuclear facilities and to place all its civil nuclear facilities under the International Atomic Energy Agency safeguards; the United States, on its part, agreed to work towards full civil nuclear cooperation with India. This Agreement took more than three years to come to fruition.

When the 22-page-long text of the India–US nuclear cooperation agreement, 'frozen' in Washington on 22 July 2006, was finally 'unveiled' on 3 August that year, it was to the applause, albeit cautious, of even diehard sceptics. They included those in government, the atomic energy establishment and the media. It was seen as 'a deal the country could live with'.

Understandably, ***Dr Manmohan Singh*** *(the then Prime Minister) – who, as a top government source told this writer, 'invested a great deal of personal capital' in the deal – expected that this would be seen as a momentous 'turning point' in Indian history and the high point of his prime ministership. Even if the BJP, as the principal Opposition party, did not cross the floor to congratulate him, he had thought the Left parties – the ruling UPA's chief ally – would thank him for delivering on the promises he had made to them in his speech in the Rajya Sabha on 17 August 2006.*

Although the Agreement eventually led to the Left parties withdrawing support, thus weakening the UPA government, Dr Singh was right in believing that it would mark the high point of his prime ministership. The general elections of 2009 were won not just on the strength of his stewardship of the Indian economy in the difficult years of 2008–09, but also on the signing of the India–US Civil Nuclear Agreement. For a while, Singh was king.

During that period, Dr Manmohan Singh made several speeches on the India–US Civil Nuclear Agreement in Parliament. In this speech, he spells out the big picture: he talks of India's place in the world and 'where we ought to be moving, and how we are going to move in that direction'. He stresses that India can realize its destiny only by becoming a major player in the evolving global economy, and by ensuring its development is not stunted by the shortage of energy.

MANMOHAN SINGH

(Rajya Sabha: Assam)

Lok Sabha: 23 August 2006

Foreign Policy Discussion Under Rule 193 (on India–US nuclear deal)

Mr. Speaker, Sir, as I listened to the debate, I felt proud to be an Indian. This debate has clearly shown that when it comes to safeguarding India's supreme national interests, there are no party differences. There are concerns, there can be worries, but the nation will speak with one voice in defence of its interests and that is the message that comes out loud and clear. Let me say that I take pride in that. But I also recognize that it casts on me a great responsibility that I should be worthy of this trust that the House has displayed in the motivation behind this deal.

Sir, I will take some time to spell out the big picture as I see it, where India is in the world and where we ought to be moving, and how we are going to move in that direction. I do recognize that we live in a world of unequal powers and those who are strong have always a tendency to twist the arms of others. Sir, I recall that as a young boy, I once heard Man Singh who, along with Netaji Subhas Chandra Bose, was the founder of the INA. In a speech he said in Punjabi: Duniya Mardi Zoran Noon-Lakh Lasnst Kamzoron Noon. The world worships the mighty and the powerful; the weak and feeble are always at the receiving end. I do recognize that we can realize our destiny only by working hard, to become a major people of the evolving global economy.

It is only then that India will acquire that respect, that credibility and that power which is our legitimate goal. After all, we are a country with a great civilizational heritage, a country of one billion people with a freedom struggle which should be the envy of every country in the world. But all these wishes can be realized only if India emerges economically as a strong nation. Today, there is a change in the mood of the world towards India. After the experiences of the last 50 to 60 years, the world today marvels that there is a country like India, a country of one billion people, a country in which you can find all great religions represented in its population mix, a country committed to the rule of law, a country committed to respect for all fundamental human freedoms. The world recognizes today that there is no country in the world of India's size, of India's diversity, of India's complexity seeking social and economic salvation in the framework of an open society and an open economy. That is why there is such great interest.

Whenever a country emerges, those who are in power get worried. But whether you like it or not, I sense today a willingness in the rest of the world to help India to realize its inherent potential because in India's civilizational heritage, our people have never gone to other countries as conquerors. They have gone as traders, they have gone as preachers, they have gone as men and women of goodwill and the world respects us for that. That is what India is about. That is what Pandit Jawaharlal Nehru said on the eve of Independence when he said: 'Our dreams are for India but they are not for India alone. They are dreams for the oppressed world as a whole.'

So, Sir, I would respectfully urge this august House to recognize the changed mood of the world towards India. This is not to say that power politics is a thing of the past; that there will never be any attempt to twist our arms. We will protect ourselves to ensure against the risks that are there. But it would be wrong for us not to take advantage of the opportunities that are now on the horizon. I sincerely believe that it is in the interest of our country to have good relations with all the major powers. I make no apology that we seek good relations with the United States. The United States is a pre-eminent power.

But, for that matter, in the last two years that I have been the Prime Minister, we have made big efforts to come closer to Russia, to come closer to the European Union, to come closer to China, to come closer to the Arab world. We had the privilege of welcoming His Majesty the King of Saudi Arabia as our honoured guest on Republic Day. When he went back, what did he say to me? He said: 'Mr. Prime Minister, the world talks about energy shortage. As long as Saudi Arabia is there, you can take it that we will take care of your energy requirements.' So, this may be a unipolar world. But we have operated in a manner which strengthens our linkages with all the big powers, with all our neighbours. We are seeking a new set of relationships with the Asian countries. Let me say that I also consider it our obligation to work hard to normalize, to expand and develop our relations with our neighbours including Pakistan, Sri Lanka, Nepal and Bangladesh. We will remain committed to that. That is our civilizational heritage. That is the meaning of our freedom struggle as I understand it.

The second thing that I do wish to say is this. I was born in a village where there was no electricity. I never saw any electricity until I went to study in the neighbouring tehsil headquarters. Our women in rural homes use wood. They spoil their eyesight in the process. Development will remain a mirage for millions and millions of our people unless we change that picture. In the old days, whenever one went to the old Soviet Union, it used to be written boldly everywhere that socialism is Soviets plus electricity. The Soviets may have disappeared, but the role of electricity in modernization and in expansion of economic and social opportunities for the people is a reality and, therefore, if India's struggle for its economic and social development is to succeed, we need ever-increasing amounts of energy.

There are two types of things which are at work today which determine the demand for energy in our country. First is the normal growth process. As growth takes place, the commercial energy demand increases roughly at the same rate, if not more than the rate of growth of the national income. But in our country, there is the other revolution and that is the modernization of our rural economy and the replacement of non-commercial energy, like firewood and other non-commercial sources of energy, by commercial energy. So, history tells us that in the process of development, if our economy is to grow at the rate of 8 to 10 per cent, our demand for commercial energy will probably increase at the minimum at the same rate or probably even more. Sir, questions have been raised on whether we need nuclear power.

I think Shri Suresh Prabhu knows this area as nobody else does. There have been important studies. I am not claiming that nuclear energy is the only way out for meeting the demand for energy in our country. We have important reserves of coal; we must exploit them. But as I look at the demand for energy, our coal reserves would be exhausted in about 45 years. We have a sizeable amount of hydel resources, but they are in distant areas and we all know the type of problems that arise when you make use of hydro-potential like resettlement cost, relief operation and also, I think, the costs associated with the risks arising out of being in unsafe seismic zones. We now know at least that there is an uncertain future for hydrocarbons. There is uncertainty about supplies, there is uncertainty about prices. The price of oil has increased from less than \$30 per barrel two years ago to \$75 per barrel and there are very many people who tell me that, probably in a very short period of time, it will increase to \$100 per barrel. We are short of hydrocarbons. We consume about 110 million tonnes of oil. We produce only 30 million tonnes. We have not increased our oil production in the last 10–15 years.

In this environment, if India's development is not to be frustrated by the shortage of energy, I think, it is incumbent on any Government to think of widening its options with regard to the supply of energy. All that I am saying as to why we need a nuclear deal is that we must ensure that the development of our economy will not be hampered by a lack of adequate commercial energy. I am, therefore, seeking to enlarge the energy options that are available to our country. We must utilize those options even if what I am saying about the future of hydrocarbons does not materialize.

But it would be imprudent on the part of the Government not to make use of opportunities to widen development options, to widen the energy options. This is the reason why we thought it is necessary to look around if this ambition of ours can be satisfied. We are short of uranium. Our uranium is also relatively high-cost compared to the cost of production in the rest of the world. The available estimates as of now are that we have uranium only for the production of nuclear energy equal to 10,000 MW and that, too, for a period of only 30 years. I believe, we must take a long-term view of our future possibilities. If that is the picture, if there are international trading opportunities to increase the availability of uranium for us, if there are opportunities through international trade to promote a mutually beneficial exchange of technologies, that will help India's ambitions to emerge as a major pole of the evolving global economy. We should exploit these opportunities.

That is the vision which inspires us to look for opportunities, to remove this nuclear apartheid regime which has stifled the growth of India's nuclear power for the last three decades or more.

Mr. Speaker, Sir, hon'ble Gen. Khanduri quoted to me what I had said in the other House that India's nuclear programme began with an emphasis on nuclear energy, and that Defence came later. That, I believe, is a correct statement. If you read Panditji's statements, if you read Dr. Bhabha's statements, I think our emphasis, by and large, has always been on peaceful uses of atomic energy. That is the reason why as early as 1960, India championed the cause of a comprehensive test ban in the United Nations. We remain committed to the vision of Rajiv Gandhi for a nuclear free world.

It must be said of the vision of Pandit Jawaharlal Nehru, of Indira Gandhi, of Rajiv Gandhi that they were idealists, but they also recognized that we live in a very uncertain world. We do not control our environment and who can today say that they were not wise men and women. In the uncertain world that we live in, in a world of unequal power, the nuclear weapons are a reality. This country must keep its strategic option and that is why India's programme for strategic assets, nuclear assets was a precious heritage which came to this country, thanks to the efforts of Pandit Jawaharlal Nehru, Indira Gandhi and Rajiv Gandhi.

You have my assurance, Sir, that we will do nothing to hurt this national heritage as long as we will work steadfastly for universal, nuclear disarmament ... I know that the day is not going to come tomorrow, the day after but hopefully some day, it will materialize. But until then, we cannot give up this strategic option. I assure you and through you, Sir, the House and the country that there is nothing in this nuclear deal which will hurt the strategic autonomy that this country must have with regard to the management of its nuclear weapons programme.

Sir, a number of issues have been raised and I do not think it would be proper for me to go one by one, the ground which I covered in the other House, but some broad concerns, which have figured in the debate here, I will take them on board. The first one is the autonomy of our foreign policy. I wish to assure you, Sir – as I said a few moments ago – that this nuclear deal is not a device to be subservient to any country, whether it is the United States or any other country. We have a proud heritage, a heritage from our freedom struggle. Mahatma Gandhi said once: 'I want to build in this country a house open on all four sides so that winds of change may blow in from each and every direction. But I refuse to be blown off my feet by any one influence. I must have the courage and the ability to stand on my own feet.' That is the motivation, that is the inspiration for our foreign policy.

Reference has been made to a particular vote on Iran. We have civilizational ties and links with Iran as we have with the Arab world. We will work hard to strengthen those civilizational and cultural links, give them a new orientation, strengthen our economic links. And the gas pipeline project is a part of that process. We will work to make it a reality. But that particular vote was in the context of one particular thing that we had to determine, and that is – the international community asked this question – Iran is a signatory to the NPT. Therefore, our view is that it must enjoy all the rights it has as a member of the NPT; it must also honour all the obligations that go with the members of NPT, nothing more and nothing less. Fortunately, things have moved in this direction. Right from the beginning, whether it is in the International Atomic Energy Agency or in the United Nations, we have consistently taken a view that this is not a matter to be resolved by coercive methods; debate, dialogue and discussion is the answer. I am glad, for example, that things are moving in that direction. The Iranian Government, for example, have responded constructively to various proposals made by the P-5. And I sincerely hope that this will promote a constructive dialogue among all the interested parties. The problems relating to Iran's nuclear programme can be resolved without exercise of coercive elements which we do not approve of.

Further, Sir, our record in the last two years is an open record. We have made efforts to promote good relations with China. I am very happy that last year Premier Wen came here; this year we are hoping to welcome the President of China, President Hu Jintao. The Prime Minister of Japan, Mr. Koizumi came here last year. Russian President Putin came here. Our relations with Russia, our relations with China, our relations with Japan, our relations with the European Union, and with ASEAN countries have taken a turn for the better. So, the House has my assurance that independence of our foreign policy and making it subservient only to our national interest will be ensured by us.

A number of questions have been raised with regard to our fast breeder programme. The House has my assurance that the prototype fast breeder programme, that is under way now, will be totally kept out of the purview of any surveillance by any agency.

If, in future, our programme develops and if we produce civilian fast breeders, we will then decide whether to designate them as civilian or military. So long as they are military, there is no question of putting them under any safeguard. So, I give my assurance that nothing will be done to impinge on the autonomy of the fast breeder programme.

A reference has been made about the three-stage nuclear fuel cycle, whether we have given any commitment or is there anything in this deal which will hurt the growth of thorium as a fuel of the future. There is nothing of that sort contemplated. I do not know where this idea came from. I saw this in *The Hindu* yesterday but as far as I know, there is nothing in this deal which says that we will give up the three-tier fuel cycle. The programme to pursue research in thorium-related technology will not be compromised.

Sir, Gen. Khanduri has asked me about the veracity of certain statements made by one particular American diplomat. I am sorry, I am not able to comment on what he said or what he did not say. He did not confide in me before he went on the television channel. Therefore, I am not able to enlighten as to what did this particular gentleman mean. But I can assure you, I believe if we stick by the July 18th Statement, we have got a very good deal, a deal which I have been told was the ambition of the previous Government to negotiate but which they were not able to negotiate.

The question is, what is our status? Are we going to be regarded as a nuclear weapons State? Let me be very clear. A nuclear weapon State has a particular connotation. Since NPT cannot be negotiated until the whole Treaty can be re-negotiated, I think, it will be wrong on my part to say that we have been given the status of a nuclear weapons State, and that fact was reflected in the July 18th Statement. It does not talk of India as a nuclear weapon State. It talks of India as a country with advanced nuclear technology, which should enjoy all the rights and obligations which countries similarly placed enjoy. It will be so because the safeguards agreement that we will sign with the International Atomic Energy Agency will not be the safeguards agreement signed by all other non-nuclear weapon States. It will be a safeguards agreement unique to India because India's position is unique. We do not fall into the category of non-nuclear weapon States. The July 18th Statement recognizes clearly and unambiguously that India has a strategic programme, India has a military programme, and that programme is totally out of the purview of any international inspections of any kind.

... Sir, a question was asked about the position on moratorium on production of fissile material and what we have agreed to. We have not agreed to any moratorium on the production of fissile material. All that we have agreed to is the same thing, which the previous Government had agreed to, that we will work towards a multilaterally negotiated and internationally verifiable treaty in this regard. Until that, there is no question of accepting any limit on the production of fissile material.

Sir, a question had been raised about the separation and how costly it will be. Some figures had been mentioned by some Hon'ble Members stating 40 billion dollars as the cost of separation. I do not know where this cost estimate originates. Doubts had also been raised about our accepting the separation of civil and military and nuclear facilities since nuclear weapon States do not accept such separation and retain the right to withdraw safeguards from their nuclear facilities. In our case, the July 2005 Statement acknowledges that India should be regarded as a State with advanced nuclear technology enjoying the same benefits and advantages as other States with nuclear technology, such as the United States. The July Statement did not refer to India as a nuclear weapon State as this has a particular connotation in the NPT. The July Statement, however, explicitly acknowledges the existence of India's military nuclear facility. This meant that India would not attract full scope safeguard such as those that apply to the non-nuclear weapon States that are signatories to the NPT, and there would be no curb on continuation of India's nuclear weapon-related activities.

In these important respects, India would be very much on par with the five nuclear weapon States, who are signatories to the NPT. The Separation Plan provides for India Specific Safeguards Agreement with the International Atomic Energy Agency, with assurances of uninterrupted supply of fuels to reactors together with India's right to take corrective measures, in the event fuel supplies are interrupted. There is no question of a separate agreement in this regard with the United States.

... Sir, as far as I know, we have taken all precautions in working out the Separation Plan. Whatever costs are there, they were within the realm of practical economics and political calculations. This 40 billion dollar figure, I think, is totally misleading. I do not know what is the basis of that.

... There are no unacceptable additional financial burdens, which are being placed on our nuclear programme as a result of dividing our programmes between a civilian and a military programme.

I do believe that it is a good thing for our country, for the future growth of both our civilian programme, and our military programme, that this wall should exist. We have, for example, DRDO, which deals with the missile programme. We have the Space Department which deals with peaceful uses of space technology, and I do believe it has created greater cost consciousness. It has created a greater sense of accountability and the same will apply as a result of the two programmes being kept separate. I am satisfied insofar as I have been told that the financial costs of the operations are not, I think, anywhere near the figures which are being quoted.

... Questions had been raised about the CIRUS and APSARA reactors. This has been raised in both the Houses. I think Shri Yashwant Sinha raised it in the other House as to why the CIRUS experimental reactor and the Fuel Core of the APSARA have been included in the Separation Plan and whether this will not result in a decline in the fissile material availability for our strategic programme.

That is the question. In my statement on March 7, 2006, I had explained the rationale why India had agreed to those provisions in the Separation Plan. The CIRUS reactor will be permanently shut down in 2010. The Fuel Core of APSARA was purchased from France and we have indicated our willingness to shift it from the present location and make it available for placing under safeguards in 2010. CIRUS and APSARA are located in the Bhabha Atomic Energy Centre and we do not want the Bhabha Atomic Energy Centre to be subject to any of these safeguards. That is the reason.

Therefore, we have decided to take these steps rather than allow intrusive inspections of nuclear facilities of high national security importance. I would like to assure the hon'ble Members that these steps do not impact at all the needs of our strategic programme nor will they hinder ongoing research and development. If and when required, we have the full freedom to build new facilities to cater to our national requirements.

Questions have also been raised about the detonation of nuclear tests in the future. Sir, we have made it quite clear to the United States that India is not willing to give any commitment about future tests. All that we are willing to state – and that is the position which was also stated by the previous Government – is 'unilateral moratorium on nuclear tests'.

Now the question arises, what happens if our national security considerations require us to have it? Who can contemplate all the possibilities in the future? I think in that case, we will, of course, have the sovereign right to take whatever measures we can to protect our interests.

But I cannot accept … (Interruptions.)

… So, I have stated the position. We are not willing to have it in the Treaty or the Agreement that we will sign. We are not in favour of having a bilateral CTBT. I think that position has been unambiguously made clear to the United States. About the American inspectors, I have explained that all that we will sign with the International Atomic Energy Agency is an India-specific safeguards agreement and there is no question of American inspectors roaming about our nuclear facilities.

On shifting of goalposts, I stated in the other House that no legislature of a foreign country can bind our country. The sole consideration for us will be our own perceptions of our national interest. But, by the same logic, I cannot prevent the US Congress in its deliberations. Now, if the outcome of these deliberations is a piece of legislation which introduces some extraneous element not envisaged in the July 18 statement, not envisaged in the March separation plan statement, then, of course, we will draw the appropriate conclusions, but I sincerely hope that that stage will not come. I have personally conveyed all our concerns, the concerns which I mentioned in detail in the other House. I could go on explaining them. But I think that will take an unduly long time. All these concerns have been raised with the United States Government both at the official level and at my level. President Bush has assured me that it is not his intention to change the goalposts which were agreed to in the Joint Statement of July 18.

The Congressional process is still not complete. I cannot predict which way it will go. But if it goes in the direction in which it hurts us or which introduces extraneous considerations into this matter, we will draw the appropriate conclusion. The House can be rest assured that we will do nothing which will compromise the integrity of our strategic programme. There is no scope for capping of our strategic programme. The decision about the future of our strategic programme will be determined by the people, by the Government, by this Parliament and no outside power will have any influence in this regard.

I believe, Sir, I have covered most of the points. With these words I once again thank the hon'ble Members. I think this debate has been characterized by a common assertion of national will. I thank all the hon'ble Members. I thank Khanduriji, because when Members of his Party spoke in the other House, they said that they disown even the July 18 Statement. But when I heard the hon'ble Members on the other side today, I was encouraged to believe that it is still not too late to work for a broad national consensus. I will work in that direction. It is very important that the whole country should speak with one voice when it comes to a matter as important as is sought to be covered by the nuclear deal ... (Interruptions.)

... I am not an expert in nuclear matters. I think, there is a question mark about interchangeability because we do not have the status of a nuclear weapons State, but there is the other feature that we are free to build new reactors and new facilities. It is our prerogative whether we want to call them civilian or military. So, India's options are not being limited.

Section Five

The Journey towards a Liberalized Economy

1

The Beginnings

After the partition of Pakistan and India, successive finance ministers faced evolving challenges. The early years involved trying to rebuild the post-colonial economy, and decoupling from the Pakistani economy. The next stage was trying to spur growth with a socialist tint and a human face. After that, it was a question of liberalizing the economy.

An enduring challenge has been maintaining high public expenditure to provide basic services and adequate infrastructure while the tax base has been relatively small as a ratio of the gross domestic product. This has led to persistent deficit financing, and that, in turn, has meant a huge and growing burden of interest payments for the State.

Speeches in Parliament reflect these concerns. The focus is sometimes on infrastructure development, sometimes on support for defence and sometimes on meeting basic needs. It was only after 1991 that thought was given to opening up the economy, and crafting policy that would enable industry and agriculture to become competitive globally.

The first interim Budget had to address the challenges of creating a new narrative for independent India and Partition. It was presented by Sir Ramasamy Chetty Kandasamy Shanmukham Chetty, lawyer, economist and politician. This first Budget was basically a review of the economy and no new taxes were proposed as the next Budget was just 95 days away.

But Chetty had to explain the actions of the Partition Council in disentangling the economy, society, infrastructure such as the railways, and the reconstitution of the armed forces. The Budget also made provisions for the rehabilitation of refugees.

The second Budget – the first full budget of independent India – was presented by ***John Matthai****, an economist and academic. Matthai was a member of the Indian National Congress who served as India's first railway minister, and twice thereafter as finance minister. He resigned after the presentation of the budget excerpted here because he disagreed with the increasing powers being granted to the Planning Commission and to its prominent member, the statistician and scientist P.C. Mahalanobis.*

Matthai went on to become the first Chairman of the State Bank of India when it was set up in 1955, and he was the founding president of the governing body of the National Council of Applied Economic Research in 1956.

Matthai moves from an extensive discussion on partition with Pakistan and independence from the British, to examining how to improve the functioning of government. He proposed an Estimates Committee to complement the Standing Finance Committee, where the former would examine the expenditures and revenues of each department of the government. The proposed Planning Commission also featured in this exercise.

Matthai also focused on the problem of inflation and suggested the rise in prices was being caused by the aftermath of the Second World War.

Matthai's Budget treated the princely states in the same way as the provinces from a budgetary perspective. He proposed regulating the stock market, not renewing the Dividend Limitation Act and abolishing the business profits tax. There was a need to provide some security to foreign investors in the post-colonial era. He also suggested that enabling the import of some luxury goods would help generate revenues from customs duties.

JOHN MATTHAI

(Constituent Assembly: United Province)

Lok Sabha: 28 February 1950

Budget for 1950–51

I rise to present the estimated Receipts and Expenditure of the Government of India for the year, 1950–51. This is the first Budget of the Republic of India and I consider it a great honour that it has fallen to me to present it to the House.

... All that I propose to do at this stage is to give hon'ble members a broad outline of the Budgetary position and the general economic background of the Budget.

This Budget is being presented under the new Constitution ... we propose to ask the House to set up an Estimates Committee to scrutinize the expenditure of each Department of Government and of the Government as a whole ... the suggestions and criticisms which may be made by the Estimates Committee would ... give a useful direction and guidance to the Government in the matter of regulating expenditure. Secondly, I think the knowledge that the expenditure of Government and of the various Departments of Government would be examined in detail by an independent authority set up by the House would act as a deterrent to extravagance in public expenditure.

... I would like the Standing Finance Committee to continue at the same time ... The Standing Finance Committee is concerned with specific proposals of expenditure by each Department of Government, but the Estimates Committee's business would be to make a comprehensive examination of expenditure in relation to the resources available to Government ...

The second matter is this. The Constitution of India envisages not merely the India of the Provinces, but also the India of the States ... The result of that is that the estimates of 1950–51 would not be strictly comparable with the figure of 1949–50 or the preceding years ... The year 1947, which saw the partition meant a break in the continuity of our statistics, and the integration of the States in 1950 is going to mean a further break ...

But there is ... another way of looking at this period of transition, because this period of 1947 to 1950 will ... appear to the future historian of India as a dividing line between one segment of our history, of the storied past of India, from another segment of our history, which is just opening out and which as it widens and moves forward will have witnessed the fulfilment of the aspirations of the generation that strove to build the New India of our dreams.

I want ... to take the House back to the main economic events that occurred during the year 1949 ... It has been a period of almost unprecedented difficulties ... But on an objective examination of the facts as they stand today, I feel I am in a position to tell the House that the stage of crisis at any rate is now definitely past ...

The first main economic problem ... is ... 'inflation' ... I want today to confine myself to that aspect of it which is reflected in the level of prices ... It is a world problem which has come to us as a legacy principally of the war. It is interesting to trace the difference between inflation as it was created by the First World War and ... that ... by the Second World War. In the first war ... the inflationary trends created by the war continued until 1920. In 1921, a marked downward trend began. In the ... second war, the war ended in 1945. Today, we are in the fifth year after the termination of the war; but the inflationary process set going by the war still continues in many countries ... India, therefore, is finding itself entangled in a world situation ... What exactly are the causes that distinguish inflation as it emerged from the first war and as it has emerged from the recent war? ... there was much larger destruction of national assets and productive capacity in the second war ... But the end of the second war has coincided almost immediately with talks and thought of another war ... Stockpiling has already started and increasing demand has already come into existence for basic and strategic materials. Therefore, today we are in a position much more difficult than the position created by the first war.

Taking our own country, we are necessarily affected by all these international forces ... On top of it, we have had difficult problems created by partition. We also have problems created by the fact that a large part of our expenditure during the war was met by fiduciary currency backed by foreign assets, instead of by loans and by taxes …

Now, I would like to briefly examine the movement of prices in 1949 … the Government adopted certain anti-inflationary measures towards the end of the year, 1948 … As the result of these anti-inflationary measures, prices slowly began to come down from October 1948, and that steady downward trend continued until March 1949 … I … thought … that that movement would continue … what happened was that from April 1949, for several months thereafter, the trend of prices was upward and that upward trend continued until, I think, October 1949, a few weeks after devaluation. Then we took certain special measures for countering the possible effects of devaluation … although we have not been able to bring down prices, we have, at any rate, been able substantially to hold the level of prices … Although it is perfectly true that there has been no fall in prices generally, there has been … a steady fall in prices of food grains from October 1948 till now. As far as the whole group of food articles is concerned, there has also been a fall, though not to the same extent … I am referring particularly to sugar and gur … I believe India is one of the few countries in the world which attempted devaluation in September in which there has been no rise in the general level of prices as a result of devaluation … If, Sir, you observe the trend of movements of prices in the various categories covered by our Index Number, you will find principally the recent rise in prices has been in regard to industrial raw materials.

… In 1931, when sterling was devalued, it was followed by a decline in dollar prices, the result being that prices of commodities of dollar origin in terms of sterling did not rise to the whole extent of the devaluation. What is apparently happening today is that the devaluation of sterling has, as far as America is concerned, resulted in the maintenance of the original level of the prices. Dollar prices have remained steady since September 1949 on the whole. The result is that sterling prices of industrial commodities have gone up almost to the extent of the devaluation … Therefore, the movement that we are witnessing today, the upward movement in the prices of industrial raw materials in our Index Number, is really a symptom of a world movement and the controlling of that, therefore, is not entirely in our hands.

Next, I come to the question of production … Now if you take production in 1949, I think there has been substantial increase in various important industries – steel, cement, coal, heavy chemicals, paper and generation of electricity. There are two … very important industries in our country … The first is cotton textiles and the other is jute manufacture. In both these cases, the limiting factor … is the supply of raw material, particularly as the result of the deadlock that has arisen in the trade between us and Pakistan … We have … arranged for the import of 10 lakh bales of cotton … and we are in a position to arrange for the importation of further raw cotton. I think also active steps with promising results have been taken in the matter of increasing the indigenous production of raw cotton ... the production of raw jute in the Indian Union has, during the past 2 years, definitely shown signs of improvement ...

With regard to production of food grains ... we have every expectation that in 1950, there would be an increase of 2.8 million tons over 1949 ... The procurement target for 1950 is a million tons above the target of 1949. The conclusion that I would come to is that although production still leaves a great deal of room for improvement, there is no cause for anxiety.

There are two important factors which have assisted this increase in production. The first is the marked improvement that has taken place in railway transport ... The other factor which has helped is the improvement in the labour situation ... There have been fewer labour disputes ... I want, in this connection, to pay a tribute to the great labour organizations of this country. They have grown in stature; they have gathered strength ... Along with that, it seems to me that they have also developed a spirit of patriotism and a sense of responsibility and of their duty to the other sections of the community, which to my mind, justify us in looking forward with confidence to the future of Indian industry.

The third problem that I want to refer to is the situation in the money market ... The position in the short-term market was one of acute stringency. The position in the long-term market was one of continued stagnation ... There was a marked fall in bank deposits. There was also an increase in bank advances. The result was that during the first six months of 1949, the ratio of deposits to advances which is the test by which we can judge the stringency of the market – the ratio was higher than in the preceding years. If you take a normal year in our country, in the slack season the ratio is somewhere about 45 per cent and in the busy season about 50; it varies between 45 and 50. In the first half of 1949, it rose above 55, an unhealthy situation. I am glad to say that since July 1949, the position has improved but it is not ... wholly satisfactory, because, part of the improvement is due to the fact not that the deposits have gone up but that advances have come down, because banks are more cautious and also because of the deadlock in our trade with Pakistan, but judged by the ratio test, the position is more satisfactory ... So far as the ... long-term market is concerned ... right from August 1946, when the great communal disturbances started in Calcutta, there was a continuous fall in industrial investments ... Since July 1949, there have been signs of revival of confidence ... the big problem that is facing us today: what exactly we can do to bring the genuine investor back into the investment market. One of the reasons why the genuine investor is holding aloof is that he has not got the measure of confidence which would justify his putting what little he has into investment ... Therefore ... it is necessary that the spirit of confidence should be fostered by every means in our power.

... I consider that foreign capital is necessary in this country, not merely for the purpose of supplementing our own resources, but for the purpose of instilling a spirit of confidence among our own investors ... any considerable assistance in the way of capital from foreign countries must hereafter be looked for not in the shape of fixed interest-bearing loans and bonds, but in the shape of equity capital on the basis of joint participation on strict business considerations without any political strings attached to it ...

... In the 19th century when foreign capital went out from advanced countries to undeveloped countries, they had the security born of political control. In other words, colonialism provided the necessary sense of security to the foreign investor. Today, since colonialism has disappeared, the only way in which the same sense of security could be imparted is by friendly agreement. Therefore, it is necessary that we should consider providing reasonable conditions of security and fair treatment for those who are willing to take the risk of investing their money in this country ...

May I ... refer to ... the Dividend Limitation Act ... We have now decided not to extend the Act for the following reasons. On account of the general fall in the level of profits the limit fixed in the Act is practically inoperative. Secondly, as an anti-inflationary measure the effect of the Act has been negligible. Thirdly, it has had a disproportionately depressing effect on the investment market ...

In connection with this question of balance of payments there has been a great deal of criticism regarding the Open General Licence ... the main charge against Government being that under the Open General Licence a large quantity of goods of a purely luxury character was admitted into the country ... I am satisfied that what can be called luxury goods amounted to not more than 1.5 to 2 per cent of the total imports ... the reason why it has become necessary to import articles of this kind is that in the bilateral agreements that we make with other countries, these countries generally insist upon a certain proportion of their non-essential goods being imported into India ... That is not business like: in actual practice it is not workable ... If, for example, you confine your imports to food grains and plant and machinery, food grains bear no duty at all, agricultural machinery bears no duty at all, industrial machinery bears a duty of 5 per cent, industrial raw materials bear relatively low rates of duty. If, therefore, I confined imports to these articles, the customs revenue would be exactly half of what it is today. We would be faced with a huge deficit which would create inflation in its turn ...

At the end of June 1949, our Sterling Balances stood at Rs. 820 crores ... and the latest figure that I have is Rs. 846 crores ... During this period our dollar receipts also exceeded our dollar payments ... But I think the figures of exports are sufficiently encouraging for us to hope that there has been a definite turn for the better as regards our balance of payments ... But there is no room for complacency ... A healthy balance is the sort of balance that you attain at the highest possible level of imports as well as exports ... When you come to the question of exports again, the crux of the problem is production ... In view of these facts, Government have decided to set up a Planning Commission as announced by the President ...

Before I leave this question of balance of payments, I want to make a brief reference to our position vis-à-vis Pakistan. Unfortunately, the deadlock with Pakistan over the exchange issue still continues. We have expressed our agreement to the proposal that there should be a joint discussion between the two countries. Our proposal is that that discussion should cover all matters which are relevant to the economic relations between the two countries, but so far, the Pakistan Government have not seen their way to extending the scope of the conference as we have suggested ...

... I think I must make a few relevant facts clear. Firstly, that if Pakistan has an overall favourable balance ... I doubt that favourable balance is due entirely to her favourable balance with India. Secondly, this favourable balance with India is due to a very large extent to the open-door policy in trade matters which we had adopted towards Pakistan and the restrictive policy adopted by Pakistan towards India. Thirdly ... Pakistan has recently been running a deficit both on her sterling and on her dollar accounts. In view of this, it seems to me an anomaly that Pakistan could remain in the sterling area and yet decline to devalue her currency as a means of rectifying her adverse balance like every other member of the Sterling area. Lastly, whatever rate may be agreed to by the International Monetary Fund for the Pakistan currency, it will not, in practice, result in a normal restoration of trade between India and Pakistan unless that rate fits the facts of the economic situation.

... Government have been strongly and widely criticized for the way in which they have handled the economic situation ... First of all, I think it has had a very stimulating effect on members of Government. Secondly, I think it has done a great deal of good to the people who make the criticism ... it provides a very useful and essential outlet for the suppressed emotions of people which, but for this outlet, might someday burst and break up society ...

I now turn to the revenue and expenditure of Government. As regards the current year, 1949–50 ... last year I estimated a total revenue of about Rs. 323 crores and a total expenditure of Rs. 322.50 crores, leaving a small surplus of about Rs. 49 lakh. The revised estimates now show a total revenue of a little over Rs. 332 crores and a total expenditure of a little over Rs. 336 crores, thus, converting the token surplus of Rs. 49 lakh into a deficit of Rs. 3.74 crores ... this small deficit of Rs. 3.74 crores, I regard with a sense of relief.

... The outstanding fact is this: defence expenditure during the current year went up from the estimated figure of over Rs. 157 crores to about Rs. 170 crores – an increase of about Rs. 12.66 crores. Against that, customs revenue went up by about Rs. 9 crores. The difference between the increase in the defence expenditure and the increase in customs revenue gives exactly the measure of the deficit ... When I put my estimates before the House last year, I made it clear that my estimates were based on the assumption that the 'Cease Fire Agreement' would lead to a peaceful solution of the Kashmir problem. That anticipation did not materialize ...

As regards the customs revenue, the increase is largely due to the fact that we had a very liberal import policy working over the greater part of the year, and also we have had some extra receipts from export duties levied since devaluation.

I will now come to the estimates for 1950–51 ... They boil down to this that the integrated States would be placed on exactly the same footing as the old provinces, the Centre having responsibility for Federal Subjects and Services and the Centre also taking over the Federal assets and liabilities ...

At the existing level of taxation, the total revenue for 1950–51 is estimated at Rs. 347.5 crores, and the total expenditure at Rs. 337.88 crores, leaving a surplus of Rs. 9.62 crores. On the revenue side the principal changes are: Customs show a drop of very nearly Rs. 14 crores, due to our present policy of strict limitation of imports. Income-tax shows an increase of nearly Rs. 35 crores which is due to three factors. First of all, it allows for the income-tax derived from the integrated States. Then there is the larger receipts that we expect by a prompter collection on current assessments and by better recoveries of arrears. Lastly, a considerable part of it represents the advance payments made under section 18A of the Income Tax Act which have been taken to revenue instead of deposit, maintaining the accounting change which was made two years ago and which we expect to complete in 1951–52.

On the expenditure side, in 1949–50, the revised figures of defence expenditure show an expenditure of Rs. 170 crores. We are providing for 1950–51 an expenditure of Rs. 168 crores for Defence ...

Our policy, as the Prime Minister has declared more than once, is to contribute in every way we can to the maintenance of peace and to the employment of peaceful methods in the settlement of international disputes ... If, however, contrary to our expectation, events so develop that the peace and security of this country are endangered, Government will have no hesitation in raising whatever finance may be required for meeting the situation ...

Now, I come to the estimates of Civil expenditure. The Civil expenditure estimate for 1950–51 is Rs. 169.87 crores against Rs. 166.04 crores, the revised estimate of 1949–50, showing an increase of Rs. 3.83 crores ... This figure of Rs. 169.87 crores includes expenditure under the following items: Administration of States taken over as Chief Commissionerships; Administration of Central Subjects in States and Unions, under the integration scheme; Privy Purses of Indian Rulers with whom we have made solemn agreements; and grants by the Centre under the financial integration scheme. These four items of expenditure aggregate to Rs. 26.18 crores ... My experience is: the more you spend on tax collection, the more you get in return, a good deal more ... Another item is interest charges, pensions and debt redemption charges amounting to very nearly Rs. 44 crores ... Then there are the grants-in-aid both to the States and Provinces. Then there is expenditure on various nation-building activities, scientific services, agriculture, medical, health and so on.

... The estimated surplus is, as I told the House, Rs. 9.62 crores. I will explain later how I propose to deal with it. Now I come to the capital budget. The figures for capital expenditure, meaning thereby development expenditure by the Centre, loans to States for long-term expenditure, expenditure from depreciation and Reserve Funds, stand like this: For 1949–50 the Budget estimate was Rs. 203 crores. Revised figure for 1949–50 is Rs. 155 crores. Budget figure for 1950–51 is Rs. 133 crores.

I will now take the capital receipts, meaning by that revenue taken to reserve. Borrowing in the market, small savings and foreign loans (foreign loans in this case are loans from the International Bank). The figures are – Budget for 1949–50 Rs. 140 crores. Revised figure for 1949–50 Rs. 101 crores. Budget figure for 1950–51 Rs. 148 crores.

As regards the more important of these receipts, viz., loans from the market, the House will remember that we were able to raise only Rs. 40 crores in 1949–50 against our estimate of Rs. 85 crores. From small savings I expected Rs. 37.50 crore while it yielded only Rs. 26 crores. But in view of the signs of improvement that are visible, I am estimating Rs. 75 crores for 1950–51 from market borrowings and Rs. 28 crores from small savings.

Apart from capital expenditure, we have other non-recurring expenditure to meet. There is the redemption of our permanent debt, like the 2.50 per cent loans of 1950 we are going to pay. Also, the outstanding on the 4.50 per cent loan of 1950–55. We have also to pay the first instalment of our dues to the World Bank this year and there are certain Railway Annuities falling due. Altogether the discharge of permanent debt would mean about Rs. 48 crores. Taking all our non-recurring receipts and expenditure, i.e., those outside the revenue budget, the deficit figures stand as follows:

In the 1949–50 Budget, we estimated a deficit on capital amount of Rs. 134 crores. The revised estimate shows a deficit of Rs. 120 crores. For 1950–51, I estimate a deficit of Rs. 24 crores. Taking all Government transactions and allowing for them, our Cash Balances position would be as follows: At the end of 1949–50, I expect our cash balances will stand approximately at Rs. 95 crores against a figure of Rs. 58 crore which I estimated in my budget last year. At the end of 1950–51, I expect the balances would stand at Rs. 78 crores ...

(The detailed tax proposals which followed have not been excerpted.)

2

Speaking for the Poor

Ram Manohar Lohia *was not just a brilliant intellectual and polyglot with a PhD from Berlin on taxation of salt in India, he was a freedom fighter and India's pre-eminent socialist leader. Initially in the Indian National Congress (INC), he quit the INC in 1938 along with other socialists to form his own party. Thereafter, he developed his own political standpoint, critically examining the positions taken by the Gandhian leadership of the Congress as well as those of the communists. Twice elected to the Lok Sabha, he left an indelible mark on Parliament and the politics of this country, though he died young, at the age of 57.*

One of Lohia's great contributions was that he recognized that caste, more than class, was the huge stumbling block in India's progress. Then, as today, it was politically incorrect to mention caste in public, but most people practised it in all aspects of life – birth, marriage, association and death. It was his thesis that India had suffered reverses throughout her history because people had viewed themselves as members of a caste rather than citizens of a country. Caste, as Lohia put it, was a congealed class.

Following the efforts of the early post-colonial governments to develop a suitable budget for India, there was a key moment in relation to the economics of India. At that time, 16 years after Independence, in 1963, Lohia argued in a parliamentary discussion that the government had overestimated the daily income of the poorest in India, that the government was 'fudging the budgets' and that the government was mindlessly following the advice of experts rather than drawing a course of its own to eradicate poverty and reduce inequality in India. During the debate, individual members gave up their time to Lohia as he built his case, demolishing the Planning Commission statistics, pointing out that a small number of rich people were pulling up the average to present a wholly unrealistic picture. This has come to be known as the 'Teen Anna' (three annas) speech, and its original in Hindi has a power that unfortunately is lost in translation.

RAM MANOHAR LOHIA

(Lok Sabha: Farukkhabad)

Lok Sabha: 6 September 1963

Teen Anna

The conclusion drawn from the discussion held so far is that … the daily earnings of 27 crore Indians is 3 annas according to me; the Hon'ble Prime Minister thinks it is 15 annas, whereas the Planning Minister says it is 7½ annas. Now it is between the Hon'ble Prime Minister and the Planning Minister to decide who is right.

My argument is not that the daily earnings of the common man, particularly of 27 crore Indians, is 3 annas or 3½ annas or 2½ annas … the point is that the Government has turned a blind eye to the poverty in the country, and unless there is a will to eradicate poverty, a tangible formula cannot be worked out …

Secondly, instead of taking prices prevalent in 1948–49 as base, generally current prices are taken into account … who are these statisticians who furnish these figures? When 50 lakh people died in the Bengal famine, they proved that only 5 lakhs had died. Therefore, the Ministers should remain cautious and give them some guidelines. I would not take their figures as it is … I shall use my own sense of judgement as far as possible. According to … the Planning Minister, rural expenditure comes to about Rs. 8700 crores, whereas income from agriculture which includes income from livestock … comes to about Rs. 6600 crores … I should have kept the income from livestock and agriculture separate, but even without doing so there is a variation of Rs. 2000 crores. In a way the variation is of about Rs. 3000 to Rs. 3500 crores if we take the two heads separately. The Government may say that there is a variation between the income and expenditure because donations, charity and debts are also included in the expenditure. In this connection, I would like to say that one cannot be under debt forever. Debts can be for a limited period for 2, 4, 5 or 10 years. After all, the figure for income and expenditure should be the same. There may be slight variation between the two.

A major mistake that is committed in the figures of consumer index is that the price difference is added. For example, the data pertaining to fuel and electricity which have been published so far relate to 13th series, but the Planning Minister has referred to the 17th series. We cannot verify it. On the basis of the data of the 13th series, I would like to tell that expenditure on fuel and electricity by the lowest income group has been computed as 20 p.[1] and other expenditure as 91 p. Similarly for another group, cash expenditure is 28 p. whereas other expenditure is Re. 1 and 2 paisa. For sugar, cash expenditure is 15 p. whereas other expenditure

[1] Editor's note: Paise.

is 19 p. In this way the total expenditure is inflated but if it is inflated from Rs. 6600 crores to Rs. 8700 crores, it will not be proper.

I would tell you another way of calculation. In 1960–61 the daily earnings of 32 crore agricultural labour was 45 paise; in 1961–62, the daily earnings of 35 crore agricultural labour came down to 43 paise … Therefore, the official figures prove that over 27 crore people in this country survive on 4 annas a day …

… I would like to submit that the Government has fudged the national income by 20 per cent from the very beginning. One reason might be that they wanted to show that India is rich. Another could be that they wanted to facilitate taxation, and everyone knows that the figures are fudged.

Now I would like to submit one thing more and that is about the per capita income in poor States. The figures that the Planning Minister had placed were based on the second census of the country. Uttar Pradesh, Bihar, Rajasthan, Madhya Pradesh, Orissa and Andhra Pradesh are the six poorest States. Their total rural population is 20 crores, though in fact it is 23 crores … At one time, the per capita income in rural areas was Rs. 182. We can go by the same argument that the top 10 per cent swallow 50 per cent of the income or I can adopt another method, which I generally use, viz., that the top 20 per cent consume 60 per cent of the income, whereas the remaining 80 per cent of the populace is left with 40 per cent … these figures are official whereas the calculation is personal. I would like to advise the Government not to take the figures provided by experts … there should be some guidelines, otherwise consequences can be bad. The per capita income of Uttar Pradesh would come down to Rs. 101 from Rs. 182 if we do not count the top 10 per cent who swallow 50 per cent of the income. Similarly, it would be reduced to Rs. 91 if we include those 20 per cent who swallow 60 per cent of the income. This means that the daily earnings per head remain under 4 annas. This is evident from the figures provided by the Government itself that 27 crore people in this country survive on daily earnings of less than 4 annas. Then there is another figure of Rs. 193 per head. If it may be a little more, even then it would be about 4 annas or 3½ annas or 3¼ annas. There will not be much difference. This is about Uttar Pradesh … which is so poor. The plight of the people of Orissa, Madhya Pradesh, Bihar and Rajasthan is also the same …

… The Hon'ble Prime Minister had stated on 22 August, 1960, that the national income had increased by 42%, and the per capita income by 20%. However, he was surprised to find … that increase evaporated. In a way, the Government had already accepted that it was not aware as to where that increase had gone. Thereafter, a committee on the Distribution of National Income was constituted. Now my question is as to where that Committee disappeared? … Previously I had submitted that 27 crores of Indians earn only 3 annas for their livelihood. Now I would submit that 10 to 15 crores of our people subsist on only 2 annas. I have received several letters condemning me for my statement about our people earning only 3 annas … If these figures are analysed differently, we will find that there are about 7 crore agricultural labourers in our country. We can deduct half or one crore out of this because they may be slightly better off.

As regards the small farmers, their number is at least 14 to 15 crores who own less than two and a half acres of land. The number of artisans is about 2 to 3 crores. Then in urban areas also, the plight of 20 to 25 per cent people is pitiable, who find it difficult to make both ends meet.

In fact, they live in such horrible conditions … surprising how they are surviving. They live on pavements and Jhuggi-Jhonpri clusters and somehow manage to survive by picking grains from garbage dumps. As regards those who have migrated from rural areas and have some means of income, they try to spend minimum on themselves as they have to support their families living in the rural areas. Then there are adivasis, widows and if I may be allowed to say so, the carefree monks. The total number of all these categories of people is 27 to 30 crores.

Apart from referring to the aforementioned figures, I would like to present a first-hand account of the situation which the Hon'ble Prime Minister, the Hon'ble Minister of Planning and the Government should keep in view. In Benares, I have seen cows eating corpses. In Orissa, where little fish is available in the rivers, I have seen hundreds of people spreading their fishing nets to catch fish. At Salem in Tamil Nadu, I have seen lakhs of artisans earning only 10, 12 or 14 annas per day. If calculations are made about the average income of these people, the average is bound to work out to less than 3 annas per day. Similarly, if we look into the income of the other weaker sections, we will find that they also earn the same amount per day …

These are Government figures. The statisticians also compete with each other in presenting a brighter picture. One such organization is based in Delhi and is called the National Council of Economic Research. It has given the names of 29 districts where the per capita income is less than Rs. 100. I am mentioning here the names of some of these districts – in Darbhanga it is Rs. 96; in Saran and Chapra it is Rs. 96; in Deoria it is Rs. 98; in Tehri Garhwal it is Rs. 84. If the method of calculation which I had previously submitted is applied here, that is, to deduct 50 per cent income for the 10 per cent upper strata and 60 per cent of the amount for the next 20 per cent people, the daily income of the remaining lower sections in these districts comes to less than 3 annas. I have referred to only 4 districts. There are similarly 40 districts where the income is Rs. 110, Rs. 120 and Rs. 125 …

If we refer to the thirteenth series it will become evident as to how our living standard is going down. In 1952, the per capita expenditure of 30 per cent of the population was Rs. 10 and 25 paise and in 1957–58 it was reduced to Rs. 10 and 14 paise. The figures which I have quoted are Government figures. The Hon'ble

Prime Minister should go through the publications of his own Government in order to know about the declining standards of living. Similarly, the expenditure of 30 per cent families was reduced from Rs. 15 and 70 paise to Rs. 14 and 50 paise. The expenditure of only 2 per cent families has increased from Rs. 45 to Rs. 48. This is how the standard of living of the people is constantly declining.

Previously per capita income used to increase by Rs. 7 per year. This holds good no longer. It now increases by 2 naya paisa[2] every year and if this is the price of our progress, we shall be vulnerable to outside threats. In this connection I would particularly like to refer to China and Ghana and not the USSR and USA In Ghana, the per capita income is increasing by Rs. 30 to Rs. 40 and in China it is increasing by Rs. 50 to Rs. 60. Why have we not been able to make similar progress? Because the pattern of consumption underwent change and modernization, but without a corresponding modernization in our production process, we started aping the Western countries in our consumption patterns …

If we examine the figures of the income of the people and the income-tax which they are paying, we will find that 6,52,000 persons are paying taxes and they are paying Rs. 200 crores as income tax having an income of Rs. 120 crores. But it is common knowledge that their actual income is double of this amount of Rs. 120 crores. Moreover, a very huge expenditure is being incurred on the facilities being provided to Ministers, etc. In this way, the total expenditure comes to about Rs. 250 crores. This amount is taken away by only one per cent of the population, as is evident from the Government statistics. The figures which I have collected from my own sources are, however, even more.

I think that we can easily save Rs. 100 to Rs. 120 crores, according to one way, and Rs. 150 to Rs. 200 crores according to the other by rationalizing the expenditure. The Government can function more effectively, the income-tax burden can be reduced and there can be better development of agriculture and industries. But only the person whose heart bleeds for the common man can do it.

This Government has turned into a Government of directionless experts and whatever recommendations the experts make, the Government blindly follows them. The Ministers have little knowledge about agriculture, industries, national income, etc. The Hon'ble Ministers should apply their own minds instead of blindly following the recommendations of the experts. They should think over the recommendations and then give directions, because the statisticians and the economists are like poisonous snakes who dance to the tune of the snake charmers. But if you are incapable of playing the flute, the results are bound to be disastrous.

---

[2] Editor's translation: New paisa.

I would like to claim that if the distribution of national income is rationalized, it can be increased by Rs. 20 every year and this can be done by any ordinary individual but only when everyone gets a share in the increase in the national income.

(The translation has been taken from Eminent Parliamentarians Monograph Series *entitled 'Lohia and Parliament'/Lok Sabha Secretariat/New Delhi/1991 from the chapter 'Distribution of National Income', available on Parliament Digital Library site.)*

3

Banking for the People

*In 1969, **Indira Gandhi** as Prime Minister took a controversial decision to nationalize fourteen Indian banks. Her aim was to stop the banks from merely providing financial assistance to large investors and taking speculative risks, and to instead become an instrument that provided credit to small and large borrowers based on their needs, and for the well-being of the country. This was a major step within India and seen by critics as a decision driven more by political rather than economic considerations.*

INDIRA GANDHI
(Lok Sabha: Rae Bareli)
Lok Sabha: 21 July 1969

On Bank Nationalization

Mr. Deputy Speaker, Sir, an Ordinance was promulgated the day-before-yesterday, nationalizing fourteen of the major commercial banks incorporated in India. With your permission, I should like to share with the House the considerations which weighed with Government in taking this momentous decision and the spirit in which they propose to implement it.

Nearly fifteen years ago, Parliament approved that we should set before ourselves the goal of a socialist pattern of society ... Public ownership, and the control of the commanding heights of the national economy, and of its strategic sectors, are essential and important aspects of the new social order which we are trying to build in the country. We regard this as particularly necessary in a poor country which seeks to achieve speedy economic progress, consistent with social justice, in a democratic political system – one which is free from the domination of a few, and in which opportunities are open to all.

Financial institutions are among the most important levers that any society has at its command, for the achievement of its social and economic objectives. It is in recognition of this fact that we nationalized the life insurance business and the then Imperial Bank of India over a decade ago. Since then, we have also set up in the public sector, other institutions for the provision of medium- or long-term finance to industry and agriculture. The nationalization of major banks is a significant step in this process of public control over the principal institutions for the mobilization of people's savings and canalizing them towards productive purposes.

After the serious difficulties which we have had to encounter in recent years, our economy is once again poised for fresh growth and development. There has been a notable breakthrough on the agricultural front, technologically and otherwise. The increase in our exports has been impressive. There has been substantial progress in power supply and the development of transport, as also the availability of trained manpower. Our industrial base has been strengthened and diversified …

… Our major concern has been to accelerate the tempo of investment and production, so as to improve living standards and increase employment opportunities, consistent with our determination to achieve self-reliance. It is necessary to mobilize the savings of the people to the largest possible extent; and to utilize them for productive purposes in accordance with our plans and priorities. Government believe that public ownership of the major banks, for which there has been widespread public support, will help in the most effective mobilization and deployment of national resources, so that our objectives can be realized with a greater degree of assurance …

… The Ordinance promulgated by Government provides for the nationalization of all scheduled banks, incorporated in India, which had minimum deposits of not less than Rs. 50 crores at the end of June last. The fourteen banks in this category, together with the State Bank of India and its subsidiaries which already operate under public ownership, account for more than 85% of bank deposits in this country … in view of the very nature of the measure, and to forestall any possibility of manipulations which may not be in the public interest, it was essential to make a swift and sudden move which could only be achieved through an ordinance …

So far as foreign banks are concerned, they provide, by and large, business of a specialized nature such as facilitating foreign trade and tourism. The operation of banks of one country in another, subject to the laws of the land, is mainly for such purposes and is part of an international facility … Having regard to all these factors, Government have decided to exclude branches of foreign banks incorporated outside India from the purview of the Ordinance.

… As I stated the other day, this is not the beginning of a new era of nationalization. Whatever the pattern of the economy, it is widely recognized that the operations of the banking system should be informed … by a larger social purpose, and should be subject to close public regulation. Government have come to the conclusion that the desired regulation and rate of progress consistent with the urgency of our problems could be secured only through nationalization.

I should like to reiterate my assurance that even after nationalization, the legitimate credit needs of private industry and trade, big or small, will be met … The banks will now be better placed to serve the farmer and to promote agricultural production and rural development generally. Public ownership will also help to curb the use of bank credit for speculative and other unproductive purposes. By severing the link between the major banks and the bigger industrial groups which have so far controlled them, Government believe that the step they have taken will also bring about the right atmosphere for the development of adequate professional management in the banking field. Government attach the utmost importance to modern managerial techniques and practices.

The moneys which depositors entrust to the banks are in the nature of a sacred trust. The interests of the depositors of the banks which have been nationalized will not only continue to be fully safeguarded but will now have the backing of the State itself. I should also make it clear that the emphasis on priority areas, new entrepreneurs … and relatively backward areas will not be at the expense of considerations of economic viability. Only thus can we fulfil our obligations to those who have entrusted their savings to us for the benefit of the community …

The Ordinance has also provided for the adequate protection of the interests of employees of the banks concerned. They have now become employees of a publicly owned and socially responsible banking system. This also places on them a special responsibility towards the community. The success of the programme of nationalization will, in a large measure, depend upon the efficiency, the devotion and the dedication with which they perform their daily tasks, and the courtesy and consideration with which they treat the constituents of the bank. I hope that all individual employees of these banks and their associations will now help in the successful implementation of the step which has been taken …

The Ordinance provides for a scheme of fair compensation for the take-over in accordance with a formula which Parliament approved recently while enacting the Banking Laws (Amendment) Act, 1968. The Ordinance provides that compensation will be payable in the form of Government securities.

In order to cause the least possible dislocation in the working of the banks covered by the Ordinance, and to avoid inconvenience to the public, it is proposed, for the present, to retain the identity of each bank in the form of a new corporation …

As in other matters of policy, Government have been guided in taking the present decision entirely by national interests, and the needs and aspirations of our people. The establishment of a socialist society is one of our declared goals, but we have not been guided by any doctrinaire considerations. Our sole concern has been to accelerate development and thus make a significant impact on the problems of poverty and unemployment, and to bring about progressive reduction of disparities between the rich and the poor sections of our people, and between the relatively advanced and backward areas of our country.

I realize that the test of the decision is in its effective implementation. Government are determined to take all possible steps to make this measure a success.

4

Liberalization

***Dr Manmohan Singh** is an economist and academic who held important positions in the government, including that of the governor of the Reserve Bank of India (RBI) and the chief economic adviser to the Government of India before he joined the Congress Party. In 2004, he became the prime minister, heading the UPA government. This speech was delivered in 1991–92 when he was the finance minister in Prime Minister P.V. Narasimha Rao's government. This was a landmark speech, as the economic liberalization package pushed by Singh and Rao opened the nation to foreign direct investment (FDI) and reduced the red tape that had previously impeded business growth.*

The liberalization was prompted by an acute balance of payments crisis whereby the Indian government was left without sufficient reserves to meet its obligations, and had begun preparations to mortgage its gold reserves to the Bank of England in order to obtain the cash reserves needed to run the country.

As such, Singh was instrumental in the opening up of the economy. He reduced the peak import duty from 300 plus to 50 per cent. He will also be remembered for making the rupee convertible in the current account across just two phases. Introducing the concept of 'service tax' was also his idea.

The economy was in a deep crisis because of the foreign exchange deficit and double-digit inflation. Expenditures far exceeded revenues. The government's path-breaking decision to open up the economy and liberalize it led to a series of reforms in industrial policy, trade policy, the liberalization of FDI, including encouraging investment from non-resident Indians (NRIs). On the domestic front, the focus was on developing human resources, promoting communal harmony and South–South cooperation, amongst other reforms.

*The next key speech was made by **P. Chidambaram**, a politician and Supreme Court lawyer, who has been the Union finance minister four times and home minister once. He has been a Congressman, barring a brief flirtation with the Tamil Maanila Congress in 1996.*

Chidambaram's budgetary speech for 1997–98, made on behalf of the H.D. Deve Gowda-led United Front (UF) government, was hailed by the Indian media as 'the dream budget': it was remarkable in continuing the focus on the UF government's Common Minimum Programme while pushing for liberalization. Seeking balance between planning and enabling the free market was the challenge. The internal public debt of the federal government was 55 per cent of gross domestic product (GDP) requiring interest payments of about 20 per cent of the central government's expenditure. This was exacerbated by the difficult balance of payments situation, which led to borrowings from abroad and external debt to NRIs, which was about 23 per cent of GDP at the end of 1990–91, and the debt service was about 21 per cent of current account receipts in 1990–91. With very high inflation and increasing costs, the challenge was to reduce the expenditures of the government while increasing the revenues. The tax to GDP ratio was about 10.5 per cent. Thus, the need to reduce state expenditures remained urgent. A Ways and Means Advances (WMA) Scheme of the RBI was introduced to help finance the deficit. The Disinvestment Commission would help identify areas where the government could withdraw its investments. The Ganga Kalyan Yojana Scheme was to help farmers access more groundwater and the Jan Arogya scheme was to enhance health insurance. At the same time, the government decided to enable and expose Indian industry to foreign competition in a phased manner through raising the limit of FDI in specific companies and in trading companies, encouraging FDI in selected areas, and either rehabilitating sick public enterprises or closing them down, subject to social security mechanisms. Energy production was being encouraged through the New Exploration Licensing Policy. A Swarnajayanti Fellowship for Outstanding Scientists was instituted to encourage scientific studies. Policies to encourage information technology were also introduced. In terms of raising resources, addressing the black market economy through a Voluntary Disclosure Scheme was a key element. In an economy of 900 million people, only 12 million people were paying tax and the government decided that big city residents who owned a four-wheel vehicle, occupied immovable property, owned a telephone and had travelled abroad in the previous year, should voluntarily file their tax returns. A new Estimated Income Scheme for retail traders was also introduced. The service sector would also be taxed. At the same time, corporate taxes were reduced.

The century ended with the budget by ***Yashwant Sinha*** *for 2000–01. Sinha, a career civil servant, quit the Indian Administrative Service in 1984 and joined the Janata Party. Subsequently, he joined the Janata Dal and became a member of then Prime Minister Chandra Shekhar's Cabinet. He later quit the Janata Dal and joined the Bharatiya Janata Party (BJP), where he became finance minister and later, foreign minister in then Prime Minister Atal Bihari Vajpayee's, Cabinet.*

This speech came in the aftermath of the super cyclone in Orissa, a 50-day war in Kashmir and a weak monsoon. This meant much higher costs and lower agricultural production. Sinha proposed, among other things, programmes for relieving poverty including microfinance, education and rural development, a national commission on land use policy, a technology leadership initiative, and a single-rate central value added tax.

Dr Singh's Budgets involved a serious shift in the government's approach to raising revenues. And here we have presented the direct and indirect tax and duties proposed in full, since these indicate the direction of the New Economic Policy.

Chidambaram's 'dream budget' also featured some radical tax proposals and therefore, the tax measures proposed have been presented in full. Sinha's Budget explained the thrust of government fiscal policy but the tax proposals were more in the nature of tinkering with rates and have been excluded from this excerpt.

MANMOHAN SINGH

(Rajya Sabha: Assam)

Lok Sabha: 24 July 1991

Budget for 1991–92

Sir, I rise to present the budget for 1991–92. As I rise, I am overpowered by a strange feeling of loneliness. I miss a handsome, smiling, face listening intently to the Budget Speech. Shri Rajiv Gandhi is no more. But his dream lives on; his dream of ushering India into the twenty-first century; his dream of a strong, united, technologically sophisticated but humane India. I dedicate this Budget to his inspiring memory.

The new Government, which assumed office barely a month ago, inherited an economy in deep crisis ... The foreign exchange crisis constitutes a serious threat to the sustainability of growth processes and orderly implementation of our development programmes ... The people of India have to face double digit inflation which hurts most the poorer sections of our society ... We have not experienced anything similar in the history of independent India ...

... The increasing difference between the income and expenditure of the Government has led to a widening of the gap between the income and expenditure of the economy as a whole ...

The crisis of the fiscal system is a cause for serious concern ... As a result, internal public debt of the Central Government has accumulated to about 55 per cent of Gross Domestic Product (GDP) ... Interest payments alone are about 4 per cent of GDP and constitute almost 20 per cent of the total expenditure of the Central Government. Without decisive action now, the situation will move beyond the possibility of corrective action.

The balance of payments situation is most difficult ... These persistent deficits, which were inevitably financed by borrowings from abroad, have led to a continuous increase in external debt which, including Non-resident Indian (NRI) deposits, is estimated at 23 per cent of GDP at the end of 1990–91. Consequently, the debt service burden is estimated at about 21 per cent of current account receipts in 1990–91 …

… inflation has reached a double digit level … The major worrisome feature of the inflation in 1990–91 was that it was concentrated in essential commodities … Inflation hurts everybody, more so the poorer segments of our population whose incomes are not indexed.

… Neither the Government nor the economy can live beyond its means year after year … For improving the management of the economy, the starting point … should be a credible fiscal adjustment and macro-economic stabilization during the current financial year, to be followed by continued fiscal consolidation thereafter … The people must be prepared to make necessary sacrifices to preserve our economic independence and restore the health of our economy.

… it should be our objective to progressively reduce the fiscal deficit of the Central Government to move towards a significant reduction of the revenue deficit and to reduce the current account deficit in the balance of payments … During the period of transition, it shall be our endeavour to minimize the burden of adjustment on the poor …

… The thrust of the reform process would be to increase the efficiency and international competitiveness of industrial production …

Thanks to the efforts of Pandit Jawaharlal Nehru, Indira Gandhi and Rajiv Gandhi, we have developed a well-diversified industrial structure … However, barriers to entry and limits on growth in the size of firms, have often led to a proliferation of licensing and an increase in the degree of monopoly. This has put shackles on segments of Indian industry and made them serve the interests of producers but not pay adequate attention to the interests of consumers … In the pursuit of this objective, we have announced important changes in industrial policy …

The policies for industrial development are intimately related to policies for trade … The time has come to expose Indian industry to competition from abroad in a phased manner …

… First direct foreign investment in specified high priority industries, with a raised limit for foreign equity at 51 per cent, would be given prompt approval, if equity inflows are sufficient to finance the import of capital goods at the stage of investment and if dividends are balanced by export earnings over a period of time. Second, foreign equity up to 51 per cent would be allowed for trading companies primarily engaged in export activities. Third, a special board would be constituted to negotiate with a number of large international firms and approve direct foreign investment in selected areas …

…The public sector has made an important contribution to the diversification of our industrial economy. But there have been a number of shortcomings. In particular, the public sector has not been able to generate internal surpluses on a large enough scale … In order to raise resources, encourage wider public participation and promote greater accountability, up to 20 per cent of government equity in selected public sector undertakings would be offered to mutual funds and investment institutions in the public sector, as also to workers in these firms. Public enterprises which are chronically sick and which cannot be turned around, will be referred to the Board for Industrial and Financial Reconstruction (BIFR), or to a similar high-powered body to be set up for the formulation of revival or rehabilitation schemes; a social security mechanism will be created to fully protect the interests of the workers likely to be affected by the rehabilitation packages of the BIFR …

Our banking system and financial institutions are at the very core of the financial infrastructure in the economy … The objective of reform in the financial sector would be to preserve its basic role as an essential adjunct to economic growth and competitive efficiency, while improving the health of its institutions. In this task, it is essential to ensure capital adequacy, introduce prudential norms and improve profitability of our commercial banks and financial institutions …

Interest rates are a crucial dimension of the financial sector …The Reserve Bank of India has already taken an important step in this direction, by stipulating a floor rate of interest and providing freedom to commercial banks to charge interest rates above the floor level based on their perceptions of risk. The Government proposes to extend a similar freedom to term-lending financial institutions, where the minimum interest rate would be 15 per cent, and these Institutions would be free to charge an interest rate in accordance with their perception of the creditworthiness of borrowers. With the exception of tax-free bonds for the public sector, it is also proposed to remove all restrictions on interest rates for debentures, both convertible and non-convertible, floated in the capital market … Our ultimate objective is to achieve a significant reduction both in the nominal and the real interest rates. This would be possible if the rate of inflation is reduced significantly over the next three years.

While presenting the Budget for 1987–88, our former Prime Minister, the late Shri Rajiv Gandhi had assured this House that … the Government would set up a separate Board for the regulation and orderly functioning of the Stock Exchanges and the securities industry. Although the Board was set up, legislation to give the Board adequate powers was unfortunately not enacted. This shall now be done forthwith and full statutory powers will be given to the Securities and Exchange Board of India for administering the relevant provisions of the Securities Contracts (Regulation) Act and the Companies Act …

In regard to Mutual Funds, some progress towards evolving a competitive structure has been made in the last few years with encouraging results ... The Government has now decided to further promote the development of mutual funds by throwing the field open to the private sector and joint sector mutual funds ...

A comprehensive review of policies and procedures bearing on Non-Resident Indian investments shall be carried out and further relaxations made in order to remove all procedural difficulties and impediments to the setting up of industrial and other ventures by Non-Resident Indians ...

I believe that the time has come to evolve a more transparent institutional mechanism for fixing tariffs and domestic prices in sectors where there might still be need for protecting Indian industry against foreign competition and for the determination of administered prices, particularly in the area of public utilities. For this purpose, we propose to restructure the Bureau of Industrial Costs and Prices and to transform it into a Tariff Commission.

As we enter the last decade of the twentieth century, India stands at the cross-roads ... The most important thing that comes out clearly is that we cannot realize our goal of establishing a just society, if we abandon the planning process ... I believe that without an intelligent and systematic coordinated resource use in some major sectors of our economy, development will be lopsided. It will violate deeply cherished values of equity and it will keep India well below its social, intellectual and moral potential. But our planning processes must be sensitive to the needs of a dynamic economy. Over-centralization and excessive bureaucratization of economic processes have proved to be counterproductive. We need to expand the scope and the area for the operation of market forces ... But markets can only serve those who are part of the market system. A vast number of people in our country live on the edges of a subsistence economy. We need credible programmes of direct government intervention focussing on the needs of these people. We have the responsibility to provide them with quality social services such as education, health, safe drinking water and roads. In the same way the development of capital and technology intensive sectors, characterized by long gestation periods, such as transport and communications and energy will need to be planned with much greater care than ever before. The control of land and water degradation, which threatens the livelihood of millions of poor people in this country, will also require effective Government leadership and action.

The challenge that we are facing is without precedent. In its initial stages, the Industrial Revolution in the Western world concentrated on the creation of wealth, unmindful of the social misery and inequity which characterized this process. The democratization of the polity came much later. The socialist experiment in charting a new path for accelerated industrial transformation of an under-developed economy and polity did achieve considerable success in developing technological and military capabilities, accumulation of capital for rapid industrial growth and human resources development, in countries such as the USSR. But recent developments have shown that this approach too suffered from major weaknesses, particularly in its allocative efficiency, in the management of technical change, control of environmental degradation and in harnessing the vast latent energy and talents of individuals. In India, we launched an experiment under the leadership of Pandit Jawaharlal Nehru, an experiment which sought to unite the strengths and merits of different approaches to accelerated development of our backward economy. We have achieved considerable success in the field of development, modernization and greater social equity. However, we are yet far from realizing our full potential in all these areas. We have to accomplish the unfinished task, while remaining steadfast in our allegiance to the values of a democratic system.

At the same time, we must restore to the creation of wealth its proper place in the development process. For, without it, we cannot remove the stigma of abject poverty, ignorance and disease. But we cannot accept social misery and inequity as unavoidable in the process of creation of wealth …

For the creation of wealth, we must encourage accumulation of capital. This will inevitably mean a regime of austerity … Those who create it and own it, have to hold it as a trust and use it in the interest of society, and particularly of those who are under-privileged and without means. Years ago, Gandhiji expounded the philosophy of trusteeship …. The trusteeship that he prescribed for the owners of wealth captured the idea of social responsibility.

In highlighting the significance of reform, my purpose is not to give a fillip to mindless and heartless consumerism we have borrowed from the affluent societies of the West … Our approach to development has to combine efficiency with austerity … To my mind, austerity is a way of holding our society together in pursuit of the noble goal of banishing poverty, hunger and disease from this ancient land of ours.

Let me now turn to fiscal adjustment during the current financial year …

… The Interim Budget presented to Parliament in March 1991 estimated the fiscal deficit at Rs. 38,475 crores … Indeed, past trends in revenue and expenditure suggest that without any corrective action on our part, the fiscal deficit during 1991–92 could well reach a level of more than Rs. 52,000 crores …

… Let me now present the scenario for 1991–92.

The increasing levels of non-plan expenditure, financed through borrowing, have led to an exponential increase in interest payments by the Government … If the present trends continue without any correction, then interest payments could well account for more than 50 per cent of the next revenue receipts of the Central Government by 1994–95 …

… Any attempt at fiscal correction during the current financial year can be meaningful only if non-plan expenditure is reduced by at least 10 per cent from the level it would otherwise reach.

The single largest component of non-plan expenditure is interest payments … The exponential increase in interest payments can be brought under some measure of control, by 1994–95, only through a strict discipline on Government borrowing for a period of three years.

The second largest component of non-plan expenditure is the allocation for the defence sector … We must, therefore, seek to limit expenditure without diluting the efficiency and effectiveness of our defence services …

Honourable members are aware that export subsidies have been abolished with effect from 3 July 1991. The export sector is being adequately compensated through the adjustment in the exchange rate and the expansion of the Replenishment Licensing System …

… The economic rationale for an increase in the price of fertilizers is so obvious that it does not need to be stated … Farmers will be compensated for the proposed increase in the price of fertilizers through suitable increases in procurement prices.

We would continue to ensure that 50 per cent of the plan resources are invested in the agricultural and rural sector. The provision for the continuing schemes for assistance to small and marginal farmers for dug wells and shallow tubewells would be doubled. The ceilings on assistance in difficult areas, where the water-table is very low, would be removed.

Similarly, the provision for assistance for fresh water and brackish water aquaculture and for oilseeds and pulses production would be substantially stepped up. New schemes are being drawn up to popularize small tractors and matching implements, drip and sprinkler irrigation in areas where water is scarce, and quality seeds in low yield areas … As far as possible our emphasis will be on provision of quality services to our farmers and not on hand outs and subsidies.

The sugar subsidy which is costing the Exchequer about Rs. 350 crores per annum is indeed an aberration … Government has decided that this subsidy should be abolished forthwith … The provision for food subsidies in the current year is being stepped up to Rs. 2,600 crores, as compared with only Rs. 1,800 crores provided in the interim budget and Rs. 2,450 crores provided in the revised estimates for 1990–91.

As a result of the exchange rate adjustment, at the beginning of July 1991, there would be an increase in the rupee value of the import bill for crude oil and petroleum products. It is, therefore, necessary to raise the prices of petroleum products for domestic consumers … The price of kerosene, for non-industrial use, would be reduced by 10 per cent which means a 50 per cent rollback in relation to the increase in the price that came into effect on 15 October 1990. Even in a most difficult financial situation, this is being done to protect the poor for whom kerosene is an essential source of light and fuel …

For non-plan expenditure, excluding interest payments, defence, and major subsidies, the total provision in the budget estimates for 1991–92 is Rs. 28,073 crores, reflecting a reduction of Rs. 1,538 crores compared with the provision in the revised estimates for 1990–91 … With this approach, the proposed reduction in other non-plan expenditure, which I am promising to the House, would be brought about in a more meaningful manner without leading to a reduction in the provision for plan programmes.

There is one large component of non-plan expenditure that is a burden on the Exchequer. I refer to the Government's obligation under the Rural Debt Relief Scheme … In addition to the sum of Rs. 1,500 crores provided in the revised estimates for last year, we have to provide Rs. 1,500 crores in the current year …

As a result of the major adjustments in the sphere of expenditure, which I have outlined in my speech, the budget estimate for total non-plan expenditure in 1991–92 stands at Rs. 79,697 crores … We have, thus, more than fulfilled our commitment to reduce non-plan expenditure by 10 per cent, which was stated in our Party's election manifesto.

The election manifesto of the Congress Party identifies areas for special emphasis in our strategy of development. These include a substantial augmentation of employment programmes, the construction of dwelling units for the weaker sections of our society, an expansion of the programme for irrigation wells and so on …

… I am, however, happy to inform the House that with the substantial cuts proposed in non-plan expenditure, it is now possible to protect the flow of Central Plan assistance to States and Union Territories at the level of Rs. 14,710 crores, as reflected in the interim budget for 1991–92 …

… In preparing this Budget, I have sought to ensure that the burden of fiscal adjustment does not fall on State Governments … In particular, I would urge them to ensure prompt payment of dues owed by the State Electricity Boards to the National Thermal Power Corporation, Coal India and the Indian Railways. We cannot allow State level enterprises to become an instrument of unplanned and unauthorized transfer of resources from the Centre to the States … I want them to be an active partner in the accomplishment of the difficult task of restoring the fiscal health of the country.

The process of macro-economic adjustment, which is being initiated with this budget, would take at least three years to complete. This adjustment must have a human face. Therefore, during the period of transition we shall do everything that is possible to minimize the burden of adjustment on the poor …

The plan outlay for the Ministry of Rural Development is being stepped up from Rs. 3,115 crores last year to Rs. 3,508 crores this year. Within this, the outlay for employment programmes alone is Rs. 2,100 crores … The Eighth Plan now under formulation will spell out a comprehensive strategy and programmes to achieve the long-term employment objectives, and targets such as those relating to the construction of irrigation wells, urban night shelters and Sulabh Shauchalayas, dwelling units for poor backward classes, Scheduled Castes and Scheduled Tribes in the villages, mentioned in our Party's election manifesto.

The provision for the rural water supply scheme is being stepped up to Rs. 758 crores, so as to make it possible to set aside Rs. 250 crores for ensuring complete coverage of 'no-source problem villages' by the end of 1992–93 … The programme, which is now being named after Shri Rajiv Gandhi, will be accelerated …

It is a matter of deep concern that we have still not been able to put an end to the dehumanizing practice of manual removal of night-soil … It has now been decided not only to accelerate the programme for the conversion of dry-latrines but also to step up the allocation for the rehabilitation and retraining of scavengers … The outlay for the Department of Women and Child Development, dealing with perhaps the two most disadvantaged segments of our population among the poor, is being enhanced from Rs. 330 crores last year to Rs. 400 crores this year. For Health and Family Welfare, I am providing a plan outlay of Rs. 1,051 crores in 1991–92 as compared with Rs. 950 crores in 1990–91.

The allocation of resources for investment in social sectors is of utmost importance for the development of human resources … Particular attention has to be paid to the provision of quality education to children belonging to the Scheduled Castes, the Scheduled Tribes and other economically and socially backward classes … I would have liked to do more but we must learn to live with the constraints on the exchequer.

We have the third largest number of scientists and technologists in the world. Yet, technology development in our country has not been commensurate … This gap would have to be bridged through a suitable reorientation of the Science and Technology Policy …

Government has also decided on five new initiatives. The first of these is the establishment of a Corporation for the welfare of the backward classes …

Government will establish a National Renewal Fund, with a substantial corpus … to ensure that the cost of technical change and modernization of the productive apparatus does not devolve on the workers …

The third programme relates to the care of children of families affected by communal riots …

The fourth programme is to promote national integration through a scheme for enabling the youth of each part of the country to go in large numbers and work for short periods in other parts of the country, giving them an opportunity to mingle with people of different regions and languages …

The fifth programme relates to promotion of South–South cooperation … It is our hope to arrange for participation of at least 500 volunteers in different nation-building tasks in selected developing countries in the coming year …

The House will also be pleased to learn that in acceptance of a recommendation of the South Commission presided over by Dr. Julius K. Nyerere, the former President of Tanzania, we propose to set up a National Committee under the chairmanship of the Prime Minister for mobilizing public opinion in support of South–South cooperation and for advising our Government for devising concrete action programmes in this regard …

… In the sphere of revenue receipts, at the existing rates of taxation, gross tax revenues are estimated at Rs. 66,218 crores during the current financial year, compared to Rs. 58,916 crores in the revised estimates of last year. The payment to States of their share of taxes is placed at Rs. 15,643 crores in 1991–92 as against Rs. 14,535 crores in the revised estimates for 1990–91. Thus, the net revenue receipts of the Centre, including non-tax revenue, are estimated to increase from Rs. 57,381 crores in 1990–91 to Rs. 65,524 crores in 1991–92.

In the sphere of capital receipts, market borrowings are placed at Rs. 7,500 crores this year, which is lower than Rs. 8,000 crores last year; this is part of a conscious effort to reduce the borrowing of the Central Government which would, in keeping with the past trends, have gone up by about 10 per cent …

The net receipts on account of external assistance, excluding grants, are placed at Rs. 3,510 crores compared to Rs. 3,984 crores in the revised estimates of 1990-91 …

Taking into account other changes in Receipts and Expenditure, total receipts at the existing rates of taxation are estimated at Rs. 1,03,698 crores, while total expenditure is estimated at Rs. 1,13,422 crores. Therefore, without additional resource mobilization, the budget deficit is estimated at Rs. 9,724 crores, the revenue deficit at Rs. 15,859 crores, and the fiscal deficit at Rs. 39,732 crores …

… I now seek the indulgence of the House to present the reliefs, the incentives and the levies in the sphere of direct taxes.

The revenue from direct taxes, both as a proportion of GDP and as a percentage of total tax revenues, has registered a steady decline over time. This trend has to be reversed, so as to restore equity in and balance to our fiscal system … I have made a conscious effort to move one step forward in this direction.

Nobody can deny the existence of large-scale tax evasion, both in terms of income and in terms of wealth … Before coming down heavily on tax evaders, I would like to give them a last opportunity to come clean. The black money so mobilized will be utilized for the achievement of social objectives such as slum clearance and low-cost housing for the rural poor …

… The Income Tax Act contains a provision under which tax payers can avail of the facility of waiver of penalty and interest on the amount disclosed once in a life-time …

The Settlement Commission was set up to provide an opportunity to assessees to declare their undisclosed income and wealth … The Settlement Commission will, however, continue to call for and take into account the Commissioner's report, provided it is furnished within a period of six months.

Our election manifesto has promised that we will promote reinvestment of profits, by suitable tax exemptions, in areas where there is crying need for massive investment such as low- and middle-income group housing, highways, roads and bridges, non-conventional energy, school buildings and supply of drinking water. I, therefore, propose to make a provision in the Income Tax Act to provide deduction, in computing taxable profits of a tax-payer carrying on a business or profession, of the entire amount paid for financing projects or schemes promoting social and economic welfare …

As a token of my commitment to education and research and in recognition of the significant role they have to play in our development process, I propose to extend certain tax concessions that will help in the funding of social science research and provide some incentive to authors and publishers.

At present, only tax-payers carrying on a business or profession get deduction for sums paid to any approved university, college or other institutions for research in social science related to the class of business carried on by them. I consider that there is a case for providing more tax incentives for social science research …

The role of books, particularly in the context of our National Literacy Mission as well as the National Education Policy cannot be overemphasized …

Off-shore country funds are emerging as important channels for attracting foreign institutional investment particularly from non-resident Indians. India made a beginning in this direction in 1989 …

In the light of our deep emotional involvement with the struggle of the Black majority in South Africa and as a further affirmation of our commitment to South–South cooperation, I propose that donations to the AFRICA FUND be entitled to 100 per cent deduction under section 80G of the Income Tax Act.

The Government is committed to the welfare of our unfortunate handicapped citizens. In an effort to mitigate in some small measure their hardship, I propose to increase the deduction available under Section 80U of the Income Tax Act in respect of totally blind or physically handicapped persons, from fifteen thousand rupees to twenty thousand rupees. The benefit of this tax concession is also proposed to be extended to partially blind persons.

Promotion of housing activity ranks high in Government's socio-economic priorities …

Our software industry has made considerable progress in recent years … It is time we make all-out efforts to capture the overseas software market. With this objective, I propose to extend the tax concession under section 80HHC of the Income Tax Act to export of software. With this concession, the exports of this industry should register rapid growth.

I also propose to extend the concession under section 80HHC to the export of processed minerals.

I consider that scientific, technical and professional skills, knowledge and experience possessed by our professionals in various fields like architecture, accounting, etc., have an increasing capacity to earn foreign exchange for the country ...

In order to encourage development of tourist infrastructure in regions where such facilities are almost non-existent today, I propose to exempt from Expenditure Tax for a period of ten years expenditure incurred in new approved hotels set up in hilly and other remote areas ...

As a token of my appreciation of the role of a healthy capital market in the development of our economy, I propose to raise the basic deduction of Rs. 10,000 now available under section 48 of the Income Tax Act in respect of long-term capital gains to Rs. 15,000.

... I now turn to my proposals for ensuring better tax compliance and mobilizing revenues through the imposition of additional taxes.

To enable the Government to identify income earners, most of whom would not otherwise declare their income or would not declare their full income, I propose to extend the scheme of tax deduction at source to cover new areas of payments in the nature of commissions, interest paid by banks on time deposits and withdrawals from the National Savings Scheme ...

The present provision for off-setting short-term capital losses against income leads to tax avoidance. I, therefore, propose that any loss on transfer of a capital asset will be set off only against gain from transfer of another capital asset ...

Over the years, those with an instinct for gambling have increasingly patronized the races. I propose to withdraw the income-tax exemption of Rs. 5,000 in respect of earnings from races, including horse races.

... We are firmly committed to a tax system which is simple, credible, yet progressive, in which people realize that honesty is the best policy ...

... For the purposes of levy of wealth-tax, the rules of valuation of assets aim at capturing their market value, or near about, as on the valuation date ... When an individual holds any asset in his name its valuation is at the market value. However, if a group of persons holds its assets through an investment company the taxable value of these assets gets reduced considerably because it is based on the book value and not on the market value. I, therefore, propose to remove this anomaly ...

I feel disappointed that the phenomenal growth in the output, value added and profits of the corporate sector, in recent years, has not been appropriately reflected in corporate tax collections ... I am, therefore, raising the corporate tax rate for widely held companies ...

The traditional distinction in corporate tax rates between trading companies and industrial companies has outlived its utility. I, therefore, propose to remove this distinction …

… In our economy, labour is abundant and capital is scarce … Yet, over the years, the Indian economy has witnessed a disturbing shift towards greater capital intensity in production … While there can be no compromise with the imperatives of technological upgradation and continuous modernization, the tendency towards excessive capital intensity in our industry must be checked.

The rates for depreciation prescribed in 1987, in relation to plant and machinery, are far too generous and provide much more than is needed to compensate for wear and tear … I think an eight-year period would be more reasonable taking into account the pace of technological change in India, the true economic life of the business assets, and the need to discourage tax induced replacement of assets … However, to encourage use of energy saving devices and renewable energy devices, I propose to continue to provide 100 per cent depreciation on such items of plant and machinery as also some others …

Tax support to special institutions may be necessary in their nascent stage … The Industrial Development Bank of India … has been enjoying complete tax exemption in respect of its income since its inception, unlike other public financial institutions. I propose to withdraw this tax exemption, which is no longer necessary.

In 1987, the Government had introduced a tax on ostentatious expenditure. It is in the form of a tax of 20 per cent of expenditure incurred in hotels where the room rent exceeds Rs. 400 per day. I propose to extend the coverage of this tax to the expenditure incurred in restaurants providing superior facilities like air-conditioning. This tax will be levied at the rate of 15 per cent of such expenditure.

In view of the binding fiscal constraints and the need to mobilize resources, I propose to revive the interest-tax which was first introduced in 1974 and withdrawn in 1978, re-introduced in a modified form in 1980 and finally withdrawn in 1985. I am enlarging, slightly, the coverage of this tax … These institutions would reimburse themselves by making necessary adjustments in the interest rates charged from borrowers. The proposed tax is expected to raise the cost of borrowing and yield revenue to the Government. It should, therefore, have both monetary and fiscal impact.

The proposed tax will be levied at the rate of 3 per cent of the gross amount of interest earned by banks, financial institutions and financial companies on loans and advances made in India …

… My proposals on direct taxes are estimated to yield a net revenue gain of Rs. 2,139 crores. Of this amount, Rs. 97 crores will accrue to the States.

... In order to attract larger inflows of foreign exchange, I propose to introduce two schemes.

Under the first scheme, I propose that remittances in foreign exchange can be made to any person in India. Even if the remittance is received as a gift by the donee in India, it would not be subjected to gift tax ...

Under the second scheme, the State Bank of India would issue India Development Bonds to be denominated in US dollars. These bonds will be available for purchase by non-resident Indians and their overseas corporate bodies. There will be no ceiling for investment in these bonds which will have a maturity period of five years. The bonds will be fully transferable among non-resident Indians. Interest from the bonds will be exempt from income tax. The bond itself would also be exempt from wealth tax until maturity ...

In formulating my proposals on indirect taxes, I have kept in mind the wider context ...

It is my intention to rationalize and simplify the procedures, rules and regulations pertaining to indirect taxes, so that the delays in the system are eliminated, and the interface between the tax collector and the tax-payer is reduced to the minimum ...

Recent years have witnessed an excessive reliance on indirect taxes for additional resource mobilization. This escalates costs, fuels inflation and is regressive in its impact. Therefore, I have not relied on indirect taxes as the major source of resource mobilization ...

In the sphere of customs duties, over time, the objective of protection for infant industries and the need to raise revenues have led to a situation where import duties prescribed for certain items are inordinately high and, in several cases, more than 300 per cent. As a measure of reform, I propose to reduce the ad valorem rate of basic plus auxiliary duties of customs to a maximum of 150 per cent where it is more than that at present, thereby eliminating the tariff peaks above 150 per cent. The only exceptions that would remain hereafter are imported alcoholic beverages and passenger baggage ...

In view of the deterioration in the fiscal situation last year auxiliary duty of customs was increased across-the-board, with effect from 15 December 1990, so as to mobilize additional resources. The increase was not quite rational and was asymmetric in its incidence ... In order to remove the anomalies which had been created and rationalize rates of duties, I propose to give a duty relief of 10 percentage points to almost every item which suffered an increase of 20 percentage points ...

The prevailing rates of import duty on capital goods for general projects and machinery are, in general, high ... I propose to reduce the level of duties from 85 per cent to 80 per cent. In tandem, the rate of duty on their components is also being reduced by 5 percentage points from the existing levels of 65 or 70 per cent ...

A technology upgradation scheme was launched in 1987 by the late Shri

Rajiv Gandhi. Under this scheme, fiscal relief was provided on import of capital equipment for the manufacture of power generation equipment, paper machinery, textile machinery and many others to promote domestic production of such machinery ... In order to give a further thrust to the scheme, I propose to expand the list of machinery items which will now attract a concessional duty of 50 per cent ...

... I would now like to outline some fiscal measures which will give a further boost to the export effort.

At present 100 per cent export-oriented undertakings or units in a free trade zone are allowed to divert a certain proportion of their production to the domestic market ... I propose to reduce the excise duty on the goods, permitted to be sold in the domestic market under the scheme, to a level which would be equivalent to half the import duty leviable on such goods subject, inter alia, to the condition that the duty would not be less than the excise duty levied on similar items produced in the domestic tariff area.

To promote the growth of the marine products industry, fiscal relief has been given by way of customs duty concession on specified machinery items required by this industry. I propose to extend the duty concession to a few more items of such machinery ...

In order to encourage the growth of the finished leather industry and also as a measure of export promotion, I propose to reduce the basic and auxiliary duties of customs on polyurethane film and foil, as well as polyols from 150 per cent to 40 per cent. The duty on isocyanates is being reduced from 120 per cent to 40 per cent. The import duty on two important leather preservatives, namely, TCMTB and PCMC, is being reduced from over 150 per cent to 50 per cent. These preservatives will replace certain other chemicals which are suspected to have carcinogenic effects ...

Synthetic cubic zirconium, which is the closest imitation of natural diamonds, has the potential to provide job opportunities for a large number of artisans ... In order to encourage indigenous manufacture of cubic zirconium, I propose to reduce the import duty on the raw materials, viz., zirconium oxide and yttrium oxide to the level of 40 per cent from the present level of over 150 per cent.

Our Government attaches the highest priority to agriculture. One of the promises made in our election manifesto is to provide a massive thrust to food processing and other agro-based industries, in an endeavour to increase the income of farmers, create employment opportunities, diversify the rural economy and foster rural industrialization.

As an important step in this direction, I propose to exempt agro-based products such as sauces, ketchup, butter, cheese, skimmed milk powder, vegetable oils, jams, jellies and juices, canned fruits and dried vegetables, certain soya products, starches and preparations of meat and fish from excise duties altogether ...

As a relief to the agro-based jute industry, which has been beset with chronic problems, I propose to reduce the excise duty on products which contain a minimum of 35 per cent of jute fibre from Rs. 660 to Rs. 330 per metric ton.

At present a number of specified bulk pesticides and pesticide intermediates enjoy concessional import and excise duties. I propose to extend the duty concession to a few more bulk pesticides and pesticide intermediates …

There is a money credit scheme in vogue to encourage the use of minor oils for the manufacture of soaps … This would also help in generating more employment for our tribal women. These proposals involve a revenue sacrifice of about Rs. 10 crores in a full year.

The MODVAT scheme was introduced in 1986 to minimize the cascading effect of indirect taxes … I expect that the benefit would be passed on to the consumers in the form of reduced prices.

I propose to rationalize the existing excise duty rates on polyester blended yarns …

In our effort to make essential drugs available to the people at affordable prices, I propose to fully exempt five specified anti-epileptic formulations from excise duty. At present, some drug intermediates and bulk drugs carry a concessional rate of import duty. I wish to extend the concession to a few more drug intermediates and bulk drugs, and grant concessions in excise duties to a few more drug intermediates.

In keeping with our commitment to give special priority to cottage khadi and village industries, I propose to give some excise duty concessions to this sector …

I would now like to outline some of the steps that I propose for the protection of our environment and for ecological security. In view of our dwindling forest cover, we must conserve our scarce resources. Therefore, as I have stated earlier, the import duty on waste paper and wood in the rough is proposed to be rolled back to the rates that were prevailing before 15 December 1990. I also propose to fully exempt from excise duty aluminium doors, windows and their frames so as to encourage the use of aluminium in the place of wood in construction activities …

Few would disagree that I am one of the most harassed Finance Ministers in recent times. To perform the onerous task before me, I need support from the Press. As a gesture of goodwill, I propose to exempt standard newsprint from import duty which is at present Rs. 450 per metric ton. I have already proposed to bring down the rates of import duty on certain specified machinery and equipment required by the printing and newspaper industry to the levels that were obtaining before 15 December 1990. The monetary limit of duty-free import of photographic goods by accredited cameramen of the press is being raised from the present level of Rs. 30,000 to 60,000. These proposals involve a revenue loss of over Rs. 9 crores in a full year. Let me add, Mr. Speaker, Sir, that I may reconsider these proposals after I see the editorials tomorrow morning.

Ever since my appointment as Finance Minister, I have had to spend long hours in office. This has quite naturally made my wife very unhappy … I propose that the total exemption from payment of excise duty currently available to utensils made of aluminium, copper and stainless steel be extended to certain other household items particularly tiffin boxes.

The same consideration has induced me to propose a reduction in the excise duty on specified tableware produced by semi-automatic process from the present level of 20 per cent to 15 per cent … Some people may not applaud my action. But I am sure most housewives harassed by the ever-rising price level will appreciate my action.

In keeping with the commitment in our election manifesto, I shall make every effort to ensure that indirect taxes do not unduly add to the prices of essential commodities …

I recognize that the tax reliefs … given, by themselves, constitute only a small step towards the realization of the objective mentioned in our manifesto in regard to prices of essential commodities …

In order to promote tourism which is an important means of earning foreign exchange, I propose to reduce the import duty on adventure sports equipment from rates ranging from about 100 to 300 per cent to 40 per cent.

In keeping with the recent exchange rate adjustments of the rupee, I propose to raise the baggage allowances including duty-free limits for bonafide gifts suitably; for instance, the general duty-free allowance for personal baggage is being raised from Rs. 2,000 to Rs. 2,400.

Let me now turn to the major proposals for additional revenue mobilization.

At present special excise duty is being levied at the rate of 5 per cent of the basic excise duty. I propose to raise it to 10 per cent …

One of the promises made in our election manifesto is to evolve policies and measures to curb conspicuous consumption. In pursuance of this, I propose to increase the excise duty rates on refrigerators, air-conditioners including compressors, motor cars, audio and video cassette tapes, video cassettes, picture tubes, colour television sets, VCRs and VCPs …

… Every Finance Minister has to do his bit to curb smoking which is injurious to health … In respect of non-filter cigarettes, I propose to raise the duties by Rs. 10 to Rs. 25 per thousand cigarettes depending upon the length. In respect of filter cigarettes, the increase will be between Rs. 35 and Rs. 125 per thousand cigarettes …

The excise duty on hand-made branded bidis is Rs. 3.75 per thousand … I accordingly propose to increase the duty on hand-made branded bidis, other than paper rolled bidis to Rs. 4.50 per thousand. Paper rolled bidis will attract a duty of Rs. 10 per thousand …

Pan masala not containing tobacco attracts a specific rate of excise duty. I propose to raise the excise duty on the same by Rs. 5 and Rs. 10 per kg depending on its value …

The excise duty on sugar, which is levied on a specific basis, has remained unchanged since 1983 with the result that the ad-valorem incidence has come down as the price of sugar has increased considerably over this period … In order to correct the situation, I propose to increase the excise duty on free sale sugar from the present level of Rs. 50 to Rs. 71 per quintal … I would like to make it clear that I am not proposing any increase in excise duty on levy sugar which is sold through the public distribution system.

I propose to exclude khandsari sugar from the list of items chargeable to additional excise duty …

Molasses which is a by-product of the sugar industry is presently subject to excise duty at the rate of Rs. 120 per metric ton … Accordingly, I propose to increase the excise duty on molasses to Rs. 150 per metric ton …

… I have also proposed certain amendments in the Finance Bill seeking to effect changes in the Customs Act, and excise and customs tariffs …

… Thus, as compared with the additional net revenue of Rs. 696.42 crores from Customs and Excise duties, the States would gain Rs. 750.04 crores, while the Centre would lose Rs. 53.62 crores in a full year …

… The proposals I have made in regard to direct taxes will yield Rs. 2,139 crores of which Rs. 97 crores will accrue to the States and Rs. 2,042 crores to the Centre. My proposals in regard to customs duties will involve a net revenue loss of Rs. 510 crores in the current year while those relating to Union excise duties are estimated to yield a net additional revenue of Rs. 988 crores in the remaining part of the current year of which Rs. 515 crores will be the share of States and Rs. 473 crores will be retained by the Centre. Taking both direct and indirect taxes into account, the net gain to the Centre in the current year is estimated at Rs. 2,005 crores and with this, the budgetary deficit of the Centre for the current year is estimated at Rs. 7,719 crores, the revenue deficit at Rs. 13,854 crores and the fiscal deficit at Rs. 37,727 crores.

Sir, I have now nearly come to the end of my labour. Before I conclude, let me end on a personal note. Years ago, in a letter which Jawaharlal Nehru wrote to the young Indira Gandhi, he advised her that in dealing with the affairs of the State one should be full of sentiment but never be sentimental. But the House will forgive me if on an occasion like this I cannot avoid being somewhat sentimental.

I was born in a poor family in a chronically drought prone village which is now part of Pakistan. University scholarships and grants made it possible for me to go to college in India as well as in England. This country has honoured me by appointing me to some of the most important public offices of our sovereign Republic. This is a debt which I can never be able to fully repay. The best I can do is to pledge myself to serve our country with utmost sincerity and dedication. This I promise to the House. A Finance Minister has to be hard-headed. This I shall endeavour to be. I shall be firm when it comes to defending the interests of this nation. But I promise that in dealing with the people of India I shall be soft hearted. I shall not in any way renege on our nation's firm and irrevocable commitment to the pursuit of equity and social justice. I shall never forget that ultimately all economic processes are meant to serve the interests of our people. It is only through a commitment to social justice and the pursuit of excellence that we can mobilize the collective will of our people for development, to give it a high moral purpose and to keep alive the spirit of national solidarity. The massive social and economic reforms needed to remove the scourge of poverty, ignorance and disease can succeed only if backed by a spirit of high idealism, self-sacrifice and dedication.

The grave economic crisis now facing our country requires determined action on the part of Government ...

Sir, I do not minimize the difficulties that lie ahead on the long and arduous journey on which we have embarked. But as Victor Hugo once said, 'no power on earth can stop an idea whose time has come'. I suggest to this august House that the emergence of India as a major economic power in the world happens to be one such idea. Let the whole world hear it loud and clear, India is now wide awake. We shall prevail. We shall overcome.

With these words, I commend the Budget to this august House.

P. CHIDAMBARAM

(Lok Sabha: Sivaganga)

Lok Sabha: 28 February 1997

Budget for 1997–98

Sir, I rise to present the Budget for the year 1997–98.

Introduction

The Government headed by Prime Minister Shri Deve Gowda completes 9 months today. When I stood before this House on 22 July 1996, this House received my proposals with a mixture of wonder, curiosity and scepticism. I was ... the Finance Minister of the first genuine coalition Government at the Centre ... the first Finance Minister who belonged to an avowed regional party, albeit with a national outlook.

Hon'ble members will indulge me … while I reflect on those eventful days in May 1996. One national party acknowledged that it had lost its claim to form the Government. Another tried, but failed. It is in that situation that regional parties, and certain parties with a larger national presence, came together to form the United Front Government. These parties – long regarded as children of a lesser God – have demonstrated that given the opportunity, they can form a Government not only at the State level but also at the Centre. Inspired by the idea of a truly cooperative federal polity Chief Ministers have assembled, more often than ever before, at the Inter-State Council, the National Development Council and at Special Conferences to formulate national policies … our efforts to take decisions by a national consensus, in the fiftieth year of India's independence, have deepened and broadened Indian democracy.

… The foundation of the Budget remains the Common Minimum Programme … Drawing on the CMP, my first Budget articulated seven broad objectives … growth, basic minimum services, employment, macro-economic stability, investment (particularly in infrastructure), human development and a viable balance of payments …

July 1996 Budget Promises

On the last occasion, I had made over forty specific promises on policies and programmes … I have fulfilled all these promises, save one … we have:

Provided an additional sum of Rs. 2,466 crores to the States for seven Basic Minimum Services;

- Funded the Rural Infrastructure Development Fund (RIDF)-II with Rs. 2,500 crores;
- Expanded the list of industries eligible for automatic approval for foreign equity investment;
- Set up the Disinvestment Commission and the Tariff Commission;
- Introduced the Jeevan Suraksha and the Jan Arogya insurance schemes; and
- Launched the Accelerated Irrigation Benefit Programme.

The one commitment that I have been unable to keep is to set up an Expenditure Management and Reform Commission …

Current Economic Situation

The Economic Survey 1996–97 was laid in Parliament a few days ago …

The positive features of our economic performance in 1996–97 include:

- Continued high economic growth at 6.8 per cent;

- A strong recovery of growth in agriculture and allied sectors to 3.7 per cent ...;
- Rebound in food grains production to 191 million tons;
- Manufacturing sector growth at 10.6 per cent; and
- A sizeable build up in our foreign currency reserves ... to US$19.5 billion ...

... Two areas of great concern are the sharp drop in domestic crude oil production and the sluggish performance of the power sector. Other matters of concern include a deceleration in the growth of exports, a rise in the rate of inflation and a volatile capital market ...

Macro-economic management involves, inevitably, striking a balance between various objectives and considerations ... Government has taken a number of steps to maintain price stability ... if necessary, Government will not hesitate to import wheat and other essential articles to counter the pressure on prices ...

... For the year 1997–98, Government and the RBI will act in concert towards a further reduction in the fiscal deficit, containment of the growth of money supply within 16 per cent and adoption of a liberal import policy for essential commodities. Our goal is to break inflationary expectations and reduce the rate of inflation from the present level.

Poverty Alleviation Programmes

Our fight against poverty ... revolve around the concerns of the poor. For example:

- The flagship programme of the Prime Minister is the Basic Minimum Services plan ...
- The provision for the Accelerated Irrigation Benefit Programme is being enhanced ...
- The Ganga Kalyan Yojana is intended to support farmers to take up schemes for groundwater and surface water utilization ...
- On 15 August 1997, the Prime Minister will inaugurate the Kasturba Gandhi Shiksha Yojana, a programme to establish special schools for girl children in the districts which have a particularly low female literacy rate ...

All current self-employment schemes, addressed to different target groups ... will be re-orientated to provide skill-based training, entrepreneurship development and subsidy-linked bank credit to 1 million youth to empower them to start viable small businesses ...

Rural Credit

Agriculture is the lifeblood of our economy. The Common Minimum Programme (CMP) calls for a doubling of the flow of credit to agriculture and agro-industries within five years ...

Hon'ble members will be glad to know that the Rural Infrastructure Development Fund (RIDF) has proved to be popular and successful … I urge the States to continue to make the best use of these funds.

The policy of recapitalizing the Regional Rural Banks (RRBs) will continue next year … I also intend to allow a greater role to sponsor banks in the ownership and management of RRBs.

National Bank for Agriculture and Rural Development (NABARD) is being strengthened …

Controls on Agriculture

The CMP said that all controls on agricultural products will be reviewed and, wherever found unnecessary, will be abolished … I urge State governments to follow this lead and abolish as many controls as possible.

Small Scale Industry

… In order to ensure that credit is available to all segments of the now-enlarged SSI sector, the RBI is issuing instructions that out of the funds normally available to the SSI sector, 40 per cent will be reserved for units with investment in plant and machinery up to Rs. 5 lakh, 20 per cent for units with investment between Rs. 5 lakh and Rs. 25 lakh and the remaining 40 per cent for other SSI units.

… With a view to reduce wastage in agricultural commodities, improve quality and hygiene and promote exports, the Advisory Committee on reservation and de-reservation has recommended that 14 items, now reserved for manufacture in the SSI sector, may be de-reserved. 822 items would still remain reserved for production in the SSI sector …

Housing

A constraint on adding to the housing stock of the country is the Urban Land (Ceiling and Regulation) Act, 1976. It is the intention of the Government to move a Bill for amending the Act in this session of Parliament.

Indira Awas Yojana was launched to build houses for the poor in rural areas … Loans, up to Rs. 2 lakh, will be given for building houses on freehold land in rural areas at normal rates of interest, subject to the borrower putting in one-third of the value of the house …

Employees' Provident Fund and Gratuity

The Central Board of Trustees of the Employees' Provident Fund (EPF) has made specific proposals to make the EPF schemes financially more attractive …

… In 1995, the Central Government enhanced the ceiling on the amount of gratuity payable from Rs. 1 lakh to Rs. 2.5 lakh for Central Government employees. I am now pleased to announce that the benefit will be extended to all employees covered under the Payment of Gratuity Act, 1972, which will be amended for this purpose.

Public Sector Autonomy

The CMP promised that 'the United Front Government will identify public sector companies that have comparative advantages and will support them in their drive to become global giants'. To begin with, nine well-performing public sector enterprises, the Navaratnas, have been identified ... The Industry Minister will shortly unveil a package of measures that will help them achieve this objective ...

Disinvestment

The Disinvestment Commission ... has observed, 'The essence of a long-term disinvestment strategy should be not only to enhance budgetary receipts, but also minimize budgetary support towards unprofitable units while ensuring their long-term viability and sustainable levels of employment in them' ...

Oil and Gas

The country's demand for petroleum products is growing at over 8 per cent per annum ... we must reduce our dependence on imported petroleum products. There is no real alternative to increasing the supply. Just 6 of the 26 basins that have potential for oil and gas in India have been explored, and that too only partially. The Minister of State for Petroleum and Natural Gas will be making a detailed statement on the New Exploration Licensing Policy (NELP) shortly ...

... In order to ensure that adequate domestic refining capacity is created, I propose to allow refineries to import capital goods during the Ninth Plan period at a concessional duty on par with the fertilizer sector. Domestic capital goods suppliers will also get deemed export status ...

Infrastructure

The Infrastructure Development Finance Company has been incorporated. Section 80IA of the Income Tax Act grants a five-year tax holiday for certain infrastructure projects. Last month, I announced that telecommunication will qualify as infrastructure. I now propose to add Oil Exploration and Industrial Parks to this category.

I am also glad to announce that the vexed question of assignability of telecom licences has been resolved and that tripartite agreements are proposed to be entered into among the Department of Telecommunications, the licencee and the lenders.

As Commerce Minister, I proposed in the EXIM Policy that supply of goods to oil, gas and power projects, if the supplies are made under the procedure of international competitive bidding, should be given the benefits of 'deemed exports'. As Finance Minister, I am glad to accept this wholesome proposal …

The National Highways Authority of India (NHAI) is now geared to implement the new policy on roads and highways …

Foreign Investment

Foreign Institutional Investors (FIIs) continue to repose great confidence in India … The limit of aggregate investment in a company by FIIs, NRIs and NRI-OCBs is now 24 per cent. I propose to allow companies to raise this limit to 30 per cent, subject to the condition that the Board of Directors of the company approves the limit and the general body of the company passes a special resolution in this behalf.

Venture capital funds are important vehicles for stimulating investments in new ventures. Under the present guidelines they can invest up to 5 per cent of their corpus in the equity of any single company … The limit is being increased to 20 per cent.

Capital Market

Over 20 million Indians have invested their savings in the capital market … I propose to accept five recommendations:

- The principle of buy-back of shares by companies subject to certain conditions will be introduced in the Companies Act;
- The provisions of Sections 370 and 372 of the Companies Act will be merged and an overall ceiling of 60 per cent will be kept to intercorporate investment and loans;
- The Companies Act will be amended to provide for nomination facilities for holders of securities;
- Companies raising funds from the capital market will be required to give an annual statement disclosing the end-use of such funds; and
- One time permission will be given to stockbrokers to corporatise their businesses without attracting tax on capital gains, which will be exempted …

FEMA and Money Laundering

… I propose to introduce, later this year, a Bill titled – The Foreign Exchange Management Act (FEMA) …

… A Bill dealing with money laundering is under preparation …

Capital Account Convertibility

A little while ago I made a reference to capital account convertibility. We are proud of our foreign exchange earners. They have been given the facility of the Export Earners Foreign Currency (EEFC) Account … I propose to expand the scope …:

- To open offices abroad and to meet the expenses thereof; and
- To make investments from the balance in the account in overseas joint ventures up to the limit of US$15 million, without reference to the RBI.

I also believe that the time has come for preparatory work towards capital account convertibility …

Science and Technology

… I propose to take the following initiatives:

- The scheme to match every additional commercial rupee earned by Council for Scientific and Industrial Research (CSIR) and Indian Council of Agricultural Research (ICAR) laboratories, as well as the IITs, will continue on a permanent basis.
- The Technology Development Board, established to accelerate the commercialization of indigenous technology, has identified 16 projects that are commercially viable in the fields of agriculture, health, chemicals and pharmaceuticals …

Tomorrow's technology is based on today's science … I hold the view that an MBA – even if he is from Harvard – is not a patch on a scientist. On the occasion of the 50th anniversary of our Independence, we will launch the 'Swarnajayanti' fellowships. Outstanding scientists below the age of 45 will be assisted to attain and sustain world class levels in science …

Closer linkages have to be developed between Indian industry and publicly-funded research laboratories. Hence, I propose to allow Government-promoted societies recognized by the Department of Scientific and Industrial Research and notified under the Income Tax Act to invest in the equity of private sector companies. These institutions will invest not money but their knowledge and know-how as their equity.

… If there is one industry in which India can emerge as a world leader, it is information technology. However, for this potential to be realized, we need a completely new policy for manufacturing and marketing IT products. The Electronic Hardware Technology Park (EHTP) Scheme, presently in force, gives limited flexibility. There is an imperative need to increase production volumes and attract foreign direct investment. Accordingly, it has been decided that EHTP/

Export Oriented Unit (EOU)/Export Processing Zone (EPZ) units in electronic hardware may be permitted to sell one-half of the value of their products, during any 12 months' period, in the domestic market and export the other half. The sale in the domestic market will be on payment of excise duty equivalent to full customs duty, including the additional duty of customs …

Insurance

The CMP accords high priority to infrastructure … The critical need is funds, and that too, long-term funds … Hon'ble members are fully aware that long-term funds are in the Pension and the Insurance sectors.

Our foremost companies in the insurance sector are Life Insurance Corporation (LIC) and General Insurance Corporation (GIC) …

… After the amendments, UTI's pension fund will compete with LIC's pension schemes.

Similarly, the penetration of health insurance cover in our country is distressingly low. Just about 20 lakh Indians have some kind of health cover. The Jan Arogya Scheme, launched barely six months ago, has already attracted 4 lakh policy-holders … Accordingly, I propose to move necessary amendments to enable GIC to float joint ventures and also to allow entry of selected Indian players in the health insurance sector.

… Comprehensive regulations will be made and enforced by the Insurance Regulatory Authority (IRA) for all the service providers in the insurance industry. They would also have to meet the prudential, investment and social norms laid down by the IRA.

Phasing Out of Ad Hocs

… The system of ad hoc treasury bills to finance the Budget deficit will be discontinued with effect from 1 April 1997. A scheme of Ways and Means Advances (WMA) by the RBI to the Central Government is being introduced to accommodate temporary mismatches in the Government's receipts and payments. This will not be a permanent source of financing the Government's deficit. Besides ways and means advances, RBI's support will be available for the Government's borrowing programme. Details of the scheme are being separately announced by the RBI.

What I am effecting today is a bold and radical change which will strengthen fiscal discipline and provide greater autonomy to the RBI in the conduct of monetary policy … Therefore, it is proposed to discontinue the practice of showing the 'Budget deficit'; instead, Gross Fiscal Deficit (GFD) would become the key indicator of deficit. The extent of RBI support to the Central Government's borrowing programme will be shown as 'Monetized deficit' in the Budget documents.

Indexed Bonds

Several countries have used a variety of indexed bonds to provide investors an effective hedge against inflation and to enhance the credibility of anti-inflationary policies followed by the Government ... I, therefore, propose to introduce a capital indexed bond where the repayment of the principal amounts will be indexed to inflation.

New Devolution Formula

I have already placed in the House a discussion paper on the recommendations of the Tenth Finance Commission (TFC) on the formula to be adopted for devolution of resources from the Centre to the States ... Based on these consultations, I propose to accept the recommendation of the TFC to form a single, divisible pool of taxes to be shared between the Centre and the States ... We affirm our belief that the polity of India requires a strong Centre and strong States and, if I may add, strong local bodies.

Revised Estimates for 1996–97

... Non-Plan expenditure in the current year is placed at Rs. 1,47,404 crores ... Despite these constraints, I made an additional provision of Rs. 1,700 crores for Defence during the year. On balance, therefore, I believe we have managed our receipts and expenditure within the Budget.

My greatest satisfaction is on the Plan side. We saved a considerable amount in the Plan expenditure of the Central Government. It was, therefore, possible for me to provide an additional Rs. 2,500 crores to the States as Additional Central Assistance for externally-aided projects. I also provided Rs. 663 crores to Jammu and Kashmir during the year ...

In October 1996, the Prime Minister announced a package of initiatives for the North-East, including adequate funding for ongoing projects, which will require over Rs. 6,000 crores. Government will allocate funds for these projects in the Ninth Plan ...

... Taking into account the Revised Estimates of revenues and expenditure, the Revenue Deficit has come down from the Budget Estimate of 2.5 per cent of GDP to 2.3 per cent of GDP. There is no change in the Budget estimate of the fiscal deficit which would remain at 5 per cent of GDP. I am profoundly sorry to disappoint my well-meaning critics.

What will we do without our critics? As Saint Thiruvalluvar, said:

'Idipparai Illatha Emara Mannan Keduppar Ilanum Kedum'

(Behold the King who reposeth not on those who can rebuke him/He will perish even when he hath no enemies.)

Budget Estimates for 1997–98

I now turn to the Budget Estimates for 1997–98. The total expenditure is estimated at Rs. 2,32,481 crores of which Rs. 62,852 crores has been provided as budget support for Central, States and UT Plans and the balance Rs. 1,69,629 crores is for non-Plan expenditure … the increase in budget support for the Plan will be Rs. 7,958 crores over RE 1996–97, which is the largest increase ever.

Budgetary support to the Central Plan is being concentrated on rural development, employment and poverty alleviation programmes and in the human resource development sectors … In 1997–98, Jawahar Rozgar Yojana is estimated to generate about 520 million man days of employment. About 90,000 habitations will be provided safe drinking water during 1997–98 under the Accelerated Rural Water Supply Scheme.

The outlay for the Social Services sector is being substantially enhanced from Rs. 11,785 crores in RE 1996–97 to Rs. 15,707 crores in BE 1997–98. Significant increases are under Urban Development (Rs. 775 crores), General Education (Rs. 1,189 crores), Technical Education (Rs. 132 crores), Family Welfare (Rs. 282 crores) and Water Supply and Sanitation (Rs. 312 crores).

The Science and Technology sector is being provided Rs. 1,870 crores as against Rs. 1,584 crores in RE 1996–97.

The Maulana Azad Education Foundation is being given Rs. 40 crores. The National Minorities Development and Finance Corporation is being provided Rs. 41 crores.

Rs. 96 crore is being allocated to the National SC and ST Finance and Development Corporation. For the welfare of the handicapped, I am providing Rs. 90 crores and for the National Handicapped Finance and Development Corporation, I am giving Rs. 28 crores.

Total non-Plan expenditure in 1997–98 is estimated to be Rs. 1,69,629 crores. The interest payments are estimated to be Rs. 68,000 crores.

Fertilizer subsidy on Indigenous fertilizers is being enhanced to Rs. 5,240 crores in 1997–98 from Rs. 4,743 crores in … RE 1996–97 …

An amount of Rs. 7,500 crores is being earmarked for food grains and sugar subsidies in 1997–98 representing an increase of Rs. 1,434 crores over RE 1996–97. When the dual card system under the Targeted PDS takes effect throughout the country, if more funds are required, I shall provide the same …

I would like to make a special mention of the outlay for Defence, Rs. 35,620 crores is being provided which includes Rs. 3,620 crores for implementing the recommendations of the Fifth Pay Commission …

A provision of Rs. 4,205 crores is being made for implementing the recommendations of the Fifth Pay Commission for employees other than Defence and Railway personnel for whom separate provisions have been made in this Budget and in the Railway Budget …

The non-Plan provision for assistance to the public sector units has been on the increase. In 1996–97, we approved revival packages for Bharat Yantra Nigam, Bharat Bhari Udyog Nigam, Hindustan Paper Corporation, Scooters India, Heavy Engineering Corporation (HEC) and Bharat Refractories. For 1997–98, I am providing Rs. 1,107 crores as non-Plan loans, and I expect that we will approve more restructuring proposals during the course of next year …

PART B

Let me preface my tax proposals by saying that I have set for myself the goal of augmenting the net tax revenues of the Central Government by a healthy 15–16 per cent …

… I believe that a good tax policy should aim at moderate rates, a wider tax base, simpler procedural rules and securing greater compliance. Households and the corporate sector are our best savers; we must reward them. From another point of view, however, the tax to GDP ratio for the Central Government, which currently is only around 10.5 per cent, needs to cease to sustain the needs of public investment and social sector expenditure …

It is inexplicable that in a country of over 900 million people, only 12 million people are assessed to income-tax and, what is worse, only about 12,000 assessees are in the tax bracket of income above Rs. 10 lakh … My proposal is that residents of large metropolitan cities who satisfy any two of the following economic criteria, namely, ownership of a four-wheel vehicle, occupation of immovable property meeting certain prescribed criteria, ownership of a telephone and foreign travel in the previous year, should normally fall within the taxable slabs and should voluntarily file their tax returns …

… I also propose to introduce a new Estimated Income Scheme for retail traders. The scheme will apply to persons engaged in the business of retail trade of any goods or merchandise having a total turnover of less than Rs. 40 lakhs. A trader with a turnover of less than Rs. 8 lakhs will stand exempted, given the present exemption limit …

… last July, I had reduced the income-tax rate for the first income slab from 20 per cent to 15 per cent … It is now widely accepted that moderate rates of taxation encourage savings, foster growth and motivate voluntary compliance …

The new tax rates are so moderate that there is now little justification for increasing the exemption limit. However, salaried persons deserve some relief. I, therefore, propose to increase the limit of standard deduction to Rs. 20,000, which will, henceforth, apply uniformly to all salaried tax-payers. An employee drawing a salary of Rs. 75,000 per annum and contributing 10 per cent thereof to the provident fund would have to pay no tax at all.

During the last meeting of the National Development Council, a suggestion was made that the Government should think of a scheme to harness 'black money' for productive purposes … I believe that the time is opportune to introduce a Voluntary Disclosure Scheme … The share which becomes available to the Central Government will go entirely towards financing thc Basic Minimum Services programme and infrastructure needs.

I also propose to give some further relief to our senior citizens …

… Turning to corporate taxes, I had in my last budget reduced the rate of surcharge from 15 per cent to 7.5 per cent and had expressed the hope that I would take a similar step in my next budget. I propose to abolish the balance surcharge on companies …

… The reduction in the corporate rates, apart from better compliance, should impart an added momentum to the growth process, create multiplier beneficial effects all around and also attract greater foreign investment.

There has also been a demand from the corporate sector that the tax rate of 30 per cent on royalty and technical services fees payable to foreign companies is too high and acts as a hindrance to the transfer of technology. I, therefore, propose to reduce this rate to 20 per cent.

I have received requests from non-resident Indians that the capital gains tax rate in their case arising on transfer of securities should be at par with the rate applicable in the case of FIIs. I see merit in their demand and, accordingly, propose that the rate be reduced from the existing 20 per cent to 10 per cent.

The Minimum Alternate Tax (MAT) on companies … has been the subject of extensive debate … I, therefore, propose to make the following changes in the provisions of MAT:

(i) Export profits will be exempt from MAT and will be eligible for full deduction under section 80HHC.

(ii) A system of credit will be introduced in respect of the payment of MAT …

Another area of vigorous debate over many years relates to the issue of tax on dividends … Hence, I propose to abolish tax on dividends in the hands of the shareholder.

Some companies distribute exorbitant dividends. Ideally, they should retain the bulk of their profits and plough them into fresh investments. I intend to reward companies who invest in future growth. Hence, I propose to levy a tax on distributed profits at the moderate rate of 10 per cent on the amount so distributed. This tax shall be an incidence on the company and shall not be passed on to the shareholder.

In order to encourage investments in Government securities, called gilts, I propose to abolish Tax Deducted at Source (TDS) on such securities. I also propose to include gilts for the higher deduction limit of Rs. 15,000 under section 80L of the Income Tax Act as is available in respect of income received from the units of UTI or approved mutual funds.

I have already announced that Telecommunication will qualify as an infrastructure. I, therefore, propose to extend the following benefits to this sector:

(i) Tax holiday under section 80IA;

(ii) Amortization of licence fees; and

(iii) Inclusion of investments made in debentures and equity shares of a public company providing telecommunication services for the purposes of tax rebate under section 88.

In order to encourage the development of tourism infrastructure, I propose to give a deduction of 50 per cent of the profits in respect of new hotels which are located in a hilly area or in a rural area or a place of pilgrimage or a specified place of tourist importance …

Taxing financial intermediation goes contrary to the canons of sound public finance. Today, an interest-tax at the rate of 3 per cent is levied on the interest income of lending institutions, including banks and NBFCs. I propose to reduce the levy to 2 per cent and I hope to eliminate this levy progressively. This will help to keep down the cost of borrowing.

As a measure of simplification, I propose to amend Section 37 of the Income Tax Act to provide for the removal of artificial disallowances on account of advertisement, travelling, hotel expenses, entertainment expenses, etc. incurred for legitimate business purposes …

Now, I turn to my indirect tax proposals.

… On more than one occasion I have stated that we would achieve the average level of tariffs prevalent in ASEAN countries by the turn of century. This will give time to Indian industry to adjust to these changes. This year's proposals should be seen in this background.

I propose to reduce the peak rate of customs duty from 50 per cent to 40 per cent.

High levels of customs duties on capital goods are inconsistent with our policy of attracting the best technology. Greenfield investments in large projects should be globally competitive … I, therefore, propose a modest reduction in duty on capital goods from 25 per cent to 20 per cent … Over the next two to three years these rates would need to be further adjusted to conform to levels prevalent in other developing Asian countries …

…The customs duty on several inputs for the steel industry is being reduced …

Iron and steel products at present generally attract customs duty at 30 per cent. I do not propose to make any major changes in the duty structure this year. However, I propose to reduce the duty on Cold Rolled Coils of iron and steel from 30 per cent to 25 per cent to help the engineering industry. I further propose to reduce the duty on ships brought for breaking from 10 per cent to 5 per cent and on pig iron from 20 per cent to 10 per cent.

I propose to reduce the duty on non-cooking coal from 20 per cent to 10 per cent. This will help the power sector.

... I propose to reduce the duty on organic and inorganic chemicals from 40 per cent to 30 per cent. I also propose to make ... reductions on certain essential chemicals ...

I also propose to reduce the customs duty on dyes, pigments, paints and varnishes, glues, enzymes and modified starches from 40 per cent to 30 per cent. These reductions will significantly benefit our textile industry.

Mr. Speaker, Sir, the scheduled dismantling of quantitative restrictions under the Multi Fibre Agreement will expose all textile exporting countries to stiff competition. The Ministry of Textiles have created a 'Technology Upgradation Fund' for both the textile and jute industries to enhance the competitive efficiency of these sectors ...

As a relief to the woollen textile industry, I propose to reduce the import duty on apparel grade wool from 25 per cent to 20 per cent, on wool waste from 30 per cent to 20 per cent and on woollen and synthetic rags from 30 per cent to 25 per cent. On flax fibre, I propose to reduce the duty from 30 per cent to 20 per cent.

In order to conserve our forest resources, I propose to fully exempt wood logs, fuel wood, wood chips, etc. from customs duty.

The spread of 'Information Technology' has radically altered conventional wisdom on growth strategies. I propose several measures to encourage this industry and to reduce costs ...

... I propose to reduce the duty on watch parts and movements from 50 per cent to 25 per cent and on watch cases of base metals from 50 per cent to 30 per cent. I also propose to reduce duty on horological materials from 20 per cent to 10 per cent. This will help our watch industry to further enhance their quality.

We are all concerned about the menace of growing pollution. In order to help reduce the cost of CNG kits, I have decided to reduce the customs duty on such kits and their parts from 10 per cent to a modest 5 per cent. Similarly, I propose to reduce the customs duty sharply on catalytic converters and their parts to 5 per cent from the existing rate of 25 per cent.

To improve the quality of medical care, I propose to reduce the import duty on medical equipment from 30 per cent to 20 per cent; on linear accelerators of 15 MeV and above used for cancer treatment from 10 per cent to 0 per cent; and on ophthalmic blanks for making spectacle lenses from 50 per cent to 20 per cent.

To promote tourism, I propose to reduce the import duty on specified equipment required for hotels from 35 per cent to 25 per cent and on specified speciality food items used by foreign tourists from 50 per cent to 25 per cent.

I also propose to give some relief to the film and photographic industry by reducing the import duty on cine films and other photographic films from 30 per cent to 25 per cent and on parts of cameras from 50 per cent to 25 per cent.

I propose to reduce the customs duty on baggage from 60 per cent to 50 per cent.

Central Excise

I now come to my proposals on central excise.

... I find that, in the first instance, it is necessary to reduce the dispersion in excise rates. I believe that we can eventually gravitate towards a mean rate around 18 per cent ...

... Cotton yarn will continue to bear an excise duty of 5 per cent only ...

... In respect of a large number of products, I propose to reduce the excise duty by percentages ranging from 2 per cent to 7 per cent and apply the mean rate. Accordingly, the mean rate of 18 per cent would be applicable to many commodities ...

Agricultural and horticultural machinery are fully exempt from excise duty. I propose to extend the exemption from excise duty to milking machines, dairy machinery and their parts.

In order to revive and give a thrust to the ailing jute industry, I propose to fully exempt all jute and jute products from excise duty.

At present, import of equipment and consumables by recognized research institutions is exempt from customs duty. In the interest of the domestic producer, I propose to allow the purchase of indigenous equipment and consumables by such institutions free of excise duty.

I also propose to reduce the duties of excise on certain items in order to bring about a more balanced excise structure on the whole. The changes proposed are:

- Reduction of duty on taxis and cars for the physically handicapped from 30 per cent to 25 per cent.
- Reduction of duty on polyester filament yarn from 40 per cent to 30 per cent.
- Reduction of duty on cosmetics and toilet preparations from 40 per cent to 30 per cent.
- Reduction of duty on glazed tiles from 30 per cent to 25 per cent.
- Reduction of duty on air conditioners from 40 per cent to 30 per cent.

... The fight against cancer and respiratory diseases continues. My contribution will be to increase the excise duty on non-filter cigarettes, not exceeding 60 mm in length, popularly called mini cigarettes, from Rs. 75 per thousand to Rs. 90 per thousand. I have also increased the excise duty on other categories of cigarettes ... The impact of this duty change on the retail price would only be 2 paise for a bundle of 20 bidis. As regards cigarettes, the increase would be 15 times more for every mini cigarette.

Small Scale Sector

The small-scale sector makes an important contribution to our overall production, provides gainful employment and also contributes to our export effort …

In order to curb avoidance from payment of duty, I have decided to exclude a few items like cotton yarn and texturized man-made yarn from the purview of the Small Scale Industry (SSI) exemption scheme.

Others

… It is reported that in some sectors, like induction furnace, steel re-rolling mills, etc., evasion of excise duty is substantial and the production is not being reported correctly. I propose to tackle this problem by introducing collection of excise duty on the basis of their production capacity …

The average citizen consumes a basket of commodities. As a result of my proposals of some increases and many reductions I believe the basket will carry a significantly lower tax burden.

The services sector contributes nearly 40 per cent to the GDP. 'Services' are products as much as 'manufactured goods'. Both must bear taxes. Hence, I propose to extend the service tax to cover a number of well-known services like:

- Transportation of goods by road;
- Consulting engineers;
- Custom house, Steamer and Clearing and Forwarding agents;
- Air travel agents, tour operators and car rental agencies;
- Outdoor caterers, pandal contractors and mandap keepers;
- Manpower recruitment agencies.

… I propose to utilize the bulk of the proceeds realized from service tax on transportation of goods by road to augment the resources of the National Highways Authority.

On the conventional basis, my proposals relating to reduction in customs duties are estimated to result in a loss of Rs. 2,625 crores in a financial year and, in the case of excise duties, my proposals are broadly revenue neutral. However, the buoyancy and the growth momentum that would be imparted to the economy would more than compensate for our losses computed through the conventional calculations.

… A revision of tariffs for some postal services has become unavoidable … This modest increase is necessary for the development of postal services and in partially bridging the deficit on the numerous services being provided by the Postal Department …

… Let me look at the final outcome. The revenue deficit in 1997–98 is placed at Rs. 30,266 crores or 2.1 per cent of GDP. The fiscal deficit comes to Rs. 65,454 crores which is 4.5 per cent of GDP …

Our goal must be to achieve rapid and broad-based growth which alone can ensure higher employment, better living standards and a humane and just society. The challenges that we face today are not unique to India. Other countries, including our friends in Asia, have faced similar challenges. Japan showed the way … These countries have shown that with courage, wisdom and pragmatism they can find their rightful places in the world …

Deng Xiaoping, to whom we paid homage a few days ago, once said, 'From our experience of these last few years, it is entirely possible for economic development to reach a new stage every few years. Development is the only hard truth.' India's economy has also reached a new stage. Our beloved India is far stronger today than she was six years ago.

I would appeal to this House, and to the Indian people to heed the call of Gurudev Rabindranath Tagore:

Desha desha nandita kari mandritta tabha bheri, Aashilo jata birabrinda aashana tabha gheri, Deen aagata oyi, Bharat tabu kayi? Shay ki rahila lupta aaji shaba-jana-paschatay? Louk bishwakarmabhar mili shabar shathay.

(Thy call has sped over all countries of the world, And men have gathered around thy seat. The day is come; but where is India? Does she still remain hidden, lagging behind? Let her take up her burden and march with all.)

Mr. Speaker, Sir, with these words, I commend the Budget to this august House.

YASHWANT SINHA

(Lok Sabha: Hazaribagh)

Lok Sabha: 28 February 2001

Budget for 2000–01

Sir, I rise to present the first budget of this Millennium.

…

The year 1999–2000 has been a year of many challenges: the 50-day war in Kashmir, the super cyclone in Orissa, long months of political uncertainty before the general elections, a somewhat weak monsoon, a near tripling of world oil prices and the continued fragility in world economic recovery. Nevertheless, we have met these challenges resolutely, accomplished a great deal and the nation is stronger as a result.

… Let me just touch a few highlights. A broad-based industrial recovery is under way. Despite lower growth of agriculture due to inclement weather, overall economic growth this year is expected to be nearly 6 per cent. The infrastructure sector is performing much better. For the first time in 17 years the inflation rate has stayed below 4 per cent for 42 consecutive weeks. Even more remarkable, the Consumer Price Index (Industrial Workers) in November 1999 showed zero increase over the previous November. This is an enormous boon for the weakest sections of our society. Public food stocks are at record levels. Exports have achieved a remarkable turnaround from negative growth last year to nearly 13 per cent growth in dollar terms in April–December 1999. Our software exports are also booming. Although surging international oil prices have increased our oil import bill by more than $6 billion, our foreign exchange reserves have nevertheless attained new record levels. With the return of investor confidence our stock markets have also soared to new heights.

... With this, my third budget, I propose to put India on a sustained, equitable and job-creating growth path of 7 to 8 per cent per year in order to banish the scourge of poverty from our land within a decade ... To achieve this objective our strategy must encompass the following elements:

- Strengthen the foundations of growth of our rural economy ...
- Nurture the revolutionary potential of the new knowledge-based industries ...
- Strengthen and modernize traditional industries ... and the SSI sector.
- Mount a sustained assault on infrastructure bottlenecks ...
- Accord the highest priority to human resource development ...
- Strengthen our role in the world economy ...
- Establish a credible framework of fiscal discipline ...

... In all these areas we must pursue thorough going economic reforms to unlock the creative energies of our people and thus reap the gains of productivity growth. But our reforms must also be guided by compassion and justice ...

Fiscal Management

... A long history of high fiscal deficits has left us with a legacy of a huge public debt and an ever-growing bill of interest payments ... If we do not raise the resources and instead take recourse to even higher borrowing next year, then we will jeopardize our prospects for growth ... and place an unfair burden on the next generation.

We must put our fiscal house in order. This means hard decisions and sacrifices. At the same time, we must preserve the intrinsic dynamism of our economy, which alone can deliver sustained growth with social justice ...

Similarly, there cannot be any compromise on Defence ...

Over the years, the composition of Central Government expenditure has become highly rigid and prone to large, pre-committed increases ... Interest payments, Defence, Internal Security, Major Subsidies, Salaries, Allowances and Pensions and non-plan grants to States account for about 95 per cent of non-plan expenditure and about 70 per cent of total expenditure. To curb built-in expenditure growth … I am introducing the following initiatives:

- All ongoing schemes will be subjected to rigorous zero-base budgeting scrutiny …
- The manpower requirements of Government departments will be reassessed …
- Fresh recruitment in Government departments and institutions will be limited …
- The scheme for redeployment of surplus staff will be made more effective …
- All subsidies will be reviewed with a view to bringing in cost-based user charges wherever feasible.
- No new autonomous institutions will be created without approval of Cabinet …
- … the interest rate on General Provident Funds is being reduced by 1 per cent to 11 per cent from 1 April 2000.
- Excessive domestic borrowings to finance current expenditure has resulted in debt service payments approaching unsustainable levels. To reduce expenditure on this account, a portion of the disinvestment proceeds will be earmarked for retiring Government debt.

… We shall pursue resolutely the objective of downsizing Government and prepare a roadmap for the purpose. For medium-term management of the fiscal deficit we also need the support of a strong institutional mechanism embodied in a Fiscal Responsibility Act …

… The financial position of the State Governments has deteriorated sharply in the last few years … It will be my endeavour to take measures in the next year for promoting fiscal reforms in the States …

Agriculture and Rural Development

… We must take all necessary measures to strengthen the rural economy … In this budget I propose to strengthen the earlier programmes and launch further initiatives:

- The Rural Infrastructure Development Fund (RIDF) managed by NABARD has emerged as a popular and effective scheme for financing rural infrastructure projects … The scope of RIDF was also widened … and the interest charged on this lending will be reduced by half a per cent.
- Micro finance has emerged as an effective tool for alleviating poverty in many countries. In my last budget I had asked NABARD and SIDBI to cover 50,000 self-help groups to develop micro enterprises … To give a further boost to this programme, a Micro finance Development Fund will be created in NABARD

with a start-up contribution of Rs. 100 crores from RBI, NABARD, banks and others. This Fund will provide start-up funds to micro finance institutions ... Special emphasis will be placed on promotion of micro finance enterprises in rural areas set up by vulnerable sections including women, Scheduled Castes, Scheduled Tribes and Other Backward Classes.

- ... For rural credit, clear delineation of the supervisory role of RBI/NABARD on banking matters is also essential. To promote ... a more vibrant rural cooperative credit system, I propose to establish a Fund in NABARD ...
- The programme of Kisan Credit Cards is progressing very well ... I am asking NABARD and Commercial Banks to redouble their promotional efforts so as to issue an additional 75 lakh Kisan Credit Cards by March 2001.
- Due to our efforts at recapitalizing RRBs, 158 RRBs are posting operating profits ... In view of the importance of the RRBs in rural financing, we will continue with this programme of strengthening the RRBs.

The Planning Commission and the Ministry of Agriculture have worked out modalities to integrate 28 ongoing separate Centrally Sponsored Schemes of agricultural development into one comprehensive programme ...

There is urgent need to review and coordinate our long-term strategy at the National and the State levels on the pattern of land use in the country, development of agriculture in relation to the agro-climatic conditions in the different regions and preservation of our forest resources. We need to adopt an integrated approach to a number of related subjects such as preservation and development of the forest wealth, optimum utilization of the wasteland, watershed development, safeguarding biodiversity, etc ...

Our Government stands fully committed to ensure that the fruits of economic reforms are shared by all sections of society ... Five elements of social and economic infrastructure are critical to the quality of life, especially in rural areas: health, education, drinking water, housing and roads.

Even after 52 years of Independence, the provision of basic services in rural areas remains very unsatisfactory ... These large gaps in basic services in rural areas are not acceptable and Government is committed to removing them rapidly.

Universalization of elementary education is one of our key objectives. A new Department of Elementary Education and Literacy has already been created ... A new Department of Drinking Water Supply in the Ministry of Rural Development has been set up ... The Reproductive and Child Health programme will receive Rs. 1,051 crores as against an allocation of Rs. 695 crores in 1999–2000. For rural housing schemes a provision of Rs. 1,710 crores has been made.

... I am announcing the launching of a new scheme, the 'Pradhan Mantri Gramodaya Yojana' with the objective of undertaking time bound programmes to fulfil these critical needs of the rural people.

Rural Housing

'Housing for All' has been identified as a priority area in the Agenda for Governance ... Schemes for meeting the needs of different sections of society have been prepared ...

Social Security for the Poor

More than one-third of our population still lives below the poverty line ... I have decided to introduce a new scheme of group insurance ... This scheme will lay a firm foundation for insurance cover to the poorest in our country.

Empowerment of Women

There is an urgent need for improving the access of women to national resources and for ensuring their rightful place in the mainstream of economic development. Towards this objective, the Government will set up a Task Force ...

Population, Health and Environment

Government have recently announced a new National Population Policy, a key objective of which is to bring down total fertility rates to replacement levels by 2010 ...

Recognizing the role of the Indian systems of medicine and homeopathy in our health care, the plan allocation for the concerned Department is being doubled. Emphasis will be placed on drug standardization, quality control, modernizing the colleges, drug testing laboratories and formulations. This will also help in boosting exports of herbal formulations.

We must preserve and nurture our forests and environment for future generations. Funds are being provided for regeneration of mangroves and creation of shelter-belts along the coastal line, bamboo regeneration and afforestation programme, encouragement of medicinal plants and ecotourism. Preservation of the rural environment will raise the living standards of millions belonging to the weakest sections of our society.

Small Scale Industry

The SSI sector plays a vital role in industrial production, employment generation and exports ... For improving credit flow to SSI units, I propose the following:

- The requirement of providing collateral security is a major bottleneck to the flow of bank credit to very small units. RBI has recently issued instructions to dispense with the collateral requirement for loans up to Rs. 1 lakhs ...
- ... To promote credit flow to small borrowers, the composite loan limit is being increased from Rs. 5 lakhs to Rs. 10 lakhs.

- I am asking the public sector banks to accelerate their programme of SSI branches to ensure that every district and SSI clusters within districts are served by at least one specialized SSI bank branch …
- Last year, I had announced that a credit guarantee scheme for SSI will be launched … a new Central Scheme for this purpose has been formulated and a provision for Rs. 100 crores has been made in the Budget …

SIDBI operates the National Equity Fund Scheme under which equity support is provided for projects up to Rs. 15 lakhs. To further help SSI entrepreneurs, this limit will be raised from Rs. 15 lakhs to 25 lakhs …

… The Khadi and Village Industries Commission (KVIC) has been playing a very important role as an instrument to generate large-scale employment in the rural areas with low per capita investment. Government will continue to encourage the Khadi and Village Industry Sector so that its products can become more competitive …

Industry and Capital

In earlier millennia, India led the world on the basis of knowledge. Today history is repeating itself. Young Indian entrepreneurs are at the forefront of the infotech revolution, whether in Silicon Valley, Bangalore or Hyderabad … We must do everything possible to promote this flowering of knowledge-based enterprise and job creation.

A key ingredient for future success lies in Venture Capital Finance … I am proposing a major liberalization of the tax treatment for venture capital funds … I should add that this liberalization will give a strong boost for Non-Resident Indians in Silicon Valley and elsewhere to invest some of their capital, knowledge and enterprise in ventures in their motherland …

… Thanks to our prudent macro-economic management and calibrated approach to currency convertibility, we have successfully weathered the East Asian crisis of the past two years … We must encourage Indian firms and businesses to grow into strong, India-based multinationals … Last month, Government had announced a policy to allow Indian companies to raise funds for investments through issue of American Depositing Receipts (ADRs)/Global Deposit Receipts (GDRs) without prior Government approval … I plan to further liberalize this policy for acquisition of companies abroad to enable Indian corporates in knowledge-based sectors to grow rapidly and lay the foundation for Indian multinationals in areas where we have comparative economic advantage …

Under existing policy on portfolio investment, Foreign Institutional Investors (FIIs) are permitted to invest in a company, up to an aggregate 24 per cent of equity shares, which can be increased to 30, subject to approval by the Board of Directors and a Special Resolution of the General Body of the Company. To give our best companies greater access to foreign portfolio investment, I am increasing this limit from 30 per cent to 40 per cent …

Science and Technology

The sustained growth of our knowledge-based industries will ultimately depend on the quality and extent of scientific and technological progress and training in our society. We must harness our potential in science and technology to realize the dream of modern India …

To fully benefit from the new intellectual property rights regime, we need to encourage our scientists and R&D institutions to maximize their patenting efforts. Government have decided to allow Universities and Research Institutions to retain the revenue generated from intellectual property rights through publicly funded research and also share a part of the revenue with the inventor.

Modernization of the Patent Office and the Trade Mark Register is long overdue …

Banking and Finance

The recent East Asian crisis has underlined the critical importance of undertaking reforms to strengthen the banking sector … To facilitate this process, Government have decided to accept the recommendations of the Narasimham Committee on Banking Sector Reforms for reducing the requirement of minimum shareholding by Government in nationalized banks to 33 per cent …

As honourable members are aware, the Report of the Working Group on Restructuring Weak Public Sector Banks had suggested the constitution of a Financial Restructuring Authority (FRA). It has been decided to have a modified version of the FRA …

Government will not close down any public sector bank. As responsible owner of the banks, Government have decided to consider recapitalization of the weak banks to achieve the prescribed capital adequacy norms, provided a viable restructuring programme acceptable to the Government as the owner and the RBI as the regulator is made available by the concerned banks.

The high level of Non-Performing Assets (NPAs) in our public sector banks is a cause for continued concern. Efficient and effective mechanisms for recovery of bank dues are critically important for reducing NPAs …

… In the fast-changing world of modern finance, it has become necessary to accord greater operational flexibility to the RBI for conduct of monetary policy and regulation of the financial system …

Similarly, to facilitate development of the Government debt market the legislative framework needs to be strengthened and modernized through a Government Securities Act which I propose to bring to replace the old Public Debt Act, 1944 …

Infrastructure

Infrastructure services remain a key bottleneck to rapid and sustained growth of our economy …

The Prime Minister has announced a major initiative for road development, the National Highways Development Project (NHDP) …

The plan outlay for the Central Public Sector Undertakings (PSUs) in the power sector has been increased from Rs. 7,626 crores to Rs. 9,194 crores. Increased budgetary support has been provided for the Tehri Hydro and the Nathpa Jhakri Hydro Projects so that both these projects can be commissioned by March 2002. For commissioning of high priority projects by State Electricity Boards (SEBs)/ State generation companies, a provision of Rs. 300 crores has also been made for subsidizing interest on loans from Power Finance Corporation.

In order to give a fillip to the reform process in the power sector and for undertaking investments on renovation and modernization of old and inefficient plants and for strengthening the distribution system, a new scheme for providing assistance to State utilities will be introduced …

… Honourable members are aware that the Sethusamudram Ship Channel Project has the potential of providing a shorter route between the East and West Coast Ports. I am glad to inform that the Government have approved the undertaking of a detailed feasibility study and environmental impact assessments of the project at a total cost of Rs. 4.8 crores …

Disinvestment/Privatization/Public Sector Restructuring

Government's policy towards the public sector is clear and unambiguous. Its main elements are:

- Restructure and revive potentially viable PSUs;
- Close down PSUs which cannot be revived;
- Bring down Government equity in all non-strategic PSUs to 26 per cent lower, if necessary; and
- Fully protect the interests of workers.

In line with this policy, during the last two years financial restructuring of 20 PSUs has been approved by Government. As a result, many PSUs have been able to restructure their operations, improve productivity and achieve a turnaround in performance …

There are many PSUs which are sick and not capable of being revived. The only remaining option is to close down these undertakings after providing an acceptable safety net for the employees and workers …

The North-East Region

Government is committed to the speedy economic development of the North-Eastern States and Sikkim. Priority is being given for development of infrastructure, specially airports, railways, power and National Highways …

For realizing the potential for agricultural and horticultural development in the North-East, schemes for minor irrigation and horticulture will be encouraged …

Scheduled Castes and Scheduled Tribes

To promote literacy and to improve the education standards of persons belonging to Scheduled Castes, a new thrust will be given to the Post-Matric Scholarship Scheme …

Budget Estimates for 2000–01

In the budget estimates for 2000–01, the total expenditure is estimated at Rs. 3,38,487 crores, of which Rs. 88,100 crores is for plan and Rs. 2,50,387 crore for non-plan.

Plan Expenditure

The budget support for Central, State and UT Plans has been placed at Rs. 88,100 crore, marking an increase of Rs. 8,705 crores over revised estimates 1999–2000. Gross budgetary support for the Central Plan is being enhanced from Rs. 43,661 crores in the revised estimates 1999–2000 to Rs. 51,276 crores …

Non-Plan Expenditure

… The increase in non-plan expenditure is mainly in defence (Rs. 10,083 crores), interest payments (Rs. 9,841 crores) and in grants to States (Rs. 9,392 crores). However, this increase is sought to be partially offset by reduction in outgo on account of food and fertilizer subsidies.

… We need to target the subsidies to those who are poor and needy … Indeed, we want to expand the access to subsidized food by Below Poverty Line (BPL) families so that they can meet their basic nutritional needs …

PART B

... Growth is not just an end in itself ... Sustained, broad-based growth, combined with all our programmes for accelerating rural development, building roads, promoting housing, boosting knowledge-based industries and enhancing the quality of human resources, will impart a strong impetus to employment expansion. There can be no better cure for the problem of poverty than this in our country.

Sir, the millennium has heralded the arrival of the Indian economy on the global stage ... In two short years we have ensured that 'made in India' is a compliment for any product or service. In two short years we have sent notice to the world that India will be an economic superpower in the 21st century. The world's eyes are now upon us, and we will deliver.

Mr. Speaker, Sir, with these words, I commend the budget to this august House.

Section Six

Gender

1

The Hindu Code Bill

Syama Prasad Mookerjee, *a barrister, academic and president of the Akhil Bharat Hindu Mahasabha between 1943 and 1946, is best known for his opposition to the now-abrogated Article 370 of the Constitution that gave special status to the erstwhile state of Jammu and Kashmir.*

It was this stance that led to his iconic status in Hindu Right-wing circles. But this did not prevent Jawaharlal Nehru from appointing him minister for Industry and Supply (now known as the Ministry of Commerce and Industry) in his first Cabinet. Subsequently, the two fell out, with Mookerjee protesting against the Liaquat–Nehru Pact, and resigning from the Cabinet.

Then, with the help of the Rashtriya Swayamsevak Sangh (RSS), he founded the Bharatiya Jana Sangh (BJS), the predecessor to the Bharatiya Janata Party (BJP), in 1951. In the general elections in 1952, he became one of only three MPs to be elected on a BJS ticket.

In this speech, made in the Constituent Assembly, Mookerjee expresses his opposition to the Hindu Code Bill, articulating what was being written in the RSS periodical, Organiser, *at that time. Mookerjee wondered whether the Code should be applicable only to Hindus or to Sikhs, Jains and Buddhists as well, and, indeed, he asked why the Code should not apply to all citizens of India – in short, he mooted a Uniform Civil Code.*

The second speech in this section was made by **Seeta Parmanand,** *an MP who was part of a generation of educated women who joined the freedom struggle. These women freedom fighters were at the forefront of those who spoke passionately to refute the arguments of those who invoked religion and tradition to oppose the reforms suggested in Ambedkar's Hindu Code.*

Dr Parmanand was a BLitt., and DPhil from Oxford, and a barrister. From 1952 to 1964, she was an active member of the Rajya Sabha, not hesitating even to challenge her own party, the Indian National Congress. She raised many issues related to the underprivileged, women and children. Indeed, long before midday meals were introduced in schools in India, she made the suggestion in the first Rajya Sabha.

She is perhaps best remembered because she belongs to an elite club of 14 MPs who sponsored the Private Members' Bills that became law. Given that hundreds of Private Members' Bill have been moved every Friday since then, it is an amazing feat.

In her case, she moved an amendment to the Hindu Marriage Act, 1955, which entered the statute book. The amendment ensured that the provisions for judicial separation of a couple in the Hindu Marriage Act, 1955, were synchronized with the provisions in the Special Marriage Act.

Indeed, this Bill was so significant that members across the House felicitated her. Prakash Narain Sapru, an MP at that time, was moved to describe her as 'a model legislator'; and the then Minister for Legal Affairs, Hari Vinayak Pataskar, acknowledged her contribution, saying, 'If she had not done it there would have been many difficulties in the way of government doing it, because there is a sense of complacency once the House has passed an Act. It would take very long to move the government machinery to effect the amendment.'

Not all ministers were as generous, with many begging her to withdraw her Bills, promising her that the government would come forward with comprehensive legislation. On one Friday, when the government came forward with the by now standard response that it would bring in a comprehensive law if the Member would agree to withdraw their Bill, she could not resist the riposte that Friday, instead of being called Private Members' day, should be called 'Government assurance day for comprehensive legislation'.

The Private Members' Bill that she moved on the subject was to bridge the discrepancies between the Act as initially passed and the Special Marriage Act. The Hindu Marriage (Amendment) Bill, 1956, was introduced in the Rajya Sabha by Dr Parmanand and passed in 1956. This Bill says that when both the parties belong to the Hindu religion and are marrying under the Special Marriage Act, they will be governed by the Hindu Succession Act, 1956. She brought the Bill after she discovered that provisions for judicial separation of a couple in the Hindu Marriage Act, 1955, were not at par with the provisions in the Special Marriage Act. Therefore, she moved an amendment to the Hindu Marriage Act, 1955, which was adopted by Parliament and eventually entered the statute book.

In the speech excerpted here, Dr Parmanand demonstrates her clarity of vision while participating in a debate on The Hindu Marriage and Divorce Bill that outlawed polygamy and contained provisions dealing with inter-caste marriages and divorce procedures.

SYAMA PRASAD MOOKERJEE

(Constituent Assembly)

Provisional Parliament Debates: 17 September 1951

Hindu Code Bill

We have met here after about seven months to take up consideration of the Hindu Code Bill. Many things have happened during this period ... it is a matter of some satisfaction that Government has kept its mind open and has volunteered to make amendments in order to meet criticisms which may be made either in this House or outside. I believe never in the history of our country has a measure given rise to so much criticism in support or against it ...

The clause we are discussing now ... raises the question of the applicability of the entire Code ... The question has arisen as to whether this Code should be made applicable to Hindus as such or to such other classes of persons including Sikhs, Jains and Buddhists as have been mentioned in the amendment moved by the hon'ble Law Minister. The question has also been raised whether the Code should not apply to all citizens of India. I would certainly say that as the Chapter in the Constitution dealing with the directive policy of the State indicates, Parliament under the new Constitution has really been called upon to pass a Code which is to be applied to all citizens – an all-India Civil Code.

When this Bill was started to be discussed, we were working under a different set of circumstances altogether. It is, therefore, a matter of regret that the new Government, even after the Constitution has been passed, should proceed with a measure of this description, applicable only to one section of the community. It is said that we are a secular State. In fact, we suffer very often from a new disease which may be called 'secularitis'. How far is it open to Parliament ... how far is it desirable for Parliament to pass a law which will be applicable to only one section of the community?

... the Law Minister ... in one of his previous speeches ... said that there was no difficulty in formulating an all-India Civil Code if the country really wanted it. If that is the answer, then why not let us have such a Code? I doubt very much if some of the provisions which have been suggested in this Code can be proposed to be made applicable to other communities, in particular to Muslims. We are discussing the question of monogamy. I believe it is nobody's case that monogamy is good for Hindus alone or for Buddhists alone or for Sikhs alone. I believe those who are advocating monogamy honestly feel that this system is sound in principle and it should be made applicable to all, not to all persons in this civilized world, at least to all citizens in India who are liable to be governed under laws passed by this Parliament.

Now, why not have a separate Bill dealing only with monogamy and make it applicable to all citizens? I am not going to tread on this question because I know the weaknesses of the promoters of the Bill. They dare not touch the Muslim community. There will be so much opposition coming from many throughout India that Government will not dare to proceed with it. But, of course, you can proceed with the Hindu community in any way you like and whatever the consequences may be.

… I want to create that atmosphere where matters affecting social reform can be discussed in a method of give and take. It is not a Press Bill which the Law Minister is sponsoring on behalf of the Home Minister. We do not want the Police to stand outside this Parliament to help the smooth passage of a Bill dealing with social reform. That does not really help anybody. Any Bill whose object is to introduce social reform must have the support of the vast majority of the people of the country …

I do not share this view that Parliament has no right to deal with matters of social reform. I know the sacredness of our ancient texts – the Vedas, Smritis and Srutis. But historically, there were commentators to interpret the great theories which are propounded by the original law makers in days of yore. Gradually, the commentators also disappeared …

So far as the right of this Parliament is concerned, naturally it is a very delicate matter. For me being a Member of this body, it is rather difficult to challenge its jurisdiction, but of course so far as its right to present the will of the people goes, that is a matter which will be decided in the next few months and the people themselves will give their verdict. It is no use either for us sitting on this side or Members of Government sitting on the other side claiming for this Parliament things which may not be actually, honestly and legitimately, claimed for this body. But my point is this: that today there is a volume of opinion – a strong body of opinion, against some or many of the fundamental features of this Bill. I beg of hon'ble Members who are supporting this Bill to appreciate the depth of these criticisms.

There may be some features in this Bill with which I am in agreement, but I am trying to look at this measure from the point of view of those who are opposing it either in whole or in part. Just as we may appreciate the depth of the feelings of those who are supporting this measure, so also the depth of feelings of those who are opposing it must be appreciated. How to find a solution?

From the papers we find that for strategic reasons it has been decided to omit the consideration of some portions of this Bill … On the one side, are marriage and divorce and on the other side, is property and somehow marriage and divorce have won the day, and property has been relegated to the background for the time being. Is it possible for us, on the consideration of the amendments which are now before the House under clause 2, to devise some procedure whereby it may be left open to those who desire to come under the Code to take the fullest advantage of its provisions and, at the same time, give freedom to those who do not believe in the sanctity or legality or justice of the provisions to continue to be governed by existing Hindu Law?

That is a proposal which I am making … on the basis of the various amendments ordered to be placed before the House for consideration. I have been told by some friends that we are liable to criticism for our backwardness in many foreign countries … some people have come and said that in China they are watching when the Hindu Code Bill will be passed! In America, some people are supposed to be watching as regards the progressive nature of the Indian people – in relation to their attitude towards the Hindu Code … Let us look at the American laws … I find that in 26 different States in America they do not allow marriage between Americans and Negroes … In some States, marriage between an American and Chinese is prohibited, or a marriage between an American and a Mongolian. In practically all the States there are different marriage laws. What about uniformity? I suppose the people of the United States of America are getting on quite merrily and quite well without having complete uniformity of all marriage laws. So uniformity is not the last word on the subject. Uniformity suggests stagnation, deadness …

I would suggest that we should follow the lead given by our own country. Now take again the Roman Catholics. According to their strict law, according to their religion, divorce is not allowed. But in almost all countries they have passed civil laws which allow Roman Catholics to adopt divorce if necessary. But they have not touched their religion. They have allowed that to remain separate, but those among the Roman Catholics who desire to be governed in accordance with the civil laws, it is open to them to do so … I find that a clear distinction is made between the two systems.

Now we are confining ourselves for the present to marriage and divorce. What is it that is worrying the so-called progressives in this country, including progressive ladies? They are anxious that there should be a provision for divorce and there should be provision for monogamy. These are the two things on which great stress has been laid. Now let us take divorce for the time being. You have got your laws passed by the Indian Legislature which permit divorce. At one stage, a Hindu could not get married under the civil laws, unless he declared that he was not a Hindu. Even that has been changed. A Hindu may remain a Hindu and, at the same time, contract a marriage which will be according to his taste or that of the couple. Similarly, with regard to inter-caste marriage, you have already passed laws and made such inter-caste marriages permissible, without taking away the Hindu character of the persons involved. Even sagotra marriage,[1] which is considered

[1] Editor's note: Sagotra marriage refers to a marriage within the same lineage or marriage through inbreeding.

to be very revolting by large sections of the people, has been recognized by laws passed by Legislative Assembly.

These are indications as to how the demand for a progressive development ... of marriage laws has been met by legislatures of this country. This is a subject which is placed in our Constitution in the Concurrent List, and I believe Bombay and Madras have passed laws on the subject. There are several States where provincial laws have been passed in some form or another, making provisions which are consistent with the wishes of the people. Now the point is this. Why do you wish to make the new laws obligatory upon all Hindus? You do not wish that the system of divorce should be taken advantage of, or must be taken advantage of, by people against the will of the parties concerned. It is an enabling measure and that power is already in existence. On the other hand, what is the blow that you are giving at the feelings of millions of people? Now you have kept this form of sacramental marriage on paper. You have changed its description from sacramental to 'dharmic' in order to give it a little oriental and attractive colouring. Of course, the substance has not changed.

I would ask very seriously those Members of the House who are supporting this Bill: What is it that you are achieving by this proposal? So far as sacramental marriage goes, this is an ideology which lies deep-rooted in the minds of millions of people – educated and uneducated, literate and illiterate – about the indissoluble nature of Hindu marriage. That is a matter of religion; it is not a matter of mere body and flesh. Now that is a feeling which lies deep in the minds of millions of people and I have talked to many people not only in my own province but in various parts of India. People who have not the remotest chance of taking advantage of any divorce law for various reasons are simply shocked at this idea and many people who are well-intentioned, who are reformers, suggest that if there are Hindus in the country today who want to take advantage of the modem system of divorce or want to do away with the religious nature of Hindu marriage, there is enough opportunity given to them under the existing law.

If, however, the law has to be revised in order to make them ultra-modern and completely up-to-date, let the law be revised for their benefit. But why do away with the fundamental and sacred nature of Hindu marriage? What is it that you gain thereby? I have not been able to get any satisfactory answer to this question. Because it is nobody's case that the new methods which are being laid down will be compulsorily adopted by all Hindus ... Therefore, if an option is given and if people take advantage of that option, naturally your case is won. I was told that even in India, as India is today, there are nearly ... 90 per cent almost Shrudras amongst whom some form or other of divorce or dissolution of marriage exists. Very well then, the answer is there. You have got your Hindu Law which provides for the dissolution of marriage in castes and communities where it is wanted. You may say, well, why should about 10 or 15 per cent of the Indian population stand against these changes?

It is not a question of anybody standing against the changes. If you want to go ahead or go backwards – whatever it may be – you are welcome to do so. But why drag others who do not believe in you and also who believe in something which is perfectly morally justifiable and in accordance with the highest standards of human conduct? I have not been able to get any answer to this fundamental question. We are told very often that our system is backward. I have got with me many extracts from the writings of great Indians and great Western scholars who have admired the way in which Hindu society has carried on its existence in spite of tremendous odds and difficulties.

I am not for a moment saying that all is well with Hindu society. I know where the defects lie. But it is something amazing, something unprecedented that our religion or the great truths on which Hindus for generations past, for thousands of years, have lived, somehow have shown a degree of adaptability and vitality which is hardly to be witnessed anywhere else. What is the reason? The reason is that whatever truths were propounded by the ancient sages or rishis, or commented upon by those who came after them, were not dogmatic in character. Just as the needs of the society changed, so also the laws were altered. In a huge country like India which is one politically today – and we would undoubtedly like to see that it grows politically, socially, culturally and economically as one solid nation – at the same time we cannot forget that in this country dwell thousands and thousands of people in various parts, in towns and in villages, men educated, uneducated, men with vision and with no vision, and they have built up a structure of their own, consistent with individual and social progress and welfare. Somehow that society has developed. Do you find any other country in this world where in spite of tremendous onslaughts the social structure has remained one?

India passed through seven hundred years of Muslim rule. Now, many theories were propounded during that period which in the context of today's circumstances may appear to be rather conservative. But they were dictated by considerations for the preservation and consolidation of the society as such and that is how those particular principles were propounded by the masters who were in no circumstance less qualified to speak on matters with which they dealt than any of us sitting in this Parliament today. From time to time, movements came into this country. Reference has been made to the Brahmo Samaj, to the Arya Samaj. As soon as it appeared that the society was becoming stagnant, was becoming conservative, some outstanding personality raised his head in this land and drew upon the great sources, the fountainhead of Indian knowledge, the Vedas or the Upanishads, gave their own interpretation and thereby tried to check the growth of the evils of conservatism or the moral decay of the society. But what has happened today? The ideology for which the Brahmo Samaj stood in this country, say, about a hundred years ago, has practically been absorbed by the Hindu society as you call the Hindu society today.

The other day we were discussing about Buddhism, a matter on which Dr. Ambedkar naturally would be the best authority to speak. But in any case, some friends from outside India came. I have something to do with the Maha Bodhi Society. I happen to be its President, without being a Buddhist. I am a Hindu and yet I am its President, because I have liberality enough to admit the greatness of Buddhism and yet remain a Hindu. The point I was about to develop was this. There were friends who came from outside India and they asked with a tone of complaint, 'Well, India was the land of birth of Buddha, but India killed Buddhism.' I do not wish to go into those controversial matters now. But one point comes out very prominently and that is that when Buddha started preaching his great doctrines, India needed Buddha, not only to save the world but to save India. And Buddha succeeded in checking the growth of certain tendencies which were about to destroy the very life-blood of Hindu civilization. Buddha has been absorbed by the same Hindus as an avatar. Although there were people in India who fought with Buddhism – whether they were right or wrong is a matter into which I need not enter now – but gradually it was realized that Buddhism was a factor of growth on Indian soil and had to be absorbed in Indian culture. So far as Buddhism is concerned, it went and spread in other countries. But the tenets of Buddhism were gradually absorbed in Hindu ideology.

The reason why I am saying all this is to show that we should never tolerate any criticism from any quarter, especially from a foreign quarter when they say that Hindu civilization or Hindu culture has been of a static nature or of a stagnant nature or of a decadent nature. There is something in our culture and civilization which is of a dynamic character and which has lived from generation to generation.

Even when India was a subject nation, people were born in this country, men of our soil, who stood up for great ideals which gave a new lease of life under new and modern conditions to the eternal tenets of Hindu civilization. This code is destroying that fountain-source. I shudder to think of the effect of clause 4. You read clause 4 of the Hindu Code. You are closing the door there. You are saying that except such manners or customs which might have been recognized in the body of this Code, everything else will be taboo from today. It is these manners and customs, based upon the ancient ideology, which allowed the Hindu society to grow and prosper from time to time.

Today, this great Assembly – and all of us are honourable and learned men – is solemnly deciding that we are the fountainhead of Indian religion and Indian culture, and whatever we decide to embody in this Code is final for the time being and nothing else will be allowed to be looked into by judges and courts. Does the House know that even in 1951, after the attainment of Independence, our own

Supreme Court had to draw from the original texts or their interpretations and give their verdict on cases where questions of Hindu law were under consideration, because they could not get any analogy from judicial decisions or textbooks? You are killing today the very fountain source of your religion which had given such a wide scope to generations of people, to make it a living reality and you say that it is a forward measure; it is a backward measure; it is a measure which does not help anybody at all; it only helps in dividing the country.

I do not wish to ascribe any motive to anybody. Anyone who may be supporting it or proposing it may be acting with the highest motives. I am prepared to admit that but what I would like to say is this: do not give compulsory effect to the provisions in respect of all people. Divorce is not compulsory but the breaking away of the sacramental ties of Hindu marriage will be compulsory and that is bad enough. Whether divorce comes or not is a different question altogether; you are violently changing customs and convictions. Somebody said that south India was specially progressive and many of the laws which we are considering are already in existence there, today. I say good luck to south India. Let south India proceed from progress to progress, from divorce to divorce. I have absolutely no quarrel with south India, but why force it on others who do not want it. In fact, I have got a letter with me. I received it only two days ago – it is a postcard and I do not know the gentleman who wrote it. Here is this gentleman who writes: 'The Bill as published on the Hindu Law contains a provision rendering the marriages between a girl and her maternal uncle void as being within the prohibited degree. The aforesaid custom is widely prevalent in Andhra and Tamil Nadu and even Brahmins considered maternal uncles of girls to be the most eligible and suitable bridegrooms for their girls. The prohibition is not known perhaps to lawyers and to others. I am sure that the vast majority of our people are ignorant of it in which case marriages celebrated in ignorance of this provision would operate as a severe hardship. I therefore request you to move an amendment …'

I do not know why they had selected me in particular and not written to Dr. Ambedkar … saving the custom from the prohibition or fixing sufficient time to elapse before the chapter on marriage can be brought into force. This is just by the way for those who were talking about the progressive nature of the people living in those territories. Naturally, they have gone very far ahead. It is only a point of view. I am not challenging the wisdom or unwisdom of any State. It might have been followed by lakhs and millions of people in this vast country. Naturally, customs might have developed in a particular manner.

My proposal boils down to this. You do not make this Code applicable to all – I am talking of marriage and divorce for the time being – but leave it open to those who will be married in future to make a declaration that they would like to be governed by these provisions and not be governed by the consequences of dharmic marriage; you leave it open to them to do so. That covers the cases of those who come in future. We are not legislating, I suppose, for the purpose of helping the dissolution of marriage of the existing Members of Parliament. We are looking to the future; we are thinking of handing over something to the future generation, whereby they can live in peace and with greater comfort. But supposing you want to apply it to those who are already married ... There also you can make a provision. Supposing you want to apply it to all who are already married, there I will give a solution. You leave it open to anybody, say, within a period of one or two years to register his decision whether he would like to be governed by this Code to opt for it, if you can use that language ... Well, 'everywhere' I do not approve for this reason that you are deciding something for others for which you have no right today. You are passing a law whereby you are saying that the dharmic form of marriage will continue as now without any modification or alteration and the other form of marriage also is open to people who would like to take advantage of it. Let the people in future make their choice. There is no compulsion, and for existing people you may give a time limit or you may not give a time limit. You can say that if any particular party desires to be governed by the provision of this Code, such persons may make a declaration before the Registrar or Registrar-General or Director General or whoever he may be and get the relief as is provided for in the Code.

I ask in all seriousness what is it that you lose thereby? What you gain thereby is that you do not break the unity of the country. You destroy the indissoluble nature of Hindu marriage which is regarded as solemn and sacred by millions of people. Many people in this House may not agree. I am not quarrelling with those people who believe that marriage is a bilateral arrangement, that it is nothing but a matter of contract: I have nothing to say against them if there are people who hold that view. Let them hold it, but there are those who hold the contrary view, who genuinely and sincerely believe that this system which has been in vogue for thousands of years is something sacred, something deep-rooted in their traditions and religion. What right have you to sit in this House and say that you want by one stroke of the pen to take this great right away? Believe me, rightly or wrongly, this country has been divided tremendously on this Hindu Code Bill, I do not wish that that should be so. I want that we should go on progressing and making reforms in our social structure. But, we will do it in such a way that we can carry the bulk of the people with us not carry them by force in this House or carry them by threads of sweeping agitation outside, but carry them by appealing to their logic and to their conviction. I have discussed this matter with many people who represent this point of view and others who are not orthodox. Somehow, the country is divided today.

How to proceed in the matter? As I said, it is not a Press law, that something is in danger and so you must go and pass the Press law somehow and operate it. This is not an amendment of the Constitution. It is not a political matter. In fact, we may differ on matters of politics. But there should be a fundamental agreement with regard to the need for introducing reforms into our great country, which will make our civilization more progressive and more advanced. That should be our common ground of approach. Those who are following the existing practices, those who are abiding by the provisions of the existing laws are not retrograde. The tragedy is that many of the supporters of the Bill, who have been carried away by their notions of so-called progress and advance, in their exuberance think that what they think is the last word on the subject, that they represent progress and the others are retrograde. That is very unfortunate. We should see the other man's point of view, the point of view of the man who believes in the existing ideology, unless it can be pointed out that something is happening in the society which is absolutely rotten, immoral, backward.

If that could be pointed out, I am at one with Dr. Ambedkar and those who want to introduce reforms. But, if it is a mere difference of opinion, a mere difference in outlook, and you get whatever you want for those who share your point of view, why then do you force your opinions on millions of others, who do not share your view? That is a point of view which I would very strongly urge before the Law Minister and Government. If I had given you a formula which indicated an abandonment of the provisions of the Code for those who believe in it, you can blame me. But, I wish you godspeed; go ahead; do whatever you like for those people who believe in the ideology which you are preaching here. But, in respect of others who and whose forefathers had proceeded in accordance with the old traditions and who are no less patriotic Indians than anyone who is sponsoring this Bill, why do you force your opinions on them?

Talking of divorce, has the law of divorce solved all social problems in countries where the system of divorce is now in existence? I have been going through some … recent books on sociology. People are perturbed, because this is a complex human problem. The world has not found a solution to these problems. Those who have taken to the system of divorce, their number is leaping up. Do they find peace? Have they found happiness? On the other hand, new problems have come up. Read some of the latest books on psychoanalysis. There, it is clearly pointed out that many of the evils which face the Western countries are due to the maladjustment of the sexes. These are complex problems. Why blindly copy something from the West because some people from some part of the world have come and told you that you are backward unless you adopt this? If there are forward people in this country, who believe in this ideology, give them a long rope, sufficiently long, so that they may hang themselves. But, do not interfere with others who have found a solution of their problems through different doors altogether.

So far as monogamy is concerned, I shall support it with one reservation. Make it applicable to all the citizens of India. It is not a question that monogamy is good for the Hindus, and monogamy is not good for others. Stand for one social doctrine. If you believe that monogamy as a social system is the best that India should have, then, do not try to look at it through the Hindu door: look at it through the human door and make it applicable to all. Behave like a secular State at least in this instance. Take courage in both hands and say that monogamy will be made applicable to all citizens of India. If you cannot do it, do not do it for one section alone ... We swear by statistics, either real or manufactured ... I wanted to know how many people in India have been marrying ... a second wife when the first is alive. The number is extremely small. It is really no problem. Already, on account of advanced views, society has adjusted itself and on account of economic conditions, general public censure, etc., this system has gone out. Why make a parade of this that you are introducing a great reform and legislating for this? If you accept it as a principle, apply it, as I said just now, to the whole of India.

So far as the Hindu Code Bill is concerned, I do not know what the decision is going to be. The Prime Minister has indicated that most likely we will not proceed with the rest of the Bill and time may not permit us to do so. I am prepared to make this offer. Pass the entire Hindu Code as it is: only make it optional. Those who want it can adopt it. I have spoken to representatives belonging to the extreme orthodox school of view: I have argued with them. Although there are some amongst them who are against the passing of any such Bill whatsoever, they also realize that just as they claim to think for themselves, others also must have the liberty to do so for themselves and for their future. That would be a splendid beginning. I am prepared to admit, however much there may be opposition to the Code, that this represents a marvellous piece of work on the part of Dr. Ambedkar and those who have been associated with him. I am quite prepared to admit that this is a most thorny subject and he has gone through the matter with as much ability as anyone could have. For that, if he is prepared to accept an honorary degree to be conferred by Parliament, we are prepared to confer a degree on Dr. Ambedkar.

But, if you look upon it as a measure which has to be pushed down the throat of millions of Hindus who are opposed to it, I say that you will not be doing a service to the people of India. The only way in which you can proceed even at this late stage is this. Let us not quarrel amongst ourselves; let us agree to differ on this fundamental issue. If you are prepared to point out that there are certain matters which are immediately anti-social, or corroding into the very life of Hindu society, let us agree to make such provisions compulsory if there are any. Otherwise, this new great structure which you have prepared, keep it there for a few years and say that anyone, whether a Hindu or not, any Indian citizen, who desires to accept it can make a declaration, and the provisions regarding marriage or divorce or property, whatever it is, will be applicable to such selectors. That would be the beginning of a great era. For after all, who is going to decide ultimately? Your elections are coming. You then go forward. As the Prime Minister has said, his sweeping wind will come and blow away all opponents and … yes, the whirlwind will come. Let the whirlwind come with regard to the provisions of the Hindu Code Bill. Let them go and convince the people and tell them that they are not forcing it on them. Let them say, 'We give you the option. Here is a heaven we have created. Come into this heaven and attain moksha.' Go and explain to the people, and if they feel that it is really such a heaven … they will come and take it, and take it with open hearts. There will be ample time.

After all, Hindu civilization has existed for thousands of years, in spite of onslaughts from various quarters, cultural, political and economic invasions and so on. We have survived all that. And we are now a free country, and we propose to survive, and survive with a much more glorious future that we had attained in the past. But when you introduce social reforms, in such a vast country as this, where opinions differ, where attitudes differ and where ideologies differ, then the only way in which you can do it is to go at a slow pace. I am not asking you to abandon principles which you believe to be true. I am not asking that for the time being. But please go and convince the people, the Hindu people who still claim to live under canons and codes which are in no way inferior to those existing in any other part of the world. Give them scope to choose for themselves. That is my appeal to the House and to Government and I hope that appeal will be heeded to.

SEETA PARMANAND

(Rajya Sabha: Madhya Pradesh)

Rajya Sabha: 11 March 1954

Hindu Marriage and Divorce Bill, 1952[2]

Mr. Speaker, Sir, I am going to attempt to speak on this Bill in Hindi today because it is being said this is an attempt by educated women to force this Bill on their uneducated sisters. By expressing such sympathy for these women, I don't know whom they hope to reward. By speaking in Hindi, I hope that they will be able to understand what I am trying to say. I know my Hindi may sometimes lack clarity, and I shall experience some difficulty, but when I do so, I shall use English.

… this Bill has been placed on the House agenda after a long time, in fact after two years. It has been brought suddenly, at a time when there was no other agenda before the House … So those who are saying that this is a matter for celebration … that is not a fact.

---

[2] Editor's note: Original speech in bilingual. Partial translation by the editor.

It is being said that there is no need for a Hindu Code, especially as the Special Marriage Bill has been brought, and therefore, there is no necessity for it. But the Hindu Marriage Bill which is contained within the Hindu Code is needed by those Hindus who do not wish to get married under the Special Marriage Bill – they require a provision under which they can have a religious marriage, something that does not exist now. The second thing that is being said is that those who are already married may take undue advantage by registering their marriage under the Special Marriage Act. In reply to this, I say that getting one's marriage registered under the Special Marriage Act does not depend on the wishes of one of the two parties. Only if both husband and wife wish for it, it can happen – if the man does not want it, how can it happen?

Our Law Minister gave us some history of the Bill. I also wish to remind you of something. In 1927, the All India Women's Conference began efforts to improve the condition of women. Through Dr Deshmukh, they sought to bring back the Hindu Women's Right to Property Act on the agenda. When the Central Government raised this question in the Assembly, then it was decided that other reform-oriented, women-related legislation – connected to the Hindu Women's Right to Property Act – would also be brought. After that, the Shri Santhanam Hindu Law of Inheritance (Amendment) Bill was brought. Dr Deshmukh, created a committee for the Hindu Women's Right to Property Act. At that time, people began to feel that a system should be created through which there should first be reforms within Hindu women's right of succession, and then marriage laws should be incorporated in that … even at that time we felt that till the Hindu Succession Act was amended, a Hindu marriage law should not be attempted.

Yesterday, Shri Kishan Chand, who is a member from Hyderabad, expressed many of his views: I am in agreement with only one of his views. As for the rest, I shall respond to them later. In 1941, when the Rao committee report was made public in the Provisional Parliament, only four of its clauses were passed. This time, the Law Minister is saying … that he will create a system through which this Bill will be brought expeditiously. But the way he is saying, it appears that it will take even longer to pass it. Two years have gone by and the progress has been so good that a small portion in it relating to Hindu marriage is now coming up. Now that small portion is heading to a Joint Select Committee. And now the third budget session has arrived. It isn't that as soon as you accept the idea of a Joint Select Committee, its findings will be ready: in the other House too, time has to be found to move a motion there on this subject, time for a discussion must be found and then after that, the Joint Select Committee will begin its meetings, and after that, its report will be tabled. So what will happen in the end?

I think that an opportunity to bring this Hindu Marriage and Divorce Bill to the House will come only in the next session – August to November. As for the Succession Bill, though it is ready, it is still under consideration of the Union Cabinet, and it is learnt that it will be discussed in the inter-session period and then even be put to seek public opinion on it ... this Bill has been before the public for about 10 years now ... from 1941, no perhaps from 1937 ... So I feel it necessary to say ... that when the Law Minister moves the Motion for the Succession Bill, he won't feel the need to spend excessive time on gauging public opinion.

I wish to say that if I speak in English, I will take less time.

Mr. Deputy Chairman, this is the occasion when that argument has to be advanced. I fear I am again in the same boat about the relevancy of this question. I thought I would be in a happy position today that I would not be once again asked not to proceed with a particular argument. Only by proceeding further, I can show the relevance of the whole question.

I really think that, if I were not to mention this point now, I would not have another opportunity to do so. As you know, when a motion for any Government Bill is considered, it is already a motion made, and it is not open to a Member, particularly to a Government party member, to make any amendment. So, unless I make that submission now, it would be too late, when the occasion comes to send it for circulation because with regard to expediting this Bill we have made representations to different authorities and the result has not been very helpful. It is absolutely necessary, therefore, that the whole House should be taken into confidence about the possible fate of this Bill as a whole, as I fear extravagance of time would retard the progress of the Bill. I would very soon read out a letter which I have received from the All India Women's Conference.

I think I must now keep my word and continue my speech in Hindi.

Many of my brothers are opposing the Hindu Code and are asking why it is being brought. It will only create turmoil in society. No one has the right to say anything about religion. People who put forward this 'religion in danger' argument, I don't know how to describe them in Hindi, but in Marathi such people are described as '*dharam martand*'. I want to ask such people who say they believe in Sanatan Dharam, how far do they observe its tenets in their daily lives? They say no one has the right to interfere in their religion, but I want to know how far these believers of Sanatan Dharam observe the Vanaprastha ashram (Vānaprastha, part of the Vedic ashrama system, starts when a person hands over household responsibilities to the next generation, takes an advisory role, and gradually withdraws from the world)?

Even when they touch 50, they are not willing to accept monogamy; they still wish to embark on another marriage. Within 13 days of the death of a wife, they are ready to marry again. Do they participate in sandhya vandanam, poojan and havan? Where are they observing the rituals and behaviour connected to the caste they belong to? Are such people not just being sanctimonious when they keep shouting slogans in favour of Hinduism? I can give several such examples but I don't wish to get stuck in a controversy … People who talk like this, wear saffron and go among the people to try and influence them through false propaganda, try to influence uneducated people, take the cover of religion to do bad things and try and fool the simple folk of this country through their talk … they fly by plane and wear saffron to fool rich people into parting with their money with which they create the wrong perceptions. What we see in society is that religion is in a pathetic condition. Many Hindu temples are in a worse condition than Muslim mosques, Christian churches and Sikh gurdwaras. Is it right that the temples belonging to the majority community should be in such a pathetic condition? Should not those proud of their religion not repair these structures? Everybody knows how the monasteries, of which Shri Shankaracharya is the head, have money that is spent on them. All of you know what work is done for the welfare of people in these monasteries, how they are administered. When a plan is placed before Sri Shankaracharya on the work that can be done by the monasteries, it is possible to seek additional help from the government. In this connection, two or three conferences were held, but there were no results. The people there did not express any sympathy for this scheme … There, the discussions were limited largely to religion, and were of a narrow and constricted nature. They are in a state of religious crisis not because of the Hindu Code; they are in a state of crisis because of many acts of laxity, for mistakes committed over the years.

The second issue I wish to take up is that of codification. Some of our brothers here say that right now Hindus are in a majority, the Congress is in a majority, and so we are being forced to accept such a Bill. It is true that the Hindu community is today in a majority, that it is in a majority in Parliament, it has an old culture which it wishes to present before the country as an example, and through which everyone gets the same justice and the same rights. Women are included in this. Let me also tell you … that it is necessary to have unity in Hindu society to create one law, and a law under which men and women are given equal rights. If we can initiate such a reform for Hindu women, then we will put our entire strength behind the creation of a civil code. Let me tell you this is not a battle that one class can engage in. We need everyone's help; only then can we reach our goal.

For such a task we need courageous men like the late Sardar Patel. When he spoke of anything that was in the national interest, he would never allow other considerations to come in the way such as the destruction of institutions. He did not bother about the critics. In that same spirit, we should pass this Bill. We should not bother about which clause is being passed and which negated, but rather how far the welfare of society as a whole can be advanced. My poor sisters, oppressed by legal offences, are weeping.

The second thing I wish to address is how codification will be possible through this Bill … ordinary people have to face great difficulties, while the lawyers prosper … the rules that have been accepted by the Privy Council are also causing great difficulties to the common man. Some people are gaining a great deal through such judgments. Many laws emerge through such judgments. Before the country gained independence … many Bills were passed and, at that time, the old protectors of our religion never opposed anything. Where was the pride in their religion? The practice of Sati ended in the old days; similarly, other practices that were proving to be deadly for Hindu society were ended through legislation. Today, the Bill that will be passed, similarly, will end some bad practices.

Those opposing this Bill are those who wish to fool people in the name of religion. This is not being opposed by uneducated people. Those who claim to be defenders of their religion are those who are seen opposing this. This is hypocrisy.

Before I examine the sections of this Bill, I want to say that these are the reasons for opposition to the Bill.

Now I will express my views about those four elements in the Bill which I support … One – separation, two – permanent alimony, three – divorce and four – monogamy …

In the twentieth century … it does not make much sense to talk about monogamy, but those opposing the Bill don't think so. They are not ready for it. Our Law Minister, while enumerating 13 points, had said that when a man is unable to have a child, then he embarks on a second marriage.

(In English) The way of deciding in olden days was that no issue meant only inability of the woman; the barrenness of the woman cannot now be taken for granted as a ground for not having an issue. A man can also be … impotent.

So if you consider this, then you will be able to decide whether a man should be allowed to undertake a second marriage or not, to produce a child, to produce a son. I want to say that even today there are many men who despite having a child, despite having a wife, embark on a second marriage. So please ponder over whether this option that society has given men is right or not.

The second question is about permanent alimony. Mr. Gupta and Mr. Kishan Chand have both said that after divorce, to expect permanent alimony is inappropriate. I want to tell you that the economic condition of women in India is very bad. This may not be in all classes, but in most classes of society, women are not able to earn their own livelihood … Under these conditions where they are unable to earn a living, it is imperative that they are given money for food and clothing. If they are not given money for food and clothing, if they are not given a share of the property of their fathers or husbands, then it will be an act of great cruelty. So … as a matter of course, permanent alimony should be given. When a law is made for divorce, provision should be made for the husband to give his wife money to live her life. The court can decide how much should be given and in what form it should be given. To enable the wife to afford her own expenses, the husband should give from his money, his property.

Dr P.C. Mitra (Member from Bihar): If the wife divorces her husband, must the husband still pay?

Dr Seeta Parmanand: The court will decide all that. Yesterday, my brother, Shri Pande, spoke. Yesterday, he told me that he does not wish to be addressed as Mr., so I will address him as Shri. So Shri Tarakeshwar Pande of Ballia said that because of this Bill, more women will start getting divorced. I am surprised at the way such thoughts enter the minds of these gentlemen. They should also understand that a woman also loves her children, she loves her home. And does she not have the same feelings for her husband? They are all valuable to her. Why would she then take advantage in this way? For those who have children, and a home, why would they seek a divorce without any reason just to gain independence? Men who think that women will just start seeking divorce are wrong. No matter what problems women face, they will not pursue such a course. They will continue to live in the way they have lived so far. Just because the Constitution has given us equal rights does not mean that we will misuse that.

Take this example. We have not asked for reserved seats. To then say that women are not our equal, and therefore don't deserve equal rights because they will misuse those rights if they are given them, does not seem correct to me … If such thoughts come to their minds, then I will ask: when they know that their religion is superior, that their culture is superior, then how do such low, degenerate thoughts enter their minds? … when something is sought for a group, then the thoughtful people in that society raise that demand. It is their duty to explain that demand and assume leadership to put it forward. If our women are being oppressed, then we will have to seek justice for them. There is no question of blaming these women. It is our duty, as it is that of our brothers, to explain these matters to those women who don't understand them. I want to say that intelligent women, and who have brothers, don't seek divorce. As far as possible, they keep what they have … in three states – Madras, Bombay and Baroda – this kind of divorce law is available, but in all these years, very few divorces have taken place there … in fact, the divorces that have taken place there are of people from other states, where there is no provision for divorce; they have gone there seeking a divorce … it is our duty to explain to those people – who don't understand … the concept of independence.

… the All India Women's Conference passed several resolutions. Recently, they had a meeting and I received this letter just yesterday in which it was written: (in English) 'The All India Women's Conference representing the women of the country urges upon you to see that the Hindu Code Bills are enacted in the

Parliament without undue delay. I am sure you will remember that a large number of your supporters – and, Sir, your supporters here too, in the electorates – were women in the last General Elections and their request to you is that by voting for these social reform measures, you will stand by them and see that women get a position of equality in Hindu society.'

I want to ask: why is this considered a Bill that only concerns women? When those in government were engaged in other tasks, when the men folk were occupied with other work, the women began to consider this question. But isn't it a fact that women alone do not live in a home. Men, too, live in that home, children, too, live there. So if it concerns one, it concerns the others, too. If a mother or sister is oppressed, then its impact is felt on everyone. Disharmony is created in that home. The peace is destroyed. So the work we are involved in will help everyone ...

... when you were fighting for independence, and then moved forward to taste that independence, then why do you want to deprive women from that? ...

We take the concept of divorce from Western countries. In those countries ... when the negative impact of divorce began to be felt, then in Britain, in 1850, the Divorce Commission was set up to see if the divorce laws could not be made more stringent. In the United States, when the incidence of divorce began to grow, a Reconciliation Committee was set up so that an attempt would be made to reconcile the husband and wife before they got to the stage of filing for divorce. What I am trying to say is that you can make changes in the law depending on your experience of it.

Yesterday, my brother, Shri Bhupesh Gupta, said that the two years given to conduct a divorce was too long, but my opinion is that it is not too long, nor is three years – prescribed in this Bill – too long. Much thought has been given to preventing cases of divorce coming up after marriage, and the divorce law has been crafted in a very simple way.

I want to say to – and, indeed, remind – those brothers who say there is not much of a public agitation for this law, that all my sisters imagined that after gaining Swarajya, they would secure all their rights without a fight, without any trouble. Our sisters did not have to fight for the vote like our Suffragette sisters in Britain ...

I am afraid that the fate of this Bill will be similar to that of the Hindu Code Bill in the Provisional Parliament ... from the time of Sarojini Naidu, from 1927, the Indian Women's Conference had ... demanded that there should be some reforms in this matter, and it be taken up in a concerted manner ... Will all these efforts go in vain? I want this government to ensure that this Bill is passed this year.

Now I want to make a few comments on what my brothers have said. One of my brothers who is from Ballia and whose name is Pande had a great deal to say on this Bill yesterday. I feel that our Prime Minister, Shri Jawaharlal Nehru, had already given all the answers in this House during the debate on the Hindu

Code. The way you spoke, it appeared as though the future of the Hindu religion depended entirely on you and no one else cared for it, but when the Prime Minister spoke, you were silenced ...

Shri Pande had said that nowhere in history were women granted primacy. He had clearly forgotten the role played by Smt. Vijaya Lakshmi Pandit. It is true that women are granted fewer rights and, therefore, the positions that will be given to them will be commensurate with that. So how will you find them in the first position? Historians, litterateurs, they are all men, aren't they! The people have chosen the Congress and sent them here ... It is a test for the Congress – how far they can improve the condition of women. The first step will have to be taken through legislation.

In the other House, Shri Deshpande posed a question about the elections that the Prime Minister will face: 'Will the Congress contest the next elections on the basis of the Hindu Code?' On this, the Prime Minister said that the elections would not be fought only on the basis of the Hindu Code Bill. But this is not correct ... The Prime Minister raised the issue of the Hindu Code several times during the elections. He fought his own election on this basis. When the Congress made this its motto, then it is not right to make it an excuse. When the Congress has accepted the principle of 'Satyamev Jayate' (the truth shall prevail), then it should honour its promise.

Many of our brothers want the Hindu Code, want sagotra marriages (that is within the same clan), and they don't oppose sapinda marriages (where the two share a common ancestor) but alongside, want to preserve the old structures, and preserve their old ideas. But I want to remind my brothers that in this Bill, there has been no objection raised to the Hindu religious system. Emphasizing the fast kept by Shri Ram's wife, my brother says that since Hindu wives continue to follow their husband's wishes even in heaven, how could they possibly divorce them? But I don't understand how people who talk like them then have four wives and, even after they go to heaven, expect arrangements will be made for them to have a series of wives? These kind of arguments, and the expectation of such benefits in birth after birth, is not good. Mr. Chairman, the scales that hang behind you are a reminder that everyone must be treated fairly and equally. One law for women and another for men, on which scales are such comparisons made? One had better throw away such scales. The truth must be the truth; otherwise you will be doing great injustice.

I was happy to see yesterday evening when this Bill was being debated, that there was a bigger turnout than during the day. In the debate yesterday, the women and men who participated in the debate all supported the Bill; only one member, Shri Pande, opposed it ... I am very happy that only one member opposed the Bill.

I want to request the Law Minister to stop according this Bill the step-motherly treatment that it is getting. If you do that, this Bill will not be passed, and the promise the government made to the people to ameliorate the condition of women will not be fulfilled. Instead of going by the personal opinion of the Law Minister on this Bill, it would be better if government policy on this is implemented ... He should be aware of the difficulties and pain that our sisters are going through. This is a piece of social legislation and the quicker it goes through the better. I have asked the Law Minister several times to declare a deadline for the passage of this Bill. If the Special Marriage Bill could be passed by the Select Committee in 10–15 sittings, then, in a far shorter time span, this Bill could have been passed by the Select Committee as it is less detailed ... When I meet my sisters they say that if you can't ... get this Bill passed, then what is the use of your being in Parliament?

So I beg the Law Minister to make an announcement on when this Bill will be passed ... Our laws say that if a Bill is passed by one House and it is not passed within six months in the other House, then it lapses. My solution is that a joint session of both Houses be called and then this Bill can surely be passed by mid-1955. I am sure that when the Law Minister rises to place his views, he will give us this assurance. Thank you.

2

Legalizing Abortion

In 1973, the Roe v Wade *judgement of the US Supreme Court gave women across America the right to have an abortion before the foetus is viable outside the womb, or before the 24–28-week mark. But on 24 June 2022, the US Supreme Court overturned the constitutional right to abortion.*

In India, abortion was legalized in 1971, with the enactment of the Medical Termination of Pregnancy (MTP) Act, 1971. Since then, it has been amended several times, each time to liberalize its provisions. For instance, in 2021, the law was amended to allow women to seek safe abortion services on grounds of contraceptive failure, an increase in gestation limit to 24 weeks for special categories of women, and to take the opinion of one abortion service provider for up to 20 weeks of gestation.

The speech excerpted here is from that first debate in 1971 that preceded the passage of India's first abortion law. Until that time, termination of pregnancy was permitted under Section 312 of the Indian Penal Code only to pregnant women who were in danger of losing their lives.

***Lakshmi Kantamma** was elected to the Lok Sabha from Khammam in united Andhra Pradesh in 1962, 1967 and 1971 as a member of the Indian National Congress. She opposed the imposition of Emergency in 1975 and joined the Janata Party in 1977. In a rich and varied political career that lasted over three decades, she focused her attention on the empowerment of women – campaigning to help permit women to sit for the IAS examination, fighting to secure the right to property for them, and battling to ensure that more women were allowed to contest elections. The opportunity to become a minister came to her several times but she refused every time, saying she would better serve the people from outside the corridors of power. She did, however, influence the politics of many front-ranking politicians, the most notable being former Prime Minister P.V. Narasimha Rao.*

Here, she makes a plea for women to be allowed 'to control their destiny, in an admirably brief speech.

LAKSHMI KANTAMMA

(Lok Sabha: Khammam)

Lok Sabha: 2 August 1971

Medical Termination of Pregnancy Bill

Mr. Deputy Speaker, Sir, I welcome the Medical Termination of Pregnancy Bill. This Bill was long overdue and many countries in the world have already passed the Bill legalizing abortion. Sir, in our epics we read that Vishwamitra and Menaka had a love affair and a child named Shakuntala was born. The child Shakuntala was thrown into the wilderness, and Kanva Maharishi saw the child, took the baby and tended it with a mother's affection …

Recently we read in the papers that a four-month pregnant British woman Member of Parliament called a press conference and announced that she is pregnant but refused to tell who was responsible for it, and said that 'my morals are my private affair', and her Party has agreed to give her a party ticket and support her in the next elections.

Sir, what I have been saying is neither have we Kanva Maharishi to tend to discarded children nor is our society so forward – we are politically forward but socially we are backward – so as to say like the British woman Member of Parliament that my morals are my private affair. Sir, it is not as though only unmarried women have been seeking abortion.

According to the Report, either of the UN or the Health Ministry, 87% to 95% of abortions are among married women due to economic, social or other causes. Sir, this is what the survey revealed. The survey was conducted in a number of institutions here and abroad. As some Members have already pointed out, either you legalize abortion or leave the fate of a woman in the hands of the quacks because the medical practitioners refuse to undertake this because of fear of illegality.

Then the women go to the quacks where they are treated. Somebody said they even treat their dogs very carefully but not the lives and body of a woman who goes to these quacks. So, mostly it is a play with death. Because of these quacks there is so much mishandling of the whole thing and there is a lot of bleeding. I myself know a number of instances where a woman having six to seven children, because she is so nervous of getting another baby, goes to these quacks and there she gets an abortion and later, when she goes home, there is no medical help and … the mother dies, leaving these six or seven children. Leave aside the baby that is to come, the children that are living are made destitute.

Our friend here, I am told, is an advocate and he has brought to the notice of the House certain lacunae in the Bill. I hope the Ministry will take note of this lacunae and see that it is amended properly. When you legalize abortion, you should have more facilities, because a number of people may be going to hospitals for seeking help. So, you should provide more facilities.

Some argue that children are a treasure. Nobody questions it. For the mother they are more so. But what can she do? Should she bring up a child and make it suffer? To the moralists, the words of Edris Rice-Wray, Director of the Maternal Health Association Clinic, Mexico City, is the answer. He says : 'I would like to challenge all those of good conscience to an act of imagination. Go in straight to spend 24 hours in a poor house with many children. Sleep on the floor with meagre food, cockroaches and rats around, lack of sanitary facilities and absence of privacy. Share the desperation of the mother who cannot provide enough for the child and yet carries another in her body. Do you think you can deny her the right to control her destiny?' With these words, I support the Bill.

3

The Shah Bano Case

In April 1985, a five-judge bench headed by the then Chief Justice Yeshwant Vishnu Chandrachud ruled that Muslim women, married under the Muslim Personal Law, were entitled to maintenance after divorce from their Muslim husbands. This judgement split the community down the middle, with conservative Muslims seeing it as an intrusion on the basic tenets of the faith. 'This judgement will go down in history as a gross and shocking departure from judicial tradition … They have totally outstepped their jurisdiction,' Gulam Mehmood Banatwalla, general secretary, Indian Union Muslim League, said at the time. Subsequently, as a Member of Parliament, he moved a Private Members' Bill, seeking amendment of Sections 125 and 127 of the Code of Criminal Procedure (CrPC), which would debar courts from granting maintenance to divorced Muslim women.

*During that debate, the then 34-year-old Union Minister of State for Home and Industry **Arif Mohammed Khan** said it was deceitful on the part of anyone to accept those parts of the Shariat which suited him, and reject those parts that enjoin certain responsibilities. Khan's defence – indirect though it was – of the Supreme Court judgement was made after consultation with Rajiv Gandhi, the then Prime Minister. That historic speech is excerpted here.*

But later, as conservative Muslims raised the pitch, Rajiv Gandhi lost his nerve: he first got a conservative Muslim colleague Ziaur Rahman Ansari to oppose the judgement in Parliament. And in 1986, brought a bill to negate the Supreme Court judgement, and placed Muslim Personal Law outside the ambit of the CrPC, following which Khan resigned from the Indian National Congress.

For the Congress, this flip-flop proved to be fatal: Rajiv Gandhi's progressive image took a hit, with criticism pouring in not just from the Hindu-Right wing but from liberals as well. At around the same time, a local judge in Faizabad ordered that the locks of the Babri Masjid be opened, throwing open the complex to the worship of Lord Ram. Many believed at the time that this had been done at the behest of a central minister close to Rajiv Gandhi – and was done as a 'balancing act'. Both proved disastrous to the Congress, not just in the 1989 general elections, but in the years to follow.

ARIF MOHAMMED KHAN

(Lok Sabha: Bahraich)

Lok Sabha: 23 August 1985

On the Shah Bano Case

... Shri Banatwalla's Bill is based on the judgement of the Supreme Court ... which Banatwalla Sahib and a number of other hon'ble Members feel ... is an assault on Muslim Personal Law ... A woman ... approached the Supreme Court seeking remedy under the Criminal Procedure Code. If under that provision the court considered that she had a right, the court might grant justice to her, and if the court considered that she had no right, the court might not grant that. And if the court considered that she was not covered by that provision, the court could give its opinion accordingly. However, the Supreme Court went a step further and gave its opinion about a uniform civil code also. But, since the Supreme Court has no power to frame a uniform civil code, it simply gave its opinion. After the Supreme Court judgement ... the Prime Minister made a statement clarifying the position on behalf of Government ... that meant we had rejected that opinion. There is, thus, no further scope for discussion on a uniform civil code.

... The point which needs consideration is whether the Supreme Court judgement affects the Shariat Law ...

The basic question is whether Islamic teachings, Islamic Law and the intention of Islamic Law are in any way affected by Sections 125 and 127 of the Criminal Procedure Code, and if so, the apprehension is well-founded in that regard. But ... nothing should be looked at emotionally ... time and again, it has been decreed that we should try to understand the Quran. (Interruptions.)

First ... the Criminal Procedure Code provides that a woman (verses) who has been divorced, but who is without any means of subsistence ... is not capable of making a living, has a right to a maintenance allowance from her former husband. From which husband? From the one who is competent and has means and resources. This provision of the Criminal Procedure Code does not apply indiscriminately to every husband and wife who are separated ... but rather ... only to those women who have no means of subsistence ...

... The question now is whether the Shariat Law enjoins any responsibility on the ex-husband in regard to a woman ... who has been divorced. This ... needs to be looked at from a juristic angle … when a woman has no means of subsistence … if she, under the secular laws of some other country, gets maintenance from her ex-husband, who has been compelled to do so, then the point is whether Islamic Law is affected by it …

… Whatever be my understanding … I shall depend on the Aayats (verses) of the Holy Quran … Now I come to the question of divorce, mehr and … maintenance … These cannot be seen in isolation. These should be viewed from the point of view of what duties are enjoined upon the husband in respect of a divorced woman … Mention has been made of mehr repeatedly … the Supreme Court judgement … seems to imply that in Islam, the position of a woman … (is) a degraded one. I have laid my hands on several authorities. I wanted to quote all those authorities which show the real status of a woman in Islam, the status of equality, which put an end to cruelty and excesses.

… I need not go into what practices were prevalent here, how after birth a female child was buried alive, how women had no rights, how Islam started a crusade against these practices and secured for women a status in society. The Prophet went to the extent of saying … that in the case of one who had a daughter, and who nurtured and brought her up well – this was up to three daughters – educated them, made them cultured and taught them knowledge of crafts, between him and Hell shall He stand, i.e. for him, the fires of Hell shall be forbidden … If we accept … that Islam does not recognize the rights of women, then we shall have to accept that all these things in the Shariat concerning women's rights should be done away with.

… let us know … from what angle Islam looks at women, how it has raised the status of women … fostered a sense of pride in having a daughter born in a society where they used to be buried and regarded as a shame upon the house. Where a woman, a girl, has been elevated to this position of prestige, we shall have to see whether this prestigious position is to obtain only for upbringing or it will continue for her entire life after marriage …

… with marriage is linked mehr, and mehr is obligatory under Muslim Law. The proposed Bill provides that where a sum has been paid under … personal law, women will have no right to ask for maintenance, but the amount of money so given will not be questioned in a court of law. Sait Sahib has agreed to a 'one time transaction', what Abdullah Yusuf Ali calls 'maintenance' … I say that if the 'one-time transaction' is such that the woman can keep body and soul together, have a roof over her head, can make both ends meet, then that woman would automatically be deprived of going to court, for, under the Criminal Procedure Code, only that woman can go to court to seek maintenance who has no means to support herself.

If a woman has been given a large sum as mehr, and if the husband says that a mehr of Rs. 5 lakhs has been given, which brings so much income annually, then how can such a woman be called a destitute? ... The provision in the Criminal Procedure Code is only for those women who are without any means which, I take it, may also include a case where she has no parents, perhaps no brother, too, and even if there be one, he is not prepared to support her ...

Coming to mehr: mehr has no relation to divorce ... in practice ... it came to be of two kinds – one, prompt dower, the other, deferred dower ... According to Islam, mehr is a sum of money or that property which the wife is entitled to receive from the husband in consideration of marriage; it has nothing whatsoever to do with divorce ... Mehr is confirmed by consummation of marriage ... a valid retirement (when the husband and wife are alone together under circumstances that present no legal, moral or physical impediment to marital intercourse) ... the death of the husband or the wife ...

The Encyclopaedia of Islam says that it belongs absolutely to the wife, it is her personal property. The idea behind it is that when she leaves her home to join another, she must have so much means 'which she can operate independently of her husband and in-laws'. She should have money at her disposal to meet her needs ... In this connection, it has been said: 'Mehr was used by the Prophets to ameliorate the position of a wife in Islam and it became a settlement for the wife.' Mr. Justice Mohamood defined mehr as: ' ... a sum of money or other property promised by the husband to be paid or delivered to the wife in consideration of the marriage, and even where no dower is expressly fixed or mentioned at the time of the marriage, something in law confers the right of dower on the wife.'

Even if mehr is not mentioned in the nikahnama,[3] the woman shall be entitled to mehr, according to her social and financial position ...

... The Quran is the basis of everything. (Interruptions.) Sir, this is the only difference in the entire approach. Shri Banatwalla ... I had said in the very beginning that this was a highly sensitive subject; I must speak on it; but I would not claim that there is an element of finality in what I say. I congratulate you on your continuing to be a spokesman.

... Sir, Abdullah Yusuf Ali in his translation in Aayat 4, Surah 4, says: 'And give the women on their marriage their Dower as a free gift, but if they of their own good pleasure, remit any part of it, take it and enjoy it – with right good cheer.'

... I mean to emphasize that mehr is out of respect ... a bridal gift, and has no relation with divorce at all; mehr is related to marriage only, it has no relation with divorce. If you associate it with divorce, then we would not be doing justice with this law ...

... Now, Sir ... I would like to come to the provision about divorce. As ... regards the Surahs (chapters) and Aayats dealing with divorce – Abdullah Yusuf

[3] Editor's translation: Marriage contract.

Ali's translation, which was also used by the Supreme Court … I would like to read out the translation of 228: 'Divorced women shall wait concerning themselves for three monthly periods. Nor is it lawful for them to hide what God hath created in their wombs if they have the faith in the God and the last day their husbands have the better right to take them back in that period if they wish reconciliation.' … Maulana Abdul Majid Dariyabadi says in this regard: 'And the divorced women shall keep themselves in waiting for three courses – nor is it allowed to them that they should conceal what Allah has created in their wombs if they believe in Allah and the last day their husbands are more entitled to their restoration during the same if they seek rectification.' Then it is further said: 'And if they resolve on a divorce, then they should not forget the fact of their having decided upon – suppression will not go unnoticed by God if he heareth and knoweth.'

… the first Aayat Sura-e-Talaq (says) … : 'When ye who divorce women, divorce them at their prescribed period and count accurately their prescribed period, and fear God or Lord and turn them not out of their houses, nor shall they themselves leave.'

This relates to the post-divorce period … the period of divorce should start from the period of purity. During this period, the husband and the wife should not live in isolation from each other, rather, they should have a satisfaction to come closer. At such a time, when you come to a conclusion that you cannot live together, that you cannot maintain the limits set by the Almighty … then what should be the course of divorce in such a situation? … it would be effective only after three months, when the divorce is pronounced in the third month. The method of divorce prevailing today, as also the method adopted by the gentleman whose spouse had knocked at the door of the Supreme Court, has not been envisaged in the Quran …

… the prevalent method of giving divorce by pronouncing 'talaq' thrice is not approved by the Quran. The method was not used in the days of the Prophet. It was also not prevalent during the days of Abu Siddiq … it is an irony of fate that Umar ibn al-Khaṭṭāb had permitted it only because people knew that pronouncing ṭalaq thrice would be treated as one count. Therefore, the husband divorced thrice. Thereafter, the woman got frightened and her rights were transferred to his own name. Then, as per the order, he knew that that it would be counted only as one, therefore, he re-established contact with the woman. He followed the style pronounced in the Quran – do not force out the woman, live with her in the same style, behave with her properly, for Allah may create such circumstances as may help you meet again. When the third month approaches, the husband pronounces divorce for the third time, and the divorce then would become effective.

Hazrat Umar ibn al-Khaṭṭāb made this provision to protect the rights of the woman, and to instil a feeling of fear in those using it as a threat, that if they pronounced talaq thrice, the divorce would become effective. But, with the passage of time, the provision made for the women was used by the menfolk for their own benefit … But I have never heard from any guardian of law that this method finds no mention in the Quran and, therefore, should be discarded … This is what the Commission says: 'It is essential that this divorce should be followed by two further pronouncements in two subsequent Tohars.'

If after keeping the wife for three months during the period of purity and during the period when both of them may have attraction also for each other, they arrive at the conclusion that they cannot live together, there is recourse to divorce. But to say talaq thrice in the same breath – I am not saying that it is un-Islamic … has not been envisaged in the Quran.

… As I have said earlier … there is no doubt about the sanctity of the position of woman, her status, and her rights, under the Islamic Law … Now if we have to discharge our responsibility towards her, what would be our attitude?

The translation of Surah 229 by Abdullah Yusuf is as follows: 'A return to each other is permissible even after divorce has been pronounced twice (in two successive months). Thereafter, two ways are open before the husbands – an honourable retention or a graceful parting (after the pronouncement of divorce for the third time in the third month). And it shall not be proper for you while divorcing your wives to take away anything out of what you have given them.'

What is the option after two months? There are two alternatives – one is an honourable retention and the other is a graceful parting. It is not that she should be kicked out of the house …

Now I come to Surah 231. The translation … which I am going to quote now is … the rendering of Maulana Azad. 'When you have divorced your wife and the period of waiting is nearing its end, you have only two ways open to you, either retain them with due propriety or walk from them with propriety.'

… what is the meaning of 'propriety' and 'kindness' … Maulana Majid Daryabadi speaks about that as follows (translation of Surah 229): 'Divorce is twice. Thereafter, either retain her honourably or release her kindly, and it is not allowed to take away all of what you have given to them.' … it has been stressed in Surah 229, that either retain her honourably or let her part gracefully. In Surah 231, stress has been laid on the same thing … 'This is for the second time that husbands are enjoined to behave towards their wives honourably and generously, whether they retain them or divorce them. The duty to be kind, fair and chivalrous towards the wife is not contingent on something else; it is unconditional.'

Even if the woman is at fault, even if … divorce is being sought for this reason, yet she should be treated with kind heartedness and this kind heartedness towards her is not conditional, it is obligatory … This is … because divorce in Islam has not been envisaged as a punishment … The concept of punishment is not there in the Holy Quran.

... Now I am coming to that Aayat ... which has been quoted by the Supreme Court ... Sait Sahib says that the Supreme Court has wrongly interpreted it. My ... purely personal view is that the Supreme Court need not have gone into it. A woman had gone to seek justice under the CrPC ... Had the Supreme Court shown some judicial discretion, such a big controversy would not have arisen ... Many judgements had been delivered earlier (by) Justice Khalid ... Justice Murtaza Fazl Ali, who referred to this case ... It is being said repeatedly that Muslim judges should have the right to decide such cases ... But since it is being said that this Aayat has been wrongly interpreted, I would like to quote the translation of Abdullah Yusuf All ... : 'For divorced women maintenance should be provided on a reasonable scale. This is a duty on the righteous.'

... Even this House will have no objection if a lump sum of money is deposited as a one-time transaction in her name with which she may be able to maintain herself for the rest of her life ... The basic point is that there should be no vagrancy. It is the duty of the State ... of the Government to see what arrangement has to be made for destitute women ... Even in an Islamic State, a murderer is sent to jail (because) ... he has committed a murder. But he is not starved in the jail. When arrangements are made for even a murderer, why not for a woman who might have been at fault? ...

... The basic point is not that a postman should bring a money order on the first of every month ... (but) that the woman who has no source of livelihood should not be thrown on the street. (Interruptions.)

... In this connection, I would quote ... the Pakistan Law Commission ... (Interruptions.) ... The question before the Commission was: 'Should it be open to a matrimonial and family law court when approached to lay down that a husband shall pay maintenance to the divorced wife for life or till her remarriage?'

... The Commission opined that such discretion should be vested in the matrimonial court. This ... Commission ... consisted of jurists as well as religious scholars ... (Interruptions.) I now come to 241. I have said so because the Commission is of the opinion that the Courts should have the right to see that women are not thrown on the street: 'And that a large number of middle-aged women who are being divorced without rhyme or reason should not be thrown on the streets without a roof over their heads and without any means of sustaining themselves and their children!'

... What more could the Quran say than that there shall be a provision for a woman? Similarly, Maulana Azad says, 'Although the provisions touching marriage and divorce have been already stated, the Quran takes occasion to re-emphasize that proper consideration should be shown to the divorced woman in every circumstance ... This call was based on the reason that she was comparatively weaker than man and her interests needed to be properly safeguarded.' ...

It has been said that it is a 'one time transaction'. I am very happy about 'one time transaction', otherwise, Sait Sahib, people are not agreeable even to 'one time transaction'. They are saying it is … the responsibility of the husband to maintain his wife only for the period of iddat … The period of iddat is three months and, in the case of pregnant women, the period … will be till delivery. I want to draw specifically the attention of Shri Banatwalla, through you, Sir, to marriages where iddat is not applicable.

… Sir, what does the Holy Quran say about marriages where … iddat does not apply in case of divorce? … In such marriages, where the provision of iddat does not apply, there should be no concept of gift … Now, I come to such marriages …

… This is the case where … mehr may not have been settled for the woman, where the marriage may not have been consummated, but the woman has been divorced. In such a case … that woman … may marry that very evening or the next day, there is no period of iddat … Maintenance has to be provided for that period. Even if she is not to wait, it has been ordained – 'benefit them'. The rich should give benefits according to his status, and the poor should provide benefits according to his means. Now, in the other cases, where iddat is not due, but mehr has been settled, what happens? In that case, Surah 2, Aayat 237, says: 'And if you divorce them before you have touched them but have already settled with them a settlement, then due from you is half of what you have settled, unless the wives forgo or he in whose hand is the wedding not forgoes and that you should forgo is higher to piety. And do not forget grace among yourselves, surely Allah is the beholder of what you do.' It was translated as: 'Present them with a gift in place of dower.'

It is where mehr has not been settled … No period of iddat is involved, but a provision of a gift has been made for her. (Interruptions.) The law declares that in such a case, half the dower fixed shall be paid by the man to the woman. It is in the case of a woman where the mehr was settled, but the marriage was not consummated and she was divorced … I want to tell you … what has been stated further. 'But it is open to the woman to remit the half due to her or to the man to remit the half which he is entitled to deduct and thus pay the whole.'

The word 'piety' has been used. The man has been instructed that half of whatever amount has been settled should be given. It is a different matter if a woman wants to forgo that, but it will be better for you if you make full payment. This is the provision: 'Him in whose hands is the marriage tie! According to Hanafi doctrine, this is the husband himself, who can dissolve the marriage. It, therefore, behoves him to be all the more liberal to the woman and pay her the full dower even if the marriage was not consummated.'

When even in the case of a marriage which has not been consummated, the husband has been ordained to be all the more liberal to the woman and to pay her the full mehr, then what will become of that woman who has been living with him for thirty years? What is the reason for being displeased with her? Such liberal provisions are there in this religion. It is not proper to distort this. The women were weak and exploited and used to leading a life of inferiority. It was the crusade of Islam to secure equal rights for all. Now, it is being directed against the teachings and spirit of Islam …

The question is to what extent we should follow Shariat. I do not think that Shariat allows us to continue to follow the Shariat in so far as rights are concerned and not follow it where it enjoins upon us to perform certain duties. How can we afford to shirk our duties? In the Holy Quran, it has been clearly mentioned in Surah 2, Aayat 81: 'And remember we took your covenant (to this effect). Shed no blood amongst you. Nor turn out your Own people from your homes; and this ye solemnly ratified, and to this ye can bear witness.'

Some agreement is violated and what happened thereafter? It has been mentioned: 'After this it is ye the same people, who stay among yourselves. And banish a party of you from their homes; assist the enemies against them, in guilt and rancour. And if they come to you …' This is the translation of the Holy Quran, not its commentary, which is very important.

'As captives, ye ransom them, though it was not lawful for you to banish them. Then is it only a part of the book that ye believe in, and to ye reject the rest?' What was the object of it? You follow Shariat to the extent it suits you and do not follow where it enjoins upon you duties. The Almighty is saying this through Rasul, who had broken some promise that he had made.

Just now I have said that the method of divorce which is being followed is not in the Shariat …

I look upon the Shariat with great respect. I think the CrPC can be changed and by changing it, those Mohammedan women can be deprived of their rights who do not have any means of livelihood and who cannot go to the courts, but nobody can change the Holy Quran. The Quran bestows this right on the women that they may lead a life of honour. Even Banatwalla Sahib cannot change the Quran. We have seen very difficult days in this country; we have faced grave consequences by using religion for political benefits … (Interruptions.) In the words of Maulana Azad, as a consequence of such politics, anxiety appeared on the faces of the people and their hearts became desolate. In spite of all the sentimental slogans, those who raised those slogans went elsewhere leaving the Mohammedans of India to their fate, considering them as orphans. There is a change in the atmosphere … today; conditions are improving … We are heading towards communal harmony in this country; we should not repeat that past which created bitterness, which caused harm, which broke hearts and created hatred. We have come a long way now and we should forget the past …

... The difference is that the slogans that have been raised, the type of speeches that have been made, the type of statements that are being given in the newspapers – all these are aimed at instigating religious sentiments ... if there are differences on any matter, then we should remember that there is scope for discussion. Somewhere, you may agree to our views and somewhere, we may agree to your views, but nobody should spoil the atmosphere by raising sentimental slogans and ... instigating religious sentiments. That will benefit neither the country nor any community.

4

Triple Talaq

Former president of the All India Mahila Congress, ***Sushmita Dev*** *is a second-generation politician, and the daughter of Santosh Mohan Dev, a former Union Minister, and Bithika Dev, a former MLA of the Assam assembly. Despite her political pedigree, and her credentials as a barrister, Dev came up the political ladder gradually, first contesting local elections, then assembly polls and finally parliamentary elections, winning on all three occasions.*

Dev, currently a Rajya Sabha member from the Trinamool Congress, was a Lok Sabha Member of Parliament from the Congress, representing Silchar in Assam at the time this speech was made in 2018.

Here, she opposes the Triple Talaq law brought in by the BJP government, on the grounds that what was 'clearly and purely a matter of civil jurisdiction', was being sought to be 'criminalized', and that far from empowering Muslim women, the law was only penalizing Muslim men.

SUSHMITA DEV

(Lok Sabha: Silchar)

Lok Sabha: 27 December 2018

Disapproval of Muslim Women (Protection of Rights on Marriage), Ordinance, 2018, and Muslim Women (Protection of Rights on Marriage) Bill, 2018

Madam Speaker, as always Shri Premachandran has spoken comprehensively on what are the legal and social issues that are connected to this Bill ... But I wish to say in a few words that if it is a question of the respect and dignity of women, then my party has no objection to this Bill. But we do object to those who have Ram on their lips and a knife under their arm. That is why it is imperative that this Bill be sent to a Parliamentary Joint Select Committee.

This Bill ... was introduced on December 28, 2017 ... During that debate, we raised certain objections which the hon'ble Law Minister, in his wisdom, feels he has met ... But we stand by that statement, and say that those apprehensions, those fears and those objections have not been met by the new amendments that have been brought in the 2018 Ordinance.

The first thing we had said in the Lok Sabha when this Bill was first debated in 2017, was that we oppose a matter, which is clearly and purely a matter of civil jurisdiction, being criminalized. We had stated at that time that criminalization of instant triple talaq goes against the very basis of the Supreme Court judgement of Shayara Bano. Let me explain as to why it is so. What is it that the Supreme Court has said? It said that the instant triple talaq is void, unconstitutional, discriminatory, and un-Islamic for the simple reason that it is a unilateral act on the part of the man without giving the woman any opportunity whatsoever to reconcile her marriage.

But I am surprised to see that, repeatedly, this Government states in the Statement of Objects and Reasons that by this Bill, and the Bill of 2017, the Government is acting at the behest of the Supreme Court judgement. I am pained to say that despite the fact that the Law Minister himself is a lawyer he has completely misread the Supreme Court judgement. In support of that I would like to point out that when he replied to my arguments last December, he categorically quoted the minority judgement where one Judge said that as per Article 25, it is not for the Court to review a practice which exists in Islam but for the Parliament to legislate. Nowhere in that 300-page judgement has the Court said that the instant triple talaq needs to be criminalized.

Madam, it is very easy to give a lecture on empowerment of Muslim women. Let me take this opportunity to say that it is not the first time that Parliament is legislating on the rights of Muslim women. We saw what happened after the 1985 case of Shah Bano. In 1986, when Shri Rajiv Gandhi was the Prime Minister of India, he introduced the Muslim Women (Protection of Rights on Divorce) Act, 1986.

Today another landmark judgement has come and another Government is seeking to pass a law which is talking about the rights of Muslim women on marriage.

Madam, I would like to point out here whether this Government sincerely believes in the empowerment of Muslim women. I don't need to go very far or all over India to look at the status of Muslim women. I look at Shah Bano and Shayara Bano. These two women will always be remembered by this country for bringing a matter to the Supreme Court which led to landmark decisions.

Madam, what is the Shah Bano case? She was being paid a maintenance of Rs 200 per month. While she was married, her husband stopped that maintenance. She invoked Section 125 of the CrPC and she asked that her maintenance be continued. How did her husband react? Her husband instantly issued a *talaqnama*[4] and gave her *mehr* and arrears and said that my duties are over.

Let us look at Shayara Bano. The hon'ble Law Minister keeps praising Shayara Bano. What is the history and life of Shayara Bano? She suffered from domestic violence for 15 years. Her husband tried to poison her. Her husband demanded dowry from her. Her husband did not let her meet her family members and took away the children.

Madam, Shayara Bano left her matrimonial home and went back to her parents' house. Her husband filed a case for restitution of conjugal rights in the Allahabad High Court. She opposed that. Madam, please understand that Shayara Bano opposed it. She said, 'I will not go back to my husband because I fear for my life. There is a threat to my life.' What did her husband do? In response to a civil jurisdiction case, he issued her a *talaqnama*.

What is this Government doing? Please learn from Shah Bano and Shayara Bano's cases. Today, what are you giving to the Muslim women in the name of empowerment? You are giving nothing but a criminal case. Will the husband reconcile? Let the hon'ble Law Minister answer that. You are talking about women's empowerment. You have spoken of respect for women and rights of women, but what I want to ask of this government is: how do you define 'subsistence', the word that you have used in this Act? What is the definition of subsistence? Today, there is no definition of subsistence in the Bill. If you look at the definition of the word in the Oxford Dictionary, it says, 'bare minimum resources by which a person can stay alive'. Today, what are you doing in the name of women's empowerment? You are giving the husband a right to subvert much greater rights owed to the women under the Domestic Violence Act of 2005.

Today, you are giving the Muslim husband, under this new Ordinance, an opportunity to say that I will not go under Section 125 of the CrPC, which the Shah Bano judgement gave and which the 1986 Act gave, by saying that I will give you only mere subsistence under this 2018 Bill.

Madam, even on the last occasion when we debated in the Lok Sabha, we had asked about the subsistence allowance for Muslim women. But you did not define it. Let me put it on record today, if anybody, any law in the history of this country has given a Muslim woman on divorce, the most progressive rights, it is the Act that Shri Rajiv Gandhiji, former Prime Minister of India, brought in 1986. I'm not saying this merely as a Congress MP, but I'm placing in the House what the Supreme Court has said.

---

[4] Editor's translation: Deed of divorce.

I quote the case of Danial Latifi of 2001. In that case, the Court has said, not once but repeatedly, that the 1986 Act that followed the Shah Bano judgement of 1985, is not only Constitutional, but it gives a divorced woman the right to maintenance for her entire lifetime and, not only that, it is time-bound. It must be given within three months.

Madam, I request the Law Minister to take a leaf from Rajivji's legislation and define 'subsistence' ... Tell the Muslim women, tell Shayara Bano and tell Shah Bano that she will not be stuck with Rs. 175 or Rs. 200 a month. What is the definition of 'subsistence', there is absolutely no explanation for that.

Madam, last but not the least, in Muslim Law, all of us know, and the hon'ble Law Minister knows as he himself is a lawyer, that in Muslim Law, a marriage is a contract just like in other laws. But today, when a contract is broken, it is a civil wrong. I would like to ask the hon'ble Law Minister that today he is saying that if a man pronounces instant triple talaq, it is a criminal offence.

I draw the attention of the hon'ble Law Minister to the Hindu Marriage Act, 1955, which governs Hindus, Sikhs, Buddhists and Jains. I draw the attention of the hon'ble Minister to the Divorce Act, 1869, which governs Christians. I draw his attention to the Parsi Marriage Act and Divorce Act, 1936, and ask him that what happens to a deserted woman in every other religion, is that she has a right to file for divorce. The minimum waiting period is two years of desertion, thereafter, she can file for divorce or if she wants any immediate relief, she has to file for restitution of conjugal rights.

What is different here is that, today, when it comes to a Muslim male, the Government is criminalizing it. This law is not about empowering a Muslim woman but penalizing a Muslim man. If this Government is true to its commitment to *'Beti Bachao, Beti Padhao'*[5], please tell us what this Bill will give Shayara Bano. It will give her nothing. It will give her a criminal case in the Magistrate's Court, that is all. All they are doing is they are keeping Shayara Bano married to her husband, the same husband who filed for restitution of conjugal rights and Shayara Bano opposed it and refused to go back to her husband. Today, all you are doing is you are giving her a criminal proceeding without any definition of subsistence allowance whatsoever.

Madam, I want to ask Shri Ravi Shankar Prasadji, if in Gujarat a woman's husband deserts her and she files a petition against him either in the High Court or Supreme Court, pleading that it be considered a criminal offence as he has deserted me, what will Ravi Shankar Prasadji do? He won't do it ... because he understands that what is civil is civil and what is criminal is criminal. It is absolutely imperative, Madam. If this Government truly believes in empowerment of Muslim women,

[5] Editor's translation: Save the daughter, educate the daughter.

let this Bill go to the appropriate committee, listen to the stakeholders, listen to the people/women who are impacted, listen to the men who will be impacted, listen to the voices of the people. All of us who sit here, we have no right to play messiah. We are the representatives of the people and we must listen to the people. I urge the Government and I urge the hon'ble Law Minister to do the right thing, send it to the appropriate committee, failing which this Bill should be withdrawn. We oppose the criminalization of triple talaq and we will support every right to subsistence allowance, and every other right that will empower not only Muslim women but every woman in the country.

5

Self-Immolation

A member of the Communist Party of India (CPI), the diminutive but feisty ***Geeta Mukherjee****, was a four-time MLA from Panskura Purba (1967 to 1977) and a Lok Sabha MP a record seven times from Panskura (1980 to 2000) in West Bengal. She was also the president of the National Federation of Indian Women, the women's wing of the CPI, and led the demand for reservation of seats for women in the central and state legislatures.*

This impassioned speech was delivered by Mukherjee during the debate on the Commission of Sati (Prevention) Bill, 1987, shortly after a young widow, Roop Kanwar, was forced to commit sati, by climbing on to the pyre of her dead husband. This was followed by the 'glorification' of that act at a chunari ceremony in Deorala, Rajasthan. Here, she places the incident in the larger context of growing religious fundamentalism and stresses that ending the barbaric practice of forced self-immolation – criminalized in the nineteenth century – should not merely be viewed as a move to uphold women's rights, but as an effort to validate 'our national honour … our humanitarian existence as a nation'.

GEETA MUKHERJEE

(Lok Sabha: Panskura)

Lok Sabha: 12 November 1987

The Commission of Sati (Prevention) Bill, 1987

Sir, before I participate in the debate proper, allow me to remove one piece of disinformation which has been given to the House by one hon'ble Member with regard to the West Bengal Government's attitude, etc. Sir, I would like to tell you here that on the 11th of November, a news item appeared in … *Aajkal*, which says that there are some temples organized by people who hail from Rajasthan, and in one such temple, a mela is being contemplated … where this glorification of sati might take place.

… He should have been here and he should have had the political sagacity to quote the same newspaper of today which clearly says that the West Bengal Chief Minister has said that in this mela, if it is held, we will not allow any glorification of sati, and he has instructed the Commissioner of Police of Calcutta to take necessary action. He has said clearly that we do not want to interfere in anybody's religious function … but no glorification of sati in the name of religion will be allowed in any such mela, and if that is done, proper steps will be taken. Anybody would think that those who are really concerned about this evil practice, would put the whole truth in the House. For everybody's reference, I would like to present, with your permission, the same paper to the Minister.

… Honestly speaking, I have to hang my head in shame as an Indian woman, but no less as an Indian citizen. I really never thought – I do not know why – that … this House will have to debate the glorification of sati, burning of a young widow in the name of sati that everybody has mentioned – after 150 years of Raja Ram Mohan Roy. Since I have been in this House, I have taken part in many debates, as you know, on women's rights. I was one of those who always appealed to the people to rise above political partisanship on such questions.

Here, today … I would like to make a few observations on this question … what is all this nonsensical debate about whether she was willing or she was forced? Who cannot understand that in the society that we are in, where women have an inferior status, there this question is irrelevant, though in this case we know from various sources that this girl was forced, this girl was drunk. Is it not a fact that in those societies widows are made common property of the other male members of the household? … it has happened several times that … innocent widows are violated by family members, and later, when they conceive, then … the servant … is accused of being in collusion to produce the child. This is the atmosphere which we still have in this country. Do you not know that? In such a situation, what is this debate about voluntary or involuntary? All such acts are involuntary, basically; it cannot be otherwise. That is the first action that all of us have to admit and proceed from there.

… What has anguished me is not only the incident in Deorala, but the most distressing thing is – this has really taken this whole thing to qualitatively new heights than any other debate we have had earlier on the women rights' question – that there is an aggressive move for defending this heinous custom … I fully support Saifu (Saifuddin Choudhury) when he says that this is a new dimension. And it is also true that this dimension tortured us during the Muslim Women's

Bill. This is most disturbing. Anyone in this House having any conscience should answer why it is so. We cannot escape this. Let alone the Deorala incident, today itself in Delhi, after thirteen years of married life, one woman has been killed for dowry. So, Sir, if that is A, this is Z – the zenith of the same line. But what is new is this glorification, and its defence in the name of religion. What is new is religious fundamentalism showing its various facets, endangering our country.

This is not a question of women's rights only, to my mind; as a citizen, it is a question of our national integrity, our national honour, our humanitarian existence as a nation. Therefore, this incident should raise us to a different height to fight it out.

Now Sir, a question has been raised of rising above political partisanship. I started by saying that in many debates – they are on record – whenever I have participated in such a discussion, I have always appealed to all our hon'ble colleagues across parties to join hands. I do the same even today. But in the name of political non-partisanship, I cannot dismiss the question of political responsibility because one cannot rise above partisan politics unless one discharges the supreme political responsibility towards our Constitution, towards humanism, towards the dignity of our women. With that end in view, I will raise a few questions. If that hurts … friends on the opposite side, with folded hands, I shall ask them to be patient and search their minds.

We Communists believe in criticism and self-criticism. Before I go in for anybody's criticism, I, for myself, would go in for a little self-criticism. Not on Deorala … but thinking back, when some two, three years back, there was one incident of sati, we did protest. But we thought that that was an isolated incident. It did not occur to me at least that this was not an isolated incident; it was the forerunner of a very big thing. And there I criticized myself that we were not … aware that this is going to come … We did put up a file but that was not taken to its logical limit …

At the same time, I would like humbly to state that as soon as the Deorala incident took place, our party's General Secretaries themselves immediately came out with absolute condemnation of the event. That should also be put on record. But that does not absolve me from my self-criticism which I have offered here. But I … find that on the 4th, the Deorala incident took place, and on the 6th itself, three women's organizations of Rajasthan went to see the Rajasthan Chief Minister … so that this Chunari thing could be stopped. Those women's representatives said that the Rajasthan Chief Minister dismissed them in less than two minutes, and then they contacted the SP of Sikar.

Is it … Sir, a responsible political attitude, if I may ask? Will that be challenged as political partisanship? There are many more things … I am really shocked to read in the *Times of India* that yesterday, in the Rajasthan Assembly, after this Ordinance was debated in the Assembly, this was carried with a voice vote. But during the debate, there were two Divisions. Naturally, there were some clauses. But the *Times of India* stated that apparently 34 MLAs violated the whip at the time of the first Division in the House, and 42 did so during the Second Division. It says that the Assembly had 115 Members and, out of them, the Opposition Members were 85 and the rest were Congressmen.

Now, how did so many Members violate the whip? I tried to understand on what clauses there were Divisions in the Assembly. I could not find out. The Rajasthan Assembly Speaker was here. I asked him to tell me the position. But he could not tell me. But I understand that the clause was on the question of shifting the onus of the responsibility of proof on the accused – the question of abetment to sati. I implore the House to recall the debate here in this House on this very question of shifting the question of onus of the responsibility of proof. We, the women, had voiced our opinion in the Select Committee and here also that the onus of responsibility of such social crimes as rape and dowry murder should shift to the accused, and this House did agree with us ultimately, but not all our suggestions were taken. So, Sir, this is a very important question and the political responsibility is this that so many violated the whip. Further, the *Times of India* says that during the second Division, this is what happened. Shri Naresh Chaturvediji was arriving at the Jaipur Airport and the MLAs went to receive him. Which is to be given priority, receiving Naresh Chaturvedi, or being present in the Assembly, when the Bill was being discussed? …

Sir, standing here even at this late hour, we have some reservations about the Rajasthan Ordinance. We want to improve it. But whatever has been passed in the Assembly has this political will. Sir, with this anguish in mind, I would say … that the nation expects an explanation from our young Prime Minister. Why did he not open his mouth after 20 days of this incident? Sir, I am a mother and I am here to voice my political feelings. He is a young man and everybody might have noted that his nature has been generally not that biting, but politically 'Yes'. But really even then I feel that this is absolutely unbecoming of the leader of the House who has to give a lead to the country to fight against such things … (we) must be really honest and above all petty political considerations. I am yet to hear any self-criticism from him on this score. In the beginning, I said that he should have been present here because when such a thing is debated, the leader of the House should be present … There is no use … crying at the top of his voice without any fight or result. I would like to ask whether there is any political response to this question. Prof. Madhu Dandavate professed something and I fully appreciate and wish that we will be able to do something in this direction with all our might, with all the Opposition parties getting together. I do not want to speak about the BJP whose role is well known. In the morning … they give lectures, and in the evening inside their houses, they practise another thing. This kind of political duplicity will not do much. They should know that this has direct relationship with religious fundamentalism which is being pursued. Therefore, I would say that the question of political responsibility has to be shared squarely.

... As far as Dandavateji himself is concerned, I have nothing to say. He is all right. But in his party, there are very many people ... (Interruptions.) ... The Ruling Party must really – it is not a question of biting, it is a question of hand on heart; search your heart and see what you can do. What you are doing in Rajasthan is not only inadequate, it is duplicity. It is not only a political failure, but political duplicity. It will not carry anybody behind you if you really say this is religious fundamentalism. And I also said during the Muslim Women's Bill that capitulation started in the social sphere and this has gone forth ...

... Sir, naturally we alone can be consistently relevant on this question because we can take a purely secular stand, irrespective of all religious fundamentalist preaching. Religion is a private affair, but this fundamentalist preaching ... is really destroying our country. Can this sati episode be isolated from the communal riots that are taking place today? Can this sati episode be isolated from extremism? I mean Khalistan extremism that is raising its head today? Can this sati incident be isolated from many such other factors today which are threatening to destroy ... national integration? To my mind it cannot ...

In one way, I am glad that our women's rights question has really opened your eyes, where you either have to defend women's rights or go down in history for ... dismembering our country, for disintegrating our country. That is the challenge which we are facing ... to face that challenge, we have to take a specific stand in each sphere, in the women's rights sphere, in the political sphere, in the legislative sphere, in the education sphere, and in the mass campaign sphere ... all political leaders of consequence will have to search their hearts, and be self-critical, and admit before the nation if they have failed on any count. This is one. Secondly, Sir, the Rajasthan Government will have to be dismissed on that score not because it is a Congress Government, that is not my contention, but (because of) ... the way they have dealt with (this episode). Since many ... earlier speakers have already referred to it at length, I am not going in for substantive proof because that has been amply proved ...

Then, Sir, all political parties will have to expel such activists or leaders who are (defending) ... sati wherever they are, and I fully support the contention that while giving nomination, they will have to be stopped and asked to get out ...

Then, Sir, the Central law should be definitely promulgated. Now, here is the question that if there was no law, how could the Rajasthan Government do anything? Already, of course, under Sections 306 and 309 of the IPC, it could have been dealt with. Even then, Sir, they cannot absolve themselves of their responsibility because this law was not there. The law of the land, the Constitution, is already there. They could have taken action if they so liked. Even then, Sir, on such an occasion a specific law again has to be enacted even (though) the Penal Code covers these things. Therefore, this law has to be Centrally administered.

In the ordinance, one thing is very funny. About the sati glorification, the … Deorala Mandir and the Rs. 50 lakhs … that this trust has amassed cannot be touched … Why? … This is one of the challenges before the nation. This fund must be confiscated … whatever law we may pass, that has to cover at least the latest incident. Otherwise, it is succumbing to the incident. A serious drive must be made for separation of religion from politics without which this evil cannot be stopped. All the necessary steps for ending discrimination against women must be examined and re-examined and taken. Here, I would fully support Mr. V.C. Jain about a widow's pension. But all the social laws which we have passed are not being implemented … Women should be protected. Economically, women's status must be changed …

… Last, but not the least, with a self-critical attitude, the … secular forces have to start a frontal war against this kind of religious fundamentalism. That is the least we can do to avenge the death of Roop Kanwar who is now the epitome of the inferior status of womanhood that prevails in our country. It is a … national shame which we have to undo, if we want to do anything. This should be done in right earnest. With these words, I hope, everybody will take proper steps to see that such things do not recur.

6

Not Ready to Empower Women

In 1996, the short-lived United Front-led government with H.D. Deve Gowda as the Prime Minister, introduced the 81st Constitution (Amendment) Bill to ensure that a third of the seats in Parliament and the legislative assemblies would be reserved for women. At that time, the Indian National Congress, the BJP and the Left parties had publicly announced that they would support the Bill. In the ensuing years, regardless of which party – or combination of parties – was in power, the official line of these parties did not change. Between them, they have also always commanded the numbers to get a Constitution Amendment Bill – that requires two-thirds of those present and voting – through.

The Bill almost went through when, under the Congress-led United Progressive Alliance government, it got through the Rajya Sabha on 9 March 2010, after two days of high drama that saw suspension of seven MPs who violently disrupted the proceedings. The Constitution (108th Amendment) Bill, pushed by the government despite the threat of withdrawal of support by the Samajwadi Party and the Rashtriya Janata Dal, was passed by a two-thirds majority, a day after it was moved in the House for consideration but could not be taken up because of unruly scenes. The Bill subsequently lapsed.

Finally, 27 years later, on 21 September 2023, the Constitution (One Hundred and Sixth Amendment) Bill was passed at a special session of Parliament. For the Modi government, which is in power, it was a feather in the cap as the Bill had been hanging for close to three decades.

Why did the process take so long? It was primarily because male MPs, cutting across party lines and who still dominate the Lok Sabha, felt that if 33 per cent of the seats were set aside for women, it would shrink their share. My observation is based on hundreds of conversations that I have had with male MPs since 1996, when the Bill was first moved. The argument that MPs from the Other Backward Classes (OBCs) put forward – that only upper-caste, city-educated, short-haired women would be given tickets – is specious.

Everyone knows that tickets are distributed largely on the basis of the caste composition of constituencies – a party that wishes to field an OBC male candidate, will look for a female OBC candidate if the seat is reserved. The bottom line is: reserving a third of the seats would signal a shift in power, something male MPs found hard to come to terms with.

Indeed, the suspicions that ***Sushma Swaraj*** *– possibly BJP's most significant woman leader, who was not just a powerful speaker, both in Hindi and English, but was at different times, chief minister of Delhi, union external affairs minister and leader of the Opposition – aired in her speech about the possibility of sabotage on the day the Bill was first moved was proven right several times over the years till 2023 when the Bill was finally passed. The increase in the number of women MPs – without reservation – in these 27 years only shows how imperative the law is.*

In 1996, 7.37 per cent of the MPs in the Lok Sabha were women, numbering 40; in 2019, the most recent general elections before this Bill was passed, that figure climbed only to 14 per cent or 78 members.

SUSHMA SWARAJ

(Lok Sabha: South Delhi)

Lok Sabha: 12 September 1996

Eighty-First Constitution Amendment Bill

Mr. Speaker, Sir, the Eighty-First Constitution Amendment Bill has been put up by the hon'ble Law Minister in the House for discussion. I rise to heartily support this Bill on behalf of my party. Before I start the discussion, I, on behalf of all women of India would like to thank you ... It is a normal practice that Parliament passes Bills, but there are certain Bills which become milestones. Such Bills change the lifestyle of a particular section of society.

The 73rd, 74th and 81st Constitution Amendment Bills come in the category of such Bills which have become milestones. The 73rd and 74th Constitution Amendment Bills brought a revolutionary change in the life of women; they provide 33 per cent reservation for women in municipal corporations, municipalities and gram panchayats. The 81st Constitution Amendment Bill is going to provide 33 per cent reservation for women in the Lok Sabha and Legislative Assemblies of the States.

Mr. Speaker, Sir, it has been written in the objectives and reasons of this Bill that all leading political parties have given their consent to bring this Bill. I, therefore, would like to thank the leaders of all political parties for this. As far as the Bharatiya

Janata Party is concerned … in 1994, we included it in our national agenda. The national convention of our party was held in Vadodara. Our national party President himself had demanded there that women should be given 33 per cent reservation in Parliament and in the Legislative Assemblies of the States … It was an historic day when the BJP brought this issue on its national agenda. Afterwards, this issue became the main point in our election manifesto … the BJP Government could run only for 13 days but, at that time, in the message of the Prime Minister to the nation telecast on Doordarshan … the main issue was that if our Government lasted long, we would provide 33 per cent reservation to women …

Besides this, last Friday, our hon'ble leader, Shri Atal Bihari Vajpayee, who is also the Leader of Opposition, brought a Private Bill in the House in which there was a proposal for providing 33 per cent reservation for women …

I heartily welcome this Bill but … why has it become necessary to introduce this Bill? … In some … countries, women got the right to vote just a few years back. In the big, progressive countries, it has been said that women should be given the right to vote only after attaining the age of 30, whereas men are entitled to vote at the age of 21. But our country is one of those leading countries where women got the right to vote from the very day the Constitution came into force. India is among those countries where a woman has had the privilege of heading the Government not only for one or two years, but for 11 years. But it is unfortunate that … (though) a woman has been the Prime Minister … participation of ordinary women in politics has been negligible. Who is responsible for that?

I say, without any hesitation, the male-dominated mentality is responsible for this discrimination … this discrimination exists in every political system, and that is why it becomes necessary to provide reservation for women. Had men given this right to women easily, it would not have become necessary to bring this Bill today … it is … a matter of shame that there has been a progressive decrease in the political representation of women from Independence till today … The House comprises 543 Members of Parliament, out of which there are only 36 lady Members. If you calculate, it stands at six and half per cent. I would like to ask as to whether it is not a matter of surprise, sorrow and shame that women comprise fifty per cent population and enjoy only six and half per cent political participation? May I ask whether the capability of leadership is only men's paternal property? Whether only men have the monopoly to rule? … (Interruptions.) … I have stated that the mentality of male domination is present in every party without exception … (Interruptions.)

Mr. Speaker: Domination is taking place even in the House. (Interruptions.) …

Sushma Swaraj: They are exhibiting the same mentality … (Interruptions.) you are confirming my point … (Interruptions.) The obvious needs no evidence … I did not take my party as an exception. I said that the mentality of male domination is present in every party. That is why the need for demanding reservation was felt. Had you provided our due earlier, who would have demanded reservation and why? … (Interruptions.)

Dr. Prabin Chandra Sarma (Member from Guwahati): Sir, it is an insulting remark. This should be expunged from the proceedings … (Interruptions.)

Mr. Speaker: Let her have her say.

Sushma Swaraj: Mr. Speaker, Sir, I was stating … (Interruptions.)

Mr. Speaker: Sushmaji, passage of this Bill needs their help also. Therefore, refrain from speaking too much … (Interruptions.)

Sushma Swaraj: It would be better if they pass the Bill, accepting the truth and facing the reality. We are not asking for mercy … (Interruptions.) So far as abilities and capabilities are concerned, women do not lag behind men. Let me tell them that God, in His vast creation, did not create only man and woman but innumerable creatures and has created a female of every male. Being male, you can … put restrictions on us, stating that physically and mentally you are weak, since God has given you power of speech and wisdom. But the other creatures made by God behave as per the qualities provided by nature to them. The males of their species cannot say anything. Therefore, if you study the females of other creatures, you will find that females are neither physically weak nor lack the capability of leadership.

God created the lion, the king of the forest, but it is the lioness which goes out daily to hunt for prey … the lioness … trains her cubs for prey and God, through her, has shown that females, in no way, even physically, are weaker. Mr. Speaker, Sir, you hail from Meghalaya where elephants are in abundance. If you visit … Assam, you can have a glimpse of herds of elephants … the herds … are never led by a male elephant; instead it is led by an old female elephant. God has provided her the capability of leadership …

Santosh Mohan Dev (Member from Silchar): The female elephant never grows old.

Sushma Swaraj: Mr. Speaker, Sir, the male elephant never grows old. Not only this … in Hindu mythology, when portfolios were distributed among the Gods, the Goddesses were given important portfolios … defence, finance and education … The Gods … had given … education to Goddess Saraswati, finance to Goddess Laxmi, and defence to Goddess Durga … Therefore, the administration of these departments was run properly. This Government has made one State Minister for 33 per cent women. It is, therefore, that this Government is in such a bad condition.

P.R. Dasmunsi (Member from Raiganj): Therefore, you should utter 'Sita's Jai' instead of 'Ram's Jai'.

Sushma Swaraj: I was mentioning these points to show that women are neither physically weak nor mentally, but the mentality of our society has created this perverted thinking ... after noticing the intention of the House, it is not clear whether even after your enthusiastic contribution, this Bill will be passed since it is a Constitution Amendment Bill, which requires 50 per cent presence, and two-thirds members present and voting. At present, I do not think that there will be 50 per cent MPs, and if the rumour which I heard in Central Hall and Lobby is true, then a conspiracy is being hatched to ensure that 50 per cent Members are not present in the House at the time of voting. If 50 per cent presence is not ensured in the House, that conspiracy will be revealed ...

Discussion was going on outside the House on the 73rd and 74th Amendment which, we said, was a revolutionary step. They were saying: what will they do; why do they need reservation? See the women members who have been elected through the 73rd Amendment. They sit veiled; their husbands work for them. Brijwasi bhai was saying that it has made 'Pia' a P.A. I asked why is it strange? He said women sit veiled. I asked whether all the male Members of Parliament and Legislative Assemblies are good speakers? How effectively do they play their roles in the House?

Mr. Speaker, Sir, I want to repeat what I said to him, 'Since purdah practice is prevalent among women only, therefore, she has become speechless in her veil, but those members who do not speak in the House are dumb without veils. But nobody pays attention to them, but the woman who ... adopts the veil ... is made a showpiece ... women chairmen of municipalities, mayors of municipal corporations and sarpanchs of gram panchayats are working more effectively and, at some places, they symbolize progress ...

If in the same process, this Bill is passed, one-third women Members will be there in the Parliament as well as in the State Assemblies. Comments are being made which apparently appear to support the Bill, but their intentions are quite contrary. For example, some say, why 33 per cent, it should be 50 per cent. I say, we would be satisfied with 33 per cent only. We did not demand 50 per cent. The second is: we support the Bill but the Bill should be comprehensive and unless a comprehensive Bill is brought, we would not support the Bill.

I know there are shortcomings in the Bill. For example there is a provision for reservation in only the Lok Sabha and the Legislative Assemblies, and not in the

Rajya Sabha and the Legislative Councils. But … no Bill is perfect in one effort. The Constitution was framed after the discussions of years. We have made many Amendments for making it more relevant. This is the 81st Amendment. We would make it … more effective later on, if need be. But this Bill should be passed today in the present form because it is a historic beginning.

Mr. Speaker, Sir, you ordered from the Chair that you have not only suspended Question Hour but you would waive the rule also, but this Bill should be introduced and passed today itself. The historic beginning that you have initiated from the Chair will have its logical conclusion with the passage of the Bill … We have two hours' time for discussion. You should direct the leaders of all the political parties to issue instructions to all the Members to be present here. At least 50 per cent of the Members should be present here … I would like to make an appeal to the leaders of all the political parties to support this Bill. I thank you for allowing me to speak and conclude.

7

Transgender Rights

On 24 April 2015, the Dravida Munnetra Kazhagam's (DMK) Rajya Sabha Member of Parliament (MP) ***Tiruchi N. Siva*** *made history when his Rights of Transgender Persons Bill was unanimously passed, making it the first time in 45 years that the Upper House had passed a Private Members' Bill. He was also only the fifteenth MP (and so far, last) to have succeeded in converting a Private Members' Bill into the law of the land.*

Subsequently, his Bill received assent in the Lok Sabha, too.

In 1996, Siva won the Pudukkottai Lok Sabha seat in Tamil Nadu by a margin of nearly two lakh votes, even though the constituency was not his home ground. He is now a third-term Rajya Sabha MP, one of four DMK members of the Upper House.

Here, in his speech, he makes an impassioned plea for support to his Bill to ensure equality – and acceptance in society – for transgender people, a community for whom he had been fighting for many years, and who number 20–25 lakh in India, according to him.

TIRUCHI N. SIVA

(Rajya Sabha: Tamil Nadu)

Rajya Sabha: 24 April 2015

The Rights of Transgender Persons Bill, 2014

Our Constitution provides for the Fundamental Right to equality and tolerates no discrimination on the grounds of caste, sex, creed or religion. Sir, the Constitution also guarantees political rights and other rights and benefits to all the citizens of this country. But, Sir ... the transgender community continues to be ostracized. The Supreme Court of India in its landmark judgment on April 15, 2014, while granting legal recognition to transgenders, has held that equality and non-discrimination on the basis of gender identity or expression is increasing and gaining acceptance in international law and should be applied in India as well …

Sir, democracies across the world … have taken several decisions seeking an end to the discrimination and violence against the transgender community. Sir, around 29 countries like South Africa, Brazil, Russia, Nepal, New Zealand, Australia, Canada, Germany, UK, Switzerland, Greece, Italy, France, Mexico, Argentina, US, Singapore, Norway, Finland, Ireland, Hong Kong, Thailand, Taiwan, Ecuador, Peru, Chile, Columbia, Uruguay, Turkey, and numerous other countries have legislations protecting the rights of the transgender community.

Sir, we all have human rights. Whatever be our gender identity, whatever be our nationality, whatever be our place of residence, national or ethnic origin, colour, religion, language, we all enjoy human rights. Sir, we have to take note, at the same time, that we enjoy human rights without discrimination and this is inter-related, inter-dependent and universal and is shared by each one of us. But without protection of human rights, Sir, there can be no democracy or justification for democracy. 'Intolerance itself is a form of violence and an obstacle to the growth of true democratic spirit' was said by none but Mahatma Gandhi.

Sir, if we want to cultivate a true spirit of democracy, we cannot afford to be intolerant and intolerance betrays want of faith in one's cause. But violence based on gender identity still continues and remains a reality for lakhs of transgender persons in our country. Sir, statistics say, they are around 4.5 lakhs. But when I had the opportunity to interact with various transgender community people and those groups which are working for this community, they said that there are around 20–25 lakh people in our country without … recognition …

In my initiating speech, I mentioned that in the voter identity card, the transgender is given a vote by way of taking her as a female. But when the same person enters a train compartment, he is not allowed. They don't have access to public toilets … They say that nobody is prepared to accept them – their family deserts them, society doesn't accept them and no person comes close; so they have to resort to some trade which the society and the law don't accept. When we hear that, we are very sorry, and when we also happen to know about them we are very surprised to know that so many efficient people are there. For the information of this august House, the Thai Airlines has recruited transgenders as its air hostesses. And, such is their ability, such is their competence, as is inferior to no one else.

The State should take measures to help them regain their respect and give them a place in society which they once enjoyed in our cultural and social life. Undoing the centuries of discrimination that the transgender community has faced, we will require targeted interventions by the State. Sir, I would like to again quote Mahatma Gandhi because he was the one person who cared as much for the rural people as well as those who are neglected in society. He said, 'The future depends on what we do in the present. Man becomes great exactly in the degree in which he works for the welfare of his fellow men.'

Sir, when fellow persons ... in our country ... are being discriminated against just for their ... gender ... that disparity must be put an end to. How? Only a law ... can do it. That is what I mentioned at the outset of my speech – that various countries have taken cognizance of this issue and they are taking a strong stand in the field of transgender rights. When legislations are in place in so many developed countries, why can India not have one? ... successive Governments might have had concern, but sorry, Sir, the result is still unfelt, unrealized. That is the compulsion for bringing in this Bill.

The Father of the Nation again remarked, 'Before you do anything, stop and recall the face of the poorest, the most helpless, destitute person you have seen and ask for yourself, is what I am about to do going to help him?'

Sir, the Bill which I have introduced ... I am very happy and proud and thankful that 22 hon'ble Members in this august House, cutting across political parties, have supported and deliberated upon it. Valuable contributions have been made. Such is the wide support we have come across. Today, so many transgender community people, from across the country, have come to the gallery. They are waiting outside. They are expecting that something remarkable is going to happen in the Rajya Sabha today, which will be path-breaking and end the centuries-long discrimination they have been suffering in the same country where we hail democracy, where we say that human rights are for all. When the Constitution empowers, when it provides equal rights, why are some people neglected?

One transgender person asked me, 'I am paying the tax for this country's exchequer. The Government is running because of me, but I am deprived of my rights. Where should I go and ask? The Government takes money from me in the form of tax, but it is not giving me the rights. Where should I go? In what way, I will be accepted? Nothing is wrong with us.' They are, in no way, inferior. In fact, they challenge that they have merits and qualities of their own.

So, Sir, the Rights of Transgender Persons Bill, which I have introduced, is respectful, comprehensive yet practical. The Act will create conditions for an equal society as it recognizes and protects transgender persons in all spheres of life. The Rights of Transgender Persons Bill promises us a different future where all people born free, equal in dignity and rights, are able to fulfil the precious birth-right towards that goal. This Bill seeks to set up conditions and institutions for the integration of the marginalized into the mainstream. The world is watching India closely. Let us jointly let the world know that equality, rights and human dignity are at the forefront of our political conversation. Let our Constitution be our gate in this virtuous endeavour. Sir, I am very proud to say that I belong to the party, DMK, and the State, Tamil Nadu, which was the first State to constitute a Welfare Board for the welfare of the transgenders. West Bengal followed suit and Maharashtra also did it. Other States have still not done it. The Central Government has still not done it. My Bill envisages a national commission.

Rapolu Ananda Bhaskar (Member from Andhra Pradesh): Sir, I would like to mention one important development. The Reserve Bank of India yesterday ordered all public sector banks to include the clause of third gender. The transgenders are getting place to record their gender in all the bank forms …

Tiruchi Siva: Thank you very much, Sir. I think, this information, which my colleague, Mr. Ananda, has given is in support of what we are deliberating. When I interacted with all the Members, everyone was for it. Sir, kindly look at the gallery. Those people are with anxiety, with curiosity, with many expectations that something good is going to happen to them by way of this Bill getting through in Rajya Sabha. Sir, after a long history, something is going to happen to them. Again, I would say that my Bill envisages a national commission for the transgender community, like for the OBCs, which is a statutory body, as well as the commissions for the States, which will solve many issues. Sir, I do not want to elaborate further, I know the time constraint. It is the concluding part of my speech. I listened to the Minister.

… I listened to him very carefully. He said so many schemes are there but we are not, in practice, giving them the social recognition which they need. So, I would urge upon the Government to consider this, rather, with folded hands, I would request all the Members, cutting across Party lines, in this House, to support my cause. It is not my cause, it is the cause of a section of the people of our country, who have been discriminated against, who have been neglected, who have faced only abuse and violence for no fault of theirs. Sir, the time has come for this. When we have become such a developed, democratic country in the world, we should do this.

Sir, I think, passing a Private Members' Bill is not a new thing. In the past, eight Bills have been passed in the Parliament, and, I think, this Bill will become a path-breaking Bill for the transgender community people who have been neglected, who are depressed, who are suppressed, who are oppressed, and, hereafter, I think, they will have a new ray of hope in our country. With these words, I conclude and I request that the Bill be passed. Thank you very much, Sir.

… I am pressing that the Bill be passed … (Interruptions.) … Sir, there are so many assurances given by various Governments. The HIV/Aids Bill has been pending for years together … (Interruptions.) … It is not against the Government. I think, it will also be a part of it … (Interruptions.) … It is as per the convention. The Minister has replied. It is my concluding speech.

Mr. Deputy Chairman: Mr. Tiruchi Siva, I agree that the Minister has replied. It is your final speech. It is all agreed. But, I think, as per the practice in the Rajya Sabha, after discussion, usually, the Private Members' Bills – I do not know if there is an exception – most of the Bills are withdrawn. That is the practice, and, I also hoped that you will go by that practice.

The Bill is the property of the House. But whether to withdraw or not is his decision. Let him take that decision. If he says, he is withdrawing, then, I will. … (Interruptions.) … Please, listen … (Interruptions.) … That is for him to say … (Interruptions.). How can you say that he is not withdrawing? Let him say … (Interruptions.)

Tiruchi Siva: I am not withdrawing … (Interruptions.) …

Tiruchi Siva: No, Sir … (Interruptions.) … I am pressing that the Bill be passed … (Interruptions.) … One small reference, Sir. In the British Parliament, in the past three years, 17 Private Members' Bills have been passed. In Canada, 229 Private Members' Bills have been passed …

… In our country, 14 Private Members' Bills have been passed. There are precedents, and, therefore, I insist on it. Sir, I press that the Bill be passed.

Thawar Chand Gehlot (Member from Madhya Pradesh and the then Social Justice and Welfare Minister): Mr. Deputy Chairperson, Sir, I am in agreement with the sentiments expressed by the honourable Siva. I had responded to his earlier speech and had touched on all those points and given my heartfelt support, but there are some difficulties … When I had spoken earlier, I had said that some of the points relate to other ministries such as women and child welfare, home ministry, external affairs ministry, law and justice ministry … We had set up a special committee for this and its report has come – it had also suggested reservations in educational institutions …

Thawar Chand Gehlot: I was coming to that. I am in agreement with the Supreme Court's verdict but I want to remind you that there is a review petition that is pending … I want to give this government's assurance that we will take this up. I want to request Shri Siva that he withdraw his Bill and maintain the honour of this House.

Tiruchi Siva: I thank the hon'ble Minister, Sir, for he has gone well through my Bill … (Interruptions.)…

Yes, Sir. He gave an assurance and I told that my Bill is more or less related with the HIV/AIDS Bill. That is a Bill which has been waiting for years together.

Nearly a decade is going to end and all those people are suffering like anything. It is a very important Bill. I think, Naddaji, the new Minister, will take care of that and we are hopeful. That is different. But we had a very good experience in the past of having heard the assurances. So, I think, it is high time that instead of yielding – I respect the Minister. I have heard him fully – there is no other way for me than to press that the Bill be passed.

But, Sir, we are not convinced. I am concerned about the lakhs of transgender people in the country, who are suffering without anything … (Interruptions.) …

Sir, I respect the Ministers and I take their word but, at the same time, my concern is the feeling which the transgender community people have expressed to me in the past few days after the Bill has been initiated. I have been travelling across the country. So many people have represented and their representations have compelled me that it is high-time. I think, the Government does not lose anything if they agree to my Bill. I think, it will be a good, gentle gesture from this Government. So, I expect them to support me. As I requested in my earlier speech, I request all the Members, including the Members in the Treasury Benches, to support my Bill, Sir. So, I press the Bill to be passed.

Sir, if this Bill is passed in this House, it does not upset the Government in bringing a comprehensive Bill by them. If they bring a Bill, that will be welcomed and this Bill will automatically go away. If this Bill is passed, maybe it will expedite Government's attempt to bring in a new Bill. (Interruptions.) So, I am pressing for it.

Mr. Deputy Chairman: So, you are not withdrawing the Bill?

Tiruchi Siva: No, Sir. I am pressing for it.

Mr. Deputy Chairman: Then I have to put the motion to vote. Since the hon'ble Member is not withdrawing the Bill, I am putting it to vote. (Interruptions.) I say it very honestly. (Interruptions.) When you bring in a Bill, my Bill, which will be passed, goes away. (Interruptions.) If you show this gesture, that will send a wrong signal.

Mr. Deputy Chairman: In that case, I have to go for division because division has been asked for.

Arun Jaitley (Member from Uttar Pradesh and the then Leader of the House): Mr. Siva has raised a very important issue. I don't think the House should be divided on this important issue. We are all concerned about this segment of society. Therefore, the hon'ble Minister has said that he is willing to take it into serious consideration and bring some official policy or legislation in this regard. There are only two options available to us. One option is that even if we approve this, it does not become a law, it only expresses a sentiment. It is more like a resolution. The other option is that Mr. Siva agrees to the assurance, which the hon'ble Minister has given, and does not press it. But in any case my appeal to all the sections would be that we come to a conclusion and that should be a general consensus of the House rather than being divided on an issue because this is not an issue on which the House should at all be divided … (Interruptions.) … One option is that Mr. Siva agrees to the suggestion and assurance of the hon'ble Minister. The other option is that the House, by a voice vote, can echo the sentiment of Mr. Siva.

Mr. Deputy Chairman: Then, I am again going to put it to voice vote. I am trying it once again because I want to know the real mood of the House. Now, the question is: That the Bill to provide for the formulation and implementation of a comprehensive national policy for ensuring overall development of the transgender persons and for their welfare to be undertaken by the State and for matters connected therewith and incidental thereto, be taken into consideration. *The motion was adopted.*

Mr. Deputy Chairman: We shall now take up clause-by-clause consideration of the Bill …

Tiruchi Siva: Sir, I move: That the Bill, as amended, be passed.
The question was put and the motion was adopted.

Mr. Deputy Chairman: It is a unanimous decision of the House. It is a good thing. It is a rare thing. (Interruptions.) Certainly. I join Prof. M.V. Rajeev Gowda in congratulating the entire House, especially the Leader of the House for his timely intervention to save the situation.

Section Seven

Deepening Democracy

1

Power to the People

Mahatma Gandhi had advocated Panchayati Raj as the foundation of India's political system, as a decentralized form of government in which each village would be responsible for its own affairs. But it was not till 24 April 1993 that the Constitution (73rd Amendment) Act of 1992 came into force, providing constitutional status to Panchayati Raj institutions.

The person who laid the ground for this constitutional amendment was the former Prime Minister, the late ***Rajiv Gandhi*** *who introduced the Constitution (64th Amendment) Bill in the Lok Sabha on 15 May 1989. In this brilliant speech – inspired by his good friend, Mani Shankar Aiyar, who went on to become a central minister – he points out that constitutional safeguards are required for Panchayati Raj institutions to help deepen and widen democracy.*

RAJIV GANDHI

(Lok Sabha: Amethi)

Lok Sabha: 15 May 1989

Constitution (Sixty-Fourth Amendment) Bill

Mr. Speaker, Sir, I beg to move for leave to introduce a Bill to further amend the Constitution of India.

Democracy was the greatest gift of our freedom struggle to the people of India. Independence made the nation free. Democracy made our people free. A free people are a people who choose their own representatives. A free people are a people who are governed by their will and ruled with their consent. A free people are a people who participate in decisions affecting their lives and their destinies.

Gandhiji believed that democratic freedoms have to be founded in institutions of self-government in every village of India. He drew his inspiration and his vision from the 'Panchayats', the traditional village republics of India. Panditji established the institutions of Panchayati Raj as the primary instrument for bringing development to the doorstep of rural India. Indiraji stressed the need for the people's participation in the processes of economic and social transformation.

Yet ... in most parts of the country we have failed to fulfil the high hopes we had vested 30 years ago in the institution of Panchayati Raj. Elections have been irregular. They are often unnecessarily delayed and frequently postponed. This is not a matter of political will. The best record of regular elections to Panchayati Raj institutions is of two State Governments ... which have almost continuously been ruled by the Congress Party, Gujarat and Maharashtra. (Interruptions.)

... Sir, in recent times, some state governments run by the Opposition parties, such as the CPI(M) in West Bengal ... the Telugu Desam Party in Andhra and the Janata Party in Karnataka have held regular elections.

... In other states, the record of non-Congress parties and coalitions has not been much better than that of Congress-run state governments. This is not a matter of political parties. The essence of democracy is elections. Elections to Panchayati Raj institutions have been woefully irregular and uncertain. A mandatory provision in the Constitution is sacrosanct. A statutory provision in the state law does not have quite the same sanctity. We propose through this Bill to enshrine in the Constitution regular, periodic elections to Panchayati Raj institutions.

We also propose ... to end ... the sickness of unending suspensions and dissolutions. In the absence of any compelling provision to re-constitute Panchayats ... suspended Panchayats have remained suspended for years on end and dissolved Panchayats have remained dissolved for up to a decade or more. In the existing municipal law on the subject, State Legislatures have given the executive authority such wide powers to abort the institutions of Panchayati Raj and delay reconstituting them that these institutions have been leached of their ability to stand on their own as representative forums of the people's will. Their existence has depended less on the mandate of the people than on the whims of state governments.

Our Bill leaves it to the states to determine the grounds and conditions on which the Panchayats may be suspended or dissolved. We expect state legislatures to specify the grounds on which the Governor may suspend or dissolve a Panchayat ... Our Bill would make it mandatory through the Constitution for all Panchayats dissolved before the expiry of their term of office to be reconstituted through democratic elections based on adult suffrage within six months of the dissolution to complete the remaining term.

No more will Panchayats remain the playthings of the arbitrary exercise of executive power. It is the people who will determine within a matter of months the profile of the reconstituted Panchayat. It is the Constitution which ensures that the Lok Sabha and the state assemblies are constituted by the vote of the people on the basis of universal adult suffrage. It is the Constitution which ensures that if an Assembly is dissolved, it is reconstituted by a procedure and within a time frame specified in the Constitution itself. These are essential safeguards to ensure the strength and vitality of democratic institutions. The institutions of Panchayati Raj have lacked strength and vitality precisely because they have lacked Constitutional safeguards. Our Bill will ensure that Panchayati Raj has a democratic character similar to the Lok Sabha and the State Assemblies and Constitutional protection for their functioning as representative institutions of the people.

The single greatest event in the evolution of democracy in India was the enactment of the Constitution which established democracy in Parliament and in the State Legislatures. This historic revolutionary Bill takes its place alongside that great event as the enshrinement in the Constitution of democracy at the grassroots.

Till now, there have been weaknesses in the structure of our democracy because although the superstructure is strong, the foundation has been weak. Putting together both Houses of Parliament and all the State Legislatures, we have only about five thousand to six thousand persons representing a population of nearly 800 million. This has had two serious consequences.

First, the number of persons holding elective office in well-founded institutions of democracy has been far too small in relation to the size of our electorate. Once we accord to democracy in the Panchayats the same sanctity now enjoyed by Parliament and the State Legislatures, we will be opening the doors to the participation in democratic institutions of something like seven lakhs elected representatives. The people's stake in democracy will be increased by a factor of approximately 115.

There is a second deleterious consequence of the vast chasm that separates the general body of the electorate from the small number of its elected representatives. This gap has been occupied by the power brokers, the middle-man, the vested interests. For the minutest municipal function, the people have had to run around, finding persons with the right connection, who would intercede for them with the distant sources of power. The system has been captured by the power brokers. It is being operated in the interest of the power brokers. It is being protected by the power brokers. The power brokers have established their vice-like grip only because democracy has not functioned at the grassroots. The only way of breaking their stranglehold is for democracy to fill the vacuum, which the power brokers have occupied. Once the people have their own elected representatives from electorates as small as a hundred to five hundred persons, the source of power will lie only as far away as the Panchayat Ghar: not some distant State capital or the even more distant capital of the country. To end any role for power brokers in the system, the Bill provides for the direct election of members to Panchayats at all levels.

Every voter will have his own representative in the Gram Panchayat, in the mid-level Panchayat and in the Zila Panchayat. That representative will be responsible to a small and well-recognized electorate. If he fulfills the mandate of the people, he will be re-elected; if he fails, the people will throw him out of office. The power of the vote will become the power of enforcement. The will of the people will render the power broker superfluous.

Today, opportunity for democratic elected leadership is confined to the few thousands who succeed in entering the portals of the State Legislatures and Parliament. Once this Bill becomes an integral part of the Constitution, a huge countrywide reservoir of leadership potential will be created. At each Panchayat election, approximately half a crore men and women, most of them young, will present themselves to the electorate seeking the people's mandate. Some will succeed and some will fall by the wayside. Those who do not succeed will get another opportunity five years later.

There is a vast uncultivated field of talent lying fallow in rural India. It is that fallow field, we now propose to seed. That field will be watered by the votes of the Members of this House and of our colleagues in the Rajya Sabha. The crop of talent you raise will give us the bountiful harvest to take our nation forward to a prosperous, glorious future.

There is no country richer than ours in the most precious asset of humankind, the human resource ... This Bill makes it possible for the bulk of the nation's talent to be given opportunity. Throughout the country there will be a ferment. In every one of our 600,000 villages, in every one of our 5,000 blocks, in every one of our 400 districts, democracy will groom the men and women whose experience will subsequently become available to legislatures at the state level and to the Parliament of the Union of India.

Our proposed Constitutional amendment lays the Constitutional injunction upon the State legislatures. It is for the State legislatures to enact the appropriate law ... (Interruptions.)

A quite unnecessary controversy has been raised about the role of the Governor in the proposed Panchayati Raj system. The Constitution is unambiguous on this point. Article 154(1) states that 'The executive power of the State shall be vested in the Governor' Article 163(1) clarifies that, 'There shall be a Council of Ministers with the Chief Minister at the head to aid and advise the Governor in the exercise of his functions'. And, therefore, the word Governor in the Constitution refers to the Governor exercising his executive powers only and exclusively on the aid and advice of the Council of Ministers, with one exception. The exception is provided for in the remainder of clause (1) of Article 163 (Interruptions) which reads: 'except in so far as the Governor is ...' (Interruptions.)

... Sir, I quote 'except in so far as he is by or under this Constitution required to exercise his functions or any of them in his discretion'. The distinction between the expression 'the Governor' and the expression 'the Governor in his discretion' is such a well-known matter of Constitutional law that it is amazing that there should be any confusion on this point. After all, the expression, 'the Governor' appears at scores of places throughout the Constitution, and has nowhere been misconstrued, or misinterpreted. We are confident that in this Parliament, acting in the exercise of its inherent constituent powers, there will be no confusion between the functions of a Governor acting in accordance with the aid and advice of his Council of Ministers, and of a Governor acting in his discretion wherever the Constitution requires him to do so.

In establishing the institutions of democracy in Parliament and in the State legislatures, our founding fathers gave particular recognition to the disabilities suffered by the Scheduled Castes and the Scheduled Tribes. Provision was made for the reservation of seats for them in accordance with the proportion of their population in the total electorate. This is a principle which has not been incorporated in most of the Panchayati Raj legislation enacted by the State legislatures.

In my discussions with Panchayati Raj representatives, both during my extensive tours of rural India and in the numerous Panchayati Raj sammelans[1] we have held, it was brought home to me most forcefully that the democratic rights of the Scheduled Castes and Scheduled Tribes cannot be secured by good intentions alone. At this stage, it has to be secured ... by reservations in Panchayati Raj institutions on the same basis as reservations are given in the Lok Sabha and in the State Assemblies.

I see that a certain section of the House is not at all happy about this ... There is a widespread and justified apprehension on the part of the Scheduled Castes and the Scheduled Tribes that if their due representation in these bodies is not ensured, Panchayati Raj could become an instrument of oppression in the hands of the rural elite. Experience in different parts of the country ... (Interruptions.)

... We are waking you up; that is what we are doing. Experience in different parts of the country has shown how, in the absence of reservations, vested interests and feudal interests have been able to capture these institutions. (Interruptions.) Their hold on these institutions has been reinforced by the failure to hold regular elections. The people's mandate has been perverted into an instrument of exploitation ...

I was aware that reservation for Scheduled Castes and Scheduled Tribes would cause certain problems when we wanted to enforce them, but to be honest I did not expect the problems to come from this section of the House. (Interruptions.) Obviously, the power brokers and feudal interests stand totally exposed today. (Interruptions.) To forestall such a perversion of the process, our Bill proposes to make it mandatory for State Legislatures to ensure reservation for the Scheduled

[1] Editor's translation: Conference.

Castes and Scheduled Tribes in proportion to their population in the relevant Panchayat area. Our Bill also proposes a significant departure from the Constitution as it exists today. We propose the reservation in Panchayats at all levels of 30 per cent of the seats for women. (Interruptions.) I appreciate the interruptions from the hon'ble members; and I appreciate that this too disturbs them tremendously. (Interruptions.)

... There are three major reasons for which we believe this Constitutional innovation to be necessary. (Interruptions.) First, women constitute half the population and are involved in rather more than half the economic life of rural India. However, to our shame, their share of assets and income is much less than their share of the population. But the toil and sweat imposed upon them is rather more than half. Second, the sound finance of the household has traditionally been the responsibility of women. Financial discipline and fiscal responsibility are ingrained in the habits and outlook of the women of rural India. These are qualities badly needed in Panchayati Raj institutions. We believe the presence of women in large numbers in the Panchayats will not only make the Panchayats more representative but will also make them more efficient, more honest, more disciplined and more responsible. (Interruptions.)

... Third, it is the women of India, in their role as grandmothers and mothers, who have been the repository of India's ancient culture and traditions. It is to them that is entrusted the responsibility of transmitting to the next generation the quintessential values, standards and ideals which have enabled our civilization to survive and flourish without a break despite vicissitudes of many kinds. It is that strength of moral character which women will bring to the Panchayats. Let us give them a warm welcome ... (Interruptions.)

I now turn to the heart of the matter: devolution and sound finance. Respecting the right of the states to legislate provisions for devolution, we have deliberately refrained from tampering with their rights. We have no intention of attempting to rule the districts from the Centre. But we do expect the State legislatures to enact such measures as are required to devolve powers and authority upon the Panchayats, keeping in mind the provisions of this Bill and the spirit in which this Amendment is being brought forward.

First is the power and authority of the Panchayats to draw up plans within the framework of guidelines and conditions to be stipulated by the state governments. These plans will constitute the basic inputs for the planning process at higher levels. Thus we will ensure that the voice of the people, their felt needs, their aspirations, their priorities become the building blocks of the edifice of planning. We must put an end to planning from above. We must put an end to priorities being conceived and decided at ethereal heights far removed from the realities on the ground. We must put an end to paternalistic planning. We must initiate a process of people's planning.

Our Bill goes beyond merely planning for economic development. It lays upon the Panchayats the even heavier responsibility of planning for social justice. It will not do to romanticize life in our villages. Life there is hard. Life there is exacting, life there is in many ways exploitative and oppressive.

In driving the power brokers out of the power houses, in rendering the Panchayats to the people, we lay upon the people's representatives the solemn responsibility of turning their attention first and foremost to the needs of the poorest, the most deprived and the most in need. Each plan for economic development will be accompanied by a plan for social justice. No plan for economic development will merit attention until its social justice component is clear. This is a charter not merely for our villages to become prosperous, but also for our villages to become just.

The second major responsibility of the Panchayats, will be the implementation of development schemes assigned to them by the state governments on such conditions as may be specified by the state governments. These schemes should cover the major economic concern of rural India, commencing with agriculture and land improvement and going on to irrigation and watershed management. It must comprise the diversification of the rural economy into animal husbandry, dairying, poultry and fisheries. It must incorporate industrial activity in rural India. It must extend to minor forest produce which is the chief source of income for our entire tribal populace. It must encompass the day to day concerns of rural India, housing, drinking water, fuel and fodder. The devolution must deal with the basic infrastructure of communication and power in rural India.

We have suggested the inclusion in the Panchayats' area of competence of development schemes relating to non-conventional energy sources.

The proposed Eleventh Schedule seeks to vest in the Panchayats the major responsibility for the administration of poverty alleviation programmes. It would entrust Panchayats with education and culture as well as health and family welfare, women and child development. We propose to request the State Legislatures to make social welfare programmes for all the weaker and handicapped sections a functional responsibility of the Panchayats. We also propose to give to the Panchayats the responsibility for the public distribution system, which is so crucial for the survival of the weakest and the poorest as also for the general health of the rural economy.

... The Bill proposes that the Panchayats be entrusted with the most neglected area of our community life, namely, the maintenance of community assets. I would like to stress that the Eleventh Schedule is not an exhaustive list. We hope that the states will progressively devolve many more powers and authority upon the Panchayats so that whatever can be looked after at the local level is looked after at that level and not remitted upwards. (Interruptions.)

… The single greatest danger we have to guard against is the devolution of powers to the Panchayats being followed by the transfer of these powers out of the Panchayati Raj system into other bodies constituted outside the system and placed under the direct control of the State Governments. Almost all the State Governments whether Congress or non-Congress, who have established a good system of Panchayati Raj have seriously weakened the impact by constituting bodies outside the Panchayati Raj system where real powers of decision-making are vested and where the elected representatives of the Panchayati Raj are overshadowed by Ministers, appointed by the state government or, as in the case of Karnataka, by the MLA becoming the ex-official Chairman of the Taluka Panchayat Samiti.

It is the purpose of our Bill to ensure that powers delegated to the Panchayats remain within the Panchayats and are not channelled outside the system. By the same token, our Bill is designed to ensure that all development agencies are brought within the framework of the Panchayati Raj institutions and made responsive to the elected authority. There are two basic reasons for administration at the district and sub-district levels having become so unresponsive to the people. One is the fragmentation of the district administration into a large number of agencies vertically owing responsibility to state government without adequate coordination at a single focal point at the district level. The other has been the absence of an elected authority to function as that focal point … (Interruptions.)

… This is a manifesto for the election of the Panchayats … (Interruptions.) Let us be clear about that. This is a manifesto for the people of India … (Interruptions.) Sir, this is a manifesto to give power to the people of India and to rob some of the power brokers who are getting so agitated … (Interruptions.)

Sir, the House would recall that our Government was returned to office with the largest mandate ever accorded to any party in the history of independent India. I, as Head of that Government, pledged to make a number of structural changes. I very quickly discovered that the system could not cope with the demands which we were making upon it. There was too much ossification. Mere tinkering with the system would not do; a systemic transformation was essential. Indeed, the starting point of the exercise which has led to the presentation of this Bill was my search for a way of fulfilling the 20th point of our revised 1986 20 Point programme, which promised to the people a responsive administration. At my instance, the Department of Personnel organized a series of workshops on Responsive Administration to which were invited all the District Magistrates, Deputy Commissioners, and District Collectors of the country. I spent over 20 hours in discussion with them.

It emerged that we could not make our administration responsive merely by simplifying procedures or establishing grievance redressal machinery or opening complaint windows. Every such step only led to one more power centre for the power brokers to occupy. The sine qua non of responsive administration is representative administration, responsible to the electorate. Such responsive administration in rural India can only be secured through genuine Panchayati Raj. It is this that our Bill seeks to achieve.

Devolution of administrative powers must go hand in hand with sound finance. Too often in the past, Panchayati Raj has had functions without finances, responsibilities without funds, duties without the means of carrying them out. Our Bill empowers State Legislatures to ensure the sound finance of the Panchayats by endowing them with the revenues of taxes that might be appropriated by, or assigned to them, as also with grants in aid from the Consolidated Fund of the State.

To assist State Legislatures and the executive authority in determining which taxes to assign or leave for appropriation, as also the grants in aid to be given, the Bill proposes the establishment of a Finance Commission to make suitable recommendations.

I would stress the importance of determining the taxes which will be levied, collected and appropriated by the Panchayats. Nothing will inculcate in the Panchayats a greater sense of fiscal responsibility than the possibility of retaining with them the monies that they raise for such use as they best deem fit. Untied grants make for local-level planning. Authorization for appropriation makes for responsible local-level planning. So far, the tendency has been to confine appropriation to cesses. We hope State Legislatures will go further and identify taxes, duties, tolls and fees which might be appropriated by the Panchayats.

We are asking of the State Legislatures no more than we are ourselves ready to do as a Union Government. A beginning has been made with the Jawahar Rozgar Yojana. 80 per cent of the Funds are being devolved on the village panchayats. (Interruptions.) We propose to extend this principle to other Centrally-sponsored schemes. There can be no better way of involving the people in their own development. There can be no better way of reducing corruption and nepotism. The system we propose is a transparent system. The bulk of the electorate in a village is composed of the intended beneficiaries of development schemes. Each intended beneficiary will know what schemes are available, how much money there is in the scheme, whether and how the monies are being spent. Any Panch or Sarpanch who cheats the people will be removed by the people. There is no way he can escape the consequences of the malfeasance.

I would now like to turn to those parts of the country we are proposing to exempt from the system, or in respect of which special provision is made for modification. In the North-East, there is one sparsely populated tribal State which has no difficulty in adopting Panchayati Raj without modification. That is the State of Arunachal Pradesh. The Bill recognizes that in three other States of the North-East, Nagaland, Meghalaya and Mizoram, there are traditional systems of self-government, akin to Panchayati Raj, which must be preserved. Indeed, the rest of the country would be well-advised to study and learn from the Village Development Boards of Nagaland. In these three States, the traditional systems will be left undisturbed.

Similarly, in areas covered by the Sixth Schedule, where autonomous District Councils have been established, we would not wish to disturb the system so carefully structured. On the same principle, we are not extending the Bill to the District Council areas of Manipur and the areas covered by the Gorkha Hill Council in the Darjeeling Hill district of West Bengal.

As regards the Union Territories, the Bill empowers the President to withhold, extend or modify the application of the provisions of the Bill to a part or the whole of the Union Territories. This is designed to ensure that traditional or nascent institutions in areas like the Nicobar Islands, Lakshadweep and Pondicherry are not adversely affected and the special characteristics of Union Territories like Delhi are taken into account. Similarly, in areas covered by the Fifth Schedule, the Governor in his discretion (and not on the aid and advice of his Council of Ministers) may determine the conditions on which Panchayati Raj would be extended to these areas.

Sir, the Bill proposes that all State Legislatures bring their State legislation into conformity with the proposed Part IX of the Constitution within a year of the commencement of operation of the amendment. We recognize, however, that Panchayati Raj institutions have been elected in most states, some as recently as this year. The Bill authorizes the continuance of these Panchayats till the expiry of their terms, unless State Legislatures decide otherwise. The interregnum between the passage of this Bill and the alignment of state legislation with its provisions will, we hope, be used by state government to give deep thought to the working of the new system.

Panchayats will have to be given the staff they require. We do not propose that the Annual Confidential Reports of the bureaucracy be written by elected representatives at the Panchayat level, but the district bureaucracy will have to be trained and oriented towards discharging its new responsibilities in changed conditions. We have to build trust and mutual respect between the district bureaucracy and the elected Panchayats. At other levels of our democracy, in the states and at the Centre, the bureaucracy and the elected authority have learned to work together in mutual cooperation. Such a harmonious relationship must also subsist between the district bureaucracy and the Panchayats. We hope state governments will resist the temptation to effect a cleavage between the regulatory and development functions of district administration. There will have to be coordination because it is only through development administration that a regulating officer can establish the contacts and linkages essential to forestalling a law and order crisis or resolving it when it occurs.

We are deeply conscious that this Bill restricts itself to democracy and development at the grassroots in rural India. We must extend the same concern to the growing urban and semi-urban population of the country. To this end, Government propose to bring forward major legislation in the next session of the Lok Sabha.

We shall turn our attention to recasting, revamping and rejuvenating the cooperative movement which Panditji had always regarded as the essential complement to Panchayati Raj.

We come to this House after long consideration and a national debate without precedent. We have consulted with more than ten thousand representatives of Panchayati Raj institutions from all over the country. We have discussed Panchayati Raj with the bureaucracy at different echelons, including district officers, Chief Secretaries and Secretaries to the Government of India. We have held meetings with Panchayati Raj Ministers and the Chief Ministers of the States. We have extended the debate to political levels, within Party forums and in a Parliamentary Consultative Committee.

Our proposals are before you but our mind is not closed. In the months to come, we hope there will be intensive debate about these proposals all over the country. We are prepared to carry forward such discussions with Opposition Parties and Chief Ministers. We will of course listen with the utmost care to suggestions made on the floor of the House. We seek consensus but we are prepared to face the challenge of confrontation. We shall fight for the rights of the people, we shall fight for democracy for the people, we shall fight for development for the people. It is the people of India who are our first and foremost concern. The proposals we place before the House are not really our proposals, they are the proposals of the people of India. We have drawn upon the accumulated experience of Panchayati Raj from all over the country, the good experience as well as the bad, the experience of Congress-run governments as much as of State Governments run by other parties. This experience has been pooled and churned. Out of this manthan[2] has emerged the amrit[3] which we now propose to share.

Our democracy has reached the stage where the full participation of the people brooks no further delay. We are accused of rushing through this Bill. There has been no rush. For several years now we have been holding well-published consultation at several different levels on Panchayati Raj. No one in the public life of this country could have been unaware of our intentions. Our respected Rashtrapatiji, in his Address to both Houses of Parliament, had specifically referred to the major legislation on the subject which Government proposed to bring forward. We now fulfil that promise. Those who decry this as an election gimmick are precisely those whose feudal interest will be overthrown by power reaching the people.

[2] Editor's translation: Churning.

[3] Editor's translation: Elixir.

(Interruptions.) Sir, whenever I talk of power brokers and feudal interest, it hurts some of our friends very deeply and for that I apologize to them. But this is a fight for strengthening our people and we will fight this fight in spite of everything the Opposition has to say.

Sir, we trust the people. We have faith in the people. It is the people who must determine their own destinies and the destiny of the nation. To the people of India, let us ensure maximum democracy and maximum devolution. Let there be an end to the power brokers. Let us give power to the people. (Interruptions.)

2

The Mandal Commission

The Socially and Educationally Backward Classes (SEBC) Commission was established in 1979 by the Janata Party government with Bindheshwari Prasad Mandal as its chairperson. The Commission's mandate was to identify SEBCs and to suggest the basis and extent of reservations that could be given to them. The Mandal Commission Report that was submitted in 1980 used 11 socio-economic indicators to determine who fell into the SEBC category. The methodology used was questioned as the Commission was working on the basis of data from the 1931 Census, the last time a caste-wise enumeration had been done. The recommendations included setting aside 27 per cent of central government jobs for these Other Backward Classes (OBCs); this was in addition to the existing reservations (22.5 per cent) for the Scheduled Castes and Scheduled Tribes. It, however, took more than a decade for the Mandal Report's recommendations to be implemented. In 1990, the National Front government headed by Vishwanath Pratap Singh took the giant step, leading not just to sharp and violent protests from upper-caste students but to a transformational change in the politics of the country in the coming decades, particularly in the populous Hindi heartland.

In this section, two speeches made on the day the government announced the implementation have been excerpted. The first is by the CPI's ***Indrajit Gupta*** *who was a remarkably versatile speaker. He brought not just his formidable intellect to bear on the speeches he gave, but compassion and vision. In this speech on the acceptance of the Mandal Commission Report, he places the government's move in the larger context of the development of the country, and gives his stamp of approval for caste-based reservation despite being a communist. 'In a democratic set-up, every individual and community has a legitimate right and aspiration to participate in ruling this country. Any situation which results in a near-denial of this right to nearly 52 per cent of the country's population needs to be urgently rectified,' he points out.*

The second speech is by ***Vishwanath Pratap Singh****, the then Prime Minister, the man who staked his political career on the Mandal Commission Report. He answers the* *charges of his critics, especially the Man he replaced as Prime Minister, Rajiv Gandhi, who delivered a three-and-a-half-hour-long critique of the government's move to give reservation to the OBCs, while making an appeal to the rampaging students.*

INDRAJIT GUPTA

(Lok Sabha: Midnapore)

Lok Sabha: 6 September 1990

On Acceptance of Mandal Commission Report

Mr. Deputy Speaker, Sir, on behalf of my party I rise to extend our whole-hearted support to the decision of the Government and the Prime Minister to introduce 27 per cent reservation to the backward classes.

... Sir ... the Congress Party is in a difficulty over this issue ... no single leader of the Congress Party ... can say that they oppose ... the Mandal Commission ... But then, they have missed the bus. They were ... given a golden opportunity; they were in power for so many years. During the last 10 years in which the Mandal Commission submitted its report, it was they who were in power, and if they were really true to their promises, they could have taken the initiative. It would not have been necessary for this present Government to ... initiate this measure ... When they say that we support the Mandal Commission, it is because they cannot oppose it. They seek to qualify it with so many conditions and so many restrictions that actually there is nothing left at the end of it ...

... Sir, the atmosphere in the country is now highly emotionally surcharged and ... it is very difficult for anybody to take a ... detached and objective view of the implications of this decision ... Because people are on the streets. It is not surprising to know that the social structure, particularly the Hindu community social structure, as it existed all these years, has been given a shake up by this decision. It is only natural that those people, or those groups, or those elements who think that they are going to lose the privilege which they have enjoyed uninterruptedly for so many years, should be upset ... angry ... alarmed and ... apprehensive of the future. It always happens when a big shake-up of the whole social structure takes place, as it is going to happen now, or as it is happening. I am deeply and my party is deeply sorrowful at the loss of lives of people and, of course, the loss of public property ... which has taken place since this announcement was made ... the Government here in Delhi had ... given orders that despite all provocations, despite all difficulties, the police should not fire. In spite of that, firing has taken place ... and some precious young lives have been lost. At the same time, I wonder when … all these young people, who are after all our own sons and daughters, who are now rampaging on the streets if all of them have really understood or anybody has bothered to explain to them in a calm, dispassionate and detailed way what exactly are the dimensions of this reservation measure which has been announced. Or is it being blown out of proportion? Is it creating in the minds of young people a spectre, which is not justified at all? They have implemented … in a truncated form, the recommendations of the Mandal Commission. The only thing that they have introduced is, and that itself has set off this big commotion throughout the country, that these backward classes who constitute 52 per cent of the population should be given 27 per cent reservation … in the Central Government services and in the Central Public Sector Undertakings, nowhere else, not in the State Government services … This decision … does not apply … to any educational institution … medical college or engineering college. It does not apply to such Classes or Castes which are not common to the State List, which are not there already in various states and are common with the Mandal Commission … Also, a categorical assurance has been given that it is not going to be imposed on any State which does not want it … .to me, it appears that it is quite a modest … truncated implementation of the recommendations of the Mandal Commission. But it is thoroughly justified and it is welcome … Some people are behaving as though their children and their grandchildren, for generations to come, are going to be totally deprived, and that there is nothing further left for them … An exaggerated distorted picture has been given … Otherwise, this kind of excitement and agitation would not have taken place …

I would only plead that this conflict … – difference of opinion, conflict, clashes in some cases – … should not be allowed to degenerate into a sort of pro-reservation and anti-reservation issue. This will be extremely harmful to … society like ours with … centuries of history and traditions behind us. Mr. Sathe had spoken eloquently about the Manusmriti and the fact is, that for 3000 years of rigid caste system in which people are sealed off from each other … hermetically sealed into watertight compartments by the accident of their birth, this is the society in which we have been living. However much we may decry this caste system, and … go on hoping and pleading that we will get rid of this caste system some time, and we all realize that this is not in keeping with the development of modern society … the reality is that every day of our lives, even those amongst us, who are well educated … we are living, breathing, eating and sleeping with consciousness of caste in our heads. We have passed so many laws in this Parliament, beginning from the Constitution, down to recent days. If you go by those laws, then beginning from untouchability, the caste system has no place in the country … But how many people in this country really, effectively, loyally and sincerely are prepared to carry out all the implications of those laws in their own daily lives? When we give our daughters in marriage, do we go by them? There may be a few exceptions ... all honour to them, to those who are prepared to practise inter-caste marriages and inter-communal marriages ... How many are there? The overwhelming majority of our people, including those who are well educated, continue to practise willy-nilly, consciously or unconsciously, all the prejudices of ... caste system which are ... ingrained in our society. How many of them are willing to go to the hut of a Harijan and sit and eat with him? How many will give their daughters in marriage to people belonging to other castes?

... this limited reservation is not a ... panacea for the caste system, nor is it going to cure the problems of unemployment. It is not meant for that. But what I say is this: I am a Communist. Personally, I may say, perhaps with a touch of shame – I suppose one should be ashamed of the fact that one has never known poverty in one's life. I have not known poverty. Let me make it quite clear here, nor have I known social oppression, nor can I complain that I was not able to get access to good education. Everything that was desirable, I was able to get because of my family, my parents' position and all that. But today, one cannot but understand this fact that if these down-trodden people ... socially ... educationally ... economically backward people remain like this as a drag on our whole society, a drag on our whole future development and progress, this country can never go forward.

Therefore, those people maybe they are 15% or 17% ... who are really, consciously, because of their own interests ... opposed to this reservation, we cannot allow them to exercise a veto on this thing ... we cannot abolish the caste system. Certainly not overnight, and certainly not, for a good many years ... or a few centuries, perhaps ...

... Taking this as the reality in which we live ... we have to accept the world, the society as it is, not as we would like it to be ... But realism tells us that we have to begin from here. When you want to bring about changes ... which eventually will be in conformity with your ultimate goal, you must begin from here.

... But you must begin by taking certain concrete steps. And, therefore, I think that this confusion between castes and classes, and professions and occupations, and all that are all mixed up, jumbled together here. If you take these lists tabulated by the Mandal Commission, you will find classes there ... we cannot speak of castes openly because it is unconstitutional. There are occupations ... professions there, but I am not learned enough to question whether all those lists ... tabulated by the Mandal Commission, are all without any error ...

... Some people have complained that, for example, in Andhra Pradesh there are certain forward people who can never be considered backward ... they have been put in the backward classes list ... if that is a fact ... corrections can be made.

Somebody said the other day, I think it was the Chief Minister of Orissa, that some people who are known to be forward ... have been put in the backward list. If that is a fact, these things can be rectified … But … you cannot hedge this thing about at this stage … with all kinds of restrictions and qualifications and conditions. This idea that there should be a means test is very late. Some people have now suddenly become very … considerate for the fate of the less educated and less affluent people within each of these backward classes. They are saying, 'Oh! They will never get these benefits. All the benefits will be cornered by a few people at the top.' But that is the way our society functions … In this great industrial empire of our big businessmen and big monopoly houses, belonging to the upper classes, are they not always complaining … that small groups of people, small groups of business houses are cornering all the licences … subsidies and … export licences …? They are doing it … I do not deny the fact that some groups … who are better organized than other groups … may try to corner a larger disproportionate share of the benefits. I know what happens among the Harijans. You know it also, Sir. In your state, in Maharashtra also, we know it. After all, we have had reservations for the Scheduled Castes and the Scheduled Tribes … from the time of our independence. Within Scheduled Castes, there are groups who are better organized than others. And who, if you go into the details, you will find … are cornering a disproportionate share of the benefits and the jobs … But, from within the entire Scheduled Castes community, I do not hear … any outcry … The psyche of these people, who are backward … deprived … kept down … not educated … poor … they have been given a kind of a permanent inferiority complex. It is our job to see that they get out of this inferiority complex.

… But I say this and my party feels that at this … initial stage … this reservation is being introduced, on a limited scale, up to 27 per cent at this stage, it would not be correct … to insist on the introduction of some economic criterion or a means test.

… after this thing has worked for some time and these classes are able to make some progress and come up, then the whole matter can be gone into again. All those other side issues … whether it should apply only to recruitment or also to promotions, are different. We all know that this promotions question is the main cause of a lot of heartburning, particularly in the government services. At some stage, I think we will have to go into the whole question as to whether there should be only a one time benefit given to a particular person or his family. Once he has become a Collector … then after that his children need not get that benefit. These are all considerations which have to be gone into at some stage. But I say and my Party says that now at the initial stage when these people for the first time are being given an opportunity to feel that they will also have a share in the administration of the country, it will not be dominated and monopolized by a few people belonging to some upper classes. At this stage, it is absolutely wrong … it would be undesirable to try to insist on some kind of means test or an income ceiling. Let us consider it after some time. We have suggested in our Party Resolution that let this scheme work for ten years and after ten years, let all these things be gone into again and they can be modified.

Today ... a massive demonstration here ... ended in a rally at the Boat Club of some forty to fifty thousand youth and students all drenched in the rain. Since last night, they are living in the open at the boat club, where there is no shelter and no covering. They have come from several States of the country and their main slogans were 'Jobs for all' 'Education for all'. Incidentally, they also voiced their support for this reservation decision ... But they made it clear that reservation by itself is not going to cure anything. Therefore, it is very necessary ... the Government ... take up follow-up measures ... new opportunities must be created in the country, particularly in the rural areas. Those unemployed boys in the rural areas are not going to come and get jobs in Government offices ... or ... the Railways. They have to be given opportunities for ... useful, productive, gainful employment ... in the rural areas, where they live. For that, a massive programme ... of developing all types of new employment opportunities, self-employment and so many other things, have to be done. Land reforms in those parts of the country, where they have not been carried out, where they have been avoided and shelved, there land reforms have to be carried out. And of course, educational opportunities are dismal in our country. We have to all ... work out – it is not a party issue – how educational opportunities should be provided on an increased scale to all these people, who are deprived ... Then only this reservation will also have some concrete meaning ... we must keep in mind ... the proportion of this whole thing.

Sir, the Mandal Commission has made some very telling remarks in its recommendation. It says:

'It is not at all our contention that by offering a few thousand jobs to OBC candidates, we shall be able to make 52 per cent of the Indian population forward. (They cannot do it.) But we must recognize that an essential part of the battle against social backwardness is to be fought in the minds of the backward people themselves. In India, the Government service has always been looked upon as a symbol of prestige and power. By increasing the representation of OBCs in Government services, we give them an immediate feeling of participation in the governance of this country. When a backward class candidate becomes a Collector or a Superintendent of Police, the material benefits are to the members of his family only. But the psychological spin-off of this phenomenon is tremendous, the entire community of the backward class candidate feels socially elevated. Even when no tangible benefits may flow to the community at large, the feeling that now it has its own man in the "corridors of power" acts as morale booster.

In a democratic set-up, every individual and community has a legitimate right and aspiration to participate in ruling this country. Any situation which results in a near denial of this right to nearly 52 per cent of the country's population needs to be urgently rectified.'

So the first limited step has been taken to rectify this situation. And all this talk which is going on how merit will suffer, how the efficiency of the administrative services will be destroyed if these people are allowed to come over there and so on and so forth – an argument which we heard before independence and also from the foreign masters – is bogus. When people are given education and opportunities, they can progress and develop as well as anybody else. It does not matter to which class or which caste they belong. I do not think that our administration which is dominated by upper class people is a great model of honesty, integrity, efficiency and all that. I do not think it has acquired that reputation. There are, of course, very good officers, very efficient officers among them. The bureaucratic system, as a whole, which runs the administration of this country has not got a very high reputation for integrity and efficiency. Why not? It is not dominated by lower class people. It is dominated by upper class people. So it should not have been so ... It is wrong to think that merit must be drawn only from the narrow upper caste segment of people. That way, ultimately merit will suffer. It is necessary to bring more people into the mainstream of the administration and development of the country. Therefore, I heartily welcome the step that has been taken ... We have said openly that perhaps the modalities of implementing this thing, how to do it, when to do it and so on, could have been perhaps better considered and a broader measure of agreement could have been reached if there had been some broader consultation and discussion and if this announcement had not been done so hastily. There is no haste in taking the step. The step is long overdue. But the haste with which it was announced perhaps was not altogether wise.

Finally ... whatever the leaders of different parties may say, I think, in every party without exception there are numbers of people who, because of party discipline or because of their leaders ... may not be speaking out, but ... there are people in all parties who heartily welcome this ... unless the leaders realize this and ... attune themselves ... with the feelings of the people in their party, they will come to grief sooner or later.

Somebody has already said that 52 per cent of this population, which we are talking about at present, is supposed to enjoy only 4.5 per cent of the top grade jobs. Is this not gross injustice? And it will not be changed overnight. You know what has happened in the case of the Scheduled Castes. Tens of thousands of unfilled reserved vacancies for the Scheduled Castes and Scheduled Tribes are being carried forward. After some time, they lapse ... That is the shame on us ... there are gross inadequacies in our whole system.

I would say finally that these apprehensions regarding drop in the quality and efficiency of the Government services, owing to influx of OBCs are totally unfounded. I am sorry to see young boys and girls from colleges who are carrying out funeral ... ceremonies of merit ... young girls are going about with posters saying we do not want our husbands to be unemployed. But, there are lakhs and crores of unemployed husbands in this country who are unemployed for no fault of their own ... What kind of outlook is this in society, I do not understand specially those who are enjoying the fruits of good education, higher education. They should have some social consciousness also. I would say that let us all try, we may have differences ... But, let us all still get together, try and see that the surcharged atmosphere is calmed down. It cannot be solved on the streets. It will be solved through discussions, dialogues, exchange of opinions and all that. And everybody who is seriously concerned with the welfare and fate of this country should appeal to the agitationists ... to give up this agitation and let ... their representatives, their leaders ... come and, as strongly as they want, let them put their point of view ... across the table and not out in the street. I urge upon the Government to take more urgent measures to see that some dialogue is opened with the leaders of the student community or other youth, who are agitating ... Thus, while I deplore the instances of police repression against them, I also deplore very much the action of some forces and elements in the country who are trying deliberately to instigate and incite these people by creating all sorts of unfounded and false apprehensions in their minds and not allowing them to understand calmly what is the actual dimension of the Government decision. This is a very wrong thing to do for political and party purposes ... We will only hurt each other and ultimately hurt the country ... the agitation has probably reached its peak now ... and it may begin to decline after that. No agitation goes on forever.

... I shall finally end by saying that my friend Shri Vasant Sathe is a very clever man ... (Interruptions.) The main thrust of his argument was that you are going back to Manu ... resurrecting Manu as though Manu was not there ... and Shri V.P. Singh, you are the new Manu. This was his main thrust ... I want to raise this question ... by carrying out after all these years this measure for uplifting people of the backward classes ... whether it is ... going back to Manu? ... It is not a revolution by any means ... but it does represent the big shaking up of the social structure in favour of the weaker sections and to that extent, of course, the upper class people may feel frightened ... But ... this was a long overdue shaking up of the social structure, and it has to be carried out. My Party fully supports this and I congratulate the Government for having taken this step.

VISHWANATH PRATAP SINGH

(Lok Sabha: Fatehpur)

Lok Sabha: 6 September 1990

On Acceptance of the Mandal Commission Report

Mr. Speaker, Sir, today I listened to the speech of the leader of the opposition in this House very patiently … no national leader has given such a long speech opposing the Mandal Commission till now. It will go to every nook and corner of the country that the leader of the Opposition[4] spoke for three hours continuously against the Mandal Commission. (Interruptions.)

But I will give him credit for his support on one point … (Interruptions.)

… He had to agree that the backward castes and classes should get reservation along with other things. He could not suppress this feeling in his heart. (Interruptions.) I would like to thank the leaders of all the parties that there is no difference of opinion in regard to making special provision for the backward classes … even though we have different opinions on other issues yet we are unanimous on the issue of making special provision for backward classes. This acceptance from both the sides is of great national importance … National acceptance has also been gained that social injustice exists in our present social system. There may be some difference of opinion as to how these special provisions should be made for the backward classes …

… There is another point. Despite having a communist outlook, Shri Indrajit Gupta spoke of social reality. The Government in this country can be changed, the Prime Minister can be changed, the religion can be changed, but the caste, decided by birth, cannot be changed till death … (Interruptions.)

Sir … one who is born in a downtrodden or backward class, had to face a lot of insult throughout life. A person is burnt on the pyre … once, but they suffer indignities for their whole life … One can accept death with honour, but one would not like to lead a life full of insult. They have alleged that through reservations, society has been divided … But, in fact, there has been such a reservation for centuries. But for whom it has been there? That reservation was made with a view to ensure the continuity of a class for the disposal of their night soil because today after … 40–42 years, no such caste is prepared to undertake that job. That reservation still holds the entire society in its grip and as a result it has stalled the progress of the downtrodden, the poor and the backward. It has also divided the country. (Interruptions.)

[4] Editor's note: Rajiv Gandhi.

Mr. Speaker: Please take your seat.

Vishwanath Pratap Singh: Look at those wounds in the hearts … (Interruptions.)

Rajiv Gandhi: This is not fair at all … (Interruptions.)

Vishwanath Pratap Singh: You spoke for two hours. I will reply to your points only when you interrupt me after I have spoken for an hour. I rose only when you had spoken for an hour. (Interruptions.)

Rajiv Gandhi: They were victims of feudalism only … (Interruptions.)

Vishwanath Pratap Singh: This is related with Government jobs only … There is no question of feudalism because this is the only way we can ensure the welfare of a particular class through the provision of reservation for them in Government jobs. (Interruptions.)

There is the question of social justice also … we have to bring changes in our social set-up also … The bureaucratic set-up is made according to the society … If we want to bring changes in the society, we will have to bring changes in the bureaucracy also, which is a decision-taking institution. All the important decisions are taken by the bureaucracy. We have to place the downtrodden in the bureaucracy and only then we can think of social reforms. So, this issue can be linked with the jobs and livelihood … If they get 40 per cent of the jobs, they will also become capable like Shri Paswan. Only those who have been in power have availed of all the opportunities. What was its result? The Scheduled Castes and Scheduled Tribes were assured of 22½ per cent reservation … in class 1 posts. All … poverty alleviation schemes, Scheduled Tribes development programmes, special component schemes and scholarships etc. were continued, but only 8½ per cent could make it to class 1 posts. (Interruptions.)

It was said that package of benefits will be provided through reservation in education … But even after … 43 years, the backward classes could not get even 4½ per cent of class 1 posts. It is not only the question of providing some facilities, but the question of participation in power. The National Front Government certainly wants to let those, who have not been allowed to participate in power, share power. We are not making these reservations just for providing them some facilities or means of livelihood … we are trying to give them a share in the institutions of power …

… The question is not of money or of the amount distributed as charity. The question is that of power …

I would like to repeat that we attribute poverty to economic factors, but it is inseparably linked to power. Centuries ago, the Aryan invaders defeated the Dravidian inhabitants of this country and established their supremacy and, today, those defeated people have remained downtrodden. It is because these people never had a share in the power structure of the society. If you want to bring them at par with others, then you should have the courage to make them equal partners in the power structure. They are not at par with others, just because the Constitution says so ...

I had proposed that if you care so much for the poor and downtrodden, then you should be bold enough to provide forty per cent reservation to them in all decision-making bodies including State Legislative Assemblies, the Lok Sabha and the Rajya Sabha. These are the small things which can contribute a lot towards the amelioration of their poverty ... (Interruptions.)

... I would like to say that if you direct these questions towards Dr. Chenna Reddy, the Chief Minister of Andhra Pradesh, with even one-tenth of the passion and anger with which you were raising them here, I am sure he would tender his resignation that very moment. You have provided for reservations in Andhra Pradesh, on a purely caste basis ... (Interruptions.)

Rajiv Gandhi: Mr. Speaker, Sir, two points have been made by the Hon'ble Prime Minister. The first point he raised was when he was talking about those people who were a reserve category for thousands of years. I would like to remind him that most of that was under the feudalistic system that existed before, which the Congress broke. You were a part of that ... (Interruptions.)

Mr. Speaker: The Prime Minister has yielded to Mr. Rajiv Gandhi.

Rajiv Gandhi: Sir, he has raised a question of different types of reservation in various States ... (Interruptions.)

Vishwanath Pratap Singh: What about Andhra?

Rajiv Gandhi: Specially Andhra; I am talking of Andhra also. (Interruptions.)

Vishwanath Pratap Singh: The number of people who talk eloquently about eliminating poverty have increased considerably. Therefore, it is essential to remove those who talk of eliminating poverty and hand over power to the poor people themselves. Either they will achieve the goal of eliminating poverty or remain satisfied with their lot ... give them power with complete confidence. Don't give it to them in a piecemeal manner ... (Interruptions.)

Rajiv Gandhi: We will extend this Session and we will have your Bill.

Vishwanath Pratap Singh: Okay. I keep it on record … (Interruptions.) It is said that casteism is increasing and when these opposition leaders meet each other, they all have smiles for each other but when it comes to raising questions in the House, they give vent to their rage and fury.

Rajiv Gandhi: We are not angry with you, we are angry over your deeds.

Vishwanath Pratap Singh: They say that casteism is increasing and that we are encouraging it. In their eyes, it is a casteless society, where the representation of 52 % of the people in the higher echelons of power is a mere 4.5 per cent, and where 22.5% of the population has a representation of 8.5 per cent … (Interruptions.) … and when an effort is made to change the present equation, it is tantamount to promoting casteism. What kind of logic is this? … (Interruptions.)

Rajiv Gandhi: Sir, I said right at the beginning that many mistakes have been made … (Interruptions.)

Vishwanath Pratap Singh: Since you have realized it, will you correct the mistake?

Rajiv Gandhi: I will answer you, if your side stops making a noise.

Vishwanath Pratap Singh: No, they will not make a noise.

Rajiv Gandhi: Many mistakes have been made in many States. It is not only Andhra but almost every State has gone through the route of caste-based reservation. I think it is wrong and I categorically say this … (Interruptions.) This evening I am not talking of votes; I am talking of what is happening to our nation. I think it is more important. Whatever might have been the mistakes in the states, there is no need to compound that mistake in the Centre. What we need is national consensus. We can look at the Centre and will look at each State. Let us sit down together and develop such a national consensus. We will sit down, we will work positively and we will implement that national consensus … (Interruptions.)

Mr. Speaker: … the way you have heard Shri Rajiv Gandhi, I would like that in the interest of the dignity of the House, please give a patient hearing to the Prime Minister also. I will tell the Opposition Members also to give a patient hearing to the Prime Minister.

Vishwanath Pratap Singh: I do appreciate the courage and honesty shown by the leader of the Opposition who at least accepts his mistake …

Rajiv Gandhi: I may add one more thing: almost all these reservations … took place long before I came into politics … (Interruptions.)

Vishwanath Pratap Singh: … the leader of the Opposition is right, when he says that these things took place long before his entry into politics. It is okay. Even if he disowns Shrimati Indira Gandhi and Pandit Jawaharlal Nehru, it doesn't matter … (Interruptions.)

Rajiv Gandhi: I am not disowning anybody here … (Interruptions.) That is why I accepted it, but when you raised your finger at me, I had no option, but clarify my position … (Interruptions.)

Vishwanath Pratap Singh: Weren't you pointing towards me, when you were speaking, but now when I pointed towards you during the course of my speech, why did it irk you? (Interruptions.)

Rajiv Gandhi: I do accept that something might have been done before my entry into politics … (Interruptions.)

Vishwanath Pratap Singh: … the leader of the Opposition has accepted that the earlier decision on reservations were a mistake, and considers the present decision also as … wrong … (Interruptions.) … I sincerely hope that he would amend that mistake and give necessary directions in this regard to the Chief Minister of Andhra Pradesh. If our leader of Opposition doesn't do it, then it won't be a sincere action … (Interruptions.) … If he doesn't intend to do so, why is he getting agitated? … you should go by what you are saying, even if it means that your Government will fall in Andhra Pradesh, you should have the courage to do it, otherwise there is no meaning in giving such a lengthy speech in the House. Not only we sitting on the treasury benches, but also those occupying the Opposition benches got bored in the past three hours.

Rajiv Gandhi: I said very clearly, let us have a consensus … (Interruptions.) … You cannot isolate any State. Andhra is not the only State. Let us have a national consensus on what the parameters of reservation should be. Let the Government bring a White Paper …

Vishwanath Pratap Singh: Just now, he was talking about the urgency to save the country from peril. If one really intends to save the country, one should be prepared to face the guillotine too, but … when a reference was made to Andhra Pradesh, the leader of the Opposition started looking for excuses, and now he is talking about the need to have a national consensus. If you are bold enough, you should go alone. We have courage … and that is why we are going ahead alone, on the issue of the implementation of the Mandal Commission Report …

Rajiv Gandhi: If you are bold and resolute enough, then you should bring about a national consensus on it. We want to see whether you can do it or not? You yourself had said that the States are free to decide their course of action. Then, what is the problem?

Vishwanath Pratap Singh: Where there is consensus, there is no need for any consultation. We are going by our own consensus and we are appealing for a wider national consensus, but here you were saying about saving the country and now you are trying to save your Government (in Andhra Pradesh). This kind of bluffing and brow-beating is not going to serve any purpose … I too was in that party for twenty years. We know their games very well.

… We are not saying that reservation is a magical wand, with the simple wave of which we can solve all their problems, but … it is a step in that direction. Definitely, the path which we have chosen will lead us to a confrontation with the existing system, but only that confrontation will result in the creation and emergence of an egalitarian social order. It is … a mistake to believe that this weapon does not have any creative power … at the moment, the parameters of the society, the scales are in favour of the affluent, and the balance pan on which the poor and downtrodden are weighed, always remain low. We are just trying to balance these pans, bring them at par with each other.

… we were questioned about the timing of this announcement … about the astrological calculations on the basis of which this announcement was made and also … when the astrologer made his predictions. For the past ten years, it was gathering dust and even the Constitution has not specified any timing for bringing about this social change.

… Yes, we are prepared to discuss it in a public meeting … (Interruptions.) You, too, have been witnessing this drama for three long hours. Just two questions have punctured it, the three hour long drama has met its end with just two questions… (Interruptions.). During the tenure of your Government … that auspicious moment did not come through but at least now that opportune moment has come for the implementation of the Mandal Commission Report. The Opposition leader read excerpts from the Mandal Commission Report in detail. They did not give … emphasis on its implementation, as much as they laid stress on the need to forestall it … according to your calculation, it has been done in a wrong way at a wrong time. Had it been done according to your calculation, it would have taken another ten years to implement, and we would have reached twenty-first century by then … they say that we did not have any discussion on it … please don't confine your vision to the time of its implementation … look at the way these downtrodden people have struggled … look at the number of people who bore the marks of the police's batons and bullets, who suffered the torments of prison life. It is true that we were in the Congress and we did not participate in that struggle, but what is the harm in joining hands for a noble cause? … we cordially invite you to join us in this endeavour … (Interruptions.)

… we included it in our manifesto. Discussions were held on this not only within the Janata Dal, but also among its various constituents and other groups. It was accorded approval by all the constituents of the National Front separately as well as collectively. After that it was included in the President's Address both the times. This issue, too, was thoroughly discussed, when the President's Address was taken up for discussion …

… (Interruptions.) Earlier, those sitting on the opposition benches used to ask us when were we going to implement the Mandal Commission Report … Now, when we have implemented it, they are saying that it is a hasty decision. During the last session, I had given an assurance in the Rajya Sabha that we would implement it within one year. This is our first year in office. The next session will be held in the next year, but we fulfilled our assurance at the earliest… (Interruptions.)

… We are saying it collectively. (Interruptions.)

There was an extensive discussion on it stretching up to three hours. During the course of discussion, it was alleged that the Mandal Commission Report was not acceptable, as its recommendations were caste-based. If you look at it, carefully, you will find that the Mandal Commission has not made its recommendations on the basis of caste alone … please look at page no. 63, chapter 11 …

Social educational survey criteria for backward classes.

'In view of their relative importance 3 points were assigned to each one of the social indicators, 2 to educational indicators and 1 to economic indicators.'

Economic indicators were also taken into consideration by the Mandal Commission. The criteria for assessing backwardness were evolved on the basis of composite indicator of social, educational and economic indicators.

Rajiv Gandhi: … The dispute is not on whether economic factors was included in the selection. The problem is the … caste word is being used … Look at para 12.4. He had said very clearly,

'In fact, caste being the basic unit of social organisation of Hindu Society, castes are the only readily and clearly "recognisable and persistent collectivities".'

He has gone on to define only caste. He might have used the economic factor to see which caste was included and which caste was excluded. But it is solely by caste, which is being indicated.

Vishwanath Pratap Singh: This does not stand scrutiny for a minute. (Interruptions.) …

It is clear from this that the Mandal Commission made its recommendations not on the basis of caste alone, but also on the basis of a composite indicator of social, educational and economic indicators. Caste system is prevalent only among the Hindus. Now, the argument that the Commission's recommendations were made on caste basis doesn't hold ground, for had it been so, the Commission would not have identified some Muslim and Christian communities for this purpose. (Interruptions.) …

… Had caste been the lone factor, it would not have included the communities of Ansari, Chikwa, Jafali, Fakir, Kunjra, Manihar, Momin, Hajjam and Rangrez in the long list of backward classes of Uttar Pradesh. The same can be said about the inclusion of certain minority communities in the long lists pertaining to Tamil Nadu and Gujarat. Thus, the Mandal Commission took into consideration, social, educational and economic backwardness, irrespective of caste or community … Now, had caste been the sole deciding factor, it would not have been that one caste is included in one state on the basis of its social, educational and economic backwardness, while the same caste is excluded from the list in another state because that community is not backward from the social, educational and economic point of view there. Thus, the regional factors have also been taken into consideration. Therefore, please do not give it a casteist colour … to achieve your narrow political ends and to stall the initiative taken by us. This is being done with the motives of strengthening the already existing caste system and of … misleading the masses. Your utterances both within and outside the House, leave no room for any doubt regarding your nefarious designs. It is an issue, which needs an in-depth study and a perfect understanding of the ground realities and it was for these very reasons that we held such wide ranging discussions on it. If I read further, you will start shouting. (Interruptions.) Restrain yourself for a moment and listen to me. I am quoting Shri P. Shiv Shankar. (Interruptions.)

… When Shri Shiv Shankar was the Law Minister, he had testified before the Mandal Commission. Permit us also to contest your claims, if not much, at least a bit …

… Paragraph 10.44 of the Report says:

'Shri P. Shiv Shankar (Law Minister) suggested that it would be safer to follow the criteria of social and educational backwardness already upheld by the Supreme Court in a number of cases … He also felt that the acceptance of economic criteria would give a setback to OBCs.'

Your Law Minister himself suggested that it is safer not to adopt any other criterion, as it will lead to fresh litigation and create complications. It is true. Now, comes the question of economic standard of a community and … of an individual. So far as economic standard of a community is concerned, the Mandal Commission made its recommendations on the basis of community-wise economic indicators. The denial of reservations to the financially well-off people among these communities can be done, once these communities are rescued from the vortex of poverty and destitution. We accept your suggestions about the need to include certain other parameters also, and as Shri Indrajit Gupta suggested, it should be reviewed. The Bharatiya Janata Party has also said that we should not be open-handed once a community reaches a particular stage of development, but first let them reach that stage, then we shall definitely review it. The Commission has suggested a review of the entire gamut, after every ten years, and it is acceptable to us. This is all when these communities reach a particular stage of development, but at the moment, we have not even served the food, and you are trying to walk off with the utensil containing the food … (Interruptions.)

… Now comes the question of criteria. The economic criteria of the various communities were taken into consideration by the Mandal Commission. So far as the question of individuals benefiting from reservations is concerned, once an individual benefits from it … (Interruptions.) … then his or her children (Interruptions.) … should not benefit from reservations, I would like to ask who has made such a demand? Has any backward class demanded it? Has anyone belonging to a Scheduled Caste demanded it? (Interruptions.) But they do not have any group. Had there been any collective demands, they would have also sat under a tent at the Boat Club as others do even for petty demands. They have never demanded anything. But there are classes who do not have any problem but even then they are given facilities and concessions. It is just like giving an injection to a healthy man. Truly speaking, even if some of them might have succeeded in becoming an officer, collector or Superintendent of Police, people belonging to this class would not have dared to approach the police station to lodge their report. We want to break their morale. What else do we want to do? If a few of them, whose forefathers could not even dream of imparting education to their children, have been able to give good education to their children, the vested interests say it should be stopped. Does that mean that at best this class should provide peons and no officers? Now that something is being done for the upliftment of the Scheduled Castes, Scheduled Tribes and the backward classes, the vested interests think that they should be crushed so that their economic conditions remain the same, and they are able to give bare minimum education to their children. Consequently, they will fill up only class IV and class III posts. They want to keep them away from getting top education … I agree with Shri Indrajit Gupta. (Interruptions.) …

There is an apprehension that those who have got good education among these classes would one day become strong and powerful and will capture all spheres of activities … Despite all efforts we have not been able to achieve much. (Interruptions.) The people belonging to poor sections say that out of the 22.5 per cent quota reserved for them, only 8.5 per cent quota is filled and the remaining 16.5 per cent is being passed over to those who are better off. The poor can only fill up 8.5 per cent quota, and they are being deprived of even that. Let reservation of 27 per cent and 22.5 per cent for backward classes and Scheduled Castes/ Scheduled Tribes continue for some more time. After 10–15 years, we can review it. (Interruptions.) …

… so far as capturing the maximum quota by well-to-do persons from among the backward classes is concerned, the same thing happens in general category also. Will you check the children of officers and Ministers from occupying prestigious posts? Let us allow full reservation for the poor. (Interruptions.) I believe the House is unanimous that reservation should be provided for the backward classes but the bone of contention is the percentage … The class, which forms 52 per cent of the total population, is going to get 27 per cent job reservation, i.e. near about half of their population, whereas the class which forms only 25 per cent of the total population, will avail approximately 50 per cent job opportunity, that is double their population. Thus, the ratio in job opportunity between the two classes is one to four (1:4). People say that everyone can compete in that category but the de facto position is 1:4 … (Interruptions.) …

Sir, we have taken precautionary measures in many States where there have been riots and bloodshed. (Interruptions.) There are many shortcomings in the list of backward classes recommended by Mandal Commission. Keeping that in view, we have asked for the opinion of the states and whatever is common in the lists, i.e. both Mandal Commission and States, we will do so that no State faces any difficulty in its implementation. The difficulties if any faced by the States would be taken into account later. (Interruptions.) …

So far as approval of states is concerned, most of them have prepared a list of backward classes who would get reservation in jobs. Are we creating anything new by doing just what is mentally and politically accepted in many States? We are doing nothing except bringing the Centre at par with the States which are ahead in this task … There is certainly some problem in the States where no such list exists. For that, we are asking such States for adopting it to the extent it is possible. People say the speed of implementation is very fast, but it is still slow. It is true that we should not accelerate the speed too much lest things go out of control. (Interruptions.) Another question is about merit. Where is the merit produced after all?

… The mentality behind this is that 72 per cent of the population of the country is without any capability and merit. What remains in the country if its 74 per cent population comprising 22 per cent of the Scheduled Castes and Tribes, and 52 per cent of the backward classes, are incapable? (Interruptions.) … There is a provision of little less than 70 per cent of reservation in Tamil Nadu, Andhra Pradesh. Karnataka and Kerala have also provided a high percentage of reservation for SC/ST. Whether the Central Administration is more efficient where there is only 8 per cent reservation for SC/ST in Class I posts and reservation of only 4½ per cent for the candidates of backward classes? They are not responsible for inefficiency and corruption. Then who is responsible for it? … (Interruptions.) What about talent? If we have to make progress, then we will have to give due regard to the labour class. We cannot raise the production capacity in the country without the upliftment of the labour class. We want equal participation of the labour in industry and other fields. We have to give the workers an equal share and participation in political, social and economic activities. People with a drawing room history behind them, cannot increase the production. Instead, they are more useful on … planning … Workers are a fit class to undertake labour intensive jobs, and they should be given more opportunities. It will expedite the progress of the country. There is a need for imparting proper education to these people and until they are educated, they cannot compete with the higher classes. Today, there are three systems of education … for the poor class … for the middle classes, and … for the higher classes … (Interruptions.) This system will have to be changed … (Interruptions.) Mandal Commission has recommended structural changes. But nothing has been done in this regard. We have included land reforms in the Ninth Schedule. We are making laws for agricultural labourers. All these things are related … Our friends in the Bharatiya Janata Party, Shri Somnath ji of the CPM and Shri Indrajit ji and many others on that side have asked for enhancing the opportunities of general employment. Sharing power is not the only solution of unemployment, and Government jobs are not their remedy … (Interruptions.)

Agricultural sector has the largest employment potential. So agriculture is being given priority. Industry will be brought under the small sector and programmes are also being prepared for the service sector. Nearly Rs. 265 crores have been allocated for self-employment of 20 crore youths … We want to talk to the students and discuss their grievances with them. We want to appeal to the students that they are being misguided which is very dangerous. All the things have not been presented before them in their proper perspective … we can chalk out new schemes for our youth. We propose to form a National Council for that … In the end, I would like to … appeal to the students that this decision has been taken in the interest of social justice. This is for the fulfilment of the dreams of Dr. Lohia, Chaudhari Charan Singh, Mahatmaji, Jaiprakashji, Ramasamy Periyar and all in the Opposition are requested to cooperate with us. But they talk of violence, arson and bloodshed. We have received a report from the Bihar Government that people like Shri

Mahachandra Singh. MLC, Shri Rajendra Singh Bismil, MLC, Shri Yogeswar Jha, MLA, Shri Ramendra Pratap Sahi, MLA and Shri Ramakant Pandey, MLA were behind these incidents of violence … (Interruptions.)

They are the legislators of the Congress. I will request the Congress Party and the entire Opposition that they should take disciplinary action against those people who are inciting violence and by that … prove that they have no hand in these incidents of violence.

3

The State of the Scheduled Castes

***P. Chidambaram** is best known for his stewardship of the finance ministry for more than one government. But he also had a stellar innings as home minister in the United Progressive Alliance government headed by Dr Manmohan Singh. He's remembered as a conscientious home minister who tried to transform one of the most difficult ministries. He used to be in North Block every morning at 9 a.m. – an hour ahead of everyone else – and expected his officers to emulate him. Every month, he would address a press conference where he would present a report of the month gone by and invite further questions – the only home minister to have ever done this.*

In this speech, Chidambaram, also a leading lawyer, speaks with surprising candour on the unhappy state of the Scheduled Castes and Scheduled Tribes. He spells out how the law enforcement machinery must be sensitized to deal with atrocities, while stressing that unless the community is involved, these crimes cannot be prevented or punished. He also points to the need, in the long run, to work towards 'creatively' destroying the caste structure.

P. CHIDAMBARAM

(Lok Sabha: Sivaganga)

Lok Sabha: 30 August 2010

On Increasing Atrocities Against the Scheduled Castes and the Scheduled Tribes

Madam Chairperson, I am grateful to the Hon'ble Members for the very informative debate that we have had over the last two days. On the first day, we had about 14 Members speak on the subject and today we have had another 14 or 15 Members who spoke on the subject.

… all of us should understand the historical injustice that has been heaped upon the Scheduled Castes and Scheduled Tribes. In fact, it goes back to the origins of society, as we know it, and the divisions in society. Over the years, instead of these divisions becoming narrower, these divisions have become deeply entrenched. There are other divisions in society but the most cruel, the most humiliating and the most dehumanizing are with regard certain castes as 'untouchables'. As a result of that, we, today, have a number of castes which are described as Scheduled Castes.

The Scheduled Tribes have a different kind of history of injustice because of where they live and the manner in which their societies are organized. They suffer another kind of injustice. Over the years, we have tried to find ways in which we can bring the Scheduled Castes and Scheduled Tribes into the mainstream and get rid of these divisions in our society which contribute to the injustices that continue to be heaped … Unless we understand that it is the divisions in society which cause or perpetuate these injustices, we cannot treat the injustices or deal with injustices alone …

… they have suffered socially, politically, economically in terms of development, and they are the victims of crimes and atrocities. In this debate, Hon'ble Members have highlighted general issues. They have illustrated them by specific instances and each instance must compel us to hang our heads in shame. Only in the last couple of months, we had instances in a neighbouring state. Some time ago, there was a very bad incident in which a judgment was delivered about three or four weeks ago. I do not wish to name the State or the place. Everybody knows that but each one highlights how deeply entrenched prejudices are, and how those who have wealth and power use that wealth and power to inflict atrocities upon the Scheduled Castes and Scheduled Tribes.

My colleague, Shri Mukul Wasnik, made a brief intervention the other day to inform the House about the issues that have been taken up by his Ministry and the initiatives taken by his Ministry. In fact, his Ministry is the nodal Ministry to deal with Scheduled Castes and the Ministry of Tribal Affairs is the nodal Ministry for dealing with Scheduled Tribes. We, in the Ministry of Home Affairs, look after the administration of criminal justice, that is most important when we deal with the crimes and atrocities against the Scheduled Castes and the Scheduled Tribes.

Madam, Parliament has made a number of laws, the general laws, the IPC and other laws. But we made two special laws. First is the Protection of Civil Rights Act of 1955, in short called the PCA, and the other is the Scheduled Castes and Scheduled Tribes Prevention of Atrocities Act of 1989, in short called the POA. These two Acts in my view, empower sufficiently the states to take action if the state has the intention, the mind and the will to take action. In fact, Hon'ble Members will agree with me that adding to the laws does not make the enforcement more effective.

It is the implementation of the existing laws and the intention to implement the laws; the will to implement the laws that makes enforcement of laws effective …

Madam, I must concede that the statistics do not reflect any decline in the atrocities. On the contrary, the information compiled by the Crime Records Bureau shows that the number of cases registered of atrocities against the Scheduled Castes and the Scheduled Tribes is, in fact, on the rise. I have the numbers from 2006 to 2008; subsequent years are being compiled. Take for example the case of the Scheduled Castes. The number of cases of atrocities against the Scheduled Castes registered in 2006 was 26,665. That itself is an understatement. Many of the cases are simply not registered. In 2007, it was 29,825 and in 2008, it was 33,365. So, this clearly shows the rise in trend. I can make one or two deductions from this. Firstly that there is no let-up in the atrocities committed on the Scheduled Castes. The other inference one can make is, perhaps, because of the pressure that is put on the state governments by the Central Government, by public opinion and by NGOs, now the states are showing greater willingness to deal with the problem. Therefore, more cases are being registered. That is also a possible conclusion. Whichever is the right conclusion, it is not a matter of which we can be proud about. We cannot be happy about the fact that approximately 33,000 cases are being registered as atrocities against Scheduled Castes in one year. What makes it even more disturbing is that while so many cases are registered, the conviction rate hovers around 30 per cent. What makes it doubly painful is that there is rise in atrocities, but when you try to prosecute and convict, the conviction rate is only 30 per cent … Acquittals are very high. Not only are acquittals very high; pendency is about 80 per cent. At any given time, 80 per cent of the cases are pending. So, there is a serious problem in the manner in which we are dealing with these cases. After all, in our system … the Executive can take preventive measures and if crimes are committed; if atrocities are committed, the Executive can only prosecute. It is the judiciary which has to punish. I am afraid that the disposal of the cases is low; the rate of conviction is low. Therefore, it is fair to conclude that the feeling amongst the Scheduled Castes and the Scheduled Tribes that all these laws and all these statements, all these pronouncements have really not brought any relief to them. That feeling is running high and I cannot but say that feeling is justified.

We must ask ourselves as to what can be done. Look at the kind of crimes that are committed against these people! The crimes that are committed are the worst kind of crimes. They are murder, rape, kidnapping, abduction and arson. These are not petty crimes. These are pre-meditated crimes. Some of them may be opportunistic but most of them are pre-meditated crimes. Among the worst crimes in the Indian Penal Code are murder, rape, arson, kidnapping and abduction. This shows how vulnerable the Scheduled Castes and how vulnerable the Scheduled Tribes are.

Madam ... please do not misunderstand me ... We all represent one State or another. If, in the course of my intervention, I would mention ... some States, just remind me, and I will tell you about my State also. There is no difficulty about it. In every State, the position is more or less the same.

Ultimately, we must recognize that police and public order are state subjects. It is the same people who elect the Central Government and the State Governments. We are all elected to represent the people in Parliament and to form the Central Government and the same people elect people like us to the State Legislature to form the State Government. In their wisdom, the founding fathers said that let police and public order be subjects of the State Government. So, when these atrocities are committed, why does the State not show the willingness, the determination and the firmness of purpose to punish those who are committing these atrocities?

Some of us who are here were and can be in the State Legislatures in the future. For example, Shri Munde, who started the debate, was in the State Legislature for many years. Some of them who are in the State Legislatures may move to Parliament. We are not saying that we are not responsible. All that I am pointing out is that ultimately, if the authority where the power resides – the State Government – does not take seriously the phenomenon of atrocities and crimes being committed on its own people, then that is a matter of shame. All of us representing one State or another must also, in a sense, share the responsibility that our States are not doing enough to punish those who commit atrocities.

Madam, on the 1st of April, 2010, my Ministry issued a very comprehensive advisory based on the recommendations of the National Commission and others. The advisory set out in great detail as to how the State law enforcing machinery must be sensitized to deal with crimes and atrocities against the Scheduled Castes and Scheduled Tribes. We emphasized that unless the law enforcing machinery involves the community, these atrocities and crimes cannot be prevented or punished.

I have no doubt in my mind that in every community, there are people belonging to the non-Scheduled Castes and non-Scheduled Tribes who are basically good human beings and who do not want these atrocities to be committed on SCs and STs. I cannot believe that everyone who is a non-Scheduled Caste and non-Scheduled Tribe participate in or condone these atrocities. In every community, there are people who will, if they are brought into the system, stand by the law enforcing agency and ensure that these atrocities are not committed ...

The point is that the law enforcing machinery stands completely divorced from the community. It must involve the community in enforcing these laws ... ensuring that these atrocities are not committed ... they must have a community monitoring system to check cases of violence, abuse and exploitation. If a complaint is made, there must be no delay in registration of an FIR and that FIR must be investigated promptly. If there are areas where there is a long history of atrocities and crimes, special attention must be paid to those areas and policing must be made more effective in those areas. If atrocities and crimes are committed, immediately the state must rush in and implement measures for the economic and social rehabilitation of victims of atrocities.

I had a case in one state – I shall not mention the name of the state – about two months ago. Several Members of Parliament and their friends came and reported. They said that the Scheduled Castes and the Scheduled Tribes have been driven out of the village and that they have moved 100 miles away and settled down in another place. There was a sense of fear in a number of villages surrounding that village. I deputed a team from here. They went and met those villagers. I am happy to inform you that many … who had left the village were persuaded to return to the village and we have got assurances from other members of that village that they will not commit any atrocities on these people and they will be treated with dignity and respect. But that is just one incident. I am sure there are many other cases where no effort of such a kind is made. Such effort in my view must be made primarily by the State Government.

The state must ensure that everybody can live in his or her traditional habitation or place of residence with respect, with dignity. Some of the measures that we have asked them to take is, the provisions of these two Acts must be enforced more vigorously; enforcement agencies should be instructed in unambiguous terms and must be sensitized to the rights of the weaker and vulnerable sections; the administration should play a more pro-active role in involving the community; and training must be imparted to police officers on these laws.

In fact, training has become a casualty. We are now, once again, restoring the primary place for training. Every officer must undergo training periodically. But when they undergo training, it is usually for arms training; it is usually for training in forensic investigation; but not enough hours or enough classes are devoted to training police officers to sensitize them to these laws. If you send a person for training for seven days, that is spent on giving them arms training and training on forensic investigations. These are the more glamorous aspects of policing. But the point is that they must devote enough hours, enough classes and enough lectures on this aspect too. Enough real life cases must be placed before the officers who are imparted training through case history, case study, etc. and they must be sensitized to these laws. We have now said that all training must include training where they are sensitized to the laws concerning the Scheduled Castes and the Scheduled Tribes.

Then, when you register an FIR, it cannot be left to the whim and fancy of the officer who registers the case. They must take the statement of the victim and the victim's statement must be appropriately reflected in the FIR. The victim could be an unlettered person; so, the victim says something and the officer records something else. The victim's statement must be recorded and the Section that is attracted must reflect the victim's statement, not what the police officer thinks is the minimal duty that he has to perform.

We have also recommended that we must use the media, print and electronic media, to create awareness of these laws. I have already spoken about the community monitoring system. We have said that they must also organize camps in sensitive areas for legal literacy and legal awareness among the sections of the people who are vulnerable. While they sensitize the police officers and the community, they must also create legal awareness and legal literacy among the Scheduled Castes and the Scheduled Tribes so that they can stand up for their rights and go and register these cases. We have recommended that NGOs working in the area must be associated. NGOs are available there and virtually for everything you can always find well-meaning and well-intentioned NGOs. These NGOs must be brought into the picture. They must be involved with the community. They must be encouraged to work among the vulnerable sections. We have said that the FIRs and the investigation of FIRs must be supervised at the appropriate level by senior officers. There are senior officers who do not take any interest. I can give you examples from my own experience where if the SP takes an interest in matters of atrocities against the Scheduled Castes and Scheduled Tribes, you will see a sharp dip in the crime in that district, at least, as long as that person is an SP. Each one, I am sure, has got the same experience ...

... In fact, the popular notion is that nothing can happen in the district, even crime, without the knowledge of the police station. If the SP takes special interest in atrocities against the Scheduled Castes and Scheduled Tribes, you will find a sharp decline, at least, for the two years or so that he is there ... (Interruptions.) In areas where they are particularly vulnerable, in my view, the State must make a conscious effort and post officers belonging to the Scheduled Castes and Scheduled Tribes in those districts ... They must supervise these cases. We have said that the District Magistrate/District Judge/District SP must periodically review these cases, the Judiciary cannot remain aloof by simply saying that 'I remain in a cloistered Chamber, and I will only hear the cases'. The District Judge has a special duty. He is responsible for the administration of criminal justice in a district. In fact, the Supreme Court had to tell them to periodically visit the district jail. Likewise, the District Judge and the Senior Judges must periodically review what is the state of these cases and how they can be expedited. Not only the Executive Administration but the Judicial Wing of the state must also take an interest in these matters ... (Interruptions.) They should review these cases. Then, we have said that the Districts and Sessions Judge must hold a monthly meeting and in that meeting the District Magistrate, the Superintendent of Police and the Public Prosecutor must be invited. They must review every single case which has been registered and the trial of those cases ... (Interruptions.) I concede that this is not happening ... I say that with a considerable degree of anguish and pain ... But hopefully the media will carry this ... out of the 700 District Judges or so presiding over districts, maybe a few district judges will now realize that it is not their duty merely to hear both sides and deliver the judgment. It is their duty to ensure that the administration of criminal justice in their jurisdiction takes place effectively. So, it is my sincere hope that the District Judges will please hold a meeting once a month or once in two months and review the trial of these cases, expedite these cases and ask why so many cases are ending in acquittal. I will tell you presently why so many acquittals take place.

Now, about the last part of this, we have rehabilitation. It is not enough for the State merely to enforce a law and punish 'X' for the crime against 'Y'. He can be punished. What about 'Y' who is the victim? You have to extend measures for the social and economic rehabilitation of the victim. In fact, a part of the reason why atrocities are committed is economic activity. In my experience, I have seen that in some areas, the Scheduled Caste or the Scheduled Tribe person is prosperous. My knowledge is mostly about the Scheduled Caste, not about the Scheduled Tribe. It is because of the economic activity, because of the enterprise, there are areas where the Scheduled Caste people have also become prosperous. The Scheduled Caste people are able to build brick and stone houses. The Scheduled Caste people are able to acquire vehicles. The Scheduled Caste people are able to dress better, send their children to better schools. One of the reasons why atrocities take place in those places is to cripple them economically. Every riot, every arson case cripples them economically. Therefore, it is important that the State must immediately rush in social and economic measures for the rehabilitation of those who have suffered through these atrocities.

Madam, the National Commission for the Scheduled Castes went into the matter on why cases are ending in acquittal. As I said, acquittals are running a little over 70 per cent. They found out the following are the reasons. They took a number of cases and analysed. The so-called compromise between the complainants and the accused is not genuine. I am not against compromise, but some of these compromises are forced compromises; compromises are brought about by the police themselves. So, they are not genuine compromises. If they are genuine compromises, we are happy. But some of these are forced compromises. Then, the witnesses turn hostile.

... The witnesses turn hostile or the witnesses do not appear on the date of the trial. Then, the Judge has no option but to acquit the accused because there is insufficient testimony ... (Interruptions.)

... In my experience, I think the most serious lacuna is delay. Delay leads to 'disappearance of relevant evidence'. Therefore, it is important that the case is tried within three months or six months. If you delay the case, you can be sure that the evidence will disappear; compromise will be forced; witnesses will turn hostile. After that, what is the point of blaming the Judge because he has to acquit? Therefore, it is important that - I repeat it - the District Judge must take responsibility for the administration of criminal justice in his jurisdiction. He must hold the Monitoring Committee meetings every month. He must bring the DM, the SP and others together and try to impress upon all his Judges, the Sub-Judges and the Magistrates that these cases must be tried and the judgment must be pronounced within three months or six months. It is not impossible to pronounce a judgment ...(Interruptions.)

... In fact, every High Court has a High Court Judge in charge of a district. That High Court Judge must now monitor that district.

There is another problem. We have asked the states and the High Courts to designate the Special Courts. Now, when you designate a Special Court, which is a Sessions Court, then, you do not designate it only for the Scheduled Caste, the Scheduled Tribe cases, but you designate it for a whole lot of cases. Then, the sufferer is the category of cases where the Executive or the Police no longer has a great interest, anyway, to prosecute. Therefore, the Special Courts are really not Special Courts. It is a misnomer to call them Special Courts because a Special Court is a Special Court on many special things. So, it ceases to be a Special Court ... (Interruptions.)

Then, the Special Court cannot take cognizance of an offence without being committed by the Magistrate. That is a provision in the POA Act, which, I think is a lacuna. We are intending to correct that lacuna. He must be able to take cognizance of a case even without the committal by a Magistrate.

The Ministry of Social Justice has taken a number of measures. For example, they are giving assistance for setting up of the Scheduled Caste, Scheduled Tribe Protection Cells; they are giving assistance for the setting up of Special Police Stations in the vulnerable areas.

They are giving assistance for setting up exclusive Special Courts, for awareness generation programmes, incentive for inter-caste marriages and for relief. But the budget of the Ministry of Social Justice and Empowerment has increased tremendously since the UPA came into office in 2004. I think my colleague Shri Mukul Wasnik must have given you the numbers. But I still think the funds are insufficient for these purposes. We are a very large country. So, more funds must be allocated to this Ministry so that they can intensify their efforts in the matter that I have just mentioned.

Madam, some States have done well in this regard and I must compliment those states. For example, Andhra Pradesh has set up 22 Mobile Courts in 22 districts ... (Interruptions.) After all, whether they give anticipatory bail or regular bail, pending a trial you cannot keep a man in jail forever. You know the law of the country. Bail is the rule, jail is the exception. So it is not important that they give bail. What is important is that these Mobile Courts should decide the cases quickly. Once the case is decided, there will either be a conviction or acquittal ... (Interruptions.)

... Tamil Nadu has set up four Special Courts in four districts only for Protection of Civil Rights Act. In other districts, they are burdened with some other cases. But in these four districts, which are extremely vulnerable, there are really 'Special Courts' for this purpose.

... I am giving these examples because these are good practices and they must be emulated by other states. In Tripura, the First Class Judicial Magistrate has been empowered to hold Special Courts. Kerala has specified the District Court itself as a Special Court. But, as I say, the District Court is already burdened with so many kinds of cases. I am not sure whether that is an effective way of dealing with these cases. Chandigarh has designated the Additional Sessions Judge as a Special Court. Puducherry has designated the Chief Judicial Magistrate as a Special Court. Special Police Stations have been set up in Bihar, Chhattisgarh and Madhya Pradesh and, I think, other States should also set up Special Police Stations for dealing with crimes and atrocities against the Scheduled Castes and Scheduled Tribes.

... West Bengal has designated the District Judge as a Special Court. But that, as I say, is not a very effective way of dealing with the matter ... (Interruptions.) This is a serious subject and we must go above the political differences.

The Act allows for appointment of Special Public Prosecutors and I am afraid not many states have appointed Special Public Prosecutors. Regular Public Prosecutors deal with these cases. But I am convinced that regular Public Prosecutors and regular courts are there and then you call them 'special' just because the Act requires you to call them 'special' makes them anything but 'special' ... So you have to really earmark Special Public Prosecutors and earmark Special Courts if we have to make a dent into the kind of crimes that are being committed against these people.

Madam, 23 states have set up SC/ST Protection Cells ... But the Act provides for the appointment of Nodal Officers. Such officers have been appointed in 28 States. In most states there is a State level Vigilance and Monitoring Committee chaired by the Chief Minister himself. But I wonder how often that Monitoring Committee meets and how often it gives specific directions in matters that are brought to its notice.

Now, there is a Committee under the Chairmanship of the Minister of Social Justice. That Committee was set up after the Scheduled Castes and Scheduled Tribes (Prevention of Atrocities) Act, 1989 was passed. That Committee has met, so far, 10 times. The situation in 25 states and 4 Union Territories were reviewed. That Committee has expressed that the most important areas of concern are the following five: firstly, the high rate of acquittal; secondly, the high rate of pendency of cases and very low rate of disposal; thirdly, inadequate use of the preventive provisions of the Act, while the punitive provisions are invoked and FIR is registered, preventive provisions are rarely invoked; fourthly, that the committees and other mechanisms provided in the Act have virtually not been put to use; and fifthly, the Act itself may not be deterrent, perhaps it is not being as deterrent as we thought it could be. That is why we have issued the advisory on the 1st of April 2010 drawing attention to the provisions of the Act and said that you have to enforce the Act more strictly.

Madam, the POA rules were notified in March 1995, that is, about 15 years ago. Since the Committee chaired by the Minister for Social Justice has come to the conclusion that the provisions of the Act and the rules may not have as much of a deterrent effect, we are in the process of amending the rules. Draft amendments were initiated in November 2009. We are now consulting the states, UTs, other Ministries and the National Commission for Scheduled Castes and my colleague, Shri Mukul Wasnik, informs me that very soon the rules will be amended and the rules will be updated. We will try to make the rules stricter and more stringent so that the Act can be implemented more effectively.

In the Government of India, the principal Ministry or the principal instrument that we have to deal with this matter is, of course, the Ministry of Social Justice. We have a young dynamic Minister. He is taking great interest in the matter. He has started the amendment of the rules and I am sure that he will bring about qualitative change in the manner in which these two Acts are administered throughout the country. We must extend our fullest support to him in whatever measures he takes and whatever advisory he gives to the states. Parliament must extend full support so that the country, the Governments in the states can know that he has the full backing of Parliament.

Madam, I could go on giving more statistics and details, but that is not the purpose. The purpose is that this is a matter of shame, wherever we go, whoever we talk to, both in India and abroad, ask us about how we treat our Scheduled Castes, Scheduled Tribes and the minorities. This is nothing to do with party politics or philosophies or ideologies. The point is, we cannot call ourselves a civilized nation, and we cannot call ourselves a land of Gandhi, Nehru and Sardar Patel unless we bring dignity and equal respect for our Scheduled Castes, Scheduled Tribes and Minorities and, if I may add, our largest neglected vulnerable group, women.

These are the four, which are most vulnerable in this country. Wherever you go, in academia, in the universities where human rights organizations gather, the question that is often asked is, very well you are a dynamic nation, you are a growing power, but how do you treat your Scheduled Castes, how do you treat your Scheduled Tribes, how do you treat your Minorities and how do you treat your women?

In Scheduled Castes and Scheduled Tribes, as I said, this is something very deeply connected to the way in which our society is organized. In fact, creative destruction of some of these structures in society is the only way in which we can get over these differences.

... In other countries, there are other divisions. There is a division of race, there are divisions of tribes, some tribes are considered superior, and some tribes are considered inferior. So, these divisions are there in some other countries too. But we are peculiar; we are unique in this caste system. But we have to get over these. We have to encourage people to transcend caste, to break these caste barriers and encourage our young people to think beyond caste. I am not sure whether we are doing the right thing sometimes when we deepen the entrenchment of caste. But that will open up a larger debate and I have no intention of opening up a larger debate at this hour of the day.

Some steps that we take entrench caste, and, on the other hand, we talk about how to break caste barriers and to creatively destruct the structure of our society. Be that as it may, in my view the principal responsibility lies with the State Governments. They are our Governments; they are your Government, my Governments in the State. We must impress upon the State Governments to enforce these laws. We will make these laws stronger when we amend these rules. And, if necessary, I am sure the Minister will come back to Parliament even to amend the Act itself. In the meanwhile, my sincere appeal to the State Government, to the Executive and the Judiciary, the Executive must bear great responsibility; the Chief Ministers must take special responsibility; the District Magistrates must take special responsibility in ensuring that prevention and punishment take place in the most vulnerable areas.

Finally, I would once again appeal to the District Judges, you are at the apex of the judicial system; you have the power which no other man or woman has the power to punish. That is an extraordinary power: a power that is given to the ruler alone. You alone have the power to punish. Judicial power is the most potent power in society. You have the power to punish. It is your duty to ensure that criminal justice is administered properly. You must chair these meetings once a month. You must call the DM, the SP and the Prosecutor. You must review these cases. You must improve the rate of disposal. You must ensure witnesses appear, trials take place quickly and punish the people.

As far as the victims are concerned, the Executive and the Judiciary must ensure that the victims are compensated and social and economic rehabilitation takes place. If all of us, collectively, together, demonstrate greater will and determination, I am sure, things will improve. Even if we cannot say in our lifetimes we have changed everything, I hope in our children's life time, at least, this humiliation and crimes and atrocities that we heap upon Scheduled Castes and Scheduled Tribes, I hope a day will come when we say they are free from these crimes and free from these atrocities and they can live with dignity in this country.

4

I Am a Muslim

'I am a Muslim, and I am an Indian. I see no distinction between the two ...' With those words, delivered in an emotionally high-pitched tone, as the Opposition tried to shout him down, former Jammu and Kashmir chief minister and National Conference leader – and third-generation politician – ***Omar Abdullah*** *became an overnight sensation, not in the least because there was a packed press gallery to take note. It was the evening of 22 July 2008, and he was supporting the Motion of Confidence moved by the then Prime Minister, Dr Manmohan Singh, after the India–United States Nuclear Agreement was signed. Under the Agreement, India agreed to separate its civil and military nuclear facilities and to place all its civil nuclear facilities under International Atomic Energy Agency (IAEA) safeguards; the United States, on its part, agreed to work toward full civil nuclear cooperation with India.*

In an interview later to Mint, *Abdullah said that he had been really 'keen' to speak that day because 'This whole perception had been created that the nuclear deal was anti-Muslim. And being a Muslim myself, being an MP from a Muslim-majority state, I thought it was important that I correct this perception.'*

Interestingly, in that debate in which he spoke, two other young Muslim MPs, former Jammu and Kashmir Chief Minister Mehbooba Mufti and AIMIM MP Asaduddin Owaisi, also supported Dr Manmohan Singh.

The backstory to the significance of the support extended by these Muslim MPs to Dr Manmohan Singh was the effort made by some Opposition leaders, particularly from the CPI(M), as well as the Bahujan Samaj Party (BSP), to present the India–United States Nuclear Agreement as being inimical to Muslim interests. The CPI(M), as is well-known, eventually pulled support from the Manmohan Singh-led UPA government, citing the Agreement. Some television channels, too, during that period held discussions on the subject, focusing on the Muslim angle.

But Abdullah, Mufti and Owaisi had read the Muslim pulse correctly: this writer recalls asking Muslim students in Uttar Pradesh in the run-up to the general elections of 2009 – that followed the signing of the Agreement – their views on it. They answered in one voice: they believed that Dr Manmohan Singh was a patriot, who believed in a multi-religious India, and he would therefore not take any decision that would harm the interests of the country or any of its citizens.

OMAR ABDULLAH

(Lok Sabha: Srinagar)

Lok Sabha: 22 July 2008

Motion of Confidence in the Council of Ministers Moved by Dr Manmohan Singh

Thank you, Mr. Speaker, Sir. I think that it is a matter of great misfortune for parties like mine … (Interruptions.) I do not know whether the Rs. 1 crore that was shown here is genuine or not. But I think that it is extremely unfortunate that if nothing else, this Rs. 1 crore is seeking to buy the silence of parties like mine who are not being given an opportunity to speak in a correct manner in this House … (Interruptions.) I have been a Member of this House for 10 years, and I have never disturbed this House in these 10 years. I have sat with them and I have sat on this side, and I have never disrupted a speaker and yet here they do not have the courtesy to listen to what I have to say … (Interruptions.)

I am a Muslim, and I am an Indian. I see no distinction between the two … (Interruptions.) I see no reason why I, as a Muslim, have to fear a deal between India and the United States of America (USA) … (Interruptions.) This is a deal between two countries. It is a deal between, we hope, two countries that in the future will be two equals … (Interruptions.) Sir, the enemies of Indian Muslims are not the Americans, and the enemies of the Indian Muslims are not 'deals' like this. The enemies of Indian Muslims are the same enemies that all the poor people of India face, namely, poverty and hunger, unemployment, lack of development and the absence of a voice. It is that we are against, namely, the effort being made to crush our voice.

… (Interruptions.) I am not a Member of the UPA, and I do not aspire to the membership of the UPA. But I am extremely unhappy with the way in which my friends in the Left have taken on this self-imposed position of being the certifiers of who is secular and who is not … (Interruptions.).

Until a few years ago, I was a part of the NDA and I was a Minister with them. The same Left people considered me as a political untouchable, and they considered me an outcaste because I was a part of the NDA. Today, the same Left people are telling me that all secular parties must unite with the BJP to bring down this Government … (Interruptions.) I made a mistake of standing with them once. I did not resign on the question of Gujarat when my conscience told me to do so, and my conscience has still not forgiven me. I need not make the same mistake again … (Interruptions.)

These people are talking about Amarnath; they have levelled allegations (against Kashmiris) in regard to Amarnath. (Interruptions.) Show me a single place where a Kashmiri has spoken against the Yatra, where a Kashmiri has said that we do not want pilgrims, where pilgrims have been attacked … (Interruptions.) Our issue was that of land; we fought for the land and will fight till death for our land, but we do not have a communal mindset like them. We do not demolish any mosque and we do not demolish any temple … (Interruptions.)

The Amarnath Yatra is going on over there for the last one hundred years and so long as there are Muslims in Kashmir, the Yatra will continue in Srinagar and in Amarnath. (Interruptions.)

Mr. Speaker, Sir, I would like to say with conviction that I do not shift loyalties in politics like them. We have joined hands with the secular forces and will continue to do so.

The Jammu and Kashmir National Conference will vote to support the Motion moved by the Prime Minister.

Section Eight

The Civic Space

1

On the Dangers of Detention

On 2 July 1971, Parliament enacted the draconian Maintenance of Internal Security Act (MISA). This gave the administration of the then Prime Minister, Indira Gandhi, enormous powers – such as indefinite preventive detention of individuals, search and seizure of property without warrants, and wiretapping – to crush civil and political agitations in the country.

The law was amended several times during the subsequently declared national Emergency (1975–77) and used to put down political dissent. It was eventually repealed in 1977, after Indira Gandhi lost the 1977 general elections, and the Janata Party came to power.

However, the central government, even today, retains similar powers to the one under MISA under other legislation such as the Unlawful Activities (Prevention) Act and various states have similar laws such as Maharashtra's Control of Organized Crime Act.

During the Emergency, the multifaceted **Piloo Mody** *found himself behind bars under MISA, the legislation that gained infamy for its disregard of legal and constitutional safeguards of civil rights. Mody combined a career in architecture with politics, and a passion for cooking with his felicity on the piano. He was at the time in the Swatantra Party. Here, in 1971, during the debates that led to the enactment of MISA, he expresses his implacable opposition to the 'black law', but with wit and humour.*

PILOO MODY

(Lok Sabha: Godhra)

Lok Sabha: 16 June 1971

Maintenance of Internal Security Bill

Mr. Chairman, Sir, after hearing the speech of my friend, Mr. Pandey, I am more than ever convinced that this Government and this party cannot be trusted with the powers that it is demanding today. It is very simple to create the sort of arguments that Mr. Pandey has created, to chase a red herring through the skies, and to create all manner of hypothetical situations with which he, as the keeper of the conscience of the country, is going to keep the peace over here.

First of all, I am against governing by ordinance. You know that this is the stand of our party. For years, we have been opposed to creating ordinances and then coming to Parliament, asking for their approval. Parliament meets here long enough for every conceivable law that their evil genius can think of, to be brought here and properly debated before they slap it on the whole country.

Everybody has accused us of believing in an open society. I make no apology for it. We want a democratic and healthy society to grow in this country. But what is this? They are bringing forth an Act which by any description is the blackest law that man has devised. If you were to read the history of how democratic movements have grown throughout the countries, it has been by this one principle of *habeas corpus*, and it is in order to establish *habeas corpus* that all democratic societies have evolved. What does this Bill do? It does precisely this – it snuffs out *habeas corpus* in the middle of the twentieth century in India after 25 years of Independence. How can one possibly support a law which gives the Home Minister and the Congress Party the power to withhold the freedom of people when there is no such emergency? No case has been made out.

Can the Home Minister say that it is necessary to impose this P.D. law in Lodi Estate or here or in Raj Path or in Chandni Chowk or in Connaught Place? Yet he has demanded these powers for these areas. Everybody knows that nobody more than we in the Swatantra Party have demanded from this Government that it maintain law and order and that maintenance of law and order is the first function of the Government and we have said this, not once, but we have said this umpteen times. When we blame them for not preserving law and order, they have come back with the facile Marxists' excuse that it is a socio-economic problem. Well, if it is a socio-economic problem, how are they going to tackle this problem by bringing this black law which is not going to improve the socio-economic condition of this country? Therefore, how are you going to preserve law and order – I would ask you.

I have no hesitation in giving approval to a particular law by which, for a temporary period of time and with proper safeguards and with foolproof reasons and after a case has been made out by the Government, they can seek this power for a limited area where they can demonstrate to us that the law and order is in jeopardy. We know that there is a tremendous influx of refugees from Bangladesh. We know that in these refugee camps it is quite likely that there are enemy agents. Let them demand these powers in areas surrounding the borders, in the refugee camps themselves and in the places where they want to settle them. But let them come forward with a proper case as to why they want to deprive us of our civil liberties. Make out a case. Not that 'we want to control Jyoti Basu'. Is that enough reason? Mr. Pandey cries hoarse about the feelings of the Muslims, and he looks towards Mr. Atal Bihari Vajpayee and blames the members of his Party. Against whom is this preventive law being used most? In 1965, every conceivable type of Muslim was carried away overnight and jailed for months on end. Nobody says anything about that. No case has been brought against them to this day. There are thousands of them who do not know why they were detained.

He has no right to talk about the Muslims. He has no right to talk about Jyoti Basu. He has no right to talk about the Durgapur Steel Plant. I can understand when he blames Jyoti Basu for stopping the work of the Durgapur Steel Plant. But what about the other plants, where we lose thousands of crores of rupees, where Mr Jyoti Basu is nowhere on the horizon, and which do not produce for the nation?

... With the 'Yem Yem', they have received, with 350 people thumping their desks – the 'Yem-yem' stands for the 'massive mandate' – they want to push through this black law. Sir, this law is a bad one and I appeal to them and most of all, to the Minister whose unfortunate duty it is to steer this legislation through Parliament – think for a moment about your own father. I am sure if the Hon'ble Minister did, he would realize that he would not have approved of this law. Yes, make out a case for a specific area and then demand your power. This House will be very happy to give you these powers. Last time, it was your party that backed away from enacting this law for an area where it was necessary, because of the pressures that were brought on it, in order that it could stay in power, by a very venerable leader of the Rajya Sabha. It was this very Party that backed away from bringing forward this law. It is only the 'Yem-yem' that they have received that now makes them bold enough to come forward and demand these powers because their greed for power is insatiable.

Therefore, I appeal to the Hon'ble Minister. He is so close to the centre of power that he probably does not see the historic perspective in which *habeas corpus* was brought about and established democracy throughout the world.

People are detained under this black law for some years; even after they have been released, their reputations are ruined, their business is ruined. A great deal of injustice is taking place. Does the Government do anything to rehabilitate them?

I have known some personal friends of mine, who were detained under this black law. I can personally guarantee this that they did absolutely nothing which would endanger the security of this country. When these friends of mine came out of jail, nobody has gone to them. People are afraid of associating themselves with such people, who suffer social ostracization. Will Mr. Pandey come and put his hand on their shoulders? No. This is the cruelty of these laws which are so arbitrary.

To deny this country *habeas corpus* is to rejuvenate the Star Chamber. We are not living in the reign of bloody Elizabeth I. We are living in the reign of Indira Gandhi, the last, I hope.

And therefore I suggest to the Minister not to turn this into a Star Chamber, not to turn this into the bloody dungeons of medieval times, but to remember that we are in the middle of the 20th century and without *habeas corpus* there is no democracy. I thoroughly oppose this measure.

2

The Emergency

By January 1976, the Emergency declared by the Indira Gandhi government on 25 June 1975 was already six months old, and many Opposition leaders were either behind bars, or had gone underground. Ignoring the obvious dangers, ***Somnath Chatterjee*** *of the CPI(M) decided to beard the lion in its den: he frontally attacked the Indira Gandhi government on the floor of the Lok Sabha. Sadly, censorship meant that apart from those who actually heard him, his message did not go out to the wider world. That same courage was visible all through his career which, included ten terms as a Member of Parliament and the Speakership of the Lok Sabha from 2004 to 2009. As Speaker, he voted for the Manmohan Singh government in the no-confidence vote in July 2008, even though his party voted against it, saying that as Speaker, he no longer had to abide by party rules. He was expelled from the CPI (M), even though senior party leaders reluctantly agreed that his action was in keeping with the Constitution of India, if not with the party constitution.*

SOMNATH CHATTERJEE

(Lok Sabha: Bardhaman)

Lok Sabha: 7 January 1976

Motion of Thanks on the President's Address

Mr. Chairman, Sir, starting from the Address of the President to the speech which we have heard just now, an attempt has been made to justify the Emergency on the basis of vague generalizations and mere abuses and vilification of the Opposition parties without specifying the supposed treasonable activities on the part of the Opposition parties. I am very sorry that having been swayed by emotions and probably encouraged by the presence of the Prime Minister, a sober and responsible minister as we thought him to be, Mr. Chandrajeet Yadav himself chose to use this occasion to vilify the CPI(M) ... on a wrong and misleading basis because, realizing that they cannot justify the Emergency on any positive ground, the best thing is to go on beating the Opposition with whatever stick comes handy. That is why it was said that there has been a sort of ganging up between the right reactionaries and the CPI(M). Sir, it is known that this is wrong and that this is an absolute calumny ... Only on a very important issue like ... civil liberties, there had been cooperation and we, Sir, certainly support anybody who will raise their voice of protest against the deliberate denuding of ... personal and civil liberties in the country by a repressive government. Whoever will come and support us, we shall certainly seek their support and give mutual support ...

Now, Sir, as Miss Patel rightly said, when BLD people join Congress, they become progressives overnight. When ex-rulers and ex-zamindars ... join the ruling party, they certainly become progressives. When Swatantrites and when Jana Sanghis join the Congress, they became progressive. Do not apply such double standards everywhere. This is my request.

You have declared Emergency. The people of the country know why. You declare Emergency on the plea of internal disturbances, when there was already an Emergency. Because of the powers under the Constitution of India, which you wanted to exercise or which you did not want to take the trouble of having obligations under, you could do it under the existing Emergency of 1971. All the powers, the Defence of India Rules and so on, have not been promulgated now. They were actually promulgated in 1971 and this is now being used under the new Emergency. Not a single extra-constitutional power was obtained by proclaiming this new Emergency. Then, what was this Emergency for? Was it for economic reasons? Then, there is a specific provision under the Constitution, Article 360, for declaring a financial emergency. You did not take recourse to that. When there was rampant inflation, when the whole economy was out of gear, as Dr. Rao has said, as he has reminded us, when the Government of India was not functioning so far as the finances of the country were concerned, you did not take recourse to financial emergency. And what emergency powers for internal disturbance are necessary to meet an economic situation? Sir, 'internal disturbance' has been used as a plea because the position of a particular individual became at stake. This is the reality. It should be understood. I am sure hon'ble members opposite realize it in their own heart of hearts. But they cannot say so. The press in this country has been gagged. The Opposition has been mercilessly gagged. Their own people have been gagged. Today the whole intention has been to create a fear psychosis in the country to bring about a feeling of terror in the minds of the people. People are not allowed to open their lips. This is a stark reality in this country. No good denying it. If you deny it, you are denying it for the purpose of record only not in your own heart of hearts.

What I was asking the government, the Prime Minister and others was this: What extraordinary powers did you need for which a second proclamation was made? Now, if there was internal disturbance alone, why have you brought out so many other justifications … for this emergency? How can you … take the pretext of late running of trains for internal disturbance? This party has been in power since independence in this country. If the trains had not been running in time, it is very easy to go on blaming the workers. Why have you not been able to inculcate a sense of discipline among the workers? Why have you not been able to make them feel part and parcel of this country, make them feel that they are one with the administration? Why are they alienated from you? Why are the common people alienated from you? You have no answer. You never ask yourselves those questions. For everything that is not happening properly in this country, an emasculated Opposition is supposed to be responsible. You ridicule the Opposition and say 'The people are not with you', but you hold that very emasculated and minuscule Opposition supposedly responsible for the ruination of this country. You have been in uninterrupted charge of the government of the country. You have not delivered the goods to the people. Poverty has been accentuated. People's miseries have increased a hundredfold, and you say you are not responsible for that.

This is why I say that your right to govern this country now is based on repressive powers. You cannot function without draconian laws. You cannot function under ordinary laws of the country. The Constitution of India which 25 years ago had been commended to the country by no less a person than Jawaharlal Nehru, that Constitution does not suit you, because it gives some powers even now to the people of the country. You do not like the people of this country to have any power. You do not want … the people of this country … raise a voice of protest. That is why you have come up with proposals, those obnoxious proposals … the source of which has not been denied.

As I was saying, if discipline was the reason, then a false reason has been given in the Proclamation of Emergency that internal disturbances were there which threatened the security of the country. If Mr. Jayaprakash Narayan had been guilty of treason, try him for treason. Give him exemplary punishment under the laws of the land. If Morarji Desai, or for that matter any person, has been guilty of sedition, try him. Give him an opportunity. Let the people of the country know. Mr. Jayaprakash Narayan has been arrested. He is a Right reactionary. In the name of fighting fascism and Right reaction, you have arrested MPs like Mr. Jyotirmoy Basu and Mr. Noorul Huda. Do they belong to Right reactionary parties? You have arrested trade union workers. You have dismissed trade unionists, government servants, under MISA. You have detained them. You have dismissed them under Art. 311(2) without even letting them know what is their wrong. Even the present Constitution, as it stands today, gives enormous powers to the Government. A government servant can lose his job in a minute. A person can be kept in detention indefinitely. Even his right to move the court is extremely limited. What have you done? You are afraid to face the people. The Supreme Court of India has given clearance to the Prime Minister's election. One of the Judges who upheld her election had made an observation. I do not know whether she has had the time to go through the judgment which has been delivered in her own case. Mr Justice Chandrachud has observed that law should not be what the king emperor thinks is law; it should be decided in the anvil of constitutionality; it should be tested on the principle whether it is for public good ... Today an attempt is being made to stifle popular and democratic movements, and stifle the ventilation of the people's grievances. If I say something here which is not to your liking, the people outside will not know; they do not know that there is another version possible on a particular issue. People may think: we have sent him to Parliament: we want to know whether our representative toes the line of Government or he has some alternative proposals to make. But now people will not know. Look at today's papers and see how Mr. Samar Mukherjee's speech has been reported. It is a travesty of reporting parliamentary proceedings. Is this the way you are going to take the country along the path of progress?

Mr. Chairman, I want to make this appeal to the Hon'ble Members opposite through you: do not feel that patriotism is your monopoly; or the desire to do good to the country is only your monopoly. We are as ... anxious that this country should be governed and governed properly: we want that this country should proceed on right lines. If my line is a little different does it mean that I do not have patriotism? If I do not want the zamindars, the landed gentry and the black-marketeers to control our country, does it mean that I am not patriotic? If I want to say something which the people of the country want me to say, should I not be allowed to say? If a judge delivers a judgment which you do not like, you say that the judge is wrong and therefore you want to take away the court's powers. Why are you so arrogant? You do not want anybody to judge your action. Why should not the judges decide whether you do something rightly or wrongly? It is a system which has worked for so many years. Take the last amendment of the Constitution which this Parliament adopted. We were willing parties to it. We had been demanding that the Constitution should be so amended that no vested interests can take advantage. We have enlarged the powers under Article 31 of the Constitution; we have given enormous powers to the Government. But how has this Government utilized those powers? What legislation has stood in their way? How have the courts stood in their way? ... We on this side have extended our support even to a capitalist and reactionary government as this when they thought of welfare legislation. Whether they were implementing that or not, we had extended them full support. Let them give one example of one single welfare legislation which had been held up by us in Parliament? I challenge them. On the other hand, in the name of bringing about a balanced society, egalitarian society, and welfare and socialism in this country, they have reduced the quantum of bonus without reducing the cost of living. They have taken away the rights of the workers even to hold meetings and demonstrations. They have not even the right to go to their managers to ventilate their grievances. There is a case in regard to Bank of India, I am not going into merits because the matter is sub judice. It is a nationalized bank and I want to tell the hon'ble members what happens there. The authorities there issued a circular deducting the salaries of the employees, because their representatives had gone to a meeting with the manager for ventilating employees' grievances who even entertained them. But after the meeting the manager issues a notice to them: you did not work during the time you came to see me and therefore you are not entitled to wages for that period.

Is this the way of getting the willing cooperation of the ordinary people of this country? Is this the way you want their participation in your so-called nation building? Mr. Chairman, Sir, the position is this. In the garb of Emergency, what is being sought to be done is to create and maintain a hegemony. We are opposed to that. The attempt is to create and maintain a particular attitude of government which is not in tune with the national aspirations of this country. You are utilizing this not for the betterment of the people because inflation has been contained. It is said that Emergency should remain and continue not because of inflation but because of other economic reasons and therefore elections should not be held. See how the reason is put forward by this government. Sir, what is the position in the economic field? What is the position in the small industries, small-scale industries like bulb manufacturing industries? Mr. Maurya is here. He has got the statistics fully. The small-scale industries are almost closed down. The wagon-building industries in West Bengal are completely at a standstill. J.K. Aluminium is being closed. Hindustan Motors have introduced a rotational system of layoffs of the employees.

Now, who is coming to their protection? Are you using Emergency powers against the management of Hindustan Motors? You have got all the powers under the sun. You don't care for the people's rights under Article 19 and under Article 14 you have suspended them. But you have not suspended Article 31 which guarantees property rights. You have forbidden my right to form an assembly and the right to free speech. You have taken away my right of equality to be treated equally amongst equals. But you have not taken away the rights of the propertied class. That is why Article 31 has not been touched. This is the true position of this Government.

Sir, in the jute industry, what is happening? Concession after concession has been made, but ... More layoffs and more closure and more retrenchment are continuing ... In the Jute Mills, even the jute growers are not getting concessions. Concessions have been given to the jute mills but jute growers are not getting even the support price. Same is the thing with regard to the Textile Mills. In those mills which have been taken over by the Textile Corporation, the workers are extending all support, not a single complaint has been made against workers. They are doing extra work. But they are in the doldrums because the management is still as bad as it was ... No attempt has been made to have the stocks cleared. The retailers cannot even take them, far less the consumers because of high cost of textile goods.

Sir, this is the position in this country and we are only told that something was being done for which Emergency must be imposed. Therefore, I request my friends, through you, Sir ... do not take the people of this country for a ride. Try to do something good for them. If the people are with you, why are you afraid of them?

3

If We Can't Eat Beef ...

***Gordon Gilbert Swell** played a critical role in the formation of the north-eastern state of Meghalaya, taught English literature to college students, and served as India's ambassador to several countries, and was even Deputy Speaker in the Lok Sabha. He was a Member of Parliament for six terms, five in the Lok Sabha and one in the Rajya Sabha. But he will probably be best remembered for this one short speech. The background to it is revealing: Atal Bihari Vajpayee, sworn in as Prime Minister in 1996, was seeking a vote of confidence. **G.G. Swell**, a close friend, was expected to back him, but after hearing Vajpayee that day, he made this impassioned speech in defence of Indian diversity. Most important, perhaps, is the fact that it was a defence that resonates even today, two and a half decades later. Not just that, Swell's statement that the people from his part of the country would not accept a ban on the eating of beef has been borne out by the fact that the BJP, which has banned its consumption elsewhere in the country, has made an exception for the Northeast merely to win votes.*

G.G. SWELL

(Lok Sabha: Shillong)

Lok Sabha: 28 May 1996

Motion of Confidence in the Council of Ministers

After so much of turmoil, after so much of collective display of lung power, I hope I would be able to restore some sanity to this House. I have returned to this House after a number of years. I have come here all on my own defeating all national parties with a margin that perhaps proportionately would be one of the highest in the world.

Sir, the Prime Minister, Mr. Vajpayee, has been my friend for a number of years and I have so many good friends in BJP. But I must say with anguish and not with jubilation, after a good deal of introspection and after a good deal of cogitation, that I have made this journey from approximating to a party which I now consider to be hierarchical and monolithic to the democratic forum of leaders where we meet and discuss, that is the United Front. Mr. Vajpayee has been my friend for a number of years, as I have already said. I thought I know him. Today, I do not know him. The irrational thing that he ever did was to have assumed power. I had expected that he would show himself to be a leader of this nation and that as a national leader his Government would project a national image. On the other hand, he started donning the Hindutva clothes and he started basing his Government on what we called the cow-belt. This is what I could not understand. This is why perhaps he has not only remained where he was – frozen with 194 supporters with him – and has not been able to win any more friends, but as a matter of fact, alienated many friends. The worst thing is, Mr. Vajpayee will be going out of office within a few minutes. He will be a leader lying in history, and history will not be repeated.

My friends in the BJP, especially Mr. Pramod Mahajan, were saying that after this, there will be another election in the country. We are not afraid of another election. I am not afraid of it. I am prepared to face election even tomorrow and I promise that I will beat you with double the margin that I have got now.

Having said so, I say it with considerable pain that Mr. Vajpayee has done great damage to this country. He has polarized this country. He has divided this country into the cow belt and non-cow belt. This is what is happening in this country … I do not understand his dissimulation. I do not understand why Mr. Vajpayee has taken to dissimulation. The President's Address is a string of inanities, a string of good wishes that he wishes to do. He seems to have forgotten all the fundamentals of his party. There is only one thing in which he is sincere and that is to have a total ban on cow slaughter. I have said that in the North-East – I come from that section as you come – beef is the cheapest source of protein for the majority of the people.

If you stop people … (Interruptions.). They are ashamed of us and we are ashamed of them. (Interruptions.) They can never impose their hegemony on the North-East. The Mughal emperors tried to do that by sending their army to Assam and, each time, they had been turned away from the banks of the Brahmaputra. They cannot impose their way of life on the people of North-East.

Sir, I think this is a wrong policy, economically also. We make an economic study of the cattle in this country. I make a submission that 80 per cent of the cattle population in this country is uneconomic. Very few cattle in this country give proper type or quantity of milk. Many of them just go on champing out blades of grass and leaves, leaving the country barren … turning the country into a desert. Some of them are being used as draught animals but a time comes when they are no longer used as draught animals. What do you do with all these cattle? Are you going to watch them? You are going to allow them to champ up all vegetation in the country. What are you going to do? … This is uneconomic.

I think, it is something right, and good that this Government is going out of power in a few minutes. If they follow … an economic policy which has got to be in sync with the economic developments in the world, they cannot suggest all these things. You have got to reform … the way which you approach your cattle. Treat your cattle well, get the benefit out of them. What are they going to do with all these stray cattle? Either you eat them or you kill them, do something. England today is facing what they call 'the mad cow disease ' … The destruction of these cattle and even the cost of destruction has become a big problem in that country. What are they going to do with it here? They have to think about it.

Mr. Speaker, Sir, if this is the way in which the BJP conducts its affairs, I can tell you that the whole of the North-East, from Bhutan right up to Nagaland, will be forbidding them psychologically. Nobody will listen to them. They have been able to make some progress in that area, mostly by overindulgence. But this time even that little progress will be swept out. Nobody is going to listen to them. They have nothing to do in West Bengal. They have nothing to do in Andhra Pradesh, and nowhere else in the South. The whole country is being divided between the cow belt and the non-cow belt. But even in the cow belt areas, the Muslims, the low-caste and the other people will rise against you. If you think that you are going to benefit when you go out of office, if you think that you will benefit out of a sympathy wave, it is going to be the other way … I predict that when the elections are held, you are going to do very poorly. You are not going to get even the number that you have today.

4

Mourning Rohith Vemula

The suicide in January 2016 of Rohith Vemula, a Dalit PhD student, six months after the University of Hyderabad stopped paying his monthly stipend (because he belonged to an active Ambedkarite student organization) sparked protests and outrage across India. It also gained widespread media attention as a case of state-sponsored discrimination against Dalits in Indian universities.

In February 2016, a few Jawaharlal Nehru University (JNU) students held a protest on their campus against the capital punishment meted out to the 2001 Indian Parliament attack convict Afzal Guru, and Kashmiri separatist Maqbool Bhat. The event was held despite protests by members of the Akhil Bharatiya Vidyarthi Parishad (ABVP), the students' wing, allied to the ruling BJP. Four days later, Delhi Police arrested JNU Students' Union President Kanhaiya Kumar – at that time with the students' wing of the CPI – and charged him with sedition. The arrests of two other students, including Umar Khalid, followed. This drew heavy criticism from within JNU and other universities in the country – as well as society at large, nationally and internationally – on the grounds that the BJP government was attempting to silence political dissent.

***Sugata Bose,** the Harvard historian – and grand-nephew of freedom fighter and national icon Subhas Chandra Bose – who served as a Trinamool Congress Member of Parliament for one term, spoke during the debate in the Lok Sabha on these two incidents. One commentator at the time, describing his speech – that was widely aired on social media – as 'luminous', said 'his powerful critique of the ruling party's "narrow, selfish and arrogant" nationalism was scholarly and elegant', as well as 'passionate and lyrical, radiating empathy for students painted as anti-nationals'.*

SUGATA BOSE

(Lok Sabha: Jadavpur)

Lok Sabha: 24 February 2016

Discussion on Situation Arising Out of Recent Incidents in Institutions of Higher Education

Madam Speaker, I rise to speak in this highly charged and sensitive debate as someone who has been a teacher at universities for three-and-a-half decades. I hope that my colleagues in this august House will have the patience to listen to me. This is after all a forum for debate and discussion, as the President reminded us only yesterday.

Just over a month ago, a Dalit research scholar at Hyderabad Central University, Rohith Vemula, tragically took his own life. The death of a bright young Dalit scholar is not new in Indian universities. The Thorat Committee that was appointed in 2007 to investigate the growing number of suicides among students in elite educational institutions discovered that of the 23 suicide cases, 19 were Dalits, two tribals and one Muslim. This alarming figure should have raised several questions of academic justice and freedom that our nation needed to seriously ponder.

Rohith Vemula left us a poignant message when he chose to leave this unfair world. In 'the only letter' that he was going to write, he told us: 'I always wanted to be a writer – a writer of science. Like Carl Sagan I love science ... stars.' Rohith today is not dead. He lives up in the Heavens as a star 'of purest ray serene' to serve as a beacon light to posterity. Rohith's tragedy should have stirred our collective conscience, including that of our Government. Unfortunately, we have a heartless Government that refuses to listen to the cries of despair coming from the marginalized sections of our society. Instead of assuring social justice to all, the ruling party wishes to use the student unrest in our universities to claim a monopoly on nationalism and tar all of their critics with the brush of 'anti-nationalism'.

Madam Speaker, I am not a communist. In fact, I won this seat in the Lok Sabha by defeating a prominent communist candidate. But I stand today in support of the right to freedom of expression by young students who may be inspired by Marx as well as Ambedkar.

Madam Speaker, I am a nationalist. I believe in a kind of nationalism that instils a spirit of selfless service in our people and inspires their creative efforts. But I know that nationalism can be a truly Janus-faced phenomenon and I deplore the brand of nationalism espoused by Members of the Treasury Benches that I find narrow, selfish and arrogant.

Following the unrest in Hyderabad, there were incidents that took place in Jawaharlal Nehru University, a university named after our great first Prime Minister.

Earlier this month, at one or two events on that campus very disturbing slogans were raised and deeply troubling posters were put up. We unequivocally condemn those slogans and posters. However, we strongly oppose the attempt being made to portray the entire university as a hub of anti-national activities and the onslaught of State forces on academic freedom. We were horrified to witness the scenes of students, teachers and journalists being assaulted within the court premises of Patiala House. It was not the students, but the black-coated storm-troopers affiliated with the ruling party who defiled and desecrated the image of Mother India.

The reverberations of the JNU incidents were felt in my home State, especially in Jadavpur University. There, too, unfortunate slogans were heard in the streets around the campus. But by contrast with what happened in the nation's capital, the West Bengal state administration led by Kumari Mamata Banerjee and the university administration knew how to defuse tension and to not unnecessarily escalate a crisis. It knew how not to over-react.

After all, the idea of India is not so brittle as to crumble at the echo of a few slogans. You cannot be a true nationalist if you are opposed to freedom. It is not a crime to seek freedom from caste oppression, freedom from class exploitation, freedom from gender discrimination. We must give our students and youth the freedom to think, the freedom to speak, the freedom to be idealistic, and, yes, the freedom to make mistakes, and learn from them. What must be avoided at all costs is the criminalization of dissent … (Interruptions.)

I heard the speech given by Kanhaiya Kumar on YouTube … (Interruptions.) I agreed with many things that he said. I disagreed with some of the things that he said. I agreed with him when he extolled Ambedkar's commitment to Constitutional rights and Constitutional morality. I agreed with him when he expressed admiration for our great revolutionaries like Bhagat Singh, Ashfaqulla, Sukhdev and Rajguru. He, of course, said that the RSS took no part in our freedom struggle. There, too, he was right … (Interruptions.), but as a teacher I would have liked to have a discussion with him about history, and I would have pointed out to him that even the Communists had actually taken part in the freedom struggle but also betrayed the freedom struggle at crucial moments during the 1942 movement, and during the Azad Hind Movement led by Netaji Subhash Chandra Bose. So, we condemn the vigilantism of self-appointed protectors of the nation who are trying to create a climate of fear.

… Madam Speaker, as I have said, I stand for the right to free expression of my Communist friends and they will be speaking in this House soon afterwards. But we condemn the acts of vigilantism by self-appointed protectors of the nation which foments a climate of fear. And I believe that students, teachers and university personnel must all be permitted to express opinions freely even if they conflict with the Government's political stances, and the Government must end the witch hunt for anti-nationals and the shameful scapegoating of university students. Why? It is because we believe that this witch hunt is meant to distract the nation from issues necessary to the nation's development such as employment opportunities and poverty alleviation.

We insist that no group within the Indian polity or in its diaspora is the univocal spokesperson for the nation. History shows us that State-sponsored or State-condoned campaigns against so-called anti-nationals lead to authoritarian rule and the destruction of democratic principles. If universities and students are attacked, then the legacy of the anti-colonial freedom struggle and of democratic reconstruction is gravely undermined. Madam Speaker, we learn our lessons in nationalism from great figures like Mahatma Gandhi, Jawaharlal Nehru and Subhash Chandra Bose, and those of us who are from Bengal are also inspired by what we have been taught about patriotism and nationalism by figures like Swami Vivekananda, Rabindranath Tagore, Deshbandhu Chittaranjan Das, Bipin Chandra Pal and Aurobindo Ghosh. I was wondering whose definition of nationalism might be acceptable to my friends in the Treasury Benches. I thought that at least I would try by citing before them the example of Aurobindo.

The issue of Kashmir kept coming up in the speech given by Shri Anurag Thakur. Now, it is incumbent on all of us who are the elected representatives of the Lok Sabha to give a greater sense of belonging to the Union of India among the people of Jammu and Kashmir and all of our far-flung States. The issue is about what kind of Indian Union do we want. What did Aurobindo say about this? Aurobindo touched upon 'the secret of the difficulty in the problem of unifying ancient India'. And he cited ancient texts. He said that the rishis from the Vedic age onwards, propounded the ideal of the Chakravarti, a uniting imperial rule, uniting without destroying the autonomy of India's many kingdoms and peoples 'from sea to sea'. The ruler was meant to establish a suzerainty. The 'full flowering' of this ideal, Aurobindo found in 'the great epics'. The Mahabharata narrates the legendary and quasi-historic pursuit of this ideal of empire which even 'the turbulent Shishupala' is represented as accepting in his attendance at Yudhisthira's dharmic Rajasuya sacrifice. The Ramayana too presents 'an idealised picture of such a Dharmarajya, a settled universal empire'. It is, in Aurobindo's words, 'not an autocratic despotism but a universal monarchy supported by a free assembly of the city and provinces and of all the classes that is held up as the ideal'. He goes on to say that according to his ideal, unification 'ought not to be secured at the expense of the free life of the regional people or of the communal liberties and not therefore by a centralised monarchy or a rigidly unitarian imperial State'.

Now we are not a monarchy any more. We are a democracy but the nationalism that is being talked about from the other side of the House represents centralized despotism and it is talking about a rigidly unitarian imperial State. I mentioned

Rabindranath Tagore. Tagore composed our National Anthem. But he was also a powerful critic of nationalism. He knew that nationalism could be both a boon and a curse. He wrote beautiful patriotic songs during our Swadeshi movement. But then he also saw that nationalism could lead to the carnage of war in Europe during the First World War. And that is why, when he travelled the world in 1916, he first went to Japan and then the United States of America, he gave lectures on nationalism and it was a powerful critique of nationalism that we find in those lectures. These lectures were published in a little book titled *Nationalism* by Macmillan in 1917.

I sometimes fear that those who are defining nationalism so narrowly will end up one day describing Rabindranath Tagore, the composer of our National Anthem, as anti-national if they read some of the sentences in his book on nationalism ... (Interruptions.) We always had different visions of nationhood and it is really a debate and discussion about what should be an ideal form of the Union of India that has animated the thought of all of the great figures that I have talked about. Chittaranjan Das, of course, had debates with Rabindranath Tagore, but they were respectful towards each other. Deshbandhu Chittaranjan Das felt that you could have a nationalism where you are very proud of Bengal, your region, but you can still be a very proud Indian nationalist at the same time. All of this, of course, has to flower in the garden of internationalism.

I know that Shri Anurag Thakur tried to quote Netaji Subhash Chandra Bose even though he confused the two great Bengali luminaries, Netaji and Rabindranath Tagore, the patriot and the poet. When I said that the nationalism that they represent is narrow, selfish and arrogant, I was, in fact, quoting from Netaji Subhash Chandra Bose. He spent a number of years in exile from 1933 to 1936 in Europe. As he was leaving and coming back to India to be imprisoned here, he pointed out that the new German nationalism that he had witnessed in Europe was narrow, selfish and arrogant. Then, in 1937, when Japan invaded China and at that time the Indian National Congress sent a medical mission to China, at that time too Netaji Subhash Chandra Bose said that we must pursue national fulfilment in every direction, but not at the cost of imperialism, and not at the price of self-aggrandizement. So, we must understand that nationalism can have a liberating aspect. That is what inspired generations of our freedom fighters. But nationalism in its narrow form can also be extremely oppressive. This is a topic and a concept on which we ought to be able to have healthy debates.

The President speaking to us yesterday pointed out that this Government is trying to repeal many obsolete laws. There are many colonial era laws that need to be done away with from our Statute Book. I venture to suggest that the law on sedition is one of them. This was a law that was deployed to persecute our freedom fighters. We ought to be able to have a discussion with our children, with our students, with our youth. We ought not to be subjecting them to trumped-up charges of sedition based on very dubious evidence, based on morphed visual evidence. We ought not to be doing this to our students and to our youth today. I have said what I have wanted to because it is not always necessary to make a long speech in order to stand for academic freedom. Free our universities, free our students, let our youth dream a glorious future for our country.

I have mentioned that Tagore wrote this beautiful little book on nationalism. At the end of the book, he printed an English rendering of a Bengali poem that he had composed on the last day of the 19th century. It says: 'The last Sun of the century sets amidst the blood-red clouds of the West and the whirlwind of hatred. The naked passion of self-love of nations, in its drunken delirium of greed, is dancing to the clash of steel and the howling verses of vengeance. Keep watch, India. Let your crown be of humility, your freedom the freedom of the soul. Build God's throne daily upon the ample bareness of your poverty. And know that what is huge is not great, and pride is not everlasting.' From this poem, I would like to simply underline three phrases. Let us not be deluded by the naked passion of self-love of nations, let our freedom be the freedom of the soul and let us remember the admonition of the great sentinel that what is huge is not great and pride is not everlasting. Thank you very much.

5

Invasion of Privacy

The initial objective of Aadhar, when it was conceived of by Dr Manmohan Singh's United Progressive Alliance government, was that it would be a tool to ensure the accurate targeting of subsidies for the poor. It was believed that creating one national identity card would help tackle the problem of multiple identity cards, many of which were often fake. Simultaneously, it was agreed that the Aadhar card should be made mandatory only for those receiving government subsidies; for the rest, it would be voluntary because there were other concerns, the primary one being that of privacy, the other of security.

But the Bharatiya Janata Party (BJP) government had other ideas. When they introduced the legislation, it was clear that it would be made mandatory for all citizens, because it would be required to be linked to all documents, from the PAN card to the Bank card, indeed, even be required for a mobile phone connection. When the matter of infringement of privacy came up later in the Supreme Court, senior advocate Anil Divan warned the Five Judge Bench that the Aadhaar project is 'an electronic leash' to keep people under control.

Here, in a no-holds barred verbal battle between two very articulate and well-matched rivals, one from the BJP, former Finance Minister ***Arun Jaitley*** *– who was a top lawyer as well – and the other from the Congress, former Environment and Rural Development Minister* ***Jairam Ramesh****, some of these issues are thrashed out.*

Another contentious issue that comes up in this debate is whether the BJP government was justified in designating the Aadhar Bill as a Money Bill. Money Bills are the only pieces of legislation in which the Rajya Sabha has no role in their passage. Once a Money Bill is passed by the Lok Sabha, the Rajya Sabha must perforce acquiesce: if it objects, it can go back to the Lok Sabha for a fresh look, but that House is not bound to agree to changes suggested. The Congress – and, for that matter, most of the Opposition – was of the view that since the BJP government did not enjoy a majority in the Rajya Sabha at the time, it had deliberately designated the Aadhar Bill as a Money Bill to bypass the Upper House.

ARUN JAITLEY

(Rajya Sabha: Uttar Pradesh)

Rajya Sabha March 16, 2016

The Aadhaar (Targeted Delivery of Financial and other Subsidies, Benefits and Services) Bill, 2016

Mr. Deputy Chairman, Sir, ... before I explain this Bill, I will ... deal with various ... points raised, ... not as an objection to introduction, because there is no introduction; it is only a transmission from the House of the People to this House.

One argument raised is that the Supreme Court's five judge bench is considering this issue and, therefore, Parliament suspends its own powers of legislation. It is an unprecedented argument, particularly in a democracy which is governed by separation of powers. The power to legislate belongs to Parliament; the power to legislate does not belong to the court. And, therefore, the court only has a power of judicial review ... the Government – I take Government as a continuing identity – decided by an Executive decision to constitute the UIDA (Unique Identification Authority). For some services, UID was being made mandatory. Thereafter, a Bill was introduced in 2010 in this House. The Bill was never passed. So, the UIDA functioned as an Executive Authority without a law. The Court may be concerned with different questions. But the principal challenge was that, in the absence of any due process, there could be, ... prima facie, a violation of the right of privacy and, therefore, was challenged on the ground that the right of privacy is a fundamental right, which is pending before a five-judge Bench of the Court.

Let us, first of all, deal with the right of privacy. The Constitution as a document ... does not mention privacy as a fundamental right. The original interpretation given by the Supreme Court used to be and, through the 1950s, the interpretation by a very large Bench was, particularly when ... cases came up in the context of policemen going and making midnight knocks at houses, that privacy is not a fundamental right. There were clear pronouncements. Subsequently, a smaller Bench of the Court said that probably, privacy is a fundamental right. The five-judge Bench which is now dealing with the theoretical question...

Sitaram Yechury: Sir...

Arun Jaitley: Sir, I don't think we have appointed a commentator in this House as yet! Let me have my say. Let me first give you the argument.

Mr.Deputy Chairman: Let the Minister finish his say.

Sitaram Yechury: You can't curtail my right to comment on what you are saying … (interruptions) ... I say that it is an attack on personal liberty again.

Mr. Deputy Chairman: Don't argue on that. ...(interruptions) ...

Arun Jaitley: Mr. Sitaram Yechury will sit here, give a running commentary when everybody speaks, and nobody can ask him to allow the House to proceed in order!

Sitaram Yechury: Why? It is going on in order.

Arun Jaitley: It is going on in order, … Others may also be speaking some sense. You can't have this kind of intellectual arrogance. ... (interruptions) ...

Sitaram Yechury: You are displaying an authoritative arrogance … not even willing to listen to the other point of view.

Arun Jaitley: Let me, Sir, now enlighten Mr. Sitaram Yechury and his colleagues a little. Somebody has sent me anonymously a few lines which I want to read for his benefit … This is in the context of a larger debate, and I am deviating from the point I was making. The comment which has been sent to me is … 'If you criticise me, it is your freedom of speech; if I criticise you, it is my intolerance.' ... (interruptions) ... I will pass on a copy to you to read the full text!

Sitaram Yechury: Privately, you can tell me who that anonymous person is ... (interruptions) ...

Mr. Deputy Chairman: You can do it privately.

Arun Jaitley: It is only somebody who disagrees with you.

Sir, the question the court was considering is: … is privacy a fundamental right or not? The present Bill ... is based on a premise that it is too late in the day to contend that privacy is not a fundamental right. So, I do accept that probably, privacy is a fundamental right. Now, where do you fit in privacy as a fundamental right? And that is where I want to clear the misconception behind some of the amendments which have been proposed ... when Article 21 says, 'No person shall be deprived of his right of life and liberty without procedure established by law,' then let us assume that privacy is a part of liberty, and no person shall be deprived of his privacy without procedure established by law.

The underlying point is that privacy is not an absolute right … Article 21 … can be restricted by a procedure established by law; now, that procedure established by law, obviously, has to be a fair, just and reasonable procedure. The case before the Supreme Court is, you have no law, you have not legislated, you have not laid down any guidelines and you have by an executive fiat created an authority where all the personal data and biometric information will go in. What will that be used for? Is this a fair, just and reasonable procedure?

The UPA Government, therefore, was well-advised to come out with a legislation … The UPA legislation was – and I will separately deal with the privacy provisions – that a UID authority will be created. There will be a procedure as to how the authority is created, … how personal details are taken and (stored); on the storage of those biometrics and when that information can be shared, and in what manner… That law kept on being discussed between committees, etc. The law, unfortunately, could not be passed. What that information will be eventually used for, and what the purpose of that information was, were absent in the UPA law ... Maybe, they thought, subsequently, by rules ... they could explain what that information will be used for.

I am not criticising that law because ... it was the beginning of a thought process … obviously, there were some gaps and, with the passage of time, that law, itself, could be improved. The present law, in pith and substance, is completely different. It borrows the complete idea from the UPA law that you need a Unique Identity Number and, to that extent, I give them all the credit for it … There will be some personal details and there will be some core biometric details ... The privacy law is much more tightened (now) ... the core purpose of this law is (to channelize) Government ... subsidies to the people … which are worth thousands and thousands, almost lakhs of crores. Now the purpose of these subsidies is that these have to be quantified amounts given to identifiable sections. If subsidies are given as unquantified amounts to unidentified sections, ... you will ... spend… money which does not go to the targeted people; which goes to the people who don't deserve subsidies. Today, every Central Government, every State Government, in some way or the other, is assisting the people by way of subsidies. So, you are entitled to take a UID identification. But if you want the benefit of that subsidy, production of the UID identity or any other alternative document, is a condition …

Sitaram Yechury: Sir, one minute ... we are on a point of objection on the basis of the rules. He is explaining the contents of the Bill. So, are you allowing the introduction?

Mr. Deputy Chairman: No, no ... (interruptions) ...

Sitaram Yechury: I am asking him … (interruptions) ...

Arun Jaitley: Sir, under the rules, there is no introduction. It is transmission ... (interruptions) ...

Sitaram Yechury: So, you have ruled on my point of order!

Mr. Deputy Chairman: That I have already told you.

Arun Jaitley: It is a transmission. It is not an introduction.

Mr. Deputy Chairman: Hon. Minister, one minute ... There is no provision in the rule to object to the consideration at this point of time. You can object only when a Bill is introduced in this House. ... This is not introduced in this House. This is introduced (in the Lok Sabha), passed there, and transmitted here. So, I am bound to allow it. Therefore, I have called him to move the Motion for consideration ...

Sitaram Yechury: I disagree with you on that point ... according to our own rule.

Mr. Deputy Chairman: You can; you can.

Sitaram Yechury: I disagree with you. I want that to be on record. But since you have permitted now ...

Mr. Deputy Chairman: Yes, I have already permitted.

Sitaram Yechury: My only request, through you, to the Hon. Minister is to explain ... the reasons why this had to be considered as a Money Bill.

Mr. Deputy Chairman: Yes, he will do that.

Sitaram Yechury: Why has this to be considered as a Money Bill? Please explain that ... (Interruptions) ...

Arun Jaitley: If I am entitled to an interruption-free right to address ... Parliament, I will certainly, meet all the questions that Mr. Yechury has raised. ... (Interruptions) ...

Mr. Deputy Chairman: You may continue your speech.

Arun Jaitley: Therefore, ... the pith or substance of this Bill is that Government moneys are being spent by the Centre and State Governments. When you spend that money, in order to ensure that money reaches the right man, you insist on the identity of the person. And the other provisions in the Bill are: how is that identity going to be determined? Now, there are two or three questions, on which I may, prima facie, like to satisfy theHon. Members of this House. The first is, which Mr. Yechury raised. Because to an unlegislated executive decision a challenge on Article 21 is pending, the House must suspend its power to legislate. My respectful submission is: it is an unsustainable argument. Parliament will not voluntarily abrogate, … surrender or squander its authority merely because some case is pending in a court.

Sitaram Yechury: So, the argument of sub judice is not valid here …

Arun Jaitley: 'Sub judice' on a legislation?

Sitaram Yechury: No, no. That is what I am asking you. You have used that argument so many times ... (interruptions) ... 'The matter is sub judice.'

Arun Jaitley: Sir, 'sub judice' is an argument which is available when issues of individual culpability are pending in court. You don't prejudice a trial or a hearing in a court by discussing it in a Parliamentary forum. So, tomorrow, if Article 356 is imposed, and somebody challenges it in court, you will say, 'It must not come up before Parliament for ratification because the challenge is pending, the matter is sub judice.' Can it ever be a sustainable argument?

Sitaram Yechury: So, no sub judice!

Arun Jaitley: … where important political and constitutional issues are pending challenge before the court, legislative bodies don't lose their right to discuss those issues. The 'sub judice' rule today has to be construed as applicable to matters of individual culpability so that we don't prejudice trials. Therefore, the best way, if Mr. Yechury's argument is accepted, is that somebody should file a petition challenging an issue in court, and then say, 'Parliament has lost its right to legislate because the Supreme Court has taken over.' If that were to happen, then, you would have a third chamber, the Supreme Court to legislate, and both Houses of Parliament ... would lose their authority.

Sitaram Yechury: Sir, please permit me. I entirely agree with you. But, I want ... (interruptions) ...

Mr. Deputy Chairman: Yechuryji, let him finish. (interruptions) ... Let him finish. (interruptions) ... Let him finish. After that, I will allow you. (interruptions) ... Let him finish. (interruptions) ...

Arun Jaitley: Therefore, Sir, merely because an unlegislated executive action of the Government has been challenged before a court, Parliament does not lose its right to legislate. It is absolutely clear. It is as clear as daylight.

Secondly, why is it a Money Bill? That is a question which Mr. Naresh Agrawal raised. This House, in my respectful submission, should not have been, on a matter of propriety, be discussing it since it has been raised and a contention made. Article 110 defines what a Money Bill is. Sub-clause (c) of Article 110 is absolutely clear that if moneys flow into the Consolidated Fund of India and if moneys are spent out of the Consolidated Fund of India and a law, in pith and substance, deals with that matter, it becomes a Money Bill.

What is that law? It has several other provisions. … Article 110 uses the words 'only if'. So, 'only' being a narrower phrase, must a Bill only deal with a taxation provision? Must it only deal with an expenditure provision and no other provision? ... the first Lok Sabha was confronted with this question. And Mr. Mavalankar gave a detailed ruling that there is no law which can ever be framed which is a one-section law. And that one-section law says, 'There shall be a tax for the following...' When you say that there will be a tax for the following purpose, you will need an administrative machinery for the levy of that tax, for the collection of that tax, for the appointment of tax officers, for an appeal provision, and for the general administration of the tax. Will those provisions, which provide for administration of that taxation, render a Money Bill to be a non-Money Bill? That was the question. And Mr. Mavalankar gave a clear ruling. The answer is: 'No'. It will remain a Money Bill if the principal purpose of the Bill is to impose a tax and the incidental provisions thereto. Now read Article 110(c), read with Article 110(g). Article 110(g) means, any other power incidental to the main purpose. So, the purpose of the present Bill is: moneys spent out of the Consolidated Fund of India, which go towards the expenditure of subsidies, makes it a Money Bill. The administrative machinery around it makes it, under sub-clause (g), a provision incidental to the administration of that Money Bill. And, Article 110(c) clearly says, 'In this matter, it is the satisfaction of the Speaker of the Lok Sabha which is final.' And, since it is final, on a matter of propriety, in a bicameral House. (interruptions) ...

Mr.Deputy Chairman: Okay. That's over. ... (interruptions) ... We cannot discuss that … (interruptions) ... No; no. That question cannot … (interruptions) ... The Hon. Minister has explained it … (interruptions) ... I am not allowing you to dispute whether it is a Money Bill or not. (interruptions) ... Let him complete … (interruptions) ... I have given a ruling that it is a Money Bill, as per the certification of the Speaker, Lok Sabha ... (interruptions) ...

D. Raja (Tamil Nadu): This way, every Bill will be a Money Bill ... (interruptions) ...

Mr.Deputy Chairman: I am not allowing anybody else ... (interruptions) ... I am not allowing. ... (interruptions)

Naresh Aggarwal (Uttar Pradesh): Sir, in which Bill is money not involved? ... (interruptions) In this way, all Bills will be considered Money Bills. ... (interruptions)

Mr.Deputy Chairman: Please sit down ... (interruptions) As per the certification of the Hon. Speaker, it is a Money Bill. (interruptions)

Arun Jaitley: One minute, Nareshji. I will explain this with greater clarity. The test ... is this – merely because there is a provision that we have created a particular Authority, and moneys will be provided from the Consolidated Fund of India for that Authority, will not make it a Money Bill. Supposing a Development Authority is being created, and the funds are to be met from the Consolidated Fund of India, in pith and substance, the money deals with the creation of the Development Authority and its functioning. Providing funds is incidental; it won't be a Money Bill. That is the answer to Mr. Raja's question. But if the principal purpose is that money spent out of the Consolidated Fund of India has to be spent in a particular manner, and a machinery is created for spending that money, then, Article 110 (c) read with Article 110 (g), that is, spending money out of the Consolidated Fund of India and any other matter incidental thereto, the machinery created is a matter which is incidental thereto, and, that is why it is a Money Bill. This satisfaction to that effect has to be of the Speaker. Therefore, once the Speaker satisfies herself and says, 'I certify, it is a Money Bill', this Money Bill, then, is transmitted to this House, it will be a Money Bill, and no authority in the country can question that provision.

Mr.Deputy Chairman: Yes.

Arun Jaitley: Now comes the third question: how is this Bill different from the one that the UPA brought in? The UPA Bill – because this whole thought process has grown – ... it was a welcome idea, ... I must straightaway concede. Dr. Saheb is here, well, at that time, some of my colleagues, probably, had reservations. There were several questions we used to raise. When new ideas come up, doubts will come up – that every Indian must be given a unique identity; issues of citizenship came up, and these are legitimate issues.

The UPA Bill, at that time, confined itself to creating an Authority. Mr. Nilekani ... brought in the technology; ... the expertise; then, core information, core biometric information and personal data was to be fed in, some privacy provisions. And the

Bill stopped with that. It wasn't a Money Bill. It was a Bill only for the creation of a UID Authority. That Bill today stands altered. One principal idea is borrowed from that Bill, that UIDA will be the machinery, which will be used for distribution of Government money as subsidies.

But the core purpose of the Bill will be (to ensure) the money is spent in a targeted manner, ... reach the persons ... who are entitled to the subsidies. Now, questions have been raised. I have seen, in the LPG, where direct benefit transfer has been used, 25 per cent has been saved. These five crore families which will get free gas connection will, actually, get it from the money saved from this. The state government of Telangana and the state government of Andhra Pradesh have already started using this in several other areas itself. So, every state government will, then, be able to ensure that subsidies reach the right persons ... That is the whole objective. Now, one question ... mentions the privacy provisions have been violated.

I have seen my good friend, Shri Jairam Ramesh, has proposed along with some other Members several amendments to the Bill. I have, in fact, analysed each one of his amendments, I will address the House after he moves those amendments. Most of those amendments are against the UPA Bill itself ... (interruptions) ... I think Shri Jairam Ramesh's stand on these issues depends on where he sits. If he sits this side, his stand is different and if he sits that side, his stand is different.

Jairam Ramesh (Andhra Pradesh): Unlike you, I have not changed my mind on Aadhaar. ... (interruptions) ...

Arun Jaitley: Sir, if I look at the earlier UPA Bill, on the privacy provisions, we are committed. Therefore, first of all, let us move on a constitutional premise clarity. I am moving on a premise: (a) that privacy is a fundamental right, without bothering for the Supreme Court's Constitution Bench Judgement, (b) it is a right which is a part of individual liberty, (c) that liberty, that is, a right of privacy, will depend on a procedure established by law and, therefore, this law is establishing that procedure.

The only question is: is that procedure fair, just and reasonable? Now, if you see the UPA law and if you see it from Chapter VI, clause 30 downwards, you had several provisions of confidentiality, and then you created a mechanism by which that confidentiality and privacy itself can be breached. The UPA law created this. The present law now restricts itself to two situations. A person by his consent can say that 'my personal data can be shared'. So, you need his consent. But his biometric data, the core biometric data, can't even be shared with consent. So, it is a much tighter provision.

The UPA law spoke in terms of Authorities which are created, which can then say that on grounds mentioned in the Bill, under special circumstances, some data can be shared. What have we done? The only ground on which data can be shared is 'national security'. And who will decide that 'national security'? One Authority will be created in Delhi. That Authority will be headed by an officer of a certain category, and then the decision of that Authority will be reviewed by a Committee headed by the Cabinet Secretary. So, an Authority, headed by the Cabinet Secretary, will review it, and that sharing then is also time-bound, three months. Now, all these are safeguards, additionally put, over and above the UPA Bill provisions. So, the only question is, can national security be a ground for sharing information by creating such a tight provision? Is that tight provision, which we have created, by a legislation, is that procedure established by law? Is that a fair, just and reasonable procedure? The answer is, 'Yes, it is'.

Now, if we look at the entire history of similar legislations, Sir, a legislation of this kind, for the first time, came, ... in the United States ... in 1935. So, we are already 80 years behind ...This was repeatedly challenged. The same debate took place 80 years ago, and, over 80 years, they have been adding to it. I have a list. For income-tax, they made it compulsory; for some policies, they made it compulsory; for buying bonds, they made it compulsory; for a lot of economic activities, they made it compulsory; for possessing arms, they made it compulsory. So, there is a list running into 10 pages ... they kept expanding it from time to time. Now, this has helped them in matters of national security. It has been repeatedly challenged in the U.S. – 'does this violate the due process?' In America, just as we use the expression 'procedure established by law', they use the expression 'due process of law', though I must concede that now, with the Supreme Court's interpretation, the two almost mean the same. It has repeatedly been challenged and, on every occasion, the United States, which is a liberal democracy, has conceded, and their courts have said, 'yes, national security is a good ground'. In fact, they went on to say, 'A person may need to make a choice between receiving a Government benefit and adhering to religious beliefs. So, you have to choose; if you want Government benefits, you need this. But if some information is required for national security, it can always be shared with national security. There are a series of challenges which resulted in that.

Now, Sir, ... the purpose of this Bill is distribution of Government monies by subsidies. The rest is incidental. So, it is a Money Bill. Two, merely because an Executive action challenge is pending in the Supreme Court, the Parliament cannot suspend its right to legislate. Three, learning from the UPA experience, and the kind of debate which took place, we have further tightened the privacy laws much more than ... the UPA had in its Bill. I am straightaway conceding that the debate evolves and so, we learnt from our experience and the only ground now is national security, and every Member has to agree that an individual's right has to give way to national security and, therefore, this House must accept the recommendation in relation to a Money Bill of the House of People...

JAIRAM RAMESH

(Rajya Sabha: Andhra Pradesh)

Rajya Sabha: 16 March 2016

The Aadhaar (Targeted Delivery of Financial and Other Subsidies, Benefits and Services) Bill, 2016

Sir, I rise in considerable anguish to speak and support, with amendments, the Aadhaar Bill, 2016. Yesterday, we had the ritualistic obeisance to the importance of the Rajya Sabha. Today, we are knocking a nail into the coffin of the Upper House. I say this advisably, Sir, and I am sure that Lord Krishna had Opposition Members of the Rajya Sabha in mind when he advised Arjuna in Chapter 2:

कर्मण्येवाधिकारस्ते मा फलेषु कदाचन। मा कर्मफलहेतुर्भूर्मा ते संगोस्त्वकर्मणि।।[1]

I feel in the same situation today. I am executing only my duty which is enjoined on me by Article 109 of the Constitution. I have no regard to the consequences of this debate because we all know what the end result of this debate is going to be. However, we have to do our duty and that duty has been enjoined on us by Article 109 and I am grateful for small mercies that we are, at least, having the opportunity for having a debate on this Bill in this House.

Sir, let me begin by saying that contrary to what the Leader of the House has tried to portray, I have been a strong, vocal and enthusiastic supporter of the Aadhaar idea and the Aadhaar legislation from the day it was born in the chamber of the then Prime Minister Dr. Manmohan Singh. As Union Rural Development Minister, I was the first one to use the Aadhaar idea, the Aadhaar number in the payment of wages for Mahatma Gandhi NREGA, the payment of pensions under the National Social Assistance Programme and for the delivery of food subsidies beginning in East Godavari district of Andhra Pradesh and then taken up in Chittoor district. So, I need no certificates or lectures on my commitment to Aadhaar.

Sir, the Leader of the House has given a detailed exposition on why this is a Money Bill and I will not go over those arguments. I am not a lawyer. I am not a Constitutional expert. But I am a student of Constitutional history. In Article 110, the word 'only', as the hon'ble Leader of the House has mentioned, has a special significance. Unfortunately, the former Attorney General of India, who is a Nominated Member of this House, is not present. I spent long hours with him over the weekend and he has given me … a ten page note, which I am willing to

[1] Editor's translation: Whenever, indeed, in action, your responsibility is not in the results, nor your motive be in the results of action, nor should your attachment be in inaction.

place on the Table of the House which argues that in pith and substance – the same language that the hon'ble Leader of the House has used – the Aadhaar Bill is not a Money Bill. This is the former Attorney General of India, who has said this. However, Sir, the Speaker's decision is final. We respect that decision. But I do want to raise one question here. The hon'ble Leader of the House, in this House and in the other House, said, 'Who are you to argue about the Aadhaar Bill being a Money Bill? The Juvenile Justice Bill in 1986 and the African Development Bank Bill in 1983 were declared as Money Bills. Who gives you the moral authority to argue?' Sir, I was astonished by what the hon'ble Leader of the House said. Could it be that the Juvenile Justice Bill was a Money Bill? Could it be that the African Development Bank Bill of 1983 was a Money Bill? I went to the Parliament House Library. I read 500 pages of debate on both these Bills. I contacted the officers concerned with both the Bills. And finally, Sir, I asked the Rajya Sabha Secretariat whether they were Money Bills or not. And what do I get from the Rajya Sabha Secretariat? The African Development Bank Bill, 1983 debated in this House on May 9, 1983 was not a Money Bill. The Juvenile Justice Bill debated in this House on the 18th of November 1986 was not a Money Bill. And the Leader of the House is telling us that these are Money Bills! Sir, I don't know where this information came from. This is a note I got from the Rajya Sabha Secretariat. I will authenticate it and put it on the Table of the House. But I would like the Leader of the House, once and for all, to tell us where this information was manufactured – the Juvenile Justice Bill as a Money Bill and the African Development Bank Bill as a Money Bill. This goes contrary to the information that we have. I may be wrong. But I am going by what the Rajya Sabha Secretariat has told me.

Sir, much has been made in the opening remarks of the Leader of the House on the LPG subsidy. The main justification for the Aadhaar was a Rs. 14,000 crore saving in LPG subsidy in the first year of the introduction of Aadhaar based DBT.[2]

Sir, I have here a study that has been done by a London based think tank called the International Institute for Sustainable Development which says the following:

'Publicly available information clearly demonstrates that the Aadhaar based DBT was not responsible for identifying and blocking 3.3 crore connections or even a significant fraction of that during any part of the financial year.'

Sir, where from are these numbers being manufactured? Is Make in India going to be on numbers or on goods and services? Here is a study which I will authenticate and place on the Table of the House. If this is wrong, let this be challenged. Here is a study which is calling into question one of the fundamental premises of what the hon'ble Leader of the House has said that there is Rs. 14,000 crore worth of saving on account of Aadhaar and its use for Direct Benefit Transfer in the LPG subsidy.

[2] Editor's note: Direct benefit transfer.

Sir, the hon'ble Leader of the House has compared the 2010 Bill and the 2016 Bill. I pleaded with the Chairman of the Standing Committee. The Prime Minister sent me to meet the Standing Committee Members. I pleaded with them but in 2010, the Standing Committee vetoed the Bill lock, stock and barrel.

I am glad six years later this Government is coming forward with a different Bill, similar in some respects, different in other aspects; but they are coming forward with this Bill. The hon'ble Leader of the House said, 'Where I stand depends on where I sit.' Sir, I supported GST when I stood there and I support GST when I am sitting here. I supported Aadhaar when I was there and I support Aadhaar when I am here. I supported the Land Acquisition Bill there and I support the Land Acquisition Bill here. On all these three, the former Leader of the Opposition and his Party have changed their minds when they have gone from here to there ... (Interruptions.) ... So, I need no certificates of my intellectual integrity from the Leader of the House.

Sir, I now come to the Bill proper. I support the Aadhaar Bill. I want the Aadhaar Bill. But, I am proposing some major amendments. Yes, those are amendments even to the 2010 Bill. As the hon'ble Leader of the House has admitted, we learn from experience. So, what is wrong if the amendments I am proposing go against the 2010 Bill itself?

Sir, much has been said about the Finance Minister's Budget. But, one thing that struck me in this Budget is his enormous fascination for the number 9, some numerology for number 9. In paragraph 13 in the Budget speech, the Finance Minister gives 9 objectives for economic policy. In para 90, the Finance Minister gives 9 objectives for financial sector reforms and, finally, in para 117, he gives 9 objectives for tax policy. Sir, I am a great admirer of the Leader of the House. I will give 9 objections to the Aadhaar Bill.

Sir, the fundamental departure on the Aadhaar Bill, 2016 comes from a recognition that even today Aadhaar must be used, but it must be voluntary. It must not be mandatory. Sir, let me backtrack a little ... What is Aadhaar? There is enormous confusion on what is Aadhaar and that Aadhaar will somehow identify people who are entitled for subsidy. My friend, Shri Rajeev Chandrasekhar, is shaking his head. I hope he will have the courage of his conviction and support me when his turn comes. Sir, Aadhaar does not determine who is eligible and who is not eligible. Please let us get rid of this myth. Aadhaar is proof of identity. It says if I am eligible, I am who I am. It does not determine that just because I have an Aadhaar number, I am entitled to a subsidy. No. That is not the idea ... (Interruptions.) ... It is proof of identity. It does not ... (Interruptions.) ... I am sure the hon'ble Leader of the House agrees with me ... (Interruptions.) ... It is proof of identity ... (Interruptions.) ... This Aadhaar is a subsidy sudhaar (reform) programme because fakes, duplicates are a reality. What Aadhaar does? My experience shows

… in NREGA, in PDS in old age pensions … the fake and duplicate, during my time, ranged anywhere from 8 per cent to 15 per cent, get eliminated. But it does not determine who is entitled for pension. It does not determine who is entitled for wages. It does not determine who is entitled for subsidy. It only determines, who you are … This is what Aadhaar does.

Sir, this Government comes out with beautiful phrases. They deserve Bharat Ratna for marketing, Bharat Ratna for labelling. JAM is a big naara[3] of this Government. Let alone the Government is in a jam, but that is a separate issue. But that is a Derek[4] type joke. So, don't laugh. Jan Dhan Yojana, Aadhaar and Mobile (JAM). This legislation is for 'A', not for 'J', not for 'M'. It is for 'A'. But the reform is JAM. Without 'J', without 'M' that 'A' is useless bread. Aadhaar by itself does not solve the problem. So, let us understand what we are doing today. We must have a legislation for Aadhaar. We must have a legislation for the UID Authority,[5] but let us not go away from here that we have done subsidy sudhaar (reform), that we have somehow managed to solve the problem of delivering subsidies, wages and pensions. We have tackled one part of the issue which is fake identity, duplicate identity. When I complete you can do so.

… Sir, because the hon'ble Leader of the House, I know, usually has his facts right, sometimes he gives it a spin. That is why when he said it, I went to cross-check … (Interruptions.) … (Interruptions.) you will soon take over his job … (Interruptions.) …

… Sir, the fundamental difference is mandatory versus voluntary. We do not believe – I do not believe and my Party does not believe – that Aadhaar should be made mandatory across the board from day one. However, this Bill, if you look at clause 57 and clause 7, certainly gives the interpretation and opens the door for mandatory use of the Aadhaar Number. The Bill is being brought to target subsidies. So, let the Bill be confined to the targeting of subsidies. Sir, I don't have an Aadhaar Number. And I don't need one, because I am not a beneficiary of a subsidy. But tomorrow if I were to want a mobile connection, if I were to go and buy an airline ticket, or if I were to go somewhere and the guy asks for my Aadhaar Number, then, you have made it mandatory. The whole idea of Aadhaar is subsidy reform. The whole idea of Aadhaar is to remove fake, duplicate identities, which we support. Now, I believe that if you read this legislation, as currently drafted, it certainly widens this ambit of Aadhaar and it certainly makes it a mandatory proposition as opposed to a voluntary proposition, which was the intention of the UPA from day one.

---

3 Editor's translation: Slogan.

4 Editor's note: A reference to Trinamool Congress MP Derek O'Brien and his brand of humour.

5 Editor's note: Unique Identification Authority of India.

Sir, I have some specific amendments. At the time of taking up amendments, I will go into these changes. Every individual must have the flexibility to opt out of Aadhaar. That is what the essence of the voluntariness means. The legislation, as currently drafted, does not allow the room for manoeuvre to somebody to either opt out of Aadhaar or somebody who does not desire an Aadhaar Number.

Sir, my next problem with this legislation is on privacy … that has been dealt with extensively by the Leader of the House. This is engaging the attention of the Supreme Court; so, I will not say much on this. There are some amendments that I have proposed which will take care of some of the privacy concerns. In 2012, the hon'ble Leader of the House knows, the then Planning Commission set up an expert committee under the chairmanship of Justice A.P. Shah, a former Chief Justice of the Delhi High Court and a former Chairman of the Law Commission. Justice A.P. Shah Committee enumerated a large number of principles which the Aadhaar legislation must follow to make it privacy-compatible, and the amendments that I am proposing are basically anchored in the recommendations of the Justice A.P. Shah Committee.

Sir, the law, as presently stands, gives sweeping powers under the name of national security. The Indian Telegraph Act of 1885 does not use the word 'national security'. It uses the words 'public emergency' and 'public safety'. What I am suggesting is that we must be consistent because the word 'national security' is very broad, very amorphous, which can be misused. We have seen how it is being misused. What I am suggesting is that instead of 'national security', there should be 'public emergency' and 'public safety'. The Supreme Court has ruled on this in 1996. It has given a series of guidelines which were incorporated in this legislation. What I am suggesting is that the presence of another independent member like the CVC[6] or the CAG[7] should also be there when the Aadhaar information is being shared in the name of 'public emergency' and 'public safety'. Sir, I have already mentioned the fact that Clause 57 widens the scope of Aadhaar. I want, my Party wants, the Aadhaar to be confined to the targeting of subsidies. Clause 57 opens a Pandora's box for the widespread use of Aadhaar for any purpose to be determined, and we certainly want Clause 57 to be dropped.

Sir, there are a number of clauses which I will come to when I speak on the amendments, which give power to the UID Authority under regulation. I am opposed to this and we are opposed to this collectively. Whatever is done, must be done and passed by Parliament. No power should be delegated to the UID Authority because then the UID Authority will decide tomorrow that DNA is required, and they will then have the powers to take DNA information as well.

---

[6] Editor's note: Chief Vigilance Commission.

[7] Editor's note: Comptroller and Auditor General.

My premise and my assumption, I hope all Members will agree, is that whatever the UID Authority wants to collect, should be empowered by Parliament. There should be no delegated legislation, no delegated regulation, no suo motu powers to the UID Authority to even collect the information because we do not believe that this will be done in a manner that will inspire public confidence on all occasions. Therefore, in order to remove any ambiguity, in order to remove any doubt, whatever the UID Authority needs to do, whatever the UID Authority needs to collect, should be a part of the main law that is being passed by Parliament.

Sir, these are, in broad terms, the differences that we have. Let me straightaway concede that the 2016 law has improved on the 2010 law in many respects. But in many respects of the 2010 law, it is silent. Obviously, in 2016, we are wiser than we were in 2010. We have listened to different points of views; we have listened to different stakeholders. We have practical experience on the ground. I do not know whether the hon'ble Finance Minister knows that yesterday one of the leading newspapers of the country, reported on the conclusion of a study, a survey that was done, that 40 per cent of the Jan Dhan Account holders, who had Aadhaar Numbers, have not been able to access their accounts ... I will give a report of the study here ... This is not an argument for not using Aadhaar; this is just an argument for caution for moving slowly because we have problems of connectivity, we have problems of biometrics, we have problems associated with old people and their biometrics becoming unreliable. So, I think anybody who raises questions on Aadhaar is not anti-national, anybody who raises questions on Aadhaar is not anti-technology, and anybody who raises questions on this legislation, it is not that he does not want subsidy sudhaar. We want to reform the regime of subsidies. If you use the Aadhaar properly, the Government stands to save anywhere between Rs. 40,000 crores and Rs. 45,000 crores a year. That was an estimate which was made when Dr. Manmohan Singh was the Prime Minister and that was the impetus, Sir, that led to the creation of Aadhaar. Let me also say this, Sir, that even though ... Civil Society was deeply sceptical of Aadhaar, even though the National Advisory Council was deeply apprehensive on Aadhaar, the Aadhaar Programme would not have seen the light of the day had the Congress President Shrimati Sonia Gandhi not given her full backing to Aadhaar. The then Prime Minister is witness to this. The then Prime Minister Dr. Manmohan Singh, the President of the Party Mrs. Gandhi, and the Vice-President Mr. Gandhi, went to Kotkasim in Rajasthan when the first Aadhaar experiment was launched for Direct Benefit Transfer. And even though there was a lot of opposition coming from different segments of society, the then Prime Minister, the Congress President and the Congress Vice-President held firm. The technocrats of UID deserve full credit for what they have done. But let us be very clear, Mr. Nilekani could not have done what he did without Dr. Manmohan Singh, Mrs. Sonia Gandhi and Mr. Rahul Gandhi ... So, Sir, as I said, I stood in anguish because we are presented with a fait accompli. However, I am going to move certain significant Amendments. I hope to get the support of the House for these Amendments. I know it is a formality …

… If only the Leader of the House had been a little more magnanimous, and brought this Bill as a non-Money Bill, all we would have done is to refer it to a Select Committee, chaired by either Mr. Anil Madhav Dave or by Mr. Bhupender Yadav,[8] whose track record … (Interruptions.) … whose track record of coming out with Reports is 100 per cent. Whatever Committee they have chaired, we have agreed …

… Even now, I am requesting them, refer it to a Select Committee, have Mr. Madhav Dave or Mr. Bhupender Yadav chair it, give them time till the 25th of April. By 25th of April, we can come up with a better Bill, a Bill which all of us can be proud of. This is my humble request to the hon'ble Leader of the House. Thank you, Sir.

[8] Editor's note: Both Mr Anil Madhav Dave and Mr Bhupender Yadav belong to the BJP.

6

Who Is a Citizen?

The Citizenship (Amendment) Act, 2019 that was brought by the BJP government provides citizenship to members of religious minority groups from Pakistan, Bangladesh and Afghanistan, fleeing religious persecution. The amendment – that was passed by Parliament, prompted widespread protests in India's Northeast, which borders Bangladesh, with many people expressing the fear that they would be 'overrun' by immigrants from across the border. Other critics of the amended law said this was part of the BJP's agenda to marginalize Muslims This is because while the amendment offers citizenship to members of six religious communities – Hindu, Sikh, Buddhist, Jain, Parsi and Christian – if they can prove that they are from Pakistan, Afghanistan or Bangladesh and can prove that they have lived or worked for six years in India – it pointedly excludes Muslims. It, therefore, violates the secular principles enshrined in the Constitution and, in the words of lawyer Gautam Bhatia, by dividing alleged migrants into Muslims and non-Muslims, the bill 'explicitly and blatantly seeks to enshrine religious discrimination into law, contrary to our long-standing, secular constitutional ethos'.

In the first speech here, ***P. Chidambaram****, using his skills as a lawyer, makes a strong case against the amendment, calling it an 'unconstitutional law', and one intended only 'to advance the ruling BJP's Hindutva agenda'.*

Hishey Lachungpa*, a Rajya Sabha Member of Parliament from the Sikkim Democratic Front expresses the apprehensions of the people of the small state to which he belongs – and which became part of the Indian Union only in 1975, when he was just eight years old.*

P. CHIDAMBARAM

(Rajya Sabha: Maharashtra)

Rajya Sabha: 11 December 2019

On the Citizenship Amendment Bill

... Sir, we have a Citizenship Act in this country. It recognizes citizenship by birth, citizenship by descent, citizenship by registration, citizenship by naturalization and citizenship by incorporation of territory. These are universal principles. Now, this Government is introducing a new category called 'citizenship by arbitrary executive fiat', and asking this Parliament to support the Government in passing what is patently an unconstitutional law. My friends have spoken about it; others will speak about it.

We are elected representatives of the people. The Constitution has asked us, in the first instance, to judge the constitutionality of a Bill. We cannot pronounce on the constitutionality. But, we have a responsibility to pass what is constitutional. Not all of us are lawyers. In fact, not all of us should be lawyers. We should be from every walk of life. And, from every walk of life, we must bring our collective wisdom and common sense to say is this constitutional or not? What are we doing in this House? What we did in the other House and what we are doing in this House is abdicating our primary responsibility in favour of another of the three entities/end organs of the Constitution. What we are doing is: You are pushing the issue to the lap of the Judges. Do you think it will stop here? It will not stop here. It will eventually go before the Judges. And, the Judges are respectable people. But, they are unelected Judges. Unelected Judges and unelected lawyers will ultimately decide what we do is constitutional or not! This is a slap on the face of Parliament. Parliamentarians are being asked to do something unconstitutional and then the baby is passed on to the judiciary and, in the judiciary, lawyers and Judges will decide what you have done is constitutional or not. Knowing this is unconstitutional, I am afraid, this Government is ramming through this Bill in order to advance its Hindutva agenda. This is a sad day. Thankfully, we are not amending the Constitution; we are only making a law. And, I am absolutely confident and I am absolutely clear in my mind that this law will be struck-off.

Sir, I have a few questions and I wanted to know who in the Government found answers to these questions. If the Law Department has advised answers to these questions, please ask the Hon'ble Home Minister to lay the opinion of the Law Ministry on the Table of the House. If it is the Home Ministry itself, in its wisdom, found answers to these questions, let us see the final note placed by the Secretary before the Hon'ble Home Minister. If it is the Attorney General who has been consulted – the Constitution has a provision to invite the Attorney

General – please call the Attorney General to this House. We will ask him these questions. But, somebody has to take responsibility for the answers to these questions. These questions are well-known. Let me read it very rapidly. How do you group three countries – Afghanistan, Pakistan and Bangladesh – and leave out the other neighbours? How do you identify only six religious groups Hindu, Sikh, Buddhist, Jain, Parsi and Christian – and leave out others like Ahmadis, Hazaras and Rohingyas? Abrahamic religions are three – Christianity, Judaism and Islam. Why have you included Christianity and left the other two? Why have you excluded Sri Lankan Hindus and Bhutan's Christians? Look at the exclusionary, inclusionary hyphenation. Sri Lanka is excluded, Hindus are included! Bhutan is excluded, Christians are included! When you hyphenate the effectives, Sri Lankan Hindus are excluded, Bhutan's Christians are excluded. This exclusionary, inclusionary hyphenation is beyond common sense and logic. Why only religious persecution? Are people not persecuted for political reasons? Are people not persecuted on linguistic grounds? Are people not persecuted by unleashing internal wars against them? Why only religious persecution? Why not every kind of persecution?

Six, does or does not the Bill violate the three fundamental elements of Article 14 of the Constitution? First, equality before law; unequals cannot be treated as equals. Second, unreasonable or irrational classification. And, there is a third element, which most people forget, Judge-made laws are the third element. Even if unequals are not treated as equals or equals are treated unequally, even if the classification is reasonable, it can be struck down on the ground that it is arbitrary. Arbitrariness is writ large on the face of this Bill. Now, I want to know who will give answers to these questions … Why are Parliamentarians being told that you will not give answers to these questions and they can go to court and find answers? … Let somebody take responsibility for answers saying, 'Yes, the Attorney General of India has answered these questions. These are our answers and, therefore, this Bill is here.' I dare the Government to lay the opinion of the Law Department; I dare the Government to invite the Attorney General to this House to answer our questions. So, what we are doing today is wrecking the Constitution from within. A small part of the Constitution is sought to be wrecked and demolished by this insidious Bill. Fortunately, we are three organs of the State. The Executive is complicit; the Legislature is being invited to collaborate; hopefully, the Judiciary will strike it down and will save India.

HISHEY LACHUNGPA

(Rajya Sabha: Sikkim)

Rajya Sabha: 11 December 2019

On the Citizenship Amendment Bill

... We, in Sikkim, have many apprehensions ... Indian citizenship was granted to the Sikkim Subject holders in the year 1975, when we became the 22nd State of the Indian Union. The Sikkim Subject is therefore a sacrosanct identity of those who were the citizens of Sikkim, under the erstwhile Chogyal. Today, we are deliberating on a Bill that has many ramifications nationally, as well as locally in the North East Region and within Sikkim, which is also a part of the North East Region. Sir, from the point of view of Sikkim, we oppose this Bill from the standpoint of its potential dilution of Article 371(F).[9] This captures the essence of the provisions under which the Sikkim kingdom was merged with the Indian Union in the year 1975, after a referendum. All that the people of Sikkim know is the Sikkim Subject Register and under this we stand protected. Though, the assurance given by Hon'ble Home Minister, that all the provisions of Article 371 will not be diluted by the CAB is certainly welcomed. However, this must be in both letter and spirit. The CAB, in its present form, will go against the very nature of the spirit of Article 371(F). The rest of the North Eastern States, have been exempted either by means of Inner Line Permit (ILP) system or as the Sixth Schedule areas, whilst Sikkim stands unprotected by either of these two exemptions given. In Sikkim, we have both RAP/PAP[10] and ILP for foreigners and hence no foreigner can come and seek ... citizenship without entering Sikkim. To that extent, we are protected. I appeal to the Hon'ble Home Minister to extend the ILP, under the Bengal Act, to Sikkim as well. Since it is also being extended to the State of Manipur, it should also not be difficult as we already have a framework in place, as already stated by me. In this regard, I seek the assurance from the Hon'ble Home Minister, on the floor of this House, during the reply. Thank you. Jai Hind.

---

[9] Editor's note: Special provisions with respect to the State of Sikkim in the Constitution.

[10] Editor's note: Protected Area Permit (PAP)/Restricted Area Permit (RAP).

7

The Right to Protest

Shortly after she took oath as a first-time Member of Parliament, the international investment banker turned politician ***Mahua Moitra*** *demonstrated that she could pack a punch. With her very first speech in the Lok Sabha on 26 June 2019 on 'the seven early signs of fascism', the Trinamool Congress MP trained her guns on the Narendra Modi government – and became a social media star. In the speech used here, she once again takes the BJP dispensation to task for introducing a discriminatory amendment in the Citizenship Law, for arbitrarily using the sedition and other laws against its critics, violating the principle of cooperative federalism, for its lack of sympathy for ordinary people for imposing a 'national lockdown at only four-hour notice causing untold misery, countless deaths', and its similar lack of concern for farmers', who protested for over a year in the open under the most appalling weather conditions. The speech will also be remembered for what she had to say about the judiciary, and especially about a former Chief Justice of India, most of which was expunged by the Speaker.*

MAHUA MOITRA

(Lok Sabha: Krishnanagar)

Lok Sabha: 8 February 2021

Discussion on the Motion of Thanks on the President's Address

... Far too many of our fellow citizens today languish in jail or bear the burden of judicial and police harassment simply for asking questions of this Government or choosing to voice an opinion on the state of affairs in our country. So, I, as a Parliamentarian, garbed in parliamentary privilege, now choose to use this platform that the people have given me to ask the questions that the people want to ask and to give voice to their thoughts so that this Government may know that arresting, attacking, and repressing voices will not hold. I trust my hon'ble colleagues in the Treasury Benches will not shout me down and you, Hon'ble Chairperson, Sir, will let me speak for the entirety of my allotted time and that the Lok Sabha TV, paid by my taxpayers' money, will not turn the screens off.

The American journalist Elmer Davis's words about the United States are just as relevant for the celebrations of the 72nd anniversary of the birth of our Republic, that this Republic was not created by cowards and cowards would not preserve it. Today, I speak of cowardice and courage, and of the difference between the two; of those cowards who hide behind the false bravado of authority, of power, of hate, of bigotry, of untruth, and dare to call it courage. After all, this Government has turned propaganda and disinformation into a cottage industry.

The biggest success of the Government is the recasting of cowardice as courage. I will lay out various instances where this Government has demonstrated courage.

The Government claims that it has shown courage to bring in a law that questions on arbitrary parameters who is or who is not an Indian. The Citizenship (Amendment) Act was passed in 2019 in this House on the pretext of granting citizenship to persecuted Hindus and other minorities in the neighbouring countries. At the same time, it threw into an abyss of insecurity millions of Indians who have been living in this land for generations. But the rules by which this Act will be implemented were not yet prepared by December 2020, according to the Ministry of Home Affairs. The deadline has yet again been extended till April 2020. If indeed this Government cares so much for those persecuted in neighbouring countries, why does it miss the deadline after deadline to notify these rules? Meanwhile, very many of us have mustered the courage to tell the Government, 'Kagaz nahin dikhayenge'[11] ... Only a small portion of Jana Gana Mana was adopted as our National Anthem. I urge the Government to read the rest of it. Maybe, it will help them understand Tagore ... and Bengal a little better. My colleague, the respected floor leader of the Congress Party, happened to also quote these very words. But I do think repeating them over and over again would do our nation some good.

'Ohoroho Tobo Aahbaano Prachaarito, Shuni Tabo Udaaro Baani Hindu Bauddho Shikho Jaino,Parashiko Musholmaano Christaani Purabo Pashchimo Aashey,Tabo Singhaasano Paashey Premohaaro Hawye Gaanthaa Jano Gano Oikyo Bidhaayako Jayo Hey.'[12]

---

[11] Editor's translation: We won't show our documents.

[12] Editor's translation: Your call is announced continuously, we heed your gracious call.
The Hindus, Buddhists, Sikhs, Jains, Parsis, Muslims and Christians,
The east and the west come, to your throne.
And weave the garland of love ...
Oh! You who bring in the unity of the people!
Victory be to you, dispenser of the destiny of India!

'"Hail Unity, Hail Religious Diversity".'

This is the courage to make India the world's greatest democracy into a virtual police state whereby a single dubious complaint under which both an eminent Member of this House and one of India's most veteran journalists are charged with sedition. This is the courage to try and take over every State Government by hook or by crook whether they have won the popular mandate or not. They claimed they were wedded to constructive cooperation and cooperative federalism. Instead of partnering with the State Governments, they try and muscle them out at every opportunity. Does the Ruling Party wish that its legacy be that it governed the largest democracy in the world or that it imposed a one-party rule in India? They should ask themselves. This is the courage to announce the national lockdown at only four-hour notice causing untold misery, countless deaths, the sight of thousands walking for hundreds of miles with no food or money. This Government spent less than 2 per cent on social transfers in contrast to OECD countries which spent 20 per cent and 6 per cent was spent by middle income countries. This is the courage, no! This is the brazen audacity to announce the economic rebound.

India was the single worst performer among developing countries in the year 2020. Even if we believe this Government's *Economic Survey*, the economy lowered by 7.7 per cent in 2020 and will rise by 11 per cent in 2021. So, in effect, by 2022, i.e. over a two-year time span, the economy will be flat just as the 2019 GDP number. This Survey proclaims that the growth is the biggest poverty alleviator. Hon'ble Members of this House, we are going to have no growth for two whole years. I do not understand the celebration.

I come from a rural constituency and a source of migrant workers. The distress in the MSME sector is real. This rebound is one where large and strong enterprises have become stronger. It is not V-shaped, it is K-shaped. One per cent of rich and successful citizens have become richer and the pains of the MSMEs have only increased. The Government had the courage to say that it gave Rs. 1,13,000 crores via the Direct Benefit Transfer Scheme only to take the same money away from those very same people and the middle class in the way of increased cess on petrol and diesel. We are not a nation that is growing and sharing its wealth, we seem to be a nation that is only finding ways to share our poverty.

The hype today is that post budget, the sensex jumped. In a country where only six crore people pay taxes, only 4.6 per cent of the total population, how many do you think are the investors in the sensex that they should jump for joy when the sensex jumps? This is the courage to use … the Ministry of External Affairs to respond to social media posts by an eighteen-year-old climate activist and an American pop star where not even one single ministry has been deputed by this Government to try and look out for food, water, and basic sanitation needs of the farmers and their families who have been camping at the border for almost ninety days.

And finally, this is the courage to bring in three farm laws when the Opposition, farmers across the country, as well as the Government's oldest ally warned it was unacceptable.

I wish to remind this Government that India under Prime Minister Lal Bahadur Shastri committed three things to Sant Fateh Singh, the Akali leader – the creation of a Punjabi-speaking State, open-ended public procurement, and an assured return on agricultural produce. These farm laws threaten to snatch away two of these guarantees. These laws were arrived at without consensus, tabled without scrutiny, and rammed down this nation's throat with the brute force of the Treasury Benches. They have firmly established this Government's motto of brutality over morality. And everyone else in this country has been portrayed as a coward or a terrorist – from the farmers, to the students, to the old ladies of Shaheen Bagh.

You say you have courage! You claim you have done so many things that no other Government before you has done. Yes, that is true! In true fascist fashion, you have made every act of pettiness, of vengeance, of hate, of bigotry, a part of your narrative of courage. The reason no one has done it before you is not because no one had the courage, but simply because it was not the right thing to do. Has that thought ever struck you?

And India's tragedy today is not just that her government has failed her but that her other democratic pillars, the media and the judiciary, have failed her, too. Lord Hain, the Labour Peer, said in the House of Lords, 'What is the point of being a Member of Parliament either in the Commons or in the Lords if you do not discharge your responsibilities and where appropriate use of the privileges that you have in order to promote justice and liberty?'

So, today, like a true child of Bengal, I will stand here and be courageous. Trust me, Mr. Baalu, we have not lost the fighting spirit. Even though the Government's spin factories will later portray it as cowardice or even plagiarism, I will lay out a few home truths by using my Parliamentary privilege that guards me from charges of sedition and contempt for anything I say in this House. And Mr. Law Minister, Sir, if you are present on the premises, with all due respect, this time you have neither the right to shut me up nor to try and get my words expunged from the record.

...*[13] The judiciary stopped being sacred when it chose to squander the greatest opportunity that any bench of the highest court of this land has ever seen to reinforce the founding principles of our democratic republic and to uphold the rights enshrined in Part 3 of our Constitution ... (Interruptions.)

Hon'ble Chairperson, Sir, it is extremely important that I not only not avoid them, but I bring them up because I did not accuse the hon'ble gentleman ... ** Let me put it on record that it is a great ... ** I did not do it ... (Interruptions.)

[13] Editor's note: The * in the speech stands for 'expunged by Speaker'.

Instead, it let our migrants walk to their deaths; it let our greatest activists and modern writers rot in jail … (Interruptions.) …

Sir, let me continue my speech. Instead, the judiciary stopped being sacred when it chose to squander the greatest opportunity that any bench of the highest court of this land has ever seen …

Sir, the Judiciary stopped being sacred when it chose to squander the greatest opportunity that any Bench of the highest court of this land has ever seen to reinforce the founding principles of our democratic republic and to uphold the rights enshrined in Part III of our Constitution. Instead, it let migrants walk to their deaths. It let our greatest activists and modern writers rot in jail. It now sits back as a mute spectator when our young are prosecuted for cracking a joke. The Judiciary seems to have forgotten the Constitutional principle of separation of powers that Parliament, and Parliament alone, can legislate. If something is bad in law, then the courts can strike it down or stay it on grounds of unconstitutionality. But unless it is so, the courts must do nothing. The Government alone must face the consequences. If the Government has brought in the farm laws which are not acceptable to people, then either the Government will repeal the laws or the people will vote the Government out. We urgently need the sagacity and courage shown by the High Courts during the Emergency when they delivered the ADM Jabalpur and like decisions. The Supreme Court, unfortunately, is failing the common citizen and is being perceived as protecting the privileged and ironically, only itself. A very large section of the Indian media has plummeted to new depths both in terms of lack of factual reporting as well as the total absence of journalistic ethics. Yet, even when the bar is so low, the WhatsApp chat leaks detailing correspondence between a large Government leaning media channel and the head of the TV ratings agency expose the utter filth and the crony capitalism that ironically this Government claim to be saving us from. What is left of the resolute media is being targeted with the provisions of the UAPA and other draconian laws. You keep taunting the Congress about the Emergency. But India today is in a state of undeclared emergency. But the Government has miscalculated. There is a fundamental difference between cowardice and courage. The coward is brave only when armed with power and authority. The truly courageous can fight even when unarmed. Do not forget this. Do not forget this when you tell the authorities in Ghaziabad to clear the protest site overnight with the help of the police and the bureaucracy. You are not being courageous. You are a … * wielding power. The truly brave came in droves from villages wielding nothing, but they believed that their cause is just. They were propelled by the spontaneous tears of their leader, not by the force of their water cannons. Do not forget this when you block the roads and cut the internet off in 17 of Haryana's districts. You are not being brave. You are … wielding power. The State of Haryana gives 10 per cent of India's Air Force and contributes to 11 per cent of the total strength of the Indian Navy. Its people can neither be termed anti-national, nor terrorist, nor gaddars.[14] Do not forget this when a peaceful 60-day movement is insidiously hijacked and then you slap FIRs on Punjab's farmers. You are not being courageous. You are a … * wielding power. Baghel Singh and Jassa Singh Ahluwalia … captured Delhi way back in 1783 from the Mughals. Their descendants do not need a lesson in courage from those who captured Delhi only in 2014.

Tagore in his poem 'Bandi Bir', the captive warrior, an ode to Sardar Banda Singh Bahadur, wrote: 'Eseche se ekdin; jibon mrityu payer bhritto; chitto vabonahin; eseche se ekdin.'[15] That momentous day has arrived.

In the 125th year of Subhas Chandra Bose's birth, the Central Government has made every attempt to hijack Netaji's legacy and weave it into their own fake, narrow narrative of courage. But this nation needs to know that Netaji had two clarion calls, both embodiments of his courage and his spirit. One was the salutation, 'Jai Hind'. Today, this Government has replaced this national greeting with a narrow, religious chant that it uses as a war cry to heckle, to bully and to always, always remind the minority about who is in charge. Netaji's second call was 'Dilli Chalo'. This Government falls over itself to pay lip service to Netaji. But in truth, you blocked the borders in Singhu, in Ghazipur, in Tigri with walls and spikes for all those who actually want to come to Delhi to tell you that much like Subhas Chandra Bose, they too will not accept any halfway house. Netaji told us, never to lose faith in the destiny of India. And it is not India's destiny to be ruled by cowards. The time has come for us to show courage …

Repeal or nothing. Thank you.

[14] Editor's translation: Traitors.

[15] Editor's translation: A day such as this has never been seen
A million hearts know not what fear means
Nor feel that they owe another.
Life and death are but servants at one's call.

Section Nine

The Religious Fault Line

1

Whose Ayodhya Was It Anyway?

The religious fault lines in India pre-date Independence, but if there was one event in post-Partition India that critically deepened that divide, it was the destruction of the Babri Masjid on 6 December 1992.

In its immediate aftermath, there was shock, anger, consternation and communal violence in different parts of the country. The BJP, one of the principal protagonists of the Ram Janmabhoomi movement, which resulted in the demise of the mosque – the Hindu Right-wing prefers to describe it either as a temple or 'disputed structure' – oddly enough, decided to bring a no-confidence motion against the Congress government at the Centre, blaming it for not intervening in time in Ayodhya, even as it justified the destruction of the mosque.

In the first speech, ***Atal Bihari Vajpayee*** *– yet to become the Prime Minister – claims that neither he nor anyone in the top BJP leadership knew of the plans to destroy the mosque, while justifying its demise, and explaining at length why Muslims should give up their claims to it. Indeed, he warns all those saying that the mosque should be rebuilt or criticizing its destruction of a worse retaliation. Vajpayee's many admirers outside the political Hindu Right like to describe him as a 'moderate', but this speech is yet more proof of his strong ideological commitment to the BJP–(RSS) credo, strengthening the claims of those who named him the mukhota or mask.*

In the second speech, the then Union Parliamentary Affairs Minister ***Ghulam Nabi Azad*** *– at the time still in the Congress, in which he spent 49 years till 2021, at which point he was the longest-serving member of the Congress Working Committee (CWC), the party's most important decision-making body – speaks not just for India's minorities but for the principles of secularism and diversity, shattered on 6 December 1992. He also finds himself targeted by fellow MPs for being a Kashmiri Muslim, a sign of the growing divisions along religious lines even within Parliament.*

The third speech is by ***P.V. Narasimha Rao****, the first Prime Minister from a southern state. He had been chief minister of undivided Andhra Pradesh, and had held several key* *portfolios in the Union Cabinet before getting the top job. But for all of Rao's achievements – including his sponsorship of the liberalization of the Indian economy – the destruction of the Babri Masjid will continue to mar his legacy. At the time, he was targeted and pilloried not just by Opposition leaders but by colleagues in the Congress for not doing enough to protect the mosque. Here, he gives a precise factual account of what happened that fateful day, the options before him and how he made his choices.*

It was a turning point for the Congress, for it was after this that the Muslims turned their backs on the party. Today they vote for the Congress only if they have no other non-BJP option. It also did not earn the party the gratitude of Ram bhakts among the Hindus, who gave the credit to the BJP, which continues to earn electoral dividends from that terrible event.

ATAL BIHARI VAJPAYEE

(Lok Sabha: Lucknow)

Lok Sabha: 17 December 1992

No-confidence Motion Against the P.V. Narasimha Rao Government (After the Demolition of the Babri Masjid)

... Mr. Speaker, Sir ... No-Confidence motion is not a religious ritual. There have been some incidents in the country on, before and after the 6th December. The nation is again in a dilemma. We are unhappy on whatever happened in Ayodhya on 6th December. (Interruptions.) Mr. Speaker, Sir, if they interrupt me, then we cannot discuss it properly ...

... Mr. Speaker, Sir, when I was coming to the House, I saw something written on a dome which says, 'A meeting is not a meeting which has no elder man, An elder man is not an elder man unless he practices religion, and a religion is not a religion which does not contain the truth and a truth is not a truth if it inspires you towards deception.' Today, in the House I shall speak only truth and nothing else. I would like ... an open discussion ... today. If it concludes that we are at fault then we are ready to accept it. We had given an assurance to the Prime Minister. I realize his concern. Arjun Singhji will not realize it. Every effort was made to fulfil the commitment given to the Prime Minister. But the commitment could not be fulfilled. The top ... leaders of BJP, RSS and VHP had been trying to prevent Kar Sevaks there. Video tapes are evidence of it ... many journalists were present there. (Interruptions.) We have apologized to the journalists who were beaten ... their cameras were broken because the karsevaks did not want their action to be recorded. If it was recorded ... (Interruptions.)

… Mr. Speaker, Sir … it would be far better if the discussions are held with … sincerity rather with a sense of prejudiced feelings. The CBI is conducting an inquiry into the Ayodhya incidents. The findings … are still awaited … whatever … facts are with the Government, it should place them before the House. Whatever … facts are with us, I am placing these before the House. I am ready to go one step further and ask those karsevaks, who were … small in number to come forward and openly confess that they have demolished the structure and for that they are prepared to face the music … there were karsevaks present in a large number but they all were not involved in the demolishing.

Ram temple will not be constructed by foul or unfair means. If Ram temple is constructed it would be constructed on the basis of moral strength … Had there been an intention to demolish the structure, it would have been done easily without collecting karsevaks in large numbers. Fairs are held after every three months in Ayodhya. If the structure was to be demolished secretly and according to a plan, it did not require Karseva … we regret the incident.

We as well as the Government of Uttar Pradesh had requested the Central Government to get the matter expedited in the Court either way … The representatives of the Central Government met us as well as the Government of Uttar Pradesh; but they refused to say in the Court that the verdict … should be delivered soon … On that day … Shri Chavan said that the matter was being postponed till 11th … Karseva was scheduled to be resumed on 6th … The assembled karsevaks were of the view that they would get some opportunity for construction work … efforts were made to control the situation. We had hoped that the karsevaks would wait for the court's verdict till 11th … and our leadership made every effort in this regard. The 'Sarkaryawaha', RSS had been requesting the people in Southern languages that no karsevak should go towards the structure. He should not take part in demolition activity …

The press reporters who went there told me that Shri Advani was very sad when the structure was demolished. He was in tears. That is why he sent in his resignation, expressing his regret over the incident. Owning the responsibility, Shri Kalyan Singh also resigned. If you consider it … a drama, then it is a gross misconception, because such … misconception will neither encourage fair politics in the country nor … secularism.

… We would like to know the reality because it is a … challenge for us. Our organization was presumed a disciplined organization … The same image is causing trouble for us.

We would like to know who … organized it. I repeat it again that the karsevaks who took part in demolishing the structure should come forward and reveal their participation in demolition. If punishment is given they should accept it. The temple of Lord Rama cannot be built without making sacrifice …

But there are other aspects also of this issue. It was not only a structure which was demolished. There was a temple as well. 'Namaz' was not offered in the mosque. Even the entry to the mosque was prohibited. But prayer was offered in the temple by orders of the court. Now some hon'ble Member can object that the mosque already existed there, and statues of deities were installed there later on … Statues were installed there, but I do not want to go into the history. I would like to ask the hon'ble Members whether statues were not kept there with this belief that it was the birthplace of Lord Rama? There was no Jana Sangh, Vishwa Hindu Parishad or Bajrang Dal those days. But the people of that area had a strong feeling. Mr. Speaker, Sir, through you, I am constrained to say that the intensity of the sentiments of the majority community is not being understood.

I, too, did not understand it earlier. When Shri Advani went on the Rath Yatra, I had my reservations. If I expressed my feelings, the press would have said that the Bharatiya Janata Party (BJP) has worn two countenances. Sometimes, it displays its countenance of moderates, and sometimes that of hardliners. Mr. Speaker, Sir, excuse me, sometimes I deviate from the issue … the way people supported the cause, the mistakes that were committed by the ruling party particularly, the arbitrary decision by the then Chief Minister Shri Mulayam Singh Yadav to deal with the agitation, the way communalism was incited by the announcement that a particular community had the right to have arms, worsened the situation … (Interruptions.)

… I would say that the then Chief Minister was soft by name (Mulayam), but very cruel in his actions … (Interruptions.)

Mr. Speaker, Sir, why did the situation deteriorate? People gathered in a large number there. I understand the crisis of the Central Government, and the crisis continued during the Kalyan Singh Government also. If people assemble in a large number and do something violently rash, how can it be controlled? (Interruptions.) Shri Rajesh Pilot rightly said that day that if such a large number of people assemble there, it will go beyond control. But we did not feel like that … (Interruptions.)

… Mr. Speaker, Sir, we had trust in the people. Therefore, we said that if the trust of the hon'ble Prime Minister has been betrayed, we too are shocked. Shri Kalyan Singh and Shri Advani resigned, but nobody from the Central Government is ready to take the blame for it. Shri Arjun Singh said that he had already warned about it. Why did he not resign from the Cabinet? It was felt that the hon'ble Prime Minister is on the right path. The NIC (National Integration Council) had given a free hand to the hon'ble Prime Minister. The hon'ble Prime Minister did what he considered right. That day in the evening I met him and I am ready to say, even if all the members of my party do not agree that the hon'ble Prime Minister tried his best to stave off any incidents … resume the Kar Seva peacefully and maintain the security of the structure, though it is a fact that he cannot escape from his responsibility …

… But the reaction to the happening in Ayodhya throughout the country and abroad is more or less overreaction … our outlook and the approach of Government to the problem is no less a factor to be blamed for it. We did not point out to the world that it was a disputed structure. It was repeatedly stated that there was a mosque. We never clarified that along with the structure of the mosque there is also a temple, in which prayer and worship is being done and this dispute has been going on for the last 500 years. There are umpteen examples like this throughout the world. When Russia occupied Warsaw, a church was built there. When Poland became independent, the first thing it did was demolition of the church … When Toynbee visited India, he taunted us that it is possible in India alone that a mosque has been erected after demolishing the temple. We have allowed wrong propaganda in the world. I attend the General Assembly of the United Nations as a delegate every year. It is discussed there, also. They do not know the root of the dispute. They do not know whether there was a temple. They do not know that the remnants which have been excavated after demolition now confirm that there was a temple at the site hundreds of years ago … Had they known … that an ancient temple was raised to the ground in order to build this mosque, then they must have asked the Muslims to settle this issue amicably. If this is the fact, then should not the issue be settled with mutual understanding?

The Government … brought a Bill … to this effect that there will be status quo in respect of all the shrines and places of worship as on 15 August 1947. What does it mean? Does it mean that time will stop running and cycle of change will stop? Does it mean secularism is in danger so everything should remain as is … ? These places of worship have been there for centuries. The rocks … and … monuments … also tell a tale … They have close links to our feelings. The Government had also to accept this … so it had put Ayodhya in an exceptional category … It could have included Ayodhya also and said that its position would remain intact as we have passed it because we are Parliament. But it did not do so. Because it knows that the … issue of Ram Temple is different, but after saying this much, what has it done? Even other parties have also left this issue to the Government to settle it amicably. I am also of this opinion that the Ayodhya issue is different … My friend, Mr. Chauhan, is sitting here, I had been to his place, Amroha, for delivering a speech. I had said … that this incident is a misfortune. It is my submission that the rulers who came were not true representatives of Islam. That day I was listening to the radio speech of Shri Ghulam Nabi Azad. He said if temples were being demolished in Pakistan and Bangladesh, they were not being demolished in accordance with the tenets of Islam. Were the temples demolished in this country as per the tenets of Islam? Even this was … against Islam. That is why I do not consider Aurangzeb or the persons demolishing the temples the true representatives of Islam. Therefore, we were expecting our Muslim brethren to deplore such excesses, but they ... want to stick to this ... In the meantime, certain incidents have taken place in the country which have shaken the ... Hindus ... impinged their psyche, be it ... the secessionists of Kashmir or ... the people of Punjab who are bent upon disintegrating the country through violence and raising arms or a crisis in Assam due to infiltration there, all such incidents are creating a feeling in the majority ...

The case of Shah Bano has also underlined it ... We, in the Bharatiya Jana Sangh did not ask for a common civil code. We had wide discussions with our ex-Sarsanghchalak, Param Pujya Guruji, in this regard. We used to say that Article 44 of the Constitution (under the Directive Principles) is about the uniform civil code. Marriage law should be uniform as it will strengthen the unity of the country. He persuaded us that every society has its own law regarding marriage and then he quoted Smritis and said that until the society does not ask for it, itself or gets ready for it, the king should not intervene ... I also apprised Shri Chandra Shekharji of it. We said that we would not make a demand for it, but the intention of the makers of the Constitution was quite conspicuous.

I have, attentively, gone through the debates of the Constituent Assembly ... The present and previous members of Muslim League have all along held that they would not tolerate any intervention by Indian State or Indian Republic or Indian Parliament in the matters of marriage. Why would they not abide by law? Do they have a different type of citizenship? Will family planning also not be implemented for the same reasons? Will the small family norm change on the basis of religion? Family Planning is the first and foremost problem, but the main obstacle to it is that Hindus, who do not wish to adopt it, say that others are being permitted for marrying with as many as four women, what does this Family Planning mean then? I know they are not marrying as many as four women because married persons know that it is difficult to maintain even one wife. (Interruptions.) I watch their plight. Mr. Narasimha Rao is asking how I ... know about it. Mr. Speaker, Sir, in order to know that fire burns, one does not need to put his finger in fire ...

That time, we did not press for ... a common civil code but in the meantime a case of an old woman from Indore came up before the Supreme Court. The Supreme Court gave its verdict and on its basis the Congress Party decided to have a common civil code. Mr. Arif Mohammad gave a beautiful speech that day and it was appreciated by the Congressmen, who said that it was a right decision and everybody should be governed by the same rules regarding marriage. Later on, the opinion of the Congress Party ... changed. The opinion of late Rajiv Gandhi ... changed. Everybody knows ... what happened to Mr. Arif ... people felt that it was a policy of appeasement. Do the ... majority not get affected by what is happening in the House, and outside the House? Do they not react to it? Now the world has come closer and by sitting at home we can watch the happenings around the world ...

I cite an example of Sharjah. People from Kerala went to Sharjah to earn their livelihood. They formed a club there. They staged a play there. This play has already received prizes from Kerala Government. It is a play written by a good writer but ... a rumour spread in Sharjah that this play amounts an insult to Mohammad Saheb ... depicted certain things which are anti-Islam. The actors of this play were arrested. They were awarded 6 years' imprisonment, and they are lodged in jail. Will this incident not have its repercussions? ... People could not understand the correct meaning of secularism ... I had said so ... that day and want to repeat it today as well. Mr. Speaker, Sir, Pandit Jawaharlal Nehru wrote an introduction to the book by Shri Raghunath Singh MP. I do not know how many members have read that book. Panditji wrote ... that the present Hindi translation for the word secularism ... Dharma Nirpeksha, is creating ... confusion. This is not a proper translation. He further said that secularism has only one meaning that there shall be no State religion and the State shall not discriminate against any religion. But even today the Hindi translation of the word secularism is Dharma Nirpeksha.

... You may see how this word is being used by All India Radio and Doordarshan. It should be changed. The word 'secular' does not express our traditions and culture. It was used in some other context which I am not discussing here. Do the events taking place outside the country not affect us? ... a gentleman took a copy of 'Satyarth-Prakash' with him. His baggage was checked at the airport. The copy was seized and he was put behind ... bars. The Ministry of External Affairs knows that he was ... released after a lot of efforts. I do not want to mention the name of the country. We want to have relations with such countries. We do not want to act in the same manner. But we do get such reports. Does such act on their part not aggravate fanaticism? ... reports are being received that in Pakistan, a Minister himself supervised the demolition of temples by using bulldozers. What was the provocation there for demolishing temples? Here, the Government is trying to control the situation through bullets. More than one thousand people have been killed ... how many died in Madhya Pradesh ... how many persons were killed in Maharashtra, Gujarat and West Bengal. But ... whosoever was killed, he was an Indian. I have sympathy for the bereaved families. The Government banned certain organizations and dissolved the BJP Governments. Why? What is their fault? Punishment was awarded before any crime was committed. Capital punishment has been awarded before the murder was committed. It has been the record of the BJP governments that they prevented communal riots that was a normal phenomena during the period of other parties' Governments. The figures will prove it. If the hon'ble Minister of Home Affairs speaks the truth today, he will admit that the number of communal riots in Uttar Pradesh, Madhya Pradesh and Rajasthan was very low and the police subdued them sternly wherever it erupted. No discrimination was made between a Hindu or a Muslim. To provide security for everyone is the religion of our Governments. There can be no communalism in this regard. The ruler cannot make any discrimination on the basis of a community. If he does so, it is wrong … But today whatever is happening is being done only on the basis of gross discrimination. The BJP governments were dissolved. Why? Had law and order failed there? In Himachal, there was no such incident. (Interruptions.)

… But Shri Arjun Singh is interested in Bhopal. He and Shri Patwa either do not pull on well together, or they pull on very nicely. I do not know … If he wants to throw light on it, he can do so.

… Sometimes the sun of truth is hidden by the clouds of politics. Now the truth needs to be spoken after clearing the clouds. I will see how far the Congress leaders speak the truth. I know that they will not admit their guilt. Why the BJP Governments were dissolved? Were they dissolved only because some persons in these Governments were members of the RSS? what … if they were members of the RSS? Were not they abiding by their constitutional liabilities? Were they violating the instructions issued by the Centre?

Mr. Speaker, Sir, when the Patwa government closed and sealed the office of an unlawful organization in Indore, the members of the office approached the Court, and the Indore High Court said that the office cannot be sealed. Please tell me whether this judgment goes in favour of or against the Patwa government? But when the pressure was being put on the Government here and the hon'ble Prime Minister smelled a rat … that the people are determined to dislodge either him or the BJP Governments, he preferred to dissolve the BJP Governments … You have violated the Constitution and run over the norms of ethics and sacrificed all the moral values.

Mr. Speaker, Sir, the State Governments were dislodged because they were ruled by the BJP, but why the legislative assemblies were dissolved? Was not it possible to keep them suspended? Were the assemblies not kept suspended in the past? What was the need of dissolving these assemblies? If there was any complaint, it was against those governments and that complaint, too, has no proper ground. Those Governments should have been allowed to work for some time and then have judged their functioning. After that if you had any complaint against them, it would have been proper and justified to dislodge them. But did the Central Government give them any such opportunity? Not at all … Today, there are so many articles against the Government's decision … I would like to quote one … :

'Dissolution is not the only option, When President's Rule was first imposed on Punjab in 1951, the Assembly was suspended as, indeed, it was in Rajasthan in 1967, Bihar in 1969, UP in 1970, Orissa in 1971, Andhra Pradesh and UP in 1973, Gujarat and UP in 1976, Manipur in 1977 and 1981, Assam in 1979, Punjab in 1983 and Kashmir in 1986 – when it suited the Congress.'

The author of the above lines is not a BJP man.

Mr. Speaker, Sir, these articles appeared in editorial columns in newspapers; even ... pro-Congress newspapers criticize the Congress party ... The daily *Jansatta*, which is not at all happy with the BJP, especially with Shri Advani, was compelled to publish:

'An action of the Prime Minister taken under pressure is not effective and credible. Shri Rao was playing politics for avoiding communal confrontation till now, but if the politics of Shri Arjun Singh can overrule his politics, Shri Rao should retire from politics.'

Mr. Speaker, Sir, I have the editorial comments of an editor who has played a role in trying to settle the Ayodhya issue. Its comments are very harsh against us, but after the dissolution of the Assemblies, you have compelled it to write ... an editorial having the title 'Political Nihilism'. The paper is *Indian Express* ...

... I would like to read out an extract from an article published in the *Indian Express*: 'there was no breakdown of law and order in these states that could even remotely warrant any Central action against their Governments. While 800 people died in Congress-ruled States, there were only 200 deaths in those under BJP control. Yet President Shankar Dayal Sharma accepted the reports of the Governors that they had apprehensions about maintenance of law and order in these states. The Centre itself is open to the charge of criminal inaction, provoking some politicians to demand its removal. The dance of violence that stupefied Surat and Bombay, generating fears that sense and sensibility had vanished from the corridors of power, was apt to sweep away the moronic ministries of Maharashtra and Gujarat. Mr. Narasimha Rao's protective umbrella that saved them was not available to Madhya Pradesh, Himachal Pradesh and Rajasthan where sanity was never shaken.'

Mr. Speaker, Sir, it is not our opinion, rather it is the opinion of an impartial newspaper. It should be taken into consideration. In the light of these commitments, we should try to introspect ... a little bit.

Mr. Speaker, Sir, now I come to the ... ban ... some organizations have been banned ... Before the 6th December, all those organizations were good, patriotic, disciplined, but on account of a single incident that occurred on 6th December in Ayodhya, they have been banned. The picture of the incident of the 6th December is not clear as yet. The Government is talking about appointing a Commission thereon and the CBI is holding an inquiry in this regard. But in the meantime, the Government took a decision to ban certain organizations. Anyway, the reasons given for banning those organizations are ... ridiculous.

I was going through this Bill. When the Unlawful Activities (Prevention) Bill was presented in the House in 1967, I was a member of the House. That time, Shri Yashwant Rao Chavan had moved the Bill ... I was going through Shri Yashwant Rao's speech which he had delivered while moving the Bill. The Bill was discussed thoroughly … Shri Yashwant Rao Chavan went on assuring Members that it would not be applied against them … He gave an assurance that the Government was seeking a right to take action against those who wanted to disintegrate the country.

I, too, delivered my speech. I stated my apprehension that the Government would involve all the opposition parties in the name of … integrity, and declare the opposition as unlawful, those who would be declared unlawful would go underground. You want to stop the unlawful activities, but how you can stop these activities; you have the option to arrest them … making arrests can win the battle of thoughts?

… Whatever is happening in this country is not the battle for a temple, it is … a battle of ideologies. What is the nationalism of this country? Wherein lies the base of this country? Through what roots this country will have water and life? … different kinds of people have come to this country for centuries. Many generations of people have settled here. Though there had been different states, yet the country remained one. No passport was needed to move anywhere in this country. There was no need of having any permit for pilgrims, for going from one place to another. This country was one. What was the uniting force behind it? The Ganga–Yamuna culture is often talked about. The place where Ganga and Yamuna flow together is called Sangam. But after the Sangam, the Ganga flows alone taking all with it.

That day I quoted Shri Nehru. While addressing the students of the Aligarh Muslim University, he said, 'You are Muslims, I am a Hindu. But does not the cultural heritage of this country thrill all of us?' The word used by Shri Nehru was 'thrill'. Now … even the slogan of 'Vande Mataram' is being opposed in this ill-fated country? …

This country had never witnessed the religious discrimination at any stage. But now … Mr. Speaker, Sir, I am worried … I have already spoken to my party. I request you too … whether you think that the recent incidents in Jamia Millia do not affect other youths also. I do not want to mention any names, but it does affect them. If the Government compromises with one kind of fanaticism and promotes it, it cannot suppress … another one. I am sorry for the demolition of the structure. I usually come across … people … who are of the opinion that it was a blot for 400 years and there was no alternative but to remove this blot. I am afraid of such … sentiments. Such issues should be solved peacefully through dialogue. Issues should not be hung in balance, otherwise they become a source of constant trouble. As long as the Ayodhya issue was raised, it was all right but now the position is somewhat different. When Sardar Patel reconstructed the temple of Somnath, our first hon'ble President Shri. Rajendra Prasad attended the function, but Shri Nehru was not happy … But Rajendra Babu went there, the temple was constructed, and the problems were solved. Ayodhya issue has been … pending in the court for forty years …

...The Hon'ble Prime Minister was requested to refer this issue to the Supreme Court under Article 143. But delay was made even in this regard. Then there was a proposal to not ... touch the structure and start construction over 2.77 acres of land. It will take 3–4 years during which some solution would be found. But this proposal was also not accepted. The Government did not bother to understand the changing mood of the people of the country. My friend Shri Shahabuddin is sitting here. I am calling him a friend. My party members would not like this word. However, it is a cultured way of behaviour. When I was the Minister of External Affairs, Shri Shahabuddin was working in our Ministry. He was well known as a progressive Muslim leader ... We wanted to send him to a particular country. I would not mention the name of the country. The Government of that country asked us to send someone else because that was an orthodox country and Shri Shahabuddin was known as a progressive Muslim leader. Then he left the foreign service and started practising law. My party colleagues blame me for bringing him into Janata Party ... But the change that has just taken place in Shri Shahabuddin is surprising. He is bringing out *Muslim India*. If *Muslim India* can be published, why not 'Hindu India'? ... (Interruptions.) The matter is not so simple. I know that Shri Shahabuddin is a very articulate person and would give an impressive reply to it. A lot of matter is published in that newspaper. But on the whole, it is doing nothing but spoiling the atmosphere.

Shri Shahabuddin must be remembering that I had said in a public meeting held in Bombay in 1986 that Ayodhya issue could be solved. I had given two suggestions in this regard. First, Muslims should forsake their claim on the structure in favour of Hindus saying that they were doing so because the sentiments of Hindus were attached to this place. Hindus believe that it is the birthplace of Lord Ram and there is ... evidence ... Faith is something very precious. We live in this country with you, we have to live together. If you believe that it is the birthplace of Lord Ram, we give it to you. Second suggestion was that the Hindus, after getting the structure should say that their struggle for Ram Janmabhoomi has now ended. This structure now would not be demolished. Pooja will continue to be performed there. Temple would be constructed at some other place. But Shri Shahabuddin did not accept it. He wrote me a letter to hold negotiations on the issue. I have that letter with me. This was no solution.

Mr. Speaker, Sir, I would like to conclude now. Ayodhya is a tragedy. The country is standing on a crossroad. It is not the time to level allegations on each other. The more you level charges on us, the more we would be aggressive. The more you try to suppress us, the more we would retaliate. The Government is not understanding the mood of the people. Government is not realizing as to what damage the Hon'ble Prime Minister has caused by giving the statement that mosque will be built again there. What was the hurry in giving such a statement? Was this statement given under some pressure from outside? Was it not necessary to find out first whether there existed temple or mosque earlier? Now the particular state is under the control of the Central Government, the Archaeological Survey of India should be asked to … carry out excavation at the site … to determine whether there existed temple or not. This dispute should be settled once for all. Shri Chandra Shekhar wanted to solve it, and he also got the cooperation of Shri Rajiv Gandhi. Shri Chandra Shekhar arranged for the talks. The talks were held in a cordial atmosphere and a number of documents were exchanged. Solution was about to be reached. But then his Government went out of power. The present Government also may go out of power before finding any solution … (Interruptions.) We are sure that there was a temple. If it is proved that there was a temple and the court also gives same verdict, then they will have to abide by it.

But no effort to this effect has been made. The matter was kept pending. After all, we had not performed the 'Shilanyas', it was performed during regime of Congress Government. At that time the Congress was in power both at the Centre and in the State. Is it wrong to complete … good work started during the days of Shri Rajiv Gandhi? We want to complete that good work. Will the Government put us behind the bars only because of this? What did Shri Advani do? He was arrested when the Lok Sabha was going on in the morning. Look at the allegations levelled against him. How ridiculous those allegations are! Advaniji was appealing to the karsevaks that the structure should not be demolished. You may confirm it from TV reports or inquire … from the journalists. Whereas the Government have got … reports prepared to the effect that Advaniji was inciting the karsevaks to pull down the mosque. Will it raise your credibility? … He is the Leader of the Opposition and he was arrested when the Lok Sabha was in session. He was in Ayodhya. I also wanted to hear from him the sequence of events that took place there. I believe that he is a man of integrity, and he is such a big man that he would admit it if at all he had committed any mistake … (Interruptions.) Please don't interrupt me, please be quiet, if you do not understand the sentiments, I want to express my feelings. I have always been saying this and most … members of our party are of the same view. Don't think that some are liberal and some are hardliners. Who is liberal in Congress Party? … (Interruptions.) … Perhaps Margaretji was saying that she was liberal.

Mr. Speaker, Sir, how can I make any complaint to you when I myself have made a mistake? It has never happened in my 30 years' Parliamentary career that I would … continue speaking when you are on your legs.

… If we cannot speak in the House and you are not ready to hear me, then what is the use of continuing as an MP? Sometimes there is a noise from our side too, but that is not a good thing. This should not happen. After all, we are also the citizens of this country. We are bound by the ties of democracy. The bonds of our culture are inseparable. This is just a passing phase … I am confident that India would emerge stronger and more prosperous out of this crisis. We are passing through a crisis and it would … help us if we discuss the matter sincerely.

Mr. Speaker, Sir, we did not create any difficulty on the first day. It was alleged that BJP Members sat with their heads down. We were … calm. We did not want to indulge in … any hullagulla; even then we were criticized. Our silence was misinterpreted. We asked for an opportunity to express our views … but that too was not given. We continued to plead not to suspend the Question Hour. Today, I faced … great difficulty to persuade my party members. Advaniji has not been released. I would like to know the difficulty in releasing him? The Government says that he can be released on bail, why is he not being released? Sky is not going to fall if he makes a speech here. Why … the Government is adopting an inflexible attitude? … It is clear that they do not want the discussion to take place … in normal situation you do not want Advaniji to express his views and that the facts in regard to Ayodhya to come to light. We are ready to admit our mistake if we have committed at all in Ayodhya. But at the same time the other political parties sitting here should also admit their fault. Central Government should also admit its mistake. I do not want to go into all those details as to how the Hon'ble Prime Minister complicated the matter and why he did not take any initiative for two months and to how he stated contradictory things before the sadhus, and how he tried to create rift among them. It is true that the Hon'ble Prime Minister was very particular even up to the last day that the structure should remain intact. Central Reserve Police was also dispatched there. What were they doing there? Why did the Central Government not interfere and impose President's Rule? Why did the Central Government not intervene in Ayodhya affair? The hon'ble Minister of Home Affairs may please tell us what was the report of the intelligence agencies? What was the role of the officers present there? Facts … should be brought into light. It won't do just by accusing us. The Government may take the immediate political advantage, by accusing BJP for it, but it would not solve the problem. There is a need to start a new chapter. Ayodhya incident is a challenge and it should be availed of as an opportunity for solving the tangle. It depends on our intention whether we take advantage of this opportunity or not. I do not think that the present Government would be able to do it. Because I am unable to understand whether the Hon'ble Prime Minister is unable to take decision or his subordinates do not allow him to take decision. Dhritarashtra is surrounded by Duryodhan and Dushasana, he cannot move on the path of justice, even if he intends to move. With these words, I conclude.

GHULAM NABI AZAD

(Rajya Sabha: Maharashtra)

Lok Sabha: 18 December 1992

No-confidence Motion Against the P.V. Narasimha Rao Government (After the Demolition of the Babri Masjid)

At present, Shri Vajpayee is the leader. He has moved a No-Confidence motion against the Government headed by Shri Narasimha Rao. It would have been much better if he had understood the feelings of crores of people of this country and brought this no-confidence motion against the leadership of the BJP and its office bearers instead of the Congress ... had you done so, it would have helped you to raise the image of your Party which has already been lowered to a great extent ... (Interruptions.)

... Hon'ble Speaker, Sir, it will be wrong to say that only the minorities of this country are saddened over the incident on 6th December in Ayodhya. I have myself seen the sentiments and attitudes of the people of the majority community, i.e. Hindus inside and outside this House. I am proud of being an Indian. Moreover, this mandir–masjid issue did not give rise to any bitterness in the House today.

I believe that there was some tension between the Hindus and Muslims, exactly four years back, when the dispute took a nasty turn, but today while on the one hand, in the Council of Ministers, there is anger, regret and disappointment over the demolition of the disputed structure, on the other, I am proud of the fact, that the people of India have unitedly withstood this holocaust as well; it has demonstrated its unity, the unity between the Hindu and Muslim communities. For this, I would like to congratulate the people of India, especially those belonging to the majority community.

Just now, it was stated that the BJP leaders were unaware that some people, whether they are of the BJP, VHP or RSS, or even the saints were demolishing the disputed Ram Janmabhoomi–Babri Masjid structure. Many references to the Mahabharata were made here, yesterday. I would like to ... express my gratitude to Doordarshan, for telecasting the Mahabharata serial and, in the process, providing some information about the great epic to people like me, who ... had no knowledge about it, who have never read the magnum opus.

Hon'ble Mr. Speaker, Sir, when Draupadi was being disrobed, King Dhritrashtra attributed his helplessness to his blindness, but I would like to know why the Dhritrashtras of Bharatiya Janata Party were silent, when the secular fabric of the country was being torn apart, when the modesty of secularism was being outraged in Ayodhya in broad daylight on December 6? Certainly, they were not blind.

Our Swamiji wondered as to how many Congressmen risked their lives to check the 1984 charge in Delhi, which took place during Rajiv Gandhi's tenure. Then, why didn't Advaniji come forward to protect the Babri Masjid when the structure was being demolished? I would like to mention here that the late Rajiv Gandhi went to the streets and bylanes of the capital to extinguish the raging fire that had engulfed Delhi, unmindful of the fact that the mortal remains of his mother were lying in his house. He was more concerned about the safety of his people, than about performing the last rites of his mother. He felt that any delay in the funeral of his mother won't make much difference, and he went to every nook and corner of the capital to protect the unarmed, to defend the unity and integrity of Mother India.

... our Swamiji says Congressmen were not injured during the 1984 riots. Mr. Speaker, Sir, I regret that such a comparison is being made. So far as the 1984 riots are concerned, nobody knew that Indiraji would be assassinated. It was a spontaneous reaction. That people belonging to one community would attack members of another community was most unexpected, but here the plan to demolish the disputed structure was going on since the past four years and everyone knew ... what would happen. Here, the leader of the Opposition himself had gone to Uttar Pradesh, and he knew very well, the reason for the assembly of such a large number of people. He was told repeatedly both within and outside the House including the National Integration Council meeting, that it could cause ... serious damage but he assured everyone, including this House, the people of India, the Supreme Court and the Union Home Ministry that nothing untoward will happen. Now, it is not proper on his part to say that he was in the dark about the whole issue and to compare this incident with the 1984 riots.

Hon'ble Mr. Speaker, Sir, we have ... learnt from the annals of history that '*Lamhon ne khata ki thi, sadiyon ne saja payi* (Moments made the mistakes, centuries were punished)'. Generations have to bear the brunt for the mistakes committed in moments. I never understood the meaning of this couplet till the December 6 incident at Ayodhya and specially, in the wake of its aftermath ...

Mr. Speaker, Sir, India's unity has a history of five thousand years and that was destroyed due to our carelessness in six hours. My dear friend Swamiji said today that he is prepared to kiss the hangman's noose, if his death can provide the soothing balm to anyone's wounds. I would like to tell Swamiji that we are not murderers, even if he is serious about what he says. We don't want to take anyone's life, nor do we want to pronounce death on anyone. We want a change of hearts, a change of minds. Unless a change of heart and mind is brought about, nothing can be done in future. Even if three persons come forward and offer themselves to be hanged, the wound is too deep to be healed.

Shri Chandra Shekharji had said yesterday that hearts have broken like glasses due to the December 6 incident. The latest available scientific and technological methods have made it possible to put together the broken pieces but ... the scars remain. Temples and mosques have been destroyed in the past, are being destroyed now, and will continue to be destroyed in the future as well ...

Shyam Bihari Mishra (Member from Bilhaur): Always temples and not mosques have been demolished and destroyed.

Ghulam Nabi Azad: Your utterances are regrettable. I see both the temples and the mosques, but you can see only the temples. You don't see both of them being destroyed, while I see both of them being destroyed. Temples and mosques are destroyed in riots. In India, Hindus, Muslims, Sikhs and Christians have been killed in riots, but one feels sad when people belonging to a particular community are singled out and slaughtered, as if in a State-sponsored manner. The matter takes a serious turn and becomes shameful, when a political party, especially one which nurtures the ambition to administer the entire nation, which holds the reins of power in four major states of the country, whose leaders trot the globe speaking of their dream to capture power at the Centre and be torchbearers of India's future, single out any particular community, especially the minorities and attempts to break their hearts.

The country was partitioned in 1947. I was not born at that time. Nevertheless, it is a fact that Indian Muslims refused to go out of India. Some people did leave, but the rest chose to hitch their destiny with that of India. They outrightly rejected the call given by Jinnah on religious lines. They rejected the two-nation theory, based on religious intolerance. They chose to live and die with their Hindu brethren.

Kashmir, which is a Muslim-majority state, also rejected the concept of Pakistan and acceded to India. Now, if the minorities of this country, Sikhs, Muslims and Christians, have made India their home and hearth, whose responsibility is it to guarantee them safety, security and respectability? Obviously, the majority community, our Hindu brethren have to shoulder this enormous responsibility of protecting the lives and property of the minorities. It is their duty.

... I will talk about Kashmir. I will answer point by point, and I challenge the BJP leader, to provide even 1/10th of the facility and representation we have provided to the minority community in Kashmir. (Interruptions.) Let me give you the figures. Minorities constitute two per cent of Kashmir's population ... Our Congress Party is responsible for not putting the facts across the table. In 1947, when rivers of blood flowed across the length and breadth of the subcontinent, not a single person belonging to the minority community was even touched. It is a matter of record ... I am even prepared to quit the Cabinet, in defence of this fact. If you are throwing a challenge, you should be daring enough to listen to us as well ...

Until the advent of terrorism into the valley 3–4 years ago, not a single Hindu was harmed, unmindful of the fact that riots occurred throughout the country, in ... Moradabad ... Hyderabad ... Bhiwandi ... Assam. Not a single state remained untouched by communal frenzy. I am prepared to resign if you cite me a single instance, where a single Hindu was killed in Kashmir. (Interruptions.) What are you talking about? I am talking about representation. As per the 1981 census, minorities constituted 2 per cent of the valley's population ... in the State Government, the minorities constituted 45 per cent of the Gazetted officers and 30 per cent of the Non-Gazetted officers. Moreover, 92 per cent of the staff manning the Central Government's offices in Kashmir, including Radio, Telecommunications etc., belong to the minorities. Is the BJP prepared to provide a similar percentage in jobs to the minority community across the country? Can you pick up the gauntlet? If you can, then do it. If the party can provide even 1/10th of this percentage for the minorities, throughout the country, I will never challenge the credibility of your party.

Hon'ble Vajpayee ji, I have a great regard for you. Please don't blame the Kashmiri Muslims for the misdeeds being committed by Pakistan in Kashmir. Pakistan is the enemy of the entire country, the Muslims, the Muslims of Kashmir. You associate the Muslims of Kashmir with those of Pakistan, it is a great injustice on your part. So long as the Government of the Congress party or the Government of Dr. Farooq Abdullah was in power in Kashmir, not a single incident of discrimination took place there, we crossed the heights of secularism ... (Interruptions.)

Mr. Speaker, Sir, I know several temples were demolished during the last three years in Kashmir, and I regret ... it. Terrorism has been prevailing there for the last three years and temples were demolished by militants. I would not have any grudge if BJP wants to be equated ... with the terrorists, I would not have any regret if BJP wants to move on the path on which the militants are moving. If you wish to make a comparison with us, you should compare the things being done by the Government, rather the activities of the terrorists. Terrorists have demolished temples and thus they are equally enemy for us. Do not say that only Hindus are killed. You can go through the records, Vajpayee ji, you have a lot of contacts, please go through the records. If 300 Hindus were killed by the terrorists, 1900 Muslims were also the victims. These Muslims were killed by militants and not by security forces ... You will again say that only Hindus were killed ... you may get political benefit out of this propaganda in elections, but please don't mislead the House, don't divide the country.

... Mr. Speaker, Sir, I will repeat that it would not be proper to equate the terrorists with us. If the terrorists are the enemies of Hindus in the region, they are as much an enemy to Ghulam Nabi Azad too; they are as ... blood thirsty for my relatives, and thus do not spare me at all. I would like to submit that the BJP is unaware of the disadvantage of our being ... Indian, we know how we raise slogans in favour of India in the shadow of bullets in Kashmir. It would not be an act of bravery if such a slogan is raised in Ayodhya.

Our Kashmiri families, whether Hindus or Muslims, our Kashmiri secular forces whether they are in Delhi, Maharashtra or Karnataka, have been going from place to place in search of shelter but still believe in India and its secularism. I would like to submit that the BJP should not take any step which may demoralize the remaining patriots in Kashmir who are few in number.

Mr. Speaker, Sir, BJP has given ... good material to Pakistan to defame India through the Ayodhya incident that occurred on the 6th December. Pakistan attacked our country thrice since 1947 and tried its best to defame our country in the world, but I think it could not ... harm ... the prestige of our country as much as BJP did on December 6. Pakistan may have the capacity to prepare bombs which can claim several thousand lives, but BJP has given a neutron bomb to Pakistan, and with the help of this bomb, it would spoil the image of the country in the world.

Dear colleagues that is why I had said that '*Lamhon ne khataa ki hai, sadiyon ne saza pai hai*'. BJP's misdeeds committed on 6th December for six hours only has brought a great disgrace to us, to you, to the Members of all political parties, to 90 crore citizens of the country, to our culture, to the unity and the freedom of our country, and we cannot wash this blot for ... centuries to come. Whatever sermons, speeches we may deliver, but this act cannot be undone. Yesterday, Atalji ... said that India has the culture of Ganga and Yamuna, but I will emphasize that this Ganga–Yamuni culture can only continue and remain intact in its true sense when it absorbs the small springs or the rivers of minority communities in it.

The Chief Minister gave an assurance in the National Integration Council, the leaders of Opposition assured us, and the Public Prosecutor of Uttar Pradesh also gave an affidavit to the Supreme Court to the effect that they would protect the structure. The Home Secretary of UP government also gave an affidavit and third is given by the Chief Minister himself. In such a case, where UP government gives three affidavits, the state government writes 12 letters, gives assurance in this regard in National Integration Council and the Leader of the Opposition assures the highest place of Democracy – the House – that they will protect the structure. Mr. Speaker. Sir, even if any mischievous person or a thief gives an affidavit in the court, the court honours it and releases that person. But it is ... very surprising ... that an elected Government betrayed us, despite writing 12 assurance letters, making promises in the NIC meetings and giving three affidavits. You may call it our mistake, foolishness, innocence or whatever you like. You may term it as our blind faith also ... (Interruptions.) But if we had not believed the assurances of the State Government and had dismissed the Government earlier, then probably they would have been given this data against us which I am giving against them ... (Interruptions.)

… Mr. Speaker, Sir, I would like to state that if my BJP colleagues want to see the results of their mistake, committed on 6th December, then they may see … what happened in Kanpur, Surat, Bombay and Seelampur? Who are after these riots?

It would not be a Ganga–Yamuni culture, if it pushes even one stream out. Panditji had said: 'Communalism as such is very bad but communalism by the majority is worse.'

That is why my submission is that even parents treat equally … their children. But if one child is weak or physically handicapped, the parents pay more attention to him. They feel that their other child is wise and strong enough to protect himself, whereas their handicapped child needs their support … Today, that weak child lacks education, wealth or means of earning. Are you not ready to spare even his life? Are you not ready to protect him?

… I had told Indiraji ten years ago what Chandra Shekharji stated yesterday … discrimination … against the minorities in Central Government offices here would force Kashmiri youth to take up arms after 10–12 years … I am very sorry to state that my predictions came true suddenly within a span of 10–12 years only … If the … minorities feel that there is none to protect them and their children and they have no future in this country, they may take up arms in self-defence … then none of us would remain safe. Therefore, I would like to submit to you that we do not want killings. We do not want any sort of violence, rather we want a change in hearts and minds … I pray to God to bring this change so as to protect the unity and integrity of the country …

P.V. NARASIMHA RAO

(Lok Sabha: Nandyal)

Lok Sabha: 21 December 1992

No-confidence Motion Against the P.V. Narasimha Rao Government

Mr. Speaker, Sir, I am indeed grateful to the large number of hon'ble Members who have participated in this discussion and made valuable contributions. The debate has rightly been exhaustive and many Members were able to express themselves with anguish, with anger, with reason and with so much of patriotism that this debate, perhaps, will go down as one of the debates of a highest order in the history of Parliament.

… The occasion itself is one of introspection, seriousness, gravity and perhaps, an occasion where each one of us has to set our sights on the vision of the future.

This country has been a great country, it has risen to great heights, it has seen aberrations but from every aberration it has come out stronger and not weaker. I do hope that this great tragedy, this act of betrayal and vandalism which occurred on the 6th of December will be obliterated as quickly as possible from the public mind. I wish to God that this happens. Even the slightest remnant of the memory of this would be harmful to the country, and I would appeal to all sections of the people, all sections of the House to help in this process, the process of living down this shameful event of the 6th December and prove to the world once again that this is just an aberration, otherwise the country is one full of harmony, full of brotherhood and this has been so for thousands of years; it will be so for thousands of years to come.

It is rather strange, Mr. Speaker, Sir, that this discussion should come in the form of a No-Confidence Motion. The Bharatiya Janata Party has no confidence in the Government of India. Why? Because the Government of India reposed confidence in the State Government of the Bharatiya Janata Party. Maybe, this is … justice meted out to the Government of India. I have to own that … But how do we run the country? How do Centre–State relations run? On the basis of suspicion? On the basis of mistrust? How do we run the governments of the states which are so inextricably linked with the Centre, that they have to run a three-legged race all the time? One of them cannot run in advance, leaving the other behind.

In the National Development Council, in the National Integration Council, in the Chief Ministers' Conference … every problem is so intractable if seen in isolation, but becomes easy when seen comprehensively with the States and the Centre both Governments sitting together and trying to sort it out. During the last one and a half years the National Development Council has been functioning this way. Several sub-committees of the Council headed by Chief Ministers of whichever party, have been constituted and they have been doing excellent work. There has been no dissension of any kind and the National Development Council … has acquitted itself admirably as a result of this functioning. This is how a federal State has to function.

But is it possible, is it conceivable for the Central Government of any federation to … imagine that one of the units, a State Government, would keep giving affidavit after affidavit after affidavit, giving solemn assurances, and finally violate those assurances in a manner that until the last moment, it cannot be detected? That is why my first reaction was that … it was pre-planned. There is going to be an inquiry. I would not like to anticipate the … findings of the inquiry. But it was so planned, it cannot be an accident, it just cannot be an accident.

Sir, I have been arraigned, I have been criticized for believing. That is the only sin I seem to have committed. I agree. I plead guilty for believing a State Government … But the point is that I believed it not only as Central Government; I found that there was nothing else but to believe the assurance of the State Government. Was there any other way when the Supreme Court believes it? The Supreme Court hearing after hearing places more reliance on the State Government; asked the state government to come back with more affidavits; asked me at some point of time to keep out because they would like to try the State Government. They have full faith in the State Government. I am not party. The Central Government is not a party before the Supreme Court nor in the High Court for that matter. But I was called for a particular purpose. We said: 'We are prepared to help the Supreme Court in whatever manner the Supreme Court wants us.' That was all the role we played. And ultimately on the 6th itself, the Supreme Court had been shocked, what they said is revealing. I do not remember any State Government in a federal set-up having behaved this way. So, those who told me and tell me now, did we not tell you? Yes, they have been proved right. But I was proved right in July. So, it is not a question of who is proved right. The question is what has happened to the Constitution of India in this process. It lies shattered. What happens to Article 356? It lies shattered ... Where is it that the President of the Union finds that a situation has arisen whereby the governance of the State cannot be carried on, according to the provisions of the Constitution. What is that precise point? We have dismissed State Governments times without number. Most ... State Governments dismissed or removed have been Congress Governments belonging to the same party as the Central Government. It was easy to tender the chief minister's resignation. We send advisers from here and the State Government gets President's Rule. In those few cases, where other Governments were also dismissed, similar procedure not quite beginning with the resignation, but some other procedure was followed. But in no case was the practical implication of Article 356 tested. You send the advisers. They take over at leisure ... But here in the Ayodhya matter, I cannot do a thing without dismissing the State Government. I send my troops, paramilitary forces. I sent them because I wanted them to be available to the State Government. At no point of time do the State Government tell me that they will not use them. Yet they do not use them. I have yet to come across a scrap of paper from Shri Kalyan Singhji to say that he refuses to use the Paramilitary forces sent by the Centre. The Home Minister will bear me out. But he has not used them. Ultimately, on the last day, when we say please use them, please use them, please use them, the Home Secretary who is sitting with the Chief Minister says – it is so unfortunate – unthinkable and unfortunate.

'At 2.20 p.m. DG, ITBP[1] informed MHA[2] that three battalions which had moved from DRC had met resistance and obstructions en route, there were a lot of

[1] Editor's note: Director General Indo-Tibetan Border Police.

[2] Editor's note: Ministry of Home Affairs.

road blocks and people stopped vehicles. After talking to the people en route, the convoy reached with great difficulty … Saket Degree college where the forces were again stopped and the road was blocked. Minor pelting of stones also took place. The Magistrate asked them in writing to return. DG, ITBP further informed that three battalions had returned accordingly. The Commissioner had been contacted, who informed, the Chief Minister, Uttar Pradesh had ordered that there will be no firing under any circumstances.'

(Interruptions.) Earlier, the Home Secretary spoke to Principal Secretary, Home, Government of Uttar Pradesh, at Chief Minister's residence, asking him to persuade the Chief Minister to accept the assistance of the Central forces. The Principal Secretary, Home, Government of Uttar Pradesh said that he would requisition central forces after consulting the Chief Minister. At no point of time was it refused? This is what I am trying to impress. When does that moment arise when we come to the conclusion that the governance of the State cannot be carried on according to the provisions of the Constitution? … Article 356 … says, 'a situation has arisen – if after that it could have been added – is likely to arise.' Then the Governor gets, the President gets a greater leeway … This is the first time in the history of the Constitution, in the history of Article 356 when it has been put to a time-based test, it was never put to before and it has not been able to stand the test. Never mind who used it, never mind who did not use it, howsoever you look at it you will find that there is a lacuna and that would have to be made good.

On one side these are the reasons why I have to trust the State Government (Interruptions.) …

… There is no variance between the IB report and what I have read … three days before the date, the Governor of Uttar Pradesh writes in categorical terms, that the Central Government should not, I repeat, should not, think of imposing President's rule in the State. He also adds that if any such thing is contemplated, the safety of the Babri mosque can become questionable. I have got the letter. All these factors … stop me from invoking Article 356. On the other side is, of course, the private advice tendered by more supposedly knowledgeable persons …

… On the other hand … was the advice that these people might let us down, and some statements … not from the Government but from some leaders, saying that they would not do Kar Seva only by sweeping … I say in all sincerity that the Government had to weigh the evidence on both sides and we came to the conclusion that it was not possible to impose President's Rule, in the face of all this, at the time at which it would have been of some use. And I would also like to add – I do not know whether I should say this – that the situation in Ayodhya was such that one had to be very careful, extremely careful. The Babri Masjid – that structure – was a hostage. On one side was the possibility of its being saved by negotiation, by further commitment of the State Government, on the other side, you had absolutely no lead time to save it by the central forces in spite of the State Government … It could have been blown up in a matter of minutes, seconds, by one bomb the size of a tennis ball, detonated from two hundred yards, if the State Government connived at it. There were the real possibilities. This is like the mother stabbing the child … poisoning the child. You do not expect it to happen but when it does happen, no one can save it. This is my case … (Interruptions.)

… In July, I succeeded. You all heard … my statement here in this House. We discussed it. It worked. I was taking the same line … (Interruptions.) Please. I was taking the same line which I had elaborated in my statement. We had the Cell. We got the discussions going. Two meetings were held in a very good atmosphere. The third meeting was to clinch the issue of reference to the Supreme Court. It was at that point that a spanner was thrown in the works and the whole thing came back to square one. This is the situation. History will judge, people will judge. I am not really being dogmatic about it. Some of my own party people had different views. I told the party that it is possible for Congressmen to have different views. Who is proved right, who is proved wrong, is not the question. You take a decision, you stick to it, you defend it. If you win, you win, if you do not win, you do not win … (Interruptions.) …

… Sir, when Shri Kalyan Singh resigned, it was too late to do anything. He timed it like that. In fact, our information had been that the BJP very much wanted to save its State Governments. Resignation route was not expected. But when it happened contrary to our information, nothing could be done then except to dismiss the Government which was done.

What I am … trying to impress on the House is let us not go into who is right and who is wrong information wise. I have borne all the criticism from friends and from other parties. I am only trying to place some known facts. In spite of these facts, there had been a betrayal. A betrayal is … never detected. A conspiracy is something which comes to light much later, when only hindsight functions. Indiraji would not have been assassinated, Rajivji would not have been assassinated, if the knowledge about the conspiracy had been available earlier. This is one of those mishaps … Nobody can say that he is impeccably right. No plan can be absolutely hundred per cent foolproof … If the State Government does not give you 20 magistrates who are needed, do you take magistrates from Delhi? Is it possible legally? Can any legal luminary tell me?

… There is a Commission of Enquiry which will go into there. I am only placing before you some recorded, rudimentary facts which need to be taken into account …

… The first impulse of anyone who gets a report like this is to see that we save the mosque first. We ask them to make use of the forces; we go on pleading with them; we go on asking them to do it. This is all that could be done at that stage … (Interruptions.)

... By 9.10 p.m. the President had signed the papers. By 7.30 p.m. or so, Shri S.B. Chavan took the papers to him. Those are the timings if I remember right. (Interruptions.)

The inexorable logic of 6th December has started ... in right earnest, started within whatever time is necessary to take action. Action after action after action has been taken. Yes, this is a change in direction because it was warranted by the worst tragedy we could imagine, and now ... the challenge has been accepted, the battle has been joined. There is no need ... to go into history now. The need for us is to make new history and that is that for the first time after many many years, the secular forces of the country have come together, the secular parties with all their internal differences have come together ... (Interruptions.)

And we will forge ahead, we will see that the secular credentials of this country are re-established fully and what our great leaders through the Constitution and through their own example told us to do, we will do it to the hilt.

Sir, Mr. Indrajit has raised a very relevant point. In fact, I was going to read the same Resolution which he read from the Constituent Assembly, I had occasion to raise this in one of our Party meetings. In a secular democracy, what is the place of non-secular parties or what should be the composition and the programme of parties participating in that democracy, is a question which needs a national debate. I want this debate, I want thinkers, I want leaders to come together because the time has come when we can easily see that there is an irreconcilability in these forces. We tried to carry on for many, many years. Now we find that there is a party which takes a religious issue as its main plank. I have nothing against a religious issue, I have nothing against religion, but a religious issue being brought into politics election after election after election cannot be accepted. This will have to be ... effectively checked. If ... a party ... takes to arms, for instance, if the candidate of one party has an AK-47 and moves with it and the other candidate has nothing, it is an unequal fight. If a party takes Ram as the spokesman of the party and affects the minds and hearts of people day in and day out, whereas the other party ... is a secular party, does not want to make use of that as an issue, then it is ... an unequal fight and the Constitution does not, in my view, allow such unequal fight. The field has to be even for both teams, those who are participating in the elections would have to participate on the basis of certain guidelines, certain principles which are common to all and which are defined very clearly in the Constitution ... Let Ram remain where he remains, let us fight on the basis of other issues which are much more important from the point of view of the people, and that is the only way of making the Constitution work in its right spirit. I appeal to the other parties who are thinking perhaps that religious issues are going to be a permanent asset to them, they will not be a permanent asset to them. The people of India can see through the game very easily and very quickly ... I thank Mr. Inderjit, for having brought out that resolution. We will have to act on it; we will have to think about it. I will come, if possible to the House or to the leaders of the Opposition first ... and perhaps for a ... wider debate in the country, on how this aberration which has become rather menacing during the decade has to be set right. It started with small beginnings, but then it has permeated, more or less, every party. Today, when I say that something which has happened will have to be undone, there are eyebrows going up in all parties. I do not want this at all to happen in any party. If we are secular, the vandal cannot be allowed to take advantage of the act of vandalism committed by him. It is quite clear to me ... I would like to once again appeal that today, the day of balancing pluses and minuses is over, we will have to go ahead with a programme.

So far as rehabilitation and reconstruction measures are concerned, I thought I should apprise the House of what has been decided. The Government of India have advised State Governments to take strong action against officers who have been derelict in their duties in maintenance of law and order during the recent communal riots. At present, the scale of ex-gratia assistance to victims of communal riots differs from State to State. The Government of India will see to it that assistance to riot victims is given on a uniform scale by all the State Governments so that next of kin of persons killed in riots could be paid Rs. One lakh and those who are permanently incapacitated are paid Rs. 50,000/- each. For this particular incident, I would like to add that as a one-time exception, we would like to raise this amount to Rs. Two lakhs in case of death.

... A fund will be set up for repair and reconstruction of all places of worship which were damaged in the disturbances. In addition to the ex-gratia relief in the case of death, grievously hurt or damage to the property, the Government of India will recommend to the State Governments that the victims of recent communal riots may also be given the following assistance: employment to widows or wards of the families affected by the communal riots where an earning member of the family had been killed or permanently incapacitated, allotment of tenements and house sites to families rendered houseless, allotment of shops/space for kiosks to families to restart their business and bank loans ... for recommencement of industries and businesses affected in the riots. Similar measures will also be taken in the Union Territories. These are the steps that have been decided upon.

... The Supreme Court have asked the Government of India to submit its views on this particular subject within a time-frame which they have fixed. We would like to examine all aspects of this and go to the Supreme Court to make our submissions. I would like to tell the hon'ble Members that this is being looked into. (Interruptions.)

... Sir, there is a specific term of reference in the terms of reference of the Commission of Enquiry in regard to what happened to media persons. We have, meanwhile, decided to give those whose equipment, etc. were damaged, certain concessions which were asked by them. So, the Commission of Enquiry will go in great detail into what happened to the media persons.

2

Uniform Civil Code

***Bhagwati Devi**, who was born into the rat-catcher community of Musahars in Bihar, survived the deprivations of being at the bottom of the caste and economic ladder and rose to become an elected Member of the Bihar Legislative Assembly in 1969 and a Lok Sabha MP in 1996. Here she voices her strong opposition to the Uniform Civil Code, which still features high on the Bharatiya Janata Party's to-do list. Bhagwati Devi views the demand for the Uniform Civil Code through the prism of caste and power politics.*

BHAGWATI DEVI

(Lok Sabha: Gaya)

Lok Sabha: 16 May 1997

On the Uniform Civil Code Constitution Amendment Bill (Omission of Article 44, etc.)

I rise to oppose the Bill which is brought in the House ... because in India, there are people belonging to different religions. As you know that when the incarnation of Adiguru Shankaracharya and Brahma, Vishnu and Mahesh took place, many castes like Kori, Gobar, Ghuian, Chamar, Dom, Dushad, Kalwar, Teli, Dhobi, Nai came into existence. I want to know how these castes were created.

When the people in power face a crisis, they start talking in terms of caste. They have created new castes. When poor people supported Lalu, then they felt envy. Why? You have divided people into various castes. A Shudra is beaten if he drinks water in a lota, you tied a bell to his throat, you tie the handi and broom to him. All the castes have been created by you. But you start talking of uniting them today. Restrictions have always been imposed on touching the idols of Gods and Goddesses, but the temples for these Gods and Goddesses are constructed by a Ghuian Chamar, namely, Bhagwati. There are Babajis for worship of these Gods and Goddesses.

I do not know about the whole country, but there was a gold idol in the Vishwanath Temple, which was stolen. Did a Ghuian Chamar go there for worship? When only Panditji was there, then where has the idol gone, who was involved in its theft, how has all this happened and what was the modus operandi in this regard?

... I want to say that you want to unite all the people. But you make love to any girl, when you desire to do so, and if she conceives, you abandon her, saying that you are not interested in her friendship. In such circumstances, she is forced to commit suicide. She is ousted from society. What are the reasons that a minister's son is allowed to do anything to any poor girl? If you want friendship with the poor, you have to change your mentality.

But when such an occasion comes, you talk of 'roti and beti' and caste – I want to ask: in which direction do you want to take society and how? When the poor in society is moving in one direction today, you thought you need to enact a law to divert the poor from that way. Then you presented this Bill, but how will you keep everyone united? In this country, the people believe in different religions. Some are Kabir-panthis, some are Christians, some people believe in the Sikh religion of Guru Nanak Dev.

You say that inter-caste marriages should be encouraged, but because of the wrong path you are following, we are unable to persuade our children to follow that way. For the sake of religion, where do you want to take us and, how do you want to take us that way? You do not allow us the right to worship. Has untouchability vanished? We have huts and when Laluji[3] brought some improvement in the condition of those huts, it pinched the rich people.

... When Laluji tried to improve our houses, all the persons became restless. Some people live in 'pucca' houses and some in khaprails. You will have to reduce the difference between the status of the poor and the rich. Tulsidas said that one day 'Kaliyug' will come, the Kshatriya will step down and the Shudra will rule. When you think so, I must be enthroned as Prime Minister ... (Interruptions.)

... I will take only one minute. I want to make it clear that this Bill should not be passed in the name of religion. Hindustan is a garden, where people of all religions live. All religions preach non-violence, so they should not be abolished. With these words, I conclude my speech.

---

[3] Editor's note: Lalu Prasad Yadav, former chief minister of Bihar, who transformed the social landscape of the state.

Section Ten

Politics

1

Resignation

In recent decades, there have been no resignations by ministers on matters of principle, or a genuine difference of opinion. This speech by ***Bhimrao Ramji Ambedkar****, the Father of the Indian Constitution, is reflective of an era where politics was not just about power, but about the power of ideas as well.*

Ambedkar's resignation in 1951 as the Union Law Minister from Jawaharlal Nehru's Union Cabinet was primarily prompted by the latter's inability to push through the Hindu Code Bill, that was intended to provide a civil code in place of the body of the Hindu personal law: the Hindu Right, present in the ranks of the Congress as well, brought pressure to bear upon Nehru not to legislate it. (Later, this was broken down into three specialized bills, which passed into law. The Hindu Marriage Act outlawed polygamy and contained provisions dealing with inter-caste marriages and divorce procedures. The Hindu Adoption and Maintenance Act had, as its main thrust, the adoption of girls, which till then was not much in practice. The Hindu Succession Act placed daughters on the same footing as widows and sons where the inheritance of family property was concerned.)

Morarji Desai, *who would go on to become the Prime Minister in 1977, heading the short-lived Janata Party government after the elections that followed the lifting of Emergency, resigned from the deputy prime ministership in July 1969. It was in protest against the nationalization of major banks by an ordinance, after Indira Gandhi, as Prime Minister, relieved him of the finance portfolio. He had argued that there was already criticism of the inefficient working of the public sector, in general, and of the State Bank of India, in particular, and, 'therefore, it would be unwise to burden the administration with the control of 94 private banks in the country, as it would pose enormous problems of integration and fitment of salaries, and efficient running of the banks', according to an authorized biography of the Reserve Bank of India.*

BIMRAO RAMJI AMBEDKAR

Legislative Assembly: 27 September 1951

Resignation over the Hindu Code Bill[1]

The House, I am sure, knows unofficially if not officially, that I have ceased to be a member of the Cabinet. I tendered my resignation on Thursday, the 27th September to the Prime Minister and asked him to relieve me immediately. The Prime Minister was good enough to accept the same on the very next day. If I have continued to be a Minister after Friday, the 28th, it is because the Prime Minister had requested me to continue till the end of the Session – a request to which I was, in obedience to constitutional convention, bound to assent.

Our Rules of Procedure permit a Minister who has resigned his office, to make a personal statement in explanation of his resignation. Many members of Cabinet have resigned during my tenure of office. There has been, however, no uniform practice in the matter of Ministers who have resigned making a statement. Some have gone without making a statement and others have gone after making a statement. For a few days, I was hesitant what course to follow. After taking all circumstances into consideration I came to the conclusion that making of a statement was not merely necessary, but it was a duty which a member who has resigned owes to the House.

The House has no opportunity to know how the Cabinet works from within, whether there is harmony or whether there is a conflict, for the simple reason that there is a joint responsibility under which a member who is in a minority is not entitled to disclose his differences. Consequently, the House continues to think that there is no conflict among members of Cabinet even when as a matter of fact a conflict exists. It is, therefore, a duty of a retiring Minister to make a statement informing the House why he wants to go and why he is not able to continue to take further joint responsibility.

Secondly, if a Minister goes without making a statement, people may suspect that there is something wrong with the conduct of the Minister, either in his public capacity or in his private capacity. No Minister should, I think, leave room for such suspicion and the only safe way out is a statement.

Thirdly, we have our newspapers. They have their age-old bias in favour of some and against others. Their judgements are seldom based on merits. Whenever they find an empty space, they are prone to fill the vacuum by supplying grounds for resignation which are not the real grounds but which put those whom they favour

---

1 Source: Vasant Moon, ed., *Dr. Babasaheb Ambedkar: Writings and Speeches* Volume 14 (Part 2), Dr Ambedkar Foundation, Ministry of Social Justice and Empowerment, Government of India, 2013.

in a better light and those not in their favour in a bad light. Some such thing I see has happened even in my case.

It is for these reasons that I decided to make a statement before going out.

It is now 4 years, 1 month and 26 days since I was called by the Prime Minister to accept the office of Law Minister in his Cabinet. The offer came as a great surprise to me. I was in the opposite camp and had already been condemned as unworthy of association when the interim Government was formed in August 1946. I was left to speculate as to what could have happened to bring about this change in the attitude of the Prime Minister. I had my doubts. I did not know how I could carry on with those who have never been my friends. I had doubts as to whether I could, as a Law Member, maintain the standard of legal knowledge and acumen which had been maintained by those who had preceded me as Law Ministers of the Government of India. But I kept my doubts at rest and accepted the offer of the Prime Minister on the ground that I should not deny my cooperation when it was asked for in the building up of our nation. The quality of my performance as a Member of the Cabinet and as Law Minister, I must leave it to others to judge.

I will now refer to matters which have led me to sever my connection with my colleagues. The urge to go has been growing from long past due to variety of reasons.

I will first refer to matters purely of a personal character and which are the least of the grounds which have led me to tender my resignation. As a result of my being a Member of the Viceroy's Executive Council, I knew the Law Ministry to be administratively of no importance. It gave no opportunity for shaping the policy of the Government of India. We used to call it an empty soap box only good for old lawyers to play with. When the Prime Minister made me the offer, I told him that besides being a lawyer by my education and experience, I was competent to run any administrative Department and that in the old Viceroy's Executive Council, I held two administrative portfolios, that of Labour and CPWD, where a great deal of planning projects were dealt with by me and would like to have some administrative portfolio.

The Prime Minister agreed, and said he would give me in addition to Law, the Planning Department which, he said, was intending to create. Unfortunately, the Planning Department came very late in the day and when it did come, I was left out. During my time, there have been many transfers of portfolios from one Minister to another. I thought I might be considered for any one of them. But I have always been left out of consideration. Many Ministers have been given two or three portfolios so that they have been overburdened. Others like me have been wanting more work. I have not even been considered for holding a portfolio temporarily when a Minister in charge has gone abroad for a few days.

It is difficult to understand what is the principle underlying the distribution of Government work among Ministers which the Prime Minister follows. Is it capacity? Is it trust? Is it friendship? Is it pliability? I was not even appointed to be a member of main Committees of the Cabinet such as Foreign Affairs Committee, or the Defence Committee. When the Economics Affairs Committee was formed, I expected, in view of the fact that I was primarily a student of Economics and Finance, to be appointed to this Committee. But I was left out. I was appointed to it by the Cabinet, when the Prime Minister had gone to England. But when he returned, in one of his many essays in the reconstruction of the Cabinet, he left me out. In a subsequent reconstruction my name was added to the Committee, but that was as a result of my protest.

The Prime Minister, I am sure, will agree that I have never complained to him in this connection. I have never been a party to the game of power politics inside the Cabinet or the game of snatching portfolios which goes on when there is a vacancy. I believe in service, service in the post which the Prime Minister, who as the head of the Cabinet, thought fit to assign to me. It would have, however, been quite unhuman for me not to have felt that a wrong was being done to me.

I will now refer to another matter that had made me dissatisfied with the Government. It relates to the treatment accorded to the Backward Classes and the Scheduled Castes. I was very sorry that the Constitution did not embody any safeguards for the Backward Classes. It was left to be done by the Executive Government on the basis of the recommendations of a Commission to be appointed by the President. More than a year has elapsed since we passed the Constitution. But the Government has not even thought of appointing the Commission. The year 1946 during which I was out of office, was a year of great anxiety to me, and to the leading members of the Scheduled Castes. The British had resiled from the commitments they had made in the matter of constitutional safeguards for the Scheduled Castes and the Scheduled Castes had no knowing as to what the Constituent Assembly would do in that behalf. In this period of anxiety, I had prepared a report on the condition of the Scheduled Castes for submission to the United Nations. But I did not submit it. I felt that it would be better to wait until the Constituent Assembly and the future Parliament was given a chance to deal with the matter. The provisions made in the Constitution for safeguarding the position of the Scheduled Castes were not to my satisfaction. However, I accepted them for what they were worth, hoping that Government will show some determination to make them effective. What is the Scheduled Castes today? So far as I see, it is the same as before. The same old tyranny, the same old oppression, the same old discrimination which existed before, exists now, and perhaps in a worst form. I can refer to hundreds of cases where people from the Scheduled Castes round about Delhi and adjoining places have come to me with their tales of woes against the Caste Hindus and against the Police who have refused to register their complaints and render them any help. I have been wondering whether there is any other parallel in the world to the condition of Scheduled Castes in India. I cannot find any. And yet why is no relief granted to the Scheduled Castes?

Compare the concern the Government shows over safeguarding the Muslims. The Prime Minister's whole time and attention is devoted for the protection of the Muslims. I yield to none, not even to the Prime Minister, in my desire to give the Muslims of India the utmost protection wherever and whenever they stand in need of it. But what I want to know is, are the Muslims the only people who need protection? Are the Scheduled Castes, Scheduled Tribes and the Indian Christians not in need of protection? What concern has he shown for these communities? So far as I know, none and yet these are the communities which need far more care and attention than the Muslims.

I could not contain within myself the indignation I have felt over the neglect of the Scheduled Castes by the Government and on one occasion, I gave vent to my feelings at a public meeting of the Scheduled Castes. A question was asked, from the Hon'ble Home Minister, whether my charge that the Scheduled Castes had not benefited by the rule which guaranteed to them 12½ per cent representation was true. In answer to the question the Hon'ble Home Minister was pleased to say that my charge was baseless. Subsequently for some reason – it may be for satisfying the qualms of his conscience – he, I am informed, sent round a circular to the various Departments of the Government of India asking them to report how many Scheduled Caste candidates had been recently recruited in Government service. I am informed that most Departments in reply said 'NIL' or nearly nil. If my information is correct, I need make no commentary on the answer given by the Hon'ble Home Minister.

From my early childhood I have dedicated myself to the upliftment of the Scheduled Castes among whom I was born. It is not that there were no temptations in my way. If I had considered my own interest I could have been anything I wanted to be and if I had joined the Congress I would have reached the highest place in that organization. But as I said, I had dedicated myself to the upliftment of Scheduled Castes and I have followed the adage that it is better to be narrow-minded if you wish to be enthusiastic about a cause which you wish to accomplish. You can therefore, well imagine what pain it has caused me to see that the cause of the Scheduled Castes has been relegated to the limbo of nothing.

The third matter which has given me cause, not merely for dissatisfaction but for actual anxiety and even worry, is the foreign policy of the country. Anyone, who has followed the course of our foreign policy and along with it the attitude of other countries towards India, could not fail to realize the sudden change that has taken place in their attitude towards us. On 15th of August, 1947 when we began our life as an independent country, there was no country which wished us ill. Every country in the world was our friend. Today, after four years, all our friends have deserted us. We have no friends left. We have alienated ourselves. We are pursuing a lonely furrow with no one even to second our resolutions in the UNO. When I think of our foreign policy, I am reminded of what Bismarck and Bernard Shaw have said. Bismarck has said that 'politics is not a game of realizing the ideal. Politics is the game of the possible.' Bernard Shaw not very long ago said that good ideals are good but one must not forget that it is often dangerous to be too good. Our foreign policy is in complete opposition to these words of wisdom uttered by two of the world's greatest men.

How dangerous it has been to us this policy of doing the impossible and of being too good is illustrated by the great drain on our resources made by our military expenditure, by the difficulty of getting food for our starving millions and by difficulty of getting aid for the industrialization of our country.

Out of 350 crores of rupees of revenue we raise annually, we spend about Rs.180 crores of rupees on the Army. It is a colossal expenditure which has hardly any parallel. This colossal expenditure is the direct result of our foreign policy. We have to foot the whole of our Bill for our defence ourselves because we have no friends on which we can depend for help in any emergency that may arise. I have been wondering whether this is the right sort of foreign policy.

Our quarrel with Pakistan is a part of our foreign policy about which I feel deeply dissatisfied. There are two grounds which have disturbed our relations with Pakistan – one is Kashmir and the other is the condition of our people in East Bengal. I felt that we should be more deeply concerned with East Bengal where the condition of our people seems, from all the newspapers, more intolerable than ... Kashmir. Notwithstanding this we have been staking our all on the Kashmir issue. Even then I feel we have been fighting on an unreal issue. The issue on which we have been fighting most of the time is, who is in the right and who is in the wrong. The real issue to my mind is not who is right, but what is right. Taking that to be the main question, my view has always been that the right solution is to partition Kashmir. Give the Hindu and Buddhist part to India and the Muslim part to Pakistan as we did in the case of India. We are really not concerned with the Muslim part of Kashmir. It is a matter between the Muslims of Kashmir and Pakistan. They may decide the issue as they like. Or if you like, divide into three parts; the cease fire zone, the Valley and the Jammu–Ladakh region and have a plebiscite only in the Valley. What I am afraid of is that in the proposed plebiscite, which is to be an overall plebiscite, the Hindus and Buddhists of Kashmir are likely to be dragged into Pakistan against their wishes and we may have to face the same problems as we are facing today in East Bengal.

I will now refer to the fourth matter which has a good deal to do with my resignation. The Cabinet has become a merely recording and registration office of decisions already arrived at by Committees. As I have said, the Cabinet now works by Committees. There is a Defence Committee. There is a Foreign Committee. All important matters relating to Defence are disposed of by the Defence Committee. The same members of the Cabinet are appointed by them. I am not a member of either of these Committees. They work behind an iron curtain. Others who are not members have only to take joint responsibility without any opportunity of taking part in the shaping of policy. This is an impossible position.

I will now deal with a matter which has led me finally to come to the decision that I should resign. It is the treatment which was accorded to the Hindu Code. The Bill was introduced in this House on the 11th April, 1947. After a life of four years, it was killed, and died unwept and unsung, after 4 clauses of it were passed. While it was before the House, it lived by fits and starts. For full one year, the Government did not feel it necessary to refer it to a Select Committee. It was referred to the Select Committee on 9th April 1948. The Report was presented to the House on 12th August, 1948. The motion for the consideration of the Report was made by me on 31st August 1948. It was merely for making the motion that the Bill was kept on the Agenda. The discussion of the motion was not allowed to take place until the February Session of the year 1949. Even then it was not allowed to have a continuous discussion. It was distributed over 10 months, 4 days in February, 1 day in March and 2 days in April 1949. After this, one day was given to the Bill in December, 1949, namely the 19th December, on which day the House adopted my motion that the Bill as reported by the Select Committee be taken into consideration. No time was given to the Bill in the year 1950. Next time the Bill came before the House was on 5th February, 1951 when the clause by clause consideration of the Bill was taken. Only three days 5th, 6th and 7th February were given to the Bill and left there to rot.

This being the last session of the present Parliament, Cabinet had to consider whether Hindu Code Bill should be got through before this Parliament ended or whether it should be left over to the new Parliament. The Cabinet unanimously decided that it should be put through in this Parliament. So the Bill was put on the Agenda and was taken up on the 17th September 1951 for further clause by clause consideration. As the discussion was going on, the Prime Minister put forth a new proposal, namely, that the Bill as a whole may not be got through within the time available and that it was desirable to get a part of it enacted into law rather than allow the whole of it to go to waste. It was a great wrench to me. But I agreed, for, as the proverb says 'it is better to save a part when the whole is likely to be lost'. The Prime Minister suggested that we should select the Marriage and Divorce part. The Bill in its truncated form went on. After two or three days of the discussion of the Bill, the Prime Minister came up with another proposal. This time his proposal was to drop the whole Bill even the Marriage and Divorce portion. This came to me as a great shock – a bolt from the blue. I was stunned and could not say anything. I am not prepared to accept that the dropping of this truncated Bill was due to want of time. I am sure that the truncated Bill was dropped because other and more powerful members of the Cabinet wanted precedence for their Bills. I am unable to understand how the Benares and Aligarh University Bills, how the Press Bill could have been given precedence over the Hindu Code even in its attenuated form? It is not that there was no law on the Statute Book to govern the Aligarh University or the Benares University. It is not that these Universities would have gone to wrack and ruin if the Bills had not been passed in this Session. It is not that the Press Bill was urgent. There is already a law on the Statute Book and the Bill could have waited. I got the impression that the Prime Minister, although sincere, had not the earnestness and determination required to get the Hindu Code Bill through.

In regard to this Bill, I have been made to go through the greatest mental torture. The aid of party machinery was denied to me. The Prime Minister gave freedom of vote, an unusual thing in the history of the party. I did not mind it. But I expected two things. I expected a party whip as to time limit on speeches and instruction to the Chief Whip to move closure when sufficient debate had taken place. A whip on time limit on speeches would have got the Bill through. When freedom of voting was given there could have been no objection to have given a whip for time limit on speeches. But such a whip was never issued. The conduct of the Minister for Parliamentary Affairs, who is also the Chief Whip of the Party in connection with the Hindu Code, to say the least, has been most extraordinary. He has been the deadliest opponent of the Code and has never been present to aid me by moving a closure motion. For days and hours, filibustering has gone on a single clause. But the Chief Whip, whose duty it is to economize Government time and push on Government business, has been systematically absent when the Hindu Code has been under consideration in the House. I have never seen a case of a Chief Whip so disloyal to the Prime Minister and a Prime Minister so loyal to a disloyal Whip. Notwithstanding this unconstitutional behaviour, the Chief Whip is really a darling of the Prime Minister. For notwithstanding his disloyalty he got a promotion in the party organization. It is impossible to carry on in such circumstances.

It has been said that the Bill had to be dropped because the Opposition was strong. How strong was the Opposition? This Bill has been discussed several times in the party and was carried to division by the opponents. Every time, the opponents were routed. The last time when the Bill was taken up in the party meeting, out of 120 only 20 were found to be against it. When the Bill was taken in the party for discussion, 44 clauses were passed in about 3½ hours' time. This shows how much opposition there was to the Bill within the party. In the House itself, there have been divisions on three clauses of the Bill – 2, 3 and 5. Every time there has been an overwhelming majority in favour even on clause 4 which is the soul of the Hindu Code.

I was, therefore, quite unable to accept the Prime Minister's decision to abandon the Bill on the grounds of time. I have been obliged to give this elaborate explanation for my resignation because some people have suggested that I am going because of my illness. I wish to repudiate any such suggestion. I am the last man to abandon my duty because of illness.

It may be said that my resignation is out of time and that if I was dissatisfied with the foreign policy of the Government and the treatment accorded to Backward Classes and the Scheduled Castes, I should have gone earlier. The charge may sound as true. But I had reasons which held me back. In the first place, most of the time I have been a Member of the Cabinet, I have been busy with the framing of the Constitution. It absorbed all my attention till 26th January 1950 and, thereafter, I was concerned with the People's Representation Bill and the Delimitation Orders. I had hardly any time to attend to our foreign affairs. I did not think it right to go away leaving this work unfinished.

In the second place, I thought it necessary to stay on, for the sake of the Hindu Code. In the opinion of some, it may be wrong for me to have held on for the sake of the Hindu Code. I took a different view. The Hindu Code was the greatest social reform measure ever undertaken by the legislature in this country. No law passed by the Indian legislature in the past or likely to be passed in the future can be compared to it in point of its significance.

To leave inequality between class and class, between sex and sex, which is the soul of Hindu society untouched and to go on passing legislation relating to economic problems is to make a farce of our Constitution and to build a palace on a dung heap. This is the significance I attached to the Hindu Code. It is for its sake that I stayed on notwithstanding my differences. So if I have committed a wrong, it is in the hope of doing some good. Had I no ground for such a hope, for overcoming the obstructionist tactics of the opponents? I would like in this connection to refer only to three of the statements made by the Prime Minister on the floor of the House.

On 28th November, 1949, the Prime Minister gave the following assurance. He said: 'What is more, the Government is committed to this thing (Hindu Code). It is going through with it.' 'Government would proceed with that. It is for this House to accept a measure, but if a Government takes an important measure, and the House rejects it, the House rejects that Government, and the Government goes and another Government comes in its place. It should be clearly understood that this is one of the important measures to which the Government attaches importance and on which it will stand or fall.'

Again on 19th December, 1949, the Prime Minister said: 'I do not wish the

House to think in the slightest degree that we consider that this Hindu Code Bill is not of importance, because we do attach the greatest importance to it, as I said, not because of any particular clause or anything, but because of the basic approach to this vast problem in problems, economic and social. We have achieved political freedom in this country, political independence. That is a stage in the journey, and there are other stages, economic, social and other and if society is to advance, there must be this integrated advance on all fronts.'

On the 26th September, 1951, the Prime Minister said: 'It is not necessary for me to assure the House of the desire of Government to proceed with this measure in so far as we can proceed with it within possibilities, and so far as we are concerned we consider this matter as adjourned till such time as the next opportunity – I hope it will be in this Parliament – offers itself.'

This was after the Prime Minister had announced the dropping of the Bill. Who could not have believed in these pronouncements of the Prime Minister? If I did not think that there could be a difference between the promises and performances of the Prime Minister, the fault is certainly not mine. My exit from the Cabinet may not be a matter of much concern to anybody in this country. But I must be true to myself and that can be only by going out. Before I do so, I wish to thank my colleagues for the kindness and courtesy they have shown to me during my membership of the Cabinet. While I am not resigning from my membership of Parliament, I also wish to express my gratitude to Members of Parliament for having shown great tolerance towards me.

MORARJI DESAI

(Lok Sabha: Surat)

Lok Sabha: 21 July 1969

Resignation from Union Council of Ministers

Mr. Deputy Speaker, Sir, I am grateful for the opportunity that you have given me to make a statement on my resignation from the Council of Ministers.

S.A. Dange (Member from Bombay central south): Is such a statement necessary? Why should it be made? We know it.

Mr. Deputy Speaker: It is permitted under the rules.

Morarji Desai: I consider it rather unfortunate that I should have to appear before this House to explain why I resigned as it involves the question of the relationship between me and the Prime Minister.

I came to the conclusion that I can no longer serve in the present Council of Ministers except at the cost of my self-respect and except as a silent spectator to methods that may endanger the basic principles of democracy on which our parliamentary system is established. I came to this conclusion because I was summarily relieved of the Finance portfolio without even the ordinary courtesy of a prior discussion on this matter being shown to me by the Prime Minister.

After the Fourth General Election, the Congress Party chose its leader. She then asked me to join her Cabinet as Deputy Prime Minister and Finance Minister. Even though I did not want to join the Cabinet. I did so at her own request and on the pressing advice of many colleagues and friends. It was again she herself who insisted that I should take up the Finance portfolio even though I did not want to do so.

S.A. Dange: You laid the pre-condition for joining. It is a false statement.

Morarji Desai: During the period of over two years, I have tried conscientiously to perform my duty as Finance Minister and to pursue and implement the policies that the party and the Cabinet formulated from time to time. The Prime Minister has not pointed out to me a single instance where I have not done so. I have never believed in saying one thing and doing another. It is an accepted principle of democracy that every man has a right to think and express his views freely and frankly and that every decision must be arrived at after full and frank discussion. It is this right of full and frank discussion that is the basis of the duty cast on every democratic person to stand by the decision unequivocally and to implement it conscientiously.

Holding this belief as I do, I have always considered it to be my duty to be bound by every decision that has been democratically taken and I have never accepted such decisions with any reservations. I would ask anyone to show if I have ever shown any reservation in either defending a decision or implementing it once it was taken. Anyone who cares to look at my 39 years of public life, in the organization, in the State legislature and Cabinet, in the Parliament and the Central Cabinet, will agree that this has been my record. I was, therefore, greatly surprised and pained when soon after my return from Bangalore, I received a letter from the Prime Minister, on the 16th instant, informing me that as she believed that I had strong reservations about some of the basic issues that arise, and that I had my own views about the direction and pace of the change, and that she did not want to put an unfair burden on me in implementing these decisions taken at Bangalore, she had decided to take the Finance portfolio, herself.

After I saw the letter and the notification issued by the President, I found that I was asked only for the sake of form to continue as Deputy Prime Minister. It is well known that the resolution on economic policy adopted … at Bangalore was moved by me at the instance of the Working Committee. I moved that resolution without any reservation, and I made it abundantly clear when I moved it and later when I replied to the debate on this resolution. If I accept to do a thing, I do it conscientiously and with all my heart. I believe this is known to everybody, including the Prime Minister. If, in spite of this, the Prime Minister came to the conclusion that I may not implement the decisions, it only means that she had not that confidence in my sincerity of action.

The reservations to which the Prime Minister has referred may be due to the fact that in discussions preceding a decision in the Cabinet or in the Working Committee, I may have put the pros and cons of a proposition forcefully and frankly because I have believed that it is the duty of every person taking part in the process of arriving at decisions, to express his views before a decision is taken and not subsequent to it. If these arguments are taken as reservations and the person concerned is to be penalized for them, it will only lead to a condition where people will not give their views fully and frankly. This will pose the greatest danger to the very functioning of democracy. If I were to accept this position, I would be doing injustice to my faith in democracy and would be failing in my duty.

I may be permitted to recall that I have been privileged to work as Chief Minister of Bombay State for quite some years and in the Central Council of Ministers for more than nine years, first under the leadership of the late Pandit Jawaharlal Nehru and then under the present Prime Minister. During all these years, I have left nothing undone to see that the policies of the Party and the decisions of the Cabinet are carried out fully and effectively, and also to defend them in legislatures or outside, even when they pertained to matters for which others were responsible.

Even in spite of my cooperation with the Prime Minister throughout the last two years in the implementation – without any reservation – of all the decisions that have been taken collectively or individually, if the Prime Minister now shows a want of confidence in me, it would be futile for me to remain in the Cabinet and expect to make any useful contribution.

This was not the only reason for my resignation. I have been so summarily relieved of the Finance portfolio that I felt it an act of disgrace, and my self-respect was deeply hurt. When I had discussions with the Prime Minister at her request on the 18th, I requested her to put herself in my position and to tell me what would have been her reaction. I told her that if she could realize that wrong was done to me, then it should be rectified. She was not prepared to undo the wrong. I had, therefore, no alternative left but to resign in order to uphold my self-respect.

Before I conclude, I would like to refer to the unfortunate fact that over the last several months, deliberate attempts have been made by several interested people to create an impression that I was opposed to rapid socio-economic changes and radical measures to eradicate poverty and inequality of human status in our great country. These people probably do not know that I come from a very poor family. I grew up in poverty. I know, as very few of these people know, what the pangs of poverty are and how opportunities for growth and expression are denied to millions of our poor people. I have, therefore, always considered it my duty to fight poverty everywhere and of every kind and all forms of inequality and vested interests which create that poverty which is not only economic but also social as well. I have from my young age subscribed to Gandhiji's dictum that every interest which is in conflict with the interest of the downtrodden or the daridranarayan, as Gandhiji used to call them, should be checked and Government must use its authority to ensure that poverty and inequality of status are eliminated. I, however, hold that these changes cannot be achieved as if by magic or in a very short time. Success in this direction can only result from persistent and collective efforts both through Government and society. It has been my endeavour to do this throughout my life. My conscience is, as DPM, clear and I am not worried by the attempts of those who try to malign me out of ignorance or prejudice.

If I had agreed to remain in the Cabinet as Deputy Prime Minister even with the addition of some duties which the Prime Minister may be pleased to assign to me, after the summary treatment meted out to me, it would have been dishonourable for me and it would have proved I was only hankering after office. I hope and trust that the House will see the correctness of my action. Finally, I would like, with your permission, Sir, to place on the Table of the House the correspondence I have had with the Prime Minister on this behalf, so that the House may have the facts on its record.

2

A Question of Confidence

On 27 May 1996, ***Atal Bihari Vajpayee****, who had taken oath as Prime Minister just 13 days earlier, after his BJP emerged as the single-largest outfit in the general elections, entered the Lok Sabha to face a vote of confidence. The BJP, with just 161 MPs, was woefully short of the halfway mark of 272, but the then President, Shankar Dayal Sharma, invited him to form the government, as his was the single-largest party. He gave him two weeks to secure a majority. As the 14-day deadline drew near, the BJP realized that it had miserably failed to win majority support. Indeed, it had not succeeded in winning the support of even one additional MP. He was up against a trust vote that he knew he would lose, and so, on 28 May – the day the motion was to be voted on – instead of facing the ignominy of being defeated, Vajpayee chose to resign. But not before he spoke for around an hour, exhibiting the masterful oratory that he was known for in Hindi. This, of course, is a translation.*

A little less than a year later, it was time for another Prime Minister – ***H.D. Deve Gowda*** *– to seek a vote of confidence. A provincial politician, Deve Gowda had earned his spurs in his home state of Karnataka, where he had been the Chief Minister. He had been a surprise choice for Prime Minister in 1996, when the United Front, a coalition of smaller parties, came to power in 1996, with the help of the Congress, after the BJP failed to cobble together the requisite numbers. But given the lack of expectations, and his charisma, which he deliberately worked on to project himself as a 'humble farmer', and which the media used against him – his list of achievements is considerable, given the brevity of his tenure. Deve Gowda understood this, and was canny enough to list them for posterity in his speech – in many cases, with citations!*

Deve Gowda's central target is, of course, the Congress and its then President, the wily Sitaram Kesri, who suddenly withdrew support from his United Front government. This speech that he delivered in the Lok Sabha in April 1997 was undoubtedly a career best as Prime Minister.

Perhaps, what unites the speeches – apart from a strong sense that the pride of these two men had taken a hit – is this: Vajpayee's BJP failed to secure even a single MP's support because his party was seen as a communal outfit; as far as the United Front was concerned, politically, though it was possibly the most ideologically cohesive coalition Indian politics had seen, consisting entirely of secular parties, one of the accusations the Congress hurled against Deve Gowda when it pulled out support was that it was a 'communal' dispensation.

ATAL BIHARI VAJPAYEE

(Lok Sabha: Gandhinagar)

Lok Sabha: 28 May 1996

Motion of Confidence in Council of Ministers

Mr. Speaker, Sir, I shall feel highly obliged if the House listens to me with patience after having witnessed so much uproar. I want to express my thanks to all those who have participated in the discussion on my Motion.[2] This House is meant for peaceful, restrained and rational debate. Some friends wanted that there should be no debate ... and the Motion should be put to vote right away so that they could be enthroned immediately after they left the House ... (Interruptions.)

... Such occasions have come many times ...

... But on every occasion, democracy in India has emerged stronger and I am sure, this occasion will not be an exception.

Mr. Speaker, Sir, I have been a critic to the Governments all these 40 years. Today, most of the time, I had to listen to criticism. There is a saying in Marathi:

> *Nindkache ghar asave shojari, ie.*
> *Nindak niyare rakhiye, aangan kuti chhabaye.*

> You should keep your critic near you, otherwise sycophants will spoil you. If you have a critic, he will keep you spotless without any cost ... (Interruptions.)

... Mr. Speaker, Sir, I would like to extend my special thanks to Sarvashri George Fernandes of the Samata Party, Sirpotdarji of the Shiv Sena, Barnalaji of the Akali Dal and Jai Prakashji of the Haryana Vikas Party who have supported my Motion. Those who have criticized me will get a reply ... However, I ... have a

---

[2] Editor's note: In an earlier section, 'The Civic Space', I have used an excerpt from a speech made by G.G.Swell, who was a close friend of Vajpayee. That speech was part of this debate.

special word of gratitude for my dear friend Shri Murasoli Maran (Interruptions.) ... Despite our differences on certain issues, he was generous enough to set the record straight on the issue of horse trading by stating categorically that we did not use suit-cases to convert our minority into a majority. He has ... demolished the baseless and politically motivated allegation levelled by some members. I am also glad that Thiru Maran has taken note of our resolve to restore the balance of resources in favour of States.

We have always held the opinion that the Centre cannot be strong if the States are weak. Thiru Maran is disturbed over our advocacy of one nation, one people, one culture. I am happy that he shares our perception of one nation. But I must say that he has got it all wrong on our interpretation of one people and one culture. I categorically state that the BJP does not stand for uniformity. We recognize ... India's multi-religious, multilingual and multi-ethnic character. This view is best reflected in a poem by ... one of India's greatest poets Subramaniam Bharati. That poem is entitled, 'E Thaai' i.e., 'My Mother'. I would like to read it in Tamil. It says:

Muppadhu kodi magamudaiyal
Vyyir moimburam ondruiyal
Lval cheppoumzhl pad inettudaiyal
Enil Sindhanai ondrudaiyal[3]

... I had also read something in Tamil in my Address in the United Nations. Its Hindi translation is ... :

Tees koti mukhmandalwali hai meri maan,
Ek hai uski kaya aur atma
Bhashayen wah atharah bolti hai.
Kintu ek hai uska chintan.[4]

---

[3] Editor's note and translation: Subramaniam Bharati's poetic composition 'Bharati, Mother Bharat, Rise!' was one of his great patriotic works. The excerpt translates thus:

My mother has thirty crore faces,
But her body and soul are one
Languages she speaks eighteen.
But her thinking is one.

The poem describes India, or Bharat as the mother goddess, and exhorts her to rise in response to the prayers of her children. Appreciating the political awakening of the masses, Bharati wrote that the sounds of freedom could now be heard far and wide. For Bharati, Mother India was his very essence. The poem describes how the people of India, united, were taking her name in 18 languages, and concludes with the hope that the people would be 'blessed by her reign', i.e., by freedom. The poem also compared her to the Goddess Durga, who vanquished evil demons, thus establishing an analogy between the anti-imperialist struggle and the fight between good and evil. 'Bharati, Mother Bharat, Rise!' by Subramania Bharati remains one of the most important patriotic poems composed during the freedom struggle.

[4] See footnote No. 3

Mr. Speaker, Sir, an allegation has been levelled against me that I … lust for power… This allegation has hurt me deep in my heart … I have been in Parliament for 40 years. The Hon'ble Members have seen my behaviour and my conduct. I had been in Government with my friends in the Janata Dal. I have never done anything wrong in the pursuit of power. Shri Sharad Pawar is sitting here. He was not present in the House when Shri Jaswant Singh was speaking. He said in his speech that Shri Pawar had caused a split in his party to form a Government with our support. Whether he formed the Government for the sake of power, or for the good of Maharashtra is a different thing. But the fact remains that he … split … his party and cooperated with us. But I did nothing of this sort. During … this debate, a remark has been made repeatedly … personally Vajpayee is a good leader but his party is not good.

… Then what do you intend to do for a good Vajpayee?

… If I am offered power with a new alliance at the cost of a split in my party, I would be the last person to even remotely entertain such an idea.

'Na bhito maranadasmi kewalam dusthito yash.' Lord Rama has said, 'I do not fear death, if at all I fear, I fear bad name, I fear public odium.' My political career … has been an open book. But when the electorate voted us as the single largest party, should we have rejected their mandate? When the Hon'ble President invited me to form the Government … should I have run away from shouldering the responsibility? … Isn't it a fact that we have emerged as the single largest party? … On being invited to form the Government, should I have asked the Hon'ble President to give me some time so that I may have consultations in the party?

When the President told me that the oath ceremony will take place the next day, and I would be given … up to 31st May '96 to prove majority, I offered to make best use of the time being given to me by talking to other parties in a bid to garner their support and try to create an atmosphere conducive to moving ahead on the basis of a common programme. What is objectionable in it? How does it indicate our greed of power? Moreover, the decision to form the Government was not just mine, rather it was that of the party.

Mr. Speaker, once the date i.e. 31st of May was fixed for a trial of strength … it could take place only on the floor of the House. We never subscribed to the view that this trial of strength should take place either in Rashtrapati Bhawan or Raj Bhawan – it therefore became necessary to summon the House and once the House is summoned the President's Address is a Constitutional obligation. We could have listed some other business too for the sitting, at least we could have moved a Motion of Thanks on the President's Address, but neither people on the Opposition benches permitted nor I too insisted on it lest it should create any doubts. We looked for the earliest opportunity for the trial of strength. Hence the Motion of Confidence was brought on 27th May and today is 28 May, and the matter will be decided. We could have insisted that since we have been given time up to 31st May ... we will remain in power ... (Interruptions.). Mr. Speaker, Sir, one should not be hit below the belt or be put under cloud. I never played this game not will ever play such a game in future ... Under the Westminster model of parliamentary system that our country has adopted, number of votes or the percentage thereof which a party gets is not taken into account, what counts is the number of seats that a party wins. This system cannot serve the twin objectives of the percentage of votes as well as number of seats. Our country has not adopted the List System of the proportional representation system. I, for one, have always been pointing out the defects of the Westminster system in which ... it is ... possible that a party getting a fewer number of votes on an aggregate, may corner disproportionately larger number of seats ... the vice versa is also possible. In Kerala, a coalition government has come to power with just one per cent margin of votes, dislodging the party in power ... And now the total number of votes you are having is being counted, but I can ... count ... your own percentage of votes which will be only to your disadvantage. They now say that they are uniting ... Are they uniting for the explicit purpose of providing a stable and responsible Government in the country? ... they have not chalked out a programme so far nor have they approached the electorate with a common programme. The mandate received and the vote percentage obtained about which they are now talking is for different States and for divergent reasons. In Tamil Nadu it was the Congress that was fighting against DMK ... not our party. The same situation obtained in Andhra Pradesh where we were nowhere in the picture. How can they say the mandate is against us, when it was the Congress that they were fighting against and not us. What sort of a mandate is that? Say explicitly what you are murmuring. Say openly that you will not let us come to power at any cost ... A bogey is being created in this House that India is moving towards a Hitler type of dictatorship, and fascism is raising its head in the country. This sort of fear is being created ... We have been working as a party here on democratic lines and have been contesting elections.

... The mandate is against the Congress. The strength of the Congress in the House stands reduced to just half of its previous strength here. The people have given their verdict differently in different States, disregarding which ... parties are now uniting and enlisting Congress support and the latter willing to extend its unqualified support to them. I do not want to reiterate what my friend Mr. George Fernandes said yesterday. The stand taken by the other parties seems to be that irrespective of whatever invectives they might have hurled at each other ... now they should unite and let the BJP not form the Government. If this is your collective decision, then I would not say anything. Nonetheless, such a decision would be negative, reactionary, aimed at ... stalling us from coming to power and hardly conducive to the health of democracy.

I want to caution them today. On our part, we are ready to sit in the opposition. Mr. Speaker, Sir, when I joined politics, I never dreamt of becoming an MP. I was a journalist. I am not keen on the type of politics being practised today.

I do wish to renounce politics. But politics itself refuses to part company with me.

Then I became the Leader of the Opposition; today, I am the Prime Minister and after some time I shall cease to be so. I was not overjoyed when I became the Prime Minister, and nor I shall have any qualms when I demit … office …

… Today … fresh allegations are being levelled against us that … The President's Address makes no mention of Ram Temple, Article 370 and Uniform Civil Code, and so much so that Swadeshi slogan has also been jettisoned. All this is being said in a tone as if they are … aggrieved on account of our putting aside these issues, whereas these … people … have all along been criticizing us for these issues. They have been holding us guilty because we intend to construct Ram Temple and wanted abrogation of Article 370 of the Constitution … Even though … the Constitution, and the Supreme Court has also vindicated this viewpoint that there should be a Uniform Civil Code … we cannot say the same. If one says so one is branded as a subverter of the unity of the country. We say that these issues are not part of our present programme (Interruptions.) … because we do not have a majority. (Interruptions.)

We are fighting for majority. If the people's mandate is not in your favour they have not fully accepted us either and with the mandate we have received now, we are not in a position to implement all the programmes … We have emerged as a single largest party and our endeavour is to evolve a workable system through consensus and that is why we did not touch upon the disputed issues. What objection do you have …?

Now, United Front is being formed … (Interruptions.) … but its programme is yet to be chalked out … (Interruptions.) if that has been done, then have they assimilated the philosophy and the programmes of the Marxist party in it, in totality. If they have done so, then why the Marxist party has been keeping a distance from the Government? … (Interruptions.)

When different political parties come together every party has to give up some of its programmes. In 1977 also we were supporting the demand for abrogation of Article 370 of the Constitution. Shri Ram Vilas Paswan, who is present here, was with us at that time. In 1977, we were in favour of making atom bomb also but when we realized that democracy was in danger … we kept aside many of our party programmes. Due to the imposition of Emergency, the entire country was turned into a jail. We all decided to work together to stop … authoritarianism. At that time no one asked us why we were not pressing for abrogation of Article 370 … Now, you are forming a United Front, so each one of you will have to forgo some of your party programmes. The Hon'ble President has given us time up to

31st, because he knew that we were not in a majority. But the Hon'ble President called us to form the Government because we were the single largest party in the House. He gave us time up to 31st May so that we may talk to other political parties and make efforts to form a stable Government. Such things are happening in other countries also. It was being done here.

... Is it my fault if the voters have not given a clear majority to any party? We have been given the chance as the single largest party, because people wanted ... a change. Is it also our fault?

... Earlier, you were not in favour of any discussion on this motion. But when a discussion was initiated, the Hon'ble Members took keen interest in it, and we have had a good discussion in the House. Now the time has come to take a decision on it. Even then you are feeling so perturbed. You are so anxious to come to power so soon.

... Mr. Speaker, Sir, the time which was given to me to mobilize majority support has been properly utilized by me. I have had talks with different political parties. Some parties have come to our support and some other parties expressed their difficulties. Some parties are of the opinion that they will lose some of their votes if they support us. I can understand if any political party is worried about its vote bank but how long and to what extent this game of vote banks will continue? Will they ignore the national interest for the sake of a vote bank? When we talk about minority, and say that they should get full protection, equal opportunities, equal rights, people level charges against us saying that we do not practise what we say ... Our Party Governments in the states are functioning accordingly and if you give us a chance in the Centre, we can show you as to how all these things are implemented ... every political party is talking about the biggest minority community but no one is bothered about the Sikhs who are just two per cent of the population ... you have listened to the agony of Shri Barnala. Nobody is bothered about them.

Mr. Speaker, Sir, I remember those days when Sikhs were being massacred in ... Delhi riots. One of our BJP workers came to me in the cover of darkness. I could not recognize him because he had cut his hair short and had shaved off his beard ... He told me that he could not come to me in the daylight. He could not come out of his house with his long hair. That was why he had sacrificed his hair. He had come to narrate his tale of woe to me. At that time, we advocated the cause of Sikhs. That was why we lost elections at that time, and the Congress party captured ... power by exploiting anti-Sikh sentiments of the people. We did not do that ... (Interruptions.)

... Mr. Speaker. Sir, I would like to stress on the point I mentioned in the beginning. There should not be polarization in the country, neither on ... communal nor on ... caste lines ... politics should also not be divided into two camps ... sans dialogue and discussion. Today, country is in crisis. Whenever needed, we helped the Government to tide over the situation. Being the Leader of the Opposition, I was deputed by the then Prime Minister, Shri Narasimha Rao, to represent India in Geneva. Members of the Pakistani delegation were taken aback at my inclusion in the Indian delegation. In that country, the Leader of Opposition is only interested in pulling down the Government. This has not been our tradition and moreover it is quite contrary to our nature. I wish this tradition to continue … Governments will come and go, but the nation will always remain there. The democracy of this country will live forever. Has it not become a difficult task in the present atmosphere? This discussion will conclude today but the chapter which is going to start from tomorrow requires some deliberation. The bitterness should not be allowed to grow. I do not know the basis on which the United Front selected Shri Deve Gowda as its leader because he was not the first choice of the United Front. He was their fourth choice. Now he is going to become their first choice for the Prime Ministership … (Interruptions.)

Mr. Speaker, Sir, I regret that during the discussion the names of such organizations were mentioned here which are independent and are engaged in the task of nation and character building. I am referring to RSS. One can have differences with the … RSS ideology but the … allegation levelled against the RSS were not warranted. Even the Members of Congress and other parties respect and admire the constructive work being done by the RSS and they also lend their cooperation for the same. If they … work among the poor, and … for the spread of education in tribal areas they should be felicitated for their endeavour … cooperation should be extended to them … (Interruptions.)

… Mr. Speaker, Sir, my friends should know that I have also come here after getting elected. They should also know that being the leader of the largest party I have been appointed Prime Minister by the President of India. It is at the directive of the President that I have come to seek the vote of confidence of the House.

… Mr. Speaker, I was saying that those who are patriots, rational in this country and those who wish welfare of the country from the core of their heart and have come in contact with RSS, know that this organization is dedicated to the country for its well-being …

I will cite a recent instance … after the Chinese aggression, the voluntary organizations which were invited to participate in the Republic Day parade for showing solidarity with Pandit Nehru, RSS was one among them … Communists were not there … (Interruptions.) Even during the time of Shri Lal Bahadur Shastri, who was also a popular Prime Minister of the country, when we had a war with Pakistan, educated people were needed to control the traffic in Delhi and … again, RSS volunteers … offered their services to control the traffic … (Interruptions.) Recently, a function was organized in Bangalore to commemorate the struggle against the Emergency, which was called the second struggle for freedom. Shri Deve Gowda was also present there. I have with me the excerpts of his speech ... he made on the occasion; I am quoting it.

RSS is a spotless organization. In my first years ... (Interruptions.)

... Mr. Speaker, Sir, what Shri Deve Gowda said about the RSS is as follows: 'RSS is a spotless organization. In my forty years long political life, not even once I criticized RSS.'

The Chief Minister said that he was telling this with the utmost responsibility. He said that he had no two opinions regarding the RSS's active role during Emergency. Shri Gowda further said, 'People who were with Mrs. Gandhi during Emergency, who praised her, who appreciated Emergency, they are today with us and are enjoying power, but RSS is the only organization without any black spot. Others have wavered this way or that way.'

Mr. Speaker, Sir ... Shri Deve Gowda ... made a true evaluation of RSS for which I would like to commend him. But these people want that he should not be praised ... It had been published not in any single newspaper, but in all the newspapers and as I had said nobody refuted his statement.

Mr. Speaker, Sir, I would like to reply to one more point ... It has been said that the BJP did not receive wide support from the people ... that we got support from the cow-belt. It is improper to refer to this ... as the cow-belt in the House. We won in Haryana. We received support from Karnataka. It is correct that we are not that strong in Kerala and Tamil Nadu. But we have our organization there. We have also received a little less than 10 per cent votes in West Bengal. If you talk of votes, then talk of 10 per cent votes. In this House, individual Member constitutes a party and he is trying to dislodge us by mobilizing people against us. They have every right to do so. Each of them has come alone from his constituency, and got united here in Delhi. Why have they got united? Is it for the well-being of the country? If so, they are welcome. We are also serving the nation in our own way. Are we not patriots and rendering selfless service to the country for carving a niche for ourselves in politics? We have been sincerely making efforts for the last 40 years to reach ... this position. It is not a sudden mandate. It was not a miracle. We worked hard. We went to the people, we have struggled. Ours is a party which functions round the year. Ours is not like the parties which mushroom during the elections. Today, we are unnecessarily being put in an embarrassing position, just because we could not get a few more seats. We do admit that it is our weakness. We should have got a majority. The President gave us an opportunity and we tried to avail of it. It is another matter that we did not succeed. But do not forget that even then, we are going to sit in the House as a largest party in the Opposition, and they have to run the House with our cooperation. I would like to assure them that we will extend our fullest cooperation ... in conducting the business of the House. But I do not know what type of Government they would form, on what programme it would be formed and how would it be run.

... out of the total of 77 Scheduled Caste Members, 29 belong to BJP, five members from CPI(M), 1 from CPI, 15 from the Congress Party and 7 from the Janata Dal ... We have the maximum number. Similarly, there are ... 11 Members belonging to Scheduled Tribes in the BJP out of the total of 41 Members. Please don't say that we do not have popular base ... if they think they can form the Government without us, and that Government will last, I do not see any such possibility. (Interruptions.) First ... it will be difficult for the Government to come into being. It is hardly possible that it will survive. The question is how for this Government surrounded by internal squabbles is going to benefit the country. For ... everything, they have to approach the Congress party. At present I cannot say but earlier there were some talks that the Congress party has laid down certain conditions. Then there was a tale that a Cabinet Coordinating Committee will be formed. They can also have coordination on the floor of the House. Without that, the business of the House cannot be conducted. It is very good that they want to govern the country. Our good wishes are with them. We shall continue to serve the country. We bow before the numerical strength and we assure you that we will not rest until we achieve the national objective.

Mr. Speaker. Sir, I am going to submit my resignation to the President ... (Interruptions.)

H.D. DEVE GOWDA

(Rajya Sabha: Karnataka)

Lok Sabha: 11 April 1997

Motion of Confidence in Council of Ministers

Hon'ble Speaker, Sir, with your permission, I would like to clear some of the doubts raised by the Hon'ble Members of this House.

First ... I would like to express my sincere thanks to the entire House for having agreed to pass the Finance Bill, the Vote on Account and the Appropriation Bill, on the 21st of this month.

Shri Atal Bihari Vajpayee, as a senior leader, has said that the supporting party should not be neglected in the manner in which the party which is running the administration, with the support of the Congress (I), has neglected. It is a very good suggestion. Shri Sontosh Mohan Dev has intervened to say that when this issue was raised by the Leader of the Congress, both CPP and the Party leader, nobody from the United Front met the Leader and tried to convince the Leader ...

Sir ... I would like to say something about the two letters ... forwarded to me, according to the statement made by the Hon'ble Member, Shri P.R. Dasmunsi. I have not received any letter. The President of India, with a covering letter and with an enclosure, which was handed over by the Congress(I) President on 30th March, 1997, has sent that letter to me on 31st March,1997. The letter of withdrawal, presented to the Rashtrapatiji on 30th March, 1997, was forwarded to me by Rashtrapatiji on 31st March, 1997. Till then, I have not received any communication from the Congress (I) President. On 30th March, 1997, I met the former Prime Minister, Shri P.V. Narasimha Rao.

Before my Finance Minister left Delhi for Calcutta on 29th March, he told me that the Congress (I) has not submitted its party accounts to the investigating officer, and that 31st March is the last date. There is no option except to ... levy a penalty. He said ... he was going to Calcutta and then to Goa, and coming back only on ... 31st March. Please try to sort out this problem, the Finance Minister told me. He also told me that he had tried his best to contact the Treasurer, Shri Ahmed Patel,[5] to get the necessary explanation. But he was not available. So, please see that this issue is sorted out. I went to Shri P.V. Narasimha Rao on 30th March because he was the President at that time responsible for the 1993–94 accounts ... He suggested that he would send Shri Pranab Mukherjee to discuss the matter. I came back, and I gave a phone call to Shri Sitaram Kesri, the President of the Party and the CPP Leader. I told him that I wanted to meet him to discuss some important issues ... He gave me ... time ... at 2 o'clock on 31st March.

I have some basic ethics in life. I have not come here in search of this office, with any aspiration, with any ambition. I did not aspire to become the Prime Minister of this country, leaving the Chief Minister's office. There is no need for ... manipulative politics. The people of this country, who are politically ... awakened, are aware of that. 12.40 p.m. was the time chosen to hand over the withdrawal letter, and he gave me time at two o'clock to meet him. Was Shri Sontosh Mohan Dev not there when I met his President? I met him twelve times.

The allegation is that I am meeting only Shri P.V. Narasimha Rao. I am not a person who will stab another behind the back. Shri P.V. Narasimha Rao was the Prime Minister of the country. Yes, I was here on the day when the Vote of No Confidence was moved, and I voted against him. On that day, he tried to save his Government with whatever methods and with whatever means he could. Today, those friends who want to teach sermons and morals in this country, those who

[5] Editor's note: Treasurer of the Indian National Congress at the time.

want to attribute motives against Shri Narasimha Rao, were they not enjoying … office in his Government? Today, everybody wants to raise a finger against Shri Narasimha Rao, saying that Deve Gowda is going to safeguard the interests of Shri Narasimha Rao. If he … is in … hospital, and if Deve Gowda goes to see him, he is showing extra regard and respect to him! Just because he has lost the Presidentship, lost the CPP leadership, I am not a person to belittle him. He has done something for the nation. Whether he continued in office by using various political methods or not, I do not want to go into the details … He has bailed out this country from the economic crisis. I am not going to make sweeping remarks against everybody, but how some of you, friends, have belittled him, I know that. Even though it is not my concern, even though I know that I am going to lay down … office today, but friendship is not a marketable commodity in this country. Shri Narasimha Rao must be aware of these words … On the day when he handed over the resignation letter to the CPP leadership, he was alone. I went to his house to know why this had happened.

Yes, I respect Shri Chandra Shekhar. My friendship with Shri Chandra Shekhar is very old. I had come in contact with him twenty years back. He is the seniormost leader, and I respect him. Whether … in office or not, I used to go to his house. Going to his house is a sin, going to Shri Narasimha Rao's house is a sin, meeting Shri Sharad Pawar is a sin, but meeting their President twelve times is not a sin! I have not neglected anybody in my life. Did I not go to Shri Atal Bihari Vajpayee's house? Did I not go to Shri L.K. Advani's house? We should have some basic manners in public life. It is not a question of wooing anybody or pampering anybody to continue in office. You must … respect … your elders. The office which I am holding today for another hour, is the highest office. Pandit Jawaharlal Nehru … one of the tallest leaders in the world, sat here and performed his duties as Prime Minister.

… destiny dragged me here and made me … sit in this chair. When the former Speaker of this House, Shri Shivraj Patil, was speaking, I was hearing his speech. I appreciate some of the viewpoints he expressed.

Sir, I would like to go into some detail because this is my last speech in this House. I will go to the other House, I have got five years to stay there … (Interruptions.). I only request all the Members, senior leaders, to cooperate with me. I have not interrupted even when severe attacks were made by several Members in this House …

Shri Dasmunsi has said about my going to Bangalore and coming back …

H.D. Deve Gowda: Shri Dasmunsi, you are a good friend … You took me to Calcutta. Please touch your heart and tell me: what is the performance of this Prime Minister in the last ten months? Which Prime Minister has continuously visited for seven days the North Eastern States? You are there from the days of the Youth

Congress. You are a staunch Congressman. I do not want to question your loyalty to the organization. But … tell the truth. Do not suppress your conscience. There were people like Feroze Gandhi who exposed … corruption … when his father-in-law was the Prime Minister. If you feel that the decision of your President to withdraw … support is going to help the so-called secular democracy, I welcome it … But I would like to tell you very frankly, I have not done anything else in the last ten months but to discharge my duties … (Interruptions.) …

Sir, my secular character was questioned. It is said that the Congress Working Committee is constrained to note that the United Front has failed to provide the leadership necessary to consolidate the forces of secularism and confront the forces of communalism. Am I responsible for their defeat in Punjab? Am I responsible for their defeat in the Corporation elections or the local bodies' elections in Maharashtra? Am I responsible for the defeat of the Congress candidates in all the by-elections except in the by-election of the seat vacated by me in my home state where the BJP lost the deposit and the Congress won? I do not want to say that the BJP and the Congress have come together. The BJP got 23,000 votes in the 1996 parliamentary election, and 27,000 votes in the Assembly elections. They lost their deposit and they have come together to fight against secularism.

Shri P.R. Dasmunsi, you might have come to that opinion because of the communication gap. I would like to ask about the spirit of this Working Committee resolution. Shri Mulayam Singh Yadav is also here. There were three by-elections for the Rajya Sabha. The Congress got 30 votes, the BSP 66 and the Janata Dal eight. If he had not passed on these 104 votes, could it be possible for any of these three parties, including the Janata Dal, the Congress and the BSP, to defeat the three official candidates of the BJP? You tell me. Do not regret the withdrawal. Do not worry about the withdrawal …

I do not want to quote again in this House the appreciation by the media … Later on, I am coming to … the word used by the Congress (I) President about the performance of the Government, and about the efficiency of the Government.

… I would like to clarify some of these issues because in the morning, I did not want to make a political speech.[6] Some people were under the impression that I was in a depressed mood. No. I got training from Shri Chandra Shekhar. I … never bother about … office. I have tendered resignation thrice even against his advice. Today, I would like to make it clear that the day I received this communication of withdrawal of support from the President's office, I would have tendered my resignation. But … the next day, the leaders of all the parties of the United Front

[6] Editor's note: The speech H.D. Deve Gowda made introducing the no-confidence motion. The speech excerpted here is his reply to the debate in the evening.

assembled here, and said, 'No, you should not resign. You should go before the House. We must test and we must find out who is who.' Because of that decision taken by the United Front, I bowed my head. It is because of their support that I was elected as the Leader, and it is with the support of the Congress, I am running the Government …

In the last eleven months, I have never used any occasion to belittle the Congress on any public platform. I might have addressed 66 meetings in Uttar Pradesh where the BJP, in the Lok Sabha elections, got a clear majority in 236 Assembly segments. In the Assembly elections, they got about 176 Assembly segments for their party. Is it not an achievement, Shri P.R. Dasmunsi?

P.R. Dasmunsi (Member from Raiganj): Mr. Prime Minister, you did not try to unite the secular forces at that point of time.

H.D. Deve Gowda: You do not know. That is why you are saying this … (Interruptions.) I do not want to reveal everything that has happened because it will be unethical on my part, if I say what I had done at various stages. I do not want to do it … (Interruptions.)

P.R. Dasmunsi: I did not accuse you entirely … (Interruptions.)

H.D. Deve Gowda: Shri Patwa, please do not disturb me.

Mr. Speaker, Sir, I never interrupted when the others were speaking. Now, they should please allow me to express my views in this august House as the Prime Minister, outgoing Prime Minister. All right!

Sir, somebody told me, I think my Home Minister, that the allegation was that the Prime Minister was trying to split the Congress Party. When Shri Madhavrao Scindia wanted to join the Congress Party, he came to me because he was in the United Front at that time. Did I not tell him to go and join and strengthen the Congress Party? … (Interruptions.)

Madhavrao Scindia (Member from Gwalior): You are a very nice man. But since you have taken my name, I would like to clarify that I have a very good equation with you, but I came to you out of courtesy to inform you that I may be joining the Congress Party. I did not ask your permission.

H.D. Deve Gowda: There is no need to get my permission. But when you came and said that, at least you maintained a certain dignity and political ethics. You were in the United Front at that time and you came and informed me. What did

I say? I said: 'Please go and join and strengthen the Congress Party; I have no objection.' Did I not say that?

Madhavrao Scindia: I agree. You are absolutely right. When I informed you, you said: 'Yes, certainly.'

H.D. Deve Gowda: Thank you very much.

When Shri N.D. Tiwari and Shri Arjun Singh came to me, saying that they were going back to the Congress Party since Shri P.V. Narasimha Rao had been removed from the Presidentship of the Congress Party, I said: 'Go, you are most welcome to do that, and I have no objection.' Had I ever tried to split the Congress Party? ...

Sir, another allegation made is that Deve Gowda wants to marginalize the Congress Party. When Shri Sharad Pawar asked me to attend some programmes in his constituency, did I ever say 'no'? Even to the constituency of Shri Sontosh Mohan Dev, to the former Speaker's constituency, wherever I have been called, I have gone. I have not even gone to my party workers' meetings because I did not want to create friction between the Congress party and my Party workers. I never attended any party meetings when I had gone to the Congress-ruled states to attend official programmes fixed by local MPs. How have I marginalized the Congress Party? ...

Sir, in the morning, the hon'ble Deputy Leader of the Opposition, Shri Jaswant Singh, in a very dignified manner, tried to mention the language which was used by the Congress (I) President against the Prime Minister. When the Press asked me about it, I said: 'Just ignore it.' Today, I would like to tell the nation, through this House, what ... language used by the hon'ble President of the Congress (I), who is aspiring to become the Leader ... If the House wants, if all my friends, including that of the Congress Party want, I have no objection.

Sir, I am unable to understand the meaning of the Hindi word, '*nikamma*'.

He said: 'You are foolish, cowardly and powerless. Just come into the open and let us see who is powerful.'

He has quoted in Hindi: '*Yeh vyakti nikamma aur kamunal hai.*' (This man is not only incompetent but he is also communal.)

An incompetent Prime Minister, what he has done in the last ten months, I must apprise this House and, through this House, the nation. I would just like to draw the attention of the hon'ble President of the Congress to an editorial which appeared in *The Hindu* newspaper ... It says: 'Mr. Deve Gowda's administration saw – as never before in the last few decades – the return of considerable autonomy to the Ministries. The role of the Prime Minister's Office has been substantially reduced in various areas of decision making such as foreign investment which rightly has been returned to the Ministry of Industry.'

I delegated the powers of the PMO because I am incompetent, inefficient and a foolish Prime Minister … (Interruptions.) He is not a Congress worker. He is an All India Congress (I) President. He occupies the chair where great people like Shri Motilal Nehru, Pt. Jawaharlal Nehru and Shrimati Indira Gandhi sat … (Interruptions.)

Sir, the *Washington Post* says:[7]

'India has just made a demonstration of the new sort of leadership that the South Asian subcontinent badly needs. But now by an initiative of Prime Minister, Mr. H.D. Deve Gowda, India, the issue is being treated and removed about the Bangladesh and India on sharing of river Ganga water. If the Ganges Agreement is an example of the leadership Mr. Deve Gowda can provide, let us see more of it.' …

… Sir, a foolish and incompetent Prime Minister, at least tried to do something for the nation. I have not kept quiet for ten months. I would like to recall what I … said on the day when I replied to the Confidence Motion in this very same House … Whether I remain for five days or five months or five years, it is not my concern. Every minute, I am going to use to serve the nation. That is the pledge I had taken. Yes, I did work for 18 to 19 hours a day. I am proud of it. There is no regret in vacating this office … I have not wasted a single minute. Whenever I used to get an opportunity, I did my best.

There is no need of any certificate from the present President of the Congress (I) … I have fought ten elections in my life. Has he fought any direct elections in his life? Why I have chosen to come to the Rajya Sabha, I would like to make … clear. I anticipated … the Congress would ditch me, because Shri Chandra Shekhar was the victim and Shri V.P. Singh was the victim. I know about all these things and what has happened in the past. Shri Narasimha Rao was the victim. I am going to say everything – how Shri Morarji Desai had been handled by the Congress, and how Shri Raj Narain, who was holding the Health portfolio and who fought against Madam Gandhi, was used to split the Janata Party. You know about it, I know about it and everybody knows about it. I know the game plan.

As long as Shri Narasimha Rao was the President, there was no problem. On the day Shri Sitaram Kesri became the President of the Congress Party, I called

---

7 Editor's note: The extract from the *Washington Post* reads thus: 'India has just made a demonstration of the sort of wide-view leadership that the South Asian subcontinent badly needs. It has resolved a generation-old dispute over the sharing of the waters of the great Ganges River with Bangladesh, which is not only a far weaker country but lies downstream … now by an initiative of Indian Prime Minister H.D. Deve Gowda, the issue is being treated and removed … if the Ganges Agreement is an example of the leadership Mr. Deve Gowda can provide, let us see more of it and him.'

him for lunch. I have not neglected your President. We had two hours of discussions in my house. He promised me and he also advised me as an elder statesman. But on the fourth day, when one of my Chief Ministers, Dr. Farooq Abdullah, whose colleague, Prof. Saifuddin Soz, is represented in my Cabinet, went to see Shri Sitaram Kesri, he was told not to join the United Front Government because he was going to withdraw … support. This happened within four days.

I have taken the oath in the name of God when I came to this House. Narasimha Raoji, you may swallow so many wounds because you are a cultured person … The charge levelled against me was that I had neglected Shri Sitaram Kesri after he became the President. It is not based on truth, but … on something else. There is a headline which correctly says, 'India's old man in a hurry: Now or Never.' This was not written by any of the Indian papers. It … appeared in the London *Times*.

It has been stated that we are hungry of status. But it is a question of respect. We are not hungry of power. The post of the President of the Congress (I) is a high office. The Congress (I) is one of the historic political parties having a background of 105 years … (Interruptions.) All right, it has a background of 111 or 113 years … (Interruptions.) This is a place where Pandit Jawaharlal Nehru used to sit and I am sitting here today. I will call it the Congress, not the Congress (I). The Congress Party is a Party which has served the nation in achieving freedom. It has served the nation in running the country, to see that the country's development takes place. From all angles, it has done its service … The office of the President of the Indian National Congress has no respect, has no status. Only if he comes and sits here, then only the respect and status will come. That is why it is said that that old man is in a hurry … (Interruptions.)

H.D. Deve Gowda: I only say one thing. The letter that has been received from the President of India contains so many allegations against me and against the United Front Government … It is not a question of attacking an individual. It is my responsibility to clarify the position about the allegations made against my Government … If I wanted to show disrespect, there is no need for me to go over it twelve times … But what is this *Nikamma* or *Akamma*?

The hon'ble Minister of Home Affairs wanted some clarification from the supporting party … for one and a half hours, he discussed with their Leader, but the only argument advanced by the Congress President to him was, 'Your leader must quit'. Unless I vacate this place, how can he come and sit? I think, the hon'ble Minister of Home Affairs can understand that much. So, where was the need for any explanation by the supporting Party?

They have not done anything. I would like to say very frankly that no member of the Congress Party has criticized in the last ten months – I am grateful to them – whether in this House or outside. The only ambition is that somebody else should occupy this chair, and I should vacate it. That is all the secrecy behind that … I do not find any fault with the hon'ble President of the Indian National Congress when he tried to persuade the hon'ble Minister of Home Affairs. At least, he … brought it to the notice of the House.

The hon'ble Minister of External Affairs has made a brief speech about our foreign affairs … He has narrated some of the achievements made by our Government. When I was in Russia, I got the message from one of my colleagues, Shri Srikant Jena, the hon'ble Minister of Parliamentary Affairs, that there was the likelihood that the Congress might withdraw … support. I told him, 'I am coming back. If they withdraw … support, why do you worry? There is nothing to bother. After all, as long as I am in this Office, I must do my duty for the sake of my country, whether I lose my office or I continue.'

I believe in destiny. The late Sanjiva Reddy was thrown out in 1969. He came back in 1978 and he himself administered the Oath of Office to Madam Indira Gandhi in 1980 …

I am not going to run away from Indian politics. I might not have passed in this House. I have been branded as an inefficient Prime Minister by the Congress President, but the final judgement is before the nation and 950 million people are watching us today … I would go before the people and I am not going to run away.

… The BJP also is not a monolithic party. I have got the highest regard for Shri Vajpayee … When I met him, I only requested him to help us pass the Budget.

It is because I am more concerned … An incompetent Prime Minister, for the first time, has launched several new programmes. For … slum clearance, we have provided Rs. 330 crores. Last year, they spent Rs. 250 crores for this programme. I am also in public life. I am not a new man. In the Central Budget, when money was allocated for the slums, we … launched several programmes. The Minister of Welfare is present here. The President of Congress (I) was also the Minister of Welfare. I am very anxious and eager to ensure that even if I vacate the office … the people get the benefit.

We have launched a Subsidized Food Programme. This PDS,[8] I think, is in existence only in three or four States like Tamil Nadu, Karnataka, Kerala and Andhra Pradesh. We have launched a national programme for which we have provided Rs. 7,500 crores this year in the Budget. Is it not a poverty alleviation programme? All the senior leaders who have spoken today have asked why they have chosen 30th March, before the Budget is passed. They could have decided to withdraw support in the month of May on the 9th or 10th after passing the Budget, after passing the Women's Reservation Bill on which my sister was attacking me,

---

[8] Editor's note: Public Distribution System.

and after passing the Lokpal Bill … Heavens would not have fallen if they had withdrawn … support on 10th of May. What is that you have achieved? What is the sin that I have committed?

Sir … the former Minister of Finance, Dr. Manmohan Singh … argued that we cannot give subsidy to the farmers. He said that subsidy would be removed through a phased programme in three years. He said that in this very same House. I argued from that place. Shri Shivraj Patil was presiding over the House at that time … He said, 'In the next three years, in a phased programme, we are going to remove subsidy because I must take care of the fiscal deficit. The IMF is dictating.' What he has said about the fertilizer subsidy on the floor of the House is on record. Within fifteen days, before I came to Parliament, I took a decision to provide Rs. 2,500 crores to my farming community. Do you mean to say that we are going to betray? You are under a dream. I may tell you today, knowing fully well about the problem of my fellow farmers, that they are an exploited class in society. I know it because I come from that community, and it is not a caste. It is a class. This year we went a step further, we tried to provide about Rs. 17,500 crores, including food subsidy and fertilizer subsidy for this section.

Sir, 32 crores of the population is going to be covered under the PDS. Is this the sin that I have committed? The charge is that this Prime Minister has not taken care of poverty alleviation programmes. Touch your heart and then you vote against the Confidence Motion. Touch your heart and then take a decision.

If I have betrayed the nation, then they can hang me and I would have no objection …

Sir, about the minorities – they have used them as a vote bank – I requested the hon'ble Finance Minister to provide at least Rs. 100 crores this year. It is not so simple to bring them up, and we are not going to leave them as it is at this stage.

Shri Antulay has made a solemn pledge in this House, that he is not going to withdraw and he is going to stand by me. He can go according to the whip of the party; I am not going to find fault with him. He has expressed his sincere and genuine feelings.

We have, for the first time, taken care of those people who had been totally neglected in the tribal areas. The rate of literacy is below two or 2½ per cent there. Shri Bhuria is sitting somewhere here; he represents them and he took me to Tribals' Conference. They say that I have marginalized the Congress. I told the hon'ble Finance Minister to start at least 250 residential schools. Is that the sin that I have committed for which they want to punish me?

I have told Shri Narasimha Rao that whenever he feels that his party is comfortable, he could tell me and I would hand over the resignation … I told Shri Kesri also not to mention frequently about withdrawal of support; whenever he feels that his party is comfortable to come to power, he could tell me and I would hand over the resignation. But why do they make this sort of an allegation against me? He could have told me, 'Shri Gowda, we have decided to withdraw support.' If he had said it very gentlemanly, I could have told my Members not to pursue this matter and we would close this chapter.

Firstly, did I ask for their support? They took a decision on the 12th – the Congress (I) Working Committee took a decision spontaneously when no one approached them and without anyone's request – to support us. On that day, they told the nation that they would not allow a communal party to come to power. But today what did they do? What is the outcome of their decision?

Now, they are searching for a new leader! Do you want to divide the United Front? When they are telling me not to divide the Congress, what moral right have they got to divide my United Front? They can say straightaway that because of such and such circumstances, they were behaving like that. Yes, Shri Vajpayee had said that we would go for polls. Who is responsible for this? If they have got the moral courage, they should say that in this House. They should not play dirty politics. Do they want to approach everybody individually? He says that now that the United Front is over, he would try to collect it individually; he would attract it, as if he is a magnetic force and the United Front is ready to be attracted by that magnetic force.

Let us accept – if he has got the moral courage – to go before the people. They can tell them what they have done. They can tell them that Deve Gowda's Government is not a secular Government, it is an incompetent Government. They can go to the people. Why do they want to search for a new leader? They search today, as if a new quality was found in the Defence Minister.

Have you found some new qualities in my Defence Minister? You want to split us. That is not possible. We have understood your strategy. It is a political strategy …

Let us accept with all sincerity that you have committed a mistake. If I have done a mistake, let the people punish me. I am prepared to go for the ultimate political judgement of the people of this country. Yes, I can understand the financial burden of conducting elections so frequently … But the issue has been forced … We were not going for elections. Now, you want to hang my head calling me an incompetent Prime Minister and a Prime Minister who is not secular. Yes, all right. But you want to search for somebody else.

I have met Shri Balasaheb Thackeray. You said that I was going to work as an ambassador for him, Shri Antulay. Shri Vajpayee, I can make a political speech also. You want to tell us to how to function in a coalition. I can ask, what happened to the Mayawati Government in Uttar Pradesh one year back. Do not talk about political morality. Every political party in this country is more interested in how best they could come to power. (Interruptions.)

Yes, I fought in Karnataka to become the Chief Minister. I am not a political sanyasi, but I have never, never aspired … to come to this office … I am not going to hide the facts. If all of you are sincere, then try it.

We are one political force. Which one of our parties is not a national party? Is the Janata Dal not a national party? Is the CPI not a national party? Is the CPI(M) not a national party? The BJP is a national party and has got influence in four to five States. Without the Badal group, what is the BJP in Punjab? Shri Chandra Shekhar, please tell what the reality is? You want to save your sincere friends. But there is no need … If destiny decided, I will rise again from the dust in … Indian politics, I will come back with the same force. That is what I want to prove.

I am not afraid of those who want to play … bullying politics. I may be a soft man outwardly, but if I start fighting then … I have already shown in Karnataka … what I am. Now, I am going to show what Deve Gowda is, with the support of my United Front. Somebody wants to crack it. It is because if it cracks, then only they can push through as they are the only alternative party. But we would not allow that crack. You also unite and fight. Shri Rajesh Pilot, as a sincere Party worker if you try to defend them, I have no objection. Somebody was asking you about the letter that you had written. I know that you have that courage, and you have said that, but I do not want those details.

Now, under what circumstances did I become Prime Minister? On the one side, there was the CBI enquiry … (Interruptions.) …

… There are several cases. I do not want to go into details. I have all the details … (Interruptions.) I have not ordered a single case for CBI inquiry. I have not ordered a single case against any political leader in the last ten months. All these cases were previous issues … (Interruptions.)

Col. Rao Ram Singh: (Member from Mahendragarh): What is … Shri Rajesh Pilot's letter, Mr. Prime Minister?

H.D. Deve Gowda: I do not want to go into the details of each case. I want to tell this august House and, through this august House, the nation that I have not passed orders about anybody, to hold an inquiry or to conduct an inquiry by the CBI in the last ten months. But, I have not interfered – I can say this much that I have not interfered. That is what has been expected by the House. I have not interfered in any case, including that of my own Chief Minister. My own Party's prestige is involved here. Whether things are moving in the right direction or not,

I do not want to comment on that. I must be fair. Nobody from the Congress made any influence on me about the CBI inquiry. I am not going to say that …

… When the matter is in the Court, I do not want to give details … (Interruptions.) As the matter is before the Court, I do not want to give any particulars or details … Before that, Government will go … Under what circumstances have I been asked to shoulder the responsibility of the office of Prime Minister?

When I went to see Shri Narasimha Rao, he said, 'You have accepted a stupendous task. It is very difficult.' … I agree. I totally agree. There is problem with my friendly parties … I, too, agree. That is one of the allegations. There is no cohesiveness among the Ministers. In the last five years, was there any cohesiveness, Mr. Rajesh Pilot?

Rajesh Pilot (Member from Dausa)**:** I did not point out that … (Interruptions.)

H.D. Deve Gowda: You were the Minister of State for Internal Security in the Ministry of Home. I do not want to go into the details … (Interruptions.)

Hon'ble Speaker has also made that remark. I accept it. Sitting in that high office, if he says that, we have to bow our heads. He advised me. With one party … you have witnessed such type of things, I have to manage 13 parties. You must give some grace marks … (Interruptions.)

Mr. Speaker: Please, order now.

H.D. Deve Gowda: Shri George Fernandes is sitting there. He is my old friend. Today I expected that you would speak, but you gave an opportunity to Shri Nitish Kumar. You do not want to attack your old friend. At least, you have shown that much … courtesy.

… Sir, there is the Enforcement Directorate … today, the judiciary has given the verdict that the investigative agency should directly report to the Courts. If somebody suspects me, what can I do? Shri Sontosh Mohan Dev must advise me. On the one side, the media says Deve Gowda has visited the house of Narasimha Rao … 28 times; Deve Gowda has visited the former Chief Justice's house at midnight, 2 o'clock. In the last ten months, I enjoyed all these things … (Interruptions.) …

H.D. Deve Gowda: There are no tears for our withdrawal. After the test is over, let us assemble here, in the Central Hall for an exchange of views. Let all the three teams go for the test.

Sir, all have agreed for passing the Vote on Account and the Finance Bill on the 21st. Do not try any political gimmicks again in these ten days. Do not try it. I will also honestly give my word that there is no need for them. Enough is enough. A Prime Minister of this country, whoever it may be, once the honour and dignity of that office goes, would not continue as a Prime Minister under the mercy of anybody. What is that we have to discuss again? With that courage, do you want to go outside, Shri Gujral? Somebody wants to name you. You are the senior most leader. I accept it, but not under this circumstance … (Interruptions.)

I.K. Gujral (Member from Jalandhar): I fully agree with you.

H.D. Deve Gowda: A Prime Minister of this country who represents 950 million people must have … certain dignity and … honour to represent the nation … when he goes outside, not with this type of, what is called, lease of life. I do not want that. There is no need … I have not betrayed you. I have never betrayed the nation. I have never given an occasion for a single corruption charge to be levelled against my Government in the last ten months. Go before the people with … courage and conviction. Money is not the criteria. I have not begged any industrialist to allow any scam during these ten months.

Sir, I … am a believer in destiny.

Lastly, I would like to quote *Gitanjali*. This is the first time I am quoting … Shri Chidambaram always used to quote *Thirukkural* in Tamil.

This is from *Gitanjali*.

'Leave this chanting and singing and telling of beads!

Whom dost thou worship in this lonely dark corner of a temple with doors all shut?

Open thine eyes and see thy God is not before thee!'

God will not accept this.

Mr. Speaker: Mr. Gadhvi, you do not have to demonstrate your knowledge … (Interruptions.)

H.D. Deve Gowda: Hon'ble Members, I am only speaking for … (Interruptions.) Please wait. Do not be in such a hurry … (Interruptions.)

> He is there where the tiller is tilling the hard ground and where the path-maker is breaking stones. He is with them in sun and in shower, and his garment is covered with dust. Put off thy holy mantle and even like him come down on the dusty soil?

These are the people who have been taken care of by this Government by launching several schemes. I cannot see God. I have not attained that spiritual power. I am an ordinary human being. I can see God through my people who are the worst sufferers in this country. 'Janatha Janardhan' is my philosophy. I am going to work for this. What kind of people are they?

> Come out of thy meditations and leave aside thy flowers and incense. What harm is there if thy clothes become tattered and stained? Meet him and stand by him in toil and in sweat of thy brow.

This is my conviction. I do not want to tempt others. The ambition in … my life has been to serve those people who have been neglected for the last 50 years. Shri Chandra Shekhar … made a padayatra. He was not allowed to place his Budget on the Table of the House. He was not allowed to launch new schemes. He walked 3,500 kilometres. But I did not lose my opportunity. I know the hanging sword. I wanted to prove what I am. That has been proved with the cooperation of my colleague, the Minister of Finance … The implementation part is left to the House. If everybody cooperates, as they have agreed to pass the Finance Bill, I am grateful.

I once again thank all of you and the country. Inevitably, when the issue was forced by a hasty decision, we had no option. The country was speaking … we have not solved all the problems. We tried to do something in ten months' time. The country at least started to feel a seeming stability. The country was about to take off but, unfortunately, this has happened.

Again, to restore this Government's confidence in the investors, on the 30th December last year, we invited all the industrialists. We invited the financial experts. I went to Mumbai. I met the investors. Their own party Chief Minister was there. I did not show any discrimination during my administration of this Government of ten months. I cleared all the projects irrespective of the State, irrespective of any political party in the country. Nearly 500 projects were cleared in the last ten months which touched about seven billion dollars.

Is that the sin I have committed? We have given licences to 118 new sugar mills in ten months. I can quote any number of decisions which I have taken, with the sole objective that … that the country's progress would be speeded up …

Sir, I would like to once again express my thanks to all the Members, including the Congress (I), who have supported me to allow me to do something in these ten months.

I was not … tallest man. But destiny has brought me here. I am satisfied. I have not betrayed my people, my nation or even my friendly partners in these last ten months. Today, Sir, with your cooperation and with the cooperation of the entire House, what little humble service I could do, I have done in these last ten months.

I would also like to express my sincere thanks to the media ... After the withdrawal of support to the United Front Government by the Congress (I), all the newspapers including the regional newspapers, have tried ... to give the correct version of the achievement of this Government. So, I want to sincerely express my gratitude ... to the media persons. I also want to thank you, Sir, the Deputy Speaker, and to everybody for having given me full cooperation in these last ten months.

Lastly, it is up to the House to take a decision according to their consciences about the Confidence Motion.

3

David and Goliath

On 20 July 2018, Prime Minister ***Narendra Modi*** *proved he still had the numbers in the Lok Sabha. But it was one of those rare occasions when Congress leader* ***Rahul Gandhi*** *stole the show. He set the tone, with an unequivocal message that love and tolerance, not hatred and lynchings, was the way forward for India, indeed, that there was no substitute for the Gandhian ideals of truth and non-violence.*

Towards the end of his speech, delivered in a mix of Hindi and English, during which he was interrupted repeatedly by BJP MPs, Gandhi addressed Modi directly, and then he walked across the House to Modi, bent down and gave him a hug, an embrace that literally left the latter speechless. Television viewers across the country were able to see for themselves that even eight hours after Gandhi ambushed Modi with a warm – and completely unexpected – hug on the floor of Parliament, he had not quite recovered from what the Shiv Sena's Sanjay Raut described as a 'jhatka' (shock), not a 'jhappi' (hug).

Replying to the no-confidence motion, Modi failed to deliver the speech that was intended to place the BJP's agenda front and centre for general elections barely a year away. Instead, clearly angry, visibly distracted, his close to two-hour-long diatribe was partly devoted to mocking Gandhi's prime ministerial ambitions – describing his hug as an effort to grab the Prime Minister's chair without winning an election – and the rest to by now tired statistics related to his government's achievements. What made it worse for Modi was that much of his speech had to be delivered through the steady tempo of the slogan 'We want justice, we want justice' that was being chanted by MPs of the Telugu Desam Party (TDP) – the first sponsor of the no-confidence motion – which was demanding special category status for Andhra Pradesh.

Normally an impressive orator, Modi looked dispirited on Friday night, his speech dull, repetitive and uninspiring – despite his clever use of wordplay – reflected on the faces of his BJP colleagues, who sat unsmiling, thumping their desks mechanically, from time to time. And when the motion was defeated, ruling party MPs simply got up and walked out: there was no cheering, just relief that the debate was over.

RAHUL GANDHI

(Lok Sabha: Amethi)

Lok Sabha: 20 July 2018

On No-confidence Motion in Council of Ministers

Thank you, Madam Speaker, for giving me the floor … (Interruptions.) Don't worry, I'll also speak in Hindi … (Interruptions.)

Two interesting speeches were made. One speech was made by Shri Galla from the TDP and the other speech was made from the BJP. I heard the speech of Shri Galla very carefully … In his speech, I sensed a certain anxiety … a deep feeling of pain and I want to tell him from here that he is the victim of the 21st century political weapon, a very fantastic political weapon. I want to also tell him that he is not alone. There are many victims like him in this country. The political weapon is called the *jumla*[9] strike and the symptoms are the following.

First, there is a great sense of excitement, happiness and then there is a feeling of shock and after that, there are eight-hour-long speeches. Now, who else are the victims of the *jumla* strike? They are the kisans of the country, the youngsters of the country, the Dalits, the tribals and the women of the country.

You said that the words of a Prime Minister should have a meaning and the same question is being asked by the whole country today. Jumla strike No. 1 – 'depositing Rs 15 lakhs in bank account of every person'. Jumla strike No. 2 – 'employment to 2 crore youth every year'.

Let's talk about the issue of employment. There was promise to provide employment to 2 crore youths …

… In … 2016, four lakh youth got employed in whole of India. These are the details of the Labour Bureau survey, not mine. These are their figures.

The youth of India had shown their trust in the Prime Minister. In every speech, the Prime Minister had said that two crore youths will be provided employment every year. It is a fact that only four lakh youth … got jobs … the work that China gives to fifty thousand youth to do in 24 hours, the same work they give to 400 youth for 24 hours … This is the truth … Wherever the Prime Minister goes, he speaks

---

[9] Editor's translation: Jumla is an Urdu word which means phrase or sentence. But, it has come to mean, in the context of promises that were made by the Modi government and not kept, an empty promise, a throwaway remark, even twisting the facts.

of employment. Sometimes he says, make pakodas, sometimes he says, open a shop. (Interruptions.) Who will provide employment? Employment will be provided by small and medium businessmen, small shopkeepers and the construction industry. What did they do? ... At eight o'clock in the night, the Prime Minister took action against ... black money and brought demonetisation ... (Interruptions.) Probably, he did not have the knowledge that farmers, labourers, poor people transact in cash only ... (Interruptions.) I went to Surat and the people of Surat told me that the Prime Minister has given us the most severe injuries ... (Interruptions.)

Today, unemployment in India is the highest since last seven years. This is true of the words of Prime Minister Shri Narendra Modi ... (Interruptions.)

... But he didn't stop there. GST was brought by the Congress party ... (Interruptions.) Gujarat Chief Minister had opposed it. We wanted one GST and petrol, diesel should be included in it. There should be one GST for the whole India with least dispersion ... (Interruptions.) GST of Prime Minister is five types of separate GST, and you have put the income tax department inside the small shopkeeper's house. You ruined millions and millions of people. (Interruptions.) ...

There is no conversation between Prime Minister and small shopkeepers (small businessmen). Prime Minister only talks to 15–20 biggest businessmen ... (Interruptions.) Whatever is in the hearts of small shopkeepers, farmers, poor ... does not reach the Prime Minister. His government damaged the entire system of employment and rendered people jobless.

As I said earlier people ... running small shops, small businesses or mid-businesses, he put his hand inside their pocket and snatched the money ... (Interruptions.) ... This truth cannot be changed.

You are absolutely right, the photo of the Prime Minister ... published on Jio's advertisement. The powers that help ... 10–20 big businessmen, he does all this for them ... (Interruptions.) but does not have even a little space in his heart for the rest of India, for the poor and the people belonging to weaker sections ... (Interruptions.)

The Prime Minister had said that he is the watchman of the country ... He said that he is not the Prime Minister, he is the watchman of the country. But when ... (Interruptions.) ...

... When the son of a friend of the Prime Minister increases his income by 16 thousand times in three months ... (Interruptions.) then the Prime Minister does not utter even a single word ... (Interruptions.)

About Rafale ... the price ... during our UPA regime was 520 crore rupees per airplane ... (Interruptions.) I do not know what happened, with whom they talked? ... (Interruptions.) The Prime Minister went to France. Whole country knows ... whom he visited there. The price of airplane magically went up to 1,600 crore rupees per airplane ... (Interruptions.) The Defence Minister is sitting here

... (Interruptions.) Earlier she publicly said she would tell the country the price of the airplanes ... (Interruptions.) Thereafter, the Defence Minister clearly said, she cannot give these figures as there is a secrecy pact between the Governments of France and India. I, myself, met the President of France ... (Interruptions.) I personally asked the President of France as to whether there was any pact between the Governments of India and France? The President of France told me that there is no such pact between the Governments of India and France ... (Interruptions.)

This is the fact he told me ... he had no hesitation in saying this and also asking me to tell this all in the entire country ...

... After coming under the pressure by the country's Prime Minister, Narendra Modiji, Nirmala Sitharaman ji[10] has told ... to the country. Prime Ministerji and Nirmalaji, please tell the country as to who is being helped and why. You told a lie ...

... The Defence Minister has clearly spoken an ...*[11]

The fact of the matter is that the French President personally has told me that there is no secret pact ... (Interruptions.)

... The fact of the matter is this ... (Interruptions.) I met the gentleman in Delhi. You can check the records. And the gentleman clearly said that there is no secret pact between the Indian Government and the French Government.

So, the Defence Minister has clearly spoken an ...* .

... Now, everybody understands the relationship the Prime Minister has with certain business people. Everybody knows it. Everybody understands, and everybody can see the amount of money that goes into the marketing of India's Prime Minister; and everybody understands where it comes from. One of those people was given the Rafale contract and he benefited thousands and thousands and thousands of crores. That contract was taken away from HAL.[12]

... And, the gentleman benefited ...* This is the truth. Now, the Prime Minister must explain. He must answer in this House whether the Cabinet Committee on Security took this decision or not.

The Prime Minister must also explain as to why this contract was taken away from HAL and the youngsters of Karnataka, and given to a businessman who had a debt of Rs. 35,000 crore and who has never ever built an aeroplane in his life ...

---

[10] Editor's note: The Defence Minister was allowed to respond to Rahul Gandhi's allegations after he completed his speech, as he did not yield to her during it, despite several appeals from the Speaker – of course, whether to yield or not to a fellow MP who wishes to interject is left to the MP who is making the speech. The Speaker at one point also admonished Rahul Gandhi: '... the No-Confidence Motion is against the entire Cabinet. I have nothing against targeting the Prime Minister, but as I remained in the very beginning, that decorum in language should be maintained.'

[11] Editor's note: The repeated asterisk refers to words expunged by the Speaker.

[12] Editor's note: Hindustan Aeronautics Limited.

(Interruptions.) Now these are the things that the Prime Minister of India must explain. He must explain why a businessman has been favoured. I know, I can see he is smiling but there is a touch of nervousness in the gentleman … (Interruptions.) There is a touch of nervousness in the gentleman and he is looking away from me … (Interruptions.) I can understand that … (Interruptions.) Now, he cannot look into my eyes. I can see that … (Interruptions.) It is because the Prime Minister has not been truthful … (Interruptions.) That is the fact … (Interruptions.) Now, let me move on … (Interruptions.) Let me go down the lists … (Interruptions.) The idea of demonetization was to damage and reduce … (Interruptions.)

… The whole country has seen just now, I have spoken clearly about the Hon'ble Prime Minister. The Hon'ble Prime Minister cannot make eye contact with me … (Interruptions.) This is the truth … (Interruptions.) no matter how much you shout now, the country has seen that moment. The country has understood the point … (Interruptions.) He is not a 'chaukidar', he is a 'bhagidar'.[13]

Now let's move to foreign policy … Our Hon'ble Prime Minister, along with the President of China, enjoyed swing rides on the banks of the river in Gujarat … (Interruptions.) At the same time, thousands of Chinese soldiers were present inside the territory of India … (Interruptions.) After that, President of China … goes back and sends his army to Doklam … (Interruptions.) … Our soldiers showed their power and stood face to face with China. But a few days later, our Prime Minister goes to China and … says in Wuhan that he is speaking without any agenda, that he will not talk Doklam here … (Interruptions.) It was not without an agenda (Interruptions.) It was China's agenda … (Interruptions.) what our soldiers did standing in front of China, our Prime Minister could not do … (Interruptions.) And Prime Minister … (Interruptions.) * the soldiers … (Interruptions.) It is the truth; no one can hide it … (Interruptions.) The farmer is saying, 'Mr. Prime Minister, you have waived off a loan of Rs 2.5 billion rupees loan of the richest twenty to twenty five industrialists of India … (Interruptions.) The farmers of India say that you waived their debt … (Interruptions.) They say with folded hands that please waive off a little bit of our loan too … (Interruptions.) And the Finance Minister says, 'No, no, no.' The farmers' debt will not be waived off … (Interruptions.) It will be waived off for the biggest industrialists, but not for the farmers … (Interruptions.) They do not wear suit-boot … (Interruptions.) The farmers are ordinary people. They ride scooters and bikes … (Interruptions.) Petrol prices are going down all over the world but rising in India, because Narendra Modi wants to put money in his friends' pockets … (Interruptions.) …

… Do not be afraid, do not be afraid of truth … (Interruptions.) Madam

[13] Editor's note: He is not a watchman, he is a partner, i.e., he has been given a share (of the loot).

Speaker, a discussion was there on the farmers. Farmers had requested … the Prime Minister to waive off their loans too. Loans of 15–20 rich persons among the richest of the country were waived off but cry of the farmers' voices was not heard … (Interruptions.)

… A few days ago a new 'jumla strike' of MSP[14] was made. I would like to inform the farmers of Haryana, Punjab and Uttar Pradesh and farmers from other States … that the Prime Minister has extended a benefit worth Rs 10,000 crores to farmers of the entire country while the Government of Karnataka alone has provided Rs 34,000 crores to farmers of the State. (Interruptions.)

Madam, now I am going to speak about the status of women in this country. Recently, the cover page of *The Economist* magazine carried a caption that India is not able to protect its women … (Interruptions.) …

… It is the opinion of the outside world that India is not able to protect her women folk for the first time in its history dating back to thousands of years … (Interruptions.) Gang rapes are committed … (Interruptions.) Atrocities are being committed against women … (Interruptions.)

… Such things were not witnessed in the entire history of the country … (Interruptions.) Wherever you see … (Interruptions.) women are being subjected to atrocities … (Interruptions.) Tribals and minorities are facing atrocities … (Interruptions.) People are being killed, beaten up, and suppressed … (Interruptions.) but not a single word is heard from the mouth of the Prime Minister … (Interruptions.) …

… Are Dalits, minorities, tribals not Indians? … (Interruptions.) Are they from other countries? Are these women not Indians? … (Interruptions.) In such cases, there comes no word from the mouth of our Prime Minister. This is my question … (Interruptions.) Please answer all this in your speech … (Interruptions.) On the contrary, their Ministers go and garland them … (Interruptions.) What will be the fate of Indian laws …? (Interruptions.)

… Wherever you go, you find … an Indian, being beaten, crushed and suppressed … (Interruptions.) and no word comes from the Prime Minister on this. (Interruptions.)

… It does not earn good name to our country … (Interruptions.) In such cases, it is the duty of our Prime Minister to explain these things to the people of the country … (Interruptions.) I have made a long speech … (Interruptions.)

… Wherever a person is killed, suppressed, beaten, it is not only an attack on a person … (Interruptions.) But it is an attack on Ambedkar's Constitution, and on this House … (Interruptions.)

… (Interruptions.) When your minister talks of changing our Constitution, they attack Ambedkarji and the whole nation. We cannot tolerate this … (Interruptions.)

---

[14] Editor's note: Minimum Support Price.

... This is an important part of my speech ... You will like it. You will enjoy this one. The Prime Minister and the President of the BJP are two very different types of politicians.

... The difference between all of us and the Prime Minister and the President of the BJP is that whereas we are okay to lose power, we can see ourselves being in power and out of power, for reasons that everybody knows here, the Prime Minister and the President of the BJP can simply not afford to lose power because the moment they lose power other processes will start against them. So, the Prime Minister and the President of the BJP act out of fear. This fear generates anger. It is this anger that the whole of India is feeling. It is this anger that is being transmitted down India, that is attempting to crush every voice in India. That is the truth ... (Interruptions.) Just now, when I entered, the hon'ble Members of opposition parties ... thanked me ... (Interruptions.) They said I spoke very well, but I was surprised that your members shook hands with me and also thanked me for my speech ... (Interruptions.) Not these people on my side but those of your side, because there is something within you also ... (Interruptions.) Akali Dal leader ... smiled at me ... (Interruptions.) Such is the feeling in the whole country ... (Interruptions.) Our duty is to connect the whole nation ... (Interruptions.)

I am here to declare that the ... opposition unitedly and most of your members are going to defeat Prime Minister in the general election ... (Interruptions.) In the end, I am going to say one thing to you ... (Interruptions.)

... You may think that I foster anger, rage and hate against the Prime Minister ... (Interruptions.) but I say to you wholeheartedly that I am so grateful to the Prime Minister, BJP and * that they ... helped me rediscover the meaning of Congress once again ... (Interruptions.)

... They have made me understand the true sense of being a Hindustani ... (Interruptions.) Being a Hindustani means whatever anybody says against you, whatever anybody does against you; one may abuse you or beat you, but you should foster love in your heart for him ... (Interruptions.) Narendra Modiji and BJP ...* You have taught me this ... (Interruptions.)

... I must really thank you for having taught me my true religion. You taught me the real meaning of God Shiva and being a Hindu ... (Interruptions.) This is a great thing ... (Interruptions.) I thank you for this ... (Interruptions.) This has been the history of our nation ... (Interruptions.) You hate me, I know. You foster anger against me, I am *pappu*[15] for you! You may abuse me the way you like ... (Interruptions.) But I do not foster even a bit of anger, rage or hate for you! I am Congress and we all are Congress. The Congress and its ... thought have built

[15] Editor's note: Naïve and foolish, a pejorative description that the BJP and its acolytes have been using for Rahul Gandhi to denigrate him publicly.

this nation … (Interruptions.) Please do not forget it. You foster a sense of hate and I will erase this … hate from your minds … (Interruptions.) I will turn you into loving people and will make all of you Congressmen! Thank you. Namaskar! (Interruptions.)

… Being a Hindu means embrace everybody! May the whole world abuse you, call you a Pappu, but you should have love in your heart for all … (Interruptions.)

… This is the history of the country and this is the future of this country. (Interruptions.)

NARENDRA MODI

(Lok Sabha: Varanasi)

Lok Sabha: 20 July 2018

On No-confidence Motion in the Council of Ministers

Madam Speaker, I express my sincere gratitude for the patience with which you have conducted the House. This No-Confidence motion bears testimony to the power of our democracy. Though the motion was moved by the TDP[16] some honourable Members associated with the party expressed their views supporting the Motion, whereas a large section has expressed their views opposing it.

I would urge all of you to reject the motion and … repose confidence in this Government which has got absolute majority after 30 years, and has worked with renewed momentum for the country. I think this is not only a good opportunity for us to express ourselves, but the country has also got to witness … what kind of negativity and grudge against development is there.

How political negativity has enveloped some of them has come out in the open in its full glory. Many are still wondering … why this No-Confidence motion has been brought in this House. There are neither the numbers nor the majority in the House, then why has this motion been brought in this House? Their impatience to topple the government has surprised me. Why could it not be suspended for 48 hours? It does not require immediate discussion. Would it cause any havoc if the No-Confidence motion is not discussed immediately? If you are not prepared for the discussion, if it was to be delayed by 48 hours, then why did you bring it? Therefore, I think they were trying to defer it, it indicates their difficulty.

Na manjhi, na rehbar, na haque mein hawayen,
Hai kashti bhi jarjar, yeh kaisa safar hai?[17]

---

[16] Editor's note: Telugu Desam Party.

[17] Editor's translation: 'Neither the boatman nor the guide nor the winds in favour
The boat is also dilapidated, what a journey this is.'

Their tone and tenor, their behaviour indicate that it did not happen ... out of ignorance, and nor did it happen due to false overconfidence. It happened because their arrogance is pushing them to indulge in such an act. Remove Modi. I am surprised, the discussion initiated this morning, voting was yet to be done, the result was yet to be announced, but their excitement to remove me knew no bounds. But they were forgetting the fact that only one hundred and twenty-five crores people of this country have the power to do so. In a democracy, it is essential to have faith in the people. Why such hurry? It is their arrogance which says that the Prime Minister cannot face them for 15 minutes if confronted.

Hon'ble Madam Speaker, I am not only standing, but standing firmly on the work we have done in four years. Our thinking is very different from theirs. We have learnt that:

Saar saar ko gahi rahe,
Thotha deyi Udaa ya[18]

Anyway, I was trying to grasp the gist, but I couldn't get that today. It is such blatant arrogance that states that they will not let us return to power in 2019. Only those who do not trust the people's mandate and consider themselves masters of destiny can utter such words. In a democracy, it's the people who are supreme. It is essential to have trust in the democratic process. If Congress comes out as the biggest party in 2019, they aspire to become the Prime Minister. What about the aspirations of others?

Madam Speaker, this is not the floor test of the Government. This is actually the floor test of the Congress, and its so-called partners. A trial run is being conducted for the dream of becoming Prime Minister with the support of 10–20 others. They have tried hard to assemble the entire clan on the pretext of this motion. Their main concern is to keep their flock intact. A serious attempt is being made to bring together strands who aren't even in regular contact, only to remove one Modi. I would like to suggest to Congress that they are free to test their potential friends, but ... not on the pretext of a no-confidence motion. At least ... that much confidence should be shown towards your prospective colleagues.

Madam Speaker, we are here because we have the numerical strength. We are blessed with the blessings of one hundred and twenty-five crore people. Do not question their blessings just because of your self-interest. We have been working on the mantra of 'Sabka Saath, Sabka Vikas' without appeasement or vote bank politics.

Hon'ble Speaker Madam, the work related to providing electricity to 18 thousand villages could have been done by the previous Governments also. Madam Speaker, out of these 18 thousand villages, 15 thousand are in eastern India and out of them, 5 thousand are ... from the North East. You can imagine who lives

---

[18] Editor's translation: The essence of the essence is getting deeper.

there – the poor tribals, Dalits, the oppressed, the exploited … deprived ones and the ones living in jungles, a major part of such people live there. Why didn't they do it? Because these people did not fit into their vote bank mathematics. They had no confidence over this population. That is why the North East was left isolated. It is not just that we have provided them electricity, we worked swiftly on the front of connectivity.

Banks were nationalized in the name of the poor, but the doors of those banks were not opened for the poor when they were in power – they remained in power for so long … The job of opening 32 crore Jan-Dhan accounts has been done by our Government and today, these poor people have deposited 80 thousand crore rupees in these Jan-Dhan accounts. This Government has constructed eight crore toilets for the dignity of our mothers and sisters. This could have been done by earlier Governments also. Four and a half crore poor women have today got a smoke-free life and better health under Ujjawala scheme – this confidence-inducing work has been done by our Government. These were the people who remained busy in the discussion of nine or twelve cylinders, and they were creating confusion among the people. According to an international report, nearly five crore people have come out of abject poverty in the last two years. Twenty crore poor people got insurance cover at a premium amount of just 90 paise per day, and only rupees one per month. This Government has given assurance to provide rupees five lakhs under the Ayushman Bharat Scheme in the coming days for helping the poor people for the treatment of disease. They do not believe in these things. We are taking steps … for doubling the income of farmers by 2022. They do not believe that either. We are improving the entire system, including seeds and markets, and making the systems seamless. They do not even believe in that. Work is going on to complete 99 irrigation schemes and all other projects pending since years … spending … more than Rs. 80,000 crores. Some schemes are about to be completed, while some have already been dedicated to the people. But they do not believe in it, too. We provided the Soil Health Card to 15 crore farmers, took the farmers towards adopting modern farming, but they do not believe this also.

Madam, they left the work after a little bit neem coating in urea, but we could not get benefit without doing it 100 per cent. We did 100% neem coating which has benefited the farmers of the country … they do not believe it also. We created confidence in farmers through the Prime Minister's Crop Insurance Scheme … We not only reduced the premium, but also expanded the coverage … For example, the farmers have paid approximately Rs. 1300 crores as insurance premium in 2016–17 while they were paid a claim amounting to more than Rs. 5500 crores as assistance. That is, the amount of claims given to the farmers is three times the amount received from them, but these people do not believe it.

Madam Speaker, they may explain why the LED bulbs were being sold for

Rs 350, 400 and 450 during the tenure of their Government, while today they are being sold for Rs 40 to 45 only. Hundred crores of the LED bulbs have been sold till date. Not only this, more than 62 lakh LED bulbs have been installed in the street lights in more than 500 urban bodies, due to which the expenditure of the municipalities has also reduced. There were only two mobile manufacturing companies during their tenure of Government. Today, there are 120 companies manufacturing mobile phones, but they do not believe it.

The educated youths were awarded certificates in the name of self-employment but they had to wander here and there for livelihood. We have provided loans to 13 crore youths under the 'Mudra' Yojana ... the times have changed; more than 10,000 start-ups are being run by ... youths ... at present and are working to take the country towards innovative India. When we started talking about digital transactions, the stalwarts in this House began to say that our country is ... illiterate ... so how can it adopt digital transactions? How can it reach the poor of our country? Madam Speaker, the person who used to undermine the power of the people of the country in this way, the public, has given a befitting reply to them. With the help of the 'BHIM' App and mobile phones, the citizens of our country are making transactions worth approximately Rs 41,000 crores, at present just within a month. But they don't trust the people of the country. They were of the view that people were illiterate and they would not be able to do this and that ...

Hon'ble Madam Speaker, ease of doing business has improved by 42 points. Now they have doubt on that also ... Global Competitive Index has improved by 31 points. They have doubts on that also. Innovation Index has improved by 24 points. Our Government is bringing cost of doing business down by improving ease of doing business. Be it 'Make in India' or 'GST', they do not have faith in them either. India has strengthened the economic growth of the world along with its own growth. India is at sixth position among the biggest fastest growing economies in the world. The credit for this does not go to the people who are running the Government, rather it goes to the hard work of 1.25 billion Indians.

They should learn to feel proud of this. But they do not know how to feel proud. The country is rapidly moving in the direction of becoming a five trillion dollars economy. We have waged a war against black money and this is not going to stop. I know what kind of people are facing problems due to this. Their wounds have not healed, that much is clear from your behaviour. We used technology and saved Rs. 90,000 crores, the money which was withdrawn from the exchequer and misused. That money was misused, and the country knows very well how and in what ways it was misused. We have banned more than 2.5 lakh shell companies, and around 2–2.5 lakh companies are on the radar, and they are likely to be banned any time. Who fostered them? Who was providing them support and through these systems their own vested interests were being fulfilled? Everyone knows this.

Benami Property Bill was passed in the House, but it was not notified even after the passage of twenty years. Why, and whom did they want to protect? We notified it and I'm happy that under this law, benami property worth Rs. 4–4.5 thousand crores has been seized till date. The country has confidence in us, the world has confidence in us, the best organizations have confidence in us, but those who do not have confidence in themselves, how will they have confidence in us? ... In our Shastras (scriptures), it is very well said about the people of such a mentality.

'Dhara naiv patani chatak mukhe meghasya kim dooshnam'

It means ... that rain water does not fall straight into the mouth of the chatak (a kind of bird), so what is the fault of clouds ...?

Madam, the Congress is not confident about itself ... Lack of confidence itself is the part of their entire work culture, cultural life. They do not have confidence in anything. They do not have confidence in Swachh Bharat, International Yoga Day, Chief Justice of the country, Reserve Bank of India, the organizations which provide the data related to the economy. The recognition of the passport is improving in the foreign countries, the country is being applauded in international forums but they do not have confidence in this also. They do not have faith in the Election Commission and the Electronic Voting Machine. Why is it so? Because they ... lack ... confidence in themselves. Why has this lack of confidence built up? Earlier, a handful of people were enjoying the privileges, they used to consider it their exclusive right. When this privilege started being challenged by the people's mandate, their problems started soaring ... When ... income from corruption stopped, their restlessness increased. When they had to appear in Court, they, too, started to suffer a little. I am surprised that such topics were touched upon here. Nowadays, everyone is talking about Lord Shiva. I also pray to Lord Shiva and I also pray to 125 crore people of the country that they should give you so much power that in the year 2024 also, you again bring a no-confidence motion. I wish them good luck.

Doklam was discussed here. I believe that the subject about which you are not aware of, sometimes speaking on that can backfire. It harms the person less but the country suffers a lot. Therefore, we should be a little informed before speaking on such topics. We must remember the event when the whole country, the whole system, the entire Government was unitedly working on the issue of Doklam and were performing their own responsibilities.

Those who talk of Doklam today, they used to sit with the ambassador of China, then. Later, it was going in a filmy style like 'Sometimes No, Sometimes Yes'. Someone used to say that he has met, someone said that he has not met. Why was there such a suspense? The Congress spokesman had clearly denied that its vice-president met the Chinese ambassador. Meanwhile a press release was issued and then the Congress was compelled to accept that yes, the meeting took place.

Is there no seriousness on issues related to the country? Will there be childish acts everywhere?

Rafale dispute was also raked up here. I cannot imagine that truth can be crushed in such a way, truth can be trounced in this way. Now again, shouting from rooftops to mislead the country. On these topics and on the issues related to the security of the country, are these issues discussed in this manner? This country will never forgive him. How sad it is that the two countries had to issue statements on the allegations levelled in this House and both the countries had to issue rebuttals. Will we keep indulging in such childish acts? Is there any responsibility or not? Those who have been in power for so many years, they are just screaming and shouting without any evidence. They are trying to thwart the truth. The people of the country know it well. Every time, the public has given a reply to you. Now there is a chance to reform, try to reform. This level of politics is not in the interest of the country.

Speaker Madam, I want to assure the countrymen through this House ... that this agreement has been signed between the two countries. It has not been signed between any business parties. It has been signed between two responsible Governments and has been done with complete transparency. My prayer is to avoid childish statements on such a sensitive issue, I insist on this.

I can only pray before the naamdar,[19] because we have seen that a mentality has set in. What kind of language has been used for the Chief of the Army? Has it ever happened? Will this type of language be used for the Chief of the army of the country? Even today, every soldier of India, either posted on the border or retired, must have felt hurt so deeply ... We can't imagine that by sitting in the House. Those who are ready to die for the country, who work for the well-being of the country, you do not have the courage to accept the feats of the troops of the army. But should they call the surgical strike a jumla strike? They called the surgical strike a jumla strike and the country will never forgive them for it. If they want to abuse, then Modi is here. He is ready to listen to all their abuse, but please stop abusing the country's jawans, who are ready to die for the country. They call the surgical strike a jumla strike and this kind of insult to the Army continues.

Honourable Speaker Madam, such no-confidence has existed for generations and it is in the nature of the Congress party. Congress has misused the constitutional arrangement of no-confidence motion to create instability in the country. We read in the newspaper that immediately after the acceptance of the no-confidence motion, a statement was given, 'who says we don't have the numbers'. Look at their ego. I want to remind this House of the year 1999, standing before the President House, it was claimed that we have the figure of 272 and others are going to join us, and Atalji's Government was voted out of power by one vote, but the claim they made

[19] Editor's note: Famous or illustrious, a sarcastic reference to Rahul Gandhi.

of 272, proved hollow and the country had to go for election within 13 months. Elections were forced on the country.

Hon'ble Madam Speaker, today the game of destabilizing the stable mandate is being played again. Fulfilling their selfishness through political instability has been the nature of the Congress. In … 1979 … they gave the illusion of giving support to the son of the soil, farmer leader Chaudhary Charan Singh, and then support was withdrawn. What can be more insulting than this for a worker, a farmer? The same modus operandi was seen in the case of Shri Chandrashekhar. First, throw the rope of support and then take it back by deceit. The game continued. The same formula was adopted once again in 1997; first, Hon'ble Deve Gowda ji was humiliated, and then it was Inder Kumar Gujral Ji's turn. Whether it was Deve Gowda ji or Mulayam Singh Yadav ji, who can forget what the Congress people did with them? The Congress cheated those parties and leaders who emerged as mass leaders and made space in the hearts of the people with their hard work and then committed the sin of forcing the country into instability time and again. How the Congress tried to buy confidence twice to save their Government. Who is not aware of the vote for note game? Today, here one more point has been raised. It has been said that the Prime Minister cannot make eye to eye contact with me.

Hon'ble Madam Speaker, it is right. Who are we to make eye to eye contact with him? I am a poor mother's son, born in a backward caste family, coming from a rural background. You are a 'naamdar' and I am a 'kaamdar'[20]. I can't dare to make eye contact with you. No, I can't. History is itself proof of what was done to Subhas Chandra Bose, who tried to do so. Morarji Bhai Desai is also an example of the same, and what was done to him also, and same has been the case with Jaiprakash Narayan ji, Choudhary Charan Singh ji, Sardar Vallabhbhai Patel ji, Chandrashekhar ji and Pranab Mukherjee and not only that, Sharad Pawar ji is another example of the same thing. I can disclose all the ins and outs. How those who dare to raise their gaze were humiliated. How to kick them out is the history of family and nobody is unaware of it in the country. We are 'kaamdar', how can we make eye to eye contact with 'naamdar'? Today, the whole country is watching the game of the eyes of those who talk about eyes, how the eyes are blinking, this is the game of eyes. Truth has been crushed again and again. Here, it has been said, why did not we bring petroleum under GST? I just want to say that there is a history of Congress outside the family. There is a history of Congress Governments outside your family too. At least take care of that. When there was the UPA Government, your Government took a decision to keep petroleum out of the GST. You do not know even that. It is also said here that I am not a 'chowkidar', but 'partner'. Hon'ble Speaker, Madam, with pride I want to say that I am 'chowkidar' and 'partner', too,

[20] Editor's note: Worker.

but we are not dealer and contractor like you … we are partner, partners of sorrow of country's poor people, we are partners of pain of country's farmers. We are partners in the aspirations of the country's youth. There are 115 aspirational districts in the country and we are partners in the dreams in their development. We are a partner of working labourers, taking the country on the new path of development. We are partners and will be partners. Sharing their sorrows, it is our participation and responsibility and we abide by it … We are proud of this. This Congress has only one mantra – either we will remain there or there will be instability in the country. The rumours will rule. You look at the entire period. Sufferers are also there. What happened with the people, everyone knows. Rumours are spread. Now technology is available in the country to spread rumours. There are rumours like reservation will be over, the law prohibiting atrocities on the oppressed has been abolished, there is a conspiracy to unleash violence in the country being hatched.

Madam Speaker, these people have been doing politics by emotional blackmailing of Dalits, victims, exploited, disadvantaged and poor people. Without worrying about the sufferings of the workers and farmers, and instead of finding ways to solve their problems, an attempt is being made to find the shortcut to win an election in this country. This is the reason that a large section of the country has been deprived of empowerment. The people who make fun of Baba Saheb Ambedkar's language and his clothes, his politics, have started singing his praise today.

Madam, the people who repeatedly abused Article 356 are teaching us a lesson of democracy. Removing undesirable Chief Ministers, creating instability, this game started immediately after Independence and never a chance was left. It is the result of the same policy that the country was dragged into elections before time in the years 1980, 1991, 1998 and 1999. Whoever came in the way of the dreams and aspirations of a family, the same treatment was meted out to him, even if the country's democracy was to be put at stake. It is natural, how can the people whose mentality is such and there is so much ego in them, will accept people like us? How can they tolerate us sitting here? We understand it very well, so it is very natural for them to dislike us.

Hon'ble Speaker Madam, Congress party has been cut off from the ground realities. They drowned and people who went with them, too, will also be drowned … The people who are always entangled in intricacies of meaning and who considered themselves great scholars and think too highly of themselves, a person who is constantly entangled in significance and insignificance has told me something, and I want to quote his words.

'Why and how did the Congress party become weak in different States? I come from a state where this party's dominance has finished. Why Congress could not understand that power has now shifted from higher classes, resourceful sections to the villagers, the intermediate castes and even to such castes, who are at the bottom of the alleged social order to those who are poor, unemployed and who do not have property, those who do not have any income. It has reached those downtrodden people who were never heard. As the power decentralizes towards the downtrodden, which should be there in a democracy, the influence of Congress decreased in many States.'

This is a quotable quote dated 11th April, 1997 when a discussion on the confidence motion of Deve Gowda ji's Government was taking place. This is the sentence of your erudite member, Shri Chidambaramji. Many … might not have understood the things said by a few scholars there.

Eighteen years ago, the Atal Bihari Vajpayee ji Government created three States – Uttarakhand, Jharkhand and Chhattisgarh. No conflicts at all. No tension at all, we sat together and sorted things out as easily as possible, and all three States are progressing peacefully and rapidly and contributing in the development of the nation. However, to gain political advantage, without taking the people of Andhra Pradesh into confidence, by closing the doors of the Rajya Sabha and by putting pressure and force, even when the House was not in order, they divided Andhra Pradesh and Telangana. This is true. Jayadeviji said this and it is true that at that time I had said, 'Telugu is our mother. We must not let the spirit of Telugu break. They saved the child and killed the mother. It is our responsibility to retain the Telugu spirit.' These were my words at that time and I still believe the same. What happened to them in the year 2014? They thought that no matter even if they lose one, they will get the other one. But the public was so clever that they neither got this nor that and they left a mess behind. This is not new for them. They divided the country into India–Pakistan, which is still creating problems for us. They have divided them like this only. If they would have taken them into confidence, then this wouldn't have happened, but they didn't think about anything. I remember very well a sort of tension prevailed in the first year between Chandrababu Naidu and Telangana CM KCR, regarding the division of the state. There were fights … The Governor, Home Minister had to sort it out and sometimes, I had to intervene. At that time, TDP's full might was against Telangana. They used to fight over this. We used to calm them down. TRS showed maturity and put their energy into development. What happened on that side, everybody knows it, problems pertaining to the distribution of resources still persist. It shows how they have divided the state and that the rift over resources is still going on there.

The NDA Government ensured that there will be no stone unturned so far as development of Telangana and Andhra Pradesh are concerned and we are fully committed to that … A Hon'ble Member of the TDP from this House said that a Special Package is far better than the Special Category Status. I would like to repeat the recommendations of the Finance Commission once again. Under this recommendation, the Commission removed the difference between Special and General Category Status. The Commission coined a new category of North Eastern and Hill State. In the process, the Commission has kept in mind that no other State suffers economically. The NDA Government respects the hopes and aspirations of Andhra Pradesh people. Please listen till the end, things of your concern are yet to come. NDA Government respects the hopes and aspirations of the people of Andhra Pradesh, but along with that we are bound by the recommendations of the 14th Finance Commission. Therefore, a new special assistance package has been made for Andhra Pradesh so that the concerned State gets the amount of financial assistance it could receive by having a Special Category Status. This decision was implemented on 8th September, 2016. On November 4th, 2016. The Chief Minister of Andhra Pradesh himself accepted this package and thanked the Finance Minister. NDA Government wanted to fulfil every commitment given under the Andhra Pradesh Reorganisation Act and special assistance package, but TDP took a U-turn to cover up its failures. Speaker Madam, when TDP decided to part from NDA, then I rang up Shri Chandrababu. This information might be new for you.

This information is useful for you. TDP opted out of NDA. I talked to Shri Chandrababu on phone and told him that he is getting trapped in the net of YSR Congress ... I said that he cannot save himself from competition. I told him this one day. I can see that. They have disputes there but are using the House for that. The people of Andhra Pradesh are observing this sheer opportunism as elections approached and appreciation turned into criticism. Whatever special incentive or package is provided, it leaves its effect on other parts as well. Shri Veerappa Moily said this in the House three years back: 'How you can create this kind of an inequality between one state and the other state? It is a major issue. After all you are an arbitrator.'

This was said by Moily ji and today I want to assure the people of Andhra that be it the case of capital or welfare of farmers, the NDA Government will not shy away from the welfare works of people of Andhra and whatever help we can give, we will keep on giving. We think that the welfare of Andhra and the welfare of the country is intertwined. We will leave no stone unturned in the development works. Our effort, our working process is for solving the problems.

Who kept pending 'One Rank, One pension, for decades? Who kept pending the issue of GST for years together? Today, it was said that the Chief Minister of Gujarat did not allow it to happen ... The letters I ... sent as Chief Minister are still available. I had told the Government of India that it cannot roll out the GST without addressing the concerns of the states ... But they were so egotistical that they were not ready to listen to even a word from the states ... non-BJP Chief Ministers, including those from Congress, used to tell me in the meetings that they would not be able to speak, so I should raise their concerns. This will benefit their states also. I raised my voice. When I became Prime Minister, the experience of being Chief Minister came handy for me. I could address the concerns of all states because of that experience. We could bring all the states on board. If you had no ego, you could have addressed the concern of the states; the GST would have rolled out five years ago. But your modus operandi is to keep … work pending.

Supreme Court had asked to constitute a SIT[21] on black money. Who kept that issue pending? You kept that pending. Who kept Benami Property Law pending?

Madam Speaker, NDA Government has taken an historic decision to increase the MSP of the Kharif crop … by 150 per cent of the input cost. Who stopped this? This report was pending with you since 2006 and you were in Government till 2014 … We had decided to increase the MSP by 1.5 times for farmers and we did that. When the UPA Government declared a National Agriculture Policy in 2007, they omitted the issue of 50 per cent. They forgot it. After that, the Congress-led Government ruled for seven years, but they kept talking about MSP and gave false assurance to the people and the farmers.

Hon'ble Speaker, today I would like to say one more thing … We came to power in … 2014. At that time, many people had asked us to bring a White Paper on the economy. This was in our mind, too … but … when we started gathering information, then one after another, we got such information that we were startled as to what is the condition of the economy.

Therefore, today, I would like to tell the story of NPA.[22] What conditions were created? This story started in 2008, and elections were scheduled in 2009. Congress thought that only one year was left, so let us squeeze the banks as much as possible … underground looting of banks continued from 2009 to 2014 …

… After sixty years of Independence, the amount as farm loan given by the banks was 18 lakh crore rupees … But from 2008 to 2014, in mere six years, this amount increased from 18 lakh crore rupees to 52 lakh crore rupees … What had happened during the last 60 years, they doubled it in six years. How did it happen?

Internet Banking was introduced … later in the world. But, Congress has such intelligent people that before the introduction of internet banking in the world, phone banking was started in India … It was the miracle of telephone banking that within six years the loan amount increased from 18 lakh crore rupees to 52 lakh crore rupees and treasures of banks were squandered for their near and dear ones. What was the modus operandi?

No documents verification required, only a call was made with regard to sanctioning of loans. And then another call was made with regard to sanctioning the

---

[21] Editor's note: Special Investigation Team.

[22] Editor's note: Non-performing assets.

second loan for the repayment of the first loan. Whatever was lost was compensated by sanctioning loans for repayment of previous loans. This very trend continued and the banks in the country were trapped … And this NPA was laid just like a land mine for the Indian banking system. We have initiated an enquiry with full transparency in this regard. And to determine the actual picture of NPA, we have initiated a new mechanism. We conducted an in-depth enquiry in this regard …

UPA Government took certain decisions which led to incessant increase in import of capital goods … the import of capital goods increased by reducing custom duty to such an extent that the same has reached the equivalent of crude oil import. All these imports were financed through bank loans. It had an adverse impact on the capital goods production in the country. The clearances were given without bank lending and project assessment. Banks extended loans even against equity in a lot of projects.

On one hand, customs duties on the imports of capital goods and Government tax for projects construction were reduced. On the other hand, a new tax was imposed for seeking Government clearance and these taxes were not credited into the Government's account. Due to this tax, there was a delay in the clearance for the projects. As a result, bank loans were not repaid and they remained stuck, and NPA kept on rising. Today, when our opposition friends constantly issue statements on the status of NPA, the Government is bound to come forward to place some new facts before the people … our Government has decided to honestly show the actual status of NPA, which are in the accounts of banks … we have taken a number of policy decisions for improvement of the banks, and I hope that these decisions will be fruitful for the economy of the country in the coming years. All NPA accounts worth more than Rs. 50 crores have been reviewed … an assessment of wilful defaulters and chances of frauds is being carried out. A new system of management of stressed assets in banks has been prepared. An amount of more than two lakhs ten thousand crore rupees is being given to banks for re-capitalization.

Our Government has chalked out insolvency and bankruptcy codes. The cases of top-12 defaulters, whose NPA forms 25 per cent of the total NPAs, have been undertaken by National Company Law Tribunal. An amount of about three lakh crore rupees are involved in these 12 big cases. Our Government has made a recovery of around 55 per cent in three cases only out of all these during the last one year. If we look at these 12 big cases, around 45 per cent has been recovered. Yesterday only, the Lok Sabha passed the Fugitive Economic Offenders Bill for such offenders. Now it has become much more difficult to escape from the law for those who do not pay bank loans. This will help in controlling NPA. Had the NDA Government not come to power in 2014 … the country could have been in great danger.

I would like to inform the country through this House that the preceding

Government had left the Special Foreign Currency Non-Resident Deposit (FCNRD) loan of around 32 million dollars. As of today, India has repaid this loan fully …

Hon'ble Speaker Madam, to carry forward the campaign of Gram Swaraj Abhiyan and to fulfil the dreams of Mahatma Gandhi, we have worked towards opening bank accounts for every person in 65 thousand villages and providing gas connection to every person, bank accounts, electricity for every household, immunization and insurance cover for all and LED bulbs in every house. These villages are in those 115 districts, wrong policies gave them cynicism of backwardness and we have given them a new confidence of aspiration.

New India's facilities are smart as well as sensitive. There were no labs in school. We have identified talent through 'Skill India', 'Khelo India' and started Atal tinkering lab. Schemes have been formulated for women, giving due attention to their needs at various stages. I say it with extreme pride that we have two women members in the Cabinet Committee on Security for the very first time, and they are part of the process of decision-making. Women have also been inducted as fighter pilots. The Government is standing firmly with Muslim women, facing Triple Talaq. The 'Beti-Bachao, Beti-Padhao' campaign has become a mass revolution. In various districts of the country, girl child birth rate has increased, and there is even a provision for capital punishment for the people committing atrocities against girls. There is no place for violence and atrocities in a democratic set-up. Even a single death in such incidents is tragic. This is against the spirit of humanity. Wherever such incidents are taking place, State Governments are taking action. I would like to urge again through you to State Governments that they should take strict action against people indulging in violence. We need to fulfil the dreams of our country in the 21st century. Highway network is being laid throughout the country under 'Bharatmata'. Port-development and port-led development is being promoted under 'Sagarmala'. Air connectivity is being provided at a fast pace in Tier-II and Tier-III cities. There is significant growth of Metro trains in the cities and work is continuing at a fast pace. Efforts are being made to provide internet to all panchayats in the country … There has been a change in the lifestyle of the poor and middle class people, right from the villages to big cities. The pace of development is quite better than under previous Governments, whether it is construction of roads, electrification of railway lines, increase in the production capacity of the country, new educational institutes, NITs, IIM increase in the number of medical seats. The employees are the same, the bureaucracy is the same, the modality of the files is the same but, in spite of this, it is political will due to which we are moving ahead, energizing the country. There is so many confusions about employment in this country. Once again, they are trying to crush the truth, indulging in baseless talk, spreading baseless rumours. It would have been better if you paid attention to the details, then you would not have committed the sin of playing politics after disappointing the youth of the country. The Government has decided to present various data available in the system related to employment in the country. The Employees Provident Fund is a way to measure the employment growth in the corporate sector or in the formal sector, i.e. contribution of employees in EPF. Around 45 lakh new subscribers were added to EPF in nine months from September, 2017 to May, 2018. 77 per cent of these are below 28 years of age. In the formal system, more than 5 lakh 68 thousand people were added to the new pension scheme, i.e. NPS, in the last two months.

Thus, while combining the figures of both EPF and NPS, over fifty lakh people were added to employment in the formal sector in the last nine months. This number will be more than 70 lakhs for the whole year. ESIC Figures have not been included in these 70 lakhs personnel because currently Aadhaar linking work is under way. Apart from this, there are many professional bodies in the country in which young professionals having professional degrees register themselves and do their work. For example, Doctors, Engineers, Architects, Lawyers, Chartered Accountants, Cost Accountants and Company Secretaries. An independent institute has conducted a survey among these professions. As per the study of this independent institute, about 17 thousand new Chartered Accountants were added in the system during 2016–17. More than 5,000 of these people have started new companies. If a Chartered Accountant institution employs 20 people, then more than one lakh people got employment in these institutions. With regard to Post-Graduate Doctors, Dental Surgeons and AYUSH Doctors, I would like to tell you that more than 80,000 postgraduate doctors, dental surgeons and AYUSH doctors pass out from the colleges every year. If sixty per cent of them practise themselves, then five people per doctor will get employment opportunities and this number will be two lakh forty thousand. In 2017, around 80,000 undergraduate and postgraduate persons became lawyers. If 60 per cent of them have started practise and given employment to two to three people, around two lakh people must have been employed through those lawyers. In 2017, more than six lakh people have got employment opportunities in these three professions.

If we talk about the informal sector, there is a lot of employment scope in the transport sector. Last year, 7 lakh 60 thousand commercial vehicles were sold in the transport sector. If the 25% sale of these vehicles is considered to replace old vehicles, then 5 lakh 70 thousand vehicles as well as new ones have landed on the road to carry the goods. If two people are employed on such a vehicle, then the number of people getting employment is 11 lakh 40 thousand.

In the same way, if we look at the sales of passenger vehicles, the number was 25 lakh 40 thousand. Of these, if twenty per cent vehicles are considered to replace old ones, then about twenty lakh new vehicles will land on the roads. If only 25 per cent of these vehicles have employed one driver, then more than five lakh people have got employment.

In the same way, last year, 2 lakh 55 thousand autos were sold. Of these, ten per cent ... is considered to replace the old ones, then around 2 lakhs 30 thousand new autos came on the road last year, because autos run in two shifts. Three people get employment from two autos. In this manner, three lakh forty thousand people got employment through new autos. Twenty lakh job opportunities have been generated in transport sector alone during the last one year through these three means. If we count EPF, NPS, Professional Transport Sector together, we will find that more than crore people have got employment during the last one year alone. This is a report of a survey conducted by an independent institution. I am quoting that independent institution. I am not giving Government data. That is why I request that do not try to suppress the truth. Do not try to mislead the country. Today, the country is at a critical stage. The 85 per cent youths of the country out of 125 crore people will decide the future of the country in next five years. New India will become the basis of the country's new hopes and aspirations. Where there will be infinite confidence in possibilities, opportunities, stability. Where there will be no lack of confidence and discrimination towards any community of the society or any area. In such an important time of change in the global scenario, there is a need to be united.

Hon'ble Speaker, I would like to thank those members who participated in this discussion. I once again reiterate that this Government will try its best for the welfare of Andhra Pradesh. We have vowed to support every person contributing in the development of India. I once again conclude by inviting these great persons to bring the No-Confidence motion in 2024, and I also urge the House to defeat this No-Confidence motion ...

4

Battle over the Constitution

As part of a year-long celebration of the 75th Anniversary of the adoption of the Constitution, a special discussion – 'Glorious journey of 75 years of the Constitution of India' – was organized in the new Parliament House in December 2024. The title suggested that it would be an occasion to remember the makers of the Constitution with gratitude for creating a document that has stood the test of time. Instead, for four days (13 and 14 December in the Lok Sabha, and 16 and 17 December in the Rajya Sabha), Parliament became an arena for scoring political points.

For the ruling Bharatiya Janata Party (BJP), in particular, the 75th anniversary provided it with the perfect moment to target the main Opposition party, the Indian National Congress (INC), that had ruled the country for 55 of its 75 years, and present its version of the Constitution. Simultaneously, the party listed its own accomplishments.

In this provocative speech, Prime Minister Narendra Modi squarely attacked the Gandhis for everything that had gone wrong in the country, and for propagating dynastic politics. He accused the family of trying to destroy the Constitution, while praising his own party for the controversial changes it had made in it, including the abrogation of Article 370 that gave the erstwhile state of Jammu and Kashmir a special status.

This accusation in Parliament came in the wake of the general elections in 2024, when the INC and other opposition parties, especially in Uttar Pradesh, had held the BJP responsible for trying to destroy the Constitution: for the BJP, it has been a sore point, as the charge stuck in many constituencies, ensuring that the party on its own failed to secure a majority and had to depend on its allies to form a government.

Mr.Modi also claimed the INC's old slogan 'Unity in diversity' as his party's 'speciality', saying that the principal opposition party only seeks contradictions in this diversity for its 'vote bank politics', and favours the Muslim community.

NARENDRA MODI

(Lok Sabha: Varanasi)

Lok Sabha: December 14, 2024

Special Discussion on the 75th Anniversary of Adoption of Constitution

This is a moment of immense pride for all of us – – not only for our fellow countrymen but also for democracy loving citizens across the world … The journey of 75 years under the Constitution is a remarkable one, and at the heart of this journey lies the divine vision of our Constitution-makers, whose contributions continue to guide us as we move forward … It brings me great joy that Parliament, too, will participate in expressing its sentiments during this celebration. I extend my gratitude to all the honourable members and congratulate everyone who took part in these celebrations …

When Bharat gained independence, there were … sceptical predictions about the country's future. However, the Indian Constitution defied … all such doubts, guiding us to where we stand today. For this remarkable accomplishment, I bow down in respect, not only to our Constitution-makers but also to the millions of citizens of this nation who … embodied its spirit and embraced this new system. Over the past 75 years, the citizens of Bharat have honoured the vision of the Constitution-makers, standing resilient in the face of every test. For this, they deserve the highest commendation …

The Constitution-makers … did not believe that Bharat was born in 1947 or that democracy began here in 1950. Instead, they recognised the greatness of Bharat's ancient traditions, its profound culture, and its heritage spanning thousands of years. They were fully cognisant of this continuity and sought to build upon it.

Bharat's democratic and republican past is extraordinarily rich and has served as an inspiration for the world … Bharat is known today as the Mother of Democracy. We are not merely a vast democracy; we are its origin …

In saying this, I wish to present before this House the words of three great visionaries. The first is Rajrishi Purushottam Das Tandon ji, who, during the Constituent Assembly debates, remarked that after centuries, our country has once again convened such a meeting. This gathering reminds us of our glorious past, of times when we were independent, when scholars would come together to deliberate on the nation's most pressing matters. The second quote is from Dr. Radhakrishnan ji, also a member of the Constituent Assembly. He observed that the republican system was not new for this great nation – – it had existed since the dawn of history. The third is from Baba Saheb Ambedkar ji, who declared that democracy was not an alien concept to Bharat. …

The Constituent Assembly had 15 honourable women members who played active roles, enriching the debates with their original perspectives. These women came from diverse backgrounds and fields, and their suggestions had a profound impact on the shaping of the Constitution. It is a matter of immense pride that, while many other nations took decades to grant rights to women, Bharat ensured their right to vote right from the inception of its Constitution …

During the recent G-20 Summit, we upheld this very spirit of our Constitution. Under Bharat's presidency, we introduced the concept of women-led development to the world, urging a shift beyond mere women's development.. all of us… came together to unanimously pass the Nari Shakti Vandan Act, taking a significant step towards ensuring greater participation of women in Indian democracy ...

Today, … women are at the centre of every major initiative … during this historic milestone, a tribal woman holds the esteemed position of President of India …

The number of women MPs in this House is steadily increasing, as is their contribution. Their involvement in the Council of Ministers is also growing … whether ... in the social sector, politics, education, sports, or the creative fields, the contributions of women in every sphere of life are a source of immense pride for the nation …

Bharat is … making strong strides towards becoming the third-largest economic power in the world in the near future. … by the time we celebrate the centenary of our independence, we will transform Bharat into a developed nation ... In the making of our Constitution, the stalwarts of this nation – freedom fighters, writers, analysts, social workers, educators, professionals, labour leaders, farmers' leaders, and representatives from every section of society – came together with an unwavering commitment to Bharat's unity. These individuals, representing diverse walks of life and regions of the country, were deeply aware of the importance of this unity. Baba Saheb Ambedkar ji had foreseen this challenge and offered a profound warning… He said: 'The problem is how to unite the diverse Indian masses; how to inspire the people of the country to take decisions in harmony with each other, so that a sense of unity is established in the country.' …

It is with great sadness that I must state that, after independence, while the Constitution-makers had unity in their hearts and minds, this unity was … attacked due to distorted mindsets or selfish motives. Unity in diversity has always been Bharat's defining strength. We celebrate diversity, and the nation's progress lies in embracing this diversity. Unfortunately, those bound by the mentality of colonial servitude, … and those who believed that Bharat was born in 1947, failed to see the inherent unity in our diversity. Instead of celebrating this invaluable heritage, attempts were made to sow seeds of discord in it …

Over the past ten years, the people of this country have entrusted us with the opportunity to serve. In reviewing our policies and decisions, … we have consistently worked towards strengthening Bharat's unity. Article 370, for instance, had become a significant obstacle to national unity, a barrier that needed to be dismantled. Guided by the spirit of our Constitution, we prioritised national unity and buried Article 370, ensuring the unity of our nation remains our foremost priority …

For a country of Bharat's size to progress economically and attract global investment, it requires favourable systems. One such significant reform was the introduction of GST, which had been discussed for years. GST has played a pivotal role in fostering economic unity. Credit also goes to the previous government for its efforts in this regard. In our tenure, we had the opportunity to advance this initiative, and we did so. The concept of 'One Nation, One Tax' is taking that role forward …

The ration card has always been a critical document for the poor. … previously, a poor person moving from one state to another could not access its benefits … To reinforce this sense of unity, we introduced the concept of 'One Nation, One Ration Card.' …

For the common citizens, especially the poor, access to free healthcare strengthens their ability to combat poverty … Committed to the mantra of national unity, we implemented the 'One Nation, One Health Card' initiative through Ayushman Bharat. Today, even if a person from a remote village in Bihar is working in Pune and falls ill, their Ayushman card ensures access to healthcare services immediately …

During the tenure of the previous government, … power shortages often resulted in international headlines portraying Bharat in a poor light … we established the 'One Nation, One Grid.' Today, electricity reaches every corner of Bharat seamlessly, ensuring that no region is left behind …

Our country's infrastructure has long suffered from disparities and discrimination … Be it the North East, Jammu and Kashmir, the Himalayan regions, or the desert areas, we have made efforts to empower infrastructure across all regions. …

Times have changed, and we are determined to ensure that the digital sector does not become a realm of 'haves' and 'have-nots.' Bharat's Digital India initiative has become a global success story. By democratising technology, we have upheld the vision of our Constitution-makers. With the aim of bolstering the 'unity in Bharat', we have extended optical fibre connectivity to every panchayat, empowering the nation.

… A nation cannot be truly cultured by suppressing its native languages … the New Education Policy gives prominence to the mother tongue. Today, even children from poor families can aspire to become doctors or engineers in their own languages. Additionally, we have honoured various Indian languages by granting them due recognition as classical languages. To nurture national unity and inculcate cultural awareness among the younger generation, we have initiated the 'Ek Bharat Shreshtha Bharat' campaign …

As the Constitution completes 75 years, it is important to reflect on its milestones. Significant anniversaries, such as 25, 50, and 60 years, carry immense importance. However, history reveals a mixed legacy. When the Constitution marked its 25th anniversary, the country witnessed one of its darkest periods. The Emergency was imposed, constitutional arrangements were suspended, the nation was turned into a prison, citizens' rights were stripped away, and press freedom was stifled. This grave injustice remains an indelible stain on the Congress party's record. Whenever democracy is discussed globally, this betrayal will be remembered as an act of strangling our Constitution …

When the Constitution completed 50 years, under the leadership of Prime Minister Atal Bihari Vajpayee, the nation celebrated this milestone with grandeur … He delivered a special message emphasising unity, public participation, and partnership, thereby bringing to life the true spirit of the Constitution and inspiring the public ...

It was during this period that I had the honour of becoming a Chief Minister. When the Constitution marked its 60th anniversary during my tenure, we celebrated it in Gujarat with unprecedented fervour. For the first time in history, the Constitution was carried in a ceremonial procession atop an elephant in a specially crafted palanquin. The 'Samvidhan Gaurav Yatra' was organised, with the Chief Minister walking alongside on foot, symbolising the reverence for our Constitution and educating the public about its significance. When we commemorated Constitution Day on 26th November in the Lok Sabha's old chamber, a senior leader questioned the need for such a celebration, citing Republic Day on 26th January. This attitude reveals how undervalued … the Constitution was at the time. However, I am delighted that in this special session, we have the opportunity to discuss the Constitution's power and diversity. Unfortunately, political compulsions have overshadowed what could have been a constructive dialogue. It would have been far better to engage in a discussion that transcended party lines and enriched the new generation's understanding of the Constitution …

It is because of the Constitution that individuals like me, without any political lineage or background, have been able to rise to positions of responsibility. It is the Constitution's power and the blessings of the people that have made this possible … This immense love and trust bestowed upon us by the people – not once, not twice, but thrice – would not have been possible without the Constitution …

I have no intention of making personal criticisms today. However, it is my duty to present the facts before the nation. One particular family from the Congress party has left no stone unturned in undermining the Constitution. I mention this family specifically because, out of the 75 years of Bharat's independence, they have ruled the country for 55 years. The people of this nation have the right to know the truth about what transpired during that time and the negative traditions, flawed policies, and harmful practices established by this family …

From 1947 to 1952, there was no elected government in this country. Instead, a temporary, selected system was in place, operating as an interim arrangement until elections could be held… the Rajya Sabha was not yet formed, nor were elections conducted in the states. There was no mandate from the people, despite the Constitution having just been created after extensive deliberations by its makers. In 1951, before an elected government was established, this interim system used an ordinance to amend the Constitution. The result? Freedom of expression was attacked. This act was a grave insult to the Constitution and its makers… It is worth noting that this was not the decision of a democratically elected Prime Minister but of someone leading an interim government. This was, undoubtedly, a grievous sin …

During that same period, the then Prime Minister, Pandit Jawaharlal Nehru, wrote a letter to a Chief Minister stating: 'If the Constitution comes in our way, then it must be changed at any cost.' These words …represent a shocking disregard for the sanctity of the Constitution ...

This … did not go unnoticed. … President Dr. Rajendra Prasad cautioned that this was a grave error. Even the Speaker of the Lok Sabha warned Pandit Nehru that he was acting against the principles of the Constitution. Prominent Congress leaders, including Acharya Kripalani and Jayaprakash Narayan, also urged him to stop. Despite receiving such sound advice from senior and respected figures, Pandit Nehru ignored their concerns, stubbornly pursuing his own version of the Constitution …

The Constitution has been amended 75 times in about six decades…

The seeds of constitutional misuse were sown by the first Prime Minister of the country and were later nurtured… by another Prime Minister, Mrs. Indira Gandhi ... In 1971, a Supreme Court decision was overturned through a constitutional amendment. This amendment not only nullified the Supreme Court's ruling but also clipped the wings of the judiciary, asserting that Parliament could amend any article of the Constitution without judicial review. The rights of the judiciary were systematically curtailed. This grave act was committed … by the then Prime Minister, Mrs. Indira Gandhi, whose government used this amendment to seize fundamental rights and exert control over the judiciary.

With no one to hold Mrs. Gandhi accountable, when the court invalidated her election for unconstitutional practices, she retaliated by imposing an Emergency to cling to her position. This misuse of constitutional provisions strangled Indian democracy. In 1975, she introduced the 39th amendment, ensuring that elections of the President, Vice President, Prime Minister, and Speaker could not be challenged in court, even retrospectively. This was not merely a shield for future misconduct but also a means to cover past transgressions ...

During the Emergency, people's fundamental rights were trampled upon, and thousands were jailed. The judiciary was gagged, and press freedoms were stifled. Mrs. Gandhi advanced the notion of a 'committed judiciary,' a concept that undermined judicial independence. Justice H.R. Khanna, a judge who upheld the Constitution and delivered a judgment against Mrs. Gandhi, was deliberately denied the position of Chief Justice of India, despite being the senior-most judge. This was a blatant assault on constitutional and democratic norms ...

Many political leaders, including those from parties present in this House today, were imprisoned during that time. Innocent citizens were brutalised, subjected to police atrocities, and many even lost their lives in jail. A ruthless government was tearing the Constitution apart with impunity ...

What began with Nehru was continued by Indira Gandhi and, later, by Rajiv Gandhi ... The Supreme Court's judgment in the Shah Bano case upheld justice and equality under the Constitution, granting an elderly woman her rightful claims. Yet, Rajiv Gandhi's government, prioritising vote-bank politics over constitutional values, overturned this judgment through legislation, bowing to fundamentalist pressures and sacrificing the spirit of justice ...

Instead of standing by an elderly woman seeking justice, he aligned with the fundamentalists. The decision of the Supreme Court was overturned through the enactment of a law in Parliament, sacrificing the spirit of the Constitution ...

The next generation of leadership was equally complicit. I would like to quote from a book that references a statement by a former Prime Minister, who was my predecessor. In this book, Manmohan Singh Ji is quoted as saying, 'I have to accept that the party president is the centre of power. The government is accountable to the party.' ...

The very concept of an elected government and an elected Prime Minister was compromised. While we had a Constitution, it was subverted by placing an unconstitutional and unsworn National Advisory Council above the Prime Minister and even the Prime Minister's Office. This gave the PMO an undeclared, diminished status, effectively undermining the principles of governance established by our Constitution ...

Under the Indian Constitution, the citizens elect the government, and the head of that government forms the cabinet. This is a fundamental constitutional process. Yet, a decision taken by this cabinet was brazenly torn up in front of journalists by individuals filled with arrogance who disrespected the Constitution... forcing the cabinet to reverse it. What kind of system operates in this manner? ...

The Congress legacy is replete with instances of constitutional violations and disregard for constitutional institutions. While Article 370 is widely known, very few are aware of Article 35A.[23] Without presenting it to Parliament, despite the constitutional mandate, Article 35A was imposed on the country...enacted without Parliamentary approval, through an order of the President, keeping the nation's Parliament in the dark. If Article 35A had not been imposed, the situation in Jammu and Kashmir would not have deteriorated to the extent it did. ...

I do not wish to delve into the bitterness and animosity that existed towards Baba Saheb Ambedkar during his time. However, when Atal Ji was in power, a decision was made to establish a memorial in honour of Baba Saheb Ambedkar ... during the ten years of UPA rule, this initiative was neither undertaken nor allowed to proceed. When our government assumed power, ... we built the Baba Saheb Memorial on Alipur Road and completed the project ...

In 1992, ... The proposal for the Ambedkar International Centre near Janpath was conceived. However, for 40 years, this idea remained confined to paper and saw no progress ... in 2015, we fulfilled this commitment and completed the work. The decision to confer the Bharat Ratna upon Baba Saheb Ambedkar also materialised only when Congress was out of power ...

Baba Saheb Ambedkar was a visionary, dedicated to uplifting the underprivileged sections of society and ensuring their inclusion in the mainstream. He firmly believed that for India to develop holistically, no region or community should

---

[23] Article 35A empowered the J and K state's legislature to define 'permanent residents' of the state and provide special rights and privileges to them including purchase of land and immovable property, the right to vote and contest elections, seek government employment and avail of state benefits such as higher education and health care. Non-permanent residents of the state, even if Indian citizens, were not entitled to these 'privileges'. The origin of this lay in a political movement in the early 20th century when residents, led by the Pandit community, launched a 'Kashmir for the Kashmiris' movement demanding that only should be employed in state government jobs. Legal provisions for the recognition of the status were enacted by the Maharaja of J and K between 1912 and 1932. The 1927 Hereditary State Subject Order granted to the state subjects the right to government office and the right to land use and ownership, which were not available to non-state subjects. Following the accession of J and K to the Indian Union, Article 370 of the Constitution and the concomitant Constitutional Order of 1950 provided for the management of defence, external affairs and communications by the Indian government. In a statement to the Lok Sabha, the then prime minister Jawaharlal Nehru explained: '...For a long time past, in the Maharaja's time, there had been laws there preventing any outsider, that is, any person from outside Kashmir, from acquiring or holding land in Kashmir .... although most of their rights were taken away from the Maharaja under the British rule, the Maharaja stuck to this that nobody from outside should acquire land there. And that continues. ... the present Government of Kashmir is very anxious to preserve that right because they are afraid, and I think rightly afraid, that Kashmir would be overrun by people whose sole qualification might be the possession of too much money and nothing else, who might buy up, and get the delectable places. Now they want to vary the old Maharaja's laws to liberalise it, but nevertheless to have checks on the acquisition of lands by persons from outside...'

remain marginalised. This vision led to the establishment of the reservation system in our country. However, those consumed by vote-bank politics exploited reservations for appeasement based on religion, causing the greatest harm to the SC, ST and OBC communities …

The story of reservation is long and fraught with challenges. From Nehru Ji to Rajiv Gandhi, successive Congress Prime Ministers vehemently opposed reservations ... Nehru Ji himself wrote extensive letters to Chief Ministers opposing reservations ... While Baba Saheb Ambedkar introduced reservations to promote equality and balanced development in India, Congress leaders consistently opposed it. The Mandal Commission's report, which sought to address these disparities, was shelved for decades. It was only after the Congress was removed from power that OBCs were granted reservation ...

When the Constitution … was being drafted, the founding members engaged in extensive discussions … on whether reservations should be granted on the basis of religion. .. it was collectively decided that, for the unity and integrity of a nation like Bharat, reservations cannot be provided on the basis of religion or sect ... However, the Congress party, driven by the hunger for power and the desire to appease its vote bank, has introduced a new game of providing reservations on the basis of religion, which is against the spirit of the Constitution. Not only that, they have even implemented it in some places, only to face setbacks from the Supreme Court ...

There is a burning issue I wish to discuss, and that is the Uniform Civil Code! …. The Constituent Assembly … After rigorous debates, … decided that it would be better for whichever government is elected in the future to take a decision on this matter and implement the Uniform Civil Code in the country… However, those who neither understand the Constitution nor the country, and have read nothing beyond their hunger for power, are unaware of what Babasaheb had actually said ...

Dr. Babasaheb Ambedkar had strongly advocated for the abolition of personal laws that were based on religious grounds … Keeping in mind the spirit of the Constitution and the sentiments of the Constitution's framers, we are fully committed and working with all our strength towards establishing a secular civil code. However, today, the Congress party is disrespecting not only the sentiments of the Constitution's framers but also the directives and aspirations of the Supreme Court. This is because such measures do not align with their political agenda. For them, the Constitution is not a sacred text; rather, it has become a tool for political manoeuvering. They have turned it into a weapon to play political games and instil fear in people …

Their veins are filled with authoritarianism and dynastic politics. Look at the chaos and lack of democratic values in their functioning. I am talking about the Congress. Twelve provincial Congress committees supported Sardar Patel for the position of Prime Minister. Not a single committee … supported Nehru … But what happened? A lack of faith in democracy, a disregard for their own party's Constitution led to Sardar Patel being sidelined and they themselves assumed power… The Congress party once had a president from an extremely backward community … Sitaram Kesri ji. And how was he treated? He was insulted. It is said that he was locked in a bathroom, and then unceremoniously thrown out onto the streets. This kind of humiliation was never written in their party's Constitution, yet they blatantly disregarded it … Over time, the Congress party became completely captive to the control of one family, discarding democratic values entirely… For us, the Constitution, its sanctity, and its integrity are supreme. This is not just rhetoric – our actions prove it. Whenever tested, we have come through with flying colours. Let me give an example. In 1996, the Bharatiya Janata Party (BJP) emerged as the single largest party in the elections. Following the Constitution's spirit, the President invited the single largest party to form the government. The government lasted only 13 days. If we did not hold the Constitution's spirit dear, we could have engaged in bargaining[24] – offering positions, deputy prime ministerships, or other incentives to secure a majority and enjoyed the fruits of power. But Atal ji did not choose the path of bargaining and instead chose to respect the Constitution. Instead he resigned after 13 days. This is the pinnacle of democratic values. Again, in 1998, under the National Democratic Alliance (NDA), we formed a stable government. However, those with the mindset of 'if not us, then no one' played their usual tricks to destabilize Atal ji's government. A trust vote was held. Even then, horse-trading was possible; the market for buying and selling votes was active. But Atal ji, committed to the Constitution's spirit, preferred losing by one vote over compromising on principles. The government fell, but we upheld the democratic and constitutional ethos. This is our history, our values, and our tradition. On the other hand, look at what happened. To save their minority government, they resorted to the infamous Cash-for-Votes scandal. Stacks of cash were brought into Parliament to buy votes. The judiciary itself has stamped this as a blatant assault on democracy. They turned Bharat's sacred Parliament into a marketplace, where votes were traded for cash …

In the 1990s, the shameful act of bribing several Members of Parliament was carried out – an unforgivable sin that trampled on the very spirit of the Constitution nurtured in the hearts of 140 crore Indians. For Congress, the pursuit of power and the hunger for power have been the only history and present of the party…

After 2014, the NDA was given the opportunity to serve. The Constitution and democracy were strengthened. We launched a campaign to free the nation from the

[24] Since the BJP came to power in 2014, it has 'changed' electoral mandates in state elections in several states that include Goa, Karnataka, Madhya Pradesh and Maharashtra.

old ailments. In the past 10 years … we have made constitutional amendments – for the unity of the nation, its integrity, and its bright future, with full dedication to the spirit of the Constitution. Why did we make these amendments? For over three decades, the OBC community in this country had been demanding constitutional status for the OBC Commission. To honour the OBC community, we made constitutional amendments to grant it constitutional status, and we take pride in this action …

In this country, there was a large section of people who, regardless of the caste they were born into, could not access opportunities due to their poverty. … There were demands, but no one took a decisive step. We made a constitutional amendment to provide 10% reservation for the poor in general categories. This was the first amendment for reservation in the country, and there was no opposition to it. … Parliament passed it with unanimous consent …

We have made amendments to the Constitution… to empower women. The old Parliament building stands witness to this – when the country was moving forward to grant reservations to women in Parliament and state assemblies, and the bill was being introduced, one of their allied parties came to the Well, snatched the papers, tore them up, and the House was adjourned. This led to the issue being stalled for 40 years.[25] And today, the same individuals who stalled progress on women's rights are considered their guides. Those who did injustice to the women of this country are now their mentors …

We made constitutional amendments for the unity of the country. Dr. Babasaheb Ambedkar's Constitution could not even reach Jammu and Kashmir due to the barrier of Article 370. We wanted Dr. Ambedkar's Constitution to apply across every part of Bharat. To honour Babasaheb and strengthen the unity of the country, we made constitutional amendments and boldly removed Article 370. Now, even the Supreme Court of Bharat has stamped its approval on this decision …

We made the amendment to remove Article 370. During the partition, senior leaders, including Mahatma Gandhi, publicly stated that this country would look after the minorities in neighbouring countries whenever they faced any crisis. Gandhi Ji's promise was never fulfilled by those who came to power in his name. We fulfilled that promise through the Citizenship Amendment Act (CAA).[26] It was

---

[25] The original was brought by H.D. Deve Gowda's United Front Government in 1996. It was eventually passed in 2023, 27 years later.

[26] The CAA expedites Indian citizenship applications of Hindus, Parsis, Sikhs, Buddhists, Jains and Christians who escaped to India from religious persecution in Muslim-majority Afghanistan, Bangladesh and Pakistan before December 31, 2014. They become eligible for citizenship in five years even if they are currently living in India without valid visas or other required paperwork. Before the CAA, India's citizenship law did not make religion a determinant of a person's eligibility for an Indian passport. All those seeking naturalisation had to show that they were in India legally, and needed to wait for the same period – 11 years

a law we brought forward, and with pride, we continue to uphold it today. We do not shy away from it, because we have stood firm in the spirit of the Constitution of this country.

The constitutional amendments we made were to correct past mistakes and to strengthen the path towards a brighter future. Time will tell whether we stood true or not. These amendments were not made for selfish power interests – they were made as a virtuous act for the nation's benefit …

… the most sensitive aspect of our Constitution has always been the people of India. 'We the people', the citizens of Bharat, the Constitution is for them, for their welfare, for their dignity. Therefore, the Constitution provides direction for a welfare state, and a welfare state means one where citizens are guaranteed a life of dignity. Our Congress colleagues hold one word very dear, and I want to use that word today. The word they are most fond of, without which they cannot live, is 'jumla'. Our Congress colleagues keep talking about 'jumla' day and night, but the people of this country know that the biggest 'jumla' in Bharat was the one that lasted for four generations: 'Garibi Hatao' (Remove Poverty). This was the 'jumla' – the slogan of removing poverty. It might have served their political interests, but the condition of the poor never improved …

Can anyone really say that after so many years of independence, a family living with dignity should not even have access to a toilet? Did you not have the time to address this? In our country, the campaign to build toilets, which was once a dream for the poor, became a reality for their dignity. … Mothers and sisters were going out to defecate in the open, either before sunrise or after sunrise, and you never felt any pain about it. …

80% of the population in this country was longing for clean drinking water. Was my Constitution supposed to stop them from getting it? The Constitution aimed for the attention to be focused on providing basic human amenities to ordinary people …We have also moved forward with this work with great dedication and commitment …

Millions of mothers in this country used to cook food on stoves, their eyes red from the smoke. It is said that cooking in smoke is like inhaling the smoke of hundreds of cigarettes, ... Their eyes used to burn, and their health would

– to become eligible for citizenship. The CAA, for the first time independent India's history has created a religious test for citizenship.

It also means that Muslim victims of religious persecution in Pakistan (like the Ahmadiyas) Afghanistan (the Hazaras) or other neighbouring nations (such as the Rohingyas in Myanmar), will still need to wait for 11 years before they become eligible for Indian citizenship. And unlike Hindus, Parsis, Sikhs, Buddhists, Jains and Christians, they need valid documentation to justify their presence in India. Many legal experts have argued, that this violates Article 14 of the Indian Constitution, which says: 'The State shall not deny to any person equality before the law or the equal protection of the laws within the territory of India.'

deteriorate. We took on the task of freeing them from the smoke. Until 2013, discussions were about giving 9 cylinders or 6 cylinders, but this country, in no time, ensured that a gas cylinder reached every household. Because for us, every citizen, especially after 70 years, deserves access to basic amenities …

If our poor families work day and night to break free from poverty and want to educate their children, but then a sickness strikes the household, all their plans are ruined, and the hard work of the entire family goes to waste. Couldn't you think of anything for the treatment of these poor families? Respecting the spirit of the Constitution, we implemented the Ayushman Bharat Scheme, ensuring free healthcare for 50 to 60 crore citizens. Today, we have also made arrangements for people above 70 years, regardless of their social class …

When we talk about providing ration to the needy, even that is ridiculed. When we say that 25 crore people have been successful in overcoming poverty, we are then asked, 'Why do you still give ration to the poor?' … Those who have come out of poverty know the reality. When a patient is discharged from the hospital after recovering, the doctor advises, 'Go home, your health is fine, the surgery was successful. But for the next month, be cautious, avoid certain things so that you don't face trouble again.' Similarly, it is essential to provide handholding to the poor to ensure they don't fall back into poverty …

In our country, there were slogans run in the name of the poor. It was in the name of the poor that the banks were nationalized. But until 2014, 50 crore citizens of this country had never even seen the door of a bank …

The poor didn't even have access to enter a bank; this injustice was done by you. But today, by opening bank accounts for 50 crore poor citizens, we have opened the doors of banks for the poor. Not only that, one Prime Minister used to say that when 1 rupee is sent from Delhi, only 15 paise reaches the recipient. But the solution was never provided by them. We showed the way, and today when 1 rupee is sent from Delhi, all 100 paise reach the … account. Why? Because we showed how to use the bank properly, how to make the right use of it …

Those who were never allowed to even approach the doors of the bank without any guarantee, today, under this government, due to our commitment to the Constitution, they can now take loans from the bank without any collateral. This power has been given to the poor by us …

Every day, our 'Divyangjans' (differently-abled citizens) struggle. It is only now that our 'Divyangjan' people have received a more accessible infrastructure, where their wheelchairs can go all the way to the train compartments. This system was created because we were deeply concerned about the marginalized, deprived members of society ...

For our 'Divyangjan' citizens, … We took the initiative to create a unified sign language system, …

The nomadic and semi-nomadic communities of our society were long ignored. We took the initiative to establish a Welfare Board for their well-being …

Everyone knows the street vendors… These people work tirelessly for 12 hours a day, sometimes taking their carts on rent, borrowing money at high interest, and buying goods with it. By the evening, they have to repay the borrowed amount and barely manage to buy a piece of bread for their children … Our government introduced the PM SVANidhi scheme, which allowed street vendors to get loans from banks without any guarantee. ...

In this country, there is hardly anyone who does not need the services of Vishwakarma. … We created a plan for the welfare of the Vishwakarma community, arranged for loans from banks, provided them with new training, gave them modern tools, and focused on helping them create new designs and strengthened them.

The transgender community, who were rejected by their families and society, and had no one to care for them, is now recognized by our government. It is under our government that we have granted them rights in the Indian Constitution. …

We often talk about Adivasi (tribal) community. When I became the Chief Minister of Gujarat, … the entire eastern belt of Gujarat, … was an Adivasi area. Even though a Congress Chief Minister, who himself was an Adivasi, had ruled for so many years, there wasn't a single school with a science stream in the entire region. … If there are no schools with science streams, no matter how much you talk about reservations, how can those children become engineers or doctors? I worked in that region, and now there are schools with science streams, and even universities have been established there …

For 60 years, 100 districts were identified as backward, and this label of 'backward districts' became so stigmatized that whenever a transfer happened, it was seen as a 'punishment posting.' No responsible officer wanted to go there. We changed this entire scenario. We introduced the concept of 'Aspirational Districts,' and we monitored them regularly online based on 40 parameters. Today, many of these Aspirational Districts have reached the level of better performing districts in their respective states, and some have even matched the national averages ...

For the welfare of the fishermen community, our government was the first to establish a separate Ministry of Fisheries. We allocated a dedicated budget for their development and addressed the concerns of this community as well …

To empower small farmers, we understood the importance of strengthening the cooperative sector, making it more capable and robust. With the small farmer's welfare in our hearts, we created a separate Ministry of Cooperation ... Similarly, we recognize that the youth of our country are our strength. While the entire world is striving to build a capable workforce, the demographic dividend presents a great opportunity. To prepare our youth for the global workforce, we established a separate Ministry of Skill Development to equip our young citizens with skills aligned to global needs …

Nobody cared for our North-East because it has fewer votes … Atal ji … established a dedicated Ministry for the welfare of the North-East. Today, we are witnessing the results of that effort as new avenues of development are being achieved in the North-East. ... railways, roads, ports and airports are being developed and progressing rapidly in this region…

Even today, many countries around the world, including developed ones, face challenges related to land records. In our villages, an ordinary person often does not possess proper ownership documents for their land or home. As a result, they face difficulties such as securing loans from banks or protecting their property from encroachment if they leave. To address this, we launched the Svamitva Yojana ... we are providing ownership documents to marginalized and underprivileged individuals in villages, thereby granting them legal ownership rights...

'Sabka Saath, Sabka Vikas' … is not merely a slogan; it is our article of faith. That is why we have worked towards implementing government schemes without any discrimination, as the Constitution does not permit bias. We have embraced the idea of saturation in governance, ensuring that the benefits of every scheme reach 100% of the eligible beneficiaries. If there is true secularism, it lies in this saturation approach. If there is genuine social justice, it lies in ensuring that everyone gets their rightful share, without discrimination …

Another essential spirit of our Constitution is its ability to guide and steer our nation forward. Politics often remains at the centre as a driving force for shaping the country's direction. Today, we must reflect and deliberate on what the trajectory of our democracy and the future course of our politics should be in the coming decades …

Some political parties, driven by their self-interest and thirst for power, have created an environment where the true spirit of democracy has been overshadowed. I wish to pose a question to all political parties – shouldn't capable leadership, irrespective of family lineage, have a fair chance in this nation? … Hasn't family-centric politics inflicted significant harm on the spirit of Indian democracy? Isn't it our constitutional responsibility to free Indian democracy from the grip of dynastic politics? … To strengthen democracy and encourage the participation of talented and capable youth, political parties must make deliberate efforts to welcome individuals without any political lineage into their ranks. … My goal is to bring 100,000 young individuals into the political domain – those who have no political family background …

… once, from the Red Fort, I spoke about the duties enshrined in our Constitution, and I was astonished to see that even the concept of duties was ridiculed by some ... Our Constitution outlines the rights of every citizen, but it also expects us to uphold our duties. The essence of our civilization lies in dharma, in our responsibilities, and in our sense of duty. Mahatma Gandhi once said … 'I learned from my uneducated but wise mother that rights naturally flow from the faithful discharge of one's duties.' … Building upon Gandhiji's message, I firmly believe that if we wholeheartedly fulfil our fundamental duties, nothing can prevent us from transforming the country into a 'Viksit Bharat' (Developed India). As we commemorate 75 years of our Constitution, let this milestone serve as a renewed call to strengthen our dedication to our duties ...

Inspired by the spirit of the Constitution, I would like to present 11 resolutions before this esteemed House for the future of Bharat: 1. First Resolution: Whether citizens or the government, all must fulfil their duties. 2. Second Resolution: Every region and every community must benefit from development, ensuring 'Sabka Saath, Sabka Vikas'. 3. Third Resolution: There must be zero tolerance towards corruption, and there should be no social acceptance of corrupt individuals. 4. Fourth Resolution: Citizens of the country should feel proud of adhering to the laws, rules, and traditions of the nation. 5. Fifth Resolution: We must be free from the mindset of slavery and take pride in our heritage. 6. Sixth Resolution: The country's politics must be free from dynastic rule. 7. Seventh Resolution: The Constitution should be respected, and it should not be used as a tool for political gain. 8. Eighth Resolution: While upholding the spirit of the Constitution, the rights of those receiving reservations should not be taken away, and all attempts to create reservations based on religion should be stopped. 9. Ninth Resolution: Bharat must become a global example in women-led development. 10. Tenth Resolution: Development of states should lead to the development of the nation. This should be our mantra for progress. 11. Eleventh Resolution: The goal of 'Ek Bharat Shreshtha Bharat' must remain supreme… .

With this resolution, if we all move forward together, the inherent spirit of the Constitution, 'We the People', and 'Sabka Prayas'(collective effort) will guide us towards the dream of a 'Viksit Bharat'. This dream should be shared by everyone in this House, as well as by the 140 crore citizens of the country. When the nation sets out with a firm resolve, it will certainly achieve its desired results. I have immense respect for the 140 crore citizens of our country, for their strength, for the 'Yuva Shakti' (youth power), and for the 'Nari Shakti' (women power). That is why I say that in 2047, when the country celebrates 100 years of independence, it will celebrate as a 'Viksit Bharat'. With this resolve, let us move forward. Once again, I extend my best wishes to everyone for advancing this great and sacred task …

Section Eleven

Trouble in Paradise

1

Kashmir Post-Independence

The integration – or accession, as the official word has it – of Jammu and Kashmir, a Muslim-dominated region, to India at the time of Independence was messy and complicated, impinging as it did on issues of territory and the belief that those who won independence for India wished to build a secular state. Seventy-five years after Independence, it remains a major sticking point in the relations between India and Pakistan.

Here, India's first Prime Minister ***Jawaharlal Nehru*** *makes a detailed speech on the situation leading up to 1952, the international complications as well as the arrangements that had to be made between Kashmir and India regarding the future Constitution of Kashmir, underscoring the need for Article 370 in the Indian Constitution, a provision that defined the special relationship between Jammu and Kashmir and the Union of India. Since then, of course, a great deal of water has flown down the Jhelum, and Nehru's critics – particularly among the members of the Hindu Right-wing – have held him responsible for the continuing instability in the region.*

In the second speech excerpted here, Nehru's foremost denigrator on the subject, **Dr Syama Prasad Mookerjee**, *the founder of the Bharatiya Jana Sangh, the precursor of the BJP, counters his arguments sharply. Indeed, the latter will be best remembered for his campaign against Jammu and Kashmir being given a special status through the insertion of Article 370 in the Indian Constitution. His battle cry at that time was 'Ek desh mein do vidhan, do nishan nahin chalenge, nahin chalenge. (Two Constitutions and two flags in one country are not acceptable)'.*

Mookerjee, a leader from West Bengal, was a member of Nehru's Cabinet until he resigned in 1950 as a mark of protest against the Nehru–Liaquat Pact – a treaty meant to secure the security and rights of minorities in both countries. Subsequently, he became one of Nehru's most vocal critics and associated himself with the Jammu and Kashmir issue, for which his admirers say he ultimately 'sacrificed' his life – he died in Srinagar on 23 June under mysterious circumstances.

JAWAHARLAL NEHRU

(Lok Sabha: Phulpur)

Lok Sabha: 24 July 1952

Statement on Kashmir

Sir, I am grateful to you for this opportunity to make a statement in regard to affairs relating to the Jammu and Kashmir state. The House has been interested and the wider public is also interested in these developments and, therefore, with your permission, Sir, I shall take a little time of the House to state not only the present position, but go somewhat into the background, because we are apt to forget what has happened in the recent past. Public memory is short and unless we remember that past it is sometimes a little difficult to understand the present.

The state of Jammu and Kashmir for long years was a delectable playground for those who could afford it, one of the famous playgrounds of the world, and though the people living there were for the great part poverty stricken, it drew many people from the rest of the world. This Kashmir, which was politically-speaking a backwater for these long years, was suddenly thrust into the current of history and since then events have happened there, many developments have taken place – good and bad – and naturally public attention has been drawn to them and it has become an international affair. For us in India it is, of course, something much more than that not only because of our long contacts ranging over a thousand years; but also because of these recent developments which have brought us nearer to one another. So, therefore, I would ask the indulgence of the House, if I may put it so, for some background information.

First of all, I would like the House just to form a mental picture of the geography – 'the geographical situation', from the southern tip of India, Kanyakumari, Kashmir is just about or a little over two thousand miles. It is a far cry. Roughly speaking, Kashmir is about a thousand miles from the sea. While a part of India it is, in fact, the heart of Asia, geographically speaking, and for countless ages great caravans have passed from India right up to Central Asia through this state. It is essentially, and it has been for two thousand years or more, very closely connected with India, culturally and politically often enough. It is also connected in various ways with Central Asia. Even now I wonder how many people realize that Kashmir is further north than Tibet. So one has to think of Kashmir in that peculiar geographical position apart from the other factors in the case.

Now Kashmir, as I said, was suddenly thrust into this current of history. This current is moving very rapidly in many parts of the world and sometimes it becomes a rushing and raging torrent in some parts. We seem, all of us or most of us all over the world, to live on a thin crust of peace and the crust threatens to crack up often enough and does crack up sometimes. Even this morning's news will bring this picture to the minds of Hon'ble. Members – the happenings in some States in Western Asia, the coup d'état[1] and the rest taking place and the lack of stability. We in India are perhaps a little fortunate in this respect, because in spite of many things that some Hon'ble Members may complain of, or protest against, there is, it is widely recognized, a large measure of stability in our machinery of Government and affairs in the country and a continuous, progressive development, without those cracks appearing. This is a matter of good fortune for us. But at the same time, nobody in this wide world can afford to forget this cracking and sometimes, as it appears, disintegrating world of ours …

Now in the State of Jammu and Kashmir, as in other Indian States of old, there were strivings for freedom against the feudal rule that existed there. As in other States again, they took their inspiration from the great nationalist movement of India. In essence, they were the outcome of that very movement and the offshoots of that movement and their ideals and objectives also very largely came from that big movement and that great leader, Mahatma Gandhi. I think I would be right in saying that of all the various State movements in India during the last twenty or thirty years, probably the State movement that developed in the Jammu and Kashmir State, the popular movement, I mean, that developed there, was the most powerful and grew up to be the best organized. It came in conflict, inevitably, with the State Government there, as all such movements did elsewhere. This movement was intimately connected with what was known as the All-India States People's Conference.[2] Thereby, it became a part of that allied movement in India which

---

1 Editor's note: The 1952 coup d'état and the 23 July Revolution in Egypt was a period of profound political, economic and societal change in that country. On 23 July 1952, the revolution began with the toppling of King Farouk in a coup d'état by the Free Officers Movement. This group of army officers was led by Mohamed Naguib and Gamal Abdel Nasser – the latter would go on to become his country's second President and subsequently, a leading figure in the Non-Aligned Movement.

2 Editor's note: The All India States Peoples' Conference (AISPC) was a conglomeration of political movements in the princely states of the British Raj, which were variously called Praja Mandals or Lok Parishads. The first session of the AISPC was held in Bombay in December 1927. The Conference looked to the Indian National Congress for support, but the Congress was reluctant to provide support until 1939, when Jawaharlal Nehru became its president, serving in this position till 1946. After Indian Independence, however, the Congress distanced itself from the movement, allying itself with the princely rulers via its national government's accession relationships. The States Peoples' Conference dissolved itself on 25 April 1948 and all its constituent units merged into the Congress, with one exception, viz., the Jammu & Kashmir National Conference. This body, under the leadership of Sheikh Abdullah, remained independent, while one section of it merged with the Congress in 1965.

affected all the States in the country. It was closely connected with it. This is the background.

There were during these years, as in the rest of India, conflicts with the State machinery and the people there and the popular organization there went through a great deal of torment and suffering. There is much to be said about that period, but I shall now come to more recent times.

When, or a little before, independence and partition came, the House will remember that we were faced by this big problem of the six hundred odd Indian States in India. It was a terrific problem and we had to solve it with great rapidity. The announcement that the British Government had made – I think it was round about early in June 1947 – had left the position of these States vague. We did not like that part of the British Government's announcement, because, in a sense it almost encouraged fissiparous tendencies in these States. It almost led some people to think or imagine in these States all over India – I am talking about the Rulers there – to think that they could function more or less independently.

So, in those months of July and August 1947 we had to face this major problem. Fortunately, we had a man big enough to face it – Sardar Patel. And then during those two or three weeks preceding Independence we saw nearly all these States in India acceding to the Union of India, or to the Dominion of India as it then was – nearly all, barring two or three, barring Hyderabad, barring Kashmir and one or two small ones. Hyderabad's case, as the House well knows, was a very special one. Kashmir, I am dealing with. The other small ones did not count much. So practically all these States acceded to India with great rapidity. And I should like to say that we were helped greatly in that process by the then Governor-General of India, Lord Mountbatten. That help had great effect because it proved to all these Rulers in these States that they could not rely upon the British Government, as against India. And so they were faced by this coming independence of India, of which they were afraid. They were faced by their own people who were dissatisfied with them and wanted a change. And when the last support which they perhaps looked up to, that is the British Government, also failed them they had no prop left, and hence the rapidity of their accession to India. They acceded on three basic subjects. Defence, Foreign Affairs and Communications. All the States did that. And so the Dominion of India started on the 15th August 1947 with all these States having acceded to it, excepting Hyderabad on the one side, Kashmir on the other, and one or two small ones.

In regard to Kashmir, even before the 15th August, I should imagine in July, the question came up before us informally. And the advice we gave was that the State of Jammu and Kashmir, for a variety of reasons, occupied a very special place. Now in the State of Jammu and Kashmir, as in other Indian States of old, there were strivings for freedom against the feudal rule that existed there. As in other States again, they took their inspiration from the great nationalist movement of India. That is to say, normally speaking there was no doubt that these States wanted to become parts of the Union of India – there was no question of consultation, no doubt – but where there was any doubt, we declared that we will consult the people and abide by their wishes. That general policy and principle applied to every State in India. But there were hardly any cases where this question arose and that is a different matter. So that, when the question of Kashmir at first informally came up before us – it was always before us in a sense, but it came up before us informally round about July or the middle of July – the advice we gave to Kashmir State was – and, if I may say so, we had contacts with the popular organization there, the National Conference, and its leaders, and we had contacts with the Maharaja's Government also, rather vague contacts, but they dealt with us – the advice we gave to both was that Kashmir is a special case and it would not be right or proper to try to rush this there, and the general principle we had laid down that the people of the State should be consulted specially applied to Kashmir. This was before Partition, before the actual coming of independence. We made it clear that even if the Maharaja and his Government then wanted to accede to India, we would like something much more, that is, popular approval of it before we took that step. We did not wish by some clever tactics to gain something on paper. We were after something much bigger, that is to gain the hearts of the people there to have a real union. Indeed, the basis and the foundation for that real union had been laid in the past – a much more enduring basis than even any legal or constitutional document. That basis had been these national movements there and here, our working together in co-operation for common ideals, and our having to endure common suffering. That was the real basis. So we made it clear in the month of July 1947 that the State of Jammu and Kashmir should not be hustled into taking any action, though many of their leaders were personally inclined, but they knew their people too and they said that the initiative should come from the people and not merely from the Maharaja's Government, only then it will endure. We accepted that entirely. And so we informed the Maharaja's Government as well as the leaders of the popular movement there that this matter of accession should not be hurried, that it should wait over till some method was found of consulting the people. And at that time what we envisaged was some kind of Constituent Assembly being elected there. In fact we envisaged that for other places, too, wherever such a question arose. And we advised that meanwhile, there should be Standstill Agreements with India and Pakistan that was going to come soon, so that no change need be made, except minor changes, and a little later, at leisure, this question could be considered further. Well, of course there was little of leisure that we had after the 15th August 1947. Upheavals took place in Pakistan, in the states of India bordering on Pakistan, and we had to pass through much pain and torment during that period. We could not think of Kashmir or any other place. We had to deal with the immediate issues that faced us from morning to evening.

Suddenly, the House will remember, in the last week of October 1947 an invasion took place of Kashmir through Pakistan. Now, it has been said in Pakistan often enough that there was some deep conspiracy on the part of India, allied with the leaders of Kashmir, to create trouble in various parts of the State, in the Poonch area and the rest. It has also been said, some people have said, that we knew all about what was happening – this invasion, I mean. The fact of the matter is that when we first heard the news of this invasion it came to us as a complete surprise. In fact, even the news did not reach us properly, because communications were not working properly. And when this dawned upon us we were taken much aback. For a day or two we gave very serious thought to this matter, and we did not quite know what we could do about it. We were far out of reach. Physically it was difficult. We were terribly busy with our own troubles here. However, as this raid and invasion developed, news came to us of rapine, killing and arson that was going on in its train, and naturally there was a great public feeling in India. Public feeling was aroused and the House can well imagine what the state of public feeling in the State of Jammu and Kashmir was at the time. At that time, we received independent appeals both from the Maharaja's Government and from the popular organization of Kashmir. The appeals were for help and for accession to India. We gave long and very anxious consideration to these, tried to consider and think out the implications, etc., and we had to come to a quick decision. I remember, it must have been the 27th of October, after practically an all-day sitting in the evening, we came to the conclusion that in spite of all the risks and dangers involved, we could not say 'No' to that appeal and that we had to go there to help them. It was not an easy matter because we could only go by air. We did not even know if the one and only temporary airfield was working or was in the hands of our foes. There was no other way to get there immediately and time was important, because every day brought further news of the depredations of those raiders. We decided to go to their help with all its consequences and within 12 hours of our decision, our troops were on the way by air. That was a fine piece of staff work on the part of our Army and Air Force. They arrived just in time; indeed it is possible that if they had arrived 24 hours late, the airfield would have been in the enemy's possession and that would have made matters much more difficult. From the airfield they went straight within a few miles to oppose these raiders. The raiders were driven back. Those raiders were supposed by us to be tribal people, no doubt, encouraged and abetted by Pakistan. At first we did not think it was a major military operation to drive out these tribal people. May I add here that before our forces reached there, probably before three or four days, the administration of Kashmir had completely collapsed. There was no administration. There was nobody – I cannot say definitely, but I hardly think there was any police force left or anything else. During these very critical days when this ruthless enemy was advancing on the famous city of Srinagar, the people of Srinagar had nobody to protect them, either big or small, and it was only the popular effort of the people, the volunteers of the National Conference that protected that city and protected it, not so much from armed forces – they could not do that because they had no arms – but they gave the necessary moral stimulus to the people and it is a fact worth remembering that when the enemy was within ten or twelve miles of Srinagar city, not a shop in Srinagar was closed. They were functioning. That showed the morale of the people and of the National movement at the moment of severe crisis. We drove back these raiders and when we drove them back to a place called Uri, where only a year or more earlier, I had been a prisoner of the Maharaja's Government.[3] Suddenly our forces discovered that a little beyond Uri they were not dealing with the tribal raiders, but with the armed might of the Pakistan army. That was a different matter that had to be dealt with on a different plane and so for the moment our armed forces stopped there.

Well, since then – this was in November 1947 – war continued there and elsewhere in the State, on the Jammu side, on the Kashmir side and on the northern side. It continued for a year and a half nearly. Round about December when we saw that we were up against the regular forces of the Pakistan army, immediately we felt that this matter was likely to become much bigger than we had imagined, that it might very well lead us to a full-scale war with Pakistan.

I should like the House to remember that time because we must judge every event in the context of that period. It was a period when soon after Partition with all the troubles we had due to the Partition and even our armies and services, everything else was split up, we wanted to settle down and apart from that, so far as we are concerned, we are averse to war, if we can help it. When we saw this matter might well develop into a full-scale war against Pakistan, we decided to refer the matter to the United Nations, I think, round about December 1947. Our reference was that certain tribal people had invaded the Kashmir State territory, behaved ruthlessly etc ... that they had come through Pakistan territory and that Pakistan had aided and abetted them in doing so. Our request to the United Nations or the Security Council was that they should inform Pakistan not to aid and abet these people. That was our request and that was the question we put. For the rest we proposed to deal with the situation ourselves. Our object was that this war should not spread in this way. We had, of course, asked Pakistan directly this question. But Pakistan had stoutly denied having anything to do with the matter. It was rather difficult

[3] Editor's note: In June 1946, Nehru was stopped at the gates of the Kashmir Valley at Kohala, the intersection where Kashmir's territory touched British India, to prevent him from reaching Srinagar. As president of the AISPC, he had come to the rescue of the incarcerated Sheikh Abdullah, but found himself jailed in the Uri dak bungalow by Maharaja Hari Singh's regime.

to understand how a few thousand people could march through Pakistan territory almost unaware so far as the Pakistan Government was concerned. However they denied that the tribal people had marched through their territory with their help at all and they denied absolutely then and for some months afterwards, that any Pakistan force or any part of the Pakistan Army had taken part in this Kashmir invasion. Later, we had plenty of evidence of this and in Delhi city, a little museum was opened by our Defence people, showing the participation of the Pakistan army when they were doing it, because we had all kinds of captured materials, diaries of soldiers, insignia, etc.

In 1948 these military operations went on fiercely throughout the winter. It is a very difficult time in those valleys of the Kashmir State during winter when you have to go up 15,000 feet or so. Simultaneously, the Security Council came into the picture. At first, for many months they talked and argued in New York. We were surprised because the question we had put was a very simple one and admitted only of a simple answer. We had not asked them to take our word for it, if it was challenged, as it was challenged, by Pakistan. The obvious course was to find out for themselves if we were telling the truth or Pakistan was telling the truth in this matter. During these four or five years of discussion, negotiation and mediation that simple question that we put at the end of 1947 has not been answered and has not been considered in that way. It has been answered in a sense rather indirectly by the Resolution of the United Nations Commission that came here in 1948, when they said that a new situation had arisen because Pakistan troops were in Kashmir. They did say that, because till the very eve of this statement, Pakistan Government had firmly denied the fact that their troops were there. That is an amazing instance of continuing to repeat what was patently false, and without foundation and which was found to be so by this United Nations Commission.

If I may just for a moment go back a little, on 31st December 1948, a cease fire was agreed to between the parties. Since then, there has been no military operation on any major scale. There have been petty raids; but, otherwise, there has been no serious fighting. That has been the position since then. Apart from local troubles and infiltrations – if you take that kind of thing, there is plenty of that – the scene has shifted to the Security Council of the United Nations, the United Nations Commission, United Nations representatives and the like, who have been visiting India from time to time. I shall not go into that history.

The latest mediator has been Dr. Graham. Dr. Graham has been here twice and has had long consultations with us and with the Pakistan Government, and is at the present moment in New York still continuing these conversations. He confined his enquiries almost entirely to what he called the demilitarization of the State. That word is hardly a happy word; but, nevertheless, for the sake of convenience we may use it. The position that we had agreed to when the United Nations Commission was here was this. In our desire to have peace, we had agreed to this, that, first of all, Pakistan armies, auxiliaries and the rest should withdraw from every inch of State territory. In fact, we had laid the greatest stress on it, not merely for military reasons, but much more so for moral reasons. They had no business to be there. They had to withdraw. They had invaded. Even if Pakistan challenged the accession of Kashmir to India, and as the House knows, they have challenged it and called it a bogus accession and all that kind of thing – even leaving it apart, I shall deal with it a little later – whatever India's position in Kashmir might be, one thing is dead clear and dead certain, that Pakistan had no position there; moral, political, constitutional or anything else, and Pakistan had no business to send any forces or abet any forces going there. So that, we made it an essential condition pre-requisite of any kind of approach to a settlement with Pakistan, their withdrawal completely from that area which they had invaded and occupied. That was the thing agreed to in that Resolution of the United Nations Commission.

Meanwhile, something else had happened and that was the building up in the Western area of the State, which was occupied by Pakistan, of forces sometimes called the Azad Kashmir forces. They had built up local levies called Azad Kashmir forces. At that time, that is in 1948, we did not have too much information about that, although we knew about it. We asked that these levies should be disbanded and disarmed. We could not ask them to go away from the State because the people lived in the State. We asked that they should be disbanded and disarmed. The form that the Commission put it later in the Resolution was, large scale disbandment and disarmament of Azad Kashmir forces. There has always been an argument between us and Pakistan on that issue. We have insisted that this meant, and we meant, a complete disbandment and disarmament: complete in the sense as far as could be. Some people may not give up arms; some may hide them, that is a different matter. Officially, it must be complete. Pakistan did not agree to that interpretation. And, this has been one of the arguments coming in the way of the conversion of the Cease Fire into a Truce Agreement. This was what Pakistan had to do. On our side, we had agreed to withdraw the bulk of our forces, mark the word 'bulk', from the State territory provided that we keep enough forces there to maintain the security of Kashmir from external invasion or any other internal troubles. It was always a condition that we must have enough forces, and we were the judges of that. We had said that we will withdraw the bulk of our forces, that is, when Pakistan armies had gone to Pakistan. We felt we could do that. This was more or less the position. Then came the cease fire and these talks are taking place. These talks had got rather struck over the interpretation of the Resolutions passed in August 1948 and January 1949, by the United Nations Commission. I shall not go into those details.

Now, Dr. Graham has been dealing solely with this so-called demilitarization problem. He laid down at one time 12 proposals. I think, as far as I can remember, we agreed to eight, about one or two, we wanted some change, and we did not agree to one or two.

May I go back a little? We had agreed to two proposals of the United Nations Commission in 1948 and 1949. The other things happened in between. But, at a later period, the Security Council passed a Resolution with which we did not agree and we made it perfectly clear in the Security Council that we could not possibly accept that Resolution because, apart from the fact that it went against all that we have stood for and all the assurances we had given to our people and the people of Kashmir, and our responsibility for the defence of Kashmir, we felt that it went against even the Resolutions passed by the Security Council itself at the instance of the Kashmir Commission. It was going back on that. So, we never accepted that Resolution, or parts of that Resolution. Dr. Graham was appointed in terms of it later. We made it clear to Dr. Graham …

L.K. Maitra (Member from Nabadwip): Dixon's report preceded that.

Jawaharlal Nehru: I am not going into all matters. Other people came in between. I am saying that we did not accept that Resolution. But, it has always been our point of view in the Security Council and elsewhere that we shall gladly – because we want peace and settlement – discuss this matter with anybody, certainly with a representative of the United Nations, and we are prepared to treat him as a mediator, but on no account are we prepared to agree to something which was imposed upon us. We are not prepared to have anything imposed upon us, and we are not prepared to accept anything that goes against our own responsibilities in this matter. So, when Dr. Graham came – he came here as a mediator, not in furtherance, so far as we are concerned, of that Resolution of the Security Council which we had not accepted. I might add that throughout his stay here, his visits here, Dr. Graham has never mentioned that Resolution here. So, he concentrates his attention on the demilitarization – what is called demilitarization – of the State, and although we agreed to many things that he said, there has always been a gap between our position and the position taken up by Pakistan. That gap has not yet been bridged.

I should like to express, if I may, my admiration for Dr. Graham and his sincere efforts and extraordinary patience. He has, undoubtedly, I believe, tried his utmost to achieve results. He desires it, and in some matters he has made progress too, but a certain gap still remains. So far as we are concerned, if I may say so with all respect, we have also been very patient, and we are prepared to match our patience with others' patience, because the consequences of being impatient are bad. So, these talks are going on, and certain reports appear in the newspapers. They are sometimes partly true, partly not true; it becomes very difficult for us to deal with these reports which are not made by any official source, but get out nevertheless. Now, that is so far as Dr. Graham is concerned.

Now, to go back to the other aspect. The position in 1948 in regard to Kashmir and all other States, the acceding States, was that they had acceded on three basic subjects – Foreign Affairs, Defence and Communications. But, then, the other States in India, all of them almost, were more closely integrated – the process of closer integration started, and was achieved, very largely again at the instance of Sardar Patel ... practically we had removed any difference between the old States and the old Provinces. It is true that provisionally some States were called B States, some were called A States, and some C States, but that is exceedingly temporary, and that goes, that must go and it is going. In effect, that difference which marked a Province and an old State was gone, and India became a much more closely integrated State.

Now, while that process was going on in regard to other States, it did not go on in regard to Jammu and Kashmir State, deliberately, for a variety of reasons. Well ... one reason was that the whole matter was in a fluid state, before the United Nations, etc. Reason number two equally important, that from the very beginning, for obvious factors, we had recognized that the position of Kashmir was somewhat different. Thirdly, that from the very beginning we had repeated that – from even before the Partition, I may inform the House – that no step will be taken about Jammu and Kashmir State without the concurrence and consent of the people of Kashmir. So, deliberately, Kashmir remained with those three subjects, and those three subjects only. Of course, when I say three subjects like Defence, Communications and Foreign Affairs, please remember that each subject itself is a category of subjects. It is not a small subject, it is a category, if you go into details. We did not touch that. And Sardar Patel was all this time dealing with these matters.

This came to an end in November, I think, of 1949 when we were designing our Constitution in the Constituent Assembly. Well, we could not leave everything quite vague and fluid there. Something had to be stated in our Constitution about Jammu and Kashmir State. That problem had to be faced by Sardar Patel. Now, he did not wish to say very much, he wanted to leave it, we all wanted to leave it in a fluid condition because of these various factors, and gradually to develop those relations, those legal and constitutional relations, and not to force the pace in any way. As a result of this, a rather unusual provision was made in our Constitution relating to Jammu and Kashmir. That provision is now in Article 370 in Part XXI, Temporary and Transitional Provisions. Now, that article if you will look into it – I will not trouble you by reading it. If you refer to it, if you are interested, you will see the position that emerged at the time of our finalizing our Constitution. And I might say that that Article 370, although it is by no means a final article, nevertheless, it defined more precisely the relationship of that unit, that constituent unit, with the Union of India. After that, on the 20th of January, the President issued an Order in terms of that Article 370, a President's Order defining the categories of subjects and parts of the Constitution that should be applicable to the Jammu and Kashmir State. Now, the position since the Constitution was framed is thus contained in Article 370 and in the President's Order following it. Article 370 was obviously of a transitional nature, and it allowed the President to make any additions to it, any variations to it, later on, the object being that if any change or addition was required, we need not have to go through the cumbrous process of amending our Constitution, but the President was given authority to amend it in the sense of adding a subject, part of a subject, whatever, it was, to the other subjects in regard to Kashmir. But in Article 370, the old principle was repeated and emphasized that all these changes or any change required the approval of the Constituent Assembly of the Jammu and Kashmir State. Now, when this was put down in our Constitution, there was no Constituent Assembly of Jammu and Kashmir State, but we envisaged it. We had envisaged it for a long time. And if the Constituent Assembly was not there, then, it required the consent of the Jammu and Kashmir Government. So, that was the position.

The House will appreciate that throughout our position has been, from before Partition, that we will not take any step which might be considered a step in the nature of compulsion or coercion, that everything should flow with the consent of the people concerned. That was the basic position. In addition to that fact, when this became an international issue, we did not wish to do anything which might be thought as if we were trying to override or bypass any assurance that we had given to the United Nations. This rather fluid condition continued, and our relationship was fluid in this sense, namely legally fluid: otherwise there was no difficulty and we carried on. It might have continued some time longer, one year, or two years, or three years. There is nothing to compel us. We were getting on in an ordinarily friendly and co-operative way. There was no other difficulty. There were minor matters. We discussed them and decided them.

Then came actually the Constituent Assembly of Kashmir into being, and it came into being with our goodwill sometime last year. When the subject that the first elections to the Constituent Assembly were going to take place was mentioned, there was a good deal of opposition to this idea in some foreign countries, which was voiced in the Security Council. And I need not say that Pakistan disliked it intensely. However, I saw no reason why and I see no reason now as to why any foreign country should interfere with the internal relationship of Kashmir with India, and what the people of Kashmir do to themselves. If other countries objected to that, we objected strongly to their objection, and we carried on. So, this Constituent Assembly came into existence last year and it has done various things, various important reforms. It has introduced but then it set down to itself the major task of drawing up a Constitution for the Jammu and Kashmir State. Now immediately we were faced with this problem. It is all right to have a fluid state for some time, but when you draw up a precise Constitution you have to be precise. This was the background and the reason for the talks we have been having amongst ourselves and with the leading members of the Jammu and Kashmir Government. We had no desire to make the relationship as a static, unchanging, or a finalized one; because the position is a dynamic one, a changing one. Nevertheless, it was perhaps too fluid and once a Constitution is going to be framed, a greater precision was necessary and it was obviously necessary that there should not be any contradictory provision in that which might not conform to the provisions of our Constitution. Hence these talks. Well, we had these talks for the last few days, and I am going to tell you now what has emerged from these talks.

But before I say that, I would like to remind you that one of the first things that this Constituent Assembly did was to tackle the land reform question, and in the course of a few months, they have successfully accomplished them or almost accomplished them. I confess that I look with some envy on the speed and celerity with which they have performed this task there, considering the enormous trouble we have had in the various States in India, the difficulties, the obstructions and the delays that we have had to face, and so I became a little envious when I saw how this was done in Kashmir State. Now I might just give you some indication of what was done there. It is said that they have expropriated the landlords there. That is not quite correct. They have put a ceiling on land holdings, the ceiling is roughly 23 acres, plus orchards. They did not touch orchards. They have allowed about 23 acres to remain with every person possessing land, plus the orchards he possesses ... And the House ought to remember that orchards are very important in Kashmir which is a great fruit-growing country. Then there are some other lands, grazing lands, etc.; they are also still with the landholders. That matter will be considered further later. I said that each person has been allowed 23 acres. It should be remembered that the average holding of land in Kashmir State is barely two acres, and so the 23 acres is a fairly generous holding ceiling that has been given.

Now in regard to the talks we have had, the position, obviously the admitted position, is that the Jammu and Kashmir State is a constituent part or unit of the Indian Republic. It is a unit of India and is, therefore, a part of the territory of India. That is the basic position.

The question of citizenship arose obviously. Full citizenship applies there. But our friends from Kashmir were very apprehensive about one or two matters. For a long time ... in the Maharaja's time, there had been laws ... preventing any outsider, that is, any person from outside Kashmir, from acquiring or holding land in Kashmir. If I may mention it, in the old days the Maharaja was very much afraid of a large number of Englishmen coming and settling down there, because the climate is delectable, and acquiring property. So, although most of their rights were taken away from the Maharaja under the British rule, the Maharaja stuck to this that nobody from outside should acquire land there. And that continues. And in the State subjects notification by the Maharaja, they have defined four grades of subjects. Class number one, Class two, Class three and Class four. And unless you come in one of these classes, you just cannot acquire land there, or any immovable property. So the present Government of Kashmir is very anxious to preserve that right because they are afraid, and I think rightly afraid, that Kashmir would be overrun by people whose sole qualification might be the possession of too much money and nothing else, who might buy up and get the delectable places. Now they want to vary the old Maharaja's law to liberalize it, but nevertheless to have checks on the acquisition of lands by persons from outside. So far as we are concerned, I agree that under Article 19, clause (5), of our Constitution, we think it is clearly permissible both in regard to the existing law and any subsequent legislation. However, we agreed that this should be cleared up. The old State's subjects definition gave certain privileges regarding this acquisition of land, the services, and other minor things, I think, state scholarships and the rest. So, we agreed and noted down this: 'The State Legislature shall have power to define and regulate the rights and privileges of the permanent residents of the State, more especially in regard to the acquisition of immovable property, appointments to services and like matters. Till then the existing State law should apply.'

Then there was another matter relating to citizenship, because owing to these troubles in Kashmir since 1947 and a little before and after, there have been large number of people who have gone out of Kashmir but want to return. So there must be provision made for them to return. In fact, in our own Constitution, some provision has been made, and I might inform the House that this question was raised early this year or last year about the inclusion of a large number of migrants from East Bengal. We could not include them in our electoral rolls, because they came too late. We are including them now. Those that fulfil the conditions will all come in. So those who had gone away from Kashmir into Pakistan or elsewhere and who normally speaking might not be eligible for citizenship should be provided for, if they want to return. So we said: 'Special provision should be made in the laws governing citizenship for the return of those permanent residents of Jammu and Kashmir State, who went to Pakistan in connection with the disturbances of 1947 or earlier in fear of them, and could not return. If they return they should be entitled to the rights and privileges and obligations of citizenship.'

Then came the question of fundamental rights. Now there was general agreement that there should be fundamental rights and these fundamental rights should apply to the State. But again there were great apprehensions in the minds of our friends from Kashmir. First of all, the question was how far these fundamental rights might not come in the way of their land legislation now or any later development of it. Certainly we did not want them to come in the way of their land legislation. We like their land legislation … We thought it was very good. In fact it is quite impossible to upset a thing that has been done, but we said the matter should be cleared. The second thing was this owing to all this business of invasion of Kashmir State, war, ceasefire, all kinds of continuing tensions, difficulties due to infiltration, etc. – constant attempts are made by infiltration, espionage cases are repeatedly heard, there is sabotage and the rest, but if you go to that State, you find normalcy there, that is to say, the State is functioning adequately normally, but behind that normalcy there is this tension, constant tension of an enemy trying to come in to create trouble, to disturb, and all that. And the State Government has to be wary and watchful all the time, and so we were told that it was possible that some part of the fundamental rights provisions might very well hamper the activities of the State Government from taking these precautions and these measures. We agreed that it was essential and in the interests of Kashmir situated as the State is now, that the State Government should have that authority. So subject to this, further consideration can be given to it as to how this could be done …

Then in regard to the Supreme Court, it was agreed that the Supreme Court should have original jurisdiction in respect of disputes mentioned in Article 131[4] of the Constitution of India. It was further agreed that the Supreme Court should have jurisdiction in regard to fundamental rights which are applied to that State. On behalf of the Government of India we recommended that the advisory tribunal in the State which is designated as His Highness's Board of Judicial Advisers should be abolished, and the jurisdiction exercised by it should be vested in the Supreme Court of India, that is to say, that the Supreme Court should be the final Court of Appeal in all civil and criminal matters as laid down in the Constitution of India. The Kashmir Government delegation had no objection to this. They were prepared to agree but they said they would like to consider the matter in some detail further.

---

[4] Editor's note: Article 131 in the Constitution of India 1949:

Original jurisdiction of the Supreme Court Subject to the provisions of this Constitution, the Supreme Court shall, to the exclusion of any other court, have original jurisdiction in any dispute

(a) between the Government of India and one or more States; or
(b) between the Government of India and any State or States on one side and one or more other States on the other; or
(c) between two or more States, if and in so far as the dispute involves any question (whether of law or fact) on which the existence or extent of a legal right depends: Provided that the said jurisdiction shall not extend to a dispute arising out of any treaty, agreement, covenant, engagements, and or other similar instrument which, having been entered into or executed before the commencement of this Constitution, continues in operation after such commencement, or which provides that the said jurisdiction shall not extend to such a dispute.

Now I come to the question which has been much discussed and referred to in the newspapers, the question of the Head of the State.

I might mention that apart from past history when this Constituent Assembly met in Kashmir, the inaugural address to that Assembly stated quite clearly some of the policies that they were going to pursue, and among these policies was the election, by democratic process, of the Head of the State. That has been the declared policy of the National Conference Organisation in Kashmir for a long time. We had no objection with regard to the enunciation of that principle then. Now, after careful consideration – because we have always had to consider two matters: firstly to give effect to the wishes of the people of the State and secondly, to give effect to our own Constitution – we have come to an agreed formula. Of course, you will not attach too much importance to the language – a word here or there. For legal and constitutional purposes the words may be changed, but it describes the way we have been thinking and what we have agreed to. Now it was agreed:

(1) that the Head of the State shall be the person recognized by the President on the recommendation of the Legislature of the State. (How the Legislature of the State recommends is a matter for the Legislature. Whether it is by the process of election or not it is for them to decide: it may be by the process of a majority, or two-thirds majority; it is entirely for them to decide. Anyhow they recommend and then it is for the President to recognize.)
(2) He, that is, the Head of the State, shall hold office during the pleasure of the President.
(3) He – the Head of the State – may by writing under his hand addressed to the President, resign his office.
(4) Subject to the foregoing provisions of this article, the Head of the State shall hold office for a term of five years from the date he enters upon his office, provided that he shall, notwithstanding the expiration of his term, continue to hold successor enters upon his office. That is so far as the Head of the State is concerned.

Then there has been a good deal of misunderstanding in regard to the National Flag. This has been cleared up, I think, adequately by public statements made. Nevertheless, we thought that this should be further cleared up. Sheikh Abdullah, the Prime Minister of Jammu and Kashmir State, had stated publicly that the question did not arise so far as they were concerned because the National Flag was the supreme flag and it had exactly the same status and position in the Jammu and Kashmir State as in any other part of India. The State Flag was in no sense a rival to the National Flag, but for historical and sentimental reasons connected with their struggle for freedom in Kashmir, they wanted this State symbol to continue. This was agreed to. It was added that this should be made clear in a formal manner, preferably by the Constituent Assembly of the State.

Then in regard to the President of India, it was agreed that the powers to reprieve and commute death sentences, etc. should belong to the President of India.

There has been some talk about financial integration. It was decided that such financial arrangements between the State and the Government of India should be considered further and details worked out. The position, as I said, is a dynamic, changing one. Matters have to be gone into in some detail; so whatever the financial arrangements might be, we shall gradually work them out.

Then there is the question of emergency powers contained in our Constitution, more especially in our Article 352 of the Constitution. It was agreed to; I will remind the House what Article 352 is: in case of invasion, external danger or internal disturbances, the President has power to declare a state of emergency, and then various consequences flow from it. This Parliament is then seized of the position. Now this was agreed to; but the friends from Kashmir were slightly apprehensive of what 'internal disturbances' meant there. For the rest, they have said, of course, if there is a grave emergency this should happen. So, with regard to adding some words to clear up, not to clear up that matter but rather to bring in the fact that in the case of internal disturbances any action taken should be with the concurrence of the Government of the State, it was agreed that Article 352 of the Constitution should apply to the State with the addition at the end of the first paragraph of the following words: 'but in regard to internal disturbances, at the request or with the concurrence of the Government of the State'.

That is, the state of emergency will be declared with the concurrence of the Government of the State.

These are the principal things that have been discussed and I think that we have arrived at very satisfactory decisions – agreements which are in consonance with the wishes of the people of Kashmir and in consonance with our Constitution. I would repeat that there is nothing final about this and gradually we can fill in other details later. I presume that at the present moment, as I said, the relationship of Kashmir with the Union of India is governed more or less by Article 370 of our Constitution. Now the accession has been complete. There is a certain confusion in people's minds. The accession is complete in law and in fact, Jammu and Kashmir State is a constituent unit like any other, it is a part of the territory of India, the people of Jammu and Kashmir are citizens of India like any other. But the fact that the subjects to which Jammu and Kashmir has acceded are limited, or less than those applying to other States, that fact produces this misunderstanding as if there was partial accession. That is not so: Accession is quite complete. In fact, all the States acceded only in regard to these three subjects to begin with. It may be that we may have more subjects later, but we are proceeding and we propose to proceed always in such matters with the consent of the other parties concerned. Now, presumably the President of the Union will have to issue some order under

Article 370 of the Constitution to give effect to any of these modifications or changes that we have suggested. I am very grateful to you, Sir, and to the House for the indulgence shown to me.

I have great pleasure, therefore, in welcoming the motion which has been moved by the Prime Minister and I only suggest that the Prime Minister, if he thinks it right in his wisdom, might go a little further and decide that it is high time we wash our hands of the United Nations as far as our appeal is concerned. I do not suggest for a moment that we should withdraw from the United Nations. It would be an absolutely suicidal step, but as far as our appeal is concerned, the United Nations has played ducks and drakes with it for over five years and it is no good proceeding with it when the Kashmiri people have come into their own, they have an appointment with destiny, and are marching towards its fulfilment. Why should we stand in their way at this time? Let us do the right thing. We have already outstretched our hand of friendship and they have clasped it. Let us not make a mess of it. Let us go forward and let us try to cement the whole of India in such a consolidated friendship as would really bring about a new heaven and a new earth in our ancient country.

SYAMA PRASAD MOOKERJEE

(Lok Sabha: Calcutta South East)

Lok Sabha: 7 August 1952

On PM's Statement on Kashmir

I agree with the Prime Minister that the matter of Kashmir is a highly complicated one and each one of us, whatever may be his point of view, must approach this problem from a constructive standpoint. I cannot share the view of the last speaker that we are creating a new heaven and a new earth[5] by accepting the scheme which has been placed before the House on the motion of the Prime Minister. The question can be divided into two parts. As the Prime Minister narrated in his own statement, one relates to the international complications arising out of Kashmir and the other relates to the arrangements that have to be made between Kashmir and ourselves regarding the future Constitution of Kashmir. Since the time is limited, I do not propose to say much on the first issue.

[5] Editor's note: The speaker that Dr S.P. Mookerjee referred to was H.N. Mukerjee, a celebrated CPI MP.

It has been said that I was a party when the decision was taken to refer the Kashmir issue to the UNO. That is an obvious fact. I have no right, and I do not wish to disclose the extraordinary circumstances under which that decision was taken and the great expectations which the Government of India had on that occasion, but it is a matter of common knowledge that we have not got fair treatment from the United Nations which we had expected. As the Prime Minister pointed out, we did not go to the UNO with regard to the question of accession, because accession then was an established fact. We went there for the purpose of getting a quick decision from the UNO regarding the raids which were then taking place by persons behind whom there was the Pakistan Government … Four years have passed. The Prime Minister paid a compliment to Dr. Graham. He may or may not deserve it. In any case, it does not seem as though we are going to get much or anything at all out of the UNO. The war started in Korea. There was aggression there, and immediately those very big countries which are dominating the UNO called upon the whole world to stand by them in defence of freedom. Those very people were the first to oppose India's very simple stand regarding the aggression on what was not merely the soil of Kashmir but the soil of India. I know that technically no case could be withdrawn from the UNO. The Hyderabad case also is still there technically. The South African dispute is also technically before the UNO. But what about these cases? They are not making any progress. Somehow, we should withdraw ourselves, so far as a consideration of the Kashmir case is concerned, from the UNO. We can tell them respectfully that we have had enough of the UNO and let us now … try to settle the matter through our own efforts. I am not suggesting that India should withdraw from the UNO. The only matter regarding which the dispute still continues is about the one-third territory of Kashmir which is in the occupation of the enemy … It is a matter of national humiliation. We say that Kashmir is a part of India … a part of India is today in the occupation of the enemy and we are helpless. We are peace-lovers, no doubt. But peace-lovers to what extent? That we will even allow a portion of our territory to be occupied by the enemy? Of course, the Prime Minister said: thus far and no further. If the raiders enter into any part of Kashmir – he repeated it today also – he held out a threat of war not in relation to Pakistan and Kashmir, but war on a bigger scale between India and Pakistan.

Now, I would like to know from the Prime Minister: is there any possibility of our getting back this territory? We shall not get it through the efforts of the United Nations: we shall not get it through peaceful methods, by negotiations with Pakistan. That means we lose it. Unless we use force and the Prime Minister is unwilling to do so. Let us face facts – are we prepared to lose it?

Now, let me come to the concessions which have been made. It has been said that there is some provision in the Constitution that we are bound by the pledges which have been given. Pledges? Undoubtedly, so many pledges we have given. We gave a pledge to Hyderabad. Did we not say that there would be a Constituent Assembly for Hyderabad? It was followed by another pledge that the future of Hyderabad would be decided by the Legislative Assembly of Hyderabad. But is not Hyderabad already a part of the Indian Union – one of the Part B States? We gave pledges also to those princes whom we are liquidating in different forms today. If we talk of pledges we have given pledges on many other occasions. We gave pledges to the minorities in East Bengal. That was given after the attainment of independence. The Prime Minister said in the Council of States the other day that even if Kashmir had not acceded to India, when Kashmir was attacked by the raiders on humanitarian grounds the Indian army could have marched to Kashmir and protected the distressed and oppressed. I felt proud. But if I make a similar statement, or even a similar suggestion for the purpose of saving the lives and honour of nine million of our fellow brethren and sisters – through whose sacrifices to some extent at least freedom has been achieved – I am a communalist, I am a reactionary, I am a war-monger!

Pledges? Undoubtedly pledges have been given. I am also anxious that pledges should be respected and honoured. What was the nature of the pledges? We did not give any new pledge to Kashmir …

As the Prime Minister explained the other day and today as well, what was the set-up we accepted when the British withdrew from India? There was the Indian India divided into India and Pakistan, and there was if I may call it the Princely India … So far as the 498 States were concerned, they came to India, acceded to India, as the Prime Minister said this morning, on the 14th August, 1947, in relation to three subjects only, but still, it was accession, full accession. Later on, they all came in in relation to all these subjects and were gradually absorbed in the Constitution of India that we have passed. Supposing some sort of fulfilment of the pledge that we are thinking of so literally in relation to Kashmir, was demanded by these states, would we have agreed to give that? We would not have because that would have destroyed India. But there was a different approach to the solution of those problems. They were made to feel that in the interest of India, in their interest, in the interest of mutual progress, they will have to accept this Constitution that we are preparing and the Constitution made elaborate provisions for naturally absorbing them into its fabric. No coercion; no compulsion. They were made to feel that they would get what they wanted from this Constitution.

May I ask – was not Sheikh Abdullah a party to this Constitution? He was a Member of the Constituent Assembly; but today he is asking for special treatment. Did he not agree to accept this Constitution in relation to the rest of India, including 497 States. If it is good enough for all of them, why should it not be good enough for him in Kashmir?

We are referred to the provision in the Constitution. The Member from Bihar in his ignorance, I will not say in his abounding knowledge, and also the new convert from Birbhum this morning said there was going to be compulsion; that we are going to hold a pistol at the head of Jammu and Kashmir saying that they must accept our terms. I have said nothing of the kind. How can we say that? What is the provision we have made in the Constitution? Article 373 – read it and read the speech of Shri Gopalaswami Ayyangar[6] when he moved the adoption of that extraordinary provision. What was the position then? All the other States had come into the picture. Kashmir could not because of special reasons which were enumerated in the speech of Shri Gopalaswami Ayyangar. They were: first, the matter was in the hands of the Security Council; secondly, there was war; thirdly, a portion of Kashmir territory was in the hands of the enemy; and lastly an assurance had been given to Kashmir that a Constituent Assembly would be allowed to be formed and the wishes of the people of Kashmir ascertained through a plebiscite. Those were the factors that had yet to be fulfilled and that was why a permanent decision could not be taken. It was a temporary provision. But read the speech of Mr. Gopalaswami Ayyangar …

He said categorically that he and also the Kashmir Government hoped that Jammu and Kashmir would accede to India just as any other State has done and accept the provisions of the Constitution. It is not a question of compulsion on our part. The Constitution of India does not say that whatever the Constituent Assembly of Jammu and Kashmir would ask for, India would give. That is not the provision. The provision is – agreement, consent. I agree.

Certain proposals have been made today. Some of us do not like them. What are we to do? If we talk we are reactionaries, we are communalists, we are enemies. If we keep quiet and if a catastrophe comes after a year, then: you were a party to it, you kept quiet – therefore, you are stopped from saying anything.

I am most anxious, as anxious as anybody else that we should have an honourable, peaceful settlement, with Kashmir. I realize the great experiment which is being made on the soil of Kashmir. Partition did not help anybody. I come from an area where sufferings are continuous, they are going on. We feel every day, every hour, the tragic effects of Partition, the tragic possibilities of approaching this national

---

[6] Editor's note: Diwan Bahadur Sir Narasimha Gopalaswami Ayyangar was an Indian civil servant and statesman, who served as the prime minister of the princely state of Jammu and Kashmir and later as a minister in the first Cabinet of independent India. He was a member of the Drafting Committee of the Constitution of India, the leader of the Rajya Sabha, a 'minister without portfolio' looking after Kashmir Affairs, and the Minister for Railways. In his Kashmir Affairs role, he represented India at the United Nations Security Council and later drafted Article 370 of the Indian Constitution that granted autonomy to Jammu and Kashmir.

problem from a narrow, communal and sectarian point of view. Why did we not utter a single word against the policy of Sheikh Abdullah so long? I could have spoken. I came out of this Government two and a half years ago. On the other hand, I supported, wherever I spoke publicly, the policy of the Kashmir Government. I said that this was a great experiment which was going on and we have to keep quiet and see that the experiment is made a success. We must be able to show that India is not only in theory, but also in fact, a country where Hindus, Muslims, Christians and everyone will be able to live without fear and with equality of rights. That is the Constitution that we have framed and which we propose to apply rigorously and scrupulously. There may be some demands to the contrary here and there. But do not regard that, whenever an attack is made on certain matters of policy, some narrow, sectarian, communal motive is prompting us. Rather it is the fear that history may repeat itself. It is the fear that what you are going to do may lead to the balkanization of India, may lead to the strengthening of the hands of those who do not want to see a strong United India, may lead to the strengthening of those like my friends to the right who do not believe that India is a nation, but is a combination of separate nationalities. That is the danger.

... Sheikh Abdullah has asked for ... certain changes to be made in the Constitution. Let us proceed coolly, cautiously, without any heat or excitement. Let us examine each of them and ask him and ask ourselves: if we make an allowance, in respect of these matters do we hurt India, do we strengthen Kashmir? ... I shall not say anything blindly because it transgresses some provisions of ... the Constitution of India ... I would have liked the Prime Minister to have sent for some of us in the Opposition when Sheikh Abdullah was here. He faces us today with his decisions. I do not like those public discussions because I know their repercussions may not be desirable in some quarters. He might not have accepted our suggestions, but I would have liked to have met him – those of us who differ from the Prime Minister's attitude on this question. I met him at a private meeting and we had a full and frank discussion. But we would have liked to have met Sheikh Abdullah and others in a friendly way and explained our point of view to them. We want to come to an agreement, an agreement which will make it possible for India to retain her unity and Kashmir to retain her separate existence from Pakistan and be merged with India.

Since when did the trouble start? Let us look at it dispassionately. Since Sheikh Abdullah's return from Paris some time ago statements started to be made by him which disturbed us. Even then we did not speak out. His first statement he made in an interview which he gave when he was abroad was about his vision of an independent Kashmir. And then when he came, he amplified it, then again retracted from it and gave an explanation, and then the speeches which he has made during the last few months were of a disturbing character. If he feels that his safety lies in remaining out of India, well, let him say so; we will be sorry for it, but it may become inevitable. But if he feels honestly otherwise, as I have always hoped and wished, then certainly it is for him also to explain why he wants these alterations to be made.

He spoke in the Constituent Assembly of Kashmir about three or four months ago, words which have not been withdrawn, but words which created a good deal of misgivings in the minds of all Indians, irrespective of party affiliations. I do not know whether the Prime Minister saw this: 'We are a hundred per cent, sovereign body. No country can put spokes in the wheel of our progress. Neither the Indian Parliament nor any other Parliament outside the State has any jurisdiction over our State.' It is an ominous statement. I shall make an offer to the Prime Minister and to Sheikh Abdullah. I shall give my full, whole-hearted support to the scheme as an interim measure. The Prime Minister said today that nothing is final. It cannot be final, because things have to be discussed in their various details. But even then I am prepared to give my support. Let two conditions be fulfilled.

Let Sheikh Abdullah declare that he accepts the Sovereignty of this Parliament. There cannot be two Sovereign Parliaments in India. You talk of Kashmir being a part of India, and Sheikh Abdullah talks of a Sovereign Parliament for Kashmir. It is inconsistent. It is contradictory. This Parliament does not mean a few of us here who are opposing this. This Parliament includes a majority of people who will not be swayed by any small considerations. And why should he be afraid of accepting the Sovereignty of this Parliament of Free India?

Secondly, it is not a matter of changing the provisions of the Constitution by the President's order. Let us look at some of the changes which are being sought for. The Maharaja. We are supporters of the Maharaja! That is what is said against us. I have never met the Maharaja. I do not know him personally. We are not supporters of this Maharaja, or of any Maharaja as such. But the Maharaja is there not by his own free will. The Parliament of India, the Constitution has made him what he is, namely, the constitutional head of Jammu and Kashmir. And what is the irony? At present, Sheikh Abdullah's Government is responsible to this Maharaja according to the Constitution, responsible to one who is being described as a wretched fellow who has to be turned out lock, stock and barrel. The Maharaja is there as a constitutional head. If you feel that this should be taken out, change your Constitution. Say that there will be no hereditary Rajpramukhs. It is a matter worthy of consideration. Let us consider it. But see the way in which it has been put: a Hindu Maharaja is being removed. That is one of the war cries in Pakistan. But who finished the royal powers of Hindu Maharajas? Not Sheikh Abdullah, but the Constitution of Free India. We did it. We said that no ruler would have any extraordinary powers, that he will be just head of the government which may be technically responsible to him but later on responsible to an elected legislature.

But now great credit is being taken that a unique performance is being done in Kashmir. In every speech of his, he gave it: the Maharaja, the Dogra raj is being finished. Is that propaganda? Is that necessary? You are flogging a dead horse. It is finished. What is the use of saying it?

What about the elected Governor? I have got here the proceedings of the Constituent Assembly. The Prime Minister will remember that in our own Constitution, we at first made a provision for an elected Governor, and then later on, Sardar Patel and the Prime Minister and others felt that in the democratic set-up that we contemplated an elected Governor had no place. Read the speech. It was stated that the Governor will be there to act as the representative of the President, and if the Governor is elected by the people or the legislature and the Chief Minister is also elected as such there is every likelihood of a clash, then again, the Governor will be a party man. And the Prime Minister pointed out all these considerations and claimed that there was a very special reason why in order to retain the unity of India and contact between the Centre and all the States, the Governor should be nominated by the President. You just ignore these basic points because Sheikh Abdullah says: 'I want an elected head now.' Why can you not tell him and others what you have done in the Constitution, that originally we provided for an elected Governor but after a good deal of thought we did away with that? Even then I say if today in your wisdom you feel that an elected head is a necessity and it will help you, consider it. Bring it up as a specific proposal. Let us discuss the pros and cons of it. But suddenly my friend, Mr. Hiren Mukerjee, says: people are clamouring for an elected head ... Are you going to have elected heads everywhere? In fact, as things are happening, we may abolish Governors altogether. Governorships are often reserved for various classes of persons – disappointed, defeated, rejected, unwanted Ministers and so forth. We need not have this class at all. Or if you want to have them, have them. I am not particularly interested. But this is a change for which no justification is given.

And then the flag. The flag has a significance. It will not do for the Prime Minister to say that it is a matter of sentiment. It was announced in the papers three days ago that the Indian flag will fly only on two ceremonial occasions and otherwise, the State flag alone will fly there. If you feel that the unity and integrity of India are not affected and it will not lead to fissiparous tendencies being generated, accept it and do it for all. But why do it as a matter of surrender to Sheikh Abdullah's demand?

He wanted to call himself the Prime Minister. That is how he first started. Some of us did not like it. We know one Prime Minister of India including Kashmir, that is the Prime Minister who is sitting here. How can you have two Prime Ministers, one Prime Minister in Delhi and another Prime Minister in Srinagar, who will not call himself the Chief Minister, but a Prime Minister? At first I thought it was a small matter and we should not look at it but see how the process is developing – some sort of special treatment at every step ... Look at the citizenship rights and fundamental rights. What is it that we are doing? ... Has the House discussed the pros and cons of the recommendations which have been made? You are changing without giving much thought to the provisions of the Constitution regarding citizenship. It was said that rich people are rushing to Kashmir and purchasing property. As the Prime Minister mentioned in his statement, in Article 19(5) there is a provision. We discussed this article threadbare when we framed the Constitution. There were attempts made by various provinces and they wanted to have some special protection against unauthorized purchases of land on a large scale. What is it that we have said? We have said that any State legislature may pass a law, imposing reasonable restrictions regarding acquisition of property or movement from one part to another in the public interest, or in the interest of the Scheduled Castes and Scheduled Tribes. If Sheikh Abdullah feels that in Kashmir some special restriction should be done, the clause is there. I would like to ask the Prime Minister categorically about this ... Is it intended that the restrictions which the Kashmir Assembly will impose will be in accordance with this exception or is it proposed to give it something more? There are four classes of citizens. I have got the details, but I have not the time to go through them. But those were done in the time of the much cursed Maharaja. Are they to be maintained or are they going to abolish the four different categories of citizenship? I am reminded of a story which was written by Lord Curzon in a book. A distinguished nobleman from England went to the court of the Shah of Persia 50 or 60 years ago accompanied by his wife. Both of them were presented and the Shah was a bit inattentive and the secretary asked: 'What should be the honour done to the lady?' There were three different categories of Order of Chastity and the award was made 'Order of Chastity – class three'. That is how the order came out and then it was realized that something had been done which was of a staggering character, and of course amends were made after the damage was done. Four classes of citizenship in Jammu and Kashmir – what for? They should be abolished. There should be only one class of citizenship. Would Indians take all your property? ... Supposing some Indian comes and purchases some property, you may have legislative measures. We have accepted it. What is the fear? We have a Kashmiri Prime Minister of India. We have a Kashmiri Home Minister of India. We are happy in India. We do not mind it. We welcome them ... Is it feared that Indians will go and invade Kashmir and one of them will become the Chief Minister of Jammu and Kashmir? We are not going to raid Jammu and Kashmir. I have never visited this beautiful part. I would like to go and stay there for some time. I have not got the money to purchase a house. In any case, I would like to go there ... The Prime Minister mentioned two or three things – scholarships and services, etc. What is this 'etc.'? And why services?

In services, do you want to make a difference between one citizen and another? Even there, as you know, in our Constitution, Parliament and Parliament alone has the right to make special provisions regarding entrance to services for those who have to be protected. Now there are similar demands made in the South. I have been going through their demands during the last few weeks. They also feel perturbed by the strict operation of some of these provisions. When you throw open the doors to them, they also will want similar protection.

There is another thing to which the Prime Minister has not referred ... As you know, two lakhs of people have gone away to Pakistan. There is a provision that a special law will be incorporated to get these people back to Kashmir. War is still going on. Fundamental rights regarding civil liberty are proposed to be made more strict, on the one hand then on the other, you are going to throw open the doors and allow Pakistanis to go to Kashmir; for this there is to be a special law and there is a special agreement. Why this anxiety on the part of Sheikh Abdullah to make special provision for getting back those who ran away to Pakistan, and who are not prepared to come? Is there any point in it? How will it affect security?

Maulana Masoodi (Member from Jammu and Kashmir): Did not run away; were driven away or killed.

Dr. S.P. Mookerjee: Those who have been killed cannot go back. Those who are alive can come back tomorrow if they honestly believe in India and if they really want to live in Jammu. They must be tested. Let them come back. No special provision is needed for it. So far as Jammu is concerned ... it was a most tragic state. It was done by both sides. There were Muslims who were bitter and there were Hindus who were bitter. That was a dark period when many parts of India were like that, but today, what is the position? ... Mr. Ajit Prasad Jain, I hope will be able to say how many thousands of refugees have come to India. They have come away from Jammu and Kashmir and are a burden on India. Why should there not be a special provision here in the agreement that promptly they will be taken back to Jammu and Kashmir? There are several thousand of them who have come. Why are they not going back? I do not know how many Pandits have come away from Kashmir. They also must go back to Kashmir.

A.P. Jain (Member from Uttar Pradesh): I may inform the hon'ble Member that a large number of them are going back to Jammu and Kashmir.

Dr. S.P. Mookerjee: I am glad these are all going back. They have not yet gone back ... In the one-third portion of Jammu and Kashmir which is now under Pakistani occupation ... nearly one lakh Hindus and Sikhs have ... taken shelter within the Kashmir territory. What will happen to them? They will have to be taken care of. You are thinking of those who have become Pakistanis for the time being. You will reconvert them and reconfer on them the status of Kashmiri citizens but those unfortunate beings who today have taken shelter, how will they be given accommodation? Is there land enough for them? These are matters which had not received any attention.

... If there is an emergency on account of internal disturbance, the President of India will not have the last say. Why this fear of the President of India? Can you contemplate a more gratuitous insult to the President of India? Here the Kashmir Government must conform to the Constitution. Why should they request if there is an internal disturbance which is the creation of their own misdeeds?

Why should they request you if, for instance, they are in league with others from the upper side, China or Russia, through our other friends? Why should they come and request you for your interference? I would expect the Prime Minister to tell me whether the other emergency provisions apply or not. As you know, there are two other very important emergency provisions in the Constitution. Article 354 relates to application of provisions relating to distribution of revenues while a Proclamation of Emergency is in operation and the other article is 356 relating to provisions in case of failure of Constitutional machinery in States. Has Sheikh Abdullah accepted the application of Article 356 or has he accepted the more important provision contained in Article 360 – provisions as to financial emergency. Has he accepted that provision? The Prime Minister does not make any reference to it. The Supreme Court's jurisdiction also has not yet been accepted.

I shall conclude, by making this constructive suggestion. These comments which I made, naturally I had to make without commenting in detail on the reactions of Sheikh Abdullah. He wrote to me and said that he would like to meet me when he was in Delhi last time. I was not here on that day. So I could not meet him. I sent him a friendly reply. Perhaps I would meet him sometime. It is not a question of his meeting me or I meeting him. I submit that we must proceed according to certain standards. First of all, there is no question of the President, by virtue of his power to make orders, altering the provisions of the Constitution in material respects.

If the Prime Minister feels that a case has been made out for re-examination of certain important provisions, for instance ... that land should be taken without payment of compensation, provide for it in the Constitution. You consider all these items and make your provisions so elastic that you can apply them either to the whole of India or you can apply them to only such parts where this Parliament of India will feel that such special treatment is necessary. Proceed in accordance with a constitutional manner, not just play with the Constitution. It is a sacred document, and it is a document on which much labour and much thought were bestowed. If you feel some changes are necessary in order to take into consideration the new set-up that is slowly developing in India, whether in Kashmir or other parts of India, by all means let the people of the country have a chance to express their opinion.

Lastly a charge was levelled that some of us have advocated separate consideration of Jammu and Ladakh. I would assure you and the House that I do not want that Jammu and Kashmir should be partitioned. I know the horrors of partition. I know the results which may ensue if partition comes. But the responsibility for preventing partition will rest on those who are today the masters of Jammu and Kashmir and are not prepared to adopt the Constitution of India. What is the crime if today the people of Jammu claim that they should be treated separately, in the sense that they should be allowed to join fully with India – mark it, it is not a question of running away from India – if they say that they would like to accept in toto the Constitution of free India, is there any crime that they then commit? I am not suggesting that you partition Jammu and Kashmir. I am not suggesting that you send Kashmir or Kashmir valley out of India. And it is not for me or for us sitting in this House to decide this matter. As the Prime Minister pointed out very rightly, it is the people of that territory who will have to decide. Now, suppose the people of Jammu and Ladakh feel that either it should be full accession in relation to the whole of Jammu and Kashmir, or, if that is not acceptable to Sheikh Abdullah, then, at least these two Provinces, the two separate entities could be justified historically or otherwise, that they should be allowed to join with India. Let Kashmir continue in any way that it likes, even with more autonomy, with less possibility of interference by India; that is a possibility which we cannot rule out. I hope that this question will be considered in its full possible implications.

My friend from Kashmir, Maulana Masoodi, for whom I have very great regard – I tried to follow his speech this morning – referred to Jammu, the last question which I would answer. Well, if this demand is made by Jammu, he said Jammu is a Province which in 1941 had a Muslim majority. He said that, but did not complete the story. Undoubtedly it was a Muslim majority province in 1941, but it became a Muslim majority including those districts which have now fallen into the Pakistan-occupied area. So, if you exclude those areas …

Maulana Masoodi: Are you going to surrender them?

Dr. S.P. Mookerjee: I am not going to surrender them. I am very glad he has put the question. The Prime Minister says that that area will not be re-occupied, but it is a different question. You are not going to re-occupy it, and it is not possible. In any case those people have worked against Jammu and Kashmir, they have become, as has been repeatedly said, more friendly to Pakistan, than to India.

An Hon'ble Member: Wrong.

Dr. S.P. Mookerjee: If you take the 1951 census figures – the figures have not been published, but it is on the basis of the territory that is under our occupation – 75 per cent of the population of Jammu will be Hindus. But I am not proceeding on the basis of Hindus and Muslims. Let me make it clear. I am proceeding on the basis of the will of the people to come to India either in whole or in part. If these two Provinces, Ladakh and Jammu, say that they will come to India with all these subjects, make it possible for them to do so.

The same right which you are claiming for Kashmir may also be demanded by the people of Jammu and Ladakh. Let us proceed in a friendly spirit. Sheikh Abdullah himself said about a month ago that he will have no objection if the people of Jammu and Ladakh really felt that they would go to India – I am not saying that you have it done immediately or you proceed in that way, but let it be possible for the people residing in those areas to make up their minds which way it will be good to proceed, and it will also be consistent with the same principles of self-determination which constitute the basic claims of Sheikh Abdullah, supported by the Prime Minister.

2

Abrogation of Article 370

In early August 2019, tens of thousands of additional troops were deployed in Jammu and Kashmir, the Amarnath Yatra was cancelled, schools and colleges were shut, tourists were ordered to leave, telephone and internet services were suspended and regional political leaders were placed under house arrest. There was a sense of foreboding among the people – and speculation that Article 35A of the Constitution, which gave some special privileges to the people of the state, would be scrapped. And then without any warning, on 5 August, in Parliament, the BJP-led government announced that it was revoking nearly all of Article 370, of which 35A is a part, and which has been the basis of Kashmir's complex relationship with the Indian Union.

Without any prior notice – as is the rule – the government moved the necessary bills to revoke Article 370. The protests by the Opposition – that the government should have circulated the text of the bills in advance, as is customary – fell on deaf ears. Displaying its brute strength, the government rammed through the changes.

***Ghulam Nabi Azad** (at the time a senior Congress leader and leader of Opposition in the Rajya Sabha and a former chief minister of Jammu and Kashmir) perhaps made the most moving speech of the day, opposing the revocation of Article 370. He stressed that over the years since the enactment of Article 370, Jammu and Kashmir had begun to integrate with the rest of India, through interstate and interreligious marriages, through students from the region studying in different parts of India. 'Integration is not achieved by making laws, it is achieved through winning hearts,' he said.*

GHULAM NABI AZAD

(Rajya Sabha: Jammu and Kashmir)

Rajya Sabha: 5 August, 2019

Cessation of all Clauses of Article 370 Except Clause (1), the Jammu and Kashmir Re-organization Bill, 2019, and the Jammu and Kashmir Reservation (Second Amendment) Bill, 2019

Mr. Deputy Chairman: LOP,[7] Hon'ble Ghulam Nabi Azad ji. I would request the members who are sitting in the Well to please go back to their respective seats and listen to the views of the Hon'ble LOP. (Interruptions.) … The members who are sitting in the Well are requested to go back to their respective seats and hear the views of the LOP …

Ghulam Nabi Azad: Hon'ble Deputy Chairman, Sir, the Bill on which I had to speak today and the Bill which was listed for discussion in the Rajya Sabha today was – Reservation for Economically Weaker Sections … Sir, I had certain views in my mind to be expressed while discussing this Bill today, but now it makes no sense to discuss this Bill … Jammu and Kashmir … history dates back to … 1947 when I was not even born … I had never imagined … that the State which is like the head of our India will be beheaded one day … for the last … week the entire Jammu and Kashmir and Ladakh was distressed and people were at a loss to understand the situation. I slept at 2.30 a.m. I was getting phone calls from Jammu and Kashmir and also from across the country. Different rumours were doing the rounds. Some people were saying that war has erupted, some said that the state is going to be bifurcated while … others said it's going to be divided into three parts. Some people were saying that delimitation is going to happen, someone said that Article 370 will be abrogated. There were also those who were saying that Article 370 will continue to exist, only 35(A) will be abrogated. Not only the people of Kashmir valley were worried and making phone calls, but the same was true about the people of Ladakh and Jammu. When I talk about Jammu, I refer to the region ranging from Rajouri Poonch to Jammu, from Kathua and Samba, from Udhampur to Ramban, Banihal and Kishtwar. I don't talk about Jammu city, Jammu is not only limited to the Jammu city but it has 10 districts and people belonging to all religions live there. In these 10 districts of Jammu, there is the population of Hindus, Muslims, Christians, Jains and Sikhs. Perhaps it might not be a matter of concern for a particular ideology but it is a matter of concern for all those whom I mentioned. But today what happened in the House was akin to the

[7] Editor's note: Leader of Opposition.

explosion of an atom bomb all of a sudden. When the Hon'ble Minister of Home Affairs came to the House, a kind of explosion took place. Many … apprehensions were being expressed last week. Paramilitary forces were being sent from here to Jammu and Kashmir and ADGP, JKP,[8] had asked all the SPs[9] if they had all the required material, if they did not have, it would be supplemented within 24 hours. Written advisory was being issued to the hospitals to not send any doctors on leave. I did not get any information about Leh but as regards Kargil Hill Council, I got a copy of the order of Deputy Commissioner, Kargil which prohibited all … officers … from proceeding on leave. Since this 27th … a written advisory of the Home Ministry said that all … pilgrims who had left for … Amarnath Yatra should start coming back and the tourists also should return. But for more than 500–600 students from across the country studying in the Central University, NITs[10] in the Kashmir valley, nothing was mentioned … in that advisory. For those students buses were made available on Saturday morning and they were being evacuated. Nothing was mentioned in the advisory about the lakhs of labourers from across the country who go there in the summers to work … labourers … carpenters … masons and … contractors … go there to build roads and buildings … since last week there was an atmosphere of fear … and terror in Jammu and Kashmir … I don't think there would be anyone in any corner of the world who would have thought that something like this would ever happen … There are many experts in Kashmir, but there may be higher number of experts in other countries … and perhaps none of them would have ever guessed that … the Home Minister would read out not only one but all four in one order … in the House and have them discussed and then passed the same day.

Hon'ble Chairman, Sir, this Bill runs into 57 pages. Here, even when we … get a one-page Bill … we argue … saying that we didn't get the opportunity to move amendments. As per our Parliament rules, the Bill should reach us two days prior to being introduced, so that we can read it and give amendments … We had 29 States – now you are bringing the number down to 28 so one State is eliminated … (Interruptions.) … Mr. Yadav, let me speak. I am not abusing. I am telling the truth. Are there 29 States in your Bill? If not, then one State has been eliminated. You tell me, please stand up, calculate and tell me whether after the passage of this Bill today, we will have 29 States. So, one State … has been erased from the map … (Interruptions.) … Please, try to understand.

… Sir … the State that would be erased … is not only the head and the crown of the country, it shares borders with China, Pakistan and the POK. When

[8] Editor's note: Additional Director General of Police, Jammu and Kashmir Police.

[9] Editor's note: Superintendents of Police.

[10] Editor's note: National Institute of Technology.

China attacked us, we had to fight a war against it. When we fought 3–4 wars with Pakistan, our Army protected our borders. And the people as well as the mainstream political parties of Jammu and Kashmir always stood by Army's side to fight Pakistan and China. We have our sources there – I have been the Chief Minister of that State and I can tell you that in our border States, particularly this one which shares its border with two countries – it's very important to have the support of the local people. Until and unless those people give you information, and tell you about the hideouts, you will not be able to achieve any success, no matter you keep fighting for years together. You can see what is happening in Afghanistan, because they don't get the crucial information, but here we have been successful in all the battles. Why? Because, our people who were nationalist and who wanted to live in India and considered India as their own country, always provided information to our security forces, be it Army, Army intelligence, IB or RAW. And the maximum information would come from the people of Kashmir as they were actually aware of the geography and people of the region. Whatever achievements we have made there so far, I would like to give its credit to the local Kashmiri people who have helped the forces – the armed forces, paramilitary forces and the security forces – with full conviction, as Maharaja Hari Singh did the accord and acceded to India. He did not choose Pakistan. The people of Kashmir did not consider Pakistan as their country despite its having the same religion. They consider India as their own country, they followed the secularism being practised in India. They opted for living with Hindu brethren in India rather than Muslims in Pakistan that was the trust. Today you have betrayed them. The trust with which the people of that time came to you – we were born in free India, we have full trust but I am talking about the people, who are still alive. They had a trust and they stayed here – they trusted Pandit Jawaharlal Nehru and Sardar Patel that they would protect them. They would not ruin their culture; they would not eliminate their history … their principles and they would not hurt their emotions. I would like to felicitate Motiram Baigra, Afzal Baig, Maharaja Hari Singh and then Dr. Karan Singh as well. From those days till today whenever … attempts were made to separate Kashmir, the people of Kashmir fought them bravely. The mainstream political parties have been decimated there. Hundreds of women have become widows because many people have been killed by militants while others lost their lives fighting with them. Our Army personnel have been killed, police and CRPF personnel have also been killed. After so many … sacrifices, today when the entire Jammu and Kashmir region had integrated into the mainstream, when the residents of this region were getting married to people belonging to the rest of the country, when inter-religion marriages were taking place, when the children … were studying in the medical colleges, engineering colleges and other institutes of technical education … so much … integration took place in the last 20–30 years, you have attempted to disintegrate this region. Integration is not achieved by making laws … When you win hearts, there is no need to formulate laws. No matter how many Constitutional Amendments you bring in, you will not be able to keep the people united unless you win their hearts.

I am not talking about Muslims. I am talking about Hindus, Muslims, Sikhs, Christians and Buddhists. I do not represent a particular sect or religion from Jammu and Kashmir, for me all are one. All those people belong to Jammu and Kashmir and Ladakh … after 1947, there was a Prime Minister of Jammu and Kashmir and a Sadar-i-Riyasat … Sadar-i-Riyasat is the Urdu equivalent of President. How many Prime Ministers have been there? Four, Sheikh Abdullah was Prime Minister for 5–6 years, succeeding him, Bakshi Ghulam Mohammad was Prime Minister for 14–15 years, then Khwaja Shams-ud-Din and then the, fourth Prime Minister was Ghulam Mohammad Sadiq and during his tenure, he was both the Prime Minister and the Chief Minister. We changed this system. The post of President was replaced by the post of Governor and the post of Prime Minister was replaced by the post of Chief Minister. So it started from the Maharaja, then changed to Prime Minister and President and you relegated it to Lieutenant Governor. This is a matter of shame that by installing a Lieutenant Governor, you have made Jammu and Kashmir a non-entity, so that you have the power of appointing even a peon or a clerk from here only. We can see what is happening … for the last four years the Chief Minister of Puducherry complains every day that the Lieutenant Governor is not letting him work. For every single thing, even to breathe or drink water, he needs to seek permission from the Lieutenant Governor. You have brought this law for … Jammu and Kashmir. Jammu and Kashmir was known world over for its history, its beauty, its culture and its tourism and you are going to make it a Union Territory. I would like to ask my brothers from Jammu to imagine that they are living in a UT and not in Jammu and Kashmir anymore. This has nothing to do with Hindus or Muslims. I am also from Jammu … (Interruptions.) … you try to make Gujarat a Union Territory … (Interruptions.) … Bring this Bill today only, let me see. It is very easy to say … (Interruptions.) … It is very easy to say … (Interruptions.) … Today the people of the concerned State are protesting. Try and bring the same Bill regarding your State and then see what happens. It is easy to say such things but don't take this politics so lightly. You should know that you are changing the history of India. Don't be so power drunk that you don't even realize … what you are doing. You have erased and destroyed the history of a State. You have converted it from a State to a Union Territory. You only know the geography of Jammu and Kashmir. Do you also know its history? Do you know that there are two districts in Ladakh – Leh and Kargil. Do you know that the population of Shia Muslims is 52 per cent and the population of Buddhists is 48 per cent in Ladakh? In this 52 per cent, there is 2–4 per cent population of some other religions as well, in Buddhist population there is about 2 per cent other population also. There is overwhelming majority amongst Buddhists. The history that you read twenty years ago is changed now. It is no more called a Buddhist State, population has grown tremendously after that. Now the situation has reversed. Ladakh is now a Muslim majority State ... for last thirty years our Buddhist brothers from Leh have been wanting it to be declared a Union Territory and the people from Kargil wanted to leave Ladakh and become a part of Kashmir province ... you don't read the law, history ... you read this, I am still alive. In 1991, I was a Union Minister. For months the Hill Council at Leh was on strike and there was Anti Hill Council in the Kargil. On behalf of Government of India, I went there for negotiation. Your MP was the Chairman and leader of my ... Legislative Party was the General Secretary. There was a point by you to dissolve. I had the first meeting with their forum and after a number of meetings, we reached this agreement with them that they will not be given the UT but ... the Hill Council. But the people of Kargil were demanding and they are still demanding not to stay with Ladakh. We cannot not leave Ladakh but we want to stay in Kargil. You gave Ladakh the status of a province just now, you should have taken a little bit of time to ensure its capital only in Leh. Out of compulsion you had to make both Leh and Kargil its capital. You had to do this only because the people of Kargil demand to be covered under Kashmir province. Do you know that this is a problem in one UT? Who will you appoint Chief Minister now? Ladakh was one of the most peaceful regions of Jammu and Kashmir and you have created a new rift between the Buddhists and Shia Muslims there. Now you have made Jammu and Kashmir a UT and a Lieutenant Governor will be its head. Leave us aside, from Sheikh Abdullah to Mr. Saadik, such intelligent people have been the Chief Ministers of this State. They are struggling with the politics of this region, but you will appoint an IAS Officer, a Joint Secretary or a person from your party as the Lieutenant Governor of this region and he or she will solve the problems of Jammu and Kashmir. You are very intelligent. You don't only rule India but the whole world but such a small fact you could not understand that now Jammu and Kashmir will be headed by a Lieutenant Governor ... You attempt to make a new India, so will you dismantle the old India ... and destroy it? ... in this process you will create a new India ... to garner votes please don't play with the history, unity, integrity and culture of India. Enough is enough. The day when this law is passed, will be a blot on the history of the country. In the history of India, in the history of this new India, this day will be considered as a blot when you are abrogating Article 370 and 35(A) from Jammu and Kashmir, when without the consent of the people of this region, you are bifurcating the State and applying delimitation on it ... destroying Kashmir. Before 1947 when people from outside India, people from Pakistan came, there would be one slogan 'Jis Kashmir ko khoon se seencha, woh

Kashmir hamara he'.[11] Today you are trampling upon the sacrifice done by those thousands of sisters, brothers and youth. You have erased that history. The people of India are prudent, their thinking is not only limited to votes, they think in the interest of the country, they think for the upliftment, unity, safety and progress of the country. The Hindus, Muslims, Sikhs and Christians of the country will never tolerate this black law brought by you. You might have brought this law on the basis of the majority and power that you have got, but you will not be able to align the people of this region with this law. Thank you very much.

[11] Editor's translation: The Kashmir that you have irrigated with your blood, that Kashmir is yours.

Section Twelve

Death, Disease and Famine

1

The Voice of Reason

In the first decade after Independence, as India's free government grappled with a range of issues, health was clearly a key sector. From the lack of medical facilities to a variety of diseases (some of which assumed epidemic proportions) to the all-important questions of child mortality and women's health, and indeed, to prejudices about mental health – the challenge was clearly gigantic. In his first term as Prime Minister, Jawaharlal Nehru appointed ***Rajkumari Amrit Kaur*** *as the country's first health minister, a position she held for 10 years with great distinction. In fact, she was the first woman to join the Union Cabinet. The khadi-clad Kapurthala princess, who had served as Mahatma Gandhi's secretary for close to 17 years, was also a member of the Constituent Assembly. A formidable sportswoman and a graduate of Oxford's Somerville College, she put both her lineage and education to good use – her achievements include the setting up of the All India Institute of Medical Sciences, her public campaign to tackle a massive outbreak of malaria and her efforts to bring clean drinking water to every home, her argument being that this would help check the spread of waterborne diseases. In this speech, she responds sharply and firmly to a Private Members' Bill, moved by S.V. Ramaswamy, a fellow Congress MP from Salem in Tamil Nadu. The Sterilization of the Unfit Bill was controversial as it sought 'to prevent procreation of human beings of undesirable physical and mental conditions by certain types of people ... '.*

RAJKUMARI AMRIT KAUR

(Lok Sabha: Mandi)

Lok Sabha: 30 July 1952

Sterilization of the Unfit Bill (Private Members' Bill)

Sir, I am very glad that you have given me just a few moments which I shall take to explain the attitude of Government in this matter. While I am extremely anxious, just as anxious as the hon'ble Mover of the Bill is, to eliminate the diseases that he has mentioned such as leprosy, syphilis, insanity and imbecility from the country, I wish to submit with all the emphasis at my command that this is not the way to achieve the end in view.

No Government in the world has any Act on its statute book as far as leprosy and syphilis are concerned. Syphilis, I may say, today by modern methods is absolutely curable. And then, while one child of a syphilitic may be syphilitic, there is no evidence to say that every child born of a syphilitic is going to be a syphilitic. In the matter of leprosy, medical opinion in the world is that it is not a hereditary disease. Leprosy has been eliminated from many countries, and if I have the means at my disposal, that is, the financial means, I guarantee to eliminate leprosy from this country also within a given period simply by isolating and segregating the cases of leprosy and their children. So, in regard to these two diseases, the question of sterilization should not apply.

In regard to insanity, in clause 2(5), 'unfit' has been defined as 'any person, male or female, who suffers from such a type of leprosy or syphilis, insanity or imbecility, congenital or otherwise, that he or she is likely to give birth to children like himself or herself unless sterilized'. We have not yet reached the stage that we can say what type of imbecility or even insanity is hereditary. Eugenics is a very great science, but it has not made all that progress which can enable any doctor to say that because a man today has lost his powers of reasoning, if he has a child, that child is necessarily going to be a lunatic. Therefore, I do not think that in view of all the medical evidence that is available to us, a Bill of this nature is necessary.

Sterilization of any man or woman is a very serious matter. No Government should at any time think of resorting to compulsion in this matter, unless one is absolutely certain of adverse results. Further, the Boards that have been suggested by the hon'ble Mover might even consist of those who are not experienced. Their decisions will not be conclusive. Then they go to a court where it will certainly not be wholly a legal matter. Experts will be required. Government administrative machinery will not be available for this, and I am not prepared to concede his viewpoint that it will not be expensive in regard to the consequential results, if this

Bill were made into law. Therefore, I want to oppose this Bill and reiterate that there are other ways and means of seeking the object which the hon'ble Mover would like to bring into being.

As I said, I, too, would like to eliminate so many things from this country, but the financial point of view, apart from the practical point of view, as also from the scientific point of view, the Bill is wholly unacceptable and I would ask the Mover of the Bill to withdraw it.

2

The Horror, the Horror

Officially, the 1971 war cost the Indira Gandhi government around ₹200 crore a week. The GDP growth rate for 1971–72 was severely hit as the economy grew by a mere 0.9 per cent, and with the additional expense of feeding over one crore Bangladeshi immigrants, the budgetary deficit rose. And then, the monsoons failed in successive years, in 1972 and 1973. An enormous swathe of the country faced droughts and, as a consequence, a massive shortage of foodgrains, pushing prices up. At the time, India was still importing food grains for sustenance. If the war had swallowed up a large chunk of the country's foreign exchange reserve, the rising cost of foodgrain import meant a further depletion. Inflation was at 22 per cent in 1972–73, over 20 per cent in 1974 and over 25 per cent in 1975.

It is against this backdrop that the Lok Sabha debated famine conditions in the country on 19 November 1974. In this moving speech, ***Jyotirmoy Basu****, a four-term MP, representing the CPI(M), who came to politics after seeing action in the Second World War and a stint at tea tasting, talks about 'hunger and death … stalking various parts of the country', bringing back memories of the 'spectre' of the 1943 famine in Bengal, while castigating the Indira Gandhi government for not doing enough.*

JYOTIRMOY BASU

(Lok Sabha: Diamond Harbour)

Lok Sabha: 19 November 1974

Motion for Adjournment on Famine Conditions in the Country

Today hunger and death are stalking various parts of the country. States like Assam, West Bengal, Orissa, Bihar, Gujarat, and Madhya Pradesh are the worst victims … a very reputed newspaper, *Economic Times* … in its editorial, says:

'The spectre of 1943 famine which had taken a toll of three million lives, stalks in West Bengal again. Calcutta streets are crowded with famished people, taking crumbs of food from garbage. Whatever euphemism the State Government might resort to, the stark reality can no longer be ignored. More than one third of the State's population of 45 million are facing starvation due to drought, floods and cyclone. There is obviously enough food in the countryside …'

That is the most important thing, Babu Jagjivan Ram[1]. '… conveniently hoarded under the protection of the garibi hatao Sarkar and no serious de-hoarding efforts have been made till recently. Voluntary efforts in Birbhum are reported to have led to arrests …'

That means nothing at all. In Assam, several thousands of people died of starvation in Dhubri sub-division of North Kamrup district; 74 per cent of the rural population of Assam are below the hunger line.

In West Bengal, about 17 million people by a rough estimate, are under starvation. Different figures have been given about starvation deaths, but it runs into several thousands. In Gujarat, particularly Saurashtra and Kutch, 17 out of 19 districts are worst affected. 15 million people are starving there. When Mr Morarji Desai[2] visited certain areas in Gujarat, people demanded poison from him instead of food because they could see no hope of life from the present Government. They knew they would only starve and die. North Bihar, where half the population of Bihar lives, is one of the worst affected areas; 9 out of 10 people are starving there. In Kerala, the Government have admitted there have been 550 starvation deaths. The real number is much more. In Orissa, at least 5 million people are under starvation. Conditions in MP are equally bad.

This Government is bluffing not only its own men but it is bluffing the world. I am quoting from a foreign paper, *Far Eastern Economic Review*:

'Hongkong, November 15, 1974.

India is trying its utmost to soft pedal reports of famine in some parts of the country. New Delhi has sent strict instructions to its diplomatic missions abroad that they should blindly deny stories in the international press saying that the problem is reaching serious proportions. The envoys are required to tell foreign officials that the situation has been exaggerated in the media. This is pricking some consciences …'

That is the directive. I will quote an extract from the *Time* magazine, which I am told has a circulation of 50 million:

'Nearly half a billion people are suffering from some form of hunger … India

---

1 Editor's note: Union Minister for Agriculture and Irrigation at the time.

2 Editor's note: Morarji Desai, at this time, was a member of the Opposition party, the Congress (Organization).

alone needs 8 to 10 million tons of food this year from outside sources or else as many as 30 million people might starve. Food riots have become commonplace in vast sections of India … In the Kutch district of drought stricken Gujarat, peasants patiently wait for dogs and vultures to finish picking at the carcasses of dead cattle. The hungry gather up the bones and sell them to mills where they are made into bone dust, a kind of fertilizer.'

Such articles have come out at which my head hangs down in shame, but this Government is unperturbed because they can behave like an ostrich, which can hide its head in the sand and think that others cannot see him!

Whilst Indira Gandhi is underplaying the whole thing, it could well be compared with the saying, 'When Rome was burning, Nero was fiddling'. Her crony, Sardar Swaran Singh[3] swore in a press conference in Washington that not a single starvation death has taken place … what a big lie it is! It is an organized, well-arranged narration of lies. Like Indira Gandhi, like Minister. He never tells the truth. They conveniently suppressed the details that even the State Congress President in West Bengal mentioned, namely, thousand deaths due to starvation have taken place.

I am quoting from *The Statesman*:

'At least, 1000 people had died of starvation and various diseases caused by the acute food scarcity in West Bengal, according to the reports received by the WBPCC from different districts, Mr Arun Moitra, the PCC President said here.'

It is not my saying or the saying of critics, but of a spokesman of the party in power. The Minister of Relief in West Bengal says that the food situation in West Bengal is extremely dangerous. There are so many like that. But in Cooch-Behar, the situation surpasses all civilized levels. What has happened in Cooch-Behar has been described by no less a person than an eminent journalist, writing for *The Times of India*, as follows:

'As I entered Cooch-Behar town last week, I was accosted by a man who implored me for help in cremating a boy, all skin and bone. I soon learnt that such cases are only too common. Often bodies of victims are abandoned on the roadside, at railway stations, in school verandahs, BDO's[4] offices; village markets, and even in backyards of private houses. At the present rate, they will soon stop counting the dead and official records will show nothing even to suggest that there was a disaster.'

… The report further says:

' … the authorities have thought it necessary to organize official squads to dispose of bodies, often in batches.'

---

[3] Editor's note: Swaran Singh was the defence minister when this speech was made; just before this he was external affairs minister.

[4] Editor's note: Block Development Office.

Let there be an official machinery to find out whether it is true or not …

… *The Economic and Political Weekly* report further says:

'The State's Relief Minister himself put the figure of the starving population at 15 million. Spokesmen of established political parties, including Ministers of the Congress, speak of starvation deaths by the hundreds. Despite the government's attempts to seal off Calcutta from the onslaught of hungry villagers, the city's pavements, parks and porticos are cluttered with destitute families who have managed to sneak through the police vigilance.'

It further says, 'Hunger, of course, is a perennial experience for most people in rural West Bengal during these months of the year. But it has not been experienced on the present scale for 31 years – not since the terrible days of the autumn of 1943.'

Well, if you want, I can present this copy of the *Economic and Political Weekly* to the Food Minister.

In the 24 Parganas the situation is equally bad. Half the people that come to Calcutta, I should say, come from south of 24 Parganas. In Assam, in Dhubri, North Kamrup, the position is the same. In Bankura, for the first time starvation has stalked the middle class …

… About Bankura, the people who never dreamt of living on dole have to accept chapatis prepared in gruel kitchens. But to the middle class, starvation has never been so close as today. It says: 'Ovens have not been lit in many homes for days together but out of shame the people have not approached the relief organizations.' That is the condition of the people there.

The conditions are even worse in the district of Purulia. I was talking about Assam. It says:

'Assam today is in the grip of famine. There have been reports of starvation deaths. Government sources have admitted that 74 per cent of the rural population are living below the hunger line … Despite early indications of food shortage in March and April, the Government had held out false assurances of successful procurement and adequate stocks …'

There are glaring instances of failure in Assam.

Then, this is from *Patriot*:

'Believe it or not, an eight year old boy sells in Assam for only Rs. 35, quite a bit cheaper than a medium-size goat. On 13 August, a group of newsmen visited an area of North Kamrup, said to be one of the worst flood-affected places in the State and met the eight year old Arfan Ali and his buyer Moslem Ali in the village of Kandhabari …'

… Coming to relief, it is only meeting the needs of 2 per cent of the population. Due to the in-fight amongst the ruling party members, and the stealing that goes on, even that is not reaching the common man. In relief camps that they have started in Assam, 150 gms of broken cereals, boiled, are being given once in a day.

Even there, the food is killing the people because the food is not quite good for the stomach of the starving person. So deaths are taking place.

The other day, six opposition MLAs from Assam came and they wanted to see the Prime Minister. They waited for 10 days. They were, more or less, refused an interview. Then, at my instance, they were able to see Mr. Dhar. Mr. Dhar promised to visit the Golpara District. Later on, he declined to go. They insisted that if food was not rushed to Golpara District, the death toll which is at present about 100 per day will continue.

The Government admitted that the shortage was marginal, and the per capita availability of food was much more now. I will show you from the documents that I have brought here. According to the reply given by the hon'ble Minister, only yesterday, the total production of cereals in 1972–73 was 87.1 million tonnes, and the total import of cereals was 6.97 lakh tonnes. In 1973–74, it is much higher. The total production of cereals in 1973–74 is 93.9 million tonnes, whereas the total import of cereals is 43.47 lakh tonnes. So the per capita availability is more. But the production is 93.9 million tonnes. The per capita availability of food per week should be 3000 grams or 3 kg. But in a place where there is full rationing, they're getting only 1250 grams per week, and in areas where there is modified rationing, they're given practically nothing. The rationing system is on the verge of collapse. The public distribution system is being systematically dismantled in order to make room for the jotdars[5], black marketeers and hoarders because if food is available through the public distribution system, the black marketeers cannot flourish. So the black marketeers should be given the freedom to loot in this 'Garibi Hatao', and the public distribution system should be dismantled. That is the truth.

I want to say that this is happening in total surrender of the Government to the black marketeers, hoarders and jotdars. Mrs. Indira Gandhi is running with the hare and hunting with the hound. For a 800 million population there is no food problem and the finding is by no less than a team of American scientists some of whom are Nobel Laureates. But, in this country, after 27 years of freedom, not more than 22 per cent of the cultivable land is irrigated, flood prevention measures are very little, there is no drainage system and the Emergency Agricultural Production Programme and the Rural Employment Crash Programme both have been both utilized to further the cause of the Congress Party. In fact, it has delivered nothing at all.

For the Kerala government, the Central Government promised 80,000 tonnes of rice. They have been promising year after year at the rate of 12 ounces per adult. This month, they've been given only 25,000 tonnes … 2 kg of rice per family per

[5] Editor's note: Jotedars owned relatively extensive tracts of land in Bengal; their land tenure status stood in contrast to those of under-ryots and bargadars (sharecroppers), who were landless.

week irrespective of the number of members in a family. The State produces cash crops and earns a lot of foreign exchange through sales of jute, tea, pepper, rubber and so many other commodities ... they use the land for the production of cash crops by not producing food items, they must be adequately compensated and they are not to come to the Central Government with a beggar's bowl year after year.

We have been demanding a National Food Budget. Shri Jagjivan Ram has not paid any attention to it. Who is responsible for the starvation conditions in the country? Not the natural calamity, but this pro-landlord, pro-hoarder policy of this government. What is the real way out? The Government should undertake the full responsibility of feeding the people, wholesale. States, trading in food grains, commandeering the surplus food grains belonging to persons who own more than 10 acres of land, giving up this pro-landlord and pro-hoarder policy ... stop the operation of black money and deficit financing ... Why don't you have a good procurement and distribution machinery? Because if you really strengthen the public distribution system, and if you really keep the rationing system alive and meet the requirements of people, the black-marketeers, the hoarders who are the patron saints of this party, and financiers and protectors of this party cannot survive and flourish. Therefore, they cannot remain in power. Therefore, you cannot run with the hare and hunt with the hounds ...

3

A Pandemic

*In India, one of the most disturbing visuals to emerge from the Covid-19 pandemic – if not the worst – was that of unaccounted corpses floating in the Ganges. If the pandemic affected virtually everyone in one way or the other, the government's efforts to underplay its impact was equally devastating. In July 2021, Rashtriya Janata Dal MP **Manoj Jha**, who is also his party's national spokesperson, as well as strategist, made a speech that made national headlines and became a YouTube sensation. The original in Hindi is much better, but in this translation, provided by Jha himself, some of the flavour of the original – the anger and the sorrow – comes through. As he stresses, for some minutes, he is not an MP representing his party's concerns, instead he is the voice of the people.*

MANOJ JHA

(Rajya Sabha: Bihar)

Rajya Sabha: 20 July 2021

Discussion on Management of Covid–19[6]

May my words not be mistaken for an act of heroism. Rather, it is the voice of a humble citizen of a nation where people are mourning everywhere. On their behalf, this apology is being tendered, to begin with, to those whose deaths are not being acknowledged, despite the fact that they have died. This is not a personal apology. I say this for I wrote six articles in the month of May … Parliament was not in session, so where was I to take any complaints? … my friends in the BJP, and colleagues, supported me and shared congratulatory messages, which strengthened my faith

[6] Editor's note: Translation provided by Manoj Jha.

in the House (as the most suitable venue) for tendering a collective apology to the corpses floating in the Ganges, without drifting to the many versions of the stories.

Another important aspect, which I tried to discuss with the General Secretary, Sir, the other day, is that never before in Parliamentary history between two sessions have there been 50 obituaries. Was Rajeev Satav ji[7] old enough to leave this world? Raghunath Mahapatra[8] would hug me, and greet me with, 'Jai Jagannath', whenever we met. Suddenly, he left us. This grief is personal.

I don't want to enter into any statistics – my facts, your figures. Your pain will give you the numbers. There is not a single person in this House or outside, or anywhere else in any other house who didn't suffer the loss of a near or dear one. I can empathize with everyone's grief. I could not help the people who contacted me … to help them get oxygen. People believe a Member of Parliament can help arrange oxygen. Of the hundred calls I'd receive each day, the success rate would be barely two or three. Who would then tell me the statistics? I will, therefore, refrain from talking numbers. Let us acknowledge that these deaths are live examples of our failure. I am not talking about you, for you would say no developments took place in the last 70 years, a debate I will avoid at this moment. This is the collective failure of all Governments since 1947. What have we all made? I never knew of the connection between a hospital and oxygen, I'll be honest. I don't hail from a medical background. Oxygen, oxygen, remdesivir were all I would hear from early morning. I would even check the pronunciations of medicines.

We are discussing statistics … we are … thanking Mr. X or Y. Sir, as I would go out, gigantic advertisements would shout out, 'Free Vaccine', 'Free Food', 'Free Treatment'.

I am not speaking on behalf of any party today. Instead, I am voicing the beliefs of the lakhs of people who wish to speak here. Why are we discussing this today? I am not complaining to you. Isn't this a welfare state? Sir, a poor man who purchases a soap in some village is as liable a taxpayer as Adani and Ambani. And you promise him 'Free Vaccine', 'Free Food', and 'Free Treatment'. No, Sir, nothing comes free. He has a stake in all this. It is the welfare state's commitment. Do not denigrate him. Do not demonize him. Do not force him to feel inferior, for which I shall plead.

Sir, as many other speakers have said, the coronavirus is a challenge for us. Tall claims are being made about new legislations. Why are we not addressing the Right to Health, the most basic right? There are no ifs and buts to it. The solution is sorted and constitutionally guaranteed – link the Right to Health with the Right to Life. No hospital would dare to mess with one's Right to Life. The right intent is missing. We need to prioritize the Right to Work.

---

[7] Editor's note: Congress Rajya Sabha MP who died of Covid in 2021.

[8] Editor's note: Nominated Rajya Sabha MP who died of Covid in 2021.

Sir, there have been ample discussions with regard to the population crisis. Let demography be the demographers' responsibility. That is all synthetic science, and can be dealt with in either of the Houses. Introduce legislation on the Right to Life and Right to Work so that people may benefit from such schemes at the time of a crisis. Our Leader of the House is not present at the moment. He is new to the post. I would have reminded him of the employees being laid off in the hospitality sector during these Corona times, while he was Railway Minister. I have continuously raised my voice, but everyone seems to have turned deaf to my pleas. No one is listening. Sir, when you don't pay heed to the words of a parliamentarian, who will attend to a low key employee who has been discharged?

Hon'ble Deputy Chairman, Sir, another astonishing incident took place during Corona times. I would like to mention one such event that happened amidst the hue and cry for hospital amenities, ICU beds, and medicines. And I am not just referring to the Central Government, since many state governments, too, can be faulted … How did this nation endure those one and a half months? I won't take names but many members of this House have come out of this, with much difficulty. It was such a nightmare, that it is hard to reimagine how the entire country lived through this period. My 37-year-old student died before I could arrange a hospital bed for him.

Sir, time and again, I request you to dwell on the personal losses; only then will we be able to come to a conclusion. Any tug of war, or blaming one another, will not help us. This is enough, and nothing will be gained through any display of vanity. I would just take one more minute to conclude.

Sir, I wrote a letter to the dead souls. I succumbed to helplessness, and drafted this letter to those who lost their lives. My letter had some suggestions for the government. Back then, it was said that the government didn't fail, the system did. Sir, why bring the system into this? Ever since my childhood, I have heard that there is a person and a structure behind every system. If the system failed in Delhi or in any village by-lane, let it be construed as the government's failure. Don't pass the buck to the system, for it is the government that creates the system.

Today, I do not feel inspired to say, 'Jai Hind'. My address today is not a complaint directed at anyone. To whom may we complain? I am hurt; it's my sincere effort to rise to the occasion, collectively, be it you or I, for I feel that we seek dignity in life, and even more dignity in death, particularly in the context of the corpses floating in the Ganges. We have witnessed unidentified deaths. If we don't amend this situation, our future generations shall not forgive us. It doesn't matter if you print huge advertisements and colour newspapers or say thank you to this or that, Sir, all this is a waste, if history doesn't thank us. Jai Hind, Sir. In case my words have hurt someone, I apologize on behalf of the lakhs of corpses. Jai Hind.

Acknowledgements

The idea for this book came from Chiki Sarkar, and it came in a new age way. My phone beeped, and I discovered I had a Twitter (it was still Twitter then) message from Chiki, who I didn't know at the time. For a few moments, I thought someone was playing a trick. But it turned out that it was a message from Chiki, and as I thought about the project, I got excited about it – for, as I say in the Introduction, I have spent a good part of my journalistic career in Parliament House, listening to many of the speeches excerpted here. Since then, much of the credit that this book is ready should go to her, Parth Mehrotra and my editor, Devangshu Datta – all of them prodded me to finish the book. While they were ready with suggestions, they allowed me to structure the book in my own way. I would also like to thank Arani Sinha, Devangana Ojha and Wesley D'Souza at Juggernaut.

Second, though I relied on the digital library to select the speeches, I must send out a very, very warm thank you to several members of the Parliament Library who painstakingly located speeches that I could not find in the digital library and found authentic translations when it was impossible to get them anywhere else. I also want to thank members of the Editorial Section of the Lok Sabha who guided me on the rules permitting use of speeches as well as carefully going through the excerpts to ensure there were no errors.

Third, I want to thank all those who helped me shape this book. First is my aunt, the late Supriya Roy, Tagore scholar and tech whiz, with whom I discussed the book at length while working on it, and who also helped me locate speeches. Then my friends, Nandini Mehta, Dina Vakil, Anjali Puri and Faraz Ahmed. Nandini and Anjali gave me the initial push, Dina's suggestions for the Introduction helped me give it its final shape and Faraz's phenomenal memory for dates and events came in very handy. Three others helped me with 'Section Five: The Journey Towards a Liberalized Economy': Priyaranjan Dash, my former colleague at the *Times of India*, and one of the finest economic correspondents I know; Devangshu Datta; and my sister, Joyeeta Gupta, climate change warrior and scholar, who helped me in what seemed like a matter of minutes to reduce budget speeches to manageable lengths. Finally, two other friends, Sri Krishna, who helped recall events when we had covered Parliament for our respective organizations, and Rakesh Batabyal, whose *The Penguin Book of Modern Indian Speeches: 1878 to the Present* served as a useful model, was always ready with advice.

Finally, I want to thank my mother, Shubha Gupta, who has always been a source of inspiration for me. She pushed me to finish the book through her many bouts of illnesses.

Index